THE
SOCIOLOGICAL
PERSPECTIVE

INTRODUCTORY
READINGS

THE
SOCIOLOGICAL
PERSPECTIVE

Edited by

Scott G. McNall
University of Minnesota

Boston LITTLE, BROWN AND COMPANY

PREFACE

The ultimate task of a reader for introductory sociology is to present material in such a way that students will learn what sociology is, which concepts are most significant in studying society, and how sociologists go about their work. In this reader we aim to accomplish this goal by presenting students with interesting, important, and readable articles in an integrated framework.

Another principle underlying this book is that a student should be presented with concepts, theories, *and* empirical research. Thus in each major section a research article illustrates how a sociologist answers some of the theoretical problems he raises. Further, five basic ways in which sociologists approach their data (by participant observation, social survey, community study, statistical analysis, or experimental control) are examined. Finally, this book will give students an opportunity to read materials from diverse theoretical frameworks, such as symbolic interactionism, conflict theory, and functionalism. The editorial remarks preceding each section explain which articles fulfill these criteria and how they do so.

I wish to acknowledge my debt to Alex Inkeles, who made many valuable suggestions and criticisms, and to my colleague Gregory P. Stone, for his very useful advice.

Scott G. McNall

v

To Amy who doesn't know any better.

CONTENTS

INTRODUCTION xi

PART
ONE   THE SOCIOLOGICAL PERSPECTIVE   1

I   PERSPECTIVES   5

   1   CHARLES H. COOLEY, *The Roots of Social Knowledge*   5
   2   C. WRIGHT MILLS, *The Sociological Imagination*   21 → *ready 38*

II   METHODS AND DATA   29

   3   MORRIS R. COHEN, *The Variability of Social Facts*   29   *cf interviews bk & series*
   4   SAMUEL STOUFFER, *Some Observations on Study Design*   32
   5   HARWIN L. VOSS, *Pitfalls in Social Research: A Case Study*   41

PART
TWO   BASIC PATTERNS AND IMAGES OF ORDER   53

III   CULTURE   55

   A.   Definitions and Concepts

   6   J. MILTON YINGER, *Contraculture and Subculture*   55

   B.   Processes and Examples

   7   S. K. WEINBERG AND H. AROND, *The Occupational Culture of the
      Boxer*   71
   8   EVON Z. VOGT AND THOMAS O'DEA, *A Comparative Study of the Role
      of Values in Social Action in Two Southwestern Communities*   85

IV   SYMBOLIC COMMUNICATION   98   *St Martin's Dr Who
                       Longman   EB textbk
                       NYU jrnalist legal guide bks*

   A.   Definitions and Concepts

   9   LESLIE A. WHITE, *The Symbol: The Origin and Basis of Human Be-
      havior*   98

   B.   Processes and Examples

   10   LEONARD SCHATZMAN AND ANSELM STRAUSS, *Social Class and Modes
      of Communication*   108

V   SOCIALIZATION   121

   A. Definitions and Concepts

   11 DENNIS H. WRONG, *The Oversocialized Conception of Man in Modern Sociology*   121

   B. Processes and Examples

   1. The Formation of the Self

   12 GEORGE H. MEAD, *The Genesis of the Self and Social Control*   133
   13 PHILIPPE ARIES, *Centuries of Childhood*   145
   14 HAROLD FINESTONE, *Cats, Kicks, and Color*   150

   2. Secondary Socialization and Resistance to Change

   15 MICHAEL BANTON, *The Fragility of Simple Role Systems*   163
   16 CARL W. BACKMAN, PAUL F. SECORD, AND JERRY R. PEIRCE, *Resistance to Change in the Self-concept as a Function of Consensus Among Significant Others*   165

VI ASSOCIATIONS   175

   A. Definitions and Concepts

   1. Primary and Secondary Groups

   17 KINGSLEY DAVIS, *Primary and Secondary Relationships*   176

   2. Formal Organizations

   18 MAX WEBER, *On Bureaucracy*   177

   19 DAVID RIESMAN AND REVEL DENNEY, *Football in America: A Study in Culture Diffusion*   186

   B. Processes and Examples

   1. Primary and Secondary Groups

   20 WILLIAM FOOTE WHYTE, *Corner Boys: A Study of Clique Behavior*   200

   2. Formal Organizations

   21 ROBERT K. MERTON, *Bureaucratic Structure and Personality*   215

PART
THREE   GENERAL SOCIAL PROCESSES   227

VII SOCIAL STRATIFICATION   229

   A. Definitions and Concepts

   22 REINHARD BENDIX AND SEYMOUR MARTIN LIPSET, *Karl Marx' Theory of Social Classes*   230

   23 KINGSLEY DAVIS AND WILBERT E. MOORE, *Some Principles of Stratification*   241

   B. Processes and Examples

   24 GERALD D. BERREMAN, *Caste in India and the United States*   252

↑ Jesus Cx ?
↝ ref T Mask of ---

25 A. B. HOLLINGSHEAD AND F. C. REDLICH, *Social Stratification and Psychiatric Disorders* 263

VIII SOCIAL DISORGANIZATION 273

A. Definitions and Concepts

26 KAI T. ERIKSON, *Notes on the Sociology of Deviance* 273

B. Processes and Examples

27 LEWIS A. COSER, *Social Conflict and the Theory of Social Change* 283

IX MASS BEHAVIOR 294

A. Definitions and Concepts

28 DANIEL BELL, *America as a Mass Society: A Critique* 294

B. Processes and Examples

29 C. ERIC LINCOLN, *On the Black Muslims* 310

30 GREGORY P. STONE, *Halloween and the Mass Child* 319

PART
FOUR QUALITIES OF THE SOCIAL STRUCTURE 327

X RACE 329

A. Definitions and Concepts

31 CARLETON S. COON, *New Findings on the Origin of Races* 329

B. Processes and Examples

32 STANLEY LIEBERSON AND ARNOLD R. SILVERMAN, *The Precipitants and Underlying Conditions of Race Riots* 340

XI COMMUNITIES 358

A. Definitions and Concepts

33 GIDEON SJOBERG, *Folk and "Feudal" Societies* 358

B. Processes and Examples

34 SCOTT GREER, *Urbanism Reconsidered: A Comparative Study of Local Areas in a Metropolis* 370

PART
FIVE SELECTED INSTITUTIONS 381

XII THE FAMILY 383

A. Definitions and Concepts

35 MELFORD E. SPIRO, *Is the Family Universal? — The Israeli Case* 383

2/23/86

1. American studies
2. basic personality change
; vs leviathan ?

see p. l

Gans ? T Urban Villagers

Bronfenbrenner in Cornell U on Parsons
; or Parsons coll. ?

see Conflict l ...

B. Processes and Examples

36 ALAN C. KERCKHOFF AND KEITH E. DAVIS, *Value Consensus and Need Complementarity in Mate Selection* 395

C. Relationships with Other Institutions

37 BARRINGTON MOORE, JR., *Thoughts on the Future of the Family* 407

XIII   THE POLITY 418

A. Definitions and Concepts

38 WILLIAM KORNHAUSER, *"Power Elite" or "Veto Groups"?* 418

B. Processes and Examples

39 SEYMOUR MARTIN LIPSET, *Working Class Authoritarianism* 433

C. Relationships with Other Institutions

40 RUSSELL MIDDLETON AND SNELL PUTNEY, *Student Rebellion Against Parental Political Beliefs* 461

XIV   RELIGION 471

A. Definitions and Concepts

41 MAX WEBER, *The Protestant Ethic and the Spirit of Capitalism* 471

B. Processes and Examples

42 BENTON JOHNSON, *Do Holiness Sects Socialize in Dominant Values?* 478

C. Relationships with Other Institutions

43 LISTON POPE, *Religion and the Class Structure* 491

XV   RELATIONSHIP OF INSTITUTIONS 501

44 ROBERT N. BELLAH, *Religious Aspects of Modernization in Turkey and Japan* 501

PART SIX   THE DISCIPLINE 509

XVI   APPROACHES 511

45 C. WRIGHT MILLS, *Two Styles of Research in Current Social Studies* 511

XVII   USES OF SOCIOLOGY 522

46 IRVING LOUIS HOROWITZ, *The Life and Death of Project Camelot* 522

47 LEWIS M. KILLIAN, *The Social Scientist's Role in the Preparation of the Florida Desegregation Brief* 538

XVIII   NEW DIRECTIONS 544

48 ROBERT A. NISBET, *Sociology as an Art Form* 544

49 JOHN T. GULLAHORN AND JEANNE E. GULLAHORN, *Some Computer Applications in Social Science* 558

INTRODUCTION

By starting with a very brief history of sociology's development we will begin
to see the problems that confronted the pioneers who tried to determine the
province of sociology. Now, men have always given thought to their relationships with one another, and they have always been interested in ways of controlling the world and other men. We are most directly interested in problems
of control, and in social change. J. B. Bury devised a framework that allows
us to see where sociology comes from.[1] This framework is made up of three
stages, which involve the Idea of Cycles, the Idea of Providence, and the
Idea of Progress.

For the Greek who lived at the time of Plato and Aristotle (400–300 B.C.),
the world was in chaos. The Greek city state was no longer a viable political
entity, and civil wars were weakening the country. Greece was now in the
center of trade routes, and exposed to strange peoples as well as strange ideas
and goods. In searching for a model to explain what was happening, the Greek
theorists turned to the world at hand. Here they saw plants which rose from
seed, flowered, wilted, and dropped their seeds so that the cycle could begin
again. Greece, too, once had its flowering, and from that age must descend.
Plato and Aristotle sought to arrest this change. *The Republic* is Plato's vision
of a totalitarian society in which guardians or philosophers control change.

There were, of course, many variations on this model, but it dominated the
intellectual scene for almost six hundred years. The ultimate collapse of this
model for describing change came about with the rise of Christianity. A cycli-
cal model was not acceptable to such thinkers as St. Augustine (A.D. 354–430)
or St. Thomas Aquinas (1225–1274). They could not see the events of the
world as having occurred before and likely to occur again. There was in their
view only one creation, one fall, and one redemption of mankind. However,
as Bury notes, this simple unfolding did not lead to any higher level. The
Idea of Providence involves no progression of mankind or society: man was
seen literally as at the mercy of God.

---

[1] J. B. Bury, *The Idea of Progress* (New York: Dover Publications, 1955.)

xi

This view of the world held sway until the Renaissance. Francis Bacon (1561–1626) first stressed the idea that knowledge has some utility in bettering the lot of man here on earth. The greatest impetus for the break with the old idea systems came, however, with the period described as the Enlightenment. René Descartes (1596–1650) was among those who believed in man as a reasoning being and in the invariability of nature's laws. The Idea of Providence, of "God's helping hand," is incompatible with this. Man is elevated to a new position; he is an independent thinker who can discover the laws of nature himself.

The last system of the Idea of Progress did not really come to fruition until the time of the French Revolution. In France and elsewhere on the continent men began thinking of knowledge as cumulative and relating this idea to the ultimate fate of mankind. A variety of reformers in England and in the United States were searching for natural laws of social progress.

As Bury illustrates so well, this search took two forms. There were those who believed that the laws had to be discovered so that man could put them to work for himself and speed the evolutionary development of society. Among this group were men who can be referred to as reformers and idealists. Another group of social theorists believed that one should discover the laws of social progress so that men might leave them alone and thus not interfere with social evolution. This group was made up of conservatives and laissez-faire theorists.

Among those who were searching for laws of social progress in order to manipulate them for man's benefit was the person often referred to as the father of sociology, Auguste Comte (1798–1857). Comte, a Frenchman, believed that sociologists should search for objective, experienced phenomena, and he developed a method for studying society in what he considered to be a scientific manner. Comte saw sociologists as eventually becoming the priests of a new age.

On the other hand, we have Herbert Spencer (1820–1903), described by Hofstadter[2] as the embodiment of Social Darwinism. In brief, Spencer was an English laissez-faire theorist who took the idea of the survival of the fittest and applied it to the social world. Society was seen as a working out of immutable evolutionary processes. It was the duty of sociology to discover the laws governing these processes. Although there were other productive Europeans at this time, such as the French sociologist Émile Durkheim (1858–1917) and the German sociologist Max Weber (1864–1920), their influence on sociology in the United States was not marked until sociology was quite well developed. It was Herbert Spencer, in particular, who dramatically influenced *early* American sociology. It is Hofstadter's contention that much of early American sociology can be seen as a reaction to Spencer's ideas: one tried either to refute them or to support them.

[2] Richard Hofstadter, *Social Darwinism in American Thought* (Boston: Beacon Press, 1965).

Part of the impetus for scientifically studying man's relation to man came with the Civil War and the years following, which saw rapid industrialization. Universities began to teach courses identified by such titles as "Social Ethics," utilizing the materials of people like Spencer. William Graham Sumner, who wrote such books as *Folkways* and *What Social Classes Owe to Each Other* (his answer was "Nothing"), found support for his ideology in Spencer. Others, like Lester Frank Ward, saw their duty in pointing out why Spencer was wrong and why a laissez-faire policy was not best for society. In reaction to Spencer, and in searching for laws to explain change, sociologists began to develop elaborate methodologies, theories, and terminologies. They asked such questions as: What is the proper province of sociology? What is its unique subject matter? How does one study this subject matter? The answers to these questions characterize early American sociology. Contemporary sociology cannot be so generally characterized. We will show what sociologists have done, what they are doing, and some of the directions in which the field is moving.

A sociologist's theoretical framework will very much determine how he asks his questions. And as anyone knows, how you ask something determines to some extent what answers you get. Let us look at three major theoretical perspectives dominant in the field of sociology: functionalism, conflict theories, and symbolic interactionism. There are, of course, others, but these three have accounted for more than their share of the questions asked. After examining these, we will look at the usual means by which sociologists try to answer their questions.

Sometimes students will find a work labeled "symbolic interaction *theory*," or "conflict *theory*," or "functional *theory*." Although there is a continuing debate as to whether these positions are theories or perspectives, it is generally accepted that they are perspectives: ways in which particular researchers look at the world. Different perspectives lead one to ask different questions about identical phenomena. We will illustrate what we mean by examples here and in the introductions to the articles.

Very briefly, functionalism is a perspective that sees a society as an integrated system of parts. The functionalist is concerned with what holds a society together, how conflicts are resolved, and what the "function" of any event is in maintaining social stability. This is an organic view in the sense that it takes a living organism as a closed system for analysis. Some sociologists feel that this is a "conservative" model, for it rarely takes account of change from sources outside the system, and they take it to task for ignoring change. Conflict theory is just what its name indicates. Instead of concentrating on what makes the system work and the processes of integration, conflict theorists stress the inevitability of conflict in any system, its pervasiveness, and its contribution to necessary change. A symbolic interactionist stresses attitudes and meanings and investigates the development and role in interaction of self-images.

An example of empirical behavior may make this clearer. Take the phenomenon of the urban neighborhood tavern. People come there to drink alcoholic beverages: Why? A functionalist would begin by asking: "What is the function of the neighborhood bar?" He would probably be interested in finding out why the people come and how the bar serves to integrate their lives. The bar might be a means for lonely people to meet, it could serve as an "extended primary group." This same person would also want to investigate the social function of alcohol, e.g.: Does it have a therapeutic function? Does the act of drinking actually serve as a safety valve for potential psychotics? etc. A conflict theorist, on the other hand, can start with the question: "What conflict does this bar represent?" He can go on to ask questions such as: "Does the drinking pattern of specific individuals lead to a conflict with other roles, such as employment or marital life? Is the bar itself a source of conflict in the community because of loud music, and so forth?" A symbolic interactionist would probably want to look at the act of drinking itself and the means by which the various drinkers identify themselves and make contact with one another, e.g., the symbol world of the tavern. His questions could be such things as: "How do the regulars identify a newcomer? What is the etiquette of drinking in a neighborhood tavern as opposed to a night club? How do people meet one another in a bar? How are pickups made? What are the different kinds of drinkers?" Each of these persepectives, then, can lead one to ask different questions, all of which may be equally important. This is the importance of the perspective.

The means of the sociologist are varied, but the following predominate: participant observation, "participant" reports, social survey, community study, statistical analysis, and experimental control. In participant observation, a sociologist participates in an event or situation and the other participants are not aware of his presence as a scientific observer. This technique is used when data are required that might not be forthcoming if the other members of the setting knew a sociologist or other observer was present. One of the most famous participant observer studies, done by William Foote Whyte, was called *Street Corner Society*. Whyte lived in a lower-class Italian area of a city and participated in most of the activities of a gang. He went bowling with them, drank with them, and went to dances with them. Another study making use of the same technique was Nels Anderson's study entitled *The Hobo*. This book was the result of Anderson's riding the rods with the hobos, sleeping with them, eating with them, and singing their songs.

The next technique is best described by the term "participant." Here I have in mind those studies which are the result of someone else's personal experience. In this category would be biographical materials supplied by bookies, thieves, prostitutes, and other deviants. One of the standards in the field is Edwin Sutherland's *The Professional Thief*. Sutherland collected and edited an excellent portrayal of the culture of crime, how a person learns to become a thief, and the differences between various types of criminals. Another exam-

ple is an anonymous book, *Streetwalker*, which describes the process of becoming a streetwalker, how the business is conducted, and the differences
between types of prostitutes. Usually, unless the book is edited by a sociologist who puts the book into a framework, these works are principally sources
of data rather than answers to questions.

Social surveys are best represented by the researcher who goes around
knocking on doors and asking people who they are going to vote for in the
coming election. The Gallup Poll and the Roper Poll are examples. For the
sociologist, the survey is the usual way of getting a wide and representative
measure of opinions on varied issues. Both interviewing and mailed questionnaires are consistently used in sociological research to answer questions
dealing with religion, politics, family behavior, and so forth.

The community study is usually the result of a sociologist's interest in such
issues as a town's power structure, how a rural community is integrated with
the larger society, how decisions are made. Floyd Hunter's *Community Power
Structure* is one study in which a researcher was able to detail the processes
by which important decisions are reached in a large city. Hunter's work
showed how the informal structure, the power behind the scenes, came into
play. Stein and Vidich's *Small Town in Mass Society* is an example of a community study in which the authors were able to explain in detail how a small
town relates to larger society.

Statistical analyses differ from social surveys not so much in how the data
may be gathered as the way in which they are analyzed. An example is the
United States census. Data are gathered by door-to-door representatives and
compiled according to prearranged categories, e.g., how many people live in
a given dwelling, and whether or not that dwelling is dilapidated. The U.S.
Bureau of the Census then publishes volumes of reports which contain these
summarized data. No effort is made to analyze or interpret the results; this is
left for the individual researcher who wishes to make use of the materials.

The controlled experiment is used when it is possible for the sociologist
to control and measure the influence of a test variable. One example is a study
in which Solomon E. Asch examined the effects of group pressure on the
modification of judgments. Asch presented a subject with three lines varying
in length and told him to tell which of the three lines was closest in length
to another line. The subject was in a group in which the other subjects were
stooges, people who knew what was happening, and who picked lines which
were obviously not similar in length to the other line. Asch was able to control the number of stooges, the length of the lines, and the position of the
subject's choice relative to that of the stooges. In short, it was possible for
Asch to "control" his test variables. (The subject would often pick the "wrong"
line to make his answer correspond with that of the stooges.)

These, then, are some of the principal means by which sociologists try to
answer questions that are framed by their theories or perspectives. Sometimes a combination of these methods will be adopted. A person might be a

participant observer in one tavern, might interview people in another, sample opinions of the general community regarding tavern behavior, and set up an experiment in which he could control the encounters of people in a tavern to see what changes in self-definitions might result. We will further illustrate these methods and perspectives by pointing to articles which best represent them.

PART
ONE

THE SOCIOLOGICAL
PERSPECTIVE

As we remarked in the Introduction, the study of sociology can
be regarded as a study of general social processes to which we
give form or order. It is our perspective, then, which determines
what the form will be. Although there are generally accepted
rules according to which sociologists analyze their data (e.g.,
adherence to certain principles of the scientific method), the
sociologists themselves will differ in the types of questions they
ask in the first place. This means that one's values will determine what he wishes to study and to what use, if any, he thinks
his findings should be put. This may seem at variance with the
often repeated proposition that any science is value-free. To
clearly illustrate what we mean by "value-free" let us look at
the basic assumptions, or a priori assumptions, on which science,
in the abstract, rests.

It is taken for granted that (1) events are causally related,
and (2) we can discover the cause or causes of any event.
Science is composed of empirical statements. It deals with
concrete phenomena, things that can be measured, touched,
weighed, etc. The cause of any event is therefore located in the

1

here and now, and cause is not attributed to any supernatural or spiritual phenomena. A science makes use of other criteria. Any discipline which professes to be a science uses "operational definitions." In other words, it defines its vocabulary in such a way that any other researcher will know exactly what operations were involved in arriving at the specific definition. Love is a nebulous word, and if this phenomenon is to be scientifically studied, one must specify exactly what it is he is talking about in order to allow other scientists to compare results or interpret them. To "operationalize" a concept, one could define "love" as a state of mind measured by variations in pulse rate. Notice that operational definitions say nothing about whether or not this is a meaningful way of defining "love."

A science also makes use of techniques which will yield reliable and valid results. In brief, a reliable measure is one which will give the same results time after time, such as an examination which would always have the "F" students getting "F's", and the "A's," "A's". A valid measure would allow you to measure what you want to measure. An early Italian criminologist, Cesare Lombroso, tried to develop an index of criminality based on head shapes, shape of the earlobe, and so forth. Now if his measure had been reliable, the same people would always be classified as criminal types according to his measure. Then, no matter who classified a group of people the results would always be quite similar. Unfortunately, Lombroso's scale was not reliable; it did not yield consistent results. The raters could not agree on who was a criminal-looking type. If his measure had been valid it would have allowed one to predict with accuracy — to pick the criminal from his bodily characteristics. Again, Lombroso met with failure, for judges, clerics, and ordinary citizens all appeared in the category of criminal with no consistency.

Disciplines which profess to be sciences deal with the problem of prediction. And here lies the main difference between sociology and a natural science, such as chemistry. Technically, a science is not concerned with an ad hoc description of events, which is one of the reasons why history falls outside the category of science. In the natural sciences it is possible to predict with high accuracy. For example, it can be predicted that the tides will be at a particular height on a particular day because the relationship between the moon's gravitational field and the tides is well known and is subject to little variation. In his predictions, a scientist makes use of probability statements. In predicting the height of tides, the probability is quite high. The facts are less variable in the natural sciences than in the social sciences. When the sociologist predicts the outcome of an election he is also making a probability statement, but the probability is much lower. He can say that Catholics will vote for the Democratic candidate, because there is a tendency in this country for Catholics to be Democrats. But he is not going to be right all the time, since as many as 30 per cent of Catholics in some areas are not Democrats.

If a discipline professes to be a science it must make use of all the criteria described above. To say that science is value-free, then, means that a person's values will not influence his findings or the interpretation of his findings. Though some scientists involved in the studies which resulted in the first atomic explosion were opposed to the idea of the bomb as a weapon, they used their knowledge and techniques to develop it. A sociologist studying any form of behavior does not impose his own moral framework on an interpretation of the data. Peter Berger gives a good example of what is meant by this.[1] Take the behavior of adolescents in a gang. The boys' behavior can be seen as a problem for the community; a solution would be to get the boys to participate in a neighborhood recreation center. If a sociologist were to impose this moral framework, he would miss the fact that the leaders of the gang feel that the attempts of "do-gooders" to get the gang to come to group recreation are a problem, because they spell the breakup of the gang.

Values do enter into the choice of problem. One's values will determine whether he is interested in studying social movements, delinquent gangs, religious behavior, or organizational behavior. To some extent the images that a sociologist has of society will also determine where he looks for his problems. In this first section we are concerned with these basic problems; e.g., what social knowledge is, how society should be studied, what social facts are, and what problems are involved. Let us turn to the specific articles in "Perspectives" and "Methods and Data."

[1] Peter L. Berger, *Invitation to Sociology: A Humanistic Perspective* (New York: Doubleday, 1963).

I PERSPECTIVES

Charles Horton Cooley, one of the founders of American sociology, worked at distinguishing sociology from other disciplines and isolating its unique subject matter. In this early article, which illustrates the questions that sociologists were then asking themselves, Cooley distinguishes a type of knowledge which is the result of symbolic communication. He examines the means by which this knowledge is acquired, and discusses the nature of the human mind and the means for studying it. He advances the technique of social observation for uncovering and examining the unique processes which he sees as the province of sociology. This article is a classic illustration of the problems approached by all early American sociologists, including Lester Frank Ward, Albion Woodbury Small, E. A. Ross, William Graham Sumner, and Franklin H. Giddings.

1 CHARLES H. COOLEY

The Roots of Social Knowledge

If we are to gain a large view of knowledge we should, it seems to me, consider it genetically by tracing it to its sources in human nature and human history. Knowledge is, after all, a phase of higher organic evolution, and has apparently been developed for the sake of its function in giving us adjustment to, and power over, the conditions under which we live. If these conditions present any fundamental division in kind we should expect that the

From *American Journal of Sociology*, Vol. XXXII (July, 1926), pp. 59–79. Reprinted by permission of the author and The University of Chicago Press.

capacities of the human mind and the knowledge based upon these capacities would show a corresponding division.

In fact, the conditions with which the mind has to deal, and has had to deal ever since life began to be human, divide themselves rather sharply into two kinds: the material, on the one hand, and the human or social, on the other. We have always needed to understand both things and persons, and the most primitive savage, though he may occasionally confuse them, is quite aware that they are different and must be understood in different ways.

This division lies as deep as anything in our experience, and it corresponds to a like division in our mental apparatus. For the external contacts we have our various senses, and also, in recent times, the extension and refinement of these through aptly named "instruments of precision" which have made the exact sciences possible. For the internal contacts we have a vast and obscure outfit of human susceptibilities, known as instincts, sentiments, emotions, drives, and the like, quite as firmly grounded in the evolutionary process as the senses, capable of extension and refinement in ways of their own, and giving rise to a kind of knowledge that we recognize as peculiarly human and social.

You will say, perhaps, that all knowledge, whether of things or of men, comes to us by the aid of the senses, and that the division I assert is therefore imaginary. It is true that all knowledge calls for sense activity of some sort or degree, but the function of this activity in material or spatial knowledge, on the one hand, and in human or social knowledge, on the other, is quite different. In dealing with things sensation is the main source of the raw material which the mind works up into knowledge; in dealing with men it serves chiefly as a means of communication, as an inlet for symbols which awaken a complex inner life not primarily sensuous at all. In the one case it is our principal instrument; in the other only ancillary. When I meet a stranger and judge by his face, bearing, and voice that he is a kindly and cultured man, and by his words perceive, in a measure, the working of his mind, the sensuous images are like the starting mechanism of an automobile; they set at work processes more complicated and potent than themselves, of which, mainly, the resulting knowledge consists.

For our present purpose we may, then, distinguish two sorts of knowledge: one, the development of sense contacts into knowledge of things, including its refinement into mensurative science. This I call spatial or material knowledge. The second is developed from contact with the minds of other men, through communication, which sets going a process of thought and sentiment similar to theirs and enables us to understand them by sharing their states of mind. This I call personal or social knowledge. It might also be described as sympathetic, or, in its more active forms, as dramatic, since it is apt to consist of a visualization of behavior accompanied by imagination of corresponding mental processes.

There is nothing mysterious or unfamiliar about social knowledge, except as we may be unaccustomed to recognize and think about it. It is quite as early to appear in the child and in the race as is material knowledge, quite as useful in the everyday affairs of life, and quite as universally accepted as real by common sense. If there are men of science who do not see that it is something distinct in kind, but are inclined to regard it as spatial knowledge in an imperfect state, destined in time to be perfected by more delicate measurements, this is doubtless because they approach the matter with the a priori conceptions appropriate to physical research. In relation to social phenomena the merely spatial conception of knowledge indicates an abstract way of thinking that does not envisage the facts. It is not, in this field, in accord with common sense. All of us know that the essential things in our relation to other men are not subject to numerical measurement.

I trust it will not be supposed that I am advocating any metaphysical dualism between mind and matter. It is not necessary, for my present purpose, to take a side on that question, but I have myself no doubt that all the phenomena connected with social knowledge, including introspection, have physical concomitants in the brain and nervous system. In theory these physical facts are capable of physical measurement, but when we consider their minuteness and inaccessibility, the likelihood of their being measured in a spatial sense seems quite remote. We must get at them, in practice, through consciousness and through overt behavior.

Spatial knowledge, we know, has been extended and refined by processes of measurement, calculation, and inference, and has given rise to exact science. It is generally agreed that knowledge of this sort is verifiable and cumulative, making possible that ever growing structure of ascertained fact which is among the proudest of human achievements. It may be worth while to consider for a moment to what this peculiarly verifiable character is owing.

It is owing, I take it, to the fact that this sort of knowledge consists essentially in the measurement of one material thing in terms of another, man, with his senses and his reason, serving only as a mediator between them. If, then, a group of investigators can agree upon a technique of measurement they may go ahead, achieving results and passing them on from man to man and from generation to generation, without concerning themselves with the vagaries of human nature and social life. This technical agreement is found possible, and the accumulation of knowledge goes on. But we must, of course, discriminate between the immediate results of measurement and the body of hypothesis and theory which is constantly arising out of them. Science gives us fact out of which the intellect endeavors to build truth. And what we judge to be true, even in the spatial sciences, is largely a social matter dependent upon the general movement of thought. A group of scientific men, familiar with previous investigation in a given field and armed with a sound technique, is the best instrument we have for the pursuit of truth, and is one of the most remarkable products of our social system; yet it is, of course, far from infallible. All groups have a body of beliefs which are taken for granted merely because no one disputes them, and which often turn out to be illusions. Assent is induced by conforming influences not wholly different from those operating in religion or politics. In short, no group is a trustworthy critic of its own conclusions, and only the test of time and of exacting criticism from wholly different points of view can determine the value of its contribution. There have been many groups, made up of very intelligent men working devotedly and in full assurance of being on the right track, who are now seen to have been astray. And although scientific methods are no doubt improved, it would be fatuous to suppose that they are a guaranty against group error. Some of the teachings of science are permanent truth, but only time reveals which they are.

The practical success of spatial science in enabling us to predict, and even to control, the behavior of the material world about us has given it vast prestige and brought about a feeling that the more all our mental processes are like it the more perfect they will become. A conception of what social science ought to be has accordingly grown up and gained wide vogue which is based rather upon analogy than upon scrutiny of the conditions with which we have to deal. Let us return, then, to the sources of our knowledge of mankind, and consider for a moment the development of this sort of knowledge in a child. He comes into the human world already provided with a vast complex of innate capacity for life peculiar to the human race and embracing in its potential content those processes of social emotion, sentiment, and intelligence in which men find their chief interests and motives. All this is an outcome of evolution, highly practical, the very stuff that has made man the most puissant of animals, and it has, no doubt, the same physical reality as any other nervous or mental processes. Regarding the exact content of this inborn raw material of personal and social life there has been much discussion, into which, fortunately, we need not enter. Some say that it includes quite definitely organized mechanisms, similar to the instincts of the lower animals; others, that the inborn mechanisms of man are small and indeterminate, taking on organization only under the stimulus of a particular kind of life. However this may be, no one can doubt that we are born with an inchoate world of mental capacity, existing physically as a mass of brain and nerve complexes, which requires as the main condition of its growth an interchange of stimulation with similar complexes existing in other personal organisms.

The process by which a distinctively human or social mind and a corresponding type of knowledge grows up within us was first expounded at some length in 1895 by James Mark Baldwin, who called it "the dialectic of personal growth." It resembles a game of tennis in that no one can play it alone; you must have another on the opposite side of the net to return the ball. From earliest infancy our life is passed in eager response to incitements that reach us through the expressive behavior of other people, through facial expression, gesture, spoken words, writing, printing, painting, sculpture, the symbols of science, and the mechanic arts. Every response we make is a step in our education, teaching us to act, to think, and to feel a little more humanly. Our brain and nerve complexes develop in the sense of our social surroundings. And at the same time our consciousness takes account of this inward experience and proceeds to ascribe it to other people in similar conditions. Thus by a single process we increase our understanding of persons, of society, and of ourselves. When you play golf you not only acquire spatial knowledge in the shape of a certain muscular skill, but also social knowledge through learning the pride one feels when he makes a long drive, or the humiliation when he tops the ball and gets into the creek. As you see another man do these things you repeat, sympathetically, your own inner response on former occasions and ascribe it to him. A new reach of human experience is opened to you and you enlarge your understanding of men. And you extend your knowledge of domestic life, of letters, arts, and sciences in much the same way. Consider scientific work in the laboratory and in the field. Does it give only material knowledge of the behavior of *things* in test tubes, of the look and feel of strata, of the habits of fishes, or does it also teach you to understand chemists, geologists, and zoölogists as *men,* to participate in a phase of human life, share its ideals, and learn its social methods? And is not the latter knowledge quite as important to the man of science as the former? Able men in every field excel, as a rule, in human as well as technical knowledge, because both are the fruit of a richly developed mind, and both must also be cultivated as instruments of success.

If the distinctive trait of spatial knowledge is that it is mensurative, that of social knowledge is, perhaps, that it is dramatic. As the former may be resolved into distinctions among our sensations, and hence among the material objects that condition those sensations, so the latter is based ultimately on perceptions of the intercommunicating behavior of men, and experience of the processes of mind that go with it. What you know about a man consists, in part, of flashes of vision as to what he would do in particular situations, how he would look, speak and move; it is by such flashes that you judge whether he is brave or a coward, hasty or deliberate, honest or false, kind or cruel, and so on. It also consists of inner sentiments which you yourself feel in some degree when you think of him in these situations, ascribing them to him. It is these latter sympathetic elements which make the difference between our knowledge of a man and our knowledge of a horse or a dog. The latter is almost wholly external or behavioristic, although those who associate intimately with them may acquire some measure of true sympathy. We know animals mostly as a peculiarly lively kind of thing. On the other hand, although our knowledge of people is likewise behavioristic, it has no penetration, no distinctively human insight, unless it is sympathetic also.

There is, no doubt, a way of knowing people with whom we do not sympathize which is essentially external or animal in character. An example of this is the practical but wholly behavioristic knowledge that men of much sexual experience sometimes have of women, or women of men — something that involves no true participation in thought and feeling. The more behavior in the other sex is instinctively sexual, the more our understanding of it is apt to be external rather than sympathetic. Or, to put it rather coarsely, a man sometimes understands a woman as he does a horse; not by sharing her psychic processes, but by watching what she does. There is, in fact, a complete series in our knowledge of persons, from the purely external, like our knowledge of babies, of idiots, of the wildly insane, up through all grades to the completely internal or sympathetic, as when, in reading a meditative writer like Marcus Aurelius, we know his consciousness and nothing else. For the most part, however, human knowledge is both behavioristic and sympathetic: the perception or imagination of the external trait is accompanied by sympathy with the feeling, sentiment, or idea that goes with it.

This is also the process by which we come to understand the meaning of a word, and through such understanding make ourselves at home in that vast realm of meanings to which words are the key. We may know words as mere behavior, as when a man speaks to us in a strange tongue, but in that case they do not admit us to the realm of meanings. To have human value the word and the inner experience that interprets it must go together.

In short, we learn to know human life outwardly and inwardly at the same time and by a single process continuous from infancy.

Adopting a convenient and popular term, I will call the individual human mind, including all these socially developed sentiments and understandings, the *mental-social complex.* I hope by the use of this colorless expression to escape from the traditional implications that obscure such terms as mind, consciousness, spirit, and soul.[1] About this, whatever we call it, the question of the nature and possibilities of social knowledge centers. It is our supreme gift; but for that very reason, because all the deep things of life are in it, it is the part of us about which we know least, and is least amenable to precise treatment. Can it be made available for science, or shall we try in some way to dodge it, or cancel it out, as the physical scientist does when he requires that the ideas about nature which come from it shall be verified by nature herself through physical measurement? The trouble with any such plan would seem to be that in human life the mental-social complex *is* nature. It is the very heart of what we seek to describe and make intelligible. It cannot be dodged without dodging life itself.

Suppose, for example, you secure, by a series of mental tests, detailed knowledge of what a certain person does in various situations. This may be of great value; I expect important results from such studies; but after all

---

[1] In a similar way the "group mind," that is, a collective view of individual complexes communicating with, and influencing, one another, might be called the social-mental complex.

they cannot enable you to know the person as a living whole. The social man is something more than the sum of standardized acts, no matter how many or how well chosen. You can grasp him only by the understanding and synthetic power of your own mental complex, without which any knowledge you may gain from behavior tests must remain superficial and unintelligent. Is it not a somewhat equivocal use of terms when we talk of measuring intelligence or personality? What we measure is the performance of standardized operations. To pass from these to the organic whole of intelligence or personality is always a difficult and fallible work of the constructive imagination.

Many people, agreeing perhaps with what I have said about the ultimate difference in kind between spatial and social knowledge, will hold that just because of this difference anything like social science is impossible. While spatial knowledge is precise and communicable, and hence cumulative, the dramatic and intuitive perceptions that underlie social knowledge are so individual, so subjective, that we cannot expect that men will be able to agree upon them or to build them up into an increasing structure of ascertained truth.

This is, in fact, a formidable difficulty which enthusiasts for exact social science are apt to ignore. I may say at once that I do not look for any rapid growth of science that is profound, as regards its penetration into human life, and at the same time exact and indisputable. There is a difference in kind here which it would be fatuous to overlook.

Regarding subjectivity, I may say that all knowledge is subjective in one sense: in the sense, namely, that it is mental, not the external thing, but a construct of the mind. Even the simplest perceptions of form or extent, much more the exact perceptions of science, far from being mere physical data, are the outcome of an extended process of education, interpretation, and social evolution. Your so-called physical sciences are, after all, part of the social heritage and creatures of the mental-social complex. In so far, then, spatial knowledge and social knowledge are on the same footing.

The question of more or less subjectivity, as among different kinds of knowledge, I take to be one of more or less agreement in the elementary perceptions. If the phenomena can be observed and described in such a way as to command the assent of all intelligent men, without regard to theory or to bias of any sort, then the factual basis of knowledge acquires that independence of particular minds which we call objectivity. A yardstick is objective because it provides an undisputed method of reaching agreement as to certain spatial relations. Professor Einstein has shown, I believe, that this objectivity is not absolute, but it suffices for most purposes of spatial science. Strictly speaking, there are no yardsticks in social knowledge, no elementary perceptions of distinctively social facts that are so alike in all men, and can be so precisely communicated, that they supply an unquestionable means of description and measurement. I say distinctively social facts, because there are many facts commonly regarded as social which are also material events, like marriages, and as such can be precisely observed and enumerated. But the distinctively social phenomena connected with marriage are inward and mental, such as the affection and desire of the parties, pecuniary considerations, their plans for setting up a household, and so on. These also can be known and communicated, but not with such precise agreement among observers as to make decisive measurement possible.

You may say that while it is true that the mental-social phenomena cannot be observed directly with much precision, they express themselves in behavior, which is tangible and which we may hope eventually to record and measure with great exactness. Even our inmost thoughts and feelings take form in the symbols of communication, in gesture, voice, words, and the written symbols which are preserved unchanged for ages. All this is true and much to the point: I am a behaviorist as far as I think I can be without being a fanatic. But we must not forget, as behaviorists sometimes appear to do, that the symbol is nothing in itself, but only a convenient means of developing, imparting, and recording a meaning, and that meanings are a product of the mental-social complex and known to us only through consciousness. Reliance upon symbols, therefore, in no way releases us from the difficulty arising from the unmeasurable nature of our elementary social perceptions. We can record behavior and handle the record by statistics, but I see no way of avoiding the ultimate question, What does it mean?

And how about introspection? Does not the kind of perception which I inculcate involve this disreputable practice, and if so, is it not thereby hopelessly vitiated?

The word "introspection," as commonly used, suggests a philosopher exploring his inner consciousness in more or less complete abstraction from the ordinary functions of life. While this method may have its uses it is thought to have been more relied upon in the past than it deserves. Let us observe men under more normal conditions, and preferably, it is urged, through their actions rather than through their supposed thoughts.

But just what, after all, is introspection? It is not merely the philosophic introversion I have indicated, but takes various forms, some of which, in everyday use by all of us, are indispensable to any real knowledge of the minds of other men.

That whole process of the social growth of the mind which I have mentioned involves elements introspective in character. We come to know about other people and about ourselves by watching not only the interplay of action, but also that of thought and feeling. As we perceive and remember sensuous images of gesture, voice, and facial expression, so, at the same time, we record the movements of thought and feeling in our consciousness, ascribe similar movements to others, and so gain an insight into their minds. We are not, for the most part, reflectively aware of this, but we do it and the result is social knowledge. This process is stimulated and organized by language and — indirectly, through language — by the social heritage from the past. Under the leading of words we interpret our observation, both external and introspective, according to patterns that have been found helpful by our predecessors. When we have come to use understandingly such words as "kindly," "resolute," "proud," "humble," "angry," "fearful," "lonesome," "sad," and the like, words recalling motions of the mind as well as of the body, it shows that we have not only kept a record of our inner life, but have worked up the data into definite conceptions which we can pass on to others by aid of the common symbol.

Much of our social knowledge, especially that acquired from reading, involves a process more consciously introspective. One can hardly read a play or a novel intelligently, I should say, without recalling ideas and emotions from his own past for comparison with those of the people described. The hero, as we conceive him, is fashioned out of material from our own lives. Is it not rather absurd for scientific men to repudiate introspection? Does anyone prepare a scientific report or article without first turning an inward eye upon the contents of his mind in order to see what he has to offer and how he can arrange and present it? In short, introspection, however abused by philosophers, is a normal and common process, without which we could know very little about life.

Introspection, if critical, is more objective than the usual practice of floating upon social currents without attempting to become aware of them. How can you be objective with regard to your motives unless you hold them off and look at them? I have in mind a recent book, a good book, too, in which the writer, who deprecates introspection, advances a series of opinions on social questions of the day so obviously those of his race, country, and social class that one can only smile at his naivete. Surely a little introspection would not be out of place here: one's subjectivity needs to be understood, if only to avoid it.

It seems, then, that outside and inside in human life, consciousness and behavior, mutually complement and explain each other, and that the study of external behavior as a thing by itself must, in the human field, be as barren as mere introspection, and for much the same reason, namely, that it isolates one aspect of a natural process from another. Nature has joined these things together, and I do not think that we gain anything by putting them asunder. Records of behavior without introspective interpretation are like a library of books in a strange tongue. They came from minds, and mean nothing until they find their goal in other minds.

However, I see no reason for quarreling with those extreme behaviorists who hold that we should observe men merely from the outside, as we do other animals. Let them work on this theory, if they find it helpful, and show what they can do. Even if it is wrong it may give rise to a valuable tech-

nique, as wrong theories have done in the past. It is fair to judge behaviorists by their behavior. I suspect that they will be found in practice to make
use of introspection when they need it, much like the rest of us.[2]

At the opposite pole, it would seem, from behaviorism we have the
method, or rather various methods, of mental analysis through the probing
of consciousness and memory. These all rest in great part upon sympathetic
introspection, or the understanding of another's consciousness by the aid of
your own, and give full play to the mental-social complex. They may be
used in sociology as well as in psychiatry, and, in fact, do not differ in principle from the personal interviews widely employed in the study of social
situations. Indeed, I take it that the psychoanalytic psychology owes its
vogue to its boldness in disregarding the rather narrowly spatial methods
within which laboratory psychologists were confining themselves, and ven-
turing, by the light of clinical interviews and introspective interpretation, to
explore the weird caverns of the human mind. Men saw that the sequent
revelations resembled what they knew of their own egos. The method is
quite separable from the extravagant theories associated with it and will no
doubt be largely used.

I have conceded that social observation is, on the whole, less precise and
verifiable, and hence less surely cumulative, than spatial observation, not
only because the conditions can seldom be reproduced by experiment, but
because the perceptions themselves are less alike in different persons, and so
less easy to agree upon. Experience shows, however, that these difficulties
are by no means sufficient to prevent objective and co-operative study of
social phenomena, and a cumulation of knowledge which, though not so tangible as in experimental science, is capable in time of yielding vast results.

The basis of common social perceptions, and hence of cumulation, is in
the general similarity of mental-social complexes throughout the human race,
and the much closer similarity among those formed by a common language
and culture. We become aware of this similarity by watching the behavior
of other men, including their language, and finding that this behavior can
be interpreted successfully by ascribing to them thoughts and sentiments
similar to our own. The idea that they are like us is practically true; it works.
It was generated in the experience of our earliest childhood, and we have
gone upon it all our lives. This fundamental agreement upon meanings can
be made more precise by the careful use of language and other communicative signs, something as sense-perceptions are refined by the use of instruments of precision (though probably to nothing like the same degree), and
thus allows a transmission and cumulation exact enough for practical use.

---

[2] I need hardly say that the scientific study of behavior has no necessary connection
with the group of men who call themselves "behaviorists." Their extreme doctrine of
the rejection of consciousness is best understood as a reaction against a former extreme,
in psychology, of purely introspective study. Social studies have always been mainly
behavioristic.

All history, all news, all social investigation, is a record of what men did — of such visible acts as are thought to be significant, and also of their symbolic acts, their speech, and their works of art. But what makes the record interesting is that through our likeness to them it becomes also a record of what they were, of their meanings, of their inner life, the semblance of which is awakened in us by the acts recorded.

I open Herodotus at random and find an account of how the Carthaginians, having captured many Phoceans from disabled ships, landed them and stoned them to death. But after this the sheep, oxen, or men who passed the spot were stricken with palsy. So they consulted the Delphic Oracle, who required them to institute a custom of honoring the dead Phoceans with funeral rites. Here is a record of behavior which we interpret by sympathy. We feel the cruelty of the Carthaginians, their wonder and alarm at the strange conduct of the stricken men and animals, their anxious resort to Delphi, their awed obedience to the oracle. Of the grounds for criticizing this narrative from the standpoint of a wider study of human ideas and human behavior I need not now speak. Like all social observation that comes down from the past, it must be interpreted in view of the difference in mental complexes between the men who made the records and us who read them. We must, as we say, get their background and point of view. But men are, after all, so much alike that an imagination trained by comparative study can usually make out fairly well what the records mean. The true reason why we must, in sociology, rely mainly upon contemporary rather than historical facts is the inadequacy of the record. History does not tell what we want to know, and we must look in the world about us for answers to questions which the men of old never thought of putting.

At any rate we actually have accumulations of social knowledge. Aristotle and many other early writers collected facts which are still held to be trustworthy, and interpreted them by generalizations which still command respect. In modern times the process has gone on developing in volume, diversity, and precision, and has given rise to technical groups of specially trained men. We have many kinds of history, we have social anthropology, political science, law, economics, sociology, comparative religion, comparative literature and art, and other departments, each with its own archives of recorded fact.

Indeed, as regards cumulation the study of mankind has a great advantage in that its subject matter is uniquely self-recording. Even the records of geology and paleontology do not compare in richness with those that man hands down about himself through language and the several arts. And the more he approaches and enters a civilized state, the more extensive these records become. The dinosaur may leave his skeleton and even his (or her) eggs, but man deposits a fossil mind. We know infinitely more about him than we do about any other animal, and the difficulty of accumulating knowledge, so far as primary facts are concerned, is quite imaginary. Dispute, as in other fields, is mainly about interpretation. The selection and explanation of facts has heretofore proved provisional; it has to be done over again with every change in the general current of thought. But is not this true of all science? At this moment the whole theoretical trunk of physics has been torn up by the roots and seems likely to be thrown upon the rubbish pile. A lasting structure of knowledge is hardly to be expected, except as regards the primary facts and their simpler relations, and this much we may expect in social science as well as in spatial.

It is high time that I referred to that body of knowledge and practice known as statistics. Statistics is an exact method, and it is enabled to be such precisely because it is not in itself social but mathematical. It does not directly *perceive* social facts, or any other kind of facts, but it takes standard units of some sort, which may be perceived social facts, and compiles, arranges, manipulates, and presents them in a way intended to make them yield illumination. The statistician operates between the primary observer, on the one hand, and, on the other, the theorist who demands light on certain hypotheses. Perhaps I may without offense liken him to a cook, who neither supplies the food nor consumes it, but is a specialist upon the intervening processes.

Evidently it would not be good sense to assume any antagonism between the exact methods of statistics and the more fallible procedure of sympathetic observation and interpretation. They are complementary and do not or should not overlap. The only opposition likely to arise is one due to the bias of the practitioner. A statistician, if he lacks breadth of mind, is apt to be so fond of his exact processes that he avoids and depreciates anything else, while the sympathetic observer is apt to be impatient of statistics. This difference of tastes would not do much harm if the functions were kept separate, but when a man who is fit for only one assumes both the result is unfortunate. Much statistical work, especially that based upon questionnaires or interviews, is vitiated by a lack of dramatic insight into the states of mind of the people who supply the information. A questionnaire is an instrument of social perception, and if its use is to have any scientific character, the first duty of the user is to dramatize the play of thought and feeling that takes place between the person that puts the question and the person that answers it. What was the actual state of mind of the latter, and what the human significance of his reply? Not every investigator has the insight and the conscience to perceive and report this real fact, commonly so different from the apparent fact, upon which the value of his work depends.

And so with the questions or problems used in mental tests. If they aim only to test the power to perform standardized operations they are objective, but, socially speaking, superficial; if they go beyond this and attempt to discover social or moral attitudes they are subjective, and of no value for science without sympathetic interpretation.

It is not the case that social science is becoming exact through the substitution of statistics for social sympathy and imagination. What is taking place is, rather, that the use of sympathy and imagination is becoming more competent, while statistics is being substituted for guesswork in the manipulation of data.

Another impression which I take to be erroneous is that statistics is revealing uniformities or regularities in social phenomena which indicate that these phenomena may in time prove to be subject to exact prediction in quite the same way as those of physics. It is true that statistics is revealing sequence, order, and a remarkable degree of predictability in certain social processes. By analysis of what has taken place during the past ten years, especially in the economic field, where the facts are largely material, it may be possible to forecast what will take place in the next five; and no one can say how far we may go in this direction. The whole basis of this, however, seems to be the prevalence of inertia and the rarity and slowness of the more originative processes. The greater part of human phenomena are so far routinized as to be more or less subject to calculation. Wherever men, under the impetus of habit and suggestion, are moving ahead in a mechanical manner, or where their intelligence is merely repeating what is essentially an old synthesis of motives — as, for example, in deciding whether to marry or not — exact methods are in place. The complex of human events can, to a great extent, be resolved into currents of tendency moving on definite lines at ascertainable speeds. If we can measure these lines and speeds it may be possible to predict their combined operation, much as the motion of a comet is predicted by calculating the resultant of the gravity, tangential momentum, and other forces acting upon it. The whole basis of prediction in such fields as that of the business cycle is the belief that the underlying motivation is essentially standardized or repetitive.

Probably no exact science could have foreseen the sudden rise of the automotive industry and the genius of Henry Ford, although now that this industry is developed and institutionized we may perhaps calculate with some precision what it will bring forth in the near future.

There is no good reason to think that such statistical methods can anticipate that which, after all, chiefly distinguishes human life from physical processes, namely, originative mental synthesis, whether by outstanding individuals or by groups. The kind of mechanistic theory which would exclude the unique function of human consciousness and will is not only highly speculative and unverifiable, but seems, as a speculation, to be losing ground. Recent philosophic writers (for example, our colleague Professor Sellars[3]), in so far as they accept mechanism or determinism, interpret them in such a way as to leave intact our human power of reorganizing and redirecting life in a manner that no exact science can hope to foresee.

There is indeed one way in which physical and social science may be

[3] R. W. Sellars, *Evolutionary Naturalism, passim.*

assimilated. We may find that atoms and electrons are not so uniform and reliable as has been believed, that the supposed physical laws are only statistical, covering diversity in the phenomena somewhat as social statistics cover the diversities of individual men. Indeed, we are told by men apparently competent that "the present state of physics lends no support whatever to the belief that there is a causality in physical nature which is founded on rigorously exact laws."[4] In some such way as this the gulf may be bridged, but never, I think, by reducing the human will to zero.

Having dealt so far with observation, either direct or mediated by technique, I come now to the interpretive use of the data, to the attempt to build a structure of social truth. This is, in all sciences, a work of the imagination, and a work which has always in the past proved to be provisional and to require renewal to meet the general advance of thought. I see no reason to expect anything else in the future.

At the present time all the sciences of life are, I suppose, controlled by the idea of organic development. Darwin gave these studies their orientation by making them studies of process rather than state, of what is going on rather than what is, of a drama rather than a picture. For many years, however, evolutionary ideas were applied to social phenomena chiefly in an external and analogical way; they were imposed artificially, not allowed to grow naturally out of the social processes themselves. The result was a vast body of social theory and propaganda, all claiming to be evolutionary and scientific, but none of it the work of a technical group devoted primarily and disinterestedly to the study of social facts. Even at the present time specialists in contiguous evolutionary fields contribute profusely to social literature and by no means hide their belief that they know more about what is important to society than do the so-called "sociologists." Whether they do or not, it is a fact that some of these extraneous doctrines, like the pseudo-Darwinism of Nietzsche or the hereditary determinism of the more extreme followers of Galton, have had, and still have, a wide influence.

I shall assume, however, that, after all, social phenomena are most likely to be understood by those who make the study of them their main business, and that the application of evolutionary ideas in this sphere is the task mainly of history, anthropology, ethnology, political science, economics, social psychology, sociology, and kindred disciplines. All of these studies have, in fact, a decidedly evolutionary trend, and several of them may be said to have been created by the evolutionary movement. All of them aim at the understanding of personal and social wholes in the actual process of living. All make increasing use of social psychology. They do not aim to resolve social phenomena into elements which are not social, but rather to investigate the simpler and more general social processes and use the knowledge thus gained in synthetic interpretation of larger social wholes. This may be

---

[4] Hermann Weyl, quoted by J. W. N. Sullivan, *Aspects of Science*, p. 158.

done by the use of well-chosen samples, as in studies of individual persons, of typical local or institutional conditions, and the like.

In general, the insights of sociology, if I may take that subject as representative, are imaginative reconstructions of life whose truth depends upon the competence of the mind that makes them to embrace the chief factors of the process studied and reproduce or anticipate their operation. This requires native ability, factual knowledge, social culture, and training in a particular technique.

It is sometimes supposed that pre-Darwinian studies in history, literature, art, and social theory were essentially unscientific and futile; in fact, mere rubbish needing to be swept aside by the advancing forces of science. On the contrary, many of these studies were based on common sense, had a sound empirical basis, and are even now of more value than hurried, dogmatical, and mostly analogical efforts to supplant them by something having the appearance of natural science. Such efforts have given rise to a variety of pseudo-sciences, some of which are flourishing at the present time, but they have not broken the real continuity of contemporary social knowledge with the solid work of earlier generations. Sociology, at least, recognizes whole-heartedly the value of pre-evolutionary research, and expects that its students shall know something of the great currents of historical, literary, and artistic tradition; shall have, indeed, as broad a culture in the humanities as possible. This culture affords the only access to great stores of facts with which we cannot dispense. It also affords a perspective of the development of social interpretation. Most of the generalizations now being defined, explored, tested, and developed into systematic knowledge were foreshadowed by penetrating minds of the past. How much of modern social psychology is implicit in the maxims of La Rochefoucauld, what insight into social processes had Gibbon! Sainte-Beuve, who saw literature as an organic human whole, observing the individual writer and the current of literary tendency with equal understanding, was a real sociologist in the field of criticism. Goethe was one in an even larger sense. An honest and competent student will be deferent to the achievements of the past and will lend no countenance to those shallow spirits who see scientific method as a sort of trick of laboratories and schedules by which they may avoid the slow approaches of actual social knowledge.

As to prediction, I have already pointed out that in the more mechanized processes of the social system it may be remarkably exact. We have no ground, however, to expect any such exactness in foretelling the multitudinous fluctuations of human life in general. Prediction, in any science, requires that the mind embrace the process, as the physicist, in his formula, embraces the process of a falling body, and so, through participation, foresee the outcome. Even in natural science this can usually be done with precision only when the process is artificially simplified, as in the laboratory. The social processes of actual life can be embraced only by a mind working at large, participating through intellect and sympathy with many currents of human force, and bringing them to an imaginative synthesis. This can hardly be done with much precision, nor done at all except by infusing technical methods with a total and creative spirit.

The human mind participates in social processes in a way that it does not in any other processes. It is itself a sample, a phase, of those processes, and is capable, under favorable circumstances, of so far identifying itself with the general movement of a group as to achieve a remarkably just anticipation of what the group will do. Prediction of this sort is largely intuitive rather than intellectual; it is like that of the man with a genius for business as contrasted with that of the statistician; it is not science, but it is the very process by which many of the great generalizations of science have first been perceived.

Predictions of any sort, however, are most likely to be sound when they are made by those who have the most precise familiarity with the observable processes, and it is the increase of this familiarity on the part of social observers, along with their greater insight into principles, that should make them better guessers of what is to happen than they have been in the past.

What, then, is there new in contemporary social science, what, if anything, that promises a more rapid and secure accumulation of knowledge than in the past? Mainly, I should say, the following:

1. Liberation from outworn theological and metaphysical assumptions and reorganization on the basis of factual study and an evolutionary outlook.

2. The rise of a technical group of adequately trained scholars, with those traditions and standards, that expert criticism and exacting group atmosphere, indispensable to all higher achievement.

3. The development, since 1860, and especially since 1900, of a network of factual theory, by which I mean theory springing from observation and capable of being verified or refuted by the closer study of fact. Such theory is to be distinguished from much of the older speculation, which was largely metaphysical, unverifiable, and for that reason of no use in stimulating research.

There is nothing startling in the present movement. It shows no break with the past, does not promise any phenomenal power of prediction, and is, in fact, chiefly occupied with the ascertainment of what is actually going on and with the development of technique. We are trying to describe and interpret human life in the same spirit that the life of animals and plants has been described and interpreted, but with due regard to the different character of the problem. The human material is peculiar not only in its enormous abundance and variety, but in requiring, to deal with it, a radically different theoretical and technical equipment.

C. Wright Mills authored several important works in sociology and criticisms of our society. Among these were White Collar, The Power Elite, The Causes of World War III, The Sociological Imagination, *and* Listen Yankee. *Mills' perspective led him to try to develop what he considered to be "the larger problems." Sometimes both his questions and answers did indeed reach great heights; at ·other times they did not. For Mills, sociology had a mission and that mission is aptly described in the following selection. Mills is absorbed by what man seems to be becoming; it is the sociological imagination which will allow him to understand others and take their actions into account. It is also a way of asking the "big questions."*

2 C. WRIGHT. MILLS

The Sociological Imagination

Nowadays men often feel that their private lives are a series of traps. They sense that within their everyday worlds, they cannot overcome their troubles, and in this feeling, they are often quite correct: What ordinary men are directly aware of and what they try to do are bounded by the private orbits in which they live; their visions and their powers are limited to the close-up scenes of job, family, neighborhood; in other milieux, they move vicariously and remain spectators. And the more aware they become, however vaguely, of ambitions and of threats which transcend their immediate locales, the more trapped they seem to feel.

Underlying this sense of being trapped are seemingly impersonal changes in the very structure of continent-wide societies. The facts of contemporary history are also facts about the success and the failure of individual men and women. When a society is industrialized, a peasant becomes a worker; a feudal lord is liquidated or becomes a businessman. When classes rise or fall, a man is employed or unemployed; when the rate of investment goes up or down, a man takes new heart or goes broke. When wars happen, an insurance salesman becomes a rocket launcher; a store clerk, a radar man; a wife lives alone; a child grows up without a father. Neither the life of an individual nor the history of a society can be understood without understanding both.

Yet men do not usually define the troubles they endure in terms of historical change and institutional contradiction. The well-being they enjoy, they do not usually impute to the big ups and downs of the societies in which they live. Seldom aware of the intricate connection between the patterns of their own lives and the course of world history, ordinary men do not usually know what this connection means for the kinds of men they are becoming and for the kinds of history-making in which they might take part. They do not possess the quality of mind essential to grasp the interplay of man and society, of biography and history, of self and world. They cannot cope with their personal troubles in such ways as to control the structural transformations that usually lie behind them.

Surely it is no wonder. In what period have so many men been so totally exposed at so fast a pace to such earthquakes of change? That Americans have not known such catastrophic changes as have the men and women of other societies is due to historical facts that are now quickly becoming "merely history." The history that now affects every man is world history. Within this scene and this period, in the course of a single generation, one sixth of mankind is transformed from all that is feudal and backward into all that is modern, advanced, and fearful. Political colonies are freed; new and less visible forms of imperialism installed. Revolutions occur; men feel the intimate grip of new kinds of authority. Totalitarian societies rise, and are smashed to bits — or succeed fabulously. After two centuries of ascendancy, capitalism is shown up as only one way to make society into an industrial apparatus. After two centuries of hope, even formal democracy is restricted to a quite small portion of mankind. Everywhere in the underdeveloped world, ancient ways of life are broken up and vague expectations become urgent demands. Everywhere in the overdeveloped world, the means of authority and of violence become total in scope and bureaucratic in form. Humanity itself now lies before us, the super-nation at either pole concentrating its most co-ordinated and massive efforts upon the preparation of World War Three.

The very shaping of history now outpaces the ability of men to orient themselves in accordance with cherished values. And which values? Even when they do not panic, men often sense that older ways of feeling and thinking have collapsed and that newer beginnings are ambiguous to the point of moral stasis. Is it any wonder that ordinary men feel they cannot cope with the larger worlds with which they are so suddenly confronted? That they cannot understand the meaning of their epoch for their own lives? That — in defense of selfhood — they become morally insensible, trying to remain altogether private men? Is it any wonder that they come to be possessed by a sense of the trap?

It is not only information that they need — in this Age of Fact, information often dominates their attention and overwhelms their capacities to assimilate it. It is not only the skills of reason that they need — although their struggles to acquire these often exhaust their limited moral energy.

What they need, and what they feel they need, is a quality of mind that will help them to use information and to develop reason in order to achieve lucid summations of what is going on in the world and of what may be happening within themselves. It is this quality, I am going to contend, that journalists and scholars, artists and publics, scientists and editors are coming to expect of what may be called the sociological imagination.

1

The sociological imagination enables its possessor to understand the larger historical scene in terms of its meaning for the inner life and the external career of a variety of individuals. It enables him to take into account how individuals, in the welter of their daily experience, often become falsely conscious of their social positions. Within that welter, the framework of modern society is sought, and within that framework the psychologies of a variety of men and women are formulated. By such means the personal uneasiness of individuals is focused upon explicit troubles and the indifference of publics is transformed into involvement with public issues.

The first fruit of this imagination — and the first lesson of the social science that embodies it — is the idea that the individual can understand his own experience and gauge his own fate only by locating himself within his period, that he can know his own chances in life only by becoming aware of those of all individuals in his circumstances. In many ways it is a terrible lesson; in many ways a magnificent one. We do not know the limits of man's capacities for supreme effort or willing degradation, for agony or glee, for pleasurable brutality or the sweetness of reason. But in our time we have come to know that the limits of "human nature" are frighteningly broad. We have come to know that every individual lives, from one generation to the next, in some society; that he lives out a biography, and that he lives it out within some historical sequence. By the fact of his living he contributes, however minutely, to the shaping of this society and to the course of its history, even as he is made by society and by its historical push and shove.

The sociological imagination enables us to grasp history and biography and the relations between the two within society. That is its task and its promise. To recognize this task and this promise is the mark of the classic social analyst. It is characteristic of Herbert Spencer — turgid, polysyllabic, comprehensive; of E. A. Ross — graceful, muckraking, upright; of Auguste Comte and Emile Durkheim; of the intricate and subtle Karl Mannheim. It is the quality of all that is intellectually excellent in Karl Marx; it is the clue to Thorstein Veblen's brilliant and ironic insight, to Joseph Schumpeter's many-sided constructions of reality; it is the basis of the psychological sweep of W. E. H. Lecky no less than of the profundity and clarity of Max Weber. And it is the signal of what is best in contemporary studies of man and society.

No social study that does not come back to the problems of biography, of history and of their intersections within a society has completed its intellectual journey. Whatever the specific problems of the classic social analysts, however limited or however broad the features of social reality they have examined, those who have been imaginatively aware of the promise of their work have consistently asked three sorts of questions:

1. What is the structure of this particular society as a whole? What are its essential components, and how are they related to one another? How does it differ from other varieties of social order? Within it, what is the meaning of any particular feature for its continuance and for its change?

2. Where does this society stand in human history? What are the mechanics by which it is changing? What is its place within and its meaning for the development of humanity as a whole? How does any particular feature we are examining affect, and how is it affected by, the historical period in which it moves? And this period — what are its essential features? How does it differ from other periods? What are its characteristic ways of history-making?

3. What varieties of men and women now prevail in this society and in this period? And what varieties are coming to prevail? In what ways are they selected and formed, liberated and repressed, made sensitive and blunted? What kinds of "human nature" are revealed in the conduct and character we observe in this society in this period? And what is the meaning for "human nature" of each and every feature of the society we are examining?

Whether the point of interest is a great power state or a minor literary mood, a family, a prison, a creed — these are the kinds of questions the best social analysts have asked. They are the intellectual pivots of classic studies of man in society — and they are the questions inevitably raised by any mind possessing the sociological imagination. For that imagination is the capacity to shift from one perspective to another — from the political to the psychological; from examination of a single family to comparative assessment of the national budgets of the world; from the theological school to the military establishment; from considerations of an oil industry to studies of contemporary poetry. It is the capacity to range from the most impersonal and remote transformations to the most intimate features of the human self — and to see the relations between the two. Back of its use there is always the urge to know the social and historical meaning of the individual in the society and in the period in which he has his quality and his being.

That, in brief, is why it is by means of the sociological imagination that men now hope to grasp what is going on in the world, and to understand what is happening in themselves as minute points of the intersections of biography and history within society. In large part, contemporary man's self-conscious view of himself as at least an outsider, if not a permanent stranger, rests upon an absorbed realization of social relativity and of the transformative power of history. The sociological imagination is the most fruitful form of this self-consciousness. By its use men whose mentalities have swept only a series of limited orbits often come to feel as if suddenly awakened in a house with which they had only supposed themselves to be familiar. Correctly or incorrectly, they often come to feel that they can now provide themselves with adequate summations, cohesive assessments, comprehensive orientations. Older decisions that once appeared sound now seem to them products of a mind unaccountably dense. Their capacity for astonishment is made lively again. They acquire a new way of thinking, they experience a transvaluation of values: in a word, by their reflection and by their sensibility, they realize the cultural meaning of the social sciences.

2

Perhaps the most fruitful distinction with which the sociological imagination works is between "the personal troubles of milieu" and "the public issues of social structure." This distinction is an essential tool of the sociological imagination and a feature of all classic work in social science.

Troubles occur within the character of the individual and within the range of his immediate relations with others; they have to do with his self and with those limited areas of social life of which he is directly and personally aware. Accordingly, the statement and the resolution of troubles properly lie within the individual as a biographical entity and within the scope of his immediate milieu — the social setting that is directly open to his personal experience and to some extent his willful activity. A trouble is a private matter: values cherished by an individual are felt by him to be threatened.

Issues have to do with matters that transcend these local environments of the individual and the range of his inner life. They have to do with the organization of many such milieux into the institutions of an historical society as a whole, with the ways in which various milieux overlap and interpenetrate to form the larger structure of social and historical life. An issue is a public matter: some value cherished by publics is felt to be threatened. Often there is a debate about what that value really is and about what it is that really threatens it. This debate is often without focus if only because it is the very nature of an issue, unlike even widespread trouble, that it cannot very well be defined in terms of the immediate and everyday environments of ordinary men. An issue, in fact, often involves a crisis in institutional arrangements, and often too it involves what Marxists call "contradictions" or "antagonisms."

In these terms, consider unemployment. When, in a city of 100,000, only one man is unemployed, that is his personal trouble, and for its relief we properly look to the character of the man, his skills, and his immediate opportunities. But when in a nation of 50 million employees, 15 million men are unemployed, that is an issue, and we may not hope to find its solution within the range of opportunities open to any one individual. The very structure of opportunities has collapsed. Both the correct statement of the problem and the range of possible solutions require us to consider the economic and political institutions of the society, and not merely the personal situation and character of a scatter of individuals.

Consider war. The personal problem of war, when it occurs, may be how to survive it or how to die in it with honor; how to make money out of it;

how to climb into the higher safety of the military apparatus; or how to contribute to the war's termination. In short, according to one's values, to find a set of milieux and within it to survive the war or make one's death in it meaningful. But the structural issues of war have to do with its causes; with what types of men it throws up into command; with its effects upon economic and political, family and religious institutions, with the unorganized irresponsibility of a world of nation-states.

Consider marriage. Inside a marriage a man and a woman may experience personal troubles, but when the divorce rate during the first four years of marriage is 250 out of every 1,000 attempts, this is an indication of a structural issue having to do with the institutions of marriage and the family and other institutions that bear upon them.

Or consider the metropolis — the horrible, beautiful, ugly, magnificent sprawl of the great city. For many upper-class people, the personal solution to "the problem of the city" is to have an apartment with private garage under it in the heart of the city, and forty miles out, a house by Henry Hill, garden by Garrett Eckbo, on a hundred acres of private land. In these two controlled environments — with a small staff at each end and a private helicopter connection — most people could solve many of the problems of personal milieux caused by the facts of the city. But all this, however splendid, does not solve the public issues that the structural fact of the city poses. What should be done with this wonderful monstrosity? Break it all up into scattered units, combining residence and work? Refurbish it as it stands? Or, after evacuation, dynamite it and build new cities according to new plans in new places? What should those plans be? And who is to decide and to accomplish whatever choice is made? These are structural issues; to confront them and to solve them requires us to consider political and economic issues that affect innumerable milieux.

In so far as an economy is so arranged that slumps occur, the problem of unemployment becomes incapable of personal solution. In so far as war is inherent in the nation-state system and in the uneven industrialization of the world, the ordinary individual in his restricted milieu will be powerless — with or without psychiatric aid — to solve the troubles this system or lack of system imposes upon him. In so far as the family as an institution turns women into darling little slaves and men into their chief providers and unweaned dependents, the problem of a satisfactory marriage remains incapable of purely private solution. In so far as the overdeveloped megalopolis and the overdeveloped automobile are built-in features of the overdeveloped society, the issues of urban living will not be solved by personal ingenuity and private wealth.

What we experience in various and specific milieux, I have noted, is often caused by structural changes. Accordingly, to understand the changes of many personal milieux we are required to look beyond them. And the number and variety of such structural changes increase as the institutions within which we live become more embracing and more intricately connected with one another. To be aware of the idea of social structure and to use it with sensibility is to be capable of tracing such linkages among a great variety of milieux. To be able to do that is to possess the sociological imagination.

3

What are the major issues for publics and the key troubles of private individuals in our time? To formulate issues and troubles, we must ask what values are cherished yet threatened, and what values are cherished and supported, by the characterizing trends of our period. In the case both of threat and of support we must ask what salient contradictions of structure may be involved.

When people cherish some set of values and do not feel any threat to them, they experience *well-being*. When they cherish values but *do* feel them to be threatened, they experience a crisis — either as a personal trouble or as a public issue. And if all their values seem involved, they feel the total threat of panic.

But suppose people are neither aware of any cherished values nor experience any threat? That is the experience of *indifference*, which, if it seems to involve all their values, becomes apathy. Suppose, finally, they are unaware of any cherished values, but still are very much aware of a threat? That is the experience of *uneasiness*, of anxiety, which, if it is total enough, becomes a deadly unspecified malaise.

Ours is a time of uneasiness and indifference — not yet formulated in such ways as to permit the work of reason and the play of sensibility. Instead of troubles — defined in terms of values and threats — there is often the misery of vague uneasiness; instead of explicit issues there is often merely the beat feeling that all is somehow not right. Neither the values threatened nor whatever threatens them has been stated; in short, they have not been carried to the point of decision. Much less have they been formulated as problems of social science.

In the 'thirties there was little doubt — except among certain deluded business circles — that there was an economic issue which was also a pack of personal troubles. In these arguments about "the crisis of capitalism," the formulations of Marx and the many unacknowledged re-formulations of his work probably set the leading terms of the issue, and some men came to understand their personal troubles in these terms. The values threatened were plain to see and cherished by all; the structural contradictions that threatened them also seemed plain. Both were widely and deeply experienced. It was a political age.

But the values threatened in the era after World War Two are often neither widely acknowledged as values nor widely felt to be threatened. Much private uneasiness goes unformulated; much public malaise and many decisions of enormous structural relevance never become public issues. For those who accept such inherited values as reason and freedom, it is the uneasiness itself that is the trouble; it is the indifference itself that is the issue. And it is this condition, of uneasiness and indifference, that is the signal feature of our period.

All this is so striking that it is often interpreted by observers as a shift in the very kinds of problems that need now to be formulated. We are frequently told that the problems of our decade, or even the crises of our period, have shifted from the external realm of economics and now have to do with the quality of individual life — in fact with the question of whether there is soon going to be anything that can properly be called individual life. Not child labor but comic books, not poverty but mass leisure, are at the center of concern. Many great public issues as well as many private troubles are described in terms of "the psychiatric" — often, it seems, in a pathetic attempt to avoid the large issues and problems of modern society. Often this statement seems to rest upon a provincial narrowing of interest to the Western societies, or even to the United States — thus ignoring two-thirds of mankind; often, too, it arbitrarily divorces the individual life from the larger institutions within which that life is enacted, and which on occasion bear upon it more grievously than do the intimate environments of childhood.

Problems of leisure, for example, cannot even be stated without considering problems of work. Family troubles over comic books cannot be formulated as problems without considering the plight of the contemporary family in its new relations with the newer institutions of the social structure. Neither leisure nor its debilitating uses can be understood as problems without recognition of the extent to which malaise and indifference now form the social and personal climate of contemporary American society. In this climate, no problems of "the private life" can be stated and solved without recognition of the crisis of ambition that is part of the very career of men at work in the incorporated economy.

It is true, as psychoanalysts continually point out, that people do often have "the increasing sense of being moved by obscure forces within themselves which they are unable to define." But it is *not* true, as Ernest Jones asserted, that "man's chief enemy and danger is his own unruly nature and the dark forces pent up within him." On the contrary: "Man's chief danger" today lies in the unruly forces of contemporary society itself, with its alienating methods of production, its enveloping techniques of political domination, its international anarchy — in a word, its pervasive transformations of the very "nature" of man and the conditions and aims of his life.

It is now the social scientist's foremost political and intellectual task — for here the two coincide — to make clear the elements of contemporary uneasiness and indifference. It is the central demand made upon him by other cultural workmen — by physical scientists and artists, by the intellectual community in general. It is because of this task and these demands, I believe, that the social sciences are becoming the common denominator of our cultural period, and the sociological imagination our most needed quality of mind.

II METHODS AND DATA

Morris R. Cohen involved himself throughout his career with the logical distinctions to be made between social sciences and the natural sciences. He dealt with such fundamental problems as the meaning of social statistics, the differences in the kinds of "laws" in natural and social sciences, as well as the logic of scientific analysis. In this brief selection, Cohen raises the problem which we mentioned in the introduction to this section, i.e., the variability of social facts. He also writes on the importance of using operational definitions so as not to compound the inevitable errors. Finally, he discusses a major theoretical problem: labeling. As we shall see in the next section, one can divide the world into numerous categories, but it is important that we recognize that labeling has occurred and determine whether it is theoretically fruitful.

3 Morris R. Cohen

The Variability of Social Facts

. . . The greater complexity and variability of social fact . . . make its . . . theoretical development . . . difficult. In general, social situations are networks in which one cannot change one factor without affecting a great many others. It is, therefore, difficult to determine the specific effects of any one factor. Moreover, social elements seldom admit of simple addition. The behavior of the same individuals in a large group will not in general be the

From William F. Ogburn and Alexander Goldweiser (eds.), *The Social Sciences and Their Interrelations* (Boston: Houghton Mifflin, 1927), pp. 456–459. Reprinted by permission.

same as their behavior in a smaller group. This makes it difficult to apply the mathematical methods which have proved so fruitful in the natural sciences. For these mathematical methods depend upon our ability to pass from a small number of instances to an indefinitely large number by the process of summation or integration.

Where the number of units is indefinitely large we can assume continuity in variation. But the application of continuous curves to very limited groups of figures to which our social observation is usually restricted produces pseudo-science, for example, the assertion that if our distribution is skewed we have a proof of teleology.

The relatively small number of observations that we generally have to deal with in the social sciences makes the application of the probability curve a source of grave errors. For all the mathematical theorems of probability refer only to infinite series (for which we substitute as a practical equivalent "the long run"). Where the number is small there is no assurance that we have eliminated the fallacy of selection. The mathematical errors of applying a continuous curve to a discrete number of observations, produces ludicrous results. We can see this clearly when we try to determine the fundamental unit of our investigation, to wit, when are two social events equally probable? It is vain to expect that the crudeness of our observation and the vagueness of our fundamental categories will be cured by manipulation of the paraphernalia of statistical methods.

Physical categories have themselves been clarified by analysis. The dimensions of the different entities that we talk about — energy, action, momentum, and so on — are numerically determined. In the social sciences the very categories that we use are hazy, subject to variable usage and to confusing suggestion. Does law determine the state, or the state make the law? How many thousands of learned men have discussed this and similar questions without fixing the precise meaning of the terms "state" and "law."[1]

It is a familiar observation that the difficulty of framing exact concepts in the social realm causes much confusion through ambiguity. To this it should be added that vague concepts make possible the constant appeal to vague propositions as self-evidently true. Open any book on social science at random and you will find the author trying to settle issues by appealing to what seems self-evident. Yet most of such self-evident propositions are vague, and when we ask for their precise meaning and for the evidence in their favor, our progress stops. In the natural sciences the questioning of what seems self-evident is relatively simple because when we have a simple proposition we can more readily formulate a true or an exclusive alternative.

---

[1] Before Fourier definitely established the exact "dimensions" of the various physical categories, physicists could dispute (as the Cartesians and the Leibnizians did) as to the proper measure of "living" forces. Social science likewise needs a system of categories the exact dimensions of which are so clear as to make impossible the many confusions of which the example in the text is only one illustration.

In social matters where difference of opinion is greater and demonstration more difficult, we cling all the more tenaciously to our primary assumption, so that our assumptions largely mold what we shall accept as facts.

Any one who naively believes that social facts come to us all finished and that our theories or assumptions must simply fit them, is bound to be shocked in a court of law or elsewhere to find how many facts persons honestly see because they expected them rather than because they objectively happened. That psychoanalysts, economists, sociologists, and moralists labor more or less in the same situation, the tremendous diversity of opinion among them amply indicates. Will a classical anthropologist admit that some Indians had a patriarchal form of kinship before adopting the matriarchal type? Is it a *fact* that the suppression of certain desires, deliberately or as a result of imitation, necessarily produces pathologic states of mind? One has but to scrutinize such questions to see how much must be assumed before it can be shown that any fact is involved.

Is corporal punishment in schools, or free divorce, an evil or not? Under the influence of general opinions one can readily maintain it as a fact that all the consequences of such practices are evil. But one who refuses to admit that these practices are evils can be equally consistent.

Is the same true in the natural sciences? Certainly not to the same extent. Because theories do not to the same extent influence what we shall regard as physical or biologic fact, false theorems have never been such serious obstacles to the progress of natural science. The statements in popular histories that the Ptolemaic, the phlogiston, or the caloric hypothesis stopped the progress of science have no foundation. On the contrary these and other false theories in physics were useful in suggesting new lines of research. It is this fact that led Darwin to remark that false observations (on which others rely) are much more dangerous than false theories to the progress of science. Now in the social sciences we certainly do not have the elaborate safeguards against false observation that the natural sciences with their simpler material and many instruments of precision find it necessary to cultivate. The very circumstance that social facts are apt to be more familiar makes it easier to be misled as to the amount of accurate knowledge that we have about them.

From another point of view we may express this by saying that in the social sciences we are more at the mercy of our authorities with regard to what are the facts. The social worker or field anthropologist has less opportunity to preserve his specimens than the naturalist or the laboratory worker. If a later social worker or field anthropologist finds the fact to be different from what was reported by his predecessor, there is the possibility not only that they have observed different things but also that the social facts have changed.

In this connection it is well to note that the invention of a technical term often creates facts for social science. Certain individuals become *introverts* when the term is invented, just as many persons begin to suffer from a disease the moment they read about it. Psychiatry is full of such technical terms; and if a criminal is rich enough he generally finds experts to qualify his state of mind with a sufficient number of technical terms to overawe those not used to scrutinizing authorities. The technical terms of natural science are useful precisely because they carry no aroma of approval or disapproval with them.

In the following article Samuel Stouffer, who has made important contributions to sociological methodology, gives a good example of how sociologists try to control for their test variables. By using illustrations from various studies he shows how controlled experiments are set up and conducted. In addition, he shows what the criteria for a controlled experiment are and how sociologists try to manipulate their variables so they can get as much control as possible. Note how Stouffer's interest in trying to eliminate extraneous variables relates to Cohen's discussion of the variability of social facts. We can view sociologists' attempts to control as many variables as possible as the approach to validity.

4   SAMUEL STOUFFER

Some Observations on Study Design

As a youth I read a series of vigorous essays in the *Century Magazine* by its editor, the late Glenn Frank. His theme was that the natural sciences had remade the face of the earth; now had arrived the age of the social sciences. The same techniques which had worked their miracles in physics, chemistry, and biology should, in competent hands, achieve equally dazzling miracles in economics, political science, and sociology. That was a long time ago. The disconcerting fact is that people are writing essays just like that today. Of course, the last two decades have seen considerable progress in social science — in theory, in technique, and in the accumulation of data. It is true that the number of practitioners is pitifully few; only a few hundred research studies are reported annually in sociology, for example, as compared with more than twenty thousand studies summarized annually in *Biological Abstracts*. But the bright promise of the period when Frank was writing has not been fulfilled.

From *American Journal of Sociology*, Vol. LV (January, 1950), pp. 355–361. Reprinted by permission of The University of Chicago Press.

Two of the most common reasons alleged for slow progress are cogent, indeed.

The data of social science are awfully complex, it is said. And they involve values which sometimes put a strain on the objectivity of the investigator even when they do not incur resistance from the vested interests of our society. However, an important part of the trouble has very little to do with the subject matter of social science as such but, rather, is a product of our own bad work habits. That is why this paper on the subject of study design may be relevant. So much has been spoken and written on this topic that I make no pretense to originality. But in the course of a little experience, especially in an effort during the war to apply social psychology to military problems, and in an undertaking to nurture a new program of research in my university, I have encountered some frustrations which perhaps can be examined with profit.

A basic problem — perhaps *the* basic problem — lies deeply imbedded in the thoughtways of our culture. This is the implicit assumption that anybody with a little common sense and a few facts can come up at once with the correct answer on any subject. Thus the newspaper editor or columnist, faced with a column of empty space to fill with readable English in an hour, can speak with finality and authority on any social topic, however complex. He might not attempt to diagnose what is wrong with his sick cat; he would call a veterinarian. But he knows precisely what is wrong with any social institution and the remedies.

In a society which rewards quick and confident answers and does not worry about how the answers are arrived at, the social scientist is hardly to be blamed if he conforms to the norms. Hence, much social science is merely rather dull and obscure journalism; a few data and a lot of "interpretation." The fact that the so-called "interpretation" bears little or no relation to the data is often obscured by academic jargon. If the stuff is hard to read, it has a chance of being acclaimed as profound. The rewards are for the answers, however tediously expressed, and not for rigorously marshaled evidence.

In the army no one would think of adopting a new type of weapon without trying it out exhaustively on the firing range. But a new idea about handling personnel fared very differently. The last thing anybody ever thought about was trying out the idea experimentally. I recall several times when we had schemes for running an experimental tryout of an idea in the socio-psychological field. Usually one of two things would happen: the idea would be rejected as stupid without a tryout (it may have been stupid, too) or it would be seized on and applied generally and at once. When the provost marshal wanted us to look into the very low morale of the MP's, our attitude surveys suggested that there was room for very much better selectivity in job assignment. There were routine jobs like guarding prisoners which could be given to the duller MP's, and there were a good many jobs calling for intelligence, discretion, and skill in public relations. We thought that the smarter men might be assigned to these jobs and that the prestige of these jobs would be raised further if a sprinkling of returned veterans with plenty of ribbons and no current assignment could be included among them. We proposed a trial program of a reassignment system in a dozen MP outfits for the purpose of comparing the resulting morale with that in a dozen matched outfits which were left untouched. Did we get anywhere? No. Instead, several of our ideas were put into effect immediately throughout the army without any prior testing at all.

The army cannot be blamed for behavior like that. In social relations it is not the habit in our culture to demand evidence for an idea; plausibility is enough.

To alter the folkways, social science itself must take the initiative. We must be clear in our own minds what proof consists of, and we must, if possible, provide dramatic examples of the advantages of relying on something more than plausibility. And the heart of our problem lies in study design *in advance,* such that the evidence is not capable of a dozen alternative interpretations.

Basically, I think it is essential that we always keep in mind the model of a controlled experiment, even if in practice we may have to deviate from an ideal model. Take the simple accompanying diagram. The test of whether a difference d is attributable to what we think it is attributable to is whether d is significantly larger than d'.

	Before	After	After — Before
Experimental group	x_1	x_2	$d = x_2 - x_1$
Control group	x_1'	x_2'	$d' = x_2' - x_1'$

We used this model over and over again during the war to measure the effectiveness of orientation films in changing soldiers' attitudes. These experiences are described in Volume III of our *Studies in Social Psychology in World War II.*

One of the troubles with using this careful design was that the effectiveness of a single film when thus measured turned out to be so slight. If, instead of using the complete experimental design, we simply took an unselected sample of men and compared the attitudes of those who said they had seen a film with those who said they had not, we got much more impressive differences. This was more rewarding to us, too, for the management wanted to believe the films were powerful medicine. The gimmick was the selective fallibility of memory. Men who correctly remembered seeing the films were likely to be those most sensitized to their message. Men who were bored or indifferent may have actually seen them but slept through them or just forgot.

Most of the time we are not able or not patient enough to design studies containing all four cells as in the diagram above. Sometimes we have only the top two cells, as in the accompanying diagram. In this situation we have two observations of the same individuals or groups taken at different times. This is often a very useful design. In the army, for example, we would take a group of recruits, ascertain their attitudes, and restudy the same men later. From this we could tell whose attitudes changed and in what direction (it was almost always for the worse, which did not endear us to the army!). But exactly what factors in the early training period were most responsible for deterioration of attitudes could only be inferred indirectly.

$$x_1 \quad x_2 \qquad d = x_2 - x_1$$

The panel study is usually more informative than a more frequent design, which might be pictured thus:

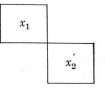

Here at one point in time we have one sample, and at a later point in time we have another sample. We observe that our measure, say, the mean, is greater for the recent sample than for the earlier one. But we are precluded from observing which men or what type of men shifted. Moreover, there is always the disturbing possibility that the populations in our two samples were initially different; hence the differences might not be attributable to conditions taking place in the time interval between the two observations. Thus we would study a group of soldiers in the United States and later ask the same questions of a group of soldiers overseas. Having matched the two groups of men carefully by branch of service, length of time in the army, rank, etc., we hoped that the results of the study would approximate what would be found if the same men could have been studied twice. But this could be no more than a hope. Some important factors could not be adequately controlled, for example, physical conditions. Men who went overseas were initially in better shape on the average than men who had been kept behind; but, if the follow-up study was in the tropics, there was a chance that unfavorable climate already had begun to take its toll. And so it went. How much men overseas changed called for a panel study as a minimum if we were to have much confidence in the findings.

A very common attempt to get the results of a controlled experiment without paying the price is with the design that might be as shown in the accompanying diagram. This is usually what we get with correlation analysis. We have two or more groups of men whom we study at the same point in time.

Thus we have men in the infantry and men in the air corps and compare their attitudes. How much of the difference between x_2' and x_2 we can attribute to experience in a given branch of service and how much is a function of attributes of the men selected for each branch we cannot know assuredly. True, we can try to rule out various possibilities by matching; we can compare men from the two branches with the same age and education, for example. But there is all too often a wide-open gate through which other uncontrolled variables can march.

Sometimes, believe it or not, we have only one cell:

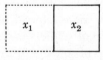

When this happens, we do not know much of anything. But we can still fill pages of social science journals with "brilliant analysis" if we use plausible conjecture in supplying missing cells from our imagination. Thus we may find that the adolescent today has wild ideas and conclude that society is going to the dogs. We fill in the dotted cell representing our own yesterdays with hypothetical data, where x_1 represents us and x_2 our offspring. The tragicomic part is that most of the public, including, I fear, many social sci-

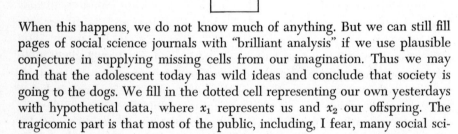

entists, are so acculturated that they ask for no better data.

I do not intend to disparage all research not conforming to the canons of the controlled experiment. I think that we will see more of full experimental design in sociology and social psychology in the future than in the past. But I am well aware of the practical difficulties of its execution, and I know that there are numberless important situations in which it is not feasible at all. What I am arguing for is awareness of the limitations of a design in which crucial cells are missing.

Sometimes by forethought and patchwork we can get approximations which are useful if we are careful to avoid overinterpretation. Let me cite an example:

In Europe during the war the army tested the idea of putting an entire platoon of Negro soldiers into a white infantry outfit. This was done in several companies. The Negroes fought beside white soldiers. After several months we were asked to find out what the white troops thought about the innovation. We found that only 7 per cent of the white soldiers in companies with Negro platoons said that they disliked the idea very much, whereas 62 per cent of the white soldiers in divisions without Negro troops said they would dislike the idea very much if it were tried in their outfits. We have:

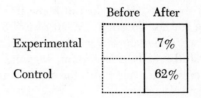

Before   After

Experimental   7%

Control   62%

Now, were these white soldiers who fought beside Negroes men who were naturally more favorable to Negroes than the cross-section of white infantrymen? We did not think so, since, for example, they contained about the same proportion of southerners. The point was of some importance, however, if we were to make the inference that actual experience with Negroes reduced hostility from 62 to 7 per cent. As a second-best substitute, we asked the white soldiers in companies with Negro platoons if they could recall how they felt when the innovation was first proposed. It happens that 67 per cent said they were initially opposed to the idea. Thus we could tentatively fill in a missing cell and conclude that, under the conditions obtaining, there probably had been a marked change in attitude.

Even if this had been a perfectly controlled experiment, there was still plenty of chance to draw erroneous inferences. The conclusions apply only to situations closely approximating those of the study. It happens, for example, that the Negroes involved were men who volunteered to leave rear-area jobs for combat duty. If other Negroes had been involved, the situation might have been different. Moreover, they had white officers. One army colonel who saw this study and whom I expected to ridicule it because he usually opposed innovations, surprised me by offering congratulations. "This proves," he said, "what I have been arguing in all my thirty years in the army — that niggers will do all right if you give 'em white officers!" Moreover, the study applied only to combat experience. Other studies would be needed to justify extending the findings to noncombat or garrison duty. In other words, one lone study, however well designed, can be a very dangerous thing if it is exploited beyond its immediate implications.

Now experiments take time and money, and there is no use denying that we in social science cannot be as prodigal with the replications as the biologist who can run a hundred experiments simultaneously by growing plants in all kinds of soils and conditions. The relative ease of experimentation in much — not all — of natural science goes far to account for the difference in quality of proof demanded by physical and biological sciences, on the one hand, and social scientists, on the other.

Though we cannot always design neat experiments when we want to, we can at least keep the experimental model in front of our eyes and behave cautiously when we fill in missing cells with dotted lines. But there is a further and even more important operation we can perform in the interest of economy. That lies in our choice of the initial problem.

Professor W. F. Ogburn always told his students to apply to a reported research conclusion the test, "How do you know it?" To this wise advice I should like to add a further question: "What of it?" I suspect that if before designing a study we asked ourselves, more conscientiously than we do, whether or not the study really is important, we would economize our energies for the few studies which are worth the expense and trouble of the kind of design I have been discussing.

Can anything be said about guides for selecting problems? I certainly think so. That is where theory comes in and where we social scientists have gone woefully astray.

Theory has not often been designed with research operations in mind. Theory as we have it in social science serves indispensably as a very broad frame of reference or general orientation. Thus modern theories of culture tell us that it is usually more profitable to focus on the learning process and the content of what is learned rather than on innate or hereditary traits. But they do not provide us with sets of interrelated propositions which can be put in the form: If x_1, given x_2 and x_3, then there is strong probability that we get x_4. Most of our propositions of that form, sometimes called "theory," are likely to be ad hoc common-sense observations which are not deducible from more general considerations and which are of the same quality as the observation, "If you stick your hand in a fire and hold it there, you will get burned."

Now in view of the tremendous cost in time and money of the ideal kind of strict empirical research operations, it is obvious that we cannot afford the luxury of conducting them as isolated fact-finding enterprises. Each should seek to be some sort of *experimentum crucis*, and, with rare exceptions, that will only happen if we see its place *beforehand* in a more general scheme of things. Especially, we need to look for situations where two equally plausible hypotheses deducible from more general theory lead to the expectation of different consequences. Then, if our evidence supports one and knocks out the other, we have accomplished something.

The best work of this sort in our field is probably being done today in laboratory studies of learning and of perception. I do not know of very good sociological examples. Yet in sociology experiments are possible. One of the most exciting, for example, was that initiated long before the war by Shaw and McKay to see whether co-operative effort by adult role models within a delinquent neighborhood would reduce juvenile delinquency. So many variables are involved in a single study like that that it is not easy to determine which were crucial. But there was theory behind the study, and the experimental design provided for controlling at least some variables.

It may be that in sociology we will need much more thinking and many more descriptive studies involving random ratlike movements on the part of the researcher before we can even begin to state our problems so that they are in decent shape for fitting into an ideal design. However, I think that we can reduce to some extent the waste motion of the exploratory period if we try to act as if we have some a priori ideas and keep our eyes on the possible relevance of data to these ideas. This is easier said than done. So many interesting rabbit tracks are likely to be uncovered in the exploratory stages of research that one is tempted to chase rabbits all over the woods and forget what his initial quarry was.

Exploratory research is of necessity fumbling, but I think that the waste motion can be reduced by the self-denying ordinance of deliberately limiting ourselves to a few variables at a time. Recently two of my colleagues and myself have been doing a little exploratory work on a problem in the general area of social mobility. We started by tabulating some school records of fifty boys in the ninth grade of one junior high school and then having members of our seminar conduct three or four interviews with each boy and his parents. We had all the interviews written up in detail, and we had enough data to fill a book — with rather interesting reading, too. But it was a very wasteful process because there were just too many intriguing ideas. We took a couple of ideas which were deducible from current general theory and tried to make some simple fourfold tables. It was obvious that, with a dozen variables uncontrolled, such tables meant little or nothing. But that led us to a second step. Now we are trying to collect school records and a short questionnaire on two thousand boys. We will not interview all these boys and their parents in detail. But, with two thousand cases to start with, we hope to take a variable in which we are interested and find fifty boys who are plus on it and fifty who are minus, yet who are approximately alike on a lot of other things. A table based on such matched comparisons should be relatively unambiguous. We can take off from there and interview those selected cases intensively to push further our exploration of the nexus between theory and observation. This, we think, will be economical, though still exploratory. Experimental manipulation is far in the future in our problem, but we do hope we can conclude the first stage with a statement of some hypotheses susceptible to experimental verification.

I am not in the least deprecating exploratory work. But I do think that some orderliness is indicated even in the bright dawn of a youthful enterprise.

One reason why we are not more orderly in our exploratory work is that all too often what is missing is a sharp definition of a given variable, such that, if we wanted to take a number of cases and even throw them into a simple fourfold table, we could.

Suppose we are studying a problem in which one of the variables we are looking for is overprotection or overindulgence of a child by his mother. We have a number of case histories or questionnaires. Now how do we know whether we are sorting them according to this variable or not? The first step, it would seem, is to have some way of knowing whether we are sorting them along any single continuum, applying the same criteria to each case. But to know this we need to have built into the study the ingredients of a scale. Unless we have some such ingredients in our data, we are defeated from the start. This is why I think the new interest social scientists are taking in scaling techniques is so crucially important to progress. In particular, the latent-structure theory developed by Paul F. Lazarsfeld, which derives Louis Guttman's scale as an important special case, is likely to be exceedingly useful, for it offers criteria by which we can make a small amount of information go a long way in telling us the logical structure of a supposed variable we are eager to identify. The details of Guttman's and Lazarsfeld's work are likely to promote a good deal of attack and controversy. Our hope is that this will stimulate others to think such problems out still better and thus make their work obsolete as rapidly as possible.

Trying to conduct a social science investigation without good criteria for knowing whether a particular variable may be treated as a single dimension is like trying to fly without a motor in the plane. Students of the history of invention point out that one reason why the airplane, whose properties had been pretty well thought out by Leonardo da Vinci, was so late in development was the unavailability of a lightweight power plant, which had to await the invention of the internal combustion motor. We are learning more and more how to make our lightweight motors in social science, and that augurs well for the future. But much work is ahead of us. In particular, we desperately need better projective techniques and better ways of getting respondents to reveal attitudes which are too emotionally charged to be accessible to direct questioning. Schemes like the latent-structure theory of Lazarsfeld should speed up the process of developing such tests.

I have tried to set forth the model of the controlled experiment as an ideal to keep in the forefront of our minds even when by necessity some cells are missing from our design. I have also tried to suggest that more economy and orderliness are made possible — even in designing the exploratory stages of a piece of research — by using theory in advance to help us decide whether a particular inquiry would be important if we made it; by narrowing down the number of variables; and by making sure that we can classify our data along a particular continuum, even if only provisionally. And a central, brooding hope is that we will have the modesty to recognize the difference between a promising idea and proof.

Oh, how we need that modesty! The public expects us to deal with great problems like international peace, full employment, maximization of industrial efficiency. As pundits we can pronounce on such matters; as citizens we have a duty to be concerned with them; but as social scientists our greatest achievement now will be to provide a few small dramatic examples that hypotheses in our field can be stated operationally and tested crucially. And we will not accomplish that by spending most of our time writing or reading papers like this one. We will accomplish it best by rolling up our sleeves and working at the intricacies of design of studies which, though scientifically strategic, seem to laymen trivial compared with the global concerns of the atomic age. Thereby, and only thereby, I believe, can we some day have the thrilling sense of having contributed to the structure of a social science which is cumulative.

This article by a criminologist illustrates some of the basic problems of empirical research. It also shows how a study is organized, some of the basic steps involved in setting up a study, carrying out the investigation, and finally altering research plans when the initial design proved to be unworkable. Voss also illustrates the general procedure of social surveys.

5 Harwin L. Voss

Pitfalls in Social Research: A Case Study

Increasingly in professional and lay circles attention is being given to the difficulties arising in the conduct of research.[1] This is a report on public reaction to a longitudinal sociological investigation done in a community in Southern California; the description of this case is intended as a commentary on the pitfalls of research in a public school setting in which administrators are subject to considerable pressure from local groups. This case

From *American Sociologist*, Vol. I (May, 1966), pp. 136–140. Reprinted by permission of the author and the American Sociological Association.

[1] "Communications to the Editor," *The American Sociologist*, 1 (November, 1965), pp. 24–27; John Lear, "Do We Need New Rules for Experiments on People?" *Saturday Review*, XLIX (February 5, 1966), pp. 61–70.

occurred in a western state characterized by a vocal right-wing political element and might be considered unique to this milieu, except that similar situations have arisen in other locales.[2]

The research was undertaken by a team of three sociologists under a grant from the National Institute of Mental Health. The aim of this research was to explore the nature of the relationship between an individual's school experiences and subsequent dropout or delinquent behavior. The research was to be conducted in schools operated by two contiguous school districts. The city district served a Negro ghetto; the suburban district had a sizeable Mexican-American population. Eight junior high schools were selected on the basis of the socio-economic and racial characteristics of the population in their attendance areas. These schools, as well as the senior high schools to which their graduates were assigned, afforded a variety of social milieux: some of the schools were homogeneous and others heterogeneous with respect to social class and race. The study incorporated a longitudinal design covering the respondents' four years of high school. In the first year questionnaires were to be administered to *all* ninth grade students in their classrooms and the mother or mother-surrogate of each child was to be interviewed. Students in the ninth grade of each school were to be enumerated; a sample was deemed inappropriate for examination of the formal and informal aspects of the school as a social system. In addition, any type of sample would allow the inference that the students selected in some way had been identified as "potential dropouts." In other words, while the results of the study would have bearing on applied or action efforts, this project was designed as basic or "pure" research in which hypotheses derived from contemporary sociological theory would be tested.

There has been a growing concern in recent years about the problem of school dropouts, although the proportion of students completing high school is increasing. Yet, in a highly complex technological society school dropout is considered a potential waste of human resources; that is to say, there is a high degree of public interest in school dropouts. In short, this research was not addressed to an esoteric sociological problem but to one with practical implications. Nevertheless, difficulties arose in the conduct of the research. The remainder of this paper is devoted to answering the question, what went wrong? To answer this query requires brief consideration of the origin of the study.

[2] There is no need to identify the city in which this experience occurred. Consequently, the names of the school districts are masked, and the names of the schools, school administrators, and politicians are fictitious. The purpose of this paper is to increase awareness of sensitive spots and the potential pitfalls of conducting research in a politically sensitive educational establishment, not retribution. Cf. Gwynn Nettler, "Test Burning in Texas," *American Psychologist*, 14 (1959), pp. 682–683; Leonard D. Eron and Leopold O. Walder, "Test Burning: II," *American Psychologist*, 16 (May, 1961), pp. 237–244.

ORIGIN OF THE STUDY

Two years prior to the initiation of the study, representatives of the city school district approached the investigators and suggested the possibility of conducting basic research concerning dropouts. Recognizing the need for such research, they were also aware that they could not obtain federal funds for basic research because they had neither the requisite facilities or personnel. A number of meetings were held and it was agreed that a study should be undertaken in which the sociologists would be in charge of the design and execution of the research. The school district would cooperate with the investigators by providing access to student respondents and records; and, the schools would benefit in that the research results would serve as a basis for deriving practical procedures for dealing with potential dropouts. The research team worked closely with the various assistant and associate superintendents and the research director of the school system in developing the research design, means of implementing the design, and in the construction of research instruments. According to these officials, the only pertinent school board policy concerning research, other than that it must be approved by the research director, was one which prohibited the use of sociometrics.[3] The closest thing to a sociometric question in the rough draft of the questionnaire was one which inquired, "What group of students here in school do you go around with most often?" We were assured that this would not be construed as a sociometric question. The school personnel maintained that it was not necessary to obtain the approval of the school board, because authority to approve research projects had been delegated to the Research Director. We recognized that approval from the highest levels was desirable, but were also informed that the organizational scheme precluded the necessity of such approval.

PITFALLS

One of the most serious pitfalls encountered in this research project was the problem of communication within a complex organization. The city district is one of the twenty largest school districts in the country; yet it did not have adequate channels of communication linking the several levels of management, namely, (1) the top administrator, the superintendent, (2) the superintendent's council or middle management, including line and staff officers, viz., the several assistant and associate superintendents, the Director of Guidance, the Research Director, and (3) the line officers, the principals. This problem was first evident in a meeting with all of the junior and senior high school principals, some fifty persons, that was arranged to provide the

---

[3] Some fifteen years earlier a teacher working on a Master's degree had employed a sociometric inventory and the students learned the results. To satisfy the irate parents, the board had prohibited the use of sociometrics.

administrators at this level with specific information concerning the procedures which the researchers had worked out with the assistant and associate
superintendents and the research director to implement the design, including
a pretest of the questionnaire. In this meeting, open hostility was encountered; the principals were only vaguely aware of the nature and purpose of
the research. For example, the principals did not understand why the researchers, as "outsiders" to the educational establishment, were conducting
the investigation, rather than school personnel. They suggested that many
parents would object to having their offspring complete the confidential, but
not anonymous, questionnaire and would, as a consequence, react negatively
to the school board's appeal to raise the property tax level.[4] The principals
were apparently unaware that the Research Director and Associate Superintendent had given formal support and approval for the research design in
a letter which accompanied the grant application some months earlier. Nor
were they apprised of the fact that the Research Director, Director of Guidance, and Associate Superintendent had given informal approval of the draft
of the questionnaire as a pretest instrument.

Despite this breakdown in communication, a pretest was arranged. The
school distributed a letter to the pretest subjects to take home to their
parents, informing them of the date that the questionnaire would be administered. This letter further stated: ". . . recognizing the value of such
knowledge, the [city] District has approved the conduct of this study, and
is arranging for information to be gathered from a cross-section of [city]
students." Approximately 200 students completed the pretest questionnaire.
There were no objections regarding procedure or the nature of the instrument and no claims were made that we did not have approval to administer
the questionnaire.

Since only informal approval of the methods of implementing the research
design, including the questionnaire, had been obtained, official clearance of
the complete study was requested. In response, the Associate Superintendent, who had been appointed liaison between the school district and the researchers, stated: "We are happy to inform you that the [city] District plans
to continue cooperating with you in the completion of the School Dropout
Project. The schedule which you outline appears satisfactory."[5] While vague,
this message apparently was not communicated to the Superintendent. An
additional pretest of the questionnaire was made in the surburban district.
Since this was a smaller district in terms of student enrollment, the re-

[4] By way of explanation, a former tax override election authorized taxation to a maximum of $2.80 per $100 valuation, but this was a temporary authorization and was due
to expire. The maximum rate would then revert to $2.00 per $100 valuation; the schools
were asking for a $3.60 maximum.

[5] At the end of the 1962 academic year the city schools abolished the research department and eliminated other services as part of an economy move; the functions of the
research department, insofar as this investigation was concerned, were assigned to an
Associate Superintendent, i.e., he was to serve as liaison between the district and the
research team.

searchers worked primarily with the Assistant Superintendent and the Supervisor of Attendance and Student Welfare. Approval was obtained from these officials, as well as from the board of education, to include schools in this district.

THE INVESTIGATION

A week before the students in the first two city schools, Alpha and Beta, were to be interviewed in normal classroom groups, notices were sent home with each of them advising the parents that their children would be participating in a study conducted by a local institution of higher learning in co-operation with the school district. The letter indicated the general nature of the study in terms of "student interests and opinions," but did not include the term "dropout." The name of one of the investigators and his campus telephone numbers were given with the suggestion that the parents call him if there was any question they wished to ask about the study. We had a few calls from parents who were concerned about the behavior of their off-spring. One or two parents were concerned about the confidentiality of the information obtained. In all such contacts with the public we were quite candid in our description of the research; and we never disguised the fact that we were interested in learning why students dropped out of high school prior to graduation. We indicated that any parent who wanted to see the questionnaire could come to our office and read through it, and we would explain the purpose of any or all items. Callers were assured that there were no questions concerning sex, religion, or politics. The only person who called who was quite negative about the study was opposed to it on the grounds that it should be done in the elementary schools rather than in the high schools.

The principal of the Alpha school, Charles Green, received a few calls from parents, and as we had previously informed the principals, these parents were told that their children would not be included in the study, if the parents so desired. Two parents called to inform the principal that they did not want their child to participate in the study; five others sent notes to the school expressing similar sentiments. One boy simply indicated to us that his parents had told him not to complete the questionnaire. Of some 550 students, 8 refusals did not seem excessive. Nevertheless, one of the investigators personally contacted the parents who had objected and informed them that their children would *not* be asked to complete a questionnaire. This appeared to be a minor problem, for a number of the people who objected identified themselves to the researcher as members of a small, militant religious sect. In fact, this accounted for 5 of the 8 refusals.

Having completed our interviewing in the Alpha school, we received a call from the Superintendent of Schools, who asked us to confer with him about the project. At this meeting, which was attended by all members of the Superintendent's council except the Superintendent, we were told that the central office had received numerous complaints about our study, and that while the schools wished to continue cooperation with us, some of the callers had threatened to make the study an issue in the forthcoming tax override election. Consequently, we agreed that it might be best to postpone further administration of the questionnaire until after the tax override election the following month. We were told that after the election, we could proceed.

A second aspect of the communication problem in the district's administrative structure appeared in the hastily called meeting with the school officials. Simply put, the line and staff officers in middle management, with whom we had worked, were not as powerful, in the sense of having access to the Superintendent, as was an Assistant Superintendent, a Mr. Black, who had been on extended sick leave. In the meeting he indicated that if he had been present, the project would have been approved only over his strenuous objection, though it was now too late to do anything. This however was not the case, for the Superintendent and the school board relied heavily upon Mr. Black's judgment.

CANCELLATION

Ten days after the meeting, we were informed by means of a letter from the Superintendent that the city schools could no longer cooperate with us in our research project. He indicated that the questionnaire could no longer be used because it violated "a district-wide policy . . . prohibiting the use of sociometric instruments within the class rooms."

A month later, public disclosure of the fact that the "dropout study was cancelled in [the city]" was made on the front page of the evening newspaper. We were given the sub-headline below the banner line indicating that Sinatra's son had been kidnapped. The Superintendent was quoted to the effect that the reasons the study was halted were two-fold: (1) We did not have approval for the research project, and (2) the questions about family life in the questionnaire were against Board of Education policy. The first issue, whether or not approval had been granted, is a thorny one. While we had the approval of the Associate Superintendent who had been appointed liaison between the school system and the project staff, we had nothing in writing from the Superintendent giving his general approval of the study, nor did we have his written approval of the questionnaire — though, as noted earlier, it had been indicated that this was unnecessary. As the Superintendent noted in the press, his staff "had made a slip-up somewhere." Two days later he said that official approval was his responsibility, though a Board of Education ruling was unnecessary. However, the notice, which the schools distributed to the parents, indicated the school's approval of the study, and according to the state's Education Code, distribution of a letter such as this implied approval of the study by the district. Further, the press noted the following: "Charles Green, principal of Alpha Junior High, said questionnaires were given to his students 'with permission of the district.

Approval came through to me from the Education Center through normal channels,' Green said."

The second point, concerning sociometrics, contained no mention of the item which inquired about the student's friends. The paper quoted the Superintendent as follows: "The sociometric questions (those about the family) are in bad taste, to put it bluntly. These are prying questions about family relationships. It is an encroachment on individual liberty and privacy." This is a rather unusual definition of the term "sociometrics," to say the least. It was clear in our earlier contacts with the school personnel that they were all using the term "sociometric" in its technical sense — questions requiring both positive and negative choices which would allow a determination of group structure, such as, What three persons would you *most* like to sit next to in class?; What three persons would you *least* like to sit next to in class? This definition apparently was not shared by the Superintendent — another problem in communication.

In the following three days, as the controversy was discussed in the press, spokesmen for the city schools revealed items from the questionnaire to the press when they could have simply stated that there was disagreement on the use of some items. Questions were thus misquoted, taken out of context, and questionable and even absurd interpretations as to their purpose or intention were made. For example, Mr. Black was quoted as saying, "The questionnaire asks children 'Do your parents always understand you?' Now what adolescent can say his parents truly understand him? So a youngster may have to answer negatively. But if he does, someone may start investigating him to see if he's a potential dropout." This question was, in fact, not asked. In addition, potential dropouts[6] would never be so identified on the basis of their response to a single item such as this. Further, this study proposed *no* special treatment or investigation for those identified as potential dropouts. The research design specified that school authorities were not to be notified which students were identified as potential dropouts. An attempt to develop a valid predictive instrument *requires* that those identified as potential dropouts receive no special treatment. In this same vein, the press incorrectly indicated that we asked students which parent they like most and whose decisions they value more.

The Superintendent appointed a seven-man committee to confer with us

---

[6] The researchers were cognizant of the issues involved in formally designating high school students as "potential deviants" and invading the privacy of individuals and families under the guise of "treatment." The theory guiding this research was that of Cohen, Cloward & Ohlin, Miller, Gordon, Coleman and Turner. Hopefully, the outcome of the study would be (1) the testing of hypotheses derived from these sources, i.e., of general sociological significance, and (2) identification of some structural sources of strain in the school situation which might be altered to permit retention of a higher proportion of intellectually capable students in the high school. In short, the goal of providing a high school education for those who could benefit by such training was explicitly recognized; however, it was *not* assumed that *all* students should remain in school or that those who terminated their education prior to high school graduation were in any sense deviants.

to see if the questionnaire might be modified to make its use permissible within the school district. Three of the members of the committee had given informal approval to our instrument; however, the chairman of the committee was Mr. Black, who previously had expressed his displeasure with the questionnaire. We met with the committee and discussed the questionnaire. Mr. Black indicated that at least one-third of the questionnaire was objectionable to some of the committee members. We proposed that the questionnaire be administered only in the two junior high schools which served the Negro community; further, since the primary objection to the questionnaire appeared to be that some of the questions "invaded the privacy" of parents and children, we offered to secure the written permission of each parent prior to the administration of the questionnaire. This clearly made participation in the study voluntary and seemed to eliminate any objection on the grounds of "invasion of privacy." While this would pose an additional difficulty, it could be handled in our efforts to obtain parental interviews. Our proposals were rejected, and a simple majority of the committee of school personnel voted that the questionnaire in its present form violated school district policies and should not be given again in the city schools.

A hearing was scheduled by the city Board of Education. Speakers, pro and con, appeared. Since each was required to state his or her name and address, it was possible to determine that, with only one or two exceptions, the speakers were not parents of children in the study population. They objected on principle to the idea of questioning students as an invasion of privacy.

Among the speakers favoring the project was an internationally known psychologist. His competence was challenged by one board member. This man then asked, "Have you met with Mr. Black and discussed this study with him? Do you think you're qualified to say that we haven't made much of a study of the dropout problem?" Undoubtedly the fact that the study consisted of basic research and did not constitute an attempt "to do something about the problem" contributed to the negative view of the board.

The researchers may have erred in not demanding board approval at the start, but the area of community support was clearly neglected. In retrospect, greater efforts to forestall complications in dealing with students should have been made, though we thought our efforts had been sufficiently extensive. It is here that the culpability of the investigators lies; as sociologists we should have been more aware of the importance of community relations, particularly the importance of special interest groups. It was just such a group that heard of the study and brought pressure to bear in the right quarters. Committed to the belief that if a few dissidents complain loudly enough they may be mistaken for a sizeable number or even a majority, the opposition besieged the office of the school district with telephone calls protesting the study. Surprisingly, few letters were sent. The deluge came after the Superintendent had temporarily halted the study. In his eagerness to avoid controversy prior to the tax election, the Superintendent indicated weakness or his vulnerability to a full scale attack by an organized pressure group. Aware that nothing sways public officials more than an avalanche of phone calls or mail, the opponents, in this case presumably part of the radical right, made the most of their opportunity, and enjoyed the advantage of having struck first. Unfortunately, those with conflicting viewpoints were neither as well organized nor as united in purpose. While greatly outnumbering their more aggressive extremist neighbors, they were far less vocal, and expressed their resentment, if any, to each other instead of making their voices heard where it counts — in the district office where the Superintendent makes decisions. While many outstanding members of the community rallied behind us when the controversy broke in the newspapers, their efforts proved unsuccessful. A succinct description which appeared in a local independent newspaper sums up what transpired:

> "[The city] provided the nation with yet another example of official gutlessness in the face of right-wing bluster this week when the city schools halted a federally financed study of the critical school dropout problem.
>
> Superintendent Brown bowed to demands by two right-of-Goldwater legislators and halted a $200,000 survey by a . . . College team trying to learn why pupils quit school before their education is completed.
>
> Brown's vague excuses notwithstanding, the real reason for the interruption is that Assemblyman White and State Senator Gray, both [City] Republicans, demanded it."

With this interpretation one must agree. Although it would be difficult to document this, the most insistent objectors apparently were members of radical right organizations, and they undoubtedly conveyed their protests directly to State Senator Gray and Assemblyman White, as well as to the school personnel. These conservative legislators apparently let their interest in the matter be known at school headquarters.

In a meeting with representatives of those opposed to the study we encountered an astonishing view. It was suggested, in all seriousness, that the federal government had contacted us because of our liberal viewpoint, and requested that we assess the personality of students so that those with right-wing tendencies could be committed to institutions as psychotic when they reached their majority. The project was conceived as a gigantic plot to obtain information on all ninth graders in the area, and that the data would be sent to a permanent file in Washington, D.C., so that it could be used in the future against anyone opposing the federal government. It was felt that in this way, in time, it would be possible for the Democrats to win control of a traditionally Republican area.

Why the alarm over questionnaires in the schools? It apparently stems from the suspicion of some that questionnaires not only invade privacy but also are a technique to weaken the moral fibre of students, thereby rendering them susceptible to Communist brainwashing and into acceptance of such evils as one-worldism, under which the United States would lose sovereignty to the United Nations. Intimate questions regarding sex, religion, and politics are usually cited and, according to the critics, these are calculated to plant seeds of doubt about the validity of old-fashioned morality, spiritualism, patriotism, and parental authority. The fact that we asked no questions about sex, religion, or politics was really immaterial. We were, after all, supported by a federal grant, and worst of all, the National Institute of *Mental Health*. While the issue was posed publicly as one of invasion of privacy, a variety of private reasons may have motivated the opponents, including generalized opposition to the federal government, federal financing of social research, and the mental health movement.

The position of the radical right was expressed in December, 1963, by Goldwater in his column, "How Do You Stand, Sir?" Goldwater begins, "As the result of a rather slick bit of parliamentary legerdemain, your child and mine may be forced to answer questions concerning the most intimate family relationships and other subjects no adult American could now be made to answer, even in court." He then notes that such investigations are often financed by the federal government. He adds that under the heading of "testing," students have been made to tell their inquisitors whether they have had sexual relations, have ever broken into warehouses, have stolen money, have fought physically with their parents. He notes, "They also have been asked which of their parents is fairer in meting out punishment and whether they wish their parents had as much money and education as do the parents of their classmates. Obviously, the replies to many of these questions could be self-incriminating, and any student would be well within his rights in refusing to answer them."

While I agree with the former Senator that the student may, if he wishes, refuse to complete a questionnaire, the answers he provides on a confidential, or as is often the case, an anonymous questionnaire, are not obviously self-incriminating. It is relevant that in 1961 and again in 1963, Goldwater introduced an amendment to the National Defense Education Act (NDEA) providing that no federal funds "shall provide for the conduct of any test, or the asking of any question in connection therewith, which is designed to elicit information dealing with the personality, environment, home life, parental or family relationships, economic status or sociological or psychological problems of the student tested."

PICKING UP THE PIECES

Cancellation of the study in the city district fortunately did not result in its termination. Upon receiving the Superintendent's letter, we contacted the suburban school district officials and magnanimously agreed to accept their earlier suggestion that we include their entire ninth grade population in the study. We requested that the study be presented to the Board of Education; the project was approved unanimously. The respondents lost through the action of the Superintendent were partially offset by inclusion of additional schools in the suburban district; with one significant exception these schools offered the same types of students which would have been obtained in the city schools. However, the vast majority of Negro respondents were to be obtained in two city schools. A school district elsewhere in the state proved to be an ideal source for this segment of the proposed study population, and this district offered full cooperation.

DISCUSSION

In this controversy the radical right raised one pertinent ethical question, and that pertains to the "invasion of privacy." While it is true that many, if not the vast majority of Americans, have no objection to the types of research in which sociologists and psychologists are interested, precautions must be taken to avoid inclusion of unwilling subjects. One costly and difficult alternative to the assumption that adults will not object to having students provide personal information is to obtain prior permission, in writing, from a parent or guardian. In the coming years such a complicating step may be necessary to avoid public controversy.

The "rights" of subjects have never been spelled out in sociology and psychology, as in law and medicine. At a minimum, a subject if he so wishes, has the right *not* to be studied, a dictum often violated when the subjects are prison inmates or college sophomores. In addition, the subject in behavioral science research has the right to expect that information provided will not be used to damage him. Damage could, of course, occur in a multitude of ways, and not all of these can be anticipated. Minor disturbance on the part of some subjects may be unavoidable, and may be tolerated if the subjects have agreed to participate in the research, perhaps in response to a vague appeal for the "advancement of knowledge." It is also apparent that the confidentiality of information gathered by means of questionnaires, interviews, and other techniques must be jealously guarded.

In addition to protecting the rights of his subjects, an investigator must recognize his obligation to his professional colleagues, i.e., he must guard his colleagues' right to conduct research.[7] This means that in his research, one must avoid, if possible, creation of suspicion and hostility toward future research. The point, of course, is that the prevailing climate of opinion among the radical right is one of suspicion; this suspicion is in part the outgrowth of previous research in which mischievous questions were asked, e.g., concerning whether it is worse to defile the American flag or the Bible. The salience of religious, familial and nationalistic commitments may be a

---

[7] At the time the notices of this study were distributed in the Beta Junior High School, an experimental sex education program under Mr. Black's supervision was concluded with a rather detailed examination of human anatomy and the mechanics of sexual reproduction. It was learned informally that the only letter received by the Board of Education at the time the study was terminated which condemned this research project referred to the testing, in depth, of junior high school students' comprehension of sexual processes. The extent to which the two studies were confused is not known.

legitimate area of inquiry; however, discretion is a prerequisite of analyses in emotion-laden areas.

Concentration on the response of the radical right in this paper might give an erroneous impression. In other contexts, the question of invasion of privacy is a basic concern of those with the diametrically opposite political stance, as, for example, the concern about adolescent's civil rights in juvenile court proceedings. This point is noted to underscore the crucial importance of carefully heeding the rights of subjects in the conduct of research.

CONCLUSION

Certain general principles concerning the conduct of research are evident in this commentary. These are noted as suggestions to other investigators interested in conducting research in conjunction with a complex organization. First, in order to avoid comparable difficulties, one must obtain formal approval for research endeavors from the highest level possible, i.e., those with final authority. The structure of a complex organization, with a system of delegated authority, may all but preclude obtaining approval from the highest echelon; yet this appears to be essential. Although one often has to work out details with middle management, in the case of research in a public school setting approval of the superintendent and board of education is mandatory to be assured of full cooperation. The approval of a staff officer assigned the function of liaison is insufficient.

Two additional suggestions are relevant to the task of obtaining adequate approval and cooperation. One must establish and maintain channels of communication with the various levels of the organization. Such channels may not be available within the organization. This was particularly evident in the principals' lack of awareness of the nature and purpose of the study and in the Superintendent's lack of familiarity with procedures agreed upon by the researchers and middle management. In addition, lack of familiarity with the structure of the organization may spell disaster. For some time sociologists have recognized that persons without portfolio may influence the decision of the titular head of the organization. The only means of avoiding such a problem is to obtain unequivocal support from the highest level possible.

As a final suggestion for future researchers, it is apparently essential, particularly in politically sensitive areas of the country, to establish a "steering committee" or some similar vehicle to inform significant figures in the community of the intent and purpose of one's research; in this way, those who might, through misinformation, become opponents of the research can be made into supporters. This approach has the additional advantage of offering the school district support from community leaders if crises occur. School districts are dependent in large measure upon the local community for financial support; as a consequence, superintendents may be expected to heed the pleadings of a special interest group unless broad support in the community has been established.

PART TWO

BASIC PATTERNS
AND IMAGES OF ORDER

In this section and all those following we will do three basic things. First, we want to give illustrations of the ideas and concepts that are being used. Usually these illustrations are non-empirical, theoretical discussions. Second, we wish to illustrate the dynamics of these ideas and concepts by referring to specific cases. Finally, we will give an example of an empirical study, using the particular concept, to show how it is operationally defined and researched.

In this part we will examine the specific ways in which sociologists have decided to look at their work and the concepts they use for this purpose. As we said above, different disciplines approach the same phenomena from different perspectives. Human society is investigated simultaneously by the anthropologist, biologist, sociologist, geographer, historian, or medical researcher. In some cases, the disciplines will have much in common, because they use similar signs, concepts, etc., to define what they see.

Culture is grist for the sociologist, for it is culture that provides the social material from which humans are made. Symbolic communication is the way in which men transmit elements of the culture to one another and from one generation to the next. Socialization includes the general manner in which the transmission takes place and the stages involved in becoming a human being. First, we will see what is transmitted; second, how humans communicate so that transmission can take place; and, finally, the general stages in transmitting and creating the self will be examined. The last basic image is that of associations. Associations are the many ways in which man relates to others. The type of association is intimately related to the type of socialization that goes on, as will be seen in an examination of primary and secondary groups. It is important to realize that society is fluid and that socialization in this society, and the methods of socialization and communication, are continually being altered. Socialization is a lifetime process.

III CULTURE

A. Definitions and Concepts

Clyde Kluckhohn, an anthropologist, was one of the first social scientists to begin to analytically investigate the concept of culture. It is culture which determines what foods a person will like, whether he will think another beautiful or ugly, what gods he will worship, what he sees in the world. Culture is learned behavior, a set of techniques allowing the individual to adapt to the world around him. This learning takes place in a group which defines the appropriate way of responding to the patterns of nature. With continued use of the concept, it was found inadequate to explain certain phenomena. In a larger society such as the United States there were ethnic groups possessing a cultural system which, though not totally at variance with the dominant culture, was different. Usually, the cultures of ethnic groups within a larger society were referred to as "subcultures." However, the word came to be applied to various groups, such as religious cults and sects, or delinquent gangs. J. Milton Yinger recognized this problem, and in the following article introduces a new concept, "contraculture," in order to deal with some of the problems in definition.

6 J. Milton Yinger

Contraculture and Subculture

In recent years there has been widespread and fruitful employment of the concept of subculture in sociological and anthropological research. The term

From *American Sociological Review*, Vol. XXV (October, 1960), pp. 625–635. Reprinted by permission of the author and the American Sociological Association.

has been used to focus attention not only on the wide diversity of norms to be found in many societies but on the normative aspects of deviant behavior. The ease with which the term has been adopted, with little study of its exact meaning or its values and its difficulties, is indicative of its utility in emphasizing a sociological point of view in research that has been strongly influenced both by individualistic and moralistic interpretations. To describe the normative qualities of an occupation, to contrast the value systems of social classes, or to emphasize the controlling power of the code of a delinquent gang is to underline a sociological aspect of these phenomena that is often disregarded.

In the early days of sociology and anthropology, a key task was to document the enormous variability of culture from society to society and to explore the significance of the overly simplified but useful idea that "the mores can make anything right." In recent years that task has been extended to the study of the enormous variability of culture *within* some societies. It is unfortunate that "subculture," a central concept in this process, has seldom been adequately defined.[1] It has been used as an ad hoc concept whenever a writer wished to emphasize the normative aspects of behavior that differed from some general standard. The result has been a blurring of the meaning of the term, confusion with other terms, and a failure frequently to distinguish between two levels of social causation.

THREE USAGES OF SUBCULTURE

Few concepts appear so often in current sociological writing. In the course of twelve months, I have noted over 100 books and articles that make some use, from incidental to elaborate, of the idea of "subculture." The usages vary so widely, however, that the value of the term is severely limited. If chemists had only one word to refer to all colorless liquids and this led them to pay attention to only the two characteristics shared in common, their analysis would be exceedingly primitive. Such an analogy overstates the diversity of ideas covered by "subculture," but the range is very wide. Nevertheless three distinct meanings can be described.

---

[1] There are a few formal definitions. For example: "The term 'subculture' refers in this paper to 'cultural variants displayed by certain segments of the population.' Subcultures are distinguished not by one or two isolated traits — they constitute relatively cohesive cultural systems. They are worlds within the larger world of our national culture." (Mirra Komarovsky and S. S. Sargent, "Research into Subcultural Influences upon Personality," in S. S. Sargent and M. W. Smith, editors, *Culture and Personality*, New York: The Viking Fund, 1949, p. 143). These authors then refer to class, race, occupation, residence, and region. After referring to sub-group values and language, Kimball Young and Raymond W. Mack state: "Such shared learned behaviors which are common to a specific group or category are called *subcultures*." (*Sociology and Social Life*, New York: American Book, 1959, p. 49.) They refer then to ethnic, occupational, and regional variations. Blaine Mercer writes: "A society contains numerous subgroups, each with its own characteristic ways of thinking and acting. These cultures within a culture are called *subcultures*." (*The Study of Society*, New York: Harcourt, Brace, 1958, p. 34.) Thereafter he discusses Whyte's *Streetcorner Society*. Although these definitions are helpful, they fail to make several distinctions which are developed below.

In some anthropological work, subculture refers to certain universal tendencies that seem to occur in all societies. They underlie culture, precede it, and set limits to the range of its variation. Thus Kroeber writes: "Indeed, such more or less recurrent near-regularities of form or process as have to date been formulated for culture are actually subcultural in nature. They are limits set to culture by physical or organic factors."[2] In *The Study of Man*, Linton uses subculture to refer to various pan-human phenomena that seem to occur everywhere. Thus good-natured and tyrannical parents may be found in societies that differ widely in their family patterns.[3] This use shades off into other concepts that are similar but not identical: Edward Sapir's "precultural" and Cooley's "human nature" refer to biological and social influences that underlie all cultures.[4] Since subculture is only rarely used today to refer to this series of ideas, I shall exclude them from further consideration, with the suggestion that the use of Sapir's term "precultural" might well clarify our thinking.

Two other usages of subculture represent a much more serious confusion. The term is often used to point to the normative systems of groups smaller than a society, to give emphasis to the ways these groups differ in such things as language, values, religion, diet, and style of life from the larger society of which they are a part. Perhaps the most common referent in this usage is an ethnic enclave (French Canadians in Maine) or a region (the subculture of the South),[5] but the distinctive norms of much smaller and more temporary groups (even a particular friendship group) may be de-

[2] A. L. Kroeber, "The Concept of Culture in Science," *Journal of General Education*, 3 (April, 1949), p. 187. See also Clyde Kluckhohn's reference to this idea in "Culture and Behavior," in Gardner Lindzey, editor, *Handbook of Social Psychology*, Cambridge: Addison-Wesley, 1954, Vol. 2, p. 954; and A. L. Kroeber in "Problems of Process: Results," in Sol Tax, *et al.*, editors, *An Appraisal of Anthropology Today*, Chicago: University of Chicago Press, 1953, p. 119.

[3] Ralph Linton, *The Study of Man*, New York: Appleton-Century, 1936, p. 486. See also his *The Cultural Background of Personality*, New York: Appleton-Century-Crofts, 1945, pp. 148–151. Elsewhere in *The Study of Man*, Linton uses subculture in a different sense, similar to the second usage described below.

[4] Edward Sapir, "Personality," in *Encyclopedia of the Social Sciences*, New York: Macmillan, 1931, Vol. 12, p. 86; Charles H. Cooley, *Human Nature and the Social Order*, revised edition, New York: Scribner, 1922.

[5] See, e.g., John K. Morland, *Millways of Kent*, Chapel Hill: University of North Carolina Press, 1958; Julian Steward, *The People of Puerto Rico*, Champaign: University of Illinois Press, 1956; Charles Wagley and Marvin Harris, "A Typology of Latin American Subcultures," *American Anthropologist*, 57 (June, 1955), pp. 428–451; Evon Z. Vogt, "American Subcultural *Continua* as Exemplified by the Mormons and Texans," *American Anthropologist*, 57 (December, 1955), pp. 1163–1172; Murray Straus, "Subcultural Variations in Ceylonese Mental Ability: A Study in National Character," *Journal of Social Psychology*, 39 (February, 1954), pp. 129–141; Joel B. Montague and Edgar G. Epps, "Attitudes Toward Social Mobility as Revealed by Samples of Negro and White Boys," *Pacific Sociological Review*, 1 (Fall, 1958), pp. 81–84; Hylan Lewis, *Blackways of Kent*, Chapel Hill: University of North Carolina Press, 1955; Robin M. Williams, Jr., *American Society*, New York: Knopf, 1951, Chapter 10; T. S. Langner, "A Test of Intergroup Prejudice Which Takes Account of Individual and Group Differences in Values," *Journal of Abnormal and Social Psychology*, 48 (October, 1953), pp. 548–554.

scribed as a subculture. Kluckhohn, for example, refers to "the subculture of anthropologists" and Riesman to "subcultures among the faculty."

This second meaning, which itself contains some ambiguities, as we shall see, must be distinguished from a third meaning associated with it when the reference is to norms that arise specifically from a frustrating situation or from conflict between a group and the larger society. Thus the emergent norms of a delinquent gang or the standards of an adolescent peer group have often been designated "subcultural." In addition to a cultural dimension, this third usage introduces a social-psychological dimension, for there is direct reference to the personality factors involved in the development and maintenance of the norms. Specifically, such personality tendencies as frustration, anxiety, feelings of role ambiguity, and resentment are shown to be involved in the creation of the subculture. The mutual influence of personality and culture is not a distinctive characteristic of this type of subculture, of course, for they are everywhere interactive. Thus:

> Tendencies for parents to respond harshly to their children's aggressive behavior, for instance, if common to the members of a society, are to be referred equally to the culture and to the modal personality of the parents. But the result in the developing child is not a foregone conclusion: present knowledge suggests that under specifiable conditions outcomes as different as rigid politeness or touchy latent hostility may follow. These consequences in turn may lead to cultural elaborations that seem superficially remote from the cultural starting point, yet are dynamically linked with it. . . .[6]

As this quotation suggests, culture and personality are always empirically tied together. Yet the nature of the relation is not the same in all cases. The term subculture, when used in the third way described here, raises to a position of prominence one particular kind of dynamic linkage between norms and personality: the creation of a series of inverse or counter values (opposed to those of the surrounding society) in face of serious frustration or conflict. To call attention to the special aspects of this kind of normative system, I suggest the term *contraculture*. Before exploring the relationship between subculture and contraculture, however, the range of meanings given subculture even when it is limited to the second usage requires comment.

SUBCULTURE AND ROLE

The variety of referents for the term subculture is very wide because the normative systems of subsocieties can be differentiated on many grounds.

---

[6] Brewster Smith, "Anthropology and Psychology," in John Gillin, editor, *For a Science of Social Man*, New York: Macmillan, 1954, p. 61. See also Talcott Parsons and Edward A. Shils, editors, *Toward a General Theory of Action*, Cambridge: Harvard University Press, 1951, esp. the monograph by the editors; and Ralph Linton's preface to Abram Kardiner, *The Psychological Frontiers of Society*, New York: Columbia University Press, 1945.

The groups involved may range from a large regional subdivision to a religious sect with only one small congregation. The distinctive norms may involve many aspects of life — religion, language, diet, moral values — or, for example, only a few separate practices among the members of an occupational group. Further distinctions among subcultures might be made on the basis of time (has the subculture persisted through a number of generations?), origin (by migration, absorption by a dominant society, social or physical segregation, occupational specialization, and other sources), and by the mode of relationship to the surrounding culture (from indifference to conflict). Such wide variation in the phenomena covered by a term can be handled by careful specification of the several grounds for subclassification. Confusion has arisen not so much from the scope of the term subculture as from its use as a substitute for "role." Only with great effort is some degree of clarity being achieved in the use of the role concept and the related terms "position" and "role behavior."[7] Were this development retarded by confusion of role with subculture it would be unfortunate. All societies have differentiating roles, but only heterogeneous societies have subcultures. Role is *that part of* a full culture that is assigned, as the appropriate rights and duties, to those occupying a given position.[8] These rights and duties usually interlock into a system with those of persons who occupy other positions. They are known to and accepted by all those who share the culture. Thus the role of a physician is known, at least in vague outline, by most persons in a society and it is seen as part of the total culture. (This is not to prejudge the question of role consensus, for there may be many non-role aspects of being a physician.) But subculture is not tied in this way into the larger cultural complex: it refers to norms that set a group apart from, not those that integrate a group with, the total society. Subcultural norms, as contrasted with role norms, are unknown to, looked down upon, or thought of as separating forces by the other members of a society. There are doubtless subcultural aspects of being a physician — normative influences affecting his behavior that are not part of his role, not culturally designated rights and duties. But the empirical mixture should not obscure the need for this analytic distinction.

Along with confusion with the role concept, subculture carries many of the ambiguities associated with the parent concept of culture. In much social scientific writing it is not at all clear whether culture refers to norms, that is, to expected or valued behavior, or to behavior that is widely followed

[7] See, e.g., Neal Gross, Ward S. Mason, and A. W. McEachern, *Explorations in Role Analysis,* New York: Wiley, 1958; F. L. Bates, "Position, Role, and Status: A Reformulation of Concepts," *Social Forces,* 34 (May, 1956), pp. 313–321; Robert K. Merton, "The Role-Set: Problems in Sociological Theory," *British Journal of Sociology,* 8 (June, 1957), pp. 106–120; S. F. Nadel, *The Theory of Social Structure,* Glencoe, Ill.: Free Press, 1957; Theodore R. Sarbin, "Role Theory," in *Handbook of Social Psychology, op. cit.,* Vol. 1, Chapter 6.

[8] It is possible, of course, for a subculture to specify roles within its own system.

and therefore normal in a statistical sense only. This dual referent is particularly likely to be found in the work of anthropologists. Perhaps because their concepts are derived largely from the study of relatively more stable and homogeneous societies, they draw less sharply the distinction between the statistically normal and the normative. Sociologists are more apt to find it necessary to explore the tensions between the social order and culture, to be alert to deviations, and they are therefore more likely to define culture abstractly as a shared normative system. Yet much of the commentary on subculture refers to behavior. In my judgment this identification is unwise. Behavior is the result of the convergence of many forces. One should not assume, when the members of a group behave in similar ways, that cultural norms produce this result. Collective behavior theory and personality theory may also help to account for the similarities.

CONTRACULTURE

Failure to distinguish between role and subculture and vagueness in the concept of culture itself are not the only difficulties in the use of the idea of subculture. Perhaps more serious is the tendency to obscure, under this one term, two levels of explanation, one sociological and the other social-psychological, with a resulting failure to understand the causal forces at work. On few topics can one get wider agreement among sociologists than on the dangers of reductionism. If a psychologist attempts to explain social facts by psychological theories, we throw the book (probably Durkheim) at him; we emphasize the "fallacy of misplaced concreteness." In view of the widespread neglect of socio-cultural factors in the explanation of behavior, this is a necessary task. It makes vitally important, however, keen awareness by sociologists that they also deal with an abstract model. Perhaps we can reverse Durkheim's dictum to say: Do not try to explain social psychological facts by sociological theories; or, more adequately, do not try to explain *behavior* (a product of the interaction of sociocultural and personality influences) by a sociological theory alone. Yablonsky has recently reminded us that an excessively sociological theory of gangs can result in our seeing a definite group structure and a clear pattern of norms where in fact there is a "near-group," with an imprecise definition of boundaries and limited agreement on norms.[9] Carelessly used, our concepts can obscure the facts we seek to understand.

To see the cultural element in delinquency or in the domination of an individual by his adolescent group, phenomena that on the surface are non-cultural or even "anti-cultural," was a long step forward in their explanation. But it is also necessary to see the non-cultural aspects of some "norms" — phenomena that on the surface seem thoroughly cultural. Our vocabulary needs to be rich enough to help us to deal with these differences. The ten-

[9] Lewis Yablonsky, "The Delinquent Gang as a Near-Group," *Social Problems*, 7 (Fall, 1959), pp. 108–117.

dency to use the same term to refer to phenomena that share *some* elements in common, disregarding important differences, is to be content with phyla names when we need also to designate genus and species.

To sharpen our analysis, I suggest the use of the term contraculture wherever the normative system of a group contains, as a primary element, a theme of conflict with the values of the total society, where personality variables are directly involved in the development and maintenance of the group's values, and wherever its norms can be understood only by reference to the relationships of the group to a surrounding dominant culture.[10] None of these criteria definitely separates contraculture from subculture because each is a continuum. Sub-societies fall along a range with respect to each criterion. The values of most subcultures probably conflict in some measure with the larger culture. In a contraculture, however, the conflict element is central; many of the values, indeed, are specifically contradictions of the values of the dominant culture. Similarly, personality variables are involved in the development and maintenance of all cultures and subcultures, but usually the influence of personality is by way of variations around a theme that is part of the culture. In a contraculture, on the other hand, the theme itself expresses the tendencies of the persons who compose it. Finally, the norms of all subcultures are doubtless affected in some degree by the nature of the relationship with the larger culture. A subculture, as a pure type, however, does not require, for its understanding, intensive analysis of inter-

---

[10] By the noun in "contraculture" I seek to call attention to the normative aspects of the phenomena under study and by the qualifying prefix to call attention to the conflict aspects. Similar terms are occasionally found in the literature, but they are either defined only by their use in context or are used differently from the meaning assigned to contraculture in this paper. Harold D. Lasswell uses the term "countermores" to refer to "culture patterns which appeal mainly to the *id* . . ." (*World Politics and Personal Insecurity*, New York: McGraw-Hill, 1935, p. 64). He then designates "revolutionists, prostitutes, prisoners, obscene and subversive talk" — which scarcely suggest a clear analytic category. In *World Revolutionary Propaganda*, New York: Knopf, 1939, Lasswell and Dorothy Blumenstock discuss the use of inverse values as a revolutionary propaganda weapon and comment on the presumed vulnerability of deprived persons to the countermores stressed in this propaganda. In *Power and Society*, New Haven: Yale University Press, 1950, p. 49, Lasswell uses the term somewhat differently: "*Countermores* are culture traits symbolized by the group as deviations from the mores, and yet are expected to occur." A certain amount of bribery, for example, is "normal" "and must be included by the candid observer as part of culture."

At various points, Talcott Parsons more nearly approaches the meaning of the concept contraculture as used here, although more by implication than by direct definition, and without distinguishing it from the concept of subculture. Referring to the ideological aspects of a subculture, he writes: "In such cases of an open break with the value-system and ideology of the wider society we may speak of a 'counter-ideology.'" (*The Social System*, Glencoe, Ill.: Free Press, 1951, p. 355.) And later: "If, however, the culture of the deviant group, like that of the delinquent gang, remains a 'counter-culture' it is difficult to find the bridges by which it can acquire influence over wider circles" (p. 522). It is not clear from these uses how counter-ideology and counterculture are to be defined; but the important place Parsons gives to the element of ambivalence in his use of the concept subculture suggests that he has in mind something similar to our concept of contraculture in his use of these various terms. (See *ibid.*, p. 286.)

action with the larger culture; that is, its norms are not, to any significant degree, a product of that interaction. But a contraculture can be understood only by giving full attention to the interaction of the group which is its bearer with the larger society. It is one thing to say that the subculture of the rural, lower-class Negro encourages slow, inefficient work. It is another thing to say, with Charles S. Johnson, that such a norm represents "pseudo-ignorant malingering," a contracultural way of describing the same phenomenon. Johnson stressed the conflict element, the extent to which the norm was a product of interaction of white and Negro. There is certainly value in emphasizing the subcultural source of some of the values of southern Negroes. Against racist views or individual explanations, the sociologist opposes the subcultural: If they strive less, have different sexual mores, or otherwise vary from standards of the dominant society, it is in part because they have been socialized in accordance with different norms. But this is not enough, for their similar behavior may be interpreted in part as a shared response to a frustrating environment.

Empirically, subcultural and contracultural influences may be mixed, of course. Delinquency and adolescent behavior almost certainly manifest both influences. The need, however, is to develop a clean analytic distinction between the two in order to interpret the wide variations in their mixture.

ADOLESCENT SUBCULTURE AND CONTRACULTURE

The utility of the distinction between contraculture and subculture can be tested by applying it to several research problems where the concept of subculture has been widely used. There is an extensive literature that interprets the behavior of adolescents substantially in these terms.[11] In the words of Havighurst and Taba: "Recent studies of adolescents have emphasized the fact that boys and girls in their teens have a culture of their own with moral standards and with moral pressures behind those standards. This culture has been called the 'adolescent peer culture.' "[12] Or Riesman: "All the morality is the group's. Indeed, even the fact that it is a morality is concealed by the confusing notion that the function of the group is to have fun, to play. . . ."[13]

[11] See Talcott Parsons, *Essays in Sociological Theory Pure and Applied*, Glencoe, Ill.: Free Press, 1949, Chapter 5; Howard Becker, *German Youth: Bond or Free*, New York: Oxford, 1946; S. N. Eisenstadt, *From Generation to Generation. Age Groups and the Social Structure*, Glencoe, Ill.: Free Press, 1956; David Riesman, *et al.*, *The Lonely Crowd*, New Haven: Yale University Press, 1950; R. J. Havighurst and Hilda Taba, *Adolescent Character and Personality*, New York: Wiley, 1949; Kingsley Davis, "The Sociology of Parent-Youth Conflict," *American Sociological Review*, 5 (August, 1940), pp. 523–534; Ralph Linton, "Age and Sex Categories," *American Sociological Review*, 7 (October, 1942), pp. 589–603; Joseph R. Gusfield, "The Problem of Generations in an Organizational Structure," *Social Forces*, 35 (May, 1957), pp. 323–330. For some contradictory evidence, see W. A. Westley and Frederick Elkin, "The Protective Environment and Adolescent Socialization," *Social Forces*, 35 (March, 1957), pp. 243–249; and Elkin and Westley, "The Myth of Adolescent Culture," *American Sociological Review*, 20 (December, 1955), pp. 680–684.

[12] *Op. cit.*, p. 35.

[13] *Op. cit.*, p. 72.

A close reading of the literature on adolescent culture reveals at least four different levels of interpretation, often only partially distinguished:

1. There is a cultural level, in which the roles of adolescent boys and girls are described, or the specialties (in Linton's sense) are designated. There is no reason to introduce concepts other than role or specialty to refer to norms that are generally accepted by elders and youths alike as appropriate to youth.

2. On the subcultural level, there are norms that manifest some separate system of values accepted within the adolescent group. These norms are not part of the role of youth. In part they are unknown to the elders; in part they conflict with standards accepted by the elders. They are learned, not by socialization in the total society, but by interaction within the sub-society of youth. Thus interests, games, speech patterns, and aesthetic tastes may be communicated among an age-group with little reference to the larger culture.

3. There are currents of fashion or of other collective behavior that sweep through an adolescent group, strongly influencing the behavior of its members.[14] Although it is difficult to distinguish fashion from culture — many empirical phenomena have aspects of both — it is wise to keep them apart conceptually. This is not always done. The terminology of Riesman is closer to that of fashion than of culture, but the net impression of his analysis is that he is thinking of control by the peer group primarily as a cultural phenomenon.[15] And the sentence following the one quoted above from Havighurst and Taba reads: "Boys and girls, desiring the approval of their age mates, follow the fashions of the peer culture in morals, dress, and speech. . . ." If the peer group influence stems from fashion, then strictly speaking it is not culture. The two differ to some degree in their origins, their functions, and their consequences.[16]

4. Many analyses of the control exercised by a youth group over its members employ the *concept* of contraculture, although the terminology and the assumptions are often those of subculture or culture. There is emphasis on the cross-pressures which young people feel: they want to be adults, yet fear to leave the securities of childhood; they experience contradictory adult treatment — a demand for grownup behavior here, the prevention of it there; ambiguity of self-image leads to efforts to prove oneself a full-fledged

---

[14] See Harold Finestone, "Cats, Kicks, and Color," *Social Problems*, 5 (July, 1957), pp. 3–13 [and pp. 150–163 in this volume]. Here the "cat" among some Negroes is seen as "the personal counterpart of an expressive social movement."

[15] See Riesman, *op. cit.*, esp. Chapter 3, "A Jury of Their Peers."

[16] The desirability of keeping distinct the analytic concepts of culture and collective behavior, including fashion, cannot be elaborated here. See Herbert Blumer, "Collective Behavior," in A. M. Lee, editor, *Principles of Sociology*, New York: Barnes and Noble, 1951; Ralph H. Turner and Lewis M. Killian, *Collective Behavior*, Englewood Cliffs, N.J.: Prentice-Hall, 1957; Edward Sapir, "Fashion," *Encyclopedia of the Social Sciences*, New York: Macmillan, 1931, Vol. 6, pp. 139–144; Georg Simmel, "Fashion," *American Journal of Sociology*, 62 (May, 1957), pp. 541–558.

adult; there is sexual frustration. The peer group may help one to struggle with these cross-pressures, as described by Parsons: "Perhaps the best single point of reference for characterizing the youth culture lies in its contrast with the dominant pattern of the adult male role. By contrast with emphasis on responsibility in this role, the orientation of the youth culture is more or less specifically irresponsible."[17] This irresponsibility cannot be understood simply as another cultural norm, as part of the "role" of youth, although these are Parsons' terms. It must be studied in the context of strain, of role ambiguity. Some sociologists explain this irresponsibility as merely a manifestation of the youth culture, thus obscuring the personality factors also involved. The description and analysis of an adolescent subculture, to be sure, are an important contribution to the sociology of youth. Many adolescents spend a great deal of time in groups that sustain norms different from those of the adult world; and adults often respond to the behavior that follows these norms in an "ethnocentric" way. To rely on a subcultural explanation alone, however, is to disregard the emergent quality of many of the standards and to minimize the fact that they are often in direct conflict with adult standards (which most adolescents themselves will soon accept).

This sharp conflict of values requires explanation. Parsons states the facts clearly. "Negatively, there is a strong tendency to repudiate interests in adult things, and to feel at least a certain recalcitrance to the pressure of adult expectations and disciplines. . . . Thus the youth culture is not only, as is true of the curricular aspects of formal education, a matter of age status as such but also shows signs of being a product of tensions in the relationship of younger people and adults."[18] At several other points Parsons develops the "reaction" theme and later uses the concept of "reaction-formation."[19] Should these various phenomena be subsumed under the concept of culture? It is one thing for a society to train its youth to certain ways of behaving. It is quite another for a youth group to develop inverse values in an effort to struggle with role ambiguities and strains. The adolescent may experience both as normative sanctions; but that should scarcely lead the social analyst to disregard their differences. I suggest the term contraculture in order to indicate the normative *and* the conflict aspects of this type of situation.

DELINQUENT CONTRACULTURE

The usefulness of separating subcultural and contracultural influences is seen particularly clearly in the analysis of delinquency and of criminality generally. Perhaps in no other field were there more substantial gains in understanding made possible by the introduction of a sociological point of view to supplement and to correct individualistic and moralistic interpretations. There is little need to review the extensive literature, from *Delinquent Gangs* to *Delinquent Boys*, to establish the importance of the normative ele-

17 Parsons, *op. cit. Essays* . . . , p. 92.
18 *Ibid.*, pp. 92–93.
19 See *ibid.*, pp. 101–102, 189–190, 342–345, 355.

ment in criminal and delinquent behavior. It is a mistake, however, to try to stretch a useful concept into a total theory. A "complex-adequate" analysis[20] may seem less sharp and definitive than one based on one factor, but it is likely to be far more useful. Cohen's excellent work,[21] although labelled as a study of the culture of the gang, does not overlook the psychogenic sources of delinquency. In fact, his explanation of the origins of the subculture (contraculture) and its functions for the lower class male makes clear that the norms of the gang are not learned, accepted, and taught in the same way that we learn what foods to eat, what clothes to wear, what language to speak. The very existence of the gang is a sign, in part, of blocked ambition. Because tensions set in motion by this blockage cannot be resolved by achievement of dominant values, such values are repressed, their importance denied, counter-values affirmed. The gang member is often ambivalent. Thwarted in his desire to achieve higher status by the criteria of the dominant society, he accepts criteria he can meet; but the reaction-formation in this response is indicated by the content of the delinquent norms — non-utilitarian, malicious, and negativistic, in Cohen's terms. This negative polarity represents the need to repress his own tendencies to accept the dominant cultural standards. This is not to say that the values of the gang cannot be explained partially by cultural analysis, by some extension of the idea that "the mores can make anything right." But I suggest that Cohen's multiple-factor analysis might have been clearer, and less subject to misinterpretation, had he introduced the concept of contraculture alongside the concept of subculture. One reviewer, for example, completely disregards the "negative polarity" theme:

> In an overall summary, cultural delinquency is a phenomenon of culture, society, and sociocultural experience. It is a positive thing: members of the several social classes are socialized, but there is a differential content in the socialization. Delinquency is not a negative thing; it is not a result of the breakdown of society, nor of the failure to curb criminal instincts, nor of the failure of the family, the church, or the school. The same set of concepts, the same social processes, and the same set of logical assumptions account for both delinquency and lawfulness. Since delinquency is of this character, it is unnecessary to invent any pathology to account for it.[22]

This statement neither adequately represents Cohen's thesis nor encourages us to explore a number of important questions: Why do only some of those who are exposed to the delinquent "subculture" learn it?[23] Why do those

[20] See Robin M. Williams, Jr., "Continuity and Change in Sociological Study," *American Sociological Review*, 23 (December, 1958), pp. 619–633.

[21] Albert K. Cohen, *Delinquent Boys*, Glencoe, Ill.: Free Press, 1955.

[22] Frank Hartung, in a review of *Delinquent Boys*, *American Sociological Review*, 20 (December, 1955), p. 752.

[23] See Solomon Kobrin, "The Conflict of Values in Delinquency Areas," *American Sociological Review*, 16 (October, 1951), pp. 653–661; Alex Inkeles, "Personality and Social Structure," in Robert K. Merton, *et al.*, editors, *Sociology Today*, New York: Basic Books, 1959, p. 254.

who follow the subculture often manifest ambivalence and guilt feelings?[24] Why do many of the same patterns of behavior occur in areas and among groups where the presence of the subculture is much less clear (middle-class delinquency)?[25] What is the significance of the fact that the delinquent subculture is not only different from but in part at least a reversal of the values of the dominant culture? The use of a purely subcultural model of analysis discourages or even prevents the raising of these questions and thus precludes adequate answers to them.

Cohen and Short have dealt with several of these issues by suggesting the need for a typology. Specifically for the study of delinquency, they propose five types of subcultures: the parent male (the central pattern described in *Delinquent Boys*), the conflict-oriented, the drug addict, the semi-professional theft, and the middle-class subcultures.[26] Although the criteria of classification are not entirely clear, these categories are primarily descriptive. The concept of contraculture might be added to this list as a type of subculture, if the one distinctive criterion used to designate a subculture is the presence in a sub-society of a normative system that separates it from the total society. Such a procedure does not seem, however, to produce an adequate taxonomy. If the shift is made from description to analysis, or from an interest in the content of norms to their etiology, an important difference emerges between subculture and contraculture: the one set of norms derives from standard socialization in a sub-society; the other stems from conflict and frustration in the experience of those who share many of the values of the whole society but are thwarted in their efforts to achieve those values.

It should be stressed once more that these are analytic concepts, no one of which is adequate to handle the empirical variations of delinquent behavior. Failure to recognize the abstract quality of our conceptual tools leads to unnecessary disagreements. When Miller describes the "Lower Class Culture as a Generating Milieu of Gang Delinquency," for example, he points to an important series of influences that derive from the value system of the lower-class community.[27] In his effort to emphasize this aspect of the etiology of delinquency, however, he tends to overlook the kind of evidence reported by Sykes and Matza, Cohen, Finestone, Yablonsky, the McCords, and others concerning collective behavior and personality variables.[28] Surely the evidence is now rich enough for us to state definitively that delinquency is a

[24] See Gresham M. Sykes and David Matza, "Techniques of Neutralization: A Theory of Delinquency," *American Sociological Review*, 22 (December, 1957), pp. 664–670.

[25] John I. Kitsuse and David C. Dietrick, "*Delinquent Boys*: A Critique," *American Sociological Review*, 24 (April, 1959), pp. 208–215.

[26] See Albert Cohen and James Short, "Research in Delinquent Subcultures," *The Journal of Social Issues*, 14, 3 (1958), pp. 20–37.

[27] Walter B. Miller, "Lower Class Culture as a Generating Milieu of Gang Delinquency," *The Journal of Social Issues*, 14, 3 (1958), pp. 5–19.

[28] In addition to the studies of Sykes and Matza, Cohen, Finestone, and Yablonsky cited above, see William McCord and Joan McCord, *Origins of Crime. A New Evaluation of the Cambridge-Somerville Youth Study*, New York: Columbia University Press, 1959.

multi-variable product. The task ahead is not to prove that it stems largely from cultural or subcultural or contracultural influences, but to spell out the conditions under which these and other factors will be found in various empirical mixtures.[29]

CONTRACULTURAL ASPECTS OF CLASS AND OCCUPATION

The same admixture of the concepts of culture, subculture, and contraculture is found in the extensive literature on occupations and classes. Doubtless all three forces are found in many instances, and the research task is to untangle their various influences. It may stretch the meaning of the term too far to speak of the *position* of the "middle-class member," with its culturally designated role specifications; although in relatively stable societies the usage seems appropriate. In such societies, many of the rights and obligations of various status levels are culturally defined. In more mobile class systems, however, subcultural and contracultural norms become important. Our understanding of the American class system has certainly been deepened in the last twenty years by the descriptions of differences, among classes, in value perspectives, time orientations, levels of aspiration, leisure-time styles, and child rearing practices.[30]

[29] In a recent manuscript, Sykes and Matza suggest that delinquent behavior can profitably be studied as an exaggerated expression of certain "subterranean values" of the dominant society (the search for excitement, the use of "pull" to get by without too much work, and aggression). This idea deserves careful study. The main research task is to discover the conditions which promote selective and exaggerated attention to these values at the cost of neglect of the more prominent "public" values. It seems likely that this task will lead to the incorporation of the "subterranean values" thesis into the larger complex of theories of delinquency. The thesis raises a question of terminology in connection with the present paper: At what point does exaggerated emphasis on a value become a counter-value by virtue of the exaggeration? *Some* cultural support can be found in a complex society for many patterns of behavior that are not fully valued. A society may accept or even applaud a pattern that is used to a limited degree while condemning its extravagant use. And the meaning of the pattern in the life of the individual when found in culturally approved degree differs from what it is when the pattern becomes a dominant theme. To discover why some subterranean values are raised into a style of life, therefore, requires more than cultural analysis. (See Gresham M. Sykes and David Matza, "Juvenile Delinquency and Subterranean Values," unpublished manuscript, 1960.)

[30] Of the many studies in this area, see Charles McArthur, "Personality Differences Between Middle and Upper Classes," *Journal of Abnormal and Social Psychology*, 50 (March, 1955), pp. 247–254; Melvin L. Kohn, "Social Class and Parental Values," *American Journal of Sociology*, 64 (January, 1959), pp. 337–351; A. B. Hollingshead and Frederick C. Redlich, *Social Class and Mental Illness*, New York: Wiley, 1958; Clyde R. White, "Social Class Differences in the Uses of Leisure," *American Journal of Sociology*, 61 (September, 1955), pp. 145–151; John A. Clausen and Melvin L. Kohn, "The Ecological Approach in Social Psychiatry," *American Journal of Sociology*, 60 (September, 1954), pp. 140–151; A. B. Hollingshead, *Elmtown's Youth*, New York: Wiley, 1949; Louis Schneider and Sverre Lysgaard, "The Deferred Gratification Pattern: A Preliminary Study," *American Sociological Review*, 18 (April, 1953), pp. 142–149; Urie Bronfenbrenner, "Socialization and Social Class Through Time and Space," in Eleanor E. Maccoby, *et al.*, editors, *Readings in Social Psychology*, New York: Holt, 1958, pp. 400–425.

The introduction of the concept of subculture has helped to avoid class derived biases in the interpretation of the wide variations in these phenomena. In class analysis as in the study of deviations, however, there may be some over-compensation in the effort to eliminate the distortions of a middle-class and often rural perspective.[31] There is evidence to suggest that differences between classes are based less upon different values and norms than the subcultural approach suggests. The "innovations" of lower-class members, to use Merton's term, are not simply subcultural acts defined as innovative by middle-class persons. They are in part responses to a frustrating situation. They are efforts to deal with the disjunction of means and ends. When the disjunction is reduced, the variations in value and behavior are reduced. Thus Rosen found, "surprisingly," that Negroes in the Northeast made higher scores on an "achievement value" test than his description of Negro "culture" led him to expect. This may indicate that the low achievement response is less the result of a subcultural norm than a protest against a difficult situation. If the situation improves, the achievement value changes.[32] Stephenson's discovery that occupational plans of lower-class youth are considerably below those of higher-class youth, but that their aspirations are only slightly lower, bears on this same point. His data suggest that the classes differ not only in norms, but also in opportunity.[33] Differences in behavior, therefore, are only partly a result of subcultural contrasts. The lower educational aspirations of lower-class members are also found to be in part situationally induced, not simply normatively induced. When the situation changes, values and behavior change, as Mulligan found in his study of the response of the sons of blue-collar workers to the educational opportunities of the GI Bill, and as Wilson reports in his investigation of the aspirations of lower-class boys attending higher-class schools and upper-class boys attending lower-class schools.[34]

In short, our thinking about differences in behavior among social classes will be sharpened if we distinguish among those differences that derive from role influences, those based on subcultural variations, and those that express contracultural responses to deprivation. The proportions will vary from so-

[31] C. Wright Mills, "The Professional Ideology of Social Pathologists," *American Journal of Sociology*, 49 (September, 1943), pp. 165–180.

[32] Bernard C. Rosen, "Race, Ethnicity, and the Achievement Syndrome," *American Sociological Review*, 24 (February, 1959), pp. 47–60. It is highly important, in aspiration studies, to compare, not absolute levels, but the extent of aspiration above the existing level of individuals or their families. A low absolute target for lower-class members may require a larger *reach* than a higher target for middle-class persons. See Leonard Reissman, "Levels of Aspiration and Social Class," *American Sociological Review*, 18 (June, 1953), pp. 233–242.

[33] Richard M. Stephenson, "Mobility Orientation and Stratification of 1,000 Ninth Graders," *American Sociological Review*, 22 (April, 1957), pp. 204–212.

[34] Raymond A. Mulligan, "Socio-Economic Background and College Enrollment," *American Sociological Review*, 16 (April, 1951), pp. 188–196; Alan B. Wilson, "Residential Segregation of Social Classes and Aspirations of High School Boys," *American Sociological Review*, 24 (December, 1959), pp. 836–845.

ciety to society; the research task is to specify the conditions under which various distributions occur. One would expect, to propose one hypothesis, to find more contracultural norms among lower-class members of an open society than in a similar group in a closed society.

The interpretation of differential behavior among the members of various occupational categories can also be strengthened by the distinctions made above. Here the contrast between role and subculture is especially useful. The role of a teacher consists of the rights and duties that *integrate* him into a system of expected and established relationships with others. The teaching subculture, on the other hand, insofar as it exists, *separates* teachers from the cultural world of others. It is either unknown to others or, if known, a source of disagreement and perhaps of conflict with others. There are also contracultural aspects of some occupational styles of life. In interpreting the differences between the values of jazz musicians and "squares," for example, Becker writes: "their rejection of commercialism in music and squares in social life was part of the casting aside of the total American culture by men who could enjoy privileged status but who were unable to achieve a satisfactory personal adjustment within it."[35] Their style of life, in other words, can be understood only by supplementing the cultural and subcultural dimensions with the conflict theme. Cameron develops the same point. Although he makes no use of the term subculture, he describes the differentiating norms of the dance-band group, presumably a result of the "esoteric" aspects of their art, the differences in their time schedule, and the like. But he also describes the *contra* aspects of some of the norms, and suggests that they derive from the fact that early recruitment ties the jazz musician to the adolescence problem.[36]

CONCLUSION

Poorly defined terms plague research in many areas, particularly in the specification of relationships between sociological and social psychological levels of analysis. Thus "anomie" is still used to refer both to a social structural fact and to a personality fact, although this confusion is gradually being reduced. "Role" may refer, alternately, to rights and duties prescribed for the occupants of a position or to individual performance of that position. And subculture, I have suggested, is used to designate both the traditional norms of a sub-society and the emergent norms of a group caught in a frustrating and conflict-laden situation. This paper indicates that there are differences in the origin, function, and perpetuation of traditional and emergent norms, and suggests that the use of the concept contraculture for the latter might improve sociological analysis.

[35] Howard S. Becker, "The Professional Dance Musician and His Audience," *American Journal of Sociology*, 57 (September, 1951), pp. 136–144.

[36] W. B. Cameron, "Sociological Notes on the Jam Session," *Social Forces*, 33 (December, 1954), pp. 177–182.

Hypotheses to guide the study of subculture can most profitably be derived from a general theory of culture. As an illustration, it may be hypothesized that a subculture will appear, in the first instance, as a result of mobility or an extension of communication that brings groups of different cultural background into membership in the same society, followed by physical or social isolation or both that prevents full assimilation.

Hypotheses concerning contracultures, on the other hand, can best be derived from social psychological theory — from the study of collective behavior, the frustration-aggression thesis, or the theory of group formation. One might hypothesize, for example, that under conditions of deprivation and frustration of major values (in a context where the deprivation is obvious because of extensive communication with the dominant group), and where value confusion and weak social controls obtain, contracultural norms will appear. One would expect to find, according to these propositions, many subcultural values among southern rural Negroes. Among first and second generation urban Negroes, however, one would expect an increase in contracultural norms. Both groups are deprived, but in the urban situation there is more "value leakage" from the dominant group, more value confusion, and weakened social controls.[37]

The subculture of the sociologist requires sophistication about the full range of human behavior. This desideratum has led to the proposition that the vast diversity of norms believed in and acted upon by the members of a modern society is not a sign of value confusion and breakdown but rather an indication that urban life brings into one system of interaction persons drawn from many cultural worlds. One unanticipated consequence of the sociological subculture may be that we exaggerate the normative insulation and solidarity of these various worlds. An important empirical question concerns the extent and results of their interaction.

[37] There are numerous alternative ways in which the protest against deprivation can be expressed. Delinquency and drug addiction often have a contracultural aspect; but somewhat less clearly, political and religious movements among disprivileged groups may also invert the values of the influential but inaccessible dominant group. Thus the concept of contraculture may help us to understand, for example, the Garveyite movement, the Ras Tafari cult, and some aspects of the value schemes of lower-class sects. (See, e.g., Liston Pope, *Millhands and Preachers*, New Haven: Yale University Press, 1942; and George E. Simpson, "The Ras Tafari Movement in Jamaica: A Study of Race and Class Conflict," *Social Forces*, 34 (December, 1955), pp. 167–170.)

B. Processes and Examples

> *As will be seen in Weinberg and Arond's description of boxing, the word "culture" can be used in a variety of settings. But, though the settings vary, the term refers to the same phenomena, i.e., a patterned set of responses. Thus, we could as well talk about the culture of the university professor or physician. We know that university professors in similar disciplines exhibit a remarkable similarity in consumption and leisure activity. Several studies in sociology have investigated specifically the culture of the physician, and here too we find similar ethics, goals, and styles of life. The article also demonstrates a variety of sociological techniques. One of the authors was a boxer, trainer, and manager; consequently, the technique is that of "participant" and participant observer. A social survey was also used in contacting other respondents.*

7   S. K. WEINBERG AND H. AROND

The Occupational Culture of the Boxer

Herein is described the culture of the professional boxer as discovered by personal experience, by reading of firsthand literature, and by interview with sixty-eight boxers and former boxers, seven trainers, and five managers.[1] The aspects covered are recruitment, practices and beliefs, and the social structure of the boxing world.

RECRUITMENT

Professional boxers are adolescents and young men. Nearly all are of low socioeconomic background. Only two of our fighters might possibly have been of middle-class family. Most are immigrants to the city and are children of such. Their residences at the time of becoming boxers are distributed like the commoner forms of social disorganization, being almost all near the center of the city. Nearly all Chicago boxers lived on the Near South and Near West sides. There is an ethnic succession of boxers which corresponds

From *American Journal of Sociology*, Vol. LVIII (March, 1952), pp. 460–469. Reprinted by permission of The University of Chicago Press.

  [1] One of us (Arond) has been a boxer, trainer, and manager. We first determined some common values, beliefs, and practices by a few unstructured interviews. We used the material thus gained to plan guided interviews which would help us sift out what is ethnic from what belongs properly to boxing culture. Mr. Leland White helped in the interviewing.

to that of the ethnic groups in these areas. First Irish, then Jewish, then Italian, were most numerous among prominent boxers; now, Negroes (Table 1).

TABLE 1. RANK ORDER OF NUMBER OF PROMINENT BOXERS OF VARIOUS ETHNIC GROUPS FOR CERTAIN YEARS[a]

| | Rank | | |
Year	1	2	3
1909	Irish	German	English
1916	Irish	German	Italian
1928	Jewish	Italian	Irish
1936	Italian	Irish	Jewish
1948	Negro	Italian	Mexican

[a] Data tabulated from *World's Annual Sporting Record* (1910 and 1917); *Everlast Boxing Record* (1929); *Boxing News Record* (1938); and *Ring* (1948 and 1949). The numbers in the succeeding years are: 103, 118, 300, 201, and 149. There may be biases in the listings, but the predominance of two or three ethnic groups is marked in all the years. The Irish were very much above others in 1909 and 1916 (about 40 per cent of all boxers listed); in 1948 nearly half of all boxers listed were Negro. The Jews and Italians did not have so marked a predominance.

The traditions of an ethnic group, as well as its temporary location at the bottom of the scale, may affect the proportion of its boys who become boxers. Many Irish, but few Scandinavians, have become boxers in this country; many Filipinos, but very few Japanese and Chinese.

The juvenile and adolescent culture of the lower socioeconomic levels provides a base for the boxing culture. Individual and gang fights are encouraged. The best fighter is often the most admired, as well as the most feared, member of a gang. A boy who lacks status tries to get it and to restore his self-esteem by fighting.[2] Successful amateur and professional boxers furnish highly visible role-models to the boys of the slum; this is especially so among urban Negroes at present. Since he has otherwise little hope of any but unskilled, disagreeable work, the boxing way to money and prestige may appear very attractive. As an old-time manager put it, "Where else can a poor kid get a stake as fast as he can in boxing?"

Since the ability to fight is a matter of status among one's peers, is learned in play, and is the accepted means of expressing hostility and settling disputes, boys learn to fight early.

> One fighter thought of becoming a boxer at the age of ten, because he could not participate in team games as a child; his mother

[2] Some juveniles who fought continually to retrieve their self-esteem and also in sheer self-defense later became boxers. One adolescent who was half-Negro and half-Indian was induced to become a boxer by a trainer who saw him beat two white opponents in a street fight. Another boxer admitted that he fought continually because other boys called him a "sissy." A third boxer fought continually because he was small and other boys picked on him. This compensatory drive among boxers is not unusual.

insisted that he had a "bad heart." He stated: "I tried to fight as soon as I got old enough, to be the roughest, toughest kid on the block." He fought so frequently and was arrested so often for fighting that one policeman told him that he might as well get paid for it. At the age of fourteen he participated in fights in vacant lots in the neighborhood. Because of his prowess as a fighter, the other boys in the neighborhood began to respect him more, and he began to associate status with fighting. When he was about seventeen, an amateur fighter told him about a gymnasium where he could learn to become a "ring fighter" instead of a "street fighter." He claimed: "I love fighting. I would rather fight than eat."

Most boxers seem to have been influenced to become "ring fighters" by a boxer in the neighborhood or by a member of the family.[3] One middleweight champion claimed that he "took after" his brother, followed him to the gymnasium, imitated him, and thus decided to be a boxer before he was fifteen years old. Another fighter was inspired by a neighbor and became his protégé into the stable. A third fighter has stated:

> I was twelve when I went to the gym first. If there's a fighter in the neighborhood, the kids always look up to him because they think he's tough. There was an amateur in my neighborhood and he was a kind of hero to all us kids. It was him that took me to the gym the first time.

A former welterweight and middleweight champion who has been boxing since he was eleven years old has written in a similar vein:

> I didn't do any boxing before I left Detroit. I was too little. But I was already interested in it, partly because I idolized a big Golden Gloves heavyweight who lived on the same block with us. I used to hang around the Brewster Center Gym all the time watching him train. His name was Joe Louis. Whenever Joe was in the gym so was I. He was my idol then just like he is today. I've always wanted to be like him.[4]

Some managers and trainers of local gymnasiums directly seek out boys who like to fight and who take fighters as their models. One such manager says that he sought boys who were considered the "toughest in the block" or "natural fighters." He would get them to come to the gym and to become amateur boxers. He entered some in tournaments, from which he received some "cut," then sifted out the most promising for professional work.

---

[3] For the last twenty-five years of boxers, we found the following brother combinations among boxers: 3 sets of five brothers, 5 sets of four brothers, 24 sets of three brothers, and 41 sets of two brothers. We also found sets of father-son combinations. This number, very likely, is less than the actual figures, because some brothers fight as amateurs only, and not as professional, and thus their records cannot be traced.

[4] "Sugar Ray" Robinson, "Fighting Is My Business," *Sport*, June, 1951, p. 18.

It is believed by many in boxing circles that those in the lower socioeconomic levels make the "best fighters":

> They say that too much education softens a man and that is why the college graduates are not good fighters. They fight emotionally on the gridiron and they fight bravely and well in our wars, but their contributions in our rings have been insignificant. The ring has been described as the refuge of the under-privileged. Out of the downtrodden have come our greatest fighters. . . . An education is an escape, and that is what they are saying when they shake their heads — those who know the fight game — as you mention the name of a college fighter. Once the bell rings, they want their fighters to have no retreat, and a fighter with an education is a fighter who does not have to fight to live and he knows it. . . . Only for the hungry fighter is it a decent gamble.[5]

It can be inferred tentatively that the social processes among juveniles and adolescents in the lower socioeconomic levels, such as individual and gang fights, the fantasies of "easy money," the lack of accessible vocational opportunities, and the general isolation from the middle-class culture, are similar for those who become professional boxers as for those who become delinquents. The difference resides in the role model the boy picks, whether criminal or boxer. The presence of one or several successful boxers in an area stimulates boys of the same ethnic groups to follow in their footsteps. Boxing, as well as other sports and certain kinds of entertainment, offers slum boys the hope of quick success without deviant behavior (although, of course, some boxers have been juvenile delinquents).[6]

Within the neighborhood the professional boxer orients his behavior and routine around the role of boxer. Usually acquiring some measure of prestige in the neighborhood, he is no longer a factory hand or an unskilled laborer. He is admired, often has a small coterie of followers, and begins to dress smartly and loudly and to conceive of himself as a neighborhood celebrity, whether or not he has money at the time. Nurtured by the praise of the trainer or manager, he has hopes that eventually he will ascend to "big-time fights" and to "big money." The money that he does make in his amateur and early professional fights by comparison with his former earnings seems a lot to him.

OCCUPATIONAL CULTURE OF THE BOXER

The intrinsic occupational culture of the boxer is composed of techniques, illusions, aspirations, and structured roles which every boxer internalizes in

---

[5] *Ring*, July, 1950, p. 45.

[6] Merton has noted that, while our culture encourages the people of lower standing to orient their conduct toward wealth, it denies them opportunities to get money in the framework of accepted institutions. This inconsistency results in a high rate of deviant behavior (Robert K. Merton, *Social Theory and Social Structure* [Glencoe, Ill.: Free Press, 1949], p. 137).

some measure and which motivate him both inside and outside the ring. At the outset of his career the boxer becomes impressed with the need for training to improve his physical condition and to acquire the skills necessary to win fights and to avoid needless injury. When he has such status as to be sought out by promoters, he assigns a specified interval for training before the bout. But in the preliminary ranks he must keep himself in excellent physical shape most of the time, because he does not know when he will be summoned to fight. He may be booked as a substitute and cannot easily refuse the match. If he does, he may find it difficult to get another bout. The particular bout may be the chance he has been hoping for. The fighter is warned persistently by tales of the ritualistic necessity of "getting in shape" and of the dire consequences if he does not. "There is no more pitiable sight," stated one boxer, "than to see a fighter get into the ring out of condition."

The boxer comes to regard his body, especially his hands, as his stock-in-trade. Boxers have varied formulas for preventing their hands from excess swelling, from excessive pain, or from being broken. This does not mean a hypochondriachal interest, because they emphasize virility and learn to slough off and to disdain punishment. But fighters continually seek nostrums and exercises for improving their bodies. One practiced Yogi, another became a physical cultist, a third went on periodic fasts; others seek out lotions, vitamins, and other means of improving their endurance, alertness, and punching power.

"You have to live up to being a fighter." This phrase justifies their deprivations and regulated living. There is also a cult of a kind of persevering courage, called a "fighting heart," which means "never admitting defeat." The fighter learns early that his exhibited courage — his ability, if necessary, to go down fighting — characterizes the respected, audience-pleasing boxer. He must cherish the lingering hope that he can win by a few more punches. One fighter was so severely beaten by another that the referee stopped the bout. The brother of the beaten fighter, a former fighter himself, became so outraged that he climbed into the ring and started to brawl with the referee. In another instance a boxer incurred a very severe eye injury, which would have meant the loss of his sight. But he insisted on continuing to fight, despite the warnings of his seconds. When the fight was stopped, he protested. This common attitude among boxers is reinforced by the demands of the spectators, who generally cheer a "game fighter." Thus the beaten fighter may become a "crowd-pleaser" and may get matches despite his defeat. On the other hand, some fighters who are influenced by friends, by wives, or by sheer experience recognize that sustained beatings may leave permanent injuries and voluntarily quit when they are beaten. But the spirit of the code is that the boxer continue to fight regardless of injuries. "If a man quits a fight, an honest fight," claimed one fighter, "he has no business there in the first place."

Fighters who remain in the sport are always hopeful of occupational climbing. This attitude may initially be due to a definite self-centeredness, but it is intensified by the character of boxing. Boxing is done by single contestants, not by teams. Emphasis is on the boxer as a distinct individual. The mores among boxers are such that fighters seldom admit to others that they are "punchy" or "washed-up."[7] One fighter said: "You can tell another fighter to quit, but you can't call him punchy. If you do, he'll punch you to show you he still has a punch." He has to keep up his front.

Further, the boxer is involved in a scheme of relationships and traditions which focus upon building confidence. The boxing tradition is full of legends of feats of exceptional fighters. Most gymnasiums have pictures of past and present outstanding boxers on the wall, and identification with them comes easy for the incoming fighters. Past fights are revived in tales. Exceptional fighters of the past and present are compared and appraised. Second, the individual boxer is continually assured and reassured that he is "great" and that he is "coming up." As a result, many fighters seem to overrate their ability and to feel that all they need are "lucky breaks" to become champions or leading contenders. Many get self-important and carry scrapbooks of their newspaper write-ups and pictures.

The process of stimulating morale among fighters is an integral accompaniment of the acquisition of boxing skills and body conditioning. The exceptions are the part-time fighters who hold outside jobs and who are in the preliminary ranks. They tend to remain on the periphery of the boxing culture and thus have a somewhat different perspective on the mobility aspects of the sport.[8]

Since most bouts are unpredictable, boxers usually have superstitions which serve to create confidence and emotional security among them. Sometimes the manager or trainer uses these superstitions to control the fighter. One fighter believed that, if he ate certain foods, he was sure to win, because these foods gave him strength.[9] Others insist on wearing the same robe in which they won their first fight: one wore an Indian blanket when he entered the ring. Many have charm pieces or attribute added importance to entering the ring after the opponent. Joe Louis insisted on using a certain dressing-room at Madison Square Garden. Some insist that, if a woman

[7] Because of the changing character of boxing at the present time, promoters or managers may sometimes tell fighters that they are "through"; but fighters, as we have indicated, seldom make these appraisals of other fighters.

[8] Since the number of local bouts has declined with the advent of television, many preliminary fighters and local club fighters are compelled to work at outside jobs in order to meet their daily expenses.

[9] According to boxing folklore, a former heavyweight champion, Max Baer, was stimulated into action by his trainer who gave him a mixture called "Go Fast," which presumably had the properties of making a "tiger" out of the one who drank it. The suggestive effects of this drink were so great that Baer knocked out his opponent. Thereafter, he demanded it in subsequent fights. This suggestive play also proved effective with a former middleweight champion, Ken Overlin. The drink itself was composed of distilled water and a little sugar.

watches them train, it is bad luck. One fighter, to show he was not superstitious, would walk under a ladder before every fight, until this became a magical rite itself. Consistent with this attitude, many intensify their religious attitudes and keep Bibles in their lockers. One fighter kept a rosary in his glove. If he lost the rosary, he would spend the morning before the fight in church. Although this superstitious attitude may be imported from local or ethnic culture, it is intensified among the boxers themselves, whether they are white or Negro, preliminary fighters or champions.

When a fighter likes the style, punch, or movement of another fighter, he may wear the latter's trunks or one of his socks or rub him on the back. In training camps some fighters make a point of sleeping in the bed that a champion once occupied. For this reason, in part, some take the names of former fighters. All these practices focus toward the perspective of "filling the place" or taking the role of the other esteemed fighter. Moreover, many fighters deliberately copy the modes of training, the style, and the general movements of role-models.

Since fighters, in the process of training, become keyed to a finely balanced physical and emotional condition and frequently are irritable, restless, and anxious, they also grow dependent and suggestible. The superstitions and the reassuring statements of the trainer and manager both unwittingly and wittingly serve to bolster their confidence.

Before and during the bout, self-confidence is essential. Fighters or their seconds try to unnerve the opponent. They may try to outstare him or may make some irritating or deflating remarks or gestures. In the ring, tactical self-confidence is expressed in the boxer's general physical condition and movements. His ability to outslug, to outspar, or to absorb punishment is part of his morale. The ability not to go down, to outmaneuver the other contestant, to change his style in, whole or in part, to retrieve his strength quickly, or to place the opponent off-balance inevitably affect the latter's confidence. A fighter can *feel* whether he will win a bout during the early rounds, but he is always wary of the dreaded single punch or the unexpected rally.

Boxers become typed by their style and manner in the ring. A "puncher" or "mauler" differs from a "boxer" and certainly from a "cream puff," who is unable to hit hard. A "miller," or continual swinger, differs from one who saves his energy by fewer movements. A "butcher" is recognized by his tendency to hit hard and ruthlessly when another boxer is helpless, inflicting needless damage. A "tanker" is one who goes down easily, sometimes in a fixed fight or "set-up." The "mechanical" fighter differs from the "smart" fighter, for among the "smart" fighters are really the esteemed fighters, those who are capable of improvising and reformulating their style, of devising original punches and leg movements, of cunningly outmaneuvering their opponents, and of possessing the compensatory hostility, deadly impulsiveness, and quick reflexes to finish off their opponents in the vital split second.

Boxers have to contend with fouls and quasi-fouls in the ring. At present, these tactics seemingly are becoming more frequent. They may have to contend with "heeling," the maneuver by which the fighter, during clinches, shoves the laced part of his glove over the opponent's wound, particularly an "eye" wound, to open or exacerbate it, with "thumbing" in the eye, with "butting" by the head, with having their insteps stepped on hard during clinches, with punches in back of the head or in the kidneys, or with being tripped. These tactics, which technically are fouls, may be executed so quickly and so cleverly that the referee does not detect them. When detected, the fighter may be warned or, at worst, may lose the round. The boxers are thus placed in a situation fraught with tension, physical punishment, and eventual fatigue. They may be harassed by the spectators. Their protection consists of their physical condition and their acquired confidence. Moreover, the outcome of the fight is decisive for their status and self-esteem.[10]

The boxer's persistent display of aggression is an aspect of status. Thus his aggression becomes impersonal, although competition is intense. Thus two boxers may be friends outside the ring, but each will try to knock the other out in a bout, and after the bout they may be as friendly as competition permits. Furthermore, the injury done to an opponent, such as maiming or killing, is quickly rationalized away by an effective trainer or manager in order to prevent an access of intense guilt, which can ruin a fighter. The general reaction is that the opponent is out to do the same thing to him and that this is the purpose of boxing: namely, to beat the opponent into submission. The exception is the "grudge fight," in which personal hostility is clearly manifest.

In a succession of bouts, if the fighter is at all successful, he goes through a fluctuating routine, in which tension mounts during training, is concentrated during the fight, and is discharged in the usual celebration, which most victorious fighters regard as their inevitable reward. Hence many boxers pursue a fast tempo of living and spend lavishly on clothes, women, gambling, and drink, practices seemingly tolerated by the manager and encouraged by the persons who are attracted to boxers. Many boxers experience intense conflict between the ordeals of training and the pursuits of pleasure.

SOCIAL STRUCTURE AND SOCIAL MOBILITY

Boxers comprise a highly stratified occupation. Rank is determined by their rating in a weight division, by their position in a match, and by their status with stablemates who have the same manager. Annually, for each weight

---

[10] Some defeated boxers, as a result of physical fatigue and self-recrimination, lapse into a condition resembling combat exhaustion or anxiety. They react by uncontrollable crying spells, tantrums, and random belligerency. The restoration of their confidence is crucial for subsequent fights. Some trainers and managers are quite skilled in accomplishing it.

division, fighters are ranked. The champion and about twenty leading contenders are listed on top.[11] The other fighters are listed into "A," "B," and "C" categories. Many local preliminary fighters are not listed. Only the first twenty contenders and the "A" category seem to have any importance. Of 1,831 fighters listed for 1950, 8.8 per cent comprised the champion and leading contenders; 10.9 per cent were in the "A" category; 74.3 per cent were in the "B" and "C" categories.

To determine the vertical mobility of fighters, the careers of 127 fighters were traced from 1938 onward.[12] Of these, 107, or 84.2 per cent, remained in the local preliminary or semiwindup category. Eleven boxers, or 8.7 per cent, became local headliners, which may be in the "A" category. They had been professional boxers for an average of almost eight years. Eight boxers, or 7.1 per cent, achieved national recognition, that is, among the first ten leading contenders. They also had been professionals for an average of almost eight years. One fighter became champion after twelve years in the ring.

The boxers who remain in the sport believe that they can ascend to the top because of the character of the boxing culture, in which the exceptional boxer is emphasized and with whom the aspiring boxer identifies. When the boxer ceases to aspire, he quits or becomes a part-time boxer. Yet the aspiring hopes of many boxers are not unfounded, because climbing in the sport does not depend upon ability only and also can be a result of a "lucky break."

RELATIONSHIPS OF THE BOXER

Boxers live in a wide social milieu of trainers, managers, and promoters. The boxer and trainer usually form the closest relationships in the boxing milieu. At one time, many managers were trainers, too; and a few owners of local gymnasiums still combine these roles, but their number has declined. Furthermore, the relationships between boxer and trainer are becoming increasingly impersonal. Consequently, the careful training and social intimacy which characterized the conditioning of many boxers by trainers in the past has also declined.[13]

Generally, the specialized trainer or trainer-manager represents the authority-figure to the boxer, transmits boxing skills to him, and becomes his anchor point of emotional security. The trainer's relationship with the boxer

[11] Data taken from *Ring*, February, 1951.

[12] These computations were made by following the fighters in every issue of *Ring* from 1938 on. This magazine lists all the fights for every month.

[13] "One of the troubles with boxing is what I call assembly line training. There are too few competent trainers and most of them have too many fighters to train. For the most part the boxers look upon training as a necessary evil. . . . [In the past], hours were spent on perfecting a movement — a feint, the proper tossing of a punch, the art of slipping a blow successfully. [This] marked the difference between a skilled craftsman and a lumbering wild-swinging tyro" (Al Buck, "Incompetency the Cause," *Ring*, September, 1950, p. 22).

becomes crucial to his development. The effective trainer polishes his skills, compels him to train regularly, and distracts him from worrying about the fight, and he can control him by withdrawing praise or can restore his morale when he has lost. For example, a trainer reviewed a lost fight to his charge so skilfully that the boxer began to believe that his opponent had won by a few lucky punches. Had he averted these "lucky" punches, the fighter felt that he would have won. His confidence restored, he renewed his training with added vigor and determination.

The trainer may be of distinct help to the boxer during the bout. Frequently his "second," he may advise him of his opponent's weaknesses and of his own faults. In addition, he can be a continuing source of confidence to the fighter. A fighter recalled that before a bout his trainer became ill. He felt alone and somewhat diffident when the fight began. He regained his confidence in the third round, when he felt that his opponent could not hurt him. Since the trainer can become so emotionally close to the fighter, he can help or hinder him, depending upon his insight and knowledge of boxing. Though very important to the fighter, the trainer is not a powerful figure in the boxing hierarchy, and some trainers are as exploited as are fighters by the managers.

One boxer has characterized managers as follows: "Some managers are interested in the money first and in the man second; other managers are interested in the man first." Our observations lead us to infer that the vast majority of managers at the present time are in the first category. They regard boxing as a business and the fighter as a commodity and are concerned mainly with making money. To do so, they are compelled to please the promoters and to sell their fighters' abilities to the promoters. Unless the manager is also a trainer, he is not concerned with the techniques of boxing, except to publicize his charge and to arrange matches which will bring the most revenue.

While the boxer devotes his aggressions to training and fighting, the manager slants his aggressions to machinations for better matches and for more money. Having few illusions about the fight business, acquainted with and often accepting its seamier side, he conforms to the standard managerial pattern of having the advantage over "his" boxers in every way. First, managers are organized into a guild, and, though some managers will try to steal boxers from one another, they usually bar fighters who run out on managers.[14] (One boxer, on the other hand, tried to organize fighters into a union. His efforts were squelched quickly, and he was informally blackballed from fighting in New York City.) Second, many managers try to keep their fighters financially and, if possible, emotionally tied to them. Some managers will encourage fighters to borrow money from them and usually will not discourage them from squandering their earnings. One manager stated characteristically: "It's good to have a fighter 'in you' for a couple of

[14] The managers' guild also serves in part as a kind of collective protection against promoters.

bucks." By having fighters financially indebted to them, they have an easy expedient for controlling individuals who are unusually headstrong. Some fighters are in the continual process of regarding every fight as an essential means for clearing their debts.

Legally managers cannot receive more than one-third of the fighters' purses, but many do not conform to this rule. Frequently, they take one-half the purse, or they may put their fighters on a flat salary and get the rest. Some managers tell their preliminary fighters that the purse was less than it was actually and thus keep the rest for themselves.

Furthermore, many managers abuse their fighters so as to make money quickly. They may overmatch them with superior fighters, "rush" them into too many fights, force them to fight when they are out of condition, and hint that the fight is "fixed" and instruct them indirectly to lose. A few managers will match their fighters in another state when they are barred in one state because of injuries; they will obtain matches before the required sixty days have elapsed after their fighters have been knocked out. Fighters may be severely hurt, even ruined, by these tactics.

Some managers, however, are concerned mainly with building up their fighters and doing everything possible to develop their maximum ability; but these managers are in the minority. In short, managers have no informal standards to protect their boxers and are guided chiefly by their own personal considerations in these activities.

Since many ruthless individuals and petty racketeers who know little about boxing are increasingly drawn into this sport with the prime purpose of making money quickly, boxers tend to have little, if any, protection from managers except that provided by boxing commissions, whose rules can be evaded without difficulty. Moreover, it is extremely difficult for a boxer to climb or get important matches unless he has an effective manager.

THE BOXER AND THE PROMOTER

The boxer's relationship with the promoter is usually indirect. Yet the promoter is the most influential person in the boxing hierarchy. He is primarily a showman and businessman, emotionally removed from the fighter, and regards him chiefly as a commodity. His aim is to get the most from his investment. Thus the "show" comes first, regardless of the boxer's welfare. To insure his direct control over many boxers, the promoter, who legally cannot be a manager, may appoint one or a series of "managers" as "fronts" and thus get shares of many boxers' earnings, as well as controlling them. Furthermore, he can reduce the amount of the fighter's share because the nominal manager will not bargain for a larger share. In effect, most boxers are relatively helpless in dealing with promoters, especially at the present time, because of the monopolistic character of boxing.

When a potentially good fighter wants to meet leading contenders, the manager may have to "cut in" the promotor or "cut in" some other manager who has connections with the promoter. Thus the mobility of the fighter depends in large part upon the manager's relationship to the promoter. When the manager does not have this acceptable relationship and is unwilling to "cut in" a third party, he will not get the desired matches.[15]

Since the promoter is concerned primarily with attracting a large audience, he tries to select and develop fighters who will draw customers.[16] Thus the fighter must have "crowd-pleasing" qualifications in addition to ability. In this connection, the race and ethnic group play a part. A good white fighter is preferred to a good Negro fighter; and in large cities, such as New York and Chicago, a Jewish fighter is considered highly desirable because the majority of fight fans are Jewish and Italian. Despite the efforts of promoters to attract white fighters, especially Jewish fighters, few Jewish fighters have emerged because the role-models and practices in the local Jewish communities have changed. Even Negro fighters, despite their dominance of the sport in quality and quantity of fighters, are increasingly turning to other sports because the role-models are slowly shifting.[17]

The fighter whom a promoter does select for grooming can easily be made mobile once he has shown crowd-pleasing tendencies. He can be, as it were, "nursed" to the top by being matched with opponents who are easy to beat or by meeting "set-ups" who are instructed to lose. Thus he builds up an impressive record and is ready for big-time fights. Hence, it is difficult to tell how competent a fighter is on his early record alone, for his record may be designed for publicity purposes. When a fighter has won all or nearly all of his early matches and then loses repeatedly to leading contenders, he has been "nursed" to the top by the promoter, unless the fighter has incurred an injury in one of his later fights. In these ways the promoter can influence decisively the occupational career of the boxer.

EFFECT UPON THE BOXER

The punitive character of boxing, as well as the social relationships in the boxing milieu, affects the boxer-participants during and after their careers in the ring.

---

[15] E.g., an outstanding light-heavyweight contender is unable to get a title match, although one whom he has defeated will get the match. He was slighted because his manager has not signed with the International Boxing Club. His manager has stated: "The I.B.C. dictates who fights who and when and where. They're big business. But I'll fight; I'm trying to keep the independents [boxers and managers] in business" (*Time*, July 9, 1951, pp. 58–59).

[16] The taste of contemporary fight fans is directed mainly toward punchers rather than boxers. In the past, clever boxers were highly appreciated.

[17] "In 1937 when [Joe] Louis won the crown from Jimmy Braddock, every Negro boy in all corners of the country worshipped him. Their thoughts centered on boxing and boxing gloves. . . . The boys who once worshipped Louis as boxer have gone daffy about a baseball hero, Jackie Robinson. . . . The eyes of the boys who once looked upon Joe Louis with pride and envy and wanted to emulate him, now are focussed on Jackie Robinson and other topnotch ballplayers" (Nat Loubet, "Jackie Robinson's Rise Blow to Boxing," *Ring*, September, 1950, p. 5).

First, the physical effects of boxing, which are intrinsic to the sport, operate to the boxer's detriment. Although boxers may cultivate strong bodies, the direct and indirect injuries from this sport are very high. In addition to the deaths in the ring, one estimate is that 60 per cent of the boxers become mildly punch-drunk and 5 per cent become severely punch-drunk.[18] The severely punch-drunk fighter can be detected by an ambling gait, thickened or retarded speech, mental stereotypy, and a general decline in efficiency. In addition, blindness and visual deficiency are so pervasive that eye injuries are considered virtually as occupational casualties, while misshaped noses and cauliflower ears are afflictions of most boxers who are in the sport for five or more years. Despite these injuries, attempts to provide safeguards, such as headguards, have been opposed by the fans and by many boxers because such devices presumably did not "protect" and did not fit into their conceptions of virility and presumed contempt for punishment.[19]

Second, the boxing culture tends to work to the eventual detriment of the boxer. Many boxers tend to continue a particular fight when they are hopelessly beaten and when they can become severely injured. Many boxers persist in fighting when they have passed their prime and even when they have been injured. For example, one boxer, blind in one eye and barred from fighting in one state, was grateful to his manager for getting him matches in other states. Another old-time boxer has admitted characteristically: "It's hard to quit. Fighting gets into your blood, and you can't get it out." Many fighters try to make one comeback, at least, and some fight until they are definitely punch-drunk.

Boxers find further that, despite their success in the sport, their careers terminate at a relatively early age.[20] Since their physical condition is so decisive to their role, when they feel a decline in their physical prowess, they tend also to acquire the premature feeling of "being old." This attitude is reinforced by others in the sport who refer to them as "old men," meaning old in the occupation. Since boxing has been the vocational medium of status attainment and since they have no other skills to retain that status, many boxers experience a sharp decline in status in their postboxing careers. As an illustration, of ninety-five leading former boxers (i.e., champions and leading contenders), each of whom earned more than $100,000 during his ring career, eighteen were found to have remained in the sport as trainers

[18] Arthur H. Steinhaus, "Boxing — Legalized Murder," *Look Magazine*, January 3, 1950, p. 36.

[19] Some precautions have been innovated recently for the boxer's protection, such as the thickness of the padding on the floor of the ring or the absence of protrusions or sharp corners in the ring.

[20] Although the boxing myths emphasize the exceptions who fought past the age of forty — e.g., Bob Fitzsimmons fought until he was about fifty-two — the average fighter is considered "old" after he is thirty years of age. At present [1952], some "old" fighters are still successfully active — e.g., Joe Louis and "Jersey Joe" Walcott, who are thirty-seven years old. In addition to being exceptions, their successful participation in the ring is also a result of the fact that few new heavyweights are entering boxing.

or trainer-managers; two became wrestlers; twenty-six worked in, "fronted for," or owned taverns;[21] two were liquor salesmen; eighteen had unskilled jobs, most commonly in the steelmills; six worked in the movies; five were entertainers; two owned or worked in gas stations; three were cab-drivers; three had newsstands; two were janitors; three were bookies; three were associated with the race tracks (two in collecting bets and one as a starter); and two were in business, one of them as a custom tailor. In short, the successful boxers have a relatively quick economic ascent at a relatively young age in terms of earning power. But the punitive character of the sport, the boxers' dependence upon their managers, and their carefree spending during their boxing careers contribute to a quicker economic descent for many boxers. Their economic descent is accompanied by a drop in status and frequently by temporary or prolonged emotional difficulties in readjusting to their new occupational roles.[22]

[21] Since successful boxers retain a reputation in their respective neighborhoods after they have quit the sport, some businessmen use their names as "fronts" for taverns or lounges. Hence it was difficult to find out whether the boxers themselves owned the taverns. In five cases they did not, although the taverns were in their names.

[22] One former champion said: "I like to hear of a boxer doing well after he leaves the ring. People think all boxers are punchy. We have a bad press. After I left the ring, I had a devil of a time telling people I wasn't punchy." The Veterans Boxing Association, an organization of former boxers, have protested occasionally against radio programs which present what they consider a false stereotype of the former boxer.

The following selection represents a community study of two South-western communities and the independent role of values in influencing action. Traditionally the Mormons have been a distinctive subgroup in this country with, for all practical purposes, their own state, religion, and value system. In short, their culture is different from that of the dominant society. Vogt and O'Dea examine the differences between a Mormon community and non-Mormon community in a similar part of the country. They attempt to explain why the Mormons developed a successful and integrated farming community with moderate affluence and the other community did not. Their answer lies in the difference between the two value systems as they influence adaptation to environment.

8 Evon Z. Vogt and Thomas O'Dea

A Comparative Study of the Role of Values in Social Action in Two Southwestern Communities

It is one of the central hypotheses of the Values Study Project that value-orientations play an important part in the shaping of social institutions and in influencing the forms of observed social action. By value-orientations are understood those views of the world, often implicitly held, which define the meaning of human life or the "life situation of man" and thereby provide the context in which day-to-day problems are solved.[1] The present article is an outgrowth of one phase of the field research carried out in western New Mexico. It presents the record of two communities composed of people with a similar cultural background and living in the same general ecological setting.

The responses of these two communities to similar problems were found to be quite different. Since the physical setting of the two villages is remarkably similar, the explanation for the differences was sought in the manner in which each group viewed the situation and the kind of social relationships and legitimate expectations which each felt appropriate in meeting situational challenges. In this sphere of value-orientations a marked difference was found. Moreover, the differences in response to situation in the two cases were found to be related to the differences between the value-orientations central to these communities.

We do not deny the importance of situational factors. Nor do we intend to disparage the importance of historical convergence of value-orientations with concrete situations in explaining the centrality of some values as against others and in leading to the deep internalization of the values we discuss. But the importance of value-orientations as an element in understanding the situation of action is inescapably clear. All the elements of what Parsons has called the action frame of reference — the actors, the means and conditions which comprise the situation, and the value-orientations of the actors enter into the act.[2] The primacy of any one in any individual case does not permit generalization. Yet the present study testifies to the great importance of the third element — the value-orientations — in shaping the final action which ensues.

From *American Sociological Review,* Vol. XVIII (December, 1953), pp. 645–654. Reprinted by permission of the authors and the American Sociological Association.

[1] Clyde Kluckhohn, "Values and Value-Orientations in the Theory of Action: an Exploration in Definition and Classification," *Toward a General Theory of Action,* edited by Talcott Parsons and E. A. Shils, Cambridge: Harvard University Press, 1951, p. 410.

[2] Talcott Parsons, *The Structure of Social Action,* Glencoe: Free Press, 1949, pp. 43–86; *Essays in Sociological Theory,* Glencoe: Free Press, 1949, pp. 32–40; *The Social System,* Glencoe: Free Press, 1951, pp. 3–24.

FOCUS OF THE INQUIRY

The inquiry is focused upon a comparison of the Mormon community of *Rimrock*[3] with the Texan community of *Homestead,* both having populations of approximately 250 and both located (forty miles apart) on the southern portion of the Colorado Plateau in western New Mexico. The natural environmental setting is virtually the same for the two villages: the prevailing elevations stand at 7,000 feet; the landscapes are characterized by mesa and canyon country; the flora and fauna are typical of the Upper Sonoran Life Zone with stands of pinyon, juniper, sagebrush, and blue gramma grass and some intrusions of Ponderosa pine, Douglas fir, Englemann spruce and Gambel oak from a higher life zone; the region has a steppe climate with an average annual precipitation of 14 inches (which varies greatly from year to year) and with killing frosts occurring late in the spring and early in the autumn.[4] The single important environmental difference between the two communities is that Rimrock is located near the base of a mountain range which has elevations rising to 9,000 feet, and a storage reservoir (fed by melting snow packs from these higher elevations) has made irrigation agriculture possible in Rimrock, while in Homestead there is only dry-land farming. Today both villages have subsistence patterns based upon combinations of farming (mainly irrigated crops of alfalfa and wheat in Rimrock, and dry-land crops of pinto beans in Homestead) and livestock raising (mainly Hereford beef cattle in both villages).

Rimrock was settled by Mormon missionaries in the 1870's as part of a larger project to plant settlements in the area of northern Arizona. Rimrock itself, unlike the Arizona sites, was established as a missionary outpost and the intention of the settlers was the conversion of the Indians, a task conceived in terms of the *Book of Mormon,* which defines the American Indian as "a remnant of Israel."

The early settlers were "called" by the Church, that is, they were selected and sent out by the Church authorities. The early years were exceedingly difficult and only the discipline of the Church and the loyalty of the settlers to its gospel kept them at the task. Drought, crop diseases, and the breaking of the earth and rock dam which they had constructed for the storage of irrigation water added to their difficulties, as did the fact that they had merely squatted on the land and were forced to purchase it at an exorbitant price to avoid eviction. The purchase money was given by the Church authorities in Salt Lake City, who also supplied 5,000 pounds of seed wheat in another period of dearth. The original settlers were largely from northern

---

[3] "Rimrock" and "Homestead" are pseudonyms used to protect the anonymity of our informants.

[4] For additional ecological details on the region see Evon Z. Vogt, *Navaho Veterans: A Study of Changing Values,* Peabody Museum of Harvard University, Papers, Vol. XLI, No. 1, 1951, pp. 11–12. . . .

Utah although there were also some converts from the southern states who had been involved in unsuccessful Arizona settlements a few years earlier.

As the emphasis shifted from missionary activities to farming, Rimrock developed into a not unusual Mormon village, despite its peripheral position to the rest of Mormondom. Irrigation farming was supplemented by cattle raising on the open range. In the early 1930's the Mormons began to buy range land, and Rimrock's economy shifted to a focus upon cattle raising. Today villagers own a total of 149 sections of range land and about four sections of irrigated or irrigable land devoted to gardens and some irrigated pastures in the immediate vicinity of the village. The family farm is still the basic economic unit, although partnerships formed upon a kinship basis and devoted to cattle raising have been important in raising the economic level of the village as a whole. In recent years some of the villagers — also on the basis of a kinship partnership — purchased the local trading post which is engaged in trading with the Indians as well as local village business. In addition to 12 family partnerships which own 111 sections of land, there is a village cooperative which owns 38 sections. Privately owned commercial facilities in the village include two stores, a boarding house, two garages, a saddle and leather shop, and a small restaurant. With this economic variety there is considerable difference in the distribution of wealth.

The Church is the central core of the village and its complex hierarchical structure, including the auxiliary organizations which activate women, youth, and young children, involves a large portion of the villagers in active participation. The church structure is backed up and impenetrated by the kinship structure. Moreover, church organization and kinship not only unify Rimrock into a social unit, they also integrate it into the larger structure of the Mormon Church and relate it by affinity and consanguinity to the rest of Mormondom.

Rimrock has been less affected by secularization than most Mormon villages in Utah and is less assimilated into generalized American patterns.[5] Its relative isolation has both kept such pressures from impinging upon it with full force and enhanced its formal and informal ties with the Church, preserving many of the characteristics of a Mormon village of a generation ago.

Homestead was settled by migrants from the South Plains area of western Texas and Oklahoma in the early 1930's. The migration represented a small aspect of that vast movement of people westward to California which was popularized in Steinbeck's *Grapes of Wrath* and which was the subject of investigation by many governmental agencies in the 1930's and 1940's.[6]

---

[5] Lowry Nelson, *The Mormon Village*. Salt Lake City: University of Utah Press, 1952, pp. 275–85.

[6] See especially the reports of the Tolan Committee, U. S. Congress, "House Committee to Investigate the Interstate Migration of Destitute Citizens," 76th Congress, 3rd Session, Volume 6, Part 6, 1940.

Instead of going on to California, these homesteaders settled in a number of semi-arid farming areas in northern and western New Mexico and proceeded to develop an economy centered around the production of pinto beans. The migration coincided with the period of national depression and was due in part to severe economic conditions on the South Plains which forced families to leave their Texas and Oklahoma communities, in part to the attraction of land available for homesteading which held out the promise of family-owned farms for families who had previously owned little or no land or who had lost their land during the depression. The land base controlled by the homesteaders comprises approximately 100 sections. Each farm unit is operated by a nuclear family; there are no partnerships. Farms now average two sections in size and are scattered as far as twenty miles from the crossroads center of the community which contains the two stores, the school, the post office, two garages, a filling station, a small restaurant, a bean warehouse, a small bar, and two church buildings. Through the years, farming technology has shifted almost completely from horse-drawn implements to mechanized equipment.

With the hazardous farming conditions (periodic droughts and early killing frosts) out-migration from Homestead has been relatively high. A few of these families have gone on to California, but more of them have moved to irrigated farms in the middle Rio Grande Valley and entered an agricultural situation which in its physical environmental aspects is similar to the situation in the Mormon community of Rimrock.

THE MORMON CASE

In broad perspective these two villages present local variations of generalized American culture. They share the common American value-orientations which emphasize the importance of achievement and success, progress and optimism, and rational mastery over nature. In the Mormon case, these were taken over from the 19th century American milieu in western New York where the Church was founded, and reinterpreted in terms of an elaborate theological conception of the universe as a dynamic process in which God and men are active collaborators in an eternal progression to greater power through increasing mastery.[7] The present life was and is conceived as a single episode in an infinity of work and mastery. The result was the heightening for the Mormons of convictions shared with most other Americans. Moreover, this conception was closely related to the belief in the reopening of divine revelation through the agency first of Joseph Smith, the original Mormon prophet, and later through the institutionalized channels of the Mormon Church. The Mormons conceived of themselves as a covenant people especially chosen for a divine task. This task was the building of the kingdom of God on earth and in this project — attempted four

[7] The data from Rimrock are based upon seven months field experience in the community during 1950–51. . . .

times unsuccessfully before the eventual migration to the west — much of the religious and secular socialism of the early 19th century found a profound reflection. The Mormon prophet proposed the "Law of Consecration" in an attempt to reconcile private initiative with cooperative endeavor. Contention led to its abandonment in 1838 after some five years of unsuccessful experiment. Yet this withdrawal did not limit, but indeed rather enhanced, its future influence in Mormon settlement. The "Law of Consecration" was no longer interpreted as a blueprint prescribing social institutions of a definite sort, but its values lent a strong cooperative bias to much of later Mormon activity.[8] In the context of the notion of peculiarity and reinforced by outgroup antagonism and persecution, these values became deeply embedded in Mormon orientations. The preference for agriculture combined with an emphasis upon community and lay participation in church activities resulted in the formation of compact villages rather than isolated family farmsteads as the typical Mormon settlement pattern.[9]

While Rimrock and Homestead share most of the central value-orientations of general American culture, they differ significantly in the values governing social relationships. Rimrock, with a stress upon community cooperation, an ethnocentrism resulting from the notion of their own peculiarity, and a village pattern of settlement, is more like the other Mormon villages of the West than it is like Homestead.

The stress upon *community cooperation* in Rimrock contrasts markedly with the stress upon *individual independence* found in Homestead. This contrast is one of emphasis, for individual initiative is important in Rimrock, especially in family farming and cattle raising, whereas cooperative activity does occur in Homestead. In Rimrock, however, the expectations are such that one must show his fellows or at least convince himself that he has good cause for *not* committing his time and resources to community efforts while in Homestead cooperative action takes place *only* after certainty has been reached that the claims of other individuals upon one's time and resources are legitimate.

Rimrock was a cooperative venture from the start, and very early the irrigation company, a mutual non-profit corporation chartered under state law, emerged from the early water association informally developed around — and in a sense within — the Church. In all situations which transcend the capacities of individual families or family combinations, Rimrock Mormons have recourse to cooperative techniques. Let us examine four examples.

---

[8] The "Law of Consecration" became the basis of the Mormon pattern of cooperative activity also known as "The United Order of Enoch." Cf. Joseph A. Geddes, *The United Order Among the Mormons,* Salt Lake City: Deseret News Press, 1924; Edward J. Allen, *The Second United Order Among the Mormons,* New York: Columbia University Press, 1936.

[9] Nelson, *op. cit.,* pp. 25–54.

The "tight" land situation. Rimrock Mormons, feeling themselves "gathered," dislike having to migrate to non-Mormon areas. However, after World War II the 32 returned veterans faced a choice between poverty and underemployment or leaving the community. This situation became the concern of the Church and was discussed in its upper lay priesthood bodies in the village. It was decided to buy land to enable the veterans to remain. The possibilities of land purchase in the area were almost nonexistent and it appeared that nothing could be done, when unexpectedly the opportunity to buy some 38 sections presented itself. At the time, the village did not have the needed $10,000 for the down payment, so the sum was borrowed from the Cooperative Security Corporation, a Church Welfare Plan agency, and the land was purchased. The patterns revealed here — community concern over a community problem, and appeal to and reception of aid from the general authorities of the Church — are typically Mormon. However, Mormon cooperation did not end here. Instead of breaking up the purchased land into plots to be individually owned and farmed, the parcel was kept as a unit, and a cooperative Rimrock Land and Cattle Company was formed. The company copied and adapted the form of the mutual irrigation company. Shares were sold in the village, each member being limited to two. A quota of cattle per share per year to be run on the land and a quota of bulls relative to cows were established. The cattle are privately owned, but the land is owned and managed cooperatively. The calves are the property of the owners of the cows. The project, which has not been limited to veterans, supplements other earnings sufficiently to keep most of the veterans in the village.

The graveling of the village streets. The streets of Rimrock were in bad repair in the fall of 1950. That summer a construction company had brought much large equipment into the area to build and gravel a section of a state highway which runs through the village. Before this company left, taking its equipment with it, villagers, again acting through the Church organization, decided that the village should avail itself of the opportunity and have the town's streets graveled. This was discussed in the Sunday priesthood meeting and announced at the Sunday sacrament meeting. A meeting was called for Monday evening, and each household was asked to send a representative. The meeting was well attended, and although not every family had a member present, practically all were represented at least by proxy. There was considerable discussion, and it was finally decided to pay $800 for the job which meant a $20 donation from each family. The local trader paid a larger amount, and, within a few days after the meeting, the total amount was collected. Only one villager raised objections to the proceedings. Although he was a man of importance locally, he was soon silenced by a much poorer man who invoked Mormon values of progress and cooperation and pledged to give $25 which was $5 above the norm.

The construction of a high school gymnasium. In 1951 a plan for the construction of a high school gymnasium was presented to the Rimrock villagers. Funds for materials and for certain skilled labor would be provided from state school appropriations, providing that the local residents would contribute the labor for construction. The plan was discussed in a Sunday priesthood meeting in the church, and later meetings were held both in the church and in the schoolhouse. Under the leadership of the principal of the school (who is also a member of the higher priesthood), arrangements were made whereby each able-bodied man in the community would either contribute at least 50 hours of labor or $50 (the latter to be used to hire outside laborers) toward the construction. The original blueprint was extended to include a row of classrooms for the high school around the large central gymnasium.

Work on the new building began in late 1951, continued through 1952, and is now (in 1953) nearing completion. The enterprise was not carried through without difficulties. A few families were sympathetic at first but failed to contribute full amounts of either labor or cash, and some were unsympathetic toward the operation from the start. The high school principal had to keep reminding the villagers about their pledges to support the enterprise. But in the end the project was successful, and it represented an important cooperative effort on the part of the majority.

The community dances. The Mormons have always considered dancing to be an important form of recreation — in fact a particularly Mormon form of recreation. Almost every Friday evening a dance is held in the village church house. These dances are family affairs and are opened and closed with prayer. They are part of the general Church recreation program and are paid for by what is called locally "the budget." The budget refers to the plan under which villagers pay $15 per family per year to cover a large number of entertainments, all sponsored by the Church auxiliary organization for youth, the Young Men's Mutual Improvement Association, and the Young Women's Mutual Improvement Association. The budget payment admits all members of the family to such entertainments.

Observation of these dances over a six-month period did not reveal any tension or fighting. Smoking and drinking are forbidden to loyal Mormons, and those who smoked did so outside and away from the building. At dances held in the local school there has been evidence of drinking, and at times fighting has resulted from the presence of non-villagers. But on the whole the Rimrock dances are peaceful family affairs.

Rimrock reveals itself responding to group problems *as a group.* The economic ethic set forth by Joseph Smith in the Law of Consecration is seen in the dual commitment to private individual initiative (family farms and family partnerships in business and agriculture) and to cooperative endeavor in larger communal problems (irrigation company, land and cattle company, graveling the streets, and construction of school gymnasium). For the Mormons, cooperation has become second nature. It has become part of the institutionalized structure of expectations, reinforced by religious conviction and social control.

THE HOMESTEADER CASE

The value-stress upon individual independence of action has deep roots in the history of the homesteader group.[10] The homesteaders were part of the westward migration from the hill country of the Southern Appalachians to the Panhandle country of Texas and Oklahoma and from there to the Southwest and California. Throughout their historical experience there has been an emphasis upon a rough and ready self-reliance and individualism, the Jacksonianism of the frontier West. The move to western New Mexico from the South Plains was made predominantly by isolated nuclear families, and Homestead became a community of scattered, individually owned farmsteads — a geographical situation and a settlement pattern which reinforced the stress upon individualism.

Let us now examine the influence of this individualistic value-orientation upon a series of situations comparable to those that were described for Rimrock.

The "tight" land situation. In 1934 the Federal Security Administration, working in conjunction with the Land Use Division of the Department of Agriculture, proposed a "unit re-organization plan." This plan would have enabled the homesteaders to acquire additional tracts of land and permit them to run more livestock and hence depend less upon the more hazardous economic pursuit of dry-land pinto bean farming. It called for the use of government funds to purchase large ranches near the Homestead area which would be managed cooperatively by a board of directors selected by the community. The scheme collapsed while it was still in the planning stages, because it was clear that each family expected to acquire its own private holdings on the range and that a cooperative would not work in Homestead.

The graveling of the village streets. During the winter of 1949–50 the construction company which was building the highway through Rimrock was also building a small section of highway north of Homestead. The construction company offered to gravel the streets of Homestead center if the residents who lived in the village would cooperatively contribute enough funds for the purpose. This community plan was rejected by the homesteaders, and an alternative plan was followed. Each of the operators of several of the service institutions — including the two stores, the bar, and the post office — independently hired the construction company truck drivers to haul a few loads of gravel to be placed in front of his own place of business, which still left the rest of the village streets a sea of mud in rainy weather.

The construction of a high school gymnasium. In 1950 the same plan for the construction of a new gymnasium was presented to the homesteaders as

[10] The data from Homestead are based upon a year's field work in the community during 1949–50. Additional data on this community will be provided in Vogt's forthcoming monograph on *The Homesteaders: A Study of Values in a Frontier Community.* See also Vogt, "Water Witching: An Interpretation of a Ritual Pattern in a Rural American Community," *Scientific Monthly,* LXXV (September, 1952).

was presented to the Mormon village of Rimrock. As noted above, this plan was accepted by the community of Rimrock, and the new building is now nearing completion. But the plan was rejected by the residents of Homestead at a meeting in the summer of 1950, and there were long speeches to the effect that "I've got to look after my own farm and my own family first; I can't be up here in town building a gymnasium." Later in the summer additional funds were provided for labor; and with these funds adobe bricks were made, the foundation was dug, and construction was started — the homesteaders being willing to work on the gymnasium on a purely business basis at a dollar an hour. But as soon as the funds were exhausted, construction stopped. Today a partially completed gymnasium, and stacks of some 10,000 adobe bricks disintegrating slowly with the rains, stand as monuments to the individualism of the homesteaders.

The community dances. As in Rimrock, the village dances in Homestead are important focal points for community activity. These affairs take place several times a year in the schoolhouse and are always well-attended. But while the dances in Rimrock are well-coordinated activities which carry through the evening, the dances in Homestead often end when tensions between rival families result in fist-fights. And there is always the expectation in Homestead that a dance (or other cooperative activity such as a picnic or rodeo) may end at any moment and the level of activity reduced to the component nuclear families which form the only solid core of social organization within the community.

The individualistic value-orientation of the homesteaders also has important functional relationships to the religious organization of the community. With the exception of two men who are professed atheists, all of the homesteaders define themselves as Christians. But denominationalism is rife, there being ten different denominations represented in the village: Baptist, Presbyterian, Methodist, Nazarene, Campbellite, Holiness, 7th Day Adventist, Mormon, Catholic, and Present Day Disciples.

In the most general terms, this religious differentiation in Homestead can be interpreted as a function of the individualistic and factionalizing tendencies in the social system. In a culture with a value-stress upon independent individual action combined with a "freedom of religion" ideology, adhering to one's own denomination becomes an important means of expressing individualism and of focusing factional disputes around a doctrine and a concrete institutional framework. In turn, the doctrinal differences promote additional factionalizing tendencies, with the result that competing churches become the battleground for a cumulative and circularly reinforcing struggle between rival small factions within the community.[11]

---

[11] This relationship between churches and factionalizing tendencies has also been observed by Bailey in his unpublished study of a community in west Texas, in the heart of the ancestral home region of the present residents of Homestead. Cf. Wilfrid C. Bailey, "A Study of a Texas Panhandle Community; A Preliminary Report on Cotton Center, Texas," Values Study Files, Harvard University.

To sum up, we may say that the strong commitment to an individualistic value-orientation has resulted in a social system in which inter-personal relations are strongly colored by a kind of factionalism and in which persons and groups become related to one another in a competitive, feuding relationship. The homesteaders do not live on their widely separated farms and ignore one another, as it might be possible to do. On the other hand, they do not cooperate in community affairs as closely as does a hive of bees. They interact, but a constant feuding tone permeates the economic, social and religious structure of the community.

RELATIONSHIP BETWEEN THE TWO COMMUNITIES

Although there is some trading in livestock, feed, and other crops, the most important contacts between the two communities are not economic but are social and recreational. The village baseball teams have scheduled games with one another for the past two decades, and there is almost always joint participation in the community dances and in the summer rodeos in the two communities. Despite Mormon objections to close associations with "gentiles," there is also considerable inter-dating between the two communities among the teen-age groups, and three intermarriages have taken place.

In general, the homesteaders envy and admire the Mormons' economic organization, their irrigated land, and more promising prospects for good crops each year. On the other hand, they regard the Mormons as cliquish and unfriendly and fail completely to understand why anyone "wants to live all bunched up the way the Mormons do." They feel that the Mormons are inbred and think they should be glad to get "new blood" from inter-marriages with homesteaders. They add, "That Mormon religion is something we can't understand at all." Finally, the homesteaders say that Mormons "used to have more than one wife, and some probably still do; they dance in the church, they're against liquor, coffee, and tobacco, and they always talk about Joseph Smith and the *Book of Mormon*."

The Mormons consider their own way of life distinctly superior to that of the homesteaders in every way. Some will admit that the homesteaders have the virtue of being more friendly and of "mixing more with others," and their efforts in the face of farming hazards are admired, but Homestead is generally regarded as a rough and in some ways immoral community, especially because of the drinking, smoking, and fighting (particularly at dances) that takes place. They also feel that Homestead is disorganized and that the churches are not doing what they should for the community. For the past few years they have been making regular missionary trips to Homestead, but to date they have made no conversions.

COMPARISONS AND CONCLUSIONS

In the case of Rimrock and Homestead, we are dealing with two communities which are comparable in population, in ecological setting, and which are variants of the same general culture. The two outstanding differences are: (1) irrigation versus dry-land farming and associated differences in settlement pattern, compact village versus isolated farmstead type;[12] (2) a value stress upon cooperative community action versus a stress upon individual action. The important question here involves the relationship (if any) between these two sets of variables. Is the cooperation in Rimrock directly a function of an irrigation agriculture situation with a compact village settlement pattern, the rugged individualism in Homestead, a function of a dry-land farming situation with a scattered settlement pattern? Or did these value-orientations arise out of earlier historical experience in each case, influence the types of communities which were established in western New Mexico, and later persist in the face of changed economic situations? We shall attempt to demonstrate that the second proposition is more in accord with the historical facts as we now know them.

Nelson has recently shown that the general pattern of the Mormon village is neither a direct function (in its beginnings) of the requirements of irrigation agriculture, nor of the need for protection against Indians on the frontier. Rather, the basic pattern was a social invention of the Mormons, motivated by a sense of urgent need to prepare a dwelling place for the "Savior" at "His Second Coming." The "Plat of the City of Zion" was invented by Joseph Smith, Sidney Rigdon, and Frederick G. Williams in 1833 and has formed the basis for the laying out of most Mormon villages, even those established in the Middle West before the Mormons migrated to Utah.[13]

It is very clear that both the compact village pattern and the cooperative social arrangements centered around the church existed before the Mormons engaged in irrigation agriculture and had a strong influence upon the development of community structure not only in Utah but in the Mormon settlements like Rimrock on the periphery of the Mormon culture area. There is no objective reason in the Rimrock ecological and cultural setting (the local Navahos and Zunis did not pose a threat to pioneer settlements in the 1880's) why the Mormons could not have set up a community which conformed more to the isolated farmstead type with a greater stress upon individualistic social relations. Once the Mormon community was established, it is clear that the cooperation required by irrigation agriculture of the Mormon type and the general organization of the church strongly reinforced the value stress upon communal social action.

It is of further significance that as the population expanded and the Rimrock Mormons shifted from irrigation agricultural pursuits to dry-land ranching in the region outside of the Rimrock valley, the earlier cooperative patterns modeled on the mutual irrigation company were applied to the solution of economic problems that are identical to those faced by the Home-

[12] Cf. Nelson, *op. cit.*, p. 4.
[13] Nelson, *op. cit.*, pp. 28–38.

steaders. Moreover, in midwestern and eastern cities to which Mormons have recently moved, church wards have purchased and cooperatively worked church welfare plan farms.

In Homestead, on the other hand, our evidence indicates that the first settlers were drawn from a westward-moving population which stressed a frontier-type of self-reliance and individualism. They were searching for a place where each man could "own his own farm and be his own boss." Each family settled on its isolated homestead claim, and there emerged from the beginning an isolated farmstead type of settlement pattern in which the nuclear family was the solidary unit. The service center which was built up later simply occupied lots that were sold to storekeepers, filling station operators, the bartender, and others, by the four families who owned the four sections which joined at a crossroads. Only two of these four family homes were located near the service center at the crossroads. The other two families continued to maintain their homes in other quarters of their sections and lived almost a mile from "town." In 1952 one of the former families built a new home located over a mile from the center of town, and commented that they had always looked forward to "getting out of town."

There is no objective reason in the Homestead ecological setting why there could not be more clustering of houses into a compact village and more community cooperation than actually exists. One would not expect those farmers whose farms are located 15 or 20 miles from the service center to live in "town" and travel out to work each day. But there is no reason why those families living within 2 or 3 miles of the village center could not live in town and work their fields from there. In typical Mormon villages a large percentage of the farms are located more than three miles from the farm homes. For example, in Rimrock over 31 per cent, in Escalante over 38 per cent, and in Ephriam over 30 per cent of the farms are located from three to eight or more miles from the center of the villages.[14]

It is clear that the homesteaders were operating with a set of individualistic property arrangements (drawn, of course, from our generalized American culture) and that their strong stress upon individualism led to a quite different utilization of these property patterns (than was the case with the Mormons) and to the establishment of a highly scattered type of community. Once Homestead was established, the individualism permitted by the scattered dry-land farming pattern, and encouraged by the emphasis upon the small nuclear family unit and upon multi-denominationalism in church affiliation reacted on and strongly reinforced the value stress upon individual independence. It is evident that the homesteaders continue to prefer this way of life, as shown by their remarks concerning the "bunched up" character of a Mormon village and the fact that a number of families have recently moved "out of town" when they built new houses.

---

[14] See Nelson, op. cit., pp. 99 and 144 for data on Escalante and Ephriam.

Of further interest is the fact that when homesteader families move to irrigated farms in the middle Rio Grande Valley, the stress upon individual action tends to persist strongly. They do not readily develop cooperative patterns to deal with this new setting which is similar to the situation in the irrigated valley of the Mormons at Rimrock. Indeed, one of the principal innovations they have been promoting in one region along the Rio Grande where they are replacing Spanish-Americans on the irrigated farming land is a system of meters on irrigation ditches. These meters will measure the water flowing into each individual farmer's ditches, and effectively eliminate the need for more highly organized cooperative arrangements for distributing the available supply of water.

In conclusion, we should like to reiterate that we are strongly cognizant of situational factors. If the Rimrock Mormons had not been able to settle in a valley which was watered by melting snow packs from a nearby mountain and which provided the possibilities for the construction of a storage reservoir, they certainly could not have developed an irrigation agricultural system at all. In the case of Rimrock, however, the actual site of settlement was selected from among several possible sites in a larger situation. The selection was largely influenced by Mormon preconceptions of the type of village they wished to establish. In fact, Mormons chose the irrigable valleys throughout the inter-montane west. On the other hand, the physical environmental features for the development of irrigation were simply not present in the Homestead setting, and the people had no alternative to dry-land farming. There is no evidence to suggest that had they found an irrigable valley, they would have developed it along Mormon lines. In fact, the homesteaders' activities in the Rio Grande Valley suggest just the opposite. It is clear that the situational facts did not determine in any simple sense the contrasting community structures which emerged. Rather, the situations set certain limits, but within these limits contrasting value-orientations influenced the development of two quite different community types. It would appear that solutions to problems of community settlement pattern and the type of concrete social action which ensues are set within a value framework which importantly influences the selections made with the range of possibilities existing within an objective situation.

IV SYMBOLIC COMMUNICATION

A. Definitions and Concepts

As we have seen, culture is composed of, among other things, symbols. For Leslie White, another anthropologist, the symbol and man's ability to use it in verbal communication are what makes him human. White distinguishes the concept of symbol from that of sign. He also points out how the context in which each of these occurs will determine its definition. In other words, such basic things as the self are dependent for their meaning on the "situational context."

9 LESLIE A. WHITE

The Symbol: The Origin and Basis of Human Behavior

I

In July, 1939, a celebration was held at Leland Stanford University to commemorate the hundredth anniversary of the discovery that the cell is the basic unit of all living tissue. Today we are beginning to realize and to appreciate the fact that the symbol is the basic unit of all human behavior and civilization.

All human behavior originates in the use of symbols. It was the symbol which transformed our anthropoid ancestors into men and made them

Reprinted with permission of the author and Farrar, Strauss & Giroux, Inc. from *The Science of Culture* by Leslie A. White. Copyright 1949 by Leslie A. White.

human. All civilizations have been generated, and are perpetuated, only by the use of symbols. It is the symbol which transforms an infant of homo sapiens into a human being, deaf mutes who grow up without the use of symbols are not human beings. All human behavior consists of, or is dependent upon, the use of symbols. Human behavior is symbolic behavior; symbolic behavior is human behavior. The symbol is the universe of humanity.

II

[handwritten: earlier fincalist]
[handwritten: White was the culture theorist par excellence qui later popn genetics types]

The great Darwin declared that "there is no fundamental difference between man and the higher mammals in their mental faculties," that the difference between them consists "solely in his [man's] almost infinitely larger power of associating together the most diversified sounds and ideas," (Ch. III, *The Descent of Man*). Thus the difference between the mind of man and that of other mammals is merely one of degree, and it is not "fundamental." *[handwritten: See Whole in T World of Math - & o]*

Essentially the same views are held by many present day students of human behavior. Professor Ralph Linton, an anthropologist, writes in *The Study of Man*:[1] "The differences between men and animals in all these [behavior] respects are enormous, but they seem to be differences in quantity rather than in quality" (p. 79; the same idea is also expressed on p. 68). *[handwritten margin: + proper Self M is Man]* "Human and animal behavior can be shown to have so much in common," Professor Linton observes, "that the gap [between them] ceases to be of great importance" (p. 60). Dr. Alexander Goldenweiser, likewise an anthropologist, believes that "In point of sheer psychology, mind as such, man is after all no more than a talented animal" and "that the difference between the mentality here displayed [by a horse and a chimpanzee] and that of man is merely one of degree."[2] *[handwritten: Duthamy of Occupational Titles vs Variety]*

That there are numerous and impressive similarities between the behavior of man and that of ape is fairly obvious; it is quite possible that even chimpanzees in zoos have noted and appreciated them. Fairly apparent, too, are man's behavioral similarities to many other kinds of animals. Almost as obvious, but not easy to define, is a difference in behavior which distinguishes man from all other living creatures. I say "obvious" because it is quite apparent to the common man that the non-human animals with which he is familiar do not and cannot enter, and participate in, the world in which he, as a human being, lives. It is impossible for a dog, horse, bird, or even an ape, ever to have *any* understanding of the meaning of the sign of the cross to a Christian, or of the fact that black (white among the Chinese) is the color of mourning. But when the scholar attempts to *define* the mental difference between animal and man he sometimes encounters difficulties which he cannot surmount and, therefore, ends up by saying

[1] (New York, 1936.)
[2] *Anthropology* (New York, 1937), p. 39.

that the difference is merely one of degree: man has a bigger mind, "larger power of association," wider range of activities, etc.[3]

There is a *fundamental* difference between the mind of man and the mind of non-man. This difference is one of kind, not one of degree. And the gap between the two types is of the greatest importance — at least to the science of comparative behavior. Man uses symbols; no other creature does. A creature either uses symbols or he does not; there are no intermediate stages.

III

A symbol is a thing the value or meaning of which is bestowed upon it by those who use it. I say "thing" because a symbol may have any kind of physical form; it may have the form of a material object, a color, a sound, an odor, a motion of an object, a taste.

The meaning, or value, of a symbol is in no instance derived from or determined by properties intrinsic in its physical form: the color appropriate to mourning may be yellow, green, or any other color; purple need not be the color of royalty; among the Manchu rulers of China it was yellow. The meaning of the word "see" is not intrinsic in its phonetic (or pictorial) properties. "Biting one's thumb at"[4] someone might mean anything. The meanings of symbols are derived from and determined by the organisms who use them; meaning is bestowed by human organisms upon physical forms which thereupon become symbols.[5]

All symbols must have a physical form otherwise they could not enter our experience.[6] But the meaning of a symbol cannot be perceived by the

---

[3] We have a good example of this in the distinguished physiologist, Anton J. Carlson. After taking note of "man's present achievements in science, in the arts (including oratory), in political and social institutions," and noting "at the same time the apparent paucity of such behavior in other animals," he, as a common man "is tempted to conclude that in these capacities, at least, man has a qualitative superiority over other mammals" ("The Dynamics of Living Processes," in *The Nature of the World and Man,* H. H. Newman, ed. (Chicago, 1926), p. 477). But, since, as a scientist, Professor Carlson cannot *define* this qualitative difference between man and other animals, since as a physiologist he cannot explain it, he refuses to admit it — ". . . the physiologist does not accept the great development of articulate speech in man as something qualitatively new; . . . (p. 478) — and suggests helplessly that some day we may find some new "building stone" an "additional lipoid, phosphatid, or potassium ion," in the human brain which will explain it, and concludes by saying that the difference between the mind of man and that of non-man is "probably only one of degree" (*op. cit.,* pp. 478–79).

[4] "Do you bite your thumb at us, sir?" — *Romeo and Juliet,* Act I, Sc. 1.

[5] "Now since sounds have no natural connection with our ideas, but have all their signification from the arbitrary imposition of men . . . ," John Locke, *Essay Concerning the Human Understanding,* Bk. III, ch. 9.

"When *I* use . . . [a] word, it means just what I choose it to mean," said Humpty Dumpty to Alice (*Through the Looking Glass*).

[6] This statement is valid regardless of our theory of experiencing. Even the exponents of "Extra-Sensory Perception," who have challenged Locke's dictum that "the knowledge of the existence of any other thing [besides ourselves and God] we can have only by sensation" (Bk. IV, ch. 11, *Essay Concerning the Human Understanding*), have been obliged to work with physical rather than ethereal forms.

senses. One cannot tell by looking at an x in an algebraic equation what it stands for; one cannot ascertain with the ears alone the symbolic value of the phonetic compound *si;* one cannot tell merely by weighing a pig how much gold he will exchange for; one cannot tell from the wave length of a color whether it stands for courage or cowardice, "stop" or "go"; nor can one discover the spirit in a fetish by any amount of physical or chemical examination. The meaning of a symbol can be communicated only by symbolic means, usually by articulate speech.

But a thing which in one context is a symbol is, in another context, not a symbol but a sign. Thus, a word is a symbol only when one is concerned with the distinction between its meaning and its physical form. This distinction *must* be made when one bestows value upon a sound-combination or when a previously bestowed value is discovered for the first time; it *may* be made at other times for certain purposes. But after value has been bestowed upon, or discovered in, a word, its meaning becomes identified, in use, with its physical form. The word then functions as a sign,[7] rather than as a symbol. Its meaning is then perceived with the senses. This fact that a thing may be both symbol (in one context) and non-symbol (in another context) has led to some confusion and misunderstanding.

Thus Darwin says: "That which distinguishes man from the lower animals is not the understanding of articulate sounds, for as everyone knows, dogs understand many words and sentences" (Ch. III, *The Descent of Man*).

It is perfectly true, of course, that dogs, apes,[8] horses, birds, and perhaps creatures even lower in the evolutionary scale, can be taught to respond in a specific way to a vocal command. But it does not follow that no difference exists between the meaning of "words and sentences" to a man and to a dog. Words are both signs and symbols to man; they are merely signs to a dog. Let us analyze the situation of vocal stimulus and response.

A dog may be taught to roll over at the command "Roll over!" A man may be taught to stop at the command "Halt!" The fact that a dog can be taught to roll over in Chinese, or that he can be taught to "go fetch" at the command "roll over" (and, of course, the same is true for a man) shows that there is no necessary and invariable relationship between a particular sound combination and a specific reaction to it. The dog or the man can be taught to respond in a certain manner to *any* arbitrarily selected combination of sounds, for example, a group of nonsense syllables, coined for the

---

[7] A *sign* is a physical form whose function is to indicate some other thing, object, quality, or event. The meaning of a sign may be intrinsic, inseparable from its physical form and nature, as in the case of the height of a column of mercury as an indication of temperature; or, it may be merely identified with its physical form, as in the case of a hurricane signal displayed by a weather bureau. But in either case, the meaning of the sign is perceived with the senses.

[8] "Surprising as it may seem, it was very clear during the first few months that the ape was considerably superior to the child in responding to human words," W. N. and L. A. Kellogg, *The Ape and the Child* (New York, 1933).

occasion. On the other hand, any one of a great number and variety of responses may become evocable by a given stimulus. Thus, so far as the *origin* of the relationship between vocal stimulus and response is concerned, the nature of the relationship, i.e., the meaning of the stimulus, is not determined by properties intrinsic in the stimulus.

But, once the relationship has been established between vocal stimulus and response, the meaning of the stimulus becomes *identified with the sounds;* it is then *as if* the meaning were intrinsic in the sounds themselves. Thus, "halt" does not have the same meaning as "hilt" or "malt." A dog may be conditioned to respond in a certain way to a sound of a given wave length. Sufficiently alter the pitch of the sound and the response will cease to be forthcoming. The meaning of the stimulus has become identified with its physical form; its value is perceived with the senses.

Thus we see that in *establishing* a relationship between a stimulus and a response the properties intrinsic in the stimulus do not determine the nature of the response. But, *after the relationship has been established* the meaning of the stimulus is *as if* it were *inherent* in its physical form. It does not make any difference what phonetic combination we select to evoke the response of terminating self-locomotion. We may teach a dog, horse, or man to stop at any vocal command we care to choose or devise. But once the relationship has been established between sound and response, the meaning of the stimulus becomes identified with its physical form and is, therefore, perceivable with the senses.

So far we have discovered no difference between the dog and the man; they appear to be exactly alike. And so they are as far as we have gone. But we have not told the whole story yet. No difference between dog and man is discoverable so far as learning to respond appropriately to a vocal stimulus is concerned. But we must not let an impressive similarity conceal an important difference. A porpoise is not yet a fish.

The man differs from the dog — and all other creatures — in that *he can and does play an active role in determining what value the vocal stimulus is to have, and the dog cannot.* As John Locke has aptly put it, "All sounds [i.e., in language] . . . have their signification from the arbitrary imposition of men." The dog does not and cannot play an active part in determining the value of the vocal stimulus. Whether he is to roll over or go fetch at a given stimulus, or whether the stimulus for roll over be one combination of sounds or another is a matter in which the dog has nothing whatever to "say." He plays a purely passive role and can do nothing else. He learns the meaning of a vocal command just as his salivary glands may learn to respond to the sound of a bell. But man plays an active role and thus becomes a creator: Let x equal three pounds of coal and it does equal three pounds of coal; let removal of the hat in a house of worship indicate respect and it becomes so. This creative faculty, that of freely, actively, and arbitrarily bestowing value upon things, is one of the most commonplace as well as *the* most important characteristic of man. Children employ it freely in their play: "Let's pretend that this rock is a wolf."

The difference between the behavior of man and other animals then, is that the lower animals may receive new values, may acquire new meanings, but they cannot create and bestow them. Only man can do this. To use a crude analogy, lower animals are like a person who has only the receiving apparatus for wireless messages: He can receive messages but cannot send them. Man can do both. And this difference is one of kind, not of degree: a creature can either "arbitrarily impose signification," to use Locke's phrase, can either create and bestow values, or he cannot. There are no intermediate stages.[9] This difference may appear slight, but, as a carpenter once told William James in discussing differences between men, "it's very important." All *human* existence depends upon it and it alone.

The confusion regarding the nature of words and their significance to men and the lower animals is not hard to understand. It arises, first of all, from a failure to distinguish between the two quite different contexts in which words function. The statements, "The meaning of a word[10] cannot be perceived with the senses," and "The meaning of a word can be perceived with the senses," though contradictory, are nevertheless equally true. In the *symbol* context the meaning cannot be perceived with the senses; in the *sign* context it can. This is confusing enough. But the situation has been made worse by using the words "symbol" and "sign" to label, not the *different contexts,* but *one and the same thing:* the word. Thus a word is a symbol *and* a sign, two different things. It is like saying that a vase is a *doli* and a *kana* — two different things — because it may function in two contexts, esthetic and commercial.[11]

That which is a *symbol* in the context of origination becomes a *sign* in use thereafter. Things may be either signs or symbols to man; they can be only signs to other creatures.

IV

Very little indeed is known of the organic basis of the symbolic faculty: we know next to nothing of the neurology of symbolizing.[12] And very few sci-

---

[9] Professor Linton speaks of "the faintest foreshadowing of language . . . at the animal level" (*op. cit.,* p. 74). But precisely what these "faintest foreshadowings" are he does not say.

[10] What we have to say here would, of course, apply equally well to gestures (e.g., the "sign of the cross," a salute), a color, a material object, etc.

[11] Like a word, the value of a vase may be perceived by the senses or imperceptible to them depending upon the context in which it is regarded. In an esthetic context its value is perceived with the senses. In the commercial context this is impossible; we must be *told* its value — in terms of price.

[12] Cf. "A Neurologist Makes Up His Mind," by C. Judson Herrick, *Scientific Monthly,* August, 1939. Professor Herrick is a distinguished one of a not too large number of scientists who are interested in the structural basis of symbol using.

entists — anatomists, neurologists, physical anthropologists — appear to be interested in the problem. Some, in fact, seem to be unaware of the existence of such a problem. The duty and task of giving an account of the organic basis of symbolizing does not fall within the province of the sociologist or the cultural anthropologist. On the contrary, he should scrupulously exclude it as irrelevant to his problems and interests; to introduce it would bring only confusion. It is enough for the sociologist or cultural anthropologist to take the ability to use symbols, possessed by man alone, as given. The use to which he puts this fact is in no way affected by his, or even the anatomist's, inability to describe the symbolic process in neurological terms. However, it is well for the social scientist to be acquainted with the little that neurologists and anatomists do know about the structural basis of "symboling." We, therefore, review briefly the chief relevant facts here.

The anatomist has not been able to discover why men can use symbols and apes cannot. So far as is known the only difference between the brain of man and the brain of an ape is a quantitative one: ". . . man has no new kinds of brain cells or brain cell connections" (A. J. Carlson, op. cit.). Nor does man, as distinguished from other animals, possess a specialized "symbol-mechanism." The so-called speech areas of the brain should not be identified with symbolizing. These areas are associated with the muscles of the tongue, larynx, etc. But symbolizing is not dependent upon these organs. One may symbolize with the fingers, the feet, or with any part of the body that can be moved at will.[13]

13 The misconception that speech is dependent upon the so-called (but mis-called) organs of speech, and, furthermore, that man alone has organs suitable for speech, is not uncommon even today. Thus Professor L. L. Bernard lists "The fourth great organic asset of man is his vocal apparatus, also characteristic of him alone" Introduction to Sociology, J. Davis and H. E. Barnes, eds. (New York, 1927), p. 399.

The great apes have the mechanism necessary for the production of articulate sounds: "It seemingly is well established that the motor mechanism of voice in this ape [chimpanzee] is adequate not only to the production of a considerable variety of sounds, but also to definite articulations similar to those of man," R. M. and A. W. Yerkes, The Great Apes (New Haven, 1929), p. 301. Also: "All of the anthropoid apes are vocally and muscularly equipped so that they could have an articulate language if they possessed the requisite intelligence," E. A. Hooton, Up from the Ape (New York, 1931), p. 167.

Furthermore, the mere production of articulate sounds would not be symbolizing any more than the mere "understanding of words and sentences" (Darwin) is. John Locke made this clear two and a half centuries ago: "Man, therefore had by nature his organs so fashioned, as to be fit to frame articulate sounds, which we call words. But this was not enough to produce language; for parrots, and several other birds, will be taught to make articulate sounds distinct enough, which yet, by no means, are capable of language. Besides articulate sounds, therefore, it was farther necessary, that he should be able to use these sounds as signs of internal conceptions; and to make them stand as marks for the ideas within his own mind, whereby they might be made known to others . . . ," Book III, Ch. 1, Secs. 2, 3, Essay Concerning the Human Understanding.

And J. F. Blumenbach, a century later, delared in his On the Natural Variety of Mankind, "That speech is the work of reason alone, appears from this, that other animals, although they have nearly the same organs of voice as man, are entirely destitute of it" (quoted by R. M. and A. W. Yerkes, op. cit., p. 23).

To be sure, the symbolic faculty was brought into existence by the natural processes of organic evolution. And we may reasonably believe that the focal point, if not the locus, of this faculty is in the brain, especially the forebrain. Man's brain is much larger than that of an ape, both absolutely and relatively.[14] And the forebrain especially is large in man as compared with ape. Now in many situations we know that quantitative changes give rise to qualitative differences. Water is transformed into steam by additional quantities of heat. Additional power and speed lift the taxiing airplane from the ground and transform terrestrial locomotion into flight. The difference between wood alcohol and grain alcohol is a qualitative expression of a quantitative difference in the proportions of carbon and hydrogen. Thus a marked growth in size of the brain in man may have brought forth a *new kind* of function.

V

All culture (civilization) depends upon the symbol. It was the exercise of the symbolic faculty that brought culture into existence and it is the use of symbols that makes the perpetuation of culture possible. Without the symbol there would be no culture, and man would be merely an animal, not a human being.

Articulate speech is the most important form of symbolic expression. Remove speech from culture and what would remain? Let us see.

Without articulate speech we would have no *human* social organization. Families we might have, but this form of organization is not peculiar to man; it is not per se, *human*. But we would have no prohibitions of incest, no rules prescribing exogamy and endogamy, polygamy or monogamy. How could marriage with a cross cousin be prescribed, marriage with a parallel cousin proscribed, without articulate speech? How could rules which prohibit plural mates possessed simultaneously but permit them if possessed one at a time, exist without speech?

Without speech we would have no political, economic, ecclesiastic, or military organization; no codes of etiquette or ethics; no laws; no science, theology, or literature; no games or music, except on an ape level. Rituals and ceremonial paraphernalia would be meaningless without articulate speech. Indeed, without articulate speech we would be all but toolless: we would have only the occasional and insignificant use of the tool such as we find today among the higher apes, for it was articulate speech that transformed the nonprogressive tool-using of the ape into the progressive, cumulative tool-using of man, the human being.

In short, without symbolic communication in some form, we would have

[14] Man's brain is about two and one-half times as large as that of a gorilla. "The human brain is about 1/50 of the entire body weight, while that of a gorilla varies from 1/150 to 1/200 part of that weight" (Hooton, *op. cit.*, p. 153).

no culture. "In the Word was the beginning" of culture — and its perpetuation also.[15]

To be sure, with all his culture man is still an animal and strives for the same ends that all other living creatures strive for: the preservation of the individual and the perpetuation of the race. In concrete terms these ends are food, shelter from the elements, defense from enemies, health, and offspring. The fact that man strives for these ends just as all other animals do has, no doubt, led many to declare that there is "no fundamental difference between the behavior of man and of other creatures." But man does differ, not in *ends* but in *means*. Man's means are cultural means: culture is simply the human animal's way of living. And, since these means, culture, are dependent upon a faculty possessed by man alone, the ability to use symbols, the difference between the behavior of man and of all other creatures is not merely great, but basic and fundamental.

VI

The behavior of man is of two distinct kinds: symbolic and nonsymbolic. Man yawns, stretches, coughs, scratches himself, cries out in pain, shrinks with fear, "bristles" with anger, and so on. Nonsymbolic behavior of this sort is not peculiar to man; he shares it not only with the other primates but with many other animal species as well. But man communicates with his fellows with articulate speech, uses amulets, confesses sins, makes laws, observes codes of etiquette, explains his dreams, classifies his relatives in designated categories, and so on. This kind of behavior is unique; only man is capable of it; it is peculiar to man because it consists of, or is dependent upon, the use of symbols. The nonsymbolic behavior of man is the behavior of man the animal; the symbolic behavior is that of man the human being.[16] It is the symbol which has transformed man from a mere animal to a human animal.

As it was the symbol that made mankind human, so it is with each member of the race. A baby is not a human being so far as his behavior is concerned. Until the infant acquires speech there is nothing to distinguish his

15 "On the whole, however, it would seem that language and culture rest, in a way which is not fully understood, on the same set of faculties . . . ," A. L. Kroeber, *Anthropology* (New York, 1923), p. 108.

It is hoped that this essay will make this matter more "fully understood."

16 It is for this reason that observations and experiments with apes, rats, etc., can tell us nothing about human behavior. They can tell us how ape-like or rat-like man is, but they throw no light upon human behavior because the behavior of apes, rats, etc., is nonsymbolic.

The title of the late George A. Dorsey's best seller, *Why We Behave Like Human Beings*, was misleading for the same reason. This interesting book told us much about vertebrate, mammalian, primate, and even man-animal behavior, but virtually nothing about symbolic, i.e., human, behavior. But we are glad to add, in justice to Dorsey, that his chapter on the function of speech in culture (Ch. II) in *Man's Own Show: Civilization* (New York, 1931), is probably the best discussion of this subject that we know of in anthropological literature.

behavior qualitatively from that of a young ape.[17] The baby becomes a human being when and as he learns to use symbols. Only by means of speech can the baby enter and take part in the human affairs of mankind. The questions we asked previously may be repeated now. How is the growing child to know of such things as families, etiquette, morals, law, science, philosophy, religion, commerce, and so on, without speech? The rare cases of children who grew up without symbols because of deafness and blindness, such as those of Laura Bridgman, Helen Keller and Marie Heurtin, are instructive.[18] Until they "got the idea" of symbolic communication they were not human beings, but animals, they did not participate in behavior which is peculiar to human beings. They were "in" human society as dogs are, but they were not *of* human society. And, although the present writer is exceedingly skeptical of the reports of the so-called "wolf children," "feral men," etc., we may note that they are described, almost without exception, as without speech, "beastly," and "inhuman."

VII

Summary. The natural processes of organic evolution brought into existence in man, and man alone, a new and distinctive ability: the ability to use symbols. The most important form of symbolic expression is articulate speech. Articulate speech means communication of ideas; communication means preservation — tradition — and preservation means accumulation and progress. The emergence of the organic faculty of symbol-using has resulted in the genesis of a new order of phenomena: a superorganic, or cultural, order. All civilizations are born of, and are perpetuated by, the use of symbols. A culture, or civilization, is but a particular kind of form (symbolic) which the biologic, life-perpetuating activities of a particular animal, man, assume.

Human behavior is symbolic behavior; if it is not symbolic, it is not human. The infant of the genus homo becomes a human being only as he is introduced into and participates in that superorganic order of phenomena which is culture. And the key to this world and the means of participation in it is — the symbol.

---

[17] In their fascinating account of their experiment with a baby chimpanzee, kept for nine months in their home and treated as their infant son was treated, Professor and Mrs. Kellogg speak of the "humanization" of the little ape: "She may thus be said to have become 'more humanized' than the human subject . . . ." (p. 315).

This is misleading. What the experiment showed so strikingly was *how like an ape* a child of homo sapiens is *before he learns to talk.* The boy even employed the ape's "food bark"! The experiment also demonstrated the ape's utter inability to learn to talk, which means an inability to become humanized at all.

[18] The reader will find a resume of the more significant facts of these cases in W. I. Thomas, *Primitive Behavior* (New York, 1937), pp. 50–54, 776–777.

B. Processes and Examples

We have seen that modes of communication differ from culture to culture. We also know that ethnic groups in this country have varied, colorful symbol systems that they use to define the world. Communication is a means of ordering experience and it was the hypothesis of two psychologists, Schatzman and Strauss, that this would also hold for different social classes. In a social survey of attitudes taken after a disaster and classified according to social class it was found that indeed classes do differ in their ways of orienting themselves to experience.

10　LEONARD SCHATZMAN AND ANSELM STRAUSS

Social Class and Modes of Communication

Common assumptions suggest that there may be important differences in the thought and communication of social classes.[1] Men live in an environment which is mediated through symbols. By naming, identifying, and classifying, the world's objects and events are perceived and handled. Order is imposed through conceptual organization, and this organization embodies not just anybody's rules but the grammatical, logical, and communicative canons of groups. Communication proceeds in terms of social requirements for comprehension, and so does "inner conversation" or thought. Both reasoning and speech meet requirements of criticism, judgment, appreciation, and control. Communication across group boundaries runs the danger — aside from sheer language difficulties — of being blocked by differential rules for the ordering of speech and thought.[2]

If these assumptions are correct, it follows that there should be observable differences in communication according to social class and that these differences should not be merely matters of degree of preciseness, elabora-

From *American Journal of Sociology*, Vol. LX (January, 1955), pp. 329–338. Reprinted by permission of the authors and The University of Chicago Press.

[1] The writers are greatly indebted to the National Opinion Research Center in Chicago, which allowed them to use data gathered during a study of responses to disaster. The disaster occurred as the result of a tornado which swept through several small Arkansas towns and adjacent rural areas.

[2] Cf. E. Cassirer, *An Essay on Man* (New Haven, 1944); S. Langer, *Philosophy in a New Key* (New York, 1948); A. R. Lindesmith and A. L. Strauss, *Social Psychology* (New York, 1949), pp. 237–52; G. Mead, *Mind, Self, and Society* (Chicago, 1934); C. W. Mills, "Language, Logic, and Culture," *American Sociological Review*, IV (1939), 670–80.

tion, vocabulary, and literary style. It follows also that the modes of thought should be revealed by modes of speaking.

Our data are the interview protocols gathered from participants in a disaster. The documents, transcribed from tape, contain a wealth of local speech. Respondents had been given a relatively free hand in reporting their experiences, and the interviews averaged twenty-nine pages. These seemed admirably suited to a study of differences between social classes in modes of communication and in the organization of perception and thought. We used them also to explore the hypothesis that substantial intraclass differences in the organization of stories and accounts existed; hence low-class respondents might fail to satisfy the interviewer's canons of communication.

Approximately 340 interviews were available, representing random sampling of several communities ravaged by a tornado. Cases were selected by extreme position on educational and income continuums. Interviewees were designated as "lower" if education did not go beyond grammar school and if the annual family income was less than two thousand dollars. The "upper" group consisted of persons with one or more years of college education and annual incomes in excess of four thousand dollars. These extremes were purposely chosen for maximum socioeconomic contrast and because it seemed probable that nothing beyond formal or ritual communication would occur between these groups.

Cases were further limited by the following criteria: age (twenty-one to sixty-five years), race (white only), residence (native of Arkansas and more than three years in the community), proximity (either in the disaster area or close by), good co-operation in interview (as rated by interviewer), and less than eight probes per page (to avoid a rigid question-answer style with consequent structuring of interview by the interviewer's questions). The use of these criteria yielded ten upper-group cases, which were then matched randomly with ten from the lower group.[3]

DIFFERENCES BETWEEN CLASSES

Differences between the lower and upper groups were striking; and, once the nature of the difference was grasped, it was astonishing how quickly a characteristic organization of communication could be detected and described from a reading of even a few paragraphs of an interview. The difference is not simply the failure or success — of lower and upper groups, respectively — in communicating clearly and in sufficient detail for the inter-

[3] Each document was scrutinized by both authors, and comprehensive notes were taken to help establish categories descriptive of the communicative style and devices of each respondent. From these notes profiles of respondents were constructed. From the notes and case profiles, there emerged the separate profiles for lower and upper groups that will be described. We had expected to code the documents to bring out the degree of overlap between groups, but it turned out that there was literally no overlap; nevertheless, each reader coded separately as he went along. Agreement upon coding scores between readers was virtually perfect.

viewer's purposes. Nor does the difference merely involve correctness or elaborateness of grammar or use of a more precise or colorful vocabulary. The difference is a considerable disparity in (1) the number and kinds of perspectives utilized in communication; (2) the ability to take the listener's role; (3) the handling of classifications; and (4) the frameworks and stylistic devices which order and implement the communication.

PERSPECTIVE OR CENTERING

By perspective or centering is meant the standpoint from which a description is made.[4] Perspectives may vary in number and scope. The flexibility with which one shifts from perspective to perspective during communication may vary also.

Lower class. Almost without exception any description offered by a lower-class respondent is a description as seen through his *own* eyes; he offers his own perceptions and images directly to the listener. His best performance is a straight, direct narrative of events as he saw and experienced them. He often locates himself clearly in time and place and indicates by various connective devices a rough progression of events in relation to his activities. But the developmental progression is only in relation to himself. Other persons and their acts come into his narrative more or less as he encountered them. In the clearest interviews other actors are given specific spatial and temporal location, and sometimes the relationships among them or between them and himself are clearly designated.

The speaker's images vary considerably in clarity but are always his own. Although he may occasionally repeat the stories of other persons, he does not tell the story as though he were the other person reconstructing events and feelings. He may describe another person's act and the motive for it, with regard to himself, but this is the extent of his role-taking — he does not assume the role of another toward still others, except occasionally in an implicit fashion: "Some people was helping other people who was hurt." This limitation is especially pronounced when the behavior of more than two or three persons is being described and related. Here the description becomes confused: At best the speaker reports some reactions, but no clear picture of interaction emerges. The interaction either is not noticed or is implicitly present in the communication ("We run over there to see about them, and they was alright"). Even with careful probing the situation is not clarified much further. The most unintelligible speakers thoroughly confound the interviewer who tries to follow images, acts, persons, and events which seem to come out of nowhere and disappear without warning.

Middle class. The middle class can equal the best performance of the lower class in communicating and elaborating a direct description. How-

---

[4] Cf. J. Piaget, *The Psychology of Intelligence* (London, 1950). See also a suggestive treatment of inadequate thinking analyzed in terms of centering in Max Wertheimer, *Productive Thinking* (New York, 1945), pp. 135–47.

ever, description is not confined to so narrow a perspective. It may be given from any of several standpoints: for instance, another person, a class of persons, an organization, an organizational role, even the whole town. The middle-class speaker may describe the behavior of others, including classes of others, from their standpoints rather than from his, and he may include sequences of acts as others saw them. Even descriptions of the speaker's own behavior often are portrayed from other points of view.

CORRESPONDENCE OF IMAGERY BETWEEN SPEAKER AND LISTENER

Individuals vary in their ability to see the necessity for mediating linguistically between their own imagery and that of their listeners. The speaker must know the limits within which he may assume a correspondence of imagery. When the context of the item under discussion is in physical view of both, or is shared because of similarity of past experience, or is implicitly present by virtue of a history of former interaction, the problem of context is largely solved.[5] But when the context is neither so provided nor offered by the speaker, the listener is confronted with knotty problems of interpretation. In the accounts of the most unintelligible respondents we found dreamlike sets of images with few connective, qualifying, explanatory, or other context-providing devices. Thus, the interviewer was hard pressed to make sense of the account and was forced to probe at every turn lest the speaker figuratively run away with the situation. The respondents were willing and often eager to tell their stories, but intention to communicate does not always bring about clear communication. The latter involves, among other requirements, an ability to hear one's words as others hear them.

Lower class. Lower-class persons displayed a relative insensitivity to disparities in perspective. At best, the respondent corrected himself on the exact time at which he performed an act or became aware that his listener was not present at the scene and so located objects and events for him. On occasion he reached a state of other-consciousness: "You can't imagine if you wasn't there what it was like." However, his assumption of a correspondence in imagery is notable. There is much surnaming of persons without genuine identification, and often terms like "we" and "they" are used without clear referents. The speaker seldom anticipates responses to his communication and seems to feel little need to explain particular features of his account. He seldom qualifies an utterance, presumably because he takes for granted that his perceptions represent reality and are shared by all who were present. Since he is apt to take so much for granted, his narrative lacks depth and richness and contains almost no qualifications and few genuine illustrations. The hearer very often is confronted with a descriptive frag-

[5] For a good discussion of this see B. Malinowski, "The Problem of Meaning in Primitive Language," in *Magic, Science and Religion and Other Essays* (Boston, 1948), pp. 228–76.

ment that supposedly represents a more complete story. The speaker may then add phrases like "and stuff like that" or "and everything." Such phrasing is not genuine summation but a substitute for detail and abstraction. Summary statements are virtually absent, since they signify that speakers are sensitive to the needs of listeners. Certain phrases that appear to be summaries — such as "That's all I know" and "That's the way it was" — merely indicate that the speaker's knowledge is exhausted. Other summary-like phraseologies, like "It was pitiful," appear to be asides, reflective of self-feeling or emotion rather than résumés of preceding detail.

Middle class. The middle-class respondent also makes certain assumptions about the correspondence of the other's images with his own. Nevertheless, in contrast with the lower group, he recognizes much more fully that imagery may be diverse and that context must be provided. Hence he uses many devices to supply context and to clarify meaning. He qualifies, summarizes, and sets the stage with rich introductory material, expands themes, frequently illustrates, anticipates disbelief, meticulously locates and identifies places and persons — all with great complexity of detail. He depends less on saying "You know"; he insists upon explaining if he realizes that a point lacks plausibility or force. Hence he rarely fails to locate an image, or series of images, in time or place. Frequent use of qualification is especially noteworthy. This indicates not only multiple centering but a very great sensitivity to listeners, actual and potential — including the speaker himself.

In short, the middle-class respondent has what might be called "communication control," at least in such a semiformal situation as the interview. Figuratively, he stands between his own images and the hearer and says, "Let me introduce you to what I saw and know." It is as though he were directing a movie, having at his command several cameras focused at different perspectives, shooting and carefully controlling the effect. By contrast, the lower-class respondent seems himself more like a single camera which unreels the scene to the audience. In the very telling of his story he is more apt to lose himself in his imagery. The middle-class person — by virtue, we would presume, of his greater sensitivity to his listener — stands more outside his experience. He does not so much tell you what he saw as fashion a story about what he saw. The story may be accurate in varying degrees, although, in so far as it is an organized account, it has both the virtues and the defects of organization. The comparative accuracies of middle- and lower-class accounts are not relevant here; the greater objectivity of the former merely reflects greater distance between narrator and event.[6]

In organizing his account, the middle-class respondent displays parallel consciousness of the other and himself. He can stop midstream, take another direction, and, in general, exert great control over the course of his

[6] Our discussion of objectivity and of mediation between self and image in communication is reminiscent of some of the literature on child, schizophrenic, and aphasic thought.

communication. The lower-class respondent seems to have much less foresight, appearing to control only how much he will say to the interviewer, or whether he will say it at all, although presumably he must have some stylistic controls not readily observable by a middle-class reader.

CLASSIFICATIONS AND CLASSIFICATORY RELATIONS

Lower class. Respondents make reference mainly to the acts and persons of particular people, often designating them by proper or family names. This makes for fairly clear denotation and description, but only as long as the account is confined to the experiences of specific individuals. There comes a point when the interviewer wishes to obtain information about classes of persons and entire organizations as well as how they impinged upon the respondent, and here the lower-class respondent becomes relatively or even wholly inarticulate. At worst he cannot talk about. categories of people or acts because, apparently, he does not think readily in terms of classes. Questions about organizations, such as the Red Cross, are converted into concrete terms, and he talks about the Red Cross "helping people" and "people helping other people" with no more than the crudest awareness of how organizational activities interlock. At most the respondent categorizes only in a rudimentary fashion: "Some people were running; other people were looking in the houses." The interviewer receives a sketchy and impressionistic picture. Some idea is conveyed of the confusion that followed upon the tornado, but the organizing of description is very poor. The respondent may mention classes in contrasting juxtaposition (rich and poor, hurt and not-hurt), or list groups of easily perceived, contrasting actions, but he does not otherwise spell out relations between these classes. Neither does he describe a scene systematically in terms of classes that are explicitly or clearly related, a performance which would involve a shifting of viewpoint.

It is apparent that the speakers think mainly in particularistic or concrete terms. Certainly classificatory thought must exist among many or all the respondents; but, in communicating to the interviewer, class terms are rudimentary or absent and class relations implicit: relationships are not spelled out or are left vague. Genuine illustrations are almost totally lacking, either because these require classifications or because we — as middle-class observers — do not recognize that certain details are meant to imply classes.

Middle class. Middle-class speech is richly interlarded with classificatory terms, especially when the narrator is talking about what he saw rather than about himself. Typically, when he describes what other persons are doing, he classifies actions and persons and more often than not explicitly relates class to class. Often his descriptions are artistically organized around what various categories of persons were doing or experiencing. When an illustration is offered, it is clear that the speaker means it to stand for a general category. Relief and other civic organizations are conceived as sets or classes of co-ordinated roles and actions; some persons couch their whole account of the disaster events in organizational terms, hardly deigning to give proper names or personal accounts. In short, concrete imagery in middle-class communication is dwarfed or overshadowed by the prevalence and richness of conceptual terminology. Organization of speech around classifications comes readily, and undoubtedly the speaker is barely conscious of it. It is part and parcel of his formal and informal education. This is not to claim that middle-class persons always think with and use classificatory terms, for doubtless this is not true. Indeed, it may be that the interview exacts from them highly conceptualized descriptions. Nonetheless, we conclude that, in general, the thought and speech of middle-class persons is less concrete than that of the lower group.

ORGANIZING FRAMEWORKS AND STYLISTIC DEVICES

One of the requirements of communication is that utterances be organized. The principle of organization need not be stated explicitly by the speaker or recognized by the listener. Organizing frames can be of various sorts. Thus an ordering of the respondent's dscription is often set by the interviewer's question, or the speaker may set his own framework ("There is one thing you should know about this"). The frame can be established jointly by both interviewer and respondent, as when the former asks an open-ended question within whose very broad limits the respondent orders his description in ways that strike him as appropriate or interesting. The respondent, indeed, may organize his account much as though he were telling a special kind of story or drama, using the interviewer's questions as hardly more than general cues to what is required. The great number of events, incidents, and images which must be conveyed to the listener may be handled haphazardly, neatly, dramatically, or sequentially; but, if they are to be communicated at all, they must be ordered somehow. Stylistic devices accompany and implement these organizing frames, and the lower and upper groups use them in somewhat different ways.

Lower class. The interviewer's opening question, "Tell me your story of the tornado," invites the respondent to play an active role in organizing his account; and this he sometimes does. However, with the exception of one person who gave a headlong personal narrative, the respondents did not give long, well-organized, or tightly knit pictures of what happened to them during and after the tornado. This kind of general depiction either did not occur to them or did not strike them as appropriate.

The frames utilized are more segmental or limited in scope than those used by the middle class. They appear to be of several kinds and their centering is personal. One is the personal narrative, with events, acts, images, persons, and places receiving sequential ordering. Stylistic devices further this kind of organization: for instance, crude temporal connectives like "then," "and," and "so" and the reporting of images or events as they are recollected or as they appear in the narrative progression. Asides may specify relationships of kinship or the individuals' location in space. But, unless the line of narrative is compelling to the speaker, he is likely to wander off into detail about a particular incident, where the incident in turn then provides a framework for mentioning further events. Likewise, when a question from the interviewer breaks into the narrative, it may set the stage for an answer composed of a number of images or an incident. Often one incident becomes the trigger for another, and, although some logical or temporal connection between them may exist for the speaker, this can scarcely be perceived by the interviewer. Hence the respondent is likely to move out of frames quickly. The great danger of probes and requests for elaboration is that the speaker will get far away from the life-line of his narrative — and frequently far away from the interviewer's question. As recompense the interviewer may garner useful and unexpectedly rich information from the digressions, although often he needs to probe this material further to bring it into context. General questions are especially likely to divert the speaker, since they suggest only loose frames; or he may answer in general, diffuse, or blurred terms which assume either that the listener was there too or that he will put meaningful content into the words. If a question is asked that concerns abstract classes or is "above" the respondent — a query, say, about relief organizations — then very general answers or concrete listing of images or triggering of images are especially noticeable. When the interviewer probes in an effort to get some elaboration of an occurrence or an expansion of idea, he commonly meets with little more than repetition or with a kind of "buckshot" listing of images or incidents which is supposed to fill out the desired picture. The lack of much genuine elaboration is probably related to the inability to report from multiple perspectives.

One requirement of the interview is that it yield a fairly comprehensive account of the respondent's actions and perceptions. With the lower-class respondent the interviewer, as a rule, must work very hard at building a comprehensive frame directly into the interview. This he does by forcing many subframes upon the respondent. He asks many questions about exact time sequence, placement and identification of persons, expansion of detail, and the like. Especially must he ask pointed questions about the relations of various personages appearing in the account. Left to his own devices, the respondent may give a fairly straightforward narrative or competently reconstruct incidents that seem only partially connected with each other or with his narrative. But the respondent seldom voluntarily gives both linear and cross-sectional pictures.

The devices used to implement communication are rather difficult to isolate, perhaps because we are middle class ourselves. Among the devices most readily observable are the use of crude chronological notations (e.g., "then, . . . and then"), the juxtaposing or direct contrasting of classes (e.g., rich and poor) and the serial locating of events. But the elaborate devices that characterize middle-class interviews are strikingly absent.

Middle class. Without exception middle-class respondents imposed overall frames of their own upon the entire interview. Although very sensitive generally to the needs of the interviewer, they made the account their own. This is evidenced sometimes from the very outset; many respondents give a lengthy picture in answer to the interviewer's invitation, "Tell me your story." The organizing frame may yield a fluid narrative that engulfs self and others in dense detail; it may give a relatively static but rich picture of a community in distress; or, by dramatic and stage-setting devices it may show a complicated web of relationships in dramatic motion. The entire town may be taken as the frame of reference and its story portrayed in time and space.

Besides the master-frame, the middle-class respondent utilizes many subsidiary frames. Like the lower-class person, he may take off from a question. But, in doing so — especially where the question gives latitude by its generality or abstractness — he is likely to give an answer organized around a subframe which orders his selection and arrangement of items. He may even shift from one image to another, but rarely are these left unrelated to the question which initially provoked them. He is much more likely also to elaborate than to repeat or merely to give a scattered series of percepts.

One prerequisite for the elaboration of a theme is an ability to depart from it while yet holding it in mind. Because he incorporates multiple perspectives, the respondent can add long asides, discuss the parallel acts of other persons in relation to himself, make varied comparisons for the enrichment of detail and comprehension — and then can return to the original point and proceed from there. Often he does this after first preparing his listener for the departure and concludes the circuit with a summary statement or a transitional phrase like "well — anyhow" that marks the end of the digression.

The stylistic devices utilized by any respondent are many and varied. But each speaker uses some devices more frequently than others, since certain ones are more or less appropriate to given frames. There is no point in spelling out the whole range of devices; they are of the sort used in any clear detailed narrative and effective exposition. If the respondent is pressed to the limit of his ability in explaining a complex point or describing a complicated scene, he calls into play resources that are of immensely high order. Sometimes a seemingly simple device will turn out on closer inspection to demand a sophisticated handling of communication — for instance, the frequent and orderly asides that break into exposition or narrative and serve with great economy to add pertinent detail.

INTRACLASS DIFFERENCES

Middle class. Although all middle-class accounts were informative, there were considerable differences of construction among them. The frames utilized by any respondent are multiple, but respondents tend to use either a frame emphasizing sequence, human drama, and personal incident or one stressing interlocking classes of civic acts. Each orientation is implemented by somewhat different stylistic techniques. There are of course different ways of narrating; thus one can dwell more upon conditions for activity than upon the acts themselves. Similarly, accounts focused upon town organization vary in such matters as the scope of description and the degree of emphasis upon temporal sequence. Both frameworks are interchangeable, and their use is a function either of the speaker's habitual orientation or of his definition of the interview situation rather than of his ability to use one or the other mode.

Lower class. Lower-class persons can best be distinguished in terms of ability to meet the minimum requirements of the interview. Some literally cannot tell a straight story or describe a simple incident coherently. At the other extreme we find an adequate self-focused narrative, with considerable detail tightly tied to sequential action, including retrospective observation about the narrator's facts as he develops them. Midway between these extremes are the people who can tell portions of narrative but are easily distracted: either an image suggests some other image, or the interviewer asks a question focusing interest and concentration elsewhere than upon the narrative or he calls for some expansion of detail. Then the interviewer must remind the speaker of the break in narrative. The interviewer constantly must be on the *qui vive* to keep the story going and to fill in gaps.

In the best accounts, also, competent description is handled by linking a variety of perceptions to the narrative. Images then appear to the listener to be in context and thus are fairly comprehensible. At the other extreme, images and incidents are free-floating. Probing improved the quality of this sort of interview but slightly. More frequently, the interviewer was confronted with fragments of the narrative and its related imagery. Then he had to piece together the general lineaments of the story by a barrage of probes: "Who?" "When?" "Where?" Even then the reader of these interviews will come across stray images and be hard pressed to fit them into the context. Competence in recounting narrative generally is accompanied by competence in making understandable departures from the narrative itself, and, lacking both skills, some lower-class respondents gave quite baffling and unintelligible reports. The best accounts are moderately clear, although subject to all the limitations already discussed.

DISCUSSION

Only if the situation in which the respondent spoke is carefully taken into account will we be on safe ground in interpreting class differences. Consider, first, the probable meaning of the interview for the middle-class respondents. Although the interviewer is a stranger, an outsider, he is a well-spoken, educated person. He is seeking information on behalf of some organization, hence his questioning not only has sanction but sets the stage for both a certain freedom of speech and an obligation to give fairly full information. The respondent may never before have been interviewed by a research organization, but he has often talked lengthily, fairly freely, and responsibly to organizational representatives. At the very least he has had some experience in talking to educated strangers. We may also suppose that the middle-class style of living often compels him to be very careful not to be misunderstood. So he becomes relatively sensitive to communication per se and to communication with others who may not exactly share his viewpoints or frames of reference.

Communication with such an audience requires alertness, no less to the meanings of one's own speech than to the possible intent of the other's. Role-taking may be inaccurate, often, but it is markedly active. Assessing and anticipating reactions to what he has said or is about to say, the individual develops flexible and ingenious ways of correcting, qualifying, making more plausible, explaining, rephrasing — in short, he assumes multiple perspectives and communicates in terms of them. A variety of perspectives implies a variety of ways of ordering or framing detail. Moreover, he is able to classify and to relate classes explicitly, which is but another way of saying that he is educated to assume multiple perspectives of rather wide scope.

It would certainly be too much to claim that middle-class persons always react so sensitively. Communication is often routinized, and much of it transpires between and among those who know each other so well or share so much in common that they need not be subtle. Nor is sensitive role-taking called forth in so-called "expressive behavior," as when hurling invective or yelling during a ball game. With the proviso that much middle-class speech is uttered under such conditions, it seems safe enough to say that people of this stratum can, if required, handle the more complex and consciously organized discourse. In addition to skill and perspicacity, this kind of discourse requires a person who can subtly keep a listener at a distance while yet keeping him in some degree informed.

Consider now, even at risk of overstating the case, how the interview appears to the lower group. The interviewer is of higher social class than the respondent, so that the interview is a "conversation between the classes." It is entirely probable that more effort and ability are demanded by cross-class conversation of this sort than between middle-class respondent and middle-class interviewer.[7] It is not surprising that the interviewer is often baffled and that the respondent frequently misinterprets what is wanted. But misunderstanding and misinterpretation are only part of the story.

Cross-class communication, while not rare, probably is fairly formalized or routinized. The communicants know the ritual steps by heart, and can assume much in the way of supporting context for phrase and gesture. The lower-class person in these Arkansas towns infrequently meets a middle-class person in a situation anything like the interview. Here he must talk at great length to a stranger about personal experiences, as well as recall for

---

[7] Somewhat like this is the I.Q. testing session which involves a middle-class test (and tester) and a lower-class subject. The many and subtle difficulties in this situation are analyzed by Allison Davis in *Social Class Influences upon Learning* (Cambridge, Mass., 1951).

his listener a tremendous number of details. Presumably he is accustomed to talking about such matters and in such detail only to listeners with whom he shares a great deal of experience and symbolism, so that he need not be very self-conscious about communicative technique. He can, as a rule, safely assume that words, phrases, and gestures are assigned approximately similar meanings by his listeners. But this is not so in the interview or, indeed, in any situation where class converses with class in nontraditional modes.

There still remains the question of whether the descriptions of perceptions and experiences given by the lower-class respondent are merely inadequate or whether this is the way he truly saw and experienced. Does his speech accurately reflect customary "concrete" modes of thought and perception, or is it that he perceives in abstract and classificatory terms, and from multiple perspectives, but is unable to convey his perceptions?[8] Unless one assumes that, when talking in familiar vein to familiar audiences, speech and gesture incorporate multiple perspectives, which is, as we have already indicated, improbable, one concludes that speech does in some sense reflect thought. The reader is perhaps best left at this point to draw his own conclusions, although we shall press upon him certain additional evidence and interpretation arising from examination of the interviews.

In any situation calling for a description of human activities it is necessary to utilize motivational terminology, either explicitly or implicitly, in the very namings of acts.[9] In the speech of those who recognize few disparities of imagery between themselves and their listeners, explicit motivational terms are sparse. The frequent use among the lower class of the expression "of course" followed by something like "They went up to see about their folks" implies that it is almost needless to say what "they" did, much less to give the reason for the act. The motive ("to see about") is implicit and terminal, requiring neither elaboration nor explanation. Where motives are explicit ("They was needin' help, so we went on up there"), they are often gratuitous and could just as well have been omitted. All this is related to preceding discussions of single centering and assumed correspondence of imagery. To the speaker it was quite clear why people did what they did. There was no need to question or to elaborate on the grounds for acts. Under probing the respondent did very little better: he used motivational terms but within a quite narrow range. The terms he used ordinarily reflected kinship obligations, concern for property, humanitarian ("help") sentiments, and action from motives of curiosity ("We went down to see"). Such a phrase as "I suppose I went to her house because I wanted reassurance" would rarely occur.

[8] "The lower class is even more concrete in its outlook than the lower-middle class. For example, a question . . . where chewing gum is usually purchased will be answered by an upper-middle person: 'At a cashier's counter or in a grocery store.' By the lower-middle: 'At the National or the corner drugstore.' By the lower class: 'From Tony'" ("Marketing Chewing Gum in New England: A Research Study" [Chicago: Social Research, Inc., 1950]).

[9] Cf. K. Burke, *Grammar of Motives* (New York, 1945).

Middle-class persons exhibit familiarity with a host of distinct "reasons" for performing particular acts. Their richness in thinking allows activities to be defined and described in a great variety of ways. Here, indeed, is an instrument for breaking down diffuse images ("They was runnin' all over") into classes of acts and events. The middle-class person is able to do this, for one thing, because he possesses an abstract motivational terminology. Then, too, the fine and subtle distinctions for rationalizing behavior require devices for insuring that they will be grasped by the hearer. In a real sense the need to explain behavior can be linked with the need to communicate well — to give a rational account as well as to be objective. Hence, there is a constant flow of qualifying and generalizing terms linked with motivational phraseology ("I don't know why, but it could be he felt there was no alternative . . .").

It is not surprising to find the middle class as familiar with elements of social structure as with individual behavior. Assuredly, this familiarity rests not only upon contact with institutions but upon the capacity to perceive and talk about abstract classes of acts. The lower-class person, on the other hand, appears to have only rudimentary notions of organizational structure — at least of relief and emergency agencies. Extended contact with representatives of them, no doubt, would familiarize him not only with organizations but with thinking in organizational, or abstract, terms. The propensity of the lower class to state concretely the activities of relief organizations corroborates the observation of Warner that the lowest strata have little knowledge or "feel" for the social structures of their communities.[10] It also suggests the difficulty of conveying to them relatively abstract information through formal media of communication.

It may be that rural townspeople of the lower class are not typical of the national or urban low strata. This raises the question — vital to urban sociology but to which currently there is no adequate answer — of whether pockets of rural-minded folk cannot live encapsulated in the city[11] and, indeed, whether lower-class persons have much opportunity to absorb middle-class culture without themselves beginning the route upward, those remaining behind remaining less urban.[12]

---

[10] W. L. Warner, *American Life: Dream and Reality* (Chicago: University of Chicago Press, 1953), pp. 193–94.

[11] David Riesman, "Urbanity and the Urban Personality," in *Proceedings of the Fourth Annual Symposium, The Human Development Bulletin* (Chicago: University of Chicago, 1953), p. 37.

[12] William Henry, of the University of Chicago, has conveyed his impression to us that urban lower-class and middle-class people perform on Thematic Apperception Tests much as our Arkansas respondents did in the interview.

We have also examined interviews about disasters in Brighton, N.Y., a middle-class suburb of Rochester, and Elizabeth, N.J., an urban community near New York City. There are no observable differences between the middle-class respondents of these areas and those of Arkansas. Four interviews with Elizabeth lower-class respondents paralleled the modes of the Arkansas lower class. A fifth exhibited considerable middle-class characteristics.

V. SOCIALIZATION

A. Definitions and Concepts

Many would classify this article by Dennis Wrong as "sociological theory." Wrong serves our purpose in this section by illustrating problems relating to the use of a particular theory, the types of questions asked, and the answers looked for. It is especially important to realize that many sociologists have a concept of man in society that is mechanical and devoid of what could be called "free-will." This, as Wrong points out, leads to an incomplete view of man. In dealing with this problem, he also introduces the processes of internalizing norms and roles, the essence of socialization, and explains which aspects are studied by many other disciplines, such as psychology. He asks us to consider these other aspects. There are various definitions of self and socialization. In Wrong's article we can see what is encompassed by a Freudian view of socialization.

11 DENNIS H. WRONG

The Oversocialized Conception of Man in Modern Sociology

Gertrude Stein, bed-ridden with a fatal illness, is reported to have suddenly muttered, "What, then, is the answer?" Pausing, she raised her head, murmured, "But what is the question?" and died. Miss Stein presumably was pondering the ultimate meaning of human life, but her brief final soliloquy

From *American Sociological Review,* Vol. XXVI (April, 1961), pp. 183–193. Reprinted by permission of the author and the American Sociological Association.

121

has a broader and humbler relevance. Its point is that answers are meaningless apart from questions. If we forget the questions, even while remembering the answers, our knowledge of them will subtly deteriorate, becoming rigid, formal, and catechistic as the sense of indeterminacy, of rival possibilities, implied by the very putting of a question is lost.

Social theory must be seen primarily as a set of answers to questions we ask of social reality. If the initiating questions are forgotten, we readily misconstrue the task of theory and the answers previous thinkers have given become narrowly confining conceptual prisons, degenerating into little more than a special, professional vocabulary applied to situations and events that can be described with equal or greater precision in ordinary language. Forgetfulness of the questions that are the starting points of inquiry leads us to ignore the substantive assumptions "buried" in our concepts and commits us to a one-sided view of reality.

Perhaps this is simply an elaborate way of saying that sociological theory can never afford to lose what is usually called a "sense of significance"; or, as it is sometimes put, that sociological theory must be "problem-conscious." I choose instead to speak of theory as a set of answers to questions because reference to "problems" may seem to suggest too close a linkage with social criticism or reform. My primary reason for insisting on the necessity of holding constantly in mind the questions that our concepts and theories are designed to answer is to preclude defining the goal of sociological theory as the creation of a formal body of knowledge satisfying the logical criteria of scientific theory set up by philosophers and methodologists of natural science. Needless to say, this is the way theory is often defined by contemporary sociologists.

Yet to speak of theory as interrogatory may suggest too self-sufficiently intellectual an enterprise. Cannot questions be satisfactorily answered and then forgotten, the answers becoming the assumptions from which we start in framing new questions? It may convey my view of theory more adequately to say that sociological theory concerns itself with questions arising out of problems that are inherent in the very existence of human societies and that cannot therefore be finally "solved" in the way that particular social problems perhaps can be. The "problems" theory concerns itself with are problems *for* human societies which, because of their universality, become intellectually problematic for sociological theorists.

Essentially, the historicist conception of sociological knowledge that is central to the thought of Max Weber and has recently been ably restated by Barrington Moore, Jr. and C. Wright Mills is a sound one. The most fruitful questions for sociology are always questions referring to the realities of a particular historical situation. Yet both of these writers, especially Mills, have a tendency to underemphasize the degree to which we genuinely wish and seek answers to trans-historical and universal questions about the nature of man and society. I do not, let it be clear, have in mind the formalistic quest for social "laws" or "universal propositions," nor the even more formalistic effort to construct all-encompassing "conceptual schemes." Moore and Mills are rightly critical of such efforts. I am thinking of such questions as, "How are men capable of uniting to form enduring societies in the first place?"; "Why and to what degree is change inherent in human societies and what are the sources of change?"; "How is man's animal nature domesticated by society?"

Such questions — and they are existential as well as intellectual questions — are the *raison d'être* of social theory. They were asked by men long before the rise of sociology. Sociology itself is an effort, under new and unprecedented historical conditions, to find novel answers to them. They are not questions which lend themselves to successively more precise answers as a result of cumulative empirical research, for they remain eternally problematic. Social theory is necessarily an interminable dialogue. "True understanding," Hannah Arendt has written, "does not tire of interminable dialogue and 'vicious circles' because it trusts that imagination will eventually catch at least a glimpse of the always frightening light of truth."

I wish briefly to review the answers modern sociological theory offers to one such question, or rather to one aspect of one question. The question may be variously phrased as, "What are the sources of social cohesion?"; or, "How is social order possible?"; or, stated in social-psychological terms, "How is it that man becomes tractable to social discipline?" I shall call this question in its social-psychological aspect the "Hobbesian question" and in its more strictly sociological aspect the "Marxist question." The Hobbesian question asks how men are capable of the guidance by social norms and goals that makes possible an enduring society, while the Marxist question asks how, assuming this capability, complex societies manage to regulate and restrain destructive conflicts between groups. Much of our current theory offers an oversocialized view of man in answering the Hobbesian question and an overintegrated view of society in answering the Marxist question.

A number of writers have recently challenged the overintegrated view of society in contemporary theory. In addition to Moore and Mills, the names of Reinhard Bendix, Lewis A. Coser, Ralf Dahrendorf, and David Lockwood come to mind. My intention, therefore, is to concentrate on the answers to the Hobbesian question in an effort to disclose the oversocialized view of man which they seem to imply.

Since my view of theory is obviously very different from that of Talcott Parsons and has, in fact, been developed in opposition to his, let me pay tribute to his recognition of the importance of the Hobbesian question — the "problem of order," as he calls it — at the very beginning of his first book, *The Structure of Social Action.* Parsons correctly credits Hobbes with being the first thinker to see the necessity of explaining why human society is not a "war of all against all"; why, if man is simply a gifted animal, men refrain from unlimited resort to fraud and violence in pursuit of their ends and maintain a stable society at all. There is even a sense in which, as Coser and Mills have both noted, Parsons' entire work represents an effort to solve the Hobbesian problem of order. His solution, however, has tended to become precisely the kind of elaboration of a set of answers in abstraction from questions that is characteristic of contemporary sociological theory.

We need not be greatly concerned with Hobbes' own solution to the problem of order he saw with such unsurpassed clarity. Whatever interest his famous theory of the origin of the state may still hold for political scientists, it is clearly inadequate as an explanation of the origin of society. Yet the pattern as opposed to the details of Hobbes' thought bears closer examination.

The polar terms in Hobbes' theory are the state of nature, where the war of all against all prevails, and the authority of Leviathan, created by social contract. But the war of all against all is not simply effaced with the creation of political authority: it remains an ever-present potentiality in human society, at times quiescent, at times erupting into open violence. Whether Hobbes believed that the state of nature and the social contract were ever historical realities — and there is evidence that he was not that simpleminded and unsociological, even in the seventeenth century — is unimportant; the whole tenor of his thought is to see the war of all against all and Leviathan dialectically, as coexisting and interacting opposites. As R. G. Collingwood has observed, "According to Hobbes . . . *a body politic is a dialectical thing*, a Heraclitean world in which at any given time there is a negative element." The first secular social theorist in the history of Western thought, and one of the first clearly to discern and define the problem of order in human society long before Darwinism made awareness of it a commonplace, Hobbes was a dialectical thinker who refused to separate answers from questions, solutions to society's enduring problems from the conditions creating the problems.

What is the answer of contemporary sociological theory to the Hobbesian question? There are two main answers, each of which has come to be understood in a way that denies the reality and meaningfulness of the question. Together they constitute a model of human nature, sometimes clearly stated, more often implicit in accepted concepts, that pervades modern sociology. The first answer is summed up in the notion of the "internalization of social norms." The second, more commonly employed or assumed in empirical research, is the view that man is essentially motivated by the desire to achieve a positive image of self by winning acceptance or status in the eyes of others.

The following statement represents, briefly and broadly, what is probably the most influential contemporary sociological conception — and dismissal — of the Hobbesian problem: "To a modern sociologist imbued with the conception that action follows institutionalized patterns, opposition of individual and common interests has only a very limited relevance or is thoroughly unsound." From this writer's perspective, the problem is an unreal one: human conduct is totally shaped by common norms or "institutionalized patterns." Sheer ignorance must have led people who were unfortunate enough not to be modern sociologists to ask, "How is order possible?" A thoughtful bee or ant would never inquire, "How is the social order of the hive or ant-hill possible?" for the opposite of that order is unimaginable when the instinctive endowment of the insects ensures its stability and built-in harmony between "individual and common interests." Human society, we are assured, is not essentially different, although conformity and stability are there maintained by non-instinctive processes. Modern sociologists believe that they have understood these processes and that they have not merely answered but disposed of the Hobbesian question, showing that, far from expressing a valid intimation of the tensions and possibilities of social life, it can only be asked out of ignorance.

It would be hard to find a better illustration of what Collingwood, following Plato, calls *eristical* as opposed to dialectical thinking: the answer destroys the question, or rather destroys the awareness of rival possibilities suggested by the question which accounts for its having been asked in the first place. A reversal of perspective now takes place and we are moved to ask the opposite question: "How is it that violence, conflict, revolution, and the individual's sense of coercion by society manage to exist at all, if this view is correct?" Whenever a one-sided answer to a question compels us to raise the opposite question, we are caught up in a dialectic of concepts which reflects a dialectic in things. But let us examine the particular processes sociologists appeal to in order to account for the elimination from human society of the war of all against all.

THE CHANGING MEANING OF INTERNALIZATION

A well-known section of *The Structure of Social Action,* devoted to the interpretation of Durkheim's thought, is entitled "The Changing Meaning of Constraint." Parsons argues that Durkheim originally conceived of society as controlling the individual from the outside by imposing constraints on him through sanctions, best illustrated by codes of law. But in Durkheim's later work he began to see that social rules do not "merely regulate 'externally' . . . they enter directly into the constitution of the actors' ends themselves." Constraint, therefore, is more than an environmental obstacle which the actor must take into account in pursuit of his goals in the same way that he takes into account physical laws: it becomes internal, psychological, and self-imposed as well. Parsons developed this view that social norms are constitutive rather than merely regulative of human nature before he was influenced by psychoanalytic theory, but Freud's theory of the superego has become the source and model for the conception of the internalization of social norms that today plays so important a part in sociological thinking. The use some sociologists have made of Freud's idea, however, might well inspire an essay entitled, "The Changing Meaning of Internalization," although, in contrast to the shift in Durkheim's view of constraint, this change has been a change for the worse.

What has happened is that internalization has imperceptibly been equated with "learning," or even with "habit-formation" in the simplest sense. Thus when a norm is said to have been "internalized" by an individual, what is frequently meant is that he habitually both affirms it and conforms to it in his conduct. The whole stress on inner conflict, on the tension between powerful impulses and superego controls the behavioral outcome of which cannot be prejudged, drops out of the picture. And it is this that is central to Freud's view, for in psychoanalytic terms to say that a norm has been internalized, or introjected to become part of the superego, is to say no more than that a person will suffer guilt-feelings if he fails to live up to it, not that he will in fact live up to it in his behavior.

The relation between internalization and conformity assumed by most sociologists is suggested by the following passage from a recent, highly-praised advanced textbook: "Conformity to institutionalized norms is, of course, 'normal.' The actor, having internalized the norms, feels something like a need to conform. His conscience would bother him if he did not." What is overlooked here is that the person who conforms may be even more "bothered," that is, subject to guilt and neurosis, than the person who violates what are not only society's norms but his own as well. To Freud, it is precisely the man with the strictest superego, he who has most thoroughly internalized and conformed to the norms of his society, who is most wracked with guilt and anxiety.

Paul Kecskemeti, to whose discussion I owe initial recognition of the erroneous view of internalization held by sociologists, argues that the relations between social norms, the individual's selection from them, his conduct, and his feelings about his conduct are far from self-evident. "It is by no means true," he writes, "to say that acting counter to one's own norms always or almost always leads to neurosis. One might assume that neurosis develops even more easily in persons who *never* violate the moral code they recognize as valid but repress and frustrate some strong instinctual motive. A person who 'succumbs to temptation,' feels guilt, and then 'purges himself' of his guilt in some reliable way (e.g., by confession) may achieve in this way a better balance, and be less neurotic, than a person who never violates his 'norms' and never feels conscious guilt."[1]

Recent discussions of "deviant behavior" have been compelled to recognize these distinctions between social demands, personal attitudes towards them, and actual conduct, although they have done so in a laboriously taxonomic fashion. They represent, however, largely the rediscovery of what was always central to the Freudian concept of the superego. The main explanatory function of the concept is to show how people repress themselves,

---

[1] Paul Kecskemeti, *Meaning, Communication, and Value,* Chicago: University of Chicago Press, 1952, pp. 244–245.

imposing checks on their own desires and thus turning the inner life into a battlefield of conflicting motives, no matter which side "wins," by successfully dictating overt action. So far as behavior is concerned, the psychoanalytic view of man is less deterministic than the sociological. For psychoanalysis is primarily concerned with the inner life, not with overt behavior, and its most fundamental insight is that the wish, the emotion, and the fantasy are as important as the act in man's experience.

Sociologists have appropriated the superego concept, but have separated it from any equivalent of the Freudian id. So long as most individuals are "socialized," that is, internalize the norms and conform to them in conduct, the Hobbesian problem is not even perceived as a latent reality. Deviant behavior is accounted for by special circumstances: ambiguous norms, anomie, role conflict, or greater cultural stress on valued goals than on the approved means for attaining them. Tendencies to deviant behavior are not seen as dialectically related to conformity. The presence in man of motivational forces bucking against the hold social discipline has over him is denied.

Nor does the assumption that internalization of norms and roles is the essence of socialization allow for a sufficient range of motives underlying conformity. It fails to allow for variable "tonicity of the superego," in Abram Kardiner's phrase. The degree to which conformity is frequently the result of coercion rather than conviction is minimized. Either someone has internalized the norms, or he is "unsocialized," a feral or socially isolated child, or a psychopath. Yet Freud recognized that many people, conceivably a majority, fail to acquire superegos. "Such people," he wrote, "habitually permit themselves to do any bad deed that procures them something they want, if only they are sure that no authority will discover it or make them suffer for it; their anxiety relates only to the possibility of detection. Present-day society has to take into account the prevalence of this state of mind." The last sentence suggests that Freud was aware of the decline of "inner-direction," of the Protestant conscience, about which we have heard so much lately. So let us turn to the other elements of human nature that sociologists appeal to in order to explain, or rather explain away, the Hobbesian problem.

MAN THE ACCEPTANCE-SEEKER

The superego concept is too inflexible, too bound to the past and to individual biography, to be of service in relating conduct to the pressures of the immediate situation in which it takes place. Sociologists rely more heavily therefore on an alternative notion, here stated — or, to be fair, overstated — in its baldest form: "People are so profoundly sensitive to the expectations of others that all action is inevitably guided by these expectations."

Parsons' model of the "complementarity of expectations," the view that in social interaction men mutually seek approval from one another by conform-

ing to shared norms, is a formalized version of what has tended to become
a distinctive sociological perspective on human motivation. Ralph Linton
states it in explicit psychological terms: "The need for eliciting favorable
responses from others is an almost constant component of [personality].
Indeed, it is not too much to say that there is very little organized human behavior which is not directed toward its satisfaction in at least some degree."

The insistence of sociologists on the importance of "social factors" easily
leads them to stress the priority of such socialized or socializing motives in
human behavior. It is frequently the task of the sociologist to call attention
to the intensity with which men desire and strive for the good opinion of
their immediate associates in a variety of situations, particularly those where
received theories or ideologies have unduly emphasized other motives such
as financial gain, commitment to ideals, or the effects on energies and aspirations of arduous physical conditions. Thus sociologists have shown that factory workers are more sensitive to the attitudes of their fellow-workers than
to purely economic incentives; that voters are more influenced by the preferences of their relatives and friends than by campaign debates on the "issues";
that soldiers, whatever their ideological commitment to their nation's cause,
fight more bravely when their platoons are intact and they stand side by
side with their "buddies."

It is certainly not my intention to criticize the findings of such studies. My
objection is that their particular selective emphasis is generalized — explicitly or, more often, implicitly — to provide apparent empirical support for
an extremely one-sided view of human nature. Although sociologists have
criticized past efforts to single out one fundamental motive in human conduct, the desire to achieve a favorable self-image by winning approval from
others frequently occupies such a position in their own thinking. The following "theorem" has been, in fact, openly put forward by Hans Zetterberg as
"a strong contender for the position as the major Motivational Theorem in
sociology":

> An actor's actions have a tendency to become dispositions that are
> related to the occurrence of favored uniform evaluations of the actor
> and-or his actions in his action system.[2]

Now Zetterberg is not necessarily maintaining that this theorem is an accurate factual statement of the basic psychological roots of social behavior.
He is, characteristically, far too self-conscious about the logic of theorizing
and "concept formation" for that. He goes on to remark that "the maximization of favorable attitudes from others would thus be the counterpart in
sociological theory to the maximization of profit in economic theory." If by
this it is meant that the theorem is to be understood as a heuristic rather
than an empirical assumption, that sociology has a selective point of view

[2] Hans L. Zetterberg, "Compliant Actions," *Acta Sociologica,* 2 (1957) p. 188.

which is just as abstract and partial as that of economics and the other social sciences, and if his view of theory as a set of logically connected formal propositions is granted provisional acceptance, I am in agreement. (Actually, the view of theory suggested at the beginning of this paper is a quite different one.)

But there is a further point to be made. Ralf Dahrendorf has observed that structural-functional theorists do not "claim that order *is based on* a general consensus of values, but that it *can be conceived of in terms of* such consensus and that, if it is conceived of in these terms, certain propositions follow which are subject to the test of specific observations." The same may be said of the assumption that people seek to maximize favorable evaluations by others; indeed this assumption has already fathered such additional concepts as "reference group" and "circle of significant others." Yet the question must be raised as to whether we really wish to, in effect, define sociology by such partial perspectives. The assumption of the maximization of approval from others is the psychological complement to the sociological assumption of a general value consensus. And the former is as selective and one-sided a way of looking at motivation as Dahrendorf and others have argued the latter to be when it determines our way of looking at social structure. The oversocialized view of man of the one is a counterpart to the over-integrated view of society of the other.

Modern sociology, after all, originated as a protest against the partial views of man contained in such doctrines as utilitarianism, classical economics, social Darwinism, and vulgar Marxism. All of the great nineteenth and early twentieth century sociologists saw it as one of their major tasks to expose the unreality of such abstractions as economic man, the gain-seeker of the classical economists; political man, the power-seeker of the Machiavellian tradition in political science; self-preserving man, the security-seeker of Hobbes and Darwin; sexual or libidinal man, the pleasure-seeker of doctrinaire Freudianism; and even religious man, the God-seeker of the theologians. It would be ironical if it should turn out that they have merely contributed to the creation of yet another reified abstraction in socialized man, the status-seeker of our contemporary sociologists.

Of course, such an image of man is, like all the others mentioned, valuable for limited purposes so long as it is not taken for the whole truth. What are some of its deficiencies? To begin with, it neglects the other half of the model of human nature presupposed by current theory: moral man, guided by his built-in superego and beckoning ego-ideal. In recent years sociologists have been less interested than they once were in culture and national character as backgrounds to conduct, partly because stress on the concept of "role" as the crucial link between the individual and the social structure has directed their attention to the immediate situation in which social interaction takes place. Man is increasingly seen as a "role-playing" creature, responding eagerly or anxiously to the expectations of other role-players in the multiple group settings in which he finds himself. Such an approach, while valuable in helping us grasp the complexity of a highly differentiated social structure such as our own, is far too often generalized to serve as a kind of ad hoc social psychology, easily adaptable to particular sociological purposes.

But it is not enough to concede that men often pursue "internalized values" remaining indifferent to what others think of them, particularly when, as I have previously argued, the idea of internalization has been "hollowed out" to make it more useful as an explanation of conformity. What of desire for material and sensual satisfactions? Can we really dispense with the venerable notion of material "interests" and invariably replace it with the blander, more integrative "social values"? And what of striving for power, not necessarily for its own sake — that may be rare and pathological — but as a means by which men are able to *impose* a normative definition of reality on others? That material interests, sexual drives, and the quest for power have often been over-estimated as human motives is no reason to deny their reality. To do so is to suppress one term of the dialectic between conformity and rebellion, social norms and their violation, man and social order, as completely as the other term is suppressed by those who deny the reality of man's "normative orientation" or reduce it to the effect of coercion, rational calculation, or mechanical conditioning.

The view that man is invariably pushed by internalized norms or pulled by the lure of self-validation by others ignores — to speak archaically for a moment — both the highest and the lowest, both beast and angel, in his nature. Durkheim, from whom so much of the modern sociological point of view derives, recognized that the very existence of a social norm implies and even creates the possibility of its violation. This is the meaning of his famous dictum that crime is a "normal phenomenon." He maintained that "for the originality of the idealist whose dreams transcend his century to find expression, it is necessary that the originality of the criminal, who is below the level of his time, shall also be possible. One does not occur without the other." Yet Durkheim lacked an adequate psychology and formulated his insight in terms of the actor's cognitive awareness rather than in motivational terms. We do not have Durkheim's excuse for falling back on what George C. Homans has called a "social mold theory" of human nature.

SOCIAL BUT NOT ENTIRELY SOCIALIZED

I have referred to forces in man that are resistant to socialization. It is not my purpose to explore the nature of these forces or to suggest how we ought best conceive of them as sociologists — that would be a most ambitious undertaking. A few remarks will have to suffice. I think we must start with the recognition that *in the beginning there is the body*. As soon as the body is mentioned the specter of "biological determinism" raises its head and sociologists draw back in fright. And certainly their view of man is sufficiently disembodied and non-materialistic to satisfy Bishop Berkeley, as well as being de-sexualized enough to please Mrs. Grundy.

Am I, then, urging us to return to the older view of a human nature divided between a "social man" and a "natural man" who is either benevolent, Rousseau's Noble Savage, or sinister and destructive, as Hobbes regarded him? Freud is usually represented, or misrepresented, as the chief modern proponent of this dualistic conception which assigns to the social order the purely negative role of blocking and re-directing man's "imperious biological drives." I say "misrepresented" because, although Freud often said things supporting such an interpretation, other and more fundamental strains in his thinking suggest a different conclusion. John Dollard, certainly not a writer who is oblivious to social and cultural "factors," saw this twenty-five years ago: "It is quite clear," he wrote, ". . . that he (Freud) does not regard the instincts as having a fixed social goal; rather, indeed, in the case of the sexual instinct he has stressed the vague but powerful and impulsive nature of the drive and has emphasized that its proper social object is not picked out in advance. His seems to be a drive concept which is not at variance with our knowledge from comparative cultural studies, since his theory does not demand that the 'instinct' work itself out with mechanical certainty alike in every varying culture."[3]

So much for Freud's "imperious biological drives"! When Freud defined psychoanalysis as the study of the "vicissitudes of the instincts," he was confirming, not denying, the "plasticity" of human nature insisted on by social scientists. The drives or "instincts" of psychoanalysis, far from being fixed dispositions to behave in a particular way, are utterly subject to social channelling and transformation and could not even reveal themselves in behavior without social molding any more than our vocal chords can produce articulate speech if we have not learned a language. To psychoanalysis man is indeed a social animal; his social nature is profoundly reflected in his bodily structure.

But there is a difference between the Freudian view on the one hand and both sociological and neo-Freudian conceptions of man on the other. To Freud, man is a *social* animal without being entirely a *socialized* animal. His very social nature is the source of conflicts and antagonisms that create resistance to socialization by the norms of any of the societies which have existed in the course of human history. "Socialization" may mean two quite distinct things; when they are confused an oversocialized view of man is the result. On the one hand socialization means the "transmission of the culture," the particular culture of the society an individual enters at birth; on the other hand the term is used to mean the "process of becoming human," of acquiring uniquely human attributes from interaction with others. All men are socialized in the latter sense, but this does not mean that they have

[3] John Dollard, *Criteria for the Life History*, New Haven: Yale University Press, 1935, p. 120.

been completely molded by the particular norms and values of their culture. All cultures, as Freud contended, do violence to man's socialized bodily drives, but this in no sense means that men could possibly exist without culture or independently of society. From such a standpoint, man may properly be called as Norman Brown has called him, the "neurotic" or the "discontented" animal and repression may be seen as the main characteristic of human nature as we have known it in history.

But isn't this psychology and haven't sociologists been taught to foreswear psychology, to look with suspicion on what are called "psychological variables" in contradistinction to the institutional and historical forces with which they are properly concerned? There is, indeed, as recent critics have complained, too much "psychologism" in contemporary sociology, largely, I think, because of the bias inherent in our favored research techniques. But I do not see how, at the level of theory, sociologists can fail to make assumptions about human nature. If our assumptions are left implicit, we will inevitably presuppose of a view of man that is tailor-made to our special needs; when our sociological theory over-stresses the stability and integration of society we will end up imagining that man is the disembodied, conscience-driven, status-seeking phantom of current theory. We must do better if we really wish to win credit outside of our ranks for special understanding of man, that plausible creature whose wagging tongue so often hides the despair and darkness in his heart.

B. Processes and Examples

1. The Formation of the Self

George Herbert Mead, another of the founding fathers of American sociology and a main proponent of symbolic interaction theory, gives us a consistent theoretical perspective on how the self develops. This selection gives a clear image of what the symbolic interactionist perspective yields. His analysis centers on the social act and the processes of exchange between individuals. The origin of the self lies in the act, since what Mead calls "self-consciousness" can only be sustained as a result of interaction with others. One maintains his self by exchanging roles with others who are, usually, significant to him. There are stages in attaining self-consciousness, and the significance of children's play in self-formation is examined.

12 Georce H. Mead

The Genesis of the Self and Social Control

2/28/6 of WH Freeman's poem + Dev of self

It is evident that a statement of the life of each individual in terms of the results of an analysis of that which is immediately experienced would offer a common plane of events, in which the experience of each would differ from the experiences of others only in their extent, and the completeness or incompleteness of their connections. These differences disappear in the generalized formulations of the social sciences. The experiences of the same individuals, in so far as each faces a world in which objects are plans of action, would implicate in each a different succession of events. In the simplest illustration, two persons approach a passing automobile. To one it is a moving object that he will pass before it reaches the portion of the street that is the meeting-place of their two paths. The other sees an object that will pass this meeting-point before he reaches it. Each slices the world from the standpoint of a different time system. Objects which in a thousand ways are identical for the two individuals, are yet fundamentally different through their location in one spatio-temporal plane, involving a certain succession of events, or in another. Eliminate the temporal dimension, and bring all events back to an instant that is timeless, and the individuality of these objects which belongs to them in behavior is lost, except in so far as they can represent the results of past conduct. But taking time seriously, we realize that the seemingly timeless character of our spatial world and its permanent objects is due to the consentient set which each one of us selects. We abstract time from this space for the purposes of our conduct. Certain objects cease to be events, cease to pass as they are in reality passing and in their permanence become the conditions of our action, and events take place with reference to them. Because a whole community selects the same consentient set does not make the selection less the attitude of each one of them. The life-process takes place in individual organisms, so that the psychology which studies that process in its creative determining function becomes a science of the objective world.

Looked at from the standpoint of an evolutionary history, not only have new forms with their different spatio-temporal environments and their objects arisen, but new characters have arisen answering to the sensitivities and capacities for response. In the terms of Alexander, they have become differently qualitied. It is as impossible to transfer these characters of the habitats to the consciousness of the forms as it is to transfer the spatio-

From *The Philosophy of the Present,* edited by Arthur E. Murphy (Chicago: Open Court, 1932), pp. 176–195. Reprinted by permission of The Open Court Publishing Company, La Salle, Illinois.

temporal structure of the things to such a so-called consciousness. If we introduce a fictitious instantaneousness into a passing universe, things fall to pieces. Things that are spatio-temporally distant from us can be brought into this instant only in terms of our immediate contact experience. They are what they would be if we were there and had our hands upon them. They take on the character of tangible matter. This is the price of their being located at the moment of our bodies' existence. But this instantaneous view has the great advantage of giving to us a picture of what the contact experience will be when we reach the distant object, and of determining conditions under which the distance characters arise. If the world existed at an instant in experience, we should be forced to find some realm such as consciousness into which to transport the distance or so-called secondary qualities of things. If consciousness in evolutionary history, then, has an unambiguous significance, it refers to that stage in the development of life in which the conduct of the individual marks out and defines the future field and objects which make up its environment, and in which emerge characters in the objects and sensitivities in the individuals that answer to each other. There is a relativity of the living individual and its environment, both as to form and content.

What I wish to trace is the fashion in which self and the mind has arisen within this conduct.

It is the implication of this undertaking that only selves have minds, that is, that cognition only belongs to selves, even in the simplest expression of awareness. This, of course, does not imply that below the stage of self-consciousness sense characters and sensitivity do not exist. This obtains in our own immediate experience in so far as we are not self-conscious. It is further implied that this development has taken place only in a social group, for selves exist only in relation to other selves, as the organism as a physical object exists only in its relation to other physical objects. There have been two fields within which social groups have arisen which have determined their environment together with that of their members, and the individuality of its members. These lie in the realm of the invertebrates and in that of the vertebrates. Among the Hymenoptera and termites there are societies whose interests determine for the individuals their stimuli and habitats, and so differentiate the individuals themselves, mainly through the sexual and alimentary processes, that the individual is what he is because of his membership within those societies. In the complex life of the group, the acts of the individuals are completed only through the acts of other individuals, but the mediation of this complex conduct is found in the physiological differentiation of the different members of the society. As Bergson has remarked of the instincts, the implements by which a complex act is carried out are found in the differentiated structure of the form. There is no convincing evidence that an ant or a bee is obliged to anticipate the act of another ant or bee, by tending to respond in the fashion of the other, in order that it may integrate its activity into the common act. And by the same mark there is no evidence of the existence of any language in their societies. Nor do we need to go to the invertebrates to discover this type of social conduct. If one picks up a little child who has fallen, he adapts his arms and attitude to the attitude of the child, and the child adapts himself to the attitude of the other; or in boxing or fencing one responds to stimulus of the other, by acquired physiological adjustment.

Among the vertebrates, apart from the differentiation of the sexes and the nurture and care of infant forms, there is little or no inherited physiological differentiation to mediate the complexities of social conduct. If we are to cooperate successfully with others, we must in some manner get their ongoing acts into ourselves to make the common act come off. As I have just indicated, there is a small range of social activity in which this is not necessary. The suckling of an infant form, or a dog fight, if this may be called a social activity, does not call for more than inherited physiological adjustment. Perhaps the so-called herding instinct should be added, but it hardly comes to more than the tendency of the herd to stick together in their various activities. The wooing and mating of forms, the care of the infant form, the bunching of animals in migrations, and fighting, about exhaust vertebrate social conduct, and beyond these seasonal processes vertebrate societies hardly exist till we reach man. They exhaust the possibilities in vertebrate structure of the mediation of social conduct, for the vertebrate organism has shown no such astonishing plasticity in physiological differentiation as that which we can trace among the insects, from isolated forms to members of the societies of the termites, the ants, and the bees.

A social act may be defined as one in which the occasion or stimulus which sets free an impulse is found in the character or conduct of a living form that belongs to the proper environment of the living form whose impulse it is. I wish, however, to restrict the social act to the class of acts which involve the cooperation of more than one individual, and whose object as defined by the act, in the sense of Bergson, is a social object. I mean by a social object one that answers to all the parts of the complex act, though these parts are found in the conduct of different individuals. The objective of the act is then found in the life-process of the group, not in those of the separate individuals alone. The full social object would not exist in the environments of the separate individuals of the societies of the Hymenoptera and termites, nor in the restricted societies of the vertebrates whose basis is found alone in physiological adjustment. A cow that licks the skin of a calf stuffed with hay, until the skin is worn away, and then eats the hay, or a woman who expends her parental impulse upon a poodle, cannot be said to have the full social object involved in the entire act in their environments. It would be necessary to piece together the environments of the different individuals or superimpose them upon each other to reach the environment and objects of the societies in question.

Where forms such as those of the Hymenoptera and the termites exhibit

great plasticity in development, social acts based on physiological adjustment, and corresponding societies, have reached astonishing complexity. But
when the limit of that plasticity is reached, the limit of the social act and
the society is reached also. Where, as among the vertebrates, that physiological adjustment which mediates a social act is limited and fixed, the
societies of this type are correspondingly insignificant. But another type of
social act, and its corresponding society and object, has been at least suggested by the description of the social act based upon physiological adjustment. Such an act would be one in which the different parts of the act which
belong to different individuals should appear in the act of each individual.
This cannot mean, however, that the single individual could carry out the
entire act, for then, even if it were possible, it would cease to be a social
act, nor could the stimulus which calls out his own part of the complex
act be that which calls out the other parts of the act in so far as they appear
in his conduct. If the social object is to appear in his experience, it must
be that the stimuli which set free the responses of the others involved in the
act should be present in his experience, not as stimuli to his response, but
as stimuli for the responses of others; and this implies that the social situation which arises after the completion of one phase of the act, which serves
as the stimulus for the next participant in the complex procedure, shall in
some sense be in the experience of the first actor, tending to call out, not
his own response, but that of the succeeding actor. Let us make the impossible assumption that the wasp, in stinging a spider which it stores with its
egg, finds in the spider a social object in the sense which I have specified.
The spider would have to exist in the experience of the wasp as live but
quiescent food for the larva when it emerges from the egg. In order that the
paralyzed spider should so appear to the wasp, the wasp would need to be
subject to the same stimulus as that which sets free the response of the
larva; in other words, the wasp would need to be able to respond in some
degree as the larva. And of course the wasp would have to view the spider
under the time dimension, grafting a hypothetical future onto its passing
present, but the occasion for this would have to lie in the wasp's tending
to respond in role of larva to the appropriate food which it is placing in
storage. This, then, presents another possible principle of social organization, as distinguished from that of physiological differentiation. If the objects that answer to the complex social act can exist spatio-temporally in the
experience of the different members of the society, as stimuli that set free
not only their own responses, but also as stimuli to the responses of those
who share in the composite act, a principle of coordination might be found
which would not depend upon physiological differentiation. Any one necessary psychological condition for this would be that the individual should
have in some fashion present in his organism the tendencies to respond as
the other participants in the act will respond. Much more than this would
be involved, but this at least would be a necessary precondition. A social

object answering to the responses of different individuals in a society could be conceived of as existing in the experiences of individuals in that society, if the different responses of these individuals in the complex acts could be found in sufficient degree in the natures of separate individuals to render them sensitive to the different values of the object answering to the parts of the act.

The cortex of the vertebrate central nervous system provides at least a part of the mechanism which might make this possible. The nervous currents from the column and the stem of the brain to the cortex can there bring the acts that go out from these lower centers into relation with each other so that more complex processes and adjustments can arise. The centers and paths of the cortex represent an indefinite number of possible actions; particularly they represent acts which, being in competition with each other, inhibit each other, and present the problem of organization and adjustment so that overt conduct may proceed. In the currents and cross-currents in the gray matter and its association fibers, there exist the tendencies to an indefinite number of responses. Answering to these adjustments are the objects organized into a field of action, not only spatially but temporally; for the tendency to grasp the distant object, while already excited, is so linked with the processes of approach that it does not get its overt expression till the intervening stretch is passed. In this vertebrate apparatus of conduct, then, the already excited predispositions to thousands of acts, that far transcend the outward accomplishments, furnish the inner attitudes implicating objects that are not immediate objectives of the individual's act.

But the cortex is not simply a mechanism. It is an organ that exists in fulfilling its function. If these tendencies to action which do not get immediate expression appear and persist, it is because they belong to the act that is going on. If, for example, property is a social object in the experience of men, as distinguished from the nut which the squirrel stores, it is because features of the food that one buys innervate the whole complex of responses by which property is not only acquired, but respected and protected, and this complex so innervated is an essential part of the act by which the man buys and stores his food. The point is not that buying food is a more complicated affair than picking it up from the ground, but that exchange is an act in which a man excites himself to give by making an offer. An offer is what it is because the presentation is a stimulus to give. One cannot exchange otherwise than by putting one's self in the attitude of the other party to the bargain. Property becomes a tangible object, because all essential phases of property appear in the actions of all those involved in exchange, and appear as essential features of the individual's action.

The individual in such an act is a self. If the cortex has become an organ of social conduct, and has made possible the appearance of social objects, it is because the individual has become a self, that is, an individual who organizes his own response by the tendencies on the part of others to respond to his act. He can do this because the mechanism of the vertebrate brain enables the individual to take these different attitudes in the formation of the act. But selves have appeared late in vertebrate evolution. The structure of the central nervous system is too minute to enable us to show the corresponding structural changes in the paths of the brain. It is only in the behavior of the human animal that we can trace this evolution. It has been customary to mark this stage in development by endowing man with a mind, or at least with a certain sort of mind. As long as consciousness is regarded as a sort of spiritual stuff out of which are fashioned sensations and affections and images and ideas or significances, a mind as a locus of these entities is an almost necessary assumption, but when these contents have been returned to things, the necessity of quarters for this furniture has disappeared also.

It lies beyond the bounds of this paper to follow out the implications of this shift for logic and epistemology, but there is one phase of all so-called mental processes which is central to this discussion, and that is self-consciousness. If the suggestions which I have made above should prove tenable, the self that is central to all so-called mental experience has appeared only in the social conduct of human vertebrates. It is just because the individual finds himself taking the attitudes of the others who are involved in his conduct that he becomes an object for himself. It is only by taking the roles of others that we have been able to come back to ourselves. We have seen above that the social object can exist for the individual only if the various parts of the whole social act carried out by other members of the society are in some fashion present in the conduct of the individual. It is further true that the self can exist for the individual only if he assumes the roles of the others. The presence in the conduct of the individual of the tendencies to act as others act may be, then, responsible for the appearance in the experience of the individual of a social object, i.e., an object answering to complex reactions of a number of individuals, and also for the appearance of the self. Indeed, these two appearances are correlative. Property can appear as an object only in so far as the individual stimulates himself to buy by a prospective offer to sell. Buying and selling are involved in each other. Something that can be exchanged can exist in the experience of the individual only in so far as he has in his own make-up the tendency to sell when he has also the tendency to buy. And he becomes a self in his experience only in so far as one attitude on his own part calls out the corresponding attitude in the social undertaking.

This is just what we imply in "self-consciousness." We appear as selves in our conduct in so far as we ourselves take the attitude that others take toward us, in these correlative activities. Perhaps as good an illustration of this as can be found is in a "right." Over against the protection of our lives or property, we assume the attitude of assent of all members in the community. We take the role of what may be called the "generalized other." And in doing this we appear as social objects, as selves. It is interesting to note that in the development of the individual child, there are two stages which present the two essential steps in attaining self-consciousness. The first stage is that of play, and the second that of the game, where these two are distinguished from each other. In play in this sense, the child is continually acting as a parent, a teacher, a preacher, a grocery man, a policeman, a pirate, or an Indian. It is the period of childish existence which Wordsworth has described as that of "endless imitation." It is the period of Froebel's kindergarten plays. In it, as Froebel recognized, the child is acquiring the roles of those who belong to his society. This takes place because the child is continually exciting in himself the responses to his own social acts. In his infant dependence upon the responses of others to his own social stimuli, he is peculiarly sensitive to this relation. Having in his own nature the beginning of the parental response, he calls it out by his own appeals. The doll is the universal type of this, but before he plays with a doll, he responds in tone of voice and in attitude as his parents respond to his own cries and chortles. This has been denominated imitation, but the psychologist now recognizes that one imitates only in so far as the so-called imitated act can be called out in the individual by his appropriate stimulation. That is, one calls or tends to call out in himself the same response that he calls out in the other.

The play antedates the game. For in a game there is a regulated procedure, and rules. The child must not only take the role of the other, as he does in the play, but he must assume the various roles of all the participants in the game, and govern his action accordingly. If he plays first base, it is as the one to whom the ball will be thrown from the field or from the catcher. Their organized reactions to him he has imbedded in his own playing of the different positions, and this organized reaction becomes what I have called the "generalized other" that accompanies and controls his conduct. And it is this generalized other in his experience which provides him with a self. I can only refer to the bearing of this childish play attitude upon so-called sympathetic magic. Primitive men call out in their own activity some simulacrum of the response which they are seeking from the world about. They are children crying in the night.

The mechanism of this implies that the individual who is stimulating others to response is at the same time arousing in himself the tendencies to the same reactions. Now, that in a complex social act, which serves as the stimulus to another individual to his response is not as a rule fitted to call out the tendency to the same response in the individual himself. The hostile demeanor of one animal does not frighten the animal himself, presumably. Especially in the complex social reactions of the ants or termites or the bees, the part of the act of one form which does call out the appropriate reaction of another can hardly be conceived of as arousing a like reaction in the form in question, for here the complex social act is dependent upon physiological differentiation, such an unlikeness in structure exists that the same stimulus could not call out like responses. For such a mechanism as has been suggested, it is necessary to find first of all some stimulus in the social conduct of the members of an authentic group that can call out in the individual that is responsible for it, the same response that it calls out in the other; and in the second place, the individuals in the group must be of such like structure that the stimulus will have the same value for one form that it has for the other. Such a type of social stimulus is found in the vocal gesture in a human society. The term gesture I am using to refer to that part of the act or attitude of one individual engaged in a social act which serves as the stimulus to another individual to carry out his part of the whole act. Illustrations of gestures, so defined, may be found in the attitudes and movements of others to which we respond in passing them in a crowd, in the turning of the head toward the glance of another's eye, in the hostile attitude assumed over against a threatening gesture, in the thousand and one different attitudes which we assume toward different modulations of the human voice, or in the attitudes and suggestions of movements in boxers or fencers, to which responses are so nicely adjusted. It is to be noted that the attitudes to which I have referred are but stages in the act as they appear to others, and include expressions of countenance, positions of the body, changes in breathing rhythm, outward evidence of circulatory changes, and vocal sounds. In general these so-called gestures belong to the beginning of the overt act, for the adjustments of others to the social process are best made early in the act. Gestures are, then, the early stages in the overt social act to which other forms involved in the same act respond. Our interest is in finding gestures which can affect the individual that is responsible for them in the same manner as that in which they affect other individuals. The vocal gesture is at least one that assails our ears who make it in the same physiological fashion as that in which it affects others. We hear our own vocal gestures as others hear them. We may see or feel movements of our hands as others see or feel them, and these sights and feels have served in the place of the vocal gestures in the case of those who are congenitally deaf or deaf and blind. But it has been the vocal gesture that has preeminently provided the medium of social organization in human society. It belongs historically to the beginning of the act, for it arises out of the change in breathing rhythm that accompanies the preparation for sudden action, those actions to which other forms must be nicely adjusted.

If, then, a vocal gesture arouses in the individual who makes it a tendency to the same response that it arouses in another, and this beginning of an act of the other in himself enters into his experience, he will find himself tending to act toward himself as the other acts toward him. In our self-conscious experience we understand what he does or says. The possibility of this entering into his experience we have found in the cortex of the human brain. There the coordinations answering to an indefinite number of acts may be excited, and while holding each other in check enter into the neural process of adjustment which leads to the final overt conduct. If one pronounces and hears himself pronounce the word "table," he has aroused in himself the organized attitudes of his response to that object, in the same fashion as that in which he has aroused it in another. We commonly call such an aroused organized attitude an idea, and the ideas of what we are saying accompany all of our significant speech. If we may trust to the statement in one of St. Paul's epistles, some of the saints spoke with tongues which had no significance to them. They made sounds which called out no response in those that made them. The sounds were without meaning. Where a vocal gesture uttered by one individual leads to a certain response in another, we may call it a symbol of that act; where it arouses in the man who makes it the tendency to the same response, we may call it a significant symbol. These organized attitudes which we arouse in ourselves when we talk to others are, then, the ideas which we say are in our minds, and in so far as they arouse the same attitudes in others, they are in their minds, in so far as they are self-conscious in the sense in which I have used that term. But it is not necessary that we should talk to another to have these ideas. We can talk to ourselves, and this we do in the inner forum of what we call thought. We are in possession of selves just in so far as we can and do take the attitudes of others toward ourselves and respond to those attitudes. We approve of ourselves and condemn ourselves. We pat ourselves upon the back and in blind fury attack ourselves. We assume the generalized attitude of the group, in the censor that stands at the door of our imagery and inner conversations, and in the affirmation of the laws and axioms of the universe of discourse. *Quod semper, quod ubique.* Our thinking is an inner conversation in which we may be taking the roles of specific acquaintances over against ourselves, but usually it is with what I have termed the "generalized other" that we converse, and so attain to the levels of abstract thinking, and that impersonality, that so-called objectivity that we cherish. In this fashion, I conceive, have selves arisen in human behavior and with the selves their minds. It is an interesting study, that of the manner in which the self and its mind arises in every child, and the indications of the corresponding manner in which it arose in primitive man. I cannot enter into a discussion of this. I do wish, however, to refer to some of the implications of this conception of the self for the theory of social control.

I wish to recur to the position, taken earlier in this paper, that, if we recognize that experience is a process continually passing into the future, objects exist in nature as the patterns of our actions. If we reduce the world to a fictitious instantaneous present, all objects fall to pieces. There is no reason to be found, except in an equally fictitious mind, why any lines should be drawn about any group of physical particles, constituting them objects. However, no such knife-edge present exists. Even in the so-called specious present there is a passage, in which there is succession, and both past and future are there, and the present is only that section in which, from the standpoint of action, both are involved. When we take this passage of nature seriously, we see that the object of perception is the existent future of the act. The food is what the animal will eat, and his refuge is the burrow where he will escape from his pursuer. Of course the future is, as future, contingent. He may not escape, but in nature it exists there as the counterpart of his act. So far as there are fixed relations there, they are of the past, and the object involves both, but the form that it has arises from the ongoing act. Evolutionary biology, in so far as it is not mere physics and chemistry, proceeds perhaps unwittingly upon this assumption, and so does social science in so far as it is not static. Its objects are in terms of the habitat, the environment. They are fashioned by reactions. I am merely affirming the existence of these objects, affirming them as existent in a passing universe answering to acts.

In so far as there are social acts, there are social objects, and I take it that social control is bringing the act of the individual into relation with this social object. With the control of the object over the act, we are abundantly familiar. Just because the object is the form of the act, in this character it controls the expression of the act. The vision of the distant object is not only the stimulus to movement toward it. It is also, in its changing distance values, a continual control of the act of approach. The contours of the object determine the organization of the act in its seizure, but in this case the whole act is in the individual and the object is in his field of experience. Barring a breakdown in the structure or function, the very existence of the object insures its control of the act. In the social act, however, the act is distributed among a number of individuals. While there is or may be an object answering to each part of the act, existing in the experience of each individual, in the case of societies dependent upon physiological differentiation the whole object does not exist in the experience of any individual. The control may be exercised through the survival of those physiological differentiations that still carry out the life-process involved in the complex act. No complication of the act which did not mediate this could survive. Or we may take refuge in a controlling factor in the act, as does Bergson, but this is not the situation that interests us. The human societies in which we are interested are societies of selves. The human individual is a self only in so far as he takes the attitude of another toward himself. In so far as this attitude is that of a number of others, and in so far as he can assume the organized attitudes of a number that are cooperating in a common activity, he takes the attitudes of the group toward himself, and in taking this or these attitudes he is defining the object of the group, that which defines and controls the response. Social control, then, will depend upon the degree to which the individual does assume the attitudes of those in the group who are involved with him in his social activities. In the illustration already used, the man who buys controls his purchase from the standpoint of a value in the object that exists for him only in so far as he takes the attitude of a seller as well as a buyer. Value exists as an object only for individuals within whose acts in exchange are present those attitudes which belong to the acts of the others who are essential to the exchange.

The act of exchange becomes very complicated; the degree to which all the essential acts involved in it enter into the acts of all those engaged therein varies enormously, and the control which the object, i.e., the value, exercises over the acts varies proportionately. The Marxian theory of state ownership of capital, i.e., of exclusive state production, is a striking illustration of the breakdown of such control. The social object, successful economic production, as presented in this theory, fails to assume the attitudes of individual initiative which successful economic production implies. Democratic government, on the theory of action through universal interest in the issues of a campaign, breaks down as a control, and surrenders the government largely to the political machine, whose object more nearly answers to the attitudes of the voters and the non-voters.

Social control depends, then, upon the degree to which the individuals in society are able to assume the attitudes of the others who are involved with them in common endeavor. For the social object will always answer to the act developing itself in self-consciousness. Besides property, all of the institutions are such objects, and serve to control individuals who find in them the organization of their own social responses.

The individual does not, of course, assume the attitudes of the numberless others who are in one way or another implicated in his social conduct, except in so far as the attitudes of others are uniform under like circumstances. One assumes, as I have said, the attitudes of generalized others. But even with this advantage of the universal over the multiplicity of its numberless instances, the number of different responses that enter into our social conduct seems to defy any capacity of any individual to assume the roles which would be essential to define our social objects. And yet, though modern life has become indefinitely more complex than it was in earlier periods of human history, it is far easier for the modern man than for his predecessor to put himself in the place of those who contribute to his necessities, who share with him the functions of government, or join with him in determining prices. It is not the number of participants, or even the number of different functions, that is of primary importance. The important question is whether these various forms of activities belong so naturally to the member of a human society that, in taking the role of another, his activities are found to belong to one's own nature. As long as the complexities of human society do not exceed those of the central nervous system, the problem of an adequate social object, which is identical with that of an adequate self-consciousness, is not that of becoming acquainted with the indefinite number of acts that are involved in social behavior, but that of so overcoming the distances in space and time, and the barriers of language and convention and social status, that we can converse with ourselves in the roles of those who are involved with us in the common undertaking of life. A journalism that is insatiably curious about the human attitudes of all of us is the sign of the times. The other curiosities as to the conditions under which other people live, and work, and fight each other, and love each other, follow from the fundamental curiosity which is the passion of self-consciousness. We must be others if we are to be ourselves. The modern realistic novel has done more than technical education in fashioning the social object that spells social control. If we can bring people together so that they can enter into each other's lives, they will inevitably have a common object, which will control their common conduct.

The task, however, is enormous enough, for it involves not simply breaking down passive barriers such as those of distance in space and time and vernacular, but those fixed attitudes of custom and status in which our selves are imbedded. Any self is a social self, but it is restricted to the group whose roles it assumes, and it will never abandon this self until it finds itself entering into the larger society and maintaining itself there. The whole history of warfare between societies and within societies shows how much more readily and with how much greater emotional thrill we realize ourselves in opposition to common enemies than in collaboration with them. All over Europe, and more specifically at Geneva, we see nationals with great distrust and constant rebounds trying to put themselves in each other's places and still preserve the selves that have existed upon enmities, that they may reach the common ground where they may avoid the horror of war, and meliorate unendurable economic conditions. A Dawes Plan is such a social object, coming painfully into existence, that may control the conflicting interests of hostile communities, but only if each can in some degree put himself in the other's place in operating it. The World Court and the League of Nations are other such social objects that sketch out common plans of action if there are national selves that can realize themselves in the collaborating attitudes of others.

If children's play is a significant stage in the development of self, children who play different "games" will have different selves. The history of children and their play indicates that childhood itself is a variable concept. Children were expected to become non-children sooner in past stages of Western history, and we know that the way in which other societies define the stages between adult and infant is different from our own. In this brief selection from Philippe Aries, we see that childhood as we know it did not exist in medieval society. The formation of the self and the socialization of the medieval child indicate quite well that the social situation, culture, or group determine what we will be.

13 PHILIPPE ARIES

Centuries of Childhood

In medieval society the idea of childhood did not exist; this is not to suggest that children were neglected, forsaken or despised. The idea of childhood is not to be confused with affection for children: it corresponds to an awareness of the particular nature of childhood, that particular nature which distinguishes the child from the adult, even the young adult. In medieval society this awareness was lacking. That is why, as soon as the child could live without the constant solicitude of his mother, his nanny or his cradle-rocker, he belonged to adult society. That adult society now strikes us as rather puerile: no doubt this is largely a matter of its mental age, but it is also due to its physical age, because it was partly made up of children and youths. Language did not give the word "child" the restricted meaning we give it today: people said "child" much as we say "lad" in everyday speech. The absence of definition extended to every sort of social activity: games, crafts, arms. There is not a single collective picture of the times in which children are not to be found, nestling singly or in pairs in the *trousse* hung round women's necks,[1] or urinating in a corner, or playing their part in a traditional festival, or as apprentices in a workshop, or as pages serving a knight, etc.

The infant who was too fragile as yet to take part in the life of adults simply "did not count": this is the expression used by Molière, who bears witness to the survival in the seventeenth century of a very old attitude of mind. Again in *Le malade imaginaire* has two daughters, one of marriageable age and little Louison who is just beginning to talk and walk. It is generally known that he is threatening to put his elder daughter in a convent to stop her philandering. His brother asks him: "How is it, Brother, that rich as you are and having only one daughter, *for I don't count the little one*, you can talk of putting her in a convent?" The little one did not count because she could disappear.

The quotation from Molière shows the continuance of the archaic attitude to childhood. But this survival, for all that it was stubborn, was precarious. From the fourteenth century on, there had been a tendency to express in art, iconography and religion (in the cult of the dead) the personality which children were seen to possess, and the poetic, familiar significance attributed to their special nature. We have followed the evolution of the *putto* and the child portrait. And we have seen that in the sixteenth and seventeenth centuries the child or infant — at least in the upper classes of society — was given a special costume which marked him out from the adults. This specialization of the dress of children and especially of little boys, in a society in which clothes and outward appearances had considerable importance, bears witness to the change which had taken place in the general attitude towards children: they counted much more than Argan's brother imagined. In fact, *Le malade imaginaire*, which seems as hard on little children as do certain remarks by La Fontaine, contains a whole conversation between Argan and little Louison: "Look at me, will you!" "What is it, papa?" "Here!" "What?" "Haven't you anything to tell me?" "If you wish, I can tell you, to amuse you, the story of the Ass's Skin, or else the fable of the Fox and the Crow which I was taught not so long ago." A new concept of childhood had appeared, in which the child, on account of his sweetness, simplicity and drollery, became a source of amusement and relaxation for the adult.

To begin with, the attitude was held by women, women whose task it was to look after children — mothers and nannies. In the sixteenth-century edition of *Le Grand Propriétaire de toutes choses* we are told about the nanny: "She rejoices when the child is happy, and feels sorry for the child when he is ill; she picks him up when he falls, she binds him when he tosses about, and she washes and cleans him when he is dirty." She brings the child up and teaches him to talk: "She pronounces the words as if she had a stammer, to teach him to talk better and more rapidly . . . , she carries him in her hands, then on her shoulder, then on her lap, to play with him when he cries; she chews the child's meat for him when he has no teeth so that he can swallow profitably and without danger; she plays with the child to make him sleep and she binds his limbs to keep them straight so that he has no stiffness in his body, and she bathes and anoints him to nourish his flesh . . . ." Thomas More dwells on the subject of the schoolboy being sent to school by his mother: "When the little boy will not rise in time for her, but lies still abed and slugg, and when he is up, weepeth because he hath lien so long, fearing to be beaten at school for his late coming thither, she telleth him then that it is but early days, and he shall come time enough, and biddeth him: 'Go, good son, I warrant thee, I have sent to thy master myself, take thy bread and butter with thee, thou shalt not be beaten at all.'" Thus she sends him off sufficiently reassured not to burst into tears at the idea of leaving her at home, but she does not get to the bottom of the trouble and the late arrival will be well and truly beaten when he gets to school.

Children's little antics must always have seemed touching to mothers, nannies and cradle-rockers, but their reactions formed part of the huge domain of unexpressed feelings. Henceforth people would no longer hesitate to recognize the pleasure they got from watching children's antics and "coddling" them. We find Mme. de Sévigné admitting, not without a certain affectation, how much time she spends playing with her granddaughter: "I am reading the story of Christopher Columbus's discovery of the Indies, which is entertaining me greatly; but your daughter entertains me even more. I do so love her . . . she strokes your portrait and caresses it in such an amusing way that I have to kiss her straight away." "I have been playing with your daughter for an hour now; she is delightful." And, as if she were afraid of some infection, she adds, with a levity which surprises us, for the death of a child is something serious for us and nothing to joke about: "I do not want her to die." For, as we have seen from Molière, this first appreciation of childhood went with a certain indifference, or rather with the indifference that was traditional.

The "coddling" attitude towards children is even better known to us by the critical reactions it provoked at the end of the sixteenth century and particularly in the seventeenth century. Peevish persons found insufferable the attention paid to children. Montaigne bristles: "I cannot abide that passion for caressing new-born children, which have neither mental activities nor recognizable bodily shape by which to make themselves lovable, and I have never willingly suffered them to be fed in my presence." He cannot accept the idea of loving children "for our amusement, like monkeys," or taking pleasure in their "frolickings, games and infantile nonsense."

Another example of this state of mind, a century later, is to be seen in Coulanges, Mme. de Sévigné's cousin. He was obviously exasperated by the way his friends and relatives fussed over their children, for he composed a song dedicated to "fathers of families," urging them not to spoil their offspring or allow them to eat with adults.

It is important to note that this feeling of exasperation was as novel as "coddling," and even more foreign than "coddling" to the indifferent attitude of people in the Middle Ages. It was precisely to the presence of children that Montaigne and Coulanges, like Mme. de Sévigné, were hypersensitive; it should be pointed out that Montaigne and Coulanges were more modern than Mme. de Sévigné in so far as they considered it necessary to keep children apart from adults. They held that it was no longer desirable that children should mingle with adults, especially at table; no doubt because if they did they were "spoiled" and became ill-mannered.

The seventeenth-century moralists and pedagogues shared the dislike felt by Montaigne and Coulanges for "coddling." Thus the austere Fleury, in his treatise on studies, speaks very much like Montaigne: "When little children are caught in a trap, when they say something foolish, drawing a correct inference from an irrelevant principle which has been given to them, people burst out laughing, rejoice at having tricked them, or kiss and caress them as if they had worked out the correct answer. It is as if the poor children had been made only to amuse the adults, like little dogs or little monkeys."

The author of *Galatée*, the manual of etiquette commonly used in the best colleges, those of the Jesuits, speaks like Coulanges: "Those persons are greatly at fault who never talk of anything but their wives, their little children and their nannies. 'My little son made me laugh so much! Just listen to this. . . .' "

M. d'Argonne, in his treatise on education, *L'Éducation de Monsieur de Moncade* (1690), likewise complains that people take an interest in very small children only for the sake of their "caresses" and "antics"; too many parents "value their children only in so far as they derive pleasure and entertainment from them."

It is important to remember that at the end of the seventeenth century this "coddling" was not practised only by people of quality, who, in fact, were beginning to disdain it. Its presence in the lower classes was noted and denounced. J.-B. de La Salle in his *Conduite des écoles chrétiennes* (1720) states that the children of the poor are particularly ill-mannered because "they do just as they please, their parents paying no attention to them, even treating them in an idolatrous manner: what the children want, they want too."

In the moralists and pedagogues of the seventeenth century, we see that fondness for childhood and its special nature no longer found expression in amusement and "coddling," but in psychological interest and moral solicitude. The child was no longer regarded as amusing or agreeable: "Every man must be conscious of that insipidity of childhood which disgusts the sane mind; that coarseness of youth which finds pleasure in scarcely anything but material objects and which is only a very crude sketch of the man of thought." Thus Balthazar Gratien in *El Discreto*, a treatise on education published in 1646 which was still being translated into French in 1723. "Only time can cure a person of childhood and youth, which are truly ages of imperfection in every respect." To be understood, these opinions need to be put back in their temporal context and compared with the other texts of the period. They have been interpreted by some historians as showing ignorance of childhood, but in fact they mark the beginning of a serious

[handwritten margin notes: 2/28/86 — Perrault's fairy tales were for t Court — left t Fabulists or Robert Graves intro to trans of Iliad — New Archaebun cherubim → copid]

and realistic concept of childhood. For they do not suggest that people should accept the levity of childhood: that was the old mistake. In order to correct the behaviour of children, people must first of all understand it, and the texts of the late sixteenth century and the seventeenth century are full of comments on child psychology. The authors show a great solicitude for children, who are seen as witnesses to baptismal innocence, comparable to the angels, and close to Christ who loved them. But this interest calls for the development in them of a faculty of reasoning which is still fragile, a determined attempt to turn them into thinking men and good Christians. The tone is sometimes grim, the emphasis being laid on strictness as opposed to the laxity and facility of contemporary manners; but this is not always the case. There is even humour in Jacqueline Pascal, and undisguised tenderness. In the texts published towards the end of the century, an attempt is made to reconcile sweetness and reason. Thus the Abbé Goussault, a counsellor at the High Court, writes in *Le Portrait d'une honnête femme:* "Familiarizing oneself with one's children, getting them to talk about all manner of things, treating them as sensible people and winning them over with sweetness, is an infallible secret for doing what one wants with them. They are young plants which need tending and watering frequently: a few words of advice offered at the right moment, a few marks of friendship and affection given now and then, touch them and bind them. A few caresses, a few little presents, a few words of cordiality and trust make an impression on their minds, and they are few in number that resist these sweet and easy methods of making them persons of honour and probity."

The first concept of childhood — characterized by "coddling" — had made its appearance in the family circle, in the company of little children. The second, on the contrary, sprang from a source outside the family: churchmen or gentlemen of the robe, few in number before the sixteenth century, and a far greater number of moralists in the seventeenth century, eager to ensure disciplined, rational manners. They too had become alive to the formerly neglected phenomenon of childhood, but they were unwilling to regard children as charming toys, for they saw them as fragile creatures of God who needed to be both safeguarded and reformed. This concept in its turn passed into family life.

In the eighteenth century, we find those two elements in the family, together with a new element: concern about hygiene and physical health. Care of the body was not ignored by seventeenth-century moralists and pedagogues. People nursed the sick devotedly (at the same time taking every precaution to unmask malingerers), but any interest shown in healthy bodies had a moral purpose behind it: a delicate body encouraged luxury, sloth, concupiscence — all the vices in fact!

General de Martange's correspondence with his wife gives us some idea of a family's private life and preoccupations about a century after Mme. de

Sévigné. Martange was born in 1722 and married in 1754. He shows great interest in everything concerning his children's life, from "coddling" to education; he watches closely over their health and even their hygiene. Everything to do with children and family life has become a matter worthy of attention. Not only the child's future but his presence and his very existence are of concern: the child has taken a central place in the family.

> *When people think of self-formation and socialization they generally think of the individual's development into a middle-class citizen. It is, however, no less important to recognize that socialization also occurs in groups which are at variance with the larger society. These groups have a distinctive culture replete with language, family patterns, music, and style of dress that are adaptive for them. Harold Finestone, a criminologist, makes use of the method of the social survey in interviewing young drug users. He describes the process by which the "cat" forms his self, and analyzes the symbols attached to his new identity. Notice how Finestone uses the concept of play to describe this developmental process in somewhat the same manner as Mead.*

14　HAROLD FINESTONE

Cats, Kicks, and Color

Growing recognition that the most recent manifestation of the use of opiates in this country has been predominantly a young peoples' problem has resulted in some speculation as to the nature of this generation of drug users. Is it possible to form an accurate conception as to what "manner of man" is represented by the current species of young drug addict? Intensive interviews between 1951 and 1953 with over fifty male colored users of heroin in their late teens and early twenties selected from several of the areas of highest incidence of drug use in Chicago served to elicit from them the expression of many common attitudes, values, schemes of behavior, and general social orientation. Moreover, since there was every reason to believe that such similarities had preceded their introduction to heroin, it appeared that it was by virtue of such shared features that they had been unusually receptive to the spread of opiate use. Methodologically, their common patterns of behavior suggested the heuristic value of the construction of a so-

From *Social Problems*, Vol. V, No. 1 (July, 1957) pp. 3–13. Reprinted by permission of the author and The Society for the Study of Social Problems.

cial type. The task of this paper is to depict this social type, and to present a hypothetical formulation to account for the form it has taken.

No special justification appears to be necessary for concentrating in this paper on the social type of the young colored drug user. One of the distinctive properties of the distribution of drug use as a social problem, at least in Chicago, is its high degree of both spatial and racial concentration. In fact, it is a problem which in this city can be pinpointed with great accuracy as having its incidence preponderantly among the young male colored persons in a comparatively few local community areas. The following delineation of the generic characteristics of young colored drug users constitutes in many respects an ideal type. No single drug addict exemplified all of the traits to be depicted but all of them revealed several of them to a marked degree.

The young drug user was a creature of contrasts. Playing the role of the fugitive and pariah as he was inevitably forced to do, he turned up for interviews in a uniformly ragged and dirty condition. And yet he talked with an air of superiority derived from his identification with an elite group, the society of "cats." He came in wearing a non-functional tie clip attached to his sport shirt and an expensive hat as the only indications that he was concerned with his appearance and yet displayed in his conversation a highly developed sense of taste in men's clothing and a high valuation upon dressing well. He came from what were externally the drabbest, most overcrowded, and physically deteriorated sections of the city and yet discussed his pattern of living as though it were a consciously cultivated work of art.

Despite the location of his social world in the "asphalt jungle" of the "Blackbelt" he strictly eschewed the use of force and violence as a technique for achieving his ends or for the settling of problematic situations. He achieved his goals by indirection, relying, rather, on persuasion and on a repertoire of manipulative techniques. To deal with a variety of challenging situations, such as those arising out of his contacts with the police, with his past or potential victims, and with jilted "chicks," etc., he used his wits and his conversational ability. To be able to confront such contingencies with adequacy and without resort to violence was to be "cool." His idea was to get what he wanted through persuasion and ingratiation; to use the other fellow by deliberately outwitting him. Indeed, he regarded himself as immeasurably superior to the "gorilla," a person who resorted to force.

The image of himself as "operator" was projected onto the whole world about him and led to a complete scepticism as to other persons' motives. He could relate to people by outsmarting them, or through openhanded and often ruinous generosity, but his world seemed to preclude any relationship which was not part of a "scheme" or did not lend itself to an "angle." The most difficult puzzle for him to solve was the "square," the honest man. On the one hand the "square" was the hard-working plodder who lived by routine and who took honesty and the other virtues at their face value. As such he constituted the prize victim for the cat. On the other hand the cat harbored the sneaking suspicion that some squares were smarter than he, because they could enjoy all the forbidden pleasures which were his stock in trade and maintain a reputation for respectability in the bargain.

The cat had a large, colorful, and discriminating vocabulary which dealt with all phases of his experience with drugs. In addition, he never seemed to content himself with the conventional word for even the most common-place objects. Thus he used "pad" for house, "pecks" for food, "flicks" for movies, "stick hall" for pool hall, "dig the scene" for observe, "box" for record player, "bread" for money, etc. In each instance the word he used was more concrete or earthier than the conventional word and such as to reveal an attitude of subtle ridicule towards the dignity and conventionality inherent in the common usage.

His soft convincing manner of speaking, the shocking earthiness and fancifulness of his vocabulary, together with the formidable gifts of charm and ingratiation which he deployed, all contributed to the dominant impression which the young drug user made as a person. Such traits would seem to have fitted naturally into a role which some cats had already played or aspired to play, that of the pimp. To be supported in idleness and luxury through the labors of one or more attractive "chicks" who shoplifted or engaged in prostitution or both and dutifully handed over the proceeds was one of his favorite fantasies. In contrast with the milieu of the white under-world, the pimp was not an object of opprobrium but of prestige.

The theme of the exploitation of the woman goes close to the heart of the cat's orientation to life, that is, his attitude towards work. Part of the cat's sense of superiority stems from his aristocratic disdain for work and for the subordination of self to superiors and to the repetitive daily routine entailed by work, which he regards as intolerable. The "square" is a person who toils for regular wages and who takes orders from his superiors without complaint.

In contrast with the "square," the cat gets by without working. Instead he keeps himself in "bread" by a set of ingenious variations on "begging, borrowing, or stealing." Each cat has his "hustle" (4), and a "hustle" is any non-violent means of "making some bread" which does not require work. One of the legendary heroes of the cat is the man who is such a skillful con-man that he can sell "State Street" to his victim. Concretely, the cat is a petty thief, pickpocket, or pool shark, or is engaged in a variety of other illegal activities of the "conning" variety. A very few cats are actually living off the proceeds of their women "on the hustle."

The main purpose of life for the cat is to experience the "kick." Just as every cat takes pride in his "hustle," so every cat cultivates his "kick." A "kick" is any act tabooed by "squares" that heightens and intensifies the present moment of experience and differentiates it as much as possible from the humdrum routine of daily life. Sex in any of its conventional expressions is not a "kick" since this would not serve to distinguish the cat from the "square," but orgies of sex behavior and a dabbling in the various perversions and byways of sex pass muster as "kicks." Some "cats" are on an alcohol "kick," others on a marihuana "kick," and others on a heroin "kick." There is some interchangeability among these various "kicks" but the tendency is so select your "kick" and stay with it. Many of these young drug users, however, had progressed from the alcohol to the marihuana to the heroin "kick." Each "kick" has its own lore of appreciation and connoisseurship into which only its devotees are initiated.

In addition to his "kick" the cat sets great store on the enjoyment of music and on proper dress. To enjoy one's "kick" without a background of popular music is inconceivable. The cat's world of music has a distinctive galaxy of stars, and the brightest luminaries in his firmament are performers such as "Yardbird" (the late Charlie Parker) and disc jockeys such as Al Benson. Almost every cat is a frustrated musician who hopes some day to get his "horn" out of pawn, take lessons, and earn fame and fortune in the field of "progressive music."

The cat places a great deal of emphasis upon clothing and exercises his sartorial talents upon a skeletal base of suit, sport shirt, and hat. The suit itself must be conservative in color. Gaiety is introduced through the selection of the sport shirt and the various accessories, all so chosen and harmonized as to reveal an exquisite sense of taste. When the cat was not talking about getting his clothes out of pawn, he talked about getting them out of the cleaners. With nonchalant pride one drug user insisted that the most expensive sport shirts and hats in the city of Chicago were sold in a certain haberdashery on the South Side. The ideal cat would always appear in public impeccably dressed and be able to sport a complete change of outfit several times a day.

The cat seeks through a harmonious combination of charm, ingratiating speech, dress, music, the proper dedication to his "kick," and unrestrained generosity to make of his day-to-day life itself a gracious work of art. Everything is to be pleasant and everything he does and values is to contribute to a cultivated aesthetic approach to living. The "cool cat" exemplifies all of these elements in proper balance. He demonstrates his ability to "play it cool" in his unruffled manner of dealing with outsiders such as the police, and in the self-assurance with which he confronts emergencies in the society of "cats." Moreover, the "cat" feels himself to be any man's equal. He is convinced that he can go anywhere and mingle easily with anyone. For example, he rejects the type of music designated "the blues" because for him it symbolizes attitudes of submission and resignation which are repugnant and alien to his customary frame of mind.

It can be seen now why heroin use should make such a powerful appeal to the cat. It was the ultimate "kick." No substance was more profoundly tabooed by conventional middle-class society. Regular heroin use provides a sense of maximal social differentiation from the "square." The cat was at last engaged, he felt, in an activity completely beyond the comprehension of the "square." No other "kick" offered such an instantaneous intensification of the immediate moment of experience and set it apart from everyday experience in such spectacular fashion. Any words used by the cat to apply to the "kick," the experience of "being high," he applied to heroin in the superlative. It was the "greatest kick of them all."

In the formulation now to be presented the cat as a social type is viewed as a manifestation of a process of social change in which a new type of self-conception has been emerging among the adolescents of the lower socio-economic levels of the colored population in large urban centers. It is a self-conception rooted in the types of accommodation to a subordinate status achieved historically by the colored race in this country, a self-conception which has become increasingly articulated as it responded to and selected various themes from the many available to it in the milieu of the modern metropolis. Blumer's classification of social movements into general, specific, or expressive, appears to provide a useful framework for the analysis of the social type of the cat. (2)

In terms of these categories the cat as a social type is the personal counterpart of an expressive social movement. The context for such a movement must include the broader community, which, by its policies of social segregation and discrimination, has withheld from individuals of the colored population the opportunity to achieve or to identify with status positions in the larger society. The social type of the cat is an expression of one possible type of adaptation to such blocking and frustration, in which a segment of the population turns in upon itself and attempts to develop within itself criteria for the achievement of social status and the rudiments of a satisfactory social life. Within his own isolated social world the cat attempts to give form and purpose to dispositions derived from but denied an outlet within the dominant social order.

What are these dispositions and in what sense may they be said to be derived from the dominant social order? Among the various interrelated facets of the life of the cat two themes are central, those of the "hustle" and the "kick." It is to be noted that they are in direct antithesis to two of the central values of the dominant culture, the "hustle" versus the paramount importance of the occupation for the male in our society, and the "kick" versus the importance of regulating conduct in terms of its future consequences. Thus, there appears to be a relationship of conflict between the central themes of the social type of the cat and those of the dominant social order. As a form of expressive behavior, however, the social type of the cat represents an indirect rather than a direct attack against central conventional values.

It is interesting to speculate on the reasons why a type such as the cat should emerge rather than a social movement with the objective of changing the social order. The forces coercing the selective process among colored male adolescents in the direction of expressive social movements are probably to be traced to the long tradition of accommodation to a subordinate status on the part of the Negro as well as to the social climate since the Second World War, which does not seem to have been favorable to the formation of specific social movements.

The themes of the "hustle" and "kick" in the social orientation of the cat are facts which appear to be overdetermined. For example, to grasp the meaning of the "hustle" to the cat one must understand it as a rejection of the obligation of the adult male to work. When asked for the reasons underlying his rejection of work the cat did not refer to the uncongenial and relatively unskilled and low paid jobs which, in large part, were the sole types of employment available to him. He emphasized rather that the routine of a job and the demand that he should apply himself continuously to his work task were the features that made work intolerable for him. The self-constraint required by work was construed as an unwarranted damper upon his love of spontaneity. The other undesirable element from his point of view was the authoritarian setting of most types of work with which he was familiar.

There are undoubtedly many reasons for the cat's rejection of work but the reasons he actually verbalized are particularly significant when interpreted as devices for sustaining his self-conception. The cat's feeling of superiority would be openly challenged were he to confront certain of the social realities of his situation, such as the discrimination exercised against colored persons looking for work and the fact that only the lowest status jobs are available to him. He avoided any mention of these factors which would have forced him to confront his true position in society and thus posed a threat to his carefully cherished sense of superiority.

In emphasizing as he does the importance of the "kick" the cat is attacking the value our society places upon planning for the future and the responsibility of the individual for such planning. Planning always requires some subordination and disciplining of present behavior in the interest of future rewards. The individual plans to go to college, plans for his career, plans for his family and children, etc. Such an orientation on the part of the individual is merely the personal and subjective counterpart of a stable social order and of stable social institutions, which not only permit but sanction an orderly progression of expectations with reference to others and to one's self. Where such stable institutions are absent or in the inchoate stages of development, there is little social sanction for such planning in the experience of the individual. Whatever studies are available strongly suggest that such are the conditions which tend to prevail in the lower socio-economic levels of the Negro urban community. (3) Stable family and community organization is lacking in those areas of the city where drug use is concentrated. A social milieu which does not encourage the subordination and disciplining of present conduct in the interests of future rewards tends by default to enhance the present. The "kick" appears to be a logical culmination of this emphasis.

Accepting the emergence of the self-conception of the cat as evidence of

a developing expressive social movement, we may phrase the central theoretical problem as follows: What are the distinctive and generic features
of the cat's social orientation? Taking a cue from the work of Huizinga as
developed in *Homo Ludens* (7), we propose that the generic characteristics
of the social type of the cat are those of play. In what follows, Huizinga's
conception of play as a distinctive type of human activity will be presented
and then applied as a tool of analysis for rendering intelligible the various
facets of the social orientation of the cat. It is believed that the concept of
play indicates accurately the type of expressive social movement which
receives its embodiment in the cat.

According to Huizinga the concept of play is a primary element of human experience and as such is not susceptible to exact definition.

"The *fun* of playing resists all analysis, all logical interpretation. . . ..
Nevertheless it is precisely this fun-element that characterizes the essence
of play." (7, p. 3) The common image of the young colored drug addict
pictures him as a pitiful figure, a trapped unfortunate. There is a certain
amount of truth in this image but it does not correspond to the conception
which the young colored addict has of himself or to the impression that he
tries to communicate to others. If it were entirely true it would be difficult
to square with the fact that substantial numbers of young colored persons
continue to become drug users. The cat experiences and manifests a certain
zest in his mode of life which is far from self-pity. This fun element seemed
to come particularly to the fore as the cat recounted his search for "kicks,"
the adventure of his life on the streets, and the intensity of his contest
against the whole world to maintain his supply of drugs. Early in the cycle
of heroin use itself there was invariably a "honeymoon" stage when the cat
abandoned himself most completely to the experience of the drug. For some
cats this "honeymoon" stage, in terms of their ecstatic preoccupation with
the drug, was perpetual. For others it passed, but the exigencies of an insa-
tiable habit never seemed to destroy completely the cat's sense of excitement in his way of life.

While Huizinga declines to define play, he does enumerate three characteristics which he considers to be proper to play. Each one of them when
applied to the cat serves to indicate a generic feature of his social orientation.

(a) "First and foremost . . . all play is a voluntary activity." (7, p. 7)
"Here we have the first main characteristic of play: that it is free, is in fact
freedom." (7, p. 8) The concept of an expressive social movement assumes
a social situation where existing social arrangements are frustrating and are
no longer accepted as legitimate and yet where collective activity directed
towards the modification of these limitations is not possible. The cat is
"free" in the sense that he is a pre-eminent candidate for new forms of social organization and novel social practices. He is attempting to escape from
certain features of the historical traditions of the Negro which he regards
as humiliating. As an adolescent or young adult he is not fully assimilated

into such social institutions as the family, school, church, or industry which may be available to him. Moreover, the social institutions which the Negroes brought with them when they migrated to the city have not as yet achieved stability or an adequate functioning relationship to the urban environment. As a Negro, and particularly as a Negro of low socio-economic status, he is excluded from many socializing experiences which adolescents in more advantaged sectors of the society take for granted. He lives in communities where the capacity of the population for effective collective action is extremely limited, and consequently there are few effective controls on his conduct besides that exercised by his peer group itself. He is fascinated by the varied "scenes" which the big city spreads out before him. Granted this setting, the cat adopts an adventurous attitude to life and is free to give his allegiance to new forms of activity.

> (b) . . . A second characteristic is closely connected with this (that is, the first characteristic of freedom), namely, that play is not "ordinary" or "real" life. It is rather a stepping out of "real" life into a temporary sphere of activity with a disposition all of its own. Every child knows perfectly well that he is "only pretending," or that it was "only for fun." . . . This "only pretending" quality of play betrays a consciousness of the inferiority of play compared with "seriousness," a feeling that seems to be something as primary as play itself. Nevertheless . . . the consciousness of play being "only a pretend" does not by any means prevent it from proceeding with the utmost seriousness, with an absorption, a devotion that passes into rapture and, temporarily at least, completely abolishes that troublesome "only" feeling. (7, p. 8)

It is implicit in the notion of an expressive social movement that, since direct collective action to modify the sources of dissatisfaction and restlessness is not possible, all such movements should appear under one guise, as forms of "escape." Persons viewing the problem of addiction from the perspective of the established social structure have been prone to make this interpretation. It is a gross oversimplification, however, as considered from the perspective of the young drug addict himself. The emergence of the self-conception of the cat is an attempt to deal with the problems of status and identity in a situation where participation in the life of the broader community is denied, but where the colored adolescent is becoming increasingly sensitive to the values, the goals, and the notions of success which obtain in the dominant social order.

> The caste pressures thus make it exceedingly difficult for an American Negro to preserve a true perspective of himself and his own group in relation to the larger white society. The increasing abstract knowledge of the world outside — of its opportunities, its rewards, its different norms of competition and cooperation — which results from the proceeding acculturation at the same time as there is increasing group isolation, only increases the tensions. (8)

Such conditions of group isolation would appear to be fairly uniform throughout the Negro group. Although this isolation may be experienced differently at different social levels of the Negro community, certain features of the adaptations arrived at in response to this problem will tend to reveal similarities. Since the struggle for status takes place on a stage where there is acute sensitivity to the values and status criteria of the dominant white group, but where access to the means through which such values may be achieved is prohibited, the status struggle turning in on itself will assume a variety of distorted forms. Exclusion from the "serious" concerns of the broader community will result in such adaptations manifesting a strong element of "play."

Frazier in *Black Bourgeoisie* discusses the social adaptation of the Negro middle class as "The World of Make-Believe." (5)

> The emphasis upon "social" life or "society" is one of the main props of the world of make-believe into which the black bourgeoisie has sought an escape from its inferiority and frustrations in American society. This world of make-believe, to be sure, is a reflection of the values of American society, but it lacks the economic basis that would give it roots in the world of reality. (5, p. 237)

In the Negro lower classes the effects of frustrations deriving from subordination to the whites may not be experienced as personally or as directly as it is by the Negro middle class, but the massive effects of residential segregation and the lack of stable social institutions and community organization are such as to reinforce strong feelings of group isolation even at the lowest levels of the society.

It is here suggested that the function performed by the emergence of the social type of the cat among Negro lower class adolescents is analogous to that performed by "The World of Make-Believe" in the Negro middle class. The development of a social type such as that of the cat is only possible in a situation where there is isolation from the broader community but great sensitivity to its goals, where the peer group pressures are extremely powerful, where institutional structures are weak, where models of success in the illegitimate world have strong appeals, where specific social movements are not possible, and where novel forms of behavior have great prestige. To give significance to his experience, the young male addict has developed the conception of a heroic figure, the "ideal cat," a person who is completely adequate to all situations, who controls his "kick" rather than letting it control him, who has a lucrative "hustle," who has no illusions as to what makes the world "tick," who is any man's equal, who basks in the admiration of his brother cats and associated "chicks," who hob-nobs with "celebs" of the musical world, and who in time himself may become a celebrity.

The cat throws himself into his way of life with a great deal of intensity but he cannot escape completely from the perspective, the judgments, and the sanctions of the dominant social order. He has to make place in his scheme of life for police, lockups, jails, and penitentiaries, to say nothing of the agonies of withdrawal distress. He is forced eventually to confront the fact that his role as a cat with its associated attitudes is largely a pose, a form of fantasy with little basis in fact. With the realization that he is addicted he comes only too well to know that he is a "junky," and he is fully aware of the conventional attitudes towards addicts as well as of the counter-rationalizations provided by his peer group. It is possible that the cat's vacillation with regard to seeking a cure for his addiction is due to a conflict of perspectives, whether to view his habit from the cat's or the dominant social order's point of view.

> (c) Play is distinct from "ordinary" life both as to locality and duration. This is the third main characteristic of play: its secludedness, its limitedness. It is "played out" within certain limits of time and place. It contains its own course and "meaning." (7, p. 9)

It is this limited, esoteric character of heroin use which gives to the cat the feeling of belonging to an elite. It is the restricted extent of the distribution of drug use, the scheming and intrigue associated with underground "connections" through which drugs are obtained, the secret lore of the appreciation of the drug's effects, which give the cat the exhilaration of participating in a conspiracy. Contrary to popular conception most drug users were not anxious to proselyte new users. Of course, spreading the habit would have the function of increasing the possible sources of supply. But an equally strong disposition was to keep the knowledge of drug use secret, to impress and dazzle the audience with one's knowledge of being "in the know." When proselyting did occur, as in jails or lockups, it was proselyting on the part of a devotee who condescended to share with the uninitiated a highly prized practice and set of attitudes.

As he elaborates his analysis of play, Huizinga brings to the fore additional aspects of the concept which also have their apt counterpart in the way of life of the cat. For instance, as was discussed earlier, the cat's appreciation of "progressive music" is an essential part of his social orientation. About this topic Huizinga remarks, "Music, as we have hinted before, is the highest and purest expression of the *facultas ludendi*." (7, p. 187) The cat's attitude toward music has a sacred, almost mystical quality. "Progressive music" opens doors to a type of highly valued experience which for him can be had in no other way. It is more important to him than eating and is second only to the "kick." He may have to give up his hope of dressing according to his standards but he never gives up music.

Huizinga also observes, "Many and close are the links that connect play with beauty." (7, p. 7) He refers to the "profoundly aesthetic quality of play." (7, p. 2) The aesthetic emphasis which seems so central to the style of living of the cat is a subtle elusive accent permeating his whole outlook but coming to clearest expression in a constellation of interests, the "kick," clothing, and music. And it certainly reaches a level of awareness in their language. Language is utilized by the cat with a conscious relish, with many variations and individual turns of phrase indicating the value placed upon creative expression in this medium.

It is to be noted that much of the description of the cat's attributes did not deal exclusively with elements unique to him. Many of the features mentioned are prevalent among adolescents in all reaches of the status scale. Dress, music, language, and the search for pleasure are all familiar themes of the adolescent world. For instance, in his description of the adolescent "youth culture" Talcott Parsons would appear to be presenting the generic traits of a "play-form" with particular reference to its expression in the middle class.

> It is at the point of emergence into adolescence that there first begins to develop a set of patterns and behavior phenomena which involve a highly complex combination of age grading and sex role elements. These may be referred to together as the phenomena of the "youth culture." . . .
>
> Perhaps the best single point of reference for characterizing the youth culture lies in its contrast with the dominant pattern of the adult male role. By contrast with the emphasis on responsibility in this role, the orientation of the youth culture is more or less specifically irresponsible. One of its dominant roles is "having a good time" . . . . It is very definitely a rounded humanistic pattern rather than one of competence in the performance of specified functions. (9)

Such significant similarities between this description and the themes of the social type of the cat only tend to reinforce the notion that the recent spread of heroin use was a problem of adolescence. The cat is an adolescent sharing many of the interests of his age-mates everywhere but confronted by a special set of problems of color, tradition, and identity.

The social orientation of the cat, with its emphasis on non-violence, was quite in contrast to the orientation of the smaller group of young white drug users who were interviewed in the course of this study. The latter's type of adjustment placed a heavy stress upon violence. Their crimes tended to represent direct attacks against persons and property. The general disposition they manifested was one of "nerve" and brashness rather than one of "playing it cool." They did not cultivate the amenities of language, music, or dress to nearly the same extent as the cat. Their social orientation was expressed as a direct rather than an indirect attack on the dominant values of our society. This indicates that the "youth culture" despite its generic features may vary significantly in different social settings.

In this paper, "Some Jewish Types of Personality," Louis Wirth made the following suggestive comments about the relationship between the social type and its setting.

> A detailed analysis of the crucial personality types in any given
> area or cultural group shows that they depend upon a set of habits
> and attitudes in the group for their existence and are the direct
> expressions of the values of the group. As the life of the group
> changes there appears a host of new social types, mainly outgrowths
> and transformations of previous patterns which have become fixed
> through experience. (11)

What are some of the sources of the various elements going to make up
the social type of the cat which may be sought in his traditions? The following suggestions are offered as little more than speculation at the present
time. The emphasis upon non-violence on the part of the cat, upon manipulative techniques rather than overt attack, is a stress upon the indirect
rather than the direct way towards one's goal. May not the cat in this
emphasis be betraying his debt to the "Uncle Tom" type of adjustment,
despite his wish to dissociate himself from earlier patterns of accommodation to the dominant white society? May not the "kick" itself be a cultural
lineal descendant of the ecstatic moment of religious possession so dear to
revivalist and store-front religion? Similarly, may not the emphasis upon
the exploitation of the woman have its origin in the traditionally greater
economic stability of the colored woman?

W. I. Thomas in one of his references to the problems raised by the city
environment stated, "Evidently the chief problem is the young American
person." (10, p. 46) In discussing the type of inquiry that would be desirable in this area he states that it should

> . . . lead to a more critical discrimination between that type of
> disorganization in the youth which is a real but frustrated tendency
> to organize on a higher plane, or one more correspondent with the
> moving environment, and that type of disorganization which is sim-
> ply the abandonment of standards. It is also along this line . . .
> that we shall gain light on the relation of fantastic phantasying to
> realistic phantasying. . . . (10, p. 47)

Posed in this way the problem becomes one of evaluating the social type
of the cat in relation to the processes of social change. This social type is
difficult to judge according to the criterion suggested by Thomas. Since
many of the cat's interests are merely an extreme form of the adolescent
"youth culture," in part the problem becomes one of determining how functional the period of adolescence is as preparation for subsequent adult
status. However, the central phases of the social orientation of the cat, the
"hustle" and the "kick," do represent a kind of disorganization which indicates the abandonment of conventional standards. The young addicted cat
is "going nowhere." With advancing age he cannot shed his addiction the
way he can many of the other trappings of adolescence. He faces only the
bleak prospect, as time goes on, of increasing demoralization. Although the
plight of the young colored addict is intimately tied to the conditions and

fate of his racial group, his social orientation seems to represent a dead-end type of adjustment. Just as Handlin in *The Uprooted* suggests that the first generation of immigrant peoples to our society tends to be a sacrificed generation (6), it may be that the unique problems of Negro migrants to our metropolitan areas will lead to a few or several sacrificed generations in the course of the tortuous process of urbanization.

The discussion of the social type of the cat leads inevitably to the issue of social control. Any attempt to intervene or modify the social processes producing the "cat" as a social type must have the objective of reducing his group isolation. For instance, because of such isolation and because of the cat's sensitivity to the gestures of his peers, the most significant role models of a given generation of cats tend to be the cats of the preceding age group. Where, in a period of rapid change, the schemes of behavior of the role models no longer correspond to the possibilities in the actual situation, it is possible for attitudes to be transmitted to a younger generation which evidence a kind of "cultural lag." Thus the condition of the labor market in Chicago is such as to suggest the existence of plentiful employment opportunities for the Negro in a variety of fields. But because such openings are not mediated to him through role models it is possible that the cat is unable to take advantage of these opportunities or of the facilities available for training for such positions.

The social type of the cat is a product of social change. The type of social orientation which it has elaborated indicates an all too acute awareness of the values of the broader social order. In an open class society where upward mobility is positively sanctioned, an awareness and sensitivity to the dominant values is the first stage in their eventual assimilation. Insofar as the social type of the cat represents a reaction to a feeling of exclusion from access to the means towards the goals of our society, all measures such as improved educational opportunities which put these means within his grasp will hasten the extinction of this social type. Just as the "hoodlum" and "gangster" types tend to disappear as the various more recently arrived white ethnic groups tend to move up in the status scale of the community (1), so it can confidently be expected that the cat as a social type will tend to disappear as such opportunities become more prevalent among the colored population.

REFERENCES

1. Bell, Daniel, "Crime as an American Way of Life," *Antioch Review*, 13 (June, 1953), 131–154.
2. Blumer, Herbert, "Social Movements," in Robert E. Park, ed., *An Outline of the Principles of Sociology* (New York: Barnes & Noble, 1939), pp. 255–278.
3. Drake, St. Clair and Horace R. Cayton, "Lower Class: Sex and Family," *Black Metropolis* (New York: Harcourt, Brace & Co., 1945), pp. 564–599.
4. Finestone, Harold, "Narcotics and Criminality," *Law and Contemporary Problems*, 22 (Winter, 1957), 60–85.
5. Frazier, E. Franklin, *Black Bourgeoisie* (Glencoe, Illinois: Free Press, 1957).

6. Handlin, Oscar, *The Uprooted* (New York: Grosset and Dunlap, 1951), p. 243.

7. Huizinga, Johan, *Homo Ludens, A Study of the Play Element in Culture* (Boston: Beacon Press, 1955).

8. Myrdal, Gunnar, *An American Dilemma* (New York: Harper & Brothers, 1944), p. 760.

9. Parsons, Talcott, "Age and Sex in the Social Structure," *Essays in Sociological Theory Pure and Applied* (Glencoe, Illinois: Free Press, 1949), pp. 220–221.

10. Thomas, William I., "The Problem of Personality in the Urban Environment," in Ernest W. Burgess, ed., *The Urban Community* (Chicago: University of Chicago Press, 1926), pp. 38–47.

11. Wirth, Louis, "Some Jewish Types of Personality," in Ernest W. Burgess, ed., *The Urban Community* (Chicago: University of Chicago Press, 1926), p. 112.

2. Secondary Socialization and Resistance to Change

Directly related to the processes of self-formation are those of secondary socialization. Secondary socialization takes place after the basic self is established. As pointed out by Wrong, part of socialization is involved with learning roles and norms. Roles usually refer to the behavioral expectations that go with a particular position. For instance, being a father, a sociologist, a husband; each is a role. Of course these roles can be fulfilled by the same person. In mass societies such as our own the possible number of roles which any one person can fill is large, and larger still is the number of different roles in the society. A small social system, on the other hand, has a limited number of roles and these are usually highly interrelated. Banton, in a few brief paragraphs, points out what happens when the role system of a small society is upset by the introduction of steel axes. Because "selves" are related to roles, we have a situation in which the self can be quite easily disorganized.

15 MICHAEL BANTON

The Fragility of Simple Role Systems

Small-scale societies organized round a few basic roles depend upon a fragile structure. Their institutions are so interrelated that they cannot absorb the consequences of other than small changes. A striking example of the effect just one technological change can have upon a simple role system is provided by a study of the introduction of steel axes among the Yir Yuront aborigines of northern Australia. Originally the Yir Yuront possessed

From *Roles: An Introduction to the Study of Social Relations*, © Michael Banton, 1965, Basic Books, Inc., Publishers, New York.

neither metals nor stone with which to make tools. Suitable kinds of stone could be found four hundred miles south and they reached the Yir Yuront through a long series of trade exchanges. Up this chain came stones suitable for use as axe heads and down it went spears tipped with the spines of the sting ray which were manufactured by aborigines living on the coast. Exchanges were made during the festivals when hunting bands assembled to initiate their youths. Only men could make and own the stone axes. Women and children could borrow them for any of the daily tasks for which axes were needed, but they must always request them from the proper male. A woman would ask her husband for his; a boy would approach his father. All loans were related to the traditional system of sex, age, and kinship roles. In this way the stone axe served as an important sign of masculinity among the Yir Yuront (like trousers or pipes in Europe). It stood for a theme that ran all through Yir Yuront culture: the superiority and rightful dominance of the male, and the greater value of things identified with him.

In 1915 a mission station was established near the mouth of the Mitchell River, about three day's march away. The missionaries prevented guns, liquor, narcotics, and diseases from reaching the aborigines while permitting them to receive suitable presents in return for work. Apart, possibly, from tobacco, no presents were in greater demand than steel axes, so a stock of these was kept for sale or giving way. The older men among the Yir Yuront refused to have anything to do with the mission, but gradually some of the women and younger people were drawn there and in one way or another obtained steel axes. No longer did they have to borrow from their husbands or fathers; indeed an old man who had only a stone axe might now go and ask one of his juniors for the loan of his superior tool. This led to the disruption of ideas about seniority and completely disorganized the role structure.

Steel axes represented technical improvement, yet it has been shown that even in the long run their introduction had only harmful effects. Any time the natives gained through using them was not put to productive use, but was given over to sleep. The supply of new axes destroyed the chain of trading relationships, for the Yir Yuront were no longer interested in acquiring hard flat stones from their neighbours. With the decline in trading went the custom of gathering for fiestas and the significance formerly attached to collective ceremonials. The new axes even upset traditional religious beliefs, for these were based upon myths which associated every skill or object with a particular clan. To which clan did the steel axe belong? Did it go to the one identified with the white man's goods, or to the one with which the stone axe was linked? The people could not agree, and for the first time a significant part of their lives was left outside their religious system. The link with the sacred past was weakened and with it the justification for their rules about land tenure and marriage. What brought them contentment has now decayed, and nothing has taken its place.

Australian aboriginal culture has a very low capacity to absorb change because the social and cultural categories are so simple and so tightly interrelated that there are few relatively independent areas in which a new practice can become established and permit other parts of the system to adapt to it gradually. The scale of a society obviously has a lot to do with this: the small island societies of the Pacific have never been able to show the resistance to Western influence displayed by the larger tribal societies in Africa.

> *It was pointed out by Mead that the self is the result of action between the individual and others and is sustained by encounters. It follows that if others who are significant to the person in question do not support his self-image, changes in it will occur, or it may be completely extinguished. Backman and his colleagues designed a controlled experiment in which it was possible to test a variation of this idea, and to see under what conditions the self-concept would resist change. Their results support the hypothesis that if an individual has little or no personal support for certain self-concepts, he is more likely to give these up than those which have strong interpersonal support.*

16 CARL W. BACKMAN, PAUL F. SECORD, AND JERRY R. PEIRCE

Resistance to Change in the Self-concept as a Function of Consensus Among Significant Others

The self-concept has been the focus of considerable research and theorizing since the early work of James,[1] Cooley,[2] and Mead.[3] All too often, however, research has not been guided except in a loose fashion by theory. Consequently the total accumulation of substantive findings has been disappointing.[4] At the same time, self-theory has remained vague and rudimentary.

From *Sociometry*, Vol. 26 (1963), pp. 102–111. Reprinted by permission.

[1] William James, *Principles of Psychology*, New York: Holt, 1890. 2 volumes.

[2] Charles H. Cooley, *Human Nature and the Social Order*, New York: Charles Scribner's Sons, 1902.

[3] George H. Mead, *Mind, Self, and Society from the Standpoint of a Social Behaviorist*, Chicago: University of Chicago Press, 1934.

[4] Ruth C. Wylie, *The Self Concept*, Lincoln, Nebraska: University of Nebraska Press, 1961.

More recently the development of a number of cognitive theories[5] closely integrated with programs of systematic research has given promise of a greater articulation between research and theory in this area. While these theories in general have been concerned with the broader problem of stability and change of attitudes, their work has implications for attitudes pertaining to the self. One of these approaches, in particular, interpersonal congruency theory, while not focusing exclusively on the self, affords it a central place, and outlines the conditions under which the self remains stable or changes.

Basic to interpersonal congruency theory is the assumption that there exists within the cognitive organization of the individual a tendency to achieve a state of congruency between three components of what has been termed the interpersonal matrix. These components include an aspect of self of an individual (S), S's interpretation of his behavior relevant to that aspect, and S's perception of the related aspects of the other person (O) with whom he is interacting. Thus an interpersonal matrix is a recurring functional relation among these three components. S strives to achieve congruency among the components of the matrix. Congruency is a cognitive phenomenon; i.e., each component enters into a state of congruency only as a perceptual-cognitive experience on the part of S. All three components of the matrix are in a *state of congruency when S perceives his behavior and that of O as implying definitions of self congruent with relevant aspects for his self-concept.*

Forces that stabilize or bring about changes in either of the other two components of the matrix will, by virtue of this principle, affect the stability of the self. Sources of stability in S's behavior as well as that of O include the residues of previous experience — learned responses — as well as constancies in the stimulus environment. These constancies in turn result not only from the expectations that constitute the social system and guide the behavior of S and O, but also from the operation of a number of interpersonal processes that stem ultimately from the tendency to achieve congruency. While the role of the social system is recognized by most theories that regard the self as a reflection of the views of other persons toward S, these interpersonal processes require further comment. Interpersonal congruency theory, while recognizing the importance of the social structure in fashioning the self, does not view S as passive in the process. Rather S is seen as

5 Charles E. Osgood and Percy H. Tannenbaum, "The Principle of Congruity in the Prediction of Attitude Change," *Psychological Review*, 62 (Jan., 1955), pp. 42–55; Dorwin Cartwright and Frank Harary, "Structural Balance: A Generalization of Heider's Theory," *Psychological Review*, 63 (Sept., 1956), pp. 277–293; Leon Festinger, *A Theory of Cognitive Dissonance*, Evanston, Illinois: Row, Peterson, 1957; Milton J. Rosenberg and Robert P. Abelson, "An Analysis of Cognitive Balancing," in Carl I. Hovland and Milton J. Rosenberg, editors, *Attitude Organization and Change*, New Haven: Yale University Press, 1960, pp. 112–163; Fritz Heider, *The Psychology of Interpersonal Relations*, New York: Wiley, 1958.

actively structuring his relations with others so as to achieve and maintain congruency. He does this in the following ways.

In the first place, he selectively interacts with other persons, preferring those who treat him in a manner congruent with his self-concept, and avoiding those who do not. Similarly, he selectively evaluates others, depending upon their attitudes toward him. He does this by liking those who treat him in a congruent fashion, and disliking those who do not. Thus he maximizes the effect of congruent actions and minimizes the effect of incongruent actions on the self-concept. He may also misperceive the actions of others toward him in the belief that they see him as he sees himself, when in actuality, their views of him are somewhat discrepant with his own. Finally, he develops certain behavior patterns that elicit from others reactions that are congruent with his self-definitions. These include not only manipulative behaviors calculated to evoke certain congruent responses, but also less self-conscious, more enduring actions that lead others to treat S in a manner congruent with his self-concept.

A final source of stability and change stems from the manner in which matrices are related to each other. A given matrix may be considered *relevant* to those matrices that contain one or more of the same or similar components as the given matrix. For example, an S who considers himself intelligent may exhibit behaviors in a variety of situations that are interpreted by him as congruent or incongruent with his belief concerning his intelligence. Thus he may obtain high grades in school, play expert chess, but may be a poor bridge player. With respect to the matrix component involving other persons, people may ask him for help in solving problems, he may generally win debates, but his father may criticize his intellectual accomplishments. Matrices having no components in common are considered irrelevant, and as having no effect upon each other.

Matrices vary with respect to *centricality*. The centricality of a matrix is a function of the number of relevant other matrices that stand in a supportive relation to it, and the value of the *O-components* in these matrices. The term *centricality* is chosen in preference to salience or centrality, since the latter terms already have several other established meanings in this field. The greater the centricality of a matrix, the more resistant it is to change, and should it change, the greater the resultant shifts in other matrices. The present study is concerned with one aspect of centricality, namely, the relative number of *O-components* having congruent relations with a given aspect of self. The contribution of S's *behavior-components* to centricality is ignored for the purposes of the present paper. Put simply, the thesis of the present paper is as follows: If a variety of significant other persons are perceived by S to agree in defining an aspect of S's self-concept congruently, their views support each other and his self-concept. If this condition were to prevail, the particular aspect of self involved would be expected to be more resistant to change than if S were to perceive less consensus among significant others. Thus, the main hypothesis of the present study may be stated as follows:

The greater the number of significant other persons who are perceived to define an aspect of an individual's self-concept congruently, the more resistant to change is that aspect of self.

The hypothesis was tested by choosing for comparison, for each S, a self-ascribed trait on which S perceived high consensus to exist among five significant other persons, and a self-ascribed trait on which perceived consensus was low. Individuals were then subjected to strong pressure to change their perception of these traits, created by means of a highly credible, but false personality assessment. The degree of change in the high consensus trait was compared with change in the low consensus trait.

METHOD

To create strong pressure toward changing certain self-cognitions, it was necessary to have an assessment of S's personality that would be highly credible. This was accomplished by using only subjects willing to volunteer two Saturday mornings for a project in personality assessment. Subjects were offered a personality assessment as a reward for serving in the experiment. In this manner, only those Ss likely to believe in the validity of personality tests would be included. In addition, high credibility was obtained by presenting a rationale emphasizing prestigious sources and serious purpose: the investigation was presented as part of a cooperative research project sponsored by the National Institute of Mental Health, of the U.S. Public Health Service, with the University of Nevada as a cooperating institution. Mention was made of the fact that several sociologists and psychologists from the University of Nevada were participating in the project. The purported purpose of the project was to discover how much insight individuals had into their own personalities.

Subjects were undergraduate students from introductory classes in several fields of study. A total of forty students attended two sessions held one week apart.

Assessment devices. The various ranking forms and checklists used were based upon the 15 needs measured by the Edwards Personal Preference Schedule (EPPS).[6] These forms contained 15 brief statements each describing one need, adapted from the need descriptions appearing in the EPPS manual. For example, the need for *nurturance* was represented by the statement, "This person enjoys helping others," and the need for *exhibition* by, "This person likes to receive a lot of attention from others; to be the center of attention."

In the first session, the following instruments were administered.

[6] Allen Edwards, *Edwards Personal Preference Schedule,* New York: Psychological Corporation, 1954.

1. Reflected-self checklist. S was asked to write down the names of five close friends or relatives whose opinion he valued. He was given one checklist form for each of these five persons. For each person, he was asked to select the five need-statements that he believed would be most likely to be assigned to him by that person. A twenty-minute break followed the completion of these forms.
2. Self-ranking form. S ranked himself from 1 to 15 on the 15 abbreviated need statements, from those he believed to be most characteristic to those he considered least characteristic.
3. Edwards Personal Preference Schedule and Gordon Personality Profile.[7] These standard tests were administered to lend credence to the assessment process. In addition, the EPPS was scored and profiles were distributed after the experiment had been completed and its real purpose explained to S.

In the second session, S was given a profile sheet indicating the rank order of the 15 needs supposedly characterizing him. Although he was told that professional psychologists had prepared the profile from a careful analysis of the personality tests and the other forms he had taken, actually the order of the needs was the same as S's initial self-ranking, except that two needs from among the highest-ranking five had been moved eight rank-steps downward. The needs on the profile were described in some detail by a psychologist while S was given time to study the profile. Finally, these profiles were placed under the chairs in which the S's were seated, and S was asked to rank himself again on the 15 needs.

The two needs were selected for each S for manipulation by the following means. For each of the five need statements ranking highest on the initial self-ranking form, a measure of consensus was obtained from the reflected self checklist. This consensus score ranged from 0 to 5 depending upon the number of significant other persons that S perceived as likely to assign the need to him. The following criteria were used to determine what two needs should be manipulated: (a) they had to be included in the five highest-ranking statements on the initial self-form, (b) one had to have relatively high consensus and the other low consensus, (c) they had to have adjacent ranks on the self-form, and (d) the needs had to be balanced for *saliency*.

The higher the ranking of the need-statement on the self-form, the more *salient* it is, and thus probably more resistant to change. But needs that rank high are also likely to be high on consensus, compared with lower-ranking needs. To control for saliency, the subjects were divided into two groups, and the needs to be manipulated selected in a counterbalanced design, as follows:

Type of need	Group I	Group II
High consensus need	High saliency	Low saliency
Low consensus need	Low saliency	High saliency

7 Leonard V. Gordon, *Gordon Personal Profile*, New York: World Book Company, 1953.

In addition, the magnitude of the difference in consensus for each need pair selected for persons in Group I was matched with the magnitude of the difference in consensus of the need pair selected for Group II. Thus any difference obtained between high and low consensus needs in susceptibility to manipulation can legitimately be attributed to the effects of consensus alone, and not saliency.

RESULTS

Several factors point to successful manipulation of the two chosen traits. The great majority of subjects (30 on the high consensus trait; 26 on the low consensus trait) ranked the two manipulated traits lower after receiving the false assessment. Moreover, on the post-experimental questionnaire most subjects indicated that they had been surprised upon reading the assessment profile, particularly stressing the point that the position of certain traits surprised them. On the other hand, only a few subjects stated that they believed any profile traits in the assessment were invalid: they found the assessment credible even though a few traits were unexpected. Somewhat inconsistently, however, subjects in general were not conscious of making deliberate changes in their self-rankings subsequent to the manipulation. The success of the experimental manipulation was also apparent from the loud sighs of relief that arose when the subjects learned that they had been deceived with respect to the assessment.

The main hypothesis of the study, as stated previously, is that an aspect of self will be more resistant to change when S believes that there is consensus among significant other persons concerning that aspect. A need high in consensus and one low in consensus for each individual were manipulated downward in an attempt to secure movement of these needs on a second self-ranking form. In general several forces could be expected to be generated by this manipulation. One is a tendency to lower one's self-ratings on these two traits. Another is the arousal of resistance to change, and some individuals in whom resistance is aroused might even rank themselves higher than they did initially on the need. Resistance of this sort would be expected because the acceptance of an incongruent self-definition not only requires a change in the matrix containing that aspect but in all related matrices in which that aspect is imbedded. Thus the threat of widespread incongruence could easily create resistance to acceptance. More frequently, of course, this resistance effect might be expected for the high consensus trait. While these two forces are represented by downward and upward movement in self-ranks, respectively, a certain amount of random movement in both directions due to error of measurement will be superimposed upon these other movements. In order to examine the movement due to acceptance or resistance to manipulation uncontaminated by random movement, the best test of the hypothesis is a comparison of the movement of the high consensus trait with the movement for the low consensus trait.

Table 1 lists in the first two columns the number of steps that the high and low consensus need was moved by each individual. Downward movements are positively labeled; upward movements are given a negative sign. Relative movement, shown in the last column of Table 1, was determined by subtracting the movement of the high consensus trait from the low. If the relative movement represented by the difference score is positive, the hypothesis is supported for that subject. This analysis allows for random effects operating to move a need upward and still permits a test of the relative effects of the degree of consensus. For example, as indicated in the first row of Table 1, deference was chosen as the low consensus need for subject 1 and autonomy as the high consensus need. From the initial self-ranking to the post-manipulation self-ranking he moved deference 8 rank steps downward and autonomy 2 rank steps upward. This yields a net change of 10 steps in the direction of the hypothesis. As may be seen by inspection of the difference column, 26 individuals produced a net difference in the direction of the hypothesis, 2 showed no change, and 12 changed in an opposite direction. Table 2 offers a more precise comparison taking into account the magnitude of the change. The low consensus need moved an average of 3.43 rank steps, and the high consensus need only 1.75 rank steps. The magnitude of the differences between the two needs is significant at the .008 level as tested by the Wilcoxon signed-ranks test[8] ($T = 229.0$, $N = 40$, $z = 2.43$). Thus it appears that the reaction to information incongruent with self-definition is a function of the perceived consensus of opinion among significant others.

As a final check on whether the movement of the manipulated traits was in fact due to the false personality appraisal, for each individual two non-manipulated traits, differing in consensus by the same amount as the previously chosen manipulated traits, were selected for analysis. These traits were compared to determine whether the low consensus trait moved to a greater extent than the high. The mean difference between them was only 0.21, and the differences were not significant ($T = 342.5$, $N = 37$, $z = .135$, $P = .44$).

DISCUSSION

The relatively greater movement in the manipulated direction of the low consensus trait supports the theoretical position that the degree of resistance to the acceptance of an incongruent self-definition is a function of the number of interpersonal matrices supporting that self-definition. In this instance, the element of each matrix supporting or weakening resistance was represented by the perceived attitude of a different significant other person toward a given aspect of an individual's self-concept. The possibility that the differing resistance of the high and low consensus needs resulted

[8] James V. Bradley, *Distribution-free Statistical Tests*. Washington, D.C.: United States Department of Commerce, Office of Technical Services, August, 1960.

Table 1. Changes in High and Low Consensus
Manipulated Traits for Each Subject

| Subject | Traits manipulated low, high | Movement of | | Difference |
		Low consensus trait	High consensus trait	
1	Def, Aut	8	—2	10
2	Aut, Aff	8	0	8
3	Def, Aba	8	1	7
4	Chg, Nur	7	0	7
5	Aba, Nur	7	0	7
6	Def, Nur	6	—1	7
7	Agg, End	8	1	7
8	Int, Nur	5	0	5
9	Suc, Aff	5	0	5
10	Exh, Chg	5	0	5
11	Def, Chg	4	—1	5
12	Def, Aba	9	5	4
13	Chg, Suc	4	1	3
14	Aff, Int	3	0	3
15	Ord, Ach	5	2	3
16	Chg, Ach	6	3	3
17	Aba, Int	2	—1	3
18	Het, Def	5	2	3
19	Int, Chg	3	1	2
20	Het, End	5	3	2
21	Chg, Aba	5	3	2
22	Het, Chg	4	2	2
23	Het, Int	—1	—3	2
24	Exh, Ach	3	1	2
25	Ord, Ach	5	4	1
26	Aba, Het	1	0	1
27	Chg, Int	0	0	0
28	Chg, Aut	3	3	0
29	Int, Aut	0	1	—1
30	Aff, End	1	2	—1
31	Ach, Nur	0	1	—1
32	Het, Chg	0	2	—2
33	Exh, Ach	7	9	—2
34	Ach, Aba	—2	0	—2
35	Suc, Ach	—2	1	—3
36	Aba, Suc	1	5	—4
37	Dom, Ord	4	8	—4
38	Het, Dom	—3	4	—7
39	End, Nur	0	7	—7
40	Int, Aff	—2	6	—8

TABLE 2. NET MEAN MOVEMENT OF MANIPULATED TRAIT

Low consensus	High consensus	Difference	P
3.43	1.75	1.68	$< .008$*

* Wilcoxon signed-ranks test: $T = 229.0$; $N = 40$; $z = 2.43$, one-tailed.

from a difference in salience (importance of the trait to S, as indicated by its self-rank position) was ruled out by equating on salience the two kinds of needs manipulated. Social desirability was presumed to be similarly controlled by the same matching process.

Encountering information contrary to self-definitions will result in a threat to congruency that must be resolved in some manner. In many instances, congruency is retained without a change in self or behavior. This is much more likely to occur when perceived consensus is high than when it is low. As described in more detail elsewhere,[9] in his attempts to restore congruency an individual may employ one or more of the following modes of resolution. He may reduce his interaction with those whose definitions of his behavior threaten congruence and increase interaction with others whose definitions he perceives as congruent. A second mode involves evaluating selected other persons positively or negatively depending upon whether they are behaving congruently with certain aspects of self: he increases his liking for those who behave in a congruent fashion and decreases his liking for those behaving incongruently. A third means of resolution is the misperception of the other person's behavior in a manner allowing congruency to be achieved. Finally, he may employ techniques permitting him to elicit congruent responses from the other person that confirm aspects of self.

For the most part, the experimental situation was designed so as to minimize the occurrence of these various forms of resolving incongruency while maintaining self unchanged. Some of these modes require situations outside the laboratory where the individual has freedom of interaction. Nevertheless, the minority of subjects who failed to change appreciably either manipulated trait may have questioned the validity of the assessment devices, the intentions, or the competence of the experimenter in order to support non-change.

Research on attitudes toward non-self objects is consistent with the findings of the present study. The well-known experiments of Asch[10] and Sherif[11] on the formation of judgments as a function of social pressure

[9] Paul F. Secord and Carl W. Backman, "Personality Theory and the Problem of Stability and Change in Individual Behavior: An Interpersonal Approach," *Psychological Review,* 68 (Jan., 1961), pp. 21–32.

[10] Solomon E. Asch, *Social Psychology,* New York: Prentice-Hall, 1952.

[11] Muzafer Sherif, *The Psychology of Social Norms,* New York: Harper and Brothers, 1936.

illustrate the effectiveness of actual consensus in the initial formation of attitudes and in resistance to change. More recent work by Festinger, Riecken, and Schachter,[12] Festinger,[13] Brehm,[14] and Cohen[15] on dissonance theory further document the point that resistance to change of attitudes is strongly tied to social support — perceived or actual — and that the behavior of individuals is often concerned with securing consonance among cognitive elements ("congruence" in the interpersonal approach).

The present study has been concerned entirely with *perceived* consensus. The assumption is made, however, that there is a high but imperfect association between actual consensus and perceived consensus. Some evidence[16] for this association has been presented in a study of a living group. The fact that the association is not perfect provides some opportunity for the individual to perceive consensus as greater than it actually is, and interpersonal congruency theory predicts that perceptual distortion will generally occur in the direction of consensus in order to maximize congruency. This prediction is also supported by data. One direction for further study, however, might be the replication of the present study, using in addition the variable of the actual consensus among significant other persons.

[12] Leon Festinger, Henry W. Riecken, and Stanley S. Schachter, *When Prophecy Fails*, Minneapolis: University of Minnesota Press, 1956.

[13] Leon Festinger, *A Theory of Cognitive Dissonance*, Evanston, Illinois: Row, Peterson, 1957.

[14] Jack W. Brehm, "A Dissonance Analysis of Attitude-discrepant Behavior," in Carl I. Hovland and Milton J. Rosenberg, editors, *Attitude Organization and Change*, New Haven: Yale University Press, 1960, pp. 164–197.

[15] Arthur R. Cohen, "Attitudinal Consequences of Induced Discrepancies Between Cognitions and Behavior," *Public Opinion Quarterly*, 24 (Summer, 1960), pp. 297–318.

[16] Paul F. Secord and Carl W. Backman, "Liking, Selective Interaction, and Misperception in Congruent Interpersonal Relations," *Sociometry*, 25 (Dec., 1962), pp. 321–335.

VI ASSOCIATIONS

A. Definitions and Concepts

1. Primary and Secondary Groups

Sociology is concerned with interaction, whether it occurs between two or two thousand people. The sociological analysis of the organization and type of groups, whatever their size, deals with the form interaction takes. Again, sociologists are interested in patterned relations and repetitive behavior, not isolated social events. The following are some of the ways in which sociologists order group phenomena.

It was the early American sociologist Charles Horton Cooley who formulated the concepts of primary and secondary relationships. His particular interest was the origin of morals or ethics in society, which he located in the primary group, of which the family was a prime example. A variety of research has been organized around the polar concepts of primary and secondary groups. Kingsley Davis, a demographer and social theorist, presents a concise summary of their characteristics in this chart.

17 KINGSLEY DAVIS

Primary and Secondary Relationships

	PRIMARY	SECONDARY
Physical Conditions	Spatial proximity	Spatial distance
	Small number	Large number
	Long duration	Short duration
Social Characteristics	Identification of ends	Disparity of ends
	Intrinsic valuation of the relation	Extrinsic valuation of the relation
	Intrinsic valuation of other person	Extrinsic valuation of other person
	Inclusive knowledge of other person	Specialized and limited knowledge of other person
	Feeling of freedom and spontaneity	Feeling of external constraint
	Operation of informal controls	Operation of formal controls
Sample Relationships	Friend-friend	Clerk-customer
	Husband-wife	Announcer-listener
	Parent-child	Performer-spectator
	Teacher-pupil	Officer-subordinate
		Author-reader
Sample Groups	Play group	Nation
	Family	Clerical hierarchy
	Village or neighborhood	Professional association
	Work-team	Corporation

2. Formal Organizations

Some associations have constitutions: principles for defining the relationships of the actors. Western industrial society is characterized by a multitude of these associations, which we refer to as bureaucratic. Bureaucracies are found at all levels, e.g., in the church, in business, or in recreation. Much of the contemporary literature on bureaucracy is grounded in the following article by Weber, the German sociologist. Notice how Weber's "characteristics of a bureaucracy" can be applied to any contemporary association.

18 Max Weber

On Bureaucracy

{2 of *on plains Quiet Common*
India 9 Galbraith's
(post office socialism ?
Dec 2 '87 NYT Mag
2/28/88

CHARACTERISTICS OF BUREAUCRACY

Modern officialdom functions in the following specific manner:

I. There is the principle of fixed and official jurisdictional areas, which are generally ordered by rules, that is, by laws or administrative regulations.

1. The regular activities required for the purposes of the bureaucratically governed structure are distributed in a fixed way as official duties.

2. The authority to give the commands required for the discharge of these duties is distributed in a stable way and is strictly delimited by rules concerning the coercive means, physical, sacerdotal, or otherwise, which may be placed at the disposal of officials.

3. Methodical provision is made for the regular and continuous fulfillment of these duties and for the execution of the corresponding rights; only persons who have the generally regulated qualifications to serve are employed.

In public and lawful government these three elements constitute "bureaucratic authority." In private economic domination, they constitute bureaucratic "management." Bureaucracy, thus understood, is fully developed in political and ecclesiastical communities only in the modern state, and, in the private economy, only in the most advanced institutions of capitalism. Permanent and public office authority, with fixed jurisdiction, is not the historical rule but rather the exception. This is so even in large political structures such as those of the ancient Orient, the Germanic and Mongolian empires of conquest, or of many feudal structures of state. In all these cases, the ruler executes the most important measures through personal trustees, table-companions, or court-servants. Their commissions and authority are not precisely delimited and are temporarily called into being for each case.

II. The principles of office hierarchy and of levels of graded authority mean a firmly ordered system of super- and subordination in which there is a supervision of the lower offices by the higher ones. Such a system offers the governed the possibility of appealing the decision of a lower office to its higher authority, in a definitely regulated manner. With the full development of the bureaucratic type, the office hierarchy is monocratically

From *Max Weber: Essays in Sociology,* edited and translated by H. H. Gerth and C. Wright Mills, pp. 196–204. Copyright 1946 by Oxford University Press, Inc. Reprinted by permission.

organized. The principle of hierarchical office authority is found in all bureaucratic structures: in state and ecclesiastical structures as well as in large party organizations and private enterprises. It does not matter for the character of bureaucracy whether its authority is called "private" or "public."

When the principle of jurisdictional "competency" is fully carried through, hierarchical subordination — at least in public office — does not mean that the "higher" authority is simply authorized to take over the business of the "lower." Indeed, the opposite is the rule. Once established and having fulfilled its task, an office tends to continue in existence and be held by another incumbent.

(III.) The management of the modern office is based upon written documents ("the files"), which are preserved in their original or draught form. There is, therefore, a staff of subaltern officials and scribes of all sorts. The body of officials actively engaged in a "public" office, along with the respective apparatus of material implements and the files, make up a "bureau." In private enterprise, "the bureau" is often called "the office."

In principle, the modern organization of the civil service separates the bureau from the private domicile of the official, and, in general, bureaucracy segregates official activity as something distinct from the sphere of private life. Public monies and equipment are divorced from the private property of the official. This condition is everywhere the product of a long development. Nowadays, it is found in public as well as in private enterprises; in the latter, the principle extends even to the leading entrepreneur. In principle, the executive office is separated from the household, business from private correspondence, and business assets from private fortunes. The more consistently the modern type of business management has been carried through the more are these separations the case. The beginnings of this process are to be found as early as the Middle Ages.

It is the peculiarity of the modern entrepreneur that he conducts himself as the "first official" of his enterprise, in the very same way in which the ruler of a specifically modern bureaucratic state spoke of himself as "the first servant" of the state. The idea that the bureau activities of the state are intrinsically different in character from the management of private economic offices is a continental European notion and, by way of contrast, is totally foreign to the American way.

(IV.) Office management, at least all specialized office management — and such management is distinctly modern — usually presupposes thorough and expert training. This increasingly holds for the modern executive and employee of private enterprises, in the same manner as it holds for the state official.

(V.) When the office is fully developed, official activity demands the full working capacity of the official, irrespective of the fact that his obligatory time in the bureau may be firmly delimited. In the normal case, this is only the product of a long development, in the public as well as in the private office. Formerly, in all cases, the normal state of affairs was reversed: official business was discharged as a secondary activity.

(VI.)The management of the office follows general rules, which are more or less stable, more or less exhaustive, and which can be learned. Knowledge of these rules represents a special technical learning which the officials possess. It involves jurisprudence, or administrative or business management.

The reduction of modern office management to rules is deeply embedded in its very nature. The theory of modern public administration, for instance, assumes that the authority to order certain matters by decree — which has been legally granted to public authorities — does not entitle the bureau to regulate the matter by commands given for each case, but only to regulate the matter abstractly. This stands in extreme contrast to the regulation of all relationships through individual privileges and bestowals of favor, which is absolutely dominant in patrimonialism, at least in so far as such relationships are not fixed by sacred tradition.

THE POSITION OF THE OFFICIAL

All this results in the following for the internal and external position of the official:

I.) Office holding is a "vocation." This is shown, first, in the requirement of a firmly prescribed course of training, which demands the entire capacity for work for a long period of time, and in the generally prescribed and special examinations which are prerequisites of employment. Furthermore, the position of the official is in the nature of a duty. This determines the internal structure of his relations, in the following manner: Legally and actually, office holding is not considered a source to be exploited for rents or emoluments, as was normally the case during the Middle Ages and frequently up to the threshold of recent times. Nor is office holding considered a usual exchange of services for equivalents, as is the case with free labor contracts. Entrance into an office, including one in the private economy, is considered an acceptance of a specific obligation of faithful management in return for a secure existence. It is decisive for the specific nature of modern loyalty to an office that, in the pure type, it does not establish a relationship to a *person*, like the vassal's or disciple's faith in feudal or in patrimonial relations of authority. Modern loyalty is devoted to impersonal and functional purposes. Behind the functional purposes, of course, "ideas of culture-values" usually stand. These are *ersatz* for the earthly or supramundane personal master: ideas such as "state," "church," "community," "party," or "enterprise" are thought of as being realized in a community; they provide an ideological halo for the master.

The political official — at least in the fully developed modern state — is not considered the personal servant of a ruler. Today, the bishop, the priest, and the preacher are in fact no longer, as in early Christian times, holders of purely personal charisma. The supra-mundane and sacred values which they offer are given to everybody who seems to be worthy of them and who asks for them. In former times, such leaders acted upon the personal command of their master; in principle, they were responsible only to him. Nowadays, in spite of the partial survival of the old theory, such religious leaders are officials in the service of a functional purpose, which in the present-day "church" has become routinized and, in turn, ideologically hallowed.

II. The personal position of the official is patterned in the following way:

1. Whether he is in a private office or a public bureau, the modern official always strives and usually enjoys a distinct *social esteem* as compared with the governed. His social position is guaranteed by the prescriptive rules of rank order and, for the political official, by special definitions of the criminal code against "insults of officials" and "contempt" of state and church authorities.

The actual social position of the official is normally highest where, as in old civilized countries, the following conditions prevail: a strong demand for administration by trained experts; a strong and stable social differentiation, where the official predominantly derives from socially and economically privileged strata because of the social distribution of power; or where the costliness of the required training and status conventions are binding upon him. The possession of educational certificates — to be discussed elsewhere — is usually linked with qualification for office. Naturally, such certificates or patents enhance the "status element" in the social position of the official. For the rest this status factor in individual cases is explicitly and impassively acknowledged; for example, in the prescription that the acceptance or rejection of an aspirant to an official career depends upon the consent ("election") of the members of the official body. This is the case in the German army with the officer corps. Similar phenomena, which promote this guild-like closure of officialdom, are typically found in patrimonial and, particularly, in prebendal officialdoms of the past. The desire to resurrect such phenomena in changed forms is by no means infrequent among modern bureaucrats. For instance, they have played a role among the demands of the quite proletarian and expert officials (the *tretyj* element) during the Russian revolution.

Usually the social esteem of the officials as such is especially low where the demand for expert administration and the dominance of status conventions are weak. This is especially the case in the United States; it is often the case in new settlements by virtue of their wide fields for profit-making and the great instability of their social stratification.

2. The pure type of bureaucratic official is *appointed* by a superior authority. An official elected by the governed is not a purely bureaucratic figure. Of course, the formal existence of an election does not by itself mean that no appointment hides behind the election — in the state, especially, appointment by party chiefs. Whether or not this is the case does not depend upon legal statutes but upon the way in which the party mechanism functions. Once firmly organized, the parties can turn a formally free election into the mere acclamation of a candidate designated by the party chief. As a rule, however, a formally free election is turned into a fight, conducted according to definite rules, for votes in favor of one of two designated candidates.

In all circumstances, the designation of officials by means of an election among the governed modifies the strictness of hierarchical subordination. In principle, an official who is so elected has an autonomous position opposite the superordinate official. The elected official does not derive his position "from above" but "from below," or at least not from a superior authority of the official hierarchy but from powerful party men ("bosses"), who also determine his further career. The career of the elected official is not, or at least not primarily, dependent upon his chief in the administration. The official who is not elected but appointed by a chief normally functions more exactly, from a technical point of view, because, all other circumstances being equal, it is more likely that purely functional points of consideration and qualities will determine his selection and career. As laymen, the governed can become acquainted with the extent to which a candidate is expertly qualified for office only in terms of experience, and hence only after his service. Moreover, in every sort of selection of officials by election, parties quite naturally give decisive weight not to expert considerations but to the services a follower renders to the party boss. This holds for all kinds of procurement of officials by elections, for the designation of formally free, elected officials by party bosses when they determine the slate of candidates, or the free appointment by a chief who has himself been elected. The contrast, however, is relative: substantially similar conditions hold where legitimate monarchs and their subordinates appoint officials, except that the influence of the followings are then less controllable.

Where the demand for administration by trained experts is considerable, and the party followings have to recognize an intellectually developed, educated, and freely moving "public opinion," the use of unqualified officials falls back upon the party in power at the next election. Naturally, this is more likely to happen when the officials are appointed by the chief. The demand for a trained administration now exists in the United States, but in the large cities, where immigrant votes are "corraled," there is, of course, no educated public opinion. Therefore, popular elections of the administrative chief and also of his subordinate officials usually endanger the expert

qualification of the official as well as the precise functioning of the bureaucratic mechanism. It also weakens the dependence of the officials upon the
hierarchy. This holds at least for the large administrative bodies that are
difficult to supervise. The superior qualification and integrity of federal
judges, appointed by the President, as over against elected judges in the
United States is well known, although both types of officials have been
selected primarily in terms of party considerations. The great changes in
American metropolitan administrations demanded by reformers have proceeded essentially from elected mayors working with an apparatus of
officials who were appointed by them. These reforms have thus come about
in a "Caesarist" fashion. Viewed technically, as an organized form of
authority, the efficiency of "Caesarism," which often grows out of democracy, rests in general upon the position of the "Caesar" as a free trustee of
the masses (of the army or of the citizenry), who is unfettered by tradition.
The "Caesar" is thus the unrestrained master of a body of highly qualified
military officers and officials whom he selects freely and personally without
regard to tradition or to any other considerations. This "rule of the personal
genius," however, stands in contradiction to the formally "democratic"
principle of a universally elected officialdom.

(3. Normally, the position of the official is held for life, at least in public
bureaucracies; and this is increasingly the case for all similar structures.
As a factual rule, *tenure for life* is presupposed, even where the giving of
notice or periodic reappointment occurs. In contrast to the worker in a
private enterprise, the official normally holds tenure. Legal or actual life-
tenure, however, is not recognized as the official's right to the possession of
office, as was the case with many structures of authority in the past. Where
legal guarantees against arbitrary dismissal or transfer are developed,
they merely serve to guarantee a strictly objective discharge of specific
office duties free from all personal considerations. In Germany, this is the
case for all juridical and, increasingly, for all administrative officials.

Within the bureaucracy, therefore, the measure of "independence," legally guaranteed by tenure, is not always a source of increased status for
the official whose position is thus secured. Indeed, often the reverse holds,
especially in old cultures and communities that are highly differentiated.
In such communities, the stricter the subordination under the arbitrary
rule of the master, the more it guarantees the maintenance of the conventional seigneurial style of living for the official. Because of the very absence
of these legal guarantees of tenure, the conventional esteem for the official
may rise in the same way as, during the Middle Ages, the esteem of the
nobility of office rose at the expense of esteem for the freemen, and as
the king's judge surpassed that of the people's judge. In Germany, the
military officer or the administrative official can be removed from office
at any time, or at least far more readily than the "independent judge,"
who never pays with loss of his office for even the grossest offense against

the "code of honor" or against social conventions of the salon. For this very reason, if other things are equal, in the eyes of the master stratum the judge is considered less qualified for social intercourse than are officers and administrative officials, whose greater dependence on the master is a greater guarantee of their conformity with status conventions. Of course, the average official strives for a civil-service law, which would materially secure his old age and provide increased guarantees against his arbitrary removal from office. This striving, however, has its limits. A very strong development of the "right to the office" naturally makes it more difficult to staff them with regard to technical efficiency, for such a development decreases the career-opportunities of ambitious candidates for office. This makes for the fact that officials, on the whole, do not feel their dependency upon those at the top. This lack of a feeling of dependency, however, rests primarily upon the inclination to depend upon one's equals rather than upon the socially inferior and governed strata. The present conservative movement among the Badenia clergy, occasioned by the anxiety of a presumably threatening separation of church and state, has been expressly determined by the desire not to be turned "from a master into a servant of the parish."

4. The official receives the regular *pecuniary* compensation of a normally fixed *salary* and the old age security provided by a pension. The salary is not measured like a wage in terms of work done, but according to "status," that is, according to the kind of function (the "rank") and, in addition, possibly, according to the length of service. The relatively great security of the official's income, as well as the rewards of social esteem, make the office a sought-after position, especially in countries which no longer provide opportunities for colonial profits. In such countries, this situation permits relatively low salaries for officials.

5. The official is set for a "career" within the hierarchical order of the public service. He moves from the lower, less important, and lower paid to the higher positions. The average official naturally desires a mechanical fixing of the conditions of promotion: if not of the offices, at least of the salary levels. He wants these conditions fixed in terms of "seniority," or possibly according to grades achieved in a developed system of expert examinations. Here and there, such examinations actually form a character *indelebilis* of the official and have lifelong effects on his career. To this is joined the desire to qualify the right to office and the increasing tendency toward status group closure and economic security. All of this makes for a tendency to consider the offices as "prebends" of those who are qualified by educational certificates. The necessity of taking general personal and intellectual qualifications into consideration, irrespective of the often subaltern character of the educational certificate, has led to a condition in which the highest political offices, especially the positions of "ministers," are principally filled without reference to such certificates.

TECHNICAL ADVANTAGES
OF BUREAUCRATIC ORGANIZATION

The decisive reason for the advance of bureaucratic organization has always been its purely technical superiority over any other form of organization. The fully developed bureaucratic mechanism compares with other organizations exactly as does the machine with the non-mechanical modes of production.

Precision, speed, unambiguity, knowledge of the files, continuity, discretion, unity, strict subordination, reduction of friction and of material and personal costs — these are raised to the optimum point in the strictly bureaucratic administration, and especially in its monocratic form. As compared with all collegiate, honorific, and avocational forms of administration, trained bureaucracy is superior on all these points. And as far as complicated tasks are concerned, paid bureaucratic work is not only more precise but, in the last analysis, it is often cheaper than even formally unremunerated honorific service.

Honorific arrangements make administrative work an avocation and, for this reason alone, honorific service normally functions more slowly; being less bound to schemata and being more formless. Hence it is less precise and less unified than bureaucratic work because it is less dependent upon superiors and because the establishment and exploitation of the apparatus of subordinate officials and filing services are almost unavoidably less economical. Honorific service is less continuous than bureaucratic and frequently quite expensive. This is especially the case if one thinks not only of the money costs to the public treasury — costs which bureaucratic administration, in comparison with administration by notables, usually substantially increases — but also of the frequent economic losses of the governed caused by delays and lack of precision. The possibility of administration by notables normally and permanently exists only where official management can be satisfactorily discharged as an avocation. With the qualitative increase of tasks the administration has to face, administration by notables reaches its limits — today, even in England. Work organized by collegiate bodies causes friction and delay and requires compromises between colliding interests and views. The administration, therefore, runs less precisely and is more independent of superiors; hence, it is less unified and slower. All advances of the Prussian administrative organization have been and will in the future be advances of the bureaucratic, and especially of the monocratic, principle.

Today, it is primarily the capitalist market economy which demands that the official business of the administration be discharged precisely, unambiguously, continuously, and with as much speed as possible. Normally, the very large, modern capitalist enterprises are themselves unequalled models of strict bureaucratic organization. Business management throughout rests on increasing precision, steadiness, and, above all, the speed of operations. This, in turn, is determined by the peculiar nature of the modern means of communication, including, among other things, the news service of the press. The extraordinary increase in the speed by which public announcements, as well as economic and political facts, are transmitted exerts a steady and sharp pressure in the direction of speeding up the tempo of administrative reaction towards various situations. The optimum of such reaction time is normally attained only by a strictly bureaucratic organization.[1]

Bureaucratization offers above all the optimum possibility for carrying through the principle of specializing administrative functions according to purely objective considerations. Individual performances are allocated to functionaries who have specialized training and who by constant practice learn more and more. The "objective" discharge of business primarily means a discharge of business according to *calculable rules* and "without regard for persons."

"Without regard for persons" is also the watchword of the "market" and, in general, of all pursuits of naked economic interests. A consistent execution of bureaucratic domination means the leveling of status "honor." Hence, if the principle of the free-market is not at the same time restricted, it means the universal domination of the "class situation." That this consequence of bureaucratic domination has not set in everywhere, parallel to the extent of bureaucratization, is due to the differences among possible principles by which polities may meet their demands.

The second element mentioned, "calculable rules," also is of paramount importance for modern bureaucracy. The peculiarity of modern culture, and specifically of its technical and economic basis, demands this very "calculability" of results. When fully developed, bureaucracy also stands, in a specific sense, under the principle of *sine ira ac studio*. Its specific nature, which is welcomed by capitalism, develops the more perfectly the more the bureaucracy is "dehumanized," the more completely it succeeds in eliminating from official business love, hatred, and all purely personal, irrational, and emotional elements which escape calculation. This is the specific nature of bureaucracy and it is appraised as its special virtue.

---

[1] Here we cannot discuss in detail how the bureaucratic apparatus may, and actually does, produce definite obstacles to the discharge of business in a manner suitable for the single case.

No organization springs into being as a full-blown, functioning unit.
There is always a period of groping for meaning, and an attempt to
lay down boundaries and define functions for the neophyte system.
Riesman and Denney, who with Nathan Glazer wrote The Lonely
Crowd, *trace the development of football and its attempt to formu-*
late rules for the interaction of those involved. If it is borne in mind
that football has become a large-scale business enterprise, it is even
easier to understand how it can be analyzed as a formal organization.

19   DAVID RIESMAN AND REVEL DENNEY

Spr/Fall 1979 Little Brown   Football + Death of an American Game   In Underwood from a Sports Illus. series
before Eduen requirements in coll

Football in America: A Study in Culture Diffusion

I

On October 9, 1951, Assistant Attorney General Graham Morrison instituted
an anti-trust action against a number of universities on account of their
efforts to limit TV broadcasts of their games — efforts dictated by the terrible burdens of what we might speak of as "industrialized football." This
action occurred only a few weeks after the scandal of the West Point student firings, which, along with the William and Mary palace revolution,
indicated that football was indeed reaching another crisis in its adaptation
to the ever-changing American environment. Small colleges such as Milligan — a church-supported school in the mountains of Eastern Tennessee —
were discovering that football was now so mechanized that they could no
longer afford the necessary entry fee for machinery and personnel. Last
year, Milligan spent $17,000, or two-thirds of its whole athletic budget —
and did not get it all back in the box-office net. Football had come to
resemble other industries or mechanized farms, into which a new firm
could not move by relying on an institutional lifetime of patient saving and
plowing back of profits, but only by large corporate investment. The production of a team involves the heavy overhead and staff personnel characteristic of high-capital, functionally rationalized industries, as the result
of successive changes in the game since its post-Civil-War diffusion from
England.[1]

Reprinted with permission of the author and The Macmillan Company from *Individualism*
Reconsidered and Other Essays by David Riesman. Copyright 1954 by The Free Press, a
Corporation.

[1] The growing scale of college football is indicated by its dollar place in the American leisure economy. In 1929, out of $4.3 billion recreation expenditures by Americans,
the college football gate accounted for $22 million. In 1950, out of $11.2 billion in
such expenditures, it accounted for $103 million. While something less than 1 per cent of
the total United States recreation account, college football had ten times the gross income
of professional football. The 1950 gate of $103 million suggests that a total capital of
perhaps $250 million is invested in the college football industry. The revenue figures,
above, of course, do not include the invisible subsidization of football, nor do they
hint at the place that football pools occupy in the American betting economy.

It would be wrong, however, to assert that football has become an impersonal market phenomenon. Rather, its rationalization as a sport and as a spectacle has served to bring out more openly the part it plays in the ethnic, class, and characterological struggles of our time — meaning, by "characterological struggle," the conflict between different styles of life. The ethnic significance of football is immediately suggested by the shift in the typical origins of player-names on the All-American Football Teams since 1889. In 1889, all but one of the names (Heffelfinger) suggested Anglo-Saxon origins. The first name after that of Heffelfinger to suggest non-Anglo-Saxon recruitment was that of Murphy, at Yale, in 1895. After 1895, it was a rare All-American team that did not include at least one Irishman (Daly, Hogan, Rafferty, Shevlin); and the years before the turn of the century saw entrance of the Jew. On the 1904 team appeared Pierkarski, of Pennsylvania. By 1927, names like Casey, Kipke, Oosterbaan, Koppisch, Garbisch, and Friedman were appearing on the All-American lists with as much frequency as names like Channing, Adams, and Ames in the 1890's.

While such a tally does little more than document a shift that most observers have already recognized in American football, it raises questions that are probably not answerable merely in terms of ethnic origins of players. There is an element of class identification running through American football since its earliest days, and the ethnic origins of players contain ample invitations to the making of theory about the class dimensions of football. Most observers would be inclined to agree that the arrival of names like Kelley and Kipke on the annual All-American list was taken by the Flanagans and the Webers as the achievement of a lower-class aspiration to be among the best at an upper-class sport. The question remains: what did the achievement mean? What did it mean at different stages in the development of the game? Hasn't the meaning worn off in the fifty-odd years, the roughly two generations since Heffelfinger and Murphy made the grade?

There are many ways to begin an answer to such questions, and here we can open only a few lines of investigation. Our method is to study the interrelations between changes in the rules of the game (since the first intercollegiate contest: Rutgers, 6 goals — Princeton, 4 goals, in 1869) and to analyze the parallel changes in football strategy and ethos. All these developments are to be seen as part of a configuration that includes changes in coaching, in the training of players, and in the no less essential training of the mass audience.

Since football is a cultural inheritance from England, such an analysis may be made in the perspective of other studies in cultural diffusion and variation. Just as the French have transformed American telephone etiquette while retaining some of its recognizable physical features, so Americans have transformed the games of Europe even when, as in track or tennis, the formalities appear to be unaltered. Even within the Western industrial culture, there are great varieties on a class and national basis, in the games, rules, strategy, etiquette, and audience structures of sport. In the case of college football — we shall leave aside the symbolically less important professional game — the documentation of sportswriters (themselves a potent factor in change) allows us to trace the stages of development.

II

A study of Anatolian peasants now under way at the Bureau of Applied Social Research indicates that these highly tradition-bound people cannot grasp the abstractness of modern sports. They lack the enterprise, in their fatalistic village cultures, to see why people want to knock themselves out for sportmanship's remote ideals; they cannot link such rituals, even by remote analogy, with their own. These peasants are similarly unable to be caught up in modern politics, or to find anything meaningful in the Voice of America. Nevertheless, football itself, like so many other games with balls and goals, originated in a peasant culture.

Football, in its earliest English form, was called the Dane's Head and it was played in the tenth and eleventh centuries as a contest in kicking a ball between towns. The legend is that the first ball was a skull, and only later a cow's bladder. In some cases, the goals were the towns themselves, so that a team entering a village might have pushed the ball several miles en route. King Henry II (1154–89) proscribed the game, on the ground that it interfered with archery practice. Played in Dublin even after the ban, football did not become respectable or legal until an edict of James I reinstated it. The reason was perhaps less ideological than practical: firearms had made the art of bowmanship obsolete.

During the following century, football as played by British schoolboys became formalized, but did not change its fundamental pattern of forceful kicking. In 1823, Ellis of Rugby made the mistake of picking up the ball and running with it towards the goal. All concerned thought it a mistake: Ellis was sheepish, his captain apologetic. The mistake turned into innovation when it was decided that a running rule might make for an interesting game. The localism, pluralism, and studied casualness of English sports made it possible to try it out without securing universal assent — three or four purely local variants of football, football-hazing and "wall games" are still played in various English schools. Rugby adopted "Rugby" in 1841, several years after Cambridge had helped to popularize it.[2]

---

[2] A commemorative stone at Rugby reads as follows:

THIS STONE
COMMEMORATES THE EXPLOIT OF
WILLIAM WEBB ELLIS
WHO WITH A FINE DISREGARD FOR THE RULES OF
FOOTBALL, AS PLAYED IN HIS TIME,
FIRST TOOK THE BALL IN HIS ARMS AND RAN WITH IT,
THUS ORIGINATING THE DISTINCTIVE FEATURE OF
THE RUGBY GAME
A.D. 1823

This establishment of the running or Rugby game, as contrasted with the earlier, kicking game, had several important results. One was that the old-style players banded themselves together for the defense of their game, and formed the London Football Association (1863). This name, abbreviated to "Assoc," appears to have been the starting point for the neologism, "Soccer," the name that the kicking game now goes by in many parts of the English-speaking world. A second result was that the English, having found a new game, continued to play it without tight rules until the Rugby Union of 1871. As we shall see, this had its effects on the American game. The third and most important result of Ellis' "mistake," of course, was that he laid the foundations for everything fundamental about the American game between about 1869 and the introduction of the forward pass. (The forward pass is still illegal in Rugby and closely related football games.)

III

In the colonial period and right down to the Civil War, Americans played variants on the kicking football game on their town greens and schoolyards. After the war, Yale and Harvard served as the culturally receptive importers of the English game. Harvard, meeting McGill in a game of Rugby football in 1874, brought the sport to the attention of collegiate circles and the press — two identifications important for the whole future development of the game. But if Harvard was an opinion leader, Yale was a technological one. A Yale student who had studied at Rugby was instrumental in persuading Yale men to play the Rugby game and was, therefore, responsible for some of Yale's early leadership in the sport.

It happened in the following way, according to Walter Camp and Lorin F. Deland.[3] The faculty in 1860, for reasons unknown, put a stop to inter-class matches of the pre-Rugby variety. "During the following years, until 1870, football was practically dead at Yale. The class of '72, however, was very fond of athletic sports, and participated especially in long hare and hound runs. The revival of football was due in a large measure to Mr. D. S. Schaft, formerly of Rugby School, who entered the class of '73 and succeeded in making the sport popular among his classmates, and eventually formed an association which sent challenges to the other classes."

Soon after the period described by Camp, it became clear that American players, having tasted the "running" game, were willing to give up the soccer form. It became equally clear that they either did not want to, or could not, play Rugby according to the British rules. "The American players found in this code [English Rugby Rules] many uncertain and knotty points which caused much trouble in their game, especially as they had no traditions, or older and more experienced players, to whom they could turn for the necessary explanations," says Camp. An example of such a problem was English rule number nine:

[3] Walter Camp and Lorin F. Deland, *Football.*

"A touchdown is when a player, putting his hand on the ball in touch or in goal, stops it so that it remains dead, or fairly so."

The ambiguity of the phrase "fairly so" was increased by the statement in rule number eight that the ball is dead "when it rests absolutely motionless on the ground."

Camp's description of these early difficulties is intensely interesting to the student of cultural diffusion not only because of what Camp observed about the situation, but also because of what he neglected to observe. Consider the fact that the development of Rugby rules in England was accomplished by admitting into the rules something that we would call a legal fiction. While an offensive runner was permitted to carry the ball, the condition of his doing so was that he should *happen* to be standing behind the swaying "scrum" (the tangled players) at the moment the ball popped back out to him. An intentional "heel out" of the ball was not permitted; and the British rules of the mid-nineteenth century appear to take it for granted that the difference between an intentional and an unintentional heel-out would be clear to everyone. Ellis' mistake became institutionalized — but still as a mistake. This aspect of Rugby rule-making had important implications for the American game.

British players, according to tradition as well as according to rules, could be expected to tolerate such ambiguity as that of the heel-out rule just as they tolerated the ambiguity of the "dead" ball. They could be expected to tolerate it not only because of their personal part in developing new rules but also (a point we shall return to) because they had an audience with specific knowledge of the traditions to assist them. In America it was quite another matter to solve such problems. No Muzafer Sherif was present[4] to solidify the perceptions of "nearly so," and the emotional tone for resolving such question without recurrent dispute could not be improvised. Rather, however, than dropping the Rugby game at that point, because of intolerance for the ambiguities involved, an effort was undertaken, at once systematic and gradual, to fill in by formal procedures the vacuum of etiquette and, in general, to adapt the game to its new cultural home.

The upshot of American procedure was to assign players to the legalized task of picking up and tossing the ball back out of scrimmage. This in turn created the role of the center, and the centering operation. This in turn led to a variety of problems in defining the situation as one of "scrimmage" or "non-scrimmage," and the whole question of the legality of passing the ball back to intended runners. American football never really solved these problems until it turned its attention, in 1880, to a definition of the scrimmage itself. The unpredictable English "scrum" or scramble for a free ball was abandoned, and a crude line of scrimmage was constructed across the field. Play was set in motion by snapping the ball. Meanwhile Americans became

[4] Cf. his *An Outline of Social Psychology,* pp. 93–182.

impatient with long retention of the ball by one side. It was possible for a team that was ahead in score to adopt tactics that would insure its retention of the ball until the end of the period. By the introduction of a minimum yardage-gain rule in 1882, the rule-makers assured the frequent interchange of the ball between sides.

The effect of this change was to dramatize the offensive-defensive symmetry of the scrimmage line, to locate it sharply in time ("downs"), and to focus attention not only on the snapping of the ball, but also on the problem of "offside" players. In the English game, with no spatially and temporally delimited "line of scrimmage," the offside player was penalized only by making him neutral in action until he could move to a position back of the position of the ball. In the American game, the new focus on centering, on a scrimmage line, and on yardage and downs, created the need for a better offside rule. From that need developed offside rules that even in the early years resembled the rules of today. American rulemakers were logically extending a native development when they decided to draw an imaginary line through the ball before it had been centered, to call this the "line of scrimmage," and to make this line, rather than the moving ball itself, the offside limit in the goalward motion of offensive players. At first, lined-up players of the two sides were allowed to stand and wrestle with each other while waiting for the ball to be centered; only later was a neutral zone introduced between the opposing lines.

Even with such a brief summary of the rule changes, we are in a position to see the operation of certain recurrent modes or patterns of adaptation. The adaptation begins with the acceptance of a single pivotal innovation (running with the ball). The problems of adaptation begin with the realization that this single innovation has been uprooted from a rich context of meaningful rules and traditions, and does not work well in their absence. Still more complex problems of adaptation develop when it is realized that the incompleteness of the adaptation will not be solved by a reference to the pristine rules. In the first place, the rules are not pristine (the English rules were in the process of development themselves). In the second place, the tradition of interpreting them is not present in experienced players. In the third place, even if it were, it might not be adaptable to the social character and mood of the adapters.

Let us put it this way. The Americans, in order to solve the heel-out problem, set in motion a redesign of the game that led ultimately to timed centering from a temporarily fixed line of scrimmage. Emphasis completely shifted from the kicking game; it also shifted away from the combined kicking and running possible under Rugby rules; it shifted almost entirely in the direction of an emphasis on ballcarrying. Meanwhile, to achieve this emphasis, the game made itself vulnerable to slowdowns caused by one team's retention of the ball. It not only lost the fluidity of the original game, but ran up against a pronounced American taste for action in sports, visible action. There is evidence that even if players had not objected to such slow-downs, the spectators would have raised a shout. The yardage rule was the way this crisis was met. This, in turn, led to an emphasis on mass play, and helped to create the early twentieth-century problems of football. But before we consider this step in the game's development we must turn to examine certain factors in the sport's audience reception.

IV

A problem posed for the student of cultural diffusion at this point can be stated as follows: What factor or factors appear to have been most influential in creating an American game possessing not only nationally distinct rules, but also rules having a specific flavor of intense legality about many a point of procedure left more or less up in the air by the British game?

We can now go beyond the rule-making aspect of the game and assert that the chief factor was the importance of the need to standardize rules to supply an ever-widening collegiate field of competition, along with the audience this implied. The English rule-makers, it appears, dealt with a situation in which amateur play was restricted to a fairly limited number of collegians and institutions. The power of localism was such that many an informality was tolerated, and intended to be tolerated, in the rules and their interpretation. American football appeared on the American campus at the beginning of a long period in which intercollegiate and interclass sportsmanship was a problem of ever-widening social participation and concern. Football etiquette itself was in the making. Thus, it appears that when early American teams met, differences of opinion could not be resolved between captains in rapid-fire agreement or penny-tossing as was the case in Britain. American teams did not delegate to their captains the role of powerful comrade-in-antagonism with opposing captains, or, if they did, they felt that such responsibilities were too grave.[5]

Into just such situations football players thrust all of the force of their democratic social ideologies, all their prejudice in favor of equalitarian and codified inter-player attitudes. Undoubtedly, similar considerations also influenced the audience. Mark Benney, a British sociologist who is familiar with the games played on both sides of the Atlantic, points out that, whereas the American game was developed in and for a student group, the English game was played before quite large crowds who, from a class standpoint, were less homogeneous than the players themselves, though they were as well informed as the latter in the "law" of the game. Rugby football was seldom played by the proletariat; it was simply enjoyed as a spectacle.

---

[5] "Fifty years ago arguments followed almost every decision the referee made. The whole team took part, so that half the time the officials scarcely knew who was captain. The player who was a good linguist was always a priceless asset." John W. Heisman, who played for both Brown and Penn in the 1890's, quoted in Frank G. Menke, *Encyclopedia of Sports*, p. 293.

Held by the critical fascination the British upper strata had for the lower strata, the audience was often hardly more interested in the result of the game than in judging the players as "gentlemen in action." "The players," Mr. Benney writes, "had to demonstrate that they were sportsmen, that they could 'take it'; and above all they had to inculcate the (politically important) ideology that legality was more important than power." The audience was, then, analogous to the skilled English jury at law, ready to be impressed by obedience to traditional legal ritual and form, and intolerant of "bad form" in their "betters." The early Yale games, played before a tiny, nonpaying audience, lacked any equivalent incentive to agree on a class-based ritual of "good form," and when the audiences came later on, their attitude towards upper-class sportsmanship was much more ambivalent — they had played the game too, and they were unwilling to subordinate themselves to a collegiate aristocracy who would thereby have been held to norms of correctness. The apparent legalism of many American arguments over the rules would strike British observers as simply a verbal power-play.

Such differences in the relation of the game to the audience, on this side of the Atlantic, undoubtedly speeded the development of the specifically American variant. Native, too, are the visual and temporal properties of the game as it developed even before 1900: its choreography could be enjoyed, if not always understood, by non-experts, and its atomistic pattern in time and space could seem natural to audiences accustomed to such patterns in other foci of the national life. The mid-field dramatization of line against line, the recurrent starting and stopping of field action around the timed snapping of a ball, the trend to a formalized division of labor between backfield and line, above all, perhaps, the increasingly precise synchronization of men in motion — these developments make it seem plausible to suggest that the whole procedural rationalization of the game which we have described was not unwelcome to Americans, and that it fitted in with other aspects of their industrial folkways.

Spurred by interest in the analysis of the athletic motions of men and animals, Eadweard Muybridge was setting out his movie-like action shorts of the body motion (more preoccupied even than Vesalius or da Vinci with the detailed anatomy of movement)[6] at about the same time that Coach Woodruff at Pennsylvania (1894) was exploring the possibilities for momentum play: linemen swinging into motion before the ball is snapped, with the offensive team, forming a wedge, charging toward an opposition held waiting by the offside rule. In Philadelphia, the painter Eakins, self-consciously following the tenets of Naturalism and his own literal American tradition, was painting the oarsmen of the Schuylkill. Nearby, at the Midvale plant of the American Steel Company, efficiency expert Frederick Winslow Taylor was experimenting with motion study and incentive pay

[6] Sigfried Giedion, *Mechanization Takes Command*, pp. 21–27.

geared to small measurable changes in output — pay that would spur but never soften the workman.[7]

Since we do not believe in historical inevitability, nor in the necessary homogeneity of a culture, we do not suggest that the American game of football developed as it did out of cultural compulsion and could not have gone off in quite different directions. Indeed, the very effectiveness of momentum play, as a mode of bulldozing the defense, led eventually to the rule that the line must refrain from motion before the ball is snapped. For the bulldozing led, or was thought to lead, to a great increase in injuries. And while these were first coped with by Walter Camp's training table (his men had their choice of beefsteak or mutton for dinner, to be washed down with milk, ale, or sherry), the public outcry soon forced further rule changes, designed to soften the game. After a particularly bloody battle between Pennsylvania and Swarthmore in 1905, President Roosevelt himself took a hand and insisted on reform.[8]

Camp's colleague at Yale, William Graham Sumner, may well have smiled wryly at this. Sumner was exhorting his students to "get capital," and cautioning them against the vices of sympathy and reformism — a theme which has given innumerable American academes a good living since — while Camp was exhorting his to harden themselves, to be stern and unafraid. In spite of them both, the reformers won out; but the end of momentum play was not the end of momentum. Rather, with an ingenuity that still dazzles, the game was gentled and at the same time speeded by a new rule favoring the forward pass. But before going on to see what changes this introduced, let us note the differences between the subjects of Sumner's and Camp's exhortations on the one hand, and Taylor's on the other.

[7] In view of the prejudice against "Taylorism" today, shared by men and management as well as the intellectuals, let us record our admiration for Taylor's achievement, our belief that he was less insensitive to psychological factors than is often claimed, and more "humane" in many ways than his no less manipulative, self-consciously psychological successors.

[8] "In a 1905 game between Pennsylvania and Swarthmore, the Pennsy slogan was 'Stop Bob Maxwell,' one of the greatest linesmen of all time. He was a mighty man, with amazing ability to roll back enemy plunges. The Penn players, realizing that Maxwell was a menace to their chances of victory, took 'dead aim' at him throughout the furious play.

"Maxwell stuck it out, but when he tottered off the field, his face was a bloody wreck. Some photographer snapped him, and the photo of the mangled Maxwell, appearing in a newspaper, caught the attention of the then President Roosevelt. It so angered him, that he issued an ultimatum that if rough play in football was not immediately ruled out, he would abolish it by executive edict." Frank G. Menke, *Encyclopedia of Sports.*

Notice here the influence of two historical factors on football development: one, the occupancy of the White House in 1905 by the first President of the United States who was a self-conscious patron of youth, sport, and the arts; two, the relative newness in 1905 of photographic sports coverage. Widespread increased photographic coverage of popular culture was the direct result of the newspaper policies of William Randolph Hearst, beginning about 1895.

Frederick Taylor, as his writings show, was already coming up against a work force increasingly drawn from non-Protestant lands, and seeking to engender in them a YMCA-morality, whereas Camp was inculcating the same morality into young men of undiluted Anglo-Saxon stock and middle- to upper-class origins. Not for another fifty years would the sons of Midvale prove harder, though fed on kale or spaghetti, and only intermittently, than the sons of Yale. Meanwhile, the sons of Yale had learned to spend summers as tracklayers or wheat harvesters in an effort to enlarge their stamina, moral toughness, and cross-class adventures.

Nevertheless, certain basic resemblances between the purposes of Taylor and those of Sumner and Camp are clearly present. In contrast with the British, the Americans demonstrated a high degree of interest in winning games and winning one's way to high production goals. The Americans, as in so many other matters, were clearly concerned with the competitive spirit that new rules might provoke and control. (British sports, like British industry, seemed to take it more for granted that competition will exist even if one does not set up an ideology for it.) Much of this seems to rest in the paradoxical belief of Americans that competition is natural — but only if it is constantly recreated by artificial systems of social rules that direct energies into it.

Back of the attitudes expressed in Taylor, Sumner, and Camp we can feel the pressure not only of a theory of competition, but also a theory of the emotional tones that ought to go along with competition. It is apparent from the brutality scandals of 1905 that President Roosevelt reacted against roughhouse not so much because it was physical violence, but for two related reasons. The first and openly implied reason was that it was connected with an unsportsmanlike attitude. The second, unacknowledged, reason was that Americans fear and enjoy their aggression at the same time, and thus have difficulty in pinning down the inner meanings of external violence. The game of Rugby as now played in England is probably as physically injurious as American football was at the turn of the century. By contrast, American attitudes toward football demonstrate a forceful need to define, limit, and conventionalize the symbolism of violence in sports.

If we look back now at England, we see a game in which shouted signals and silent counting of timed movements are unknown — a game that seems to Americans to wander in an amorphous and disorderly roughhouse. Rugby, in the very home of the industrial revolution, seems pre-industrial, seems like one of the many feudal survivals that urbanization and industrialization have altered but not destroyed. The English game, moreover, seems not to have developed anyone like Camp, the Judge Gary of football (as Rockne was to be its Henry Ford): Camp was a sparkplug in efforts to codify inter-collegiate rules; he was often the head of the important committees. His training table, furthermore, was one of the signs of the slow rise in "overhead" expense — a rise which, rather like the water in United

States Steel Stock, assumed that abundance was forthcoming and bailing out probable, as against the British need for parsimony. But at the same time the rise in costs undoubtedly made American football more vulnerable than ever to public-relations considerations: the "gate" could not be damned.

V

This public relations issue in the game first appears in the actions of the rules committee of 1906 — the introduction of the legalized forward pass in order to open up the game and reduce brutal power play. Between 1906 and 1913 the issue was generally treated as a problem centered about players and their coaches, and thus took the form of an appeal to principles rather than to audiences. However, the development of the high audience appeal that we shall show unfolding after 1913 was not autonomous and unheralded. If public relations became a dominant factor by 1915, when the University of Pittsburgh introduced numbers of players in order to spur the sale of programs, it had its roots in the 1905–13 period. The rules committee of 1906, by its defensive action on roughhouse rules, had already implicitly acknowledged a broad public vested interest in the ethos of the game. Let us turn to look at the speed with which football was soon permeated by broad social meanings unanticipated by the founders of the sport.

By 1913, the eve of the First World War, innovation in American industry had ceased to be the prerogative of Baptist, Calvinist, and North of Ireland tycoons. Giannini was starting his Bank of America; the Jews were entering the movies and the garment hegemonies. Yet these were exceptions, and the second generation of immigrants, taught in America to be dissatisfied with the manual work their fathers did, were seldom finding the easy paths of ascent promised in success literature. Where, for one thing, were they to go to college? If the sought to enter the older eastern institutions, would they face a social struggle? Such anxieties probably contributed to the fact that the game of boyish and spirited brawn played at the eastern centers of intellect and cultivation was to be overthrown by the new game of craft and field maneuver that got its first rehearsal at the hands of two second-generation poor boys attending little-known Notre Dame.

The more significant of the two boys, Knute Rockne, was, to be a sure, of Danish Protestant descent and only later became a Catholic.[9] During their summer vacation jobs as lifeguards on Lake Michigan, Rockne and Gus Dorais decided to work as a passing team. Playing West Point early in the season of 1913, they put on the first demonstration of the spiral pass that makes scientific use of the difference in shape between the round ball used in the kicking game and the oval that gradually replaced it when ball-carrying began. As the first players to exploit the legal pass, they rolled up

_____

[9] "After the church, football is the best thing we have," Rockne.

a surprise victory over Army. One of the effects of the national change in rules was to bring the second-generation boys of the early twentieth century to the front, with a craft innovation that added new elements of surprise, "system" and skull-session to a game that had once revolved about an ethos of brawn plus character-building.

With the ethnic shift, appears to have come a shift in type of hero. The work-minded glamor of an all-'round craftsman like Jim Thorpe gave way to the people-minded glamor of backfield generals organizing deceptive forays into enemy territory — of course, the older martial virtues are not so much ruled out as partially incorporated in the new image. In saying this, it must not be forgotten, as sports columnist Red Smith has pointed out, that the fictional Yale hero, Dick Merriwell, is openly and shamelessly represented as a dirty player in the first chapters of his career. But the difference is that his deviation from standard sportsmanship consisted largely of slugging, not of premeditated wiliness. In fact, the Yale Era, even into Camp's reign, was characterized by a game played youthfully, with little attention to the players' prestige outside college circles. Again, the second-generationers mark a change. A variety of sources, including letters to the sports page, indicate that a Notre Dame victory became representational in a way a Yale or Harvard victory never was, and no Irish or Polish boy on the team could escape the symbolism. And by the self-confirming process, the Yale or Harvard showing became symbolic in turn, and the game could never be returned, short of intramuralization to the players themselves and their earlier age of innocent dirtiness.[10] The heterogeneity of America which had made it impossible to play the Rugby game at Yale had finally had its effect in transforming the meaning of the game to a point where Arnold of Rugby might have difficulty in drawing the right moral or any moral from it. Its "ideal types" had undergone a deep and widespread characterological change.

For the second-generation boy, with his father's muscles but not his father's motives, football soon became a means to career ascent. So was racketeering, but football gave acceptance, too — acceptance into the democratic fraternity of the entertainment world where performance counts and ethnic origin is hardly a handicap. Moreover, Americans as onlookers

[10] One of us, while a Harvard undergraduate, sought with several friends to heal the breach between Harvard and Princeton — a breach whose bitterness could hardly be credited today. The Harvards believed Princeton played dirty — it certainly won handily in those years of the 20's —while Princetonians believed themselves snubbed by Harvard as crude parvenus trying to make a trio out of the Harvard-Yale duo. The diplomatic problems involved in seeking to repair these status slights and scars were a microcosm of the Congress of Westphalia or Vienna —whether the Harvard or Princeton athletic directors should enter the room first was an issue. A leak to the Hearst press destroyed our efforts, as alumni pressure forced denials of any attempt to resume relations, but the compromise formulas worked out were eventually accepted, about the time that the University of Chicago "solved" the problem of the intellecutal school by withdrawing from the game altogether.

welcomed the anti-traditional innovations of a Rockne, and admired the trick that worked, whatever the opposing team and alumni may have thought about the effort involved. One wonders whether Rockne and Dorais may not have gotten a particular pleasure from their craftiness by thinking of it as a counter-image to the stereotype of muscle-men applied to their fathers.

It was in 1915, at about the same time that the newcomers perfected their passing game, that the recruitment of players began in earnest. Without such recruitment, the game could not have served as a career route for many of the second generation who would not have had the cash or impetus to make the class jump that college involved.[11]

The development of the open and rationalized game has led step by step not only to the T formation, but also to the two-platoon system. These innovations call for a very different relationship among the players than was the case under the older star system. For the game is now a cooperative enterprise in which mistakes are too costly — to the head coach, the budget, even the college itself — to be left to individual initiative. At least at one institution, an anthropologist has been called in to study the morale problems of the home team, and to help in the scouting of opposing teams. To the learning of Taylor, there has been added that of Mayo, and coaches are conscious of the need to be group-dynamics leaders rather than old-line straw bosses.

Today, the semi-professionalized player, fully conscious of how many people's living depends on him, cannot be exhorted by Frank Merriwell appeals, but needs to be "handled." And the signals are no longer the barks of the first Camp-trained quarterback — hardly more differentiated than a folkdance caller's — but are cues of great subtlety and mathematical precision for situations planned in advance with camera shots and character fill-ins of the opposing team. James Worthy and other advocates of a span of control beyond the usual half-dozen of the older military and executive manuals might find support for their views in the way an eleven is managed. Industrial, military, and football teamwork have all a common cultural frame.

Yet it would be too simple to say that football has ceased to be a game for its players, and has become an industry, or a training for industry. In the American culture as a whole, no sharp line exists between work and play, and in some respects the more work-like an activity becomes, the more it can successfully conceal elements of playfulness.[12] Just because the sophisticated "amateur" of today does *not* have his manhood at stake in the antique do-or-die fashion (though his manhood may be involved, in very ambivalent ways, in his more generalized role as athlete and teammate),

[11] See George Saxon, "Immigrant Culture in a Stratified Society," *Modern Review*, II, No. 2, February 1948.
[12] Compare the discussion of Freud's playful work, pp. 331–333, below.

there can be a relaxation of certain older demands and a more detached enjoyment of perfection of play irrespective of partisanship.

The role of football tutor to the audience has been pushed heavily onto radio and TV announcers (some of whom will doubtless be mobile into the higher-status role of commentators on politics or symphony broadcasts). The managerial coalescence of local betting pools into several big oceans has also contributed to the audience stake in the game. Yet all that has so far been said does not wholly explain alumnus and subway-alumnus loyalties. It may be that we have to read into this interest of the older age groups a much more general aspect of American behavior: the pious and near-compulsory devotion of the older folks to whatever the younger folks are alleged to find important. The tension between the generations doubtless contributes to the hysterical note of solemnity in the efforts of some older age groups to control the ethics of the game, partly perhaps as a displacement of their efforts to control youthful sexuality.

And this problem in turn leads to questions about the high percentage of women in the American football audience, compared with that of any other country, and the high salience of women in football as compared with baseball imagery (in recent American football films, girls have been singled out as the most influential section of the spectators). The presence of these women heightens the sexual impact of everything in and around the game, from shoulderpads to the star system, as the popular folklore of the game recognizes. Although women are not expected to attend baseball games, when they do attend they are expected to understand them and to acquire, if not a "male" attitude, at least something approaching companionship on a basis of equality with their male escorts.[13]

For all its involvement with such elemental themes in American life, it may be that football has reached the apex of its audience appeal. With bigness comes vulnerability: "inter-industry" competition is invited, and so are rising costs — the players, though not yet unionized, learn early in high school of their market value and, like Jim in Huckleberry Finn, take pride in it.[14] The educators' counter-reformation cannot be laughed off. With the lack of ethnic worlds to conquer, we may soon find the now-decorous Irish of the Midwest embarrassed by Notre Dame's unbroken victories. Perhaps the period of innovation which began in 1823 at Rugby has about come to an end in the United States, with large changes likely to result only if the game is used as a device for acculturation to America, not by the vanishing stream of immigrants to that country, but by the rest of the world that will seek the secret of American victories on the playing fields of South Bend.

[13] Anthropologist Ray Birdwhistell convincingly argues that football players play with an eye to their prestige among teammates, other football players, and other men.

[14] Their pride varies to some extent with their place on the team. Linemen, with the exception of ends, have lower status than backfield men. Many players believe that backfields are consciously and unconsciously recruited from higher social strata than linemen.

B. Processes and Examples

1. Primary and Secondary Groups

When someone thinks of primary behavior, with its emphasis on spontaneity and informal controls, it may strike him as disorganized. However, human behavior is organized behavior, and individuals have different roles to play no matter what the relationship. Even Whyte's "Corner Boys" and their gangs are subject to certain types of organizing behavior. His Street Corner Society was a prime example of the technique of participant observation. Using this method, Whyte is able to show how clique behavior is organized, and the importance of recognizing that before one begins to analyze the individual's place in the larger society, he must first consider the individual's position in the primary group.

20   WILLIAM FOOTE WHYTE

Corner Boys: A Study of Clique Behavior

This paper presents some of the results of a study of leadership in informal groupings or gangs of corner boys in "Cornerville," a slum area of a large eastern city. The aim of the research was to develop methods whereby the position (rank or status) of the individual in his clique might be empirically determined; to study the bases of group cohesion and of the subordination and superordination of its members; and, finally, to work out means for determining the position of corner gangs in the social structure of the community.

While the explanation of behavior in informal social groupings is generally regarded as a basic problem of sociology, empirical studies of human society, comparable to those now available for animal and bird groupings,[1] are still in the early stages of development. Frederic Thrasher[2] has recognized the phenomenon of informal leadership and has presented some generalizations upon its nature in boys' gangs. F. J. Roethlisberger and W. J. Dickson,[3] in their Western Electric Company studies, have recognized the

Reprinted from *American Journal of Sociology,* Vol. XLVI (March, 1941), pp. 647–664, by permission of the author and The University of Chicago Press.

[1] Thorlief Schjelderup-Ebbe presents an authoritative discussion of research upon bird groupings in his "Social Behavior of Birds," chap. xx, pp. 947–972, in *Handbook of Social Psychology,* ed. Carl Murchison.

[2] *The Gang* (rev. ed.; Chicago: University of Chicago Press, 1936).

[3] *Management and the Worker* (Cambridge: Harvard University Press, 1939).

importance of informal groups of workers in labor relations and have contributed valuable data upon the nature of informal organization in the factory situation. J. L. Moreno[4] has developed a "sociometric" method of charting "social attraction-patterns" which has been applied by him, George Lundberg,[5] Helen Jennings,[6] and others to open a new and promising line of research. W. Lloyd Warner[7] has applied the techniques of social anthropology to the study of groups in modern American society; and, following this approach, Eliot Chapple and Conrad Arensberg[8] have developed a method of studying social behavior by means of detailed observations of interactions.

My research is a product of this period of experimentation, based in part upon the work of Arensberg and Chapple. It differs from Thrasher's gang studies in several respects. He was dealing with young boys, few of them beyond their early teens. While my subjects called themselves corner boys, they were all grown men, most of them in their twenties, and some in their thirties. He studied the gang from the standpoint of juvenile delinquency and crime. While some of the men I observed were engaged in illegal activities, I was not interested in crime as such; instead, I was interested in studying the nature of clique behavior, regardless of whether or not the clique was connected with criminal activity. While Thrasher gathered extensive material upon 1,313 gangs, I made an intensive and detailed study of 5 gangs on the basis of personal observation, intimate acquaintance, and participation in their activities for an extended period of time. Throughout three and a half years of research, I lived in Cornerville, not in a settlement house, but in tenements such as are inhabited by Cornerville people.

The population of the district is almost entirely of Italian extraction. Most of the corner boys belong to the second generation of immigrants. In general, they are men who have had little education beyond grammar school and who are unemployed, irregularly employed, or working steadily for small wages.

Their name arises from the nature of their social life. For them "the corner" is not necessarily at a street intersection. It is any part of the sidewalk which they take for their social headquarters, and it often includes a poolroom, barroom, funeral parlor, barber-shop, or clubroom. Here they

[4] *Who Shall Survive? A New Approach to the Problem of Human Interrelations* (Washington, D.C.: Nervous and Mental Disease Publishing Co., 1934).

[5] Lundberg and Margaret Lawsing, "The Sociography of Some Community Relations," *American Sociological Review*, II (1937), 318–335; Lundberg and Mary Steele, "Social Attraction-Patterns in a Village," *Sociometry*, January–April, 1938, pp. 375–419.

[6] "Structure of Leadership," *Sociometry*, July–October, 1937, pp. 99–143.

[7] [There have been several studies all reported in the volume, *Social Class in America*, Warner, *et al.* (Chicago: Science Research Associates, 1949).]

[8] *Measuring Human Relations: An Introduction to the Study of the Interaction of Individuals* ("Genetic Psychology Monographs" [Provincetown, Mass.: Journal Press, 1940]).

may be found almost any afternoon or evening, talking and joking about sex, sports, personal relations, or politics in season. Other social activities either take place "on the corner" or are planned there.

The existence of a hierarchy of personal relations in these cliques is seldom explicitly recognized by the corner boys. Asked if they have a leader or boss, they invariably reply, "No, we're all equal." It is only through the observation of actions that the group structure becomes apparent. My problem was to apply methods which would produce an objective and reasonably exact picture of such structures.

In any group containing more than two people there are subdivisions to be observed. No member is equally friendly with all other members. In order to understand the behavior of the individual member it is necessary to place him not only in his group but also in his particular position in the subgroup.

My most complete study of groupings was made from observations in the rooms of the Cornerville Social and Athletic Club. This was a club of corner boys, which had a membership of about fifty and was divided primarily into two cliques, which had been relatively independent of each other before the formation of the club. There were, of course, subdivisions in each clique.

I sought to make a record of the groupings in which I found the members whenever I went into the club. While the men were moving around, I would be unable to retain their movements for my record, but on most occasions they would settle down in certain spatial arrangements. In the accompanying example (Fig. 1) two were at a table playing checkers with one watching, four at another table playing whist and three more watching the game, and six talking together toward the back of the room. As I looked around the room, I would count the number of men present so that I should know later how many I should have to account for. Then I would say over to myself the names of the men in each grouping and try to fix in my mind their positions in relation to one another. In the course of an evening there might be a general reshuffling of positions. I would not be able to remember every movement, but I would try to observe with which members the movements began; and, when another spatial arrangement had developed, I would go through the same mental process as I had with the first. As soon as I got home from the club, I would draw a map or maps of the spatial positions I had observed and add any movements between positions which I recalled. The map (Fig. 1) indicates the sort of data that came out of these observations.

In this case I have the following notes on movements of the members:

> Eleven walked over to One and pinched his cheek hard, went out of the club rooms, returned and pinched cheek again. One pretended to threaten Eleven with an ash tray. Eleven laughed and returned to seat on couch. I [the observer] asked Eleven about the purpose

THE CORNERVILLE S & A CLUB
February 29, 1940   8–8:15 P.M.

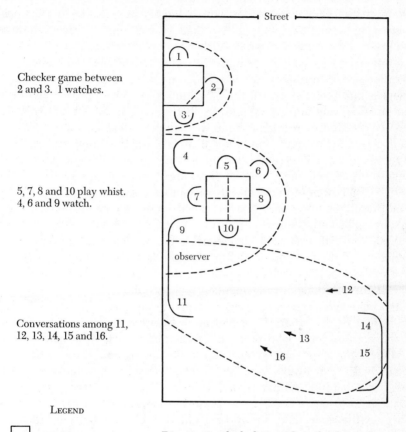

Checker game between
2 and 3. 1 watches.

5, 7, 8 and 10 play whist.
4, 6 and 9 watch.

Conversations among 11,
12, 13, 14, 15 and 16.

LEGEND

Tables

Straight chairs

Couches

Easy chairs

Direction in which chairs and couches face indicates
direction in which men face.
Arrows indicate direction in which standing men face.
Dotted lines enclose those interacting.

FIG. 1

of the club meeting. He asked Ten and Ten explained. Eleven
laughed and shrugged his shoulders. Sixteen, the janitor, served beer
for the card players.

On the basis of a number of maps such as this it is not difficult to place
most of the men in the clique and grouping within the clique to which they

belong. I did not attempt to place all the men, because the club had a fluctuating membership and some of the men were available for observation for only a short time. There were, throughout the ten months of my observation, some thirty-odd members who were active most of the time. Events in the club could be explained largely in terms of the actions of these men; and, therefore, when I had placed them in relation to one another, I did not need to press further in this direction.

Positional map-making is simply an extension of the techniques of observation and recording which have been used in the past by social anthropologists and sociologists. All these techniques require practice before they can be effectively applied. While my first maps left out a number of men, later I was able to record accurately enough so that on most occasions I could account for every man present at a particular time; and on several occasions I was able to work out two maps giving different positional arrangements during the course of the same period of observation. Beyond two I did not attempt to go, and it was not necessary to do so because there would rarely be more than two positional arrangements in the course of an evening sufficiently different from one another to require additional maps.

While the data from such maps enable one to determine groupings, they do not reveal the position or rank of the men in the groupings. For this purpose other data are needed. In practice they may be gathered at the same time as the positional arrangements are observed.

As I conceive it, position in the informal group means power to influence the actions of the group. I concentrated my attention upon the origination of action, to observe who proposed an action, to whom he made the proposal, and the steps that followed up to the completion of the action. I was dealing with "pair events" and "set events," to use the terminology of Arensberg and Chapple.[9] A "pair event" is an event between two people. A "set event" is an event in which one person originates action for two or more others at the same time. In working out the relations between men in an informal group, this is an important distinction to bear in mind. I found that observations of pair events did not provide a safe guide for the ranking of the members of the pair. At times A would originate action for B, at other times B would originate action for A. In some cases there would be a predominance of originations in one direction; but on the whole the data did not support rankings based upon quantitative comparisons of the rates of origination of action in pair events. Qualitatively one could say that when A originated action for B he used a tone of voice and words which indicated that he held a superior position. To take the extreme case, it is not difficult to tell the difference between an order and a request, although both may originate action. It is not safe, however, to rely upon such qualitative differences. The observer may read into the situation his own impres-

---

[9] *Op. cit.*

sion of the relative positions of the men and thus lose the objective basis for his conclusions.

It is observation of set events which reveals the hierarchical basis of informal group organization. As defined by Arensberg and Chapple,

> a *set* is an aggregate of relations such that every individual related in the set is a member either (*a*) of a class of individuals who only originate action, or (*b*) of an intermediate class of individuals who at some time originate action and at another time terminate action, or (*c*) of a class of individuals who only terminate action.[10]

Study of corner-boy groups reveals that the members may, indeed, be divided and ranked upon this basis. Several examples will illustrate.

INFORMAL ORGANIZATION OF THE CORNERVILLE S & A CLUB
February 1940

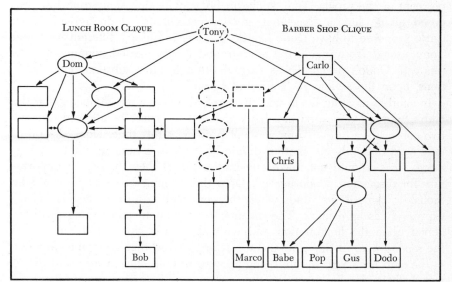

LEGEND

⬭ Members employed in the policy racket organization.

▭ Members not employed in the policy racket organization.

---- Those infrequently present.
Level of boxes indicates relative status.
Arrows indicate chief lines of influence.
For purposes of simplification, names of members not
   mentioned in text are omitted.

FIG. 2

---

[10] *Op. cit.*, p. 54. To terminate an action is to follow the initiative of another person.

At the top of the Cornerville S. and A. Club (see Fig. 2), we have Tony, Carlo, and Dom. They were the only ones who could originate action for the entire club. At the bottom were Dodo, Gus, Pop, Babe, Marco, and Bob, who never originated action in a set event involving anyone above their positions. Most of the members fell into the intermediate class. They terminated action on the part of the top men and originated action for the bottom men. Observations of the actions of the men of the intermediate class when neither top nor bottom men were present revealed that there were subdivisions or rankings within that class. This does not mean that the intermediate or bottom men never have any ideas as to what the club should do. It means that their ideas must go through the proper channels if they are to go into effect.

In one meeting of the Cornerville S. and A. Club, Dodo proposed that he be allowed to handle the sale of beer in the clubrooms in return for 75 per cent of the profits. Tony spoke in favor of Dodo's suggestion but proposed giving him a somewhat smaller percentage. Dodo agreed. Then Carlo proposed to have Dodo handle the beer in quite a different way, and Tony agreed. Tony made the motion, and it was carried unanimously. In this case Dodo's proposal was carried through, after substantial modifications, upon the actions of Tony and Carlo.

In another meeting Dodo said that he had two motions to make: that the club's funds be deposited in a bank and that no officer be allowed to serve two consecutive terms. Tony was not present at this time. Dom, the president, said that only one motion should be made at a time and that, furthermore, Dodo should not make any motions until there had been opportunity for discussion. Dodo agreed. Dom then commented that it would be foolish to deposit the funds when the club had so little to deposit. Carlo expressed his agreement. The meeting passed on to other things without action upon the first motion and without even a word of discussion on the second one. In the same meeting Chris moved that a member must be in the club for a year before being allowed to hold office. Carlo said that it was a good idea, he seconded the motion, and it carried unanimously.

All my observations indicate that the idea for group action which is carried out must originate with the top man or be accepted by him so that he acts upon the group. A follower may originate action for a leader in a pair event, but he does not originate action for the leader and other followers at the same time — that is, he does not originate action in a set event which includes the leader.

One may also observe that, when the leader originates action for the group, he does not act as if his followers were all of equal rank. Implicitly he takes the structure of the group into account. An example taken from the corner gang known as the "Millers" will illustrate this point. The Millers were a group of twenty corner boys, who were divided into two subgroups. Members of both subgroups frequently acted together; but, when two activities occupied the men at the same time, the division generally fell between the subgroups. Sam was the leader of the Millers. Joe was directly below him in one subgroup. Chichi led the other subgroup. Joe as well as Sam was in a position to originate action for Chichi and his subgroup.

It was customary for the Millers to go bowling every Saturday night. On this particular Saturday night Sam had no money, so he set out to persuade the boys to do something else. They followed his suggestion. Later Sam explained to me how he had been able to change the established social routine of the group. He said:

> I had to show the boys that it would be in their own interests to come with me — that each one of them would benefit. But I knew I only had to convince two of the fellows. If they start to do something, the other boys will say to themselves, "If Joe does it — or if Chichi does it—it must be a good thing for us too." I told Joe and Chichi what the idea was, and I got them to come with me. I didn't pay no attention to the others. When Joe and Chichi came, all the other boys came along too.

Another example from the Millers indicates what happens when the leader and the man next to him in rank disagree upon group policy. This is Sam talking again:

> One time we had a raffle to raise money to build a camp on Lake ———— [on property lent them by a local business man]. We had collected $54, and Joe and I were holding the money. . . . That week I knew Joe was playing pool, and he lost three or four dollars gambling. When Saturday came, I says to the boys, "Come on, we go out to Lake ————. We're gonna build that camp on the hill . . . ." Right away Joe said, "If yuz are gonna build the camp on the hill, I don't come. I want it on the other side. . . ." All the time I knew he had lost the money, and he was only making up excuses so he wouldn't have to let anybody know. . . . Now the hill was really the place to build that camp. On the other side, the ground was swampy. That would have been a stupid place. . . . But I knew that if I tried to make them go through with it now, the group would split up into two cliques. Some would come with me, and some would go with Joe. . . . So I let the whole thing drop for a while. . . . After, I got Joe alone, and I says to him, "Joe, I know you lost some of that money, but that's all right. You can pay up when you have it and nobody will say nothin'. But Joe, you know we shouldn't have the camp on the other side of the hill because the land is no good there. We should build it on the hill. . . ." So he said, "All right," and we got all the boys together, and we went out to build the camp.

Under ordinary circumstances the leader implicitly recognizes and helps to maintain the position of the man or men immediately below him, and the group functions smoothly. In this respect the informal organization is similar to the formal organization. If the executive in a factory attempts to pass over his immediate subordinates and give orders directly to the men on the assembly line, he creates confusion. The customary channels must be used.

The social structures vary from group to group, but each one may be represented in some form of hierarchy. The members have clearly defined relations of subordination and superordination, and each group has a leader. Since we are concerned with informal organization, the Cornerville S. and A. members must be considered as two groups, with Carlo leading the barber-shop boys, and Dom leading the lunchroom boys. Since Tony's position requires special consideration, he will be discussed later.

Observation not only serves to provide a description of the group structure. It also reveals information upon the bases of structure and the factors differentiating between the positions of members. The clique structure arises out of the habitual association of the members over a long period of time. The nuclei of most gangs can be traced back to early boyhood years when living close together provided the first opportunities for social contacts. School years modified the original pattern somewhat, but I know of no corner gangs which arose through classroom or school-playground association. The gangs grew up "on the corner" and have remained there with remarkable persistence. In the course of years some groups have been broken up by the movement of families away from Cornerville, and the remaining members have merged with gangs on near-by corners; but frequently movement out of the district does not take the corner boy away from his corner. On any evening in Cornerville on almost any corner one finds corner boys who have come in from other parts of the city or from suburbs to be with their old friends. The residence of the corner boy may also change within the district, but nearly always he retains his allegiance to his original corner.

The leader of one group spoke to me in this way about corner boys:

> Fellows around here don't know what to do except within a radius of about 300 yards. That's the truth, Bill. . . . They come home from work, hang on the corner, go up to eat, back on the corner, up (to) a show, and they come back to hang on the corner. If they're not on the corner, it's likely the boys there will know where you can find them. . . . Most of them stick to one corner. It's only rarely that a fellow will change his corner.

The stable composition of the group over a long period and the lack of social assurance felt by most of the members contribute toward producing a very high rate of social interaction within the group. The structure to be observed is a product of past interactions.

Out of these interactions there arises a system of mutual obligations which is fundamental to group cohesion. If the men are to carry on their activities as a unit, there are many occasions when they must do favors for one another. Frequently, one member must spend money to help another who does not have the money to participate in some of the group activities. This creates an obligation. If the situation is later reversed, the recipient is expected to help the man who gave him aid. The code of the corner boy requires him to help his friends when he can and to refrain from doing anything to harm them. When life in the group runs smoothly, the mutual obligations binding members to one another are not explicitly recognized. A corner boy, asked if he helped a fellow-member because of a sense of obligation, will reply, "No, I didn't have to do it. He's my friend. That's all." It is only when the relationship breaks down that the underlying obligations are brought to light. When two members of the group have a falling-out, their actions form a familiar pattern. One tells a story something like this: "What a heel Blank turned out to be. After all I've done for him, the first time I ask him to do something for me, he won't do it." The other may say: "What does he want from me? I've done plenty for him, but he wants you to do everything." In other words, the actions which were performed explicitly for the sake of friendship are now revealed as being part of a system of mutual obligations.

Not all the corner boys live up to their obligations equally well, and this factor partly accounts for the differentiation in status among the men. The man with a low status may violate his obligations without much change in his position. His fellows know that he has failed to discharge certain obligations in the past, and his position reflects his past performances. On the other hand, the leader is depended upon by all the members to meet his personal obligations. He cannot often fail to do so without causing confusion and losing his position. The relationship of status to the system of mutual obligations is most clearly revealed when we consider the use of money. While all the men are expected to be generous, the flow of money between members can be explained only in terms of the group structure.

The Millers provide an illustration of this point. During the time that I knew them, Sam, the leader, was out of work except for an occasional odd job; yet, whenever he had a little money, he spent it on Joe and Chichi, his closest friends, who were next to him in the structure of the group. When Joe or Chichi had money, which was less frequent, they reciprocated. Sam frequently paid for two members who stood close to the bottom of the structure and occasionally for others. The two men who held positions immediately below Joe and Chichi in the subgroups were considered very well off according to Cornerville standards. Sam said that he occasionally borrowed money from them, but never more than fifty cents at a time. Such loans he tried to repay at the earliest possible moment. There were four other members, with positions ranging from intermediate to the bottom, who nearly always had more money than Sam. He did not recall ever having borrowed from them. He said that the only time he had obtained a substantial sum from anyone around his corner was when he borrowed eleven dollars from a friend who was the *leader* of another corner-boy group.

The system is substantially the same for all the groups on which I have information. The leader spends more money on his followers than they on him. The farther down in the structure one looks, the fewer are the financial relations which tend to obligate the leader to a follower. This does not mean that the leader has more money than others or even that he necessarily spends more — though he must always be a free spender. It means that the financial relations must be explained in social terms. Unconsciously, and in some cases consciously, the leader refrains from putting himself under obligations to those with low status in the group.

Relations of rivalry or outright hostility with other groups are an important factor in promoting in-group solidarity, as has been well recognized in the literature. Present-day corner gangs grew up in an atmosphere of street fighting against gangs of Irish or of fellow-Italians. While actual fights are now infrequent, the spirit of gang loyalty is maintained in part through athletic contests and political rivalries.

As the structures indicate, members have higher rates of interaction with men close to their own positions in their subgroups than with men who rank much higher or much lower or belong to a different subgroup. That is a significant fact for the explanation of group cohesion.

In the case of the Millers, Sam's best friends were Joe and Chichi. As his remarks have indicated, Sam realized that the solidarity of the Millers depended in the first instance upon the existence of friendly and co-operative relations between himself, Joe, and Chichi. A Cornerville friend, who was aware of the nature of my observations, commented in this manner:

> On any corner, you would find not only a leader but probably a couple of lieutenants. They could be leaders themselves, but they let the man lead them. You would say, They let him lead because they like the way he does things. Sure, but he leans upon them for his authority. . . . Many times you find fellows on a corner that stay in the background until some situation comes up, and then they will take over and call the shots. Things like that can change fast sometimes.

Such changes are the result not of an uprising of the bottom men but of a shift in the relations between men at the top of the structure. When a gang breaks into two parts, the explanation is to be found in a conflict between the leader and one who ranked close to him in the structure of the original gang.

The distinctive functions of the top men in promoting social cohesion are readily observable in the field. Frequently, in the absence of their leader the members of a gang are divided into a number of small groups. There is no common activity or general conversation. When the leader appears, the situation changes strikingly. The small units form into one large group. The conversation becomes general, and unified action frequently follows. The leader becomes the focal point in discussion. One observes a follower start to say something, pause when he notices that the leader is not listening, and begin again when he has the leader's attention. When the leader leaves the group, unity gives way to the divisions that existed before his appearance. To a certain extent the lieutenants can perform this unifying function; but their scope is more limited because they are more closely identified with one particular subgroup than is the leader.

The same Cornerville friend summed up the point in this way:

> If we leave the followers, they'll go find some other leader. They won't know what they're doing, but that's what they'll do, because by themselves they won't know what to do. They gather around the leader, and it is the leader that keeps them together.

The leader is the man who knows what to do. He is more resourceful than his followers. Past events have shown that his ideas were right. In this sense "right" simply means satisfactory to the members. He is the most independent in judgment. While his followers are undecided as to a course of action or upon the character of a newcomer, the leader makes up his mind. When he gives his word to one of "his boys," he keeps it. The followers look to him for advice and encouragement, and he receives more of the confidences of the members than any other man. Consequently, he knows more about what is going on in the group than anyone else. Whenever there is a quarrel among the boys, he will hear of it almost as soon as it happens. Each party to the quarrel may appeal to him to work out a solution; and, even when the men do not want to compose their differences, each one will take his side of the story to the leader at the first opportunity. A man's standing depends partly upon the leader's belief that he has been conducting himself as he should.

The leader is respected for his fair-mindedness. Whereas there may be hard feelings among some of the followers, the leader cannot bear a grudge against any man in the group. He has close friends (men who stand next to him in position), and he is indifferent to some of the members; but if he is to retain his reputation for impartiality, he cannot allow personal animus to override his judgment.

The leader need not be the best baseball player, bowler, or fighter, but he must have some skill in whatever pursuits are of particular interest to the group. It is natural for him to promote activities in which he excels and to discourage those in which he is not skilful; and, in so far as he is thus able to influence the group, his competent performance is a natural consequence of his position. At the same time his performance supports his position.

It is significant to note that the leader is better known and more respected outside of his group than is any of his followers. His social mobility is greater. One of the most important functions he performs is that of relating his group to other groups in the district. His reputation outside the group tends to support his standing within the group, and his position in the group supports his reputation among outsiders.

It should not be assumed from this discussion that the corner boys compete with one another for the purpose of gaining leadership. Leadership is a product of social interaction. The men who reach the top in informal groups are those who can perform skilfully the actions required by the situation. Most such skills are performed without long premeditation.

What the leader is has been discussed in terms of what he does. I doubt whether an analysis in terms of his personality traits will add anything to such an explanation of behavior. One can find a great variety of personality traits among corner-boy leaders, just as one can among business or political leaders. Some are aggressive in social contacts, and others appear almost retiring. Some are talkative, and others have little to say. Few uniformities of this nature are to be found. On the other hand, there are marked uniformities to be observed in the functions performed by men who hold similar positions in society, and the study of them promises to provide the best clues for the understanding of social behavior.

For a community study, data upon five corner gangs are hardly more than a beginning. Two problems were involved in extending the research. First, I had to discover whether I could safely generalize my conclusions to apply them to all corner gangs in Cornerville. Second, I had to fit the corner gangs into the fabric of Cornerville society.

To accomplish the first end I solicited the aid of a number of corner-boy leaders, who made for me more or less systematic observations of their own groups and of groups about them. The generalizations, presented earlier, upon the functions of leaders, indicate why I found them the best sources of information upon their groups. This procedure could not be relied upon as a substitute for observation, for it is only through observation that the student can discover what his informants are talking about and understand their remarks in terms of group structure. Observation suggests a framework of significant behavior patterns and indicates subjects that are relevant for discussion with informants.

The student should realize that this procedure changes the attitude of the corner boy toward himself and his group. The quotations from Cornerville men presented here all show the effects of prior discussion with me. However, the effort of informants to make explicit statements upon unreflective behavior does not distort the factual picture as long as they are required to tell their stories in terms of observed interactions.

The most thorough study of this kind was made for me by Sam of the Millers upon his own group. The structure of the Millers was worked out by Sam over a period of months on the basis of such material as I have quoted. My function was to discuss Sam's observations with him, to point out gaps in his data, and to check them with some independent observations.

All the generalizations presented here have been checked against the experience and observations of four such informants. In this way I have been able to expand my study far beyond what I should have been able to cover alone.

Accomplishment of the second purpose — fitting corner gangs into the fabric of society — required study of the relations which linked group to group and the group to persons who held superior positions in Cornerville — politicians and racketeers, for example.

The observation that the leader is the person to relate his group to other people provides the most important lead for such a study. We see that the social behavior of groups pivots around the actions of certain men who hold strategic positions in them. This does not mean that the leader can make his followers do anything he desires. It does mean that he customarily leads the group activity and that outsiders, in order to influence the members, must deal with the group through him. This is to be observed particularly at the time of a political campaign when politicians seek to mobilize group support. Similar observations may be made in order to explain the position and influence of the racketeer in relation to corner-boy groups.

Brief reference to the Cornerville S. and A. study will indicate the nature of the results that may be obtained. Tony, the top man in the chart, was a prominent policy racketeer. The chart indicates that certain members were agents who turned their policy slips in to him. While Tony belonged to the club, his interests were so widespread that he had little time to spend with the members. It was recognized that he held a higher status, that he was not a corner boy.

At the time of the formation of the club, Tony knew Dom, his agent, and recognized Dom's position among the lunchroom boys. He knew Carlo only casually and was not aware of his position as leader of the barber-shop clique. In the course of a political campaign (November, 1939) a conflict arose over the indorsement of a candidate for alderman. By playing off one clique against the other, Tony was able to secure the adoption of his policy, but Carlo opposed him vigorously and lost out in a close vote. Carlo's position was strengthened when his candidate defeated the man supported by Tony. Following the election, there was a marked change in Tony's actions. He began to attend every meeting and to spend more time with the members. For his purposes Carlo was the most important man in the club, and he made every effort to cement his social relations with Carlo and to place Carlo under obligations to him. During this period a basis for co-operation between the two men was established. When Tony turned his attention to other activities, he was able to deal with the club through Carlo as well as through Dom.

This story illustrates a method of study, not a set of conclusions. Through observing the interactions between Tony and Dom, Tony and Carlo, Dom and the members of his clique, and Carlo and the members of his clique, one can establish the position and influence of the racketeer in relation to this particular organization of corner boys. Other observations establish Tony's position in the racket organization, which extends throughout the district and far beyond it. They also point out Tony's relations with certain politicians. Only in the study of such specific situations can one arrive at reliable generalizations upon the positions and influence of men in the community.

The methods I have used call for precise and detailed observation of spatial positions and of the origination of action in pair and set events between members of informal groups. Such observations provide data by means of which one may chart structures of social relations and determine the basis of the structures — a system of mutual obligations growing out of the interactions of the members over a long period of time. Observations also point out the distinctive functions of the leader, who serves as chief representative of his group and director and co-ordinator of group activity. A knowledge of the structure and of the social processes carried on through it serves to explain the behavior of individual members in a manner which could not be accomplished if one considered the men as an unstructured aggregation.

Such an understanding of clique behavior seems a necessary first step in the development of knowledge of the nature of the larger social organization into which the cliques fit. Instead of seeking to place each clique member in relation to the total social organization, the investigator may concentrate his attention upon the actions of the leader, who relates his corner boys to other groups and to persons holding superior positions. By discovering these strategic points for social integration and by extending the network of social relations through them, the investigator can place a large number of the inhabitants of his community in their social positions.

This is a painstaking and time-consuming method. While it does not produce statistics which count all the inhabitants in terms of certain characteristics, it does provide the investigator with a close-up view of the social organization in action.

2. Formal Organizations

Thorstein Veblen, best known for his Theory of the Leisure Class, *referred to the behavior of certain bureaucratic officials as "trained incapacity." A fine example would be chickens trained in the Pavlovian manner to associate the sound of a bell with meals. The bell can then be used to summon the chickens to be fed or to be killed. The bureaucratic official who is trained to respond to a phenomenon by manipulating it in a particular manner may come to believe that phenomena which cannot be classified in his traditional manner are not worthy of consideration. Robert K. Merton, a contemporary social theorist, uses the term "bureaucratic virtuoso" for the person who has transferred his sentiments from the goals of the organization to the means by which the goals are to be accomplished. This may ultimately lead to inaccurate perception of the goals or complete disregard of them.*

21   ROBERT K. MERTON

Bureaucratic Structure and Personality

A formal, rationally organized social structure involves clearly defined patterns of activity in which, ideally, every series of actions is functionally related to the purposes of the organization.[1] In such an organization there is integrated a series of offices, of hierarchized statuses, in which inhere a number of obligations and privileges closely defined by limited and specific rules. Each of these offices contains an area of imputed competence and responsibility. Authority, the power of control which derives from an acknowledged status, inheres in the office and not in the particular person who performs the official role. Official action ordinarily occurs within the framework of preexisting rules of the organization. The system of prescribed relations between the various offices involves a considerable degree of formality and clearly defined social distance between the occupants of these positions. Formality is manifested by means of a more or less complicated social ritual which symbolizes and supports the pecking order of

[1] For a development of the concept of "rational organization," see Karl Mannheim, *Mensch und Gesellschaft im Zeitalter des Umbaus* (Leiden: A. W. Sijthoff, 1935), esp. 28 ff.

the various offices. Such formality, which is integrated with the distribution of authority within the system, serves to minimize friction by largely restricting (official) contact to modes which are previously defined by the rules of the organization. Ready calculability of others' behavior and a stable set of mutual expectations is thus built up. Moreover, formality facilitates the interaction of the occupants of offices despite their (possibly hostile) private attitudes toward one another. In this way, the subordinate is protected from the arbitrary action of his superior, since the actions of both are constrained by a mutually recognized set of rules. Specific procedural devices foster objectivity and restrain the "quick passage of impulse into action."[2]

THE STRUCTURE OF BUREAUCRACY

The ideal type of such formal organization is bureaucracy and, in many respects, the classical analysis of bureaucracy is that by Max Weber.[3] As Weber indicates, bureaucracy involves a clear-cut division of integrated activities which are regarded as duties inherent in the office. A system of differentiated controls and sanctions is stated in the regulations. The assignment of roles occurs on the basis of technical qualifications which are ascertained through formalized, impersonal procedures (e.g., examinations). Within the structure of hierarchically arranged authority, the activities of "trained and salaried experts" are governed by general, abstract, and clearly defined rules which preclude the necessity for the issuance of specific instructions for each specific case. The generality of the rules requires the constant use of *categorization*, whereby individual problems and cases are classified on the basis of designated criteria and are treated accordingly. The pure type of bureaucratic official is appointed, either by a superior or through the exercise of impersonal competition; he is not elected. A measure of flexibility in the bureaucracy is attained by electing higher functionaries who presumably express the will of the electorate (e.g., a body of citizens or a board of directors). The election of higher officials is designed to affect the purposes of the organization, but the technical procedures for attaining these ends are carried out by continuing bureaucratic personnel.[4]

Most bureaucratic offices involve the expectation of life-long tenure, in the absence of disturbing factors which may decrease the size of the organization. Bureaucracy maximizes vocational security.[5] The function of

---

[2] H. D. Lasswell, *Politics* (New York: McGraw-Hill, 1936), 120–121.

[3] Max Weber, *Wirtschaft und Gesellschaft* (Tübingen: J. C. B. Mohr, 1922), Pt. III, chap. 6, 650–678. For a brief summary of Weber's discussion, see Talcott Parsons, *The Structure of Social Action*, esp. 506 ff. For a description, which is not a caricature, of the bureaucrat as a personality type, see C. Rabany, "Les types sociaux: le fonctionnaire," *Revue générale d'administration*, 1907, 88, 5–28.

[4] Karl Mannheim, *Ideology and Utopia* (New York: Harcourt, Brace, 1936), 18n., 105 ff. See also Ramsay Muir, *Peers and Bureaucrats* (London: Constable, 1910), 12–13.

[5] E. G. Cahen-Salvador suggests that the personnel of bureaucracies is largely constituted by those who value security above all else. See his "La situation matérielle et morale des fonctionnaires," *Revue politique et parlementaire* (1926), 319.

security of tenure, pensions, incremental salaries and regularized procedures for promotion is to ensure the devoted performance of official duties,
without regard for extraneous pressures.[6] The chief merit of bureaucracy
is its technical efficiency, with a premium placed on precision, speed, expert control, continuity, discretion, and optimal returns on input. The
structure is one which approaches the complete elimination of personalized
relationships and nonrational considerations (hostility, anxiety, affectual
involvements, etc.).

With increasing bureaucratization, it becomes plain to all who would see
that man is to a very important degree controlled by his social relations to
the instruments of production. This can no longer seem only a tenet of
Marxism, but a stubborn fact to be acknowledged by all, quite apart from
their ideological persuasion. Bureaucratization makes readily visible what
was previously dim and obscure. More and more people discover that to
work, they must be employed. For to work, one must have tools and equipment. And the tools and equipment are increasingly available only in
bureaucracies, private or public. Consequently, one must be employed by
the bureaucracies in order to have access to tools in order to work in order
to live. It is in this sense that bureaucratization entails separation of individuals from the instruments of production, as in modern capitalistic enterprise or in state communistic enterprise (of the midcentury variety), just
as in the post-feudal army, bureaucratization entailed complete separation
from the instruments of destruction. Typically, the worker no longer owns
his tools nor the soldier, his weapons. And in this special sense, more and
more people become workers, either blue collar or white collar or stiff shirt.
So develops, for example, the new type of scientific worker, as the scientist
is "separated" from his technical equipment — after all, the physicist does
not ordinarily own his cyclotron. To work at his research, he must be employed by a bureaucracy with laboratory resources.

Bureaucracy is administration which almost completely avoids public
discussion of its techniques, although there may occur public discussion of
its policies.[7] This secrecy is confined neither to public nor to private bureaucracies. It is held to be necessary to keep valuable information from
private economic competitors or from foreign and potentially hostile political groups. And though it is not often so called, espionage among competitors is perhaps as common, if not as intricately organized, in systems
of private economic enterprise as in systems of national states. Cost figures,
lists of clients, new technical processes, plans for production — all these
are typically regarded as essential secrets of private economic bureaucracies
which might be revealed if the bases of all decisions and policies had to be
publicly defended.

[6] H. J. Laski, "Bureaucracy," *Encyclopedia of the Social Sciences.* This article is
written primarily from the standpoint of the political scientist rather than that of the
sociologist.

[7] Weber, *op. cit.,* 671.

THE DYSFUNCTIONS OF BUREAUCRACY

In these bold outlines, the positive attainments and functions of bureaucratic organization are emphasized and the internal stresses and strains of such structures are almost wholly neglected. The community at large, however, evidently emphasizes the imperfections of bureaucracy, as is suggested by the fact that the "horrid hybrid," bureaucrat, has become an epithet, a *Schimpfwort*.

The transition to a study of the negative aspects of bureaucracy is afforded by the application of Veblen's concept of "trained incapacity," Dewey's notion of "occupational psychosis" or Warnotte's view of "professional deformation." Trained incapacity refers to that state of affairs in which one's abilities function as inadequacies or blind spots. Actions based upon training and skills which have been successfully applied in the past may result in inappropriate responses *under changed conditions*. An inadequate flexibility in the application of skills, will, in a changing milieu, result in more or less serious maladjustments.[8] Thus, to adopt a barnyard illustration used in this connection by Burke, chickens may be readily conditioned to interpret the sound of a bell as a signal for food. The same bell may now be used to summon the trained chickens to their doom as they are assembled to suffer decapitation. In general, one adopts measures in keeping with one's past training and, under new conditions which are not recognized as *significantly* different, the very soundness of this training may lead to the adoption of the wrong procedures. Again, in Burke's almost echolalic phrase, "people may be unfitted by being fit in an unfit fitness"; their training may become an incapacity.

Dewey's concept of occupational psychosis rests upon much the same observations. As a result of their day to day routines, people develop special preferences, antipathies, discriminations and emphases.[9] (The term psychosis is used by Dewey to denote a "pronounced character of the mind.") These psychoses develop through demands put upon the individual by the particular organization of his occupational role.

The concepts of both Veblen and Dewey refer to a fundamental ambivalence. Any action can be considered in terms of what it attains or what it fails to attain. "A way of seeing is also a way of not seeing — a focus upon object A involves a neglect of object B."[10] In his discussion, Weber is almost exclusively concerned with what the bureaucratic structure attains: precision, reliability, efficiency. This same structure may be examined from

---

[8] For a stimulating discussion and application of these concepts, see Kenneth Burke, *Permanence and Change* (New York: New Republic, 1935), pp. 50 ff.; Daniel Warnotte, "Bureaucratie et Fonctionnarisme," *Revue de l'Institut de Sociologie*, 1937, 17, 245.

[9] *Ibid.*, 58–59.

[10] *Ibid.*, 70.

another perspective provided by the ambivalence. What are the limitations of the organizations designed to attain these goals?

For reasons which we have already noted, the bureaucratic structure exerts a constant pressure upon the official to be "methodical, prudent, disciplined." If the bureaucracy is to operate successfully, it must attain a high degree of reliability of behavior, an unusual degree of conformity with prescribed patterns of action. Hence, the fundamental importance of discipline, which may be as highly developed in a religious or economic bureaucracy as in the army. Discipline can be effective only if the ideal patterns are buttressed by strong sentiments which entail devotion to one's duties, a keen sense of the limitation of one's authority and competence, and methodical performance of routine activities. The efficacy of social structure depends ultimately upon infusing group participants with appropriate attitudes and sentiments. As we shall see, there are definite arrangements in the bureaucracy for inculcating and reinforcing these sentiments.

At the moment, it suffices to observe that in order to ensure discipline (the necessary reliability of response), these sentiments are often more intense than is technically necessary. There is a margin of safety, so to speak, in the pressure exerted by these sentiments upon the bureaucrat to conform to his patterned obligations, in much the same sense that added allowances (precautionary overestimations) are made by the engineer in designing the supports for a bridge. But this very emphasis leads to a transference of the sentiments from the *aims* of the organization onto the particular details of behavior required by the rules. Adherence to the rules, originally conceived as a means, becomes transformed into an end-in-itself; there occurs the familiar process of *displacement of goals* whereby "an instrumental value becomes a terminal value."[11] Discipline, readily interpreted as conformance with regulations, whatever the situation, is seen not as a measure designed for specific purposes but becomes an immediate value in the life-organization of the bureaucrat. This emphasis, resulting

[11] This process has often been observed in various connections. Wundt's *heterogony of ends* is a case in point; Max Weber's *Paradoxie der Folgen* is another. See also MacIver's observations on the transformation of civilization into culture and Lasswell's remark that "the human animal distinguishes himself by his infinite capacity for making ends of his means." See Merton, "The unanticipated consequences of purposive social action," *American Sociological Review*, 1936, 1, 894–904. In terms of the psychological mechanisms involved, this process has been analyzed most fully by Gordon W. Allport, in his discussion of what he calls "the functional autonomy of motives." Allport emends the earlier formulations of Woodworth, Tolman, and William Stern, and arrives at a statement of the process from the standpoint of individual motivation. He does not consider those phases of the social structure which conduce toward the "transformation of motives." The formulation adopted in this paper is thus complementary to Allport's analysis; the one stressing the psychological mechanisms involved, the other considering the constraints of the social structure. The convergence of psychology and sociology toward this central concept suggests that it may well constitute one of the conceptual bridges between the two disciplines. See Gordon W. Allport, *Personality* (New York: Henry Holt & Co., 1937), chap. 7.

from the displacement of the original goals, develops into rigidities and an inability to adjust readily. Formalism, even ritualism, ensues with an unchallenged insistence upon punctilious adherence to formalized procedures.[12] This may be exaggerated to the point where primary concern with conformity to the rules interferes with the achievement of the purposes of the organization, in which case we have the familiar phenomenon of the technicism or red tape of the official. An extreme product of this process of displacement of goals is the bureaucratic virtuoso, who never forgets a single rule binding his action and hence is unable to assist many of his clients.[13] A case in point, where strict recognition of the limits of authority and literal adherence to rules produced this result, is the pathetic plight of Bernt Balchen, Admiral Byrd's pilot in the flight over the South Pole.

> According to a ruling of the department of labor Bernt Balchen . . . cannot receive his citizenship papers. Balchen, a native of Norway, declared his intention in 1927. It is held that he has failed to meet the condition of five years' continuous residence in the United States. The Byrd antarctic voyage took him out of the country, although he was on a ship carrying the American flag, was an invaluable member of the American expedition, and in a region to which there is an American claim because of the exploration and occupation of it by Americans, this region being Little America.
>
> The bureau of naturalization explains that it cannot proceed on the assumption that Little America is American soil. That would be *trespass on international questions* where it has no sanction. So far as the bureau is concerned, Balchen was out of the country and *technically* has not complied with the law of naturalization.[14]

STRUCTURAL SOURCES OF OVERCONFORMITY

Such inadequacies in orientation which involve trained incapacity clearly derive from structural sources. The process may be briefly recapitulated. (1) An effective bureaucracy demands reliability of response and strict devotion to regulations. (2) Such devotion to the rules leads to their transformation into absolutes; they are no longer conceived as relative to a set of purposes. (3) This interferes with ready adaptation under special conditions not clearly envisaged by those who drew up the general rules. (4) Thus, the very elements which conduce toward efficiency in general produce inefficiency in specific instances. Full realization of the inadequacy is seldom attained by members of the group who have not divorced them-

---

[12] See E. C. Hughes, "Institutional office and the person," *American Journal of Sociology*, 1937, 43, 404–413; E. T. Hiller, "Social structure in relation to the person," *Social Forces*, 1937, 16, 34–40.

[13] Mannheim, *Ideology and Utopia*, 106.

[14] Quoted from the *Chicago Tribune* (June 24, 1931, p. 10) by Thurman Arnold, *The Symbols of Government* (New Haven: Yale University Press, 1935), 201–202. (My italics.)

selves from the meanings which the rules have for them. These rules in time become symbolic in cast, rather than strictly utilitarian.

Thus far, we have treated the ingrained sentiments making for rigorous discipline simply as data, as given. However, definite features of the bureaucratic structure may be seen to conduce to these sentiments. The bureaucrat's official life is planned for him in terms of a graded career, through the organizational devices of promotion by seniority, pensions, incremental salaries, etc., all of which are designed to provide incentives for disciplined action and conformity to the official regulations.[15] The official is tacitly expected to and largely does adapt his thoughts, feelings and actions to the prospect of this career. But *these very devices* which increase the probability of conformance also lead to an over-concern with strict adherence to regulations which induces timidity, conservatism, and technicism. Displacement of sentiments from goals onto means is fostered by the tremendous symbolic significance of the means (rules).

Another feature of the bureaucratic structure tends to produce much the same result. Functionaries have the sense of a common destiny for all those who work together. They share the same interests, especially since there is relatively little competition in so far as promotion is in terms of seniority. In-group aggression is thus minimized and this arrangement is therefore conceived to be positively functional for the bureaucracy. However, the esprit de corps and informal social organization which typically develops in such situations often leads the personnel to defend their entrenched interests rather than to assist their clientele and elected higher officials. As President Lowell reports, if the bureaucrats believe that their status is not adequately recognized by an incoming elected official, detailed information will be withheld from him, leading him to errors for which he is held responsible. Or, if he seeks to dominate fully, and thus violates the sentiment of self-integrity of the bureaucrats, he may have documents brought to him in such numbers that he cannot manage to sign them all, let alone read them.[16] This illustrates the defensive informal organization which tends to arise whenever there is an apparent threat to the integrity of the group.[17]

It would be much too facile and partly erroneous to attribute such resistance by bureaucrats simply to vested interests. Vested interests oppose any new order which either eliminates or at least makes uncertain their differential advantage deriving from the current arrangements. This is undoubtedly involved in part in bureaucratic resistance to change but another pro-

[15] Mannheim, *Mensch und Gesellschaft*, 32–33. Mannheim stresses the importance of the "Lebensplan" and the "Amtskarriere." See the comments by Hughes, *op. cit.*, 413.

[16] A. L. Lowell, *The Government of England* (New York, 1908), I, 189 ff.

[17] For an instructive description of the development of such a defensive organization in a group of workers, see F. J. Roethlisberger and W. J. Dickson, *Management and the Worker* (Boston: Harvard School of Business Administration, 1934).

cess is perhaps more significant. As we have seen, bureaucratic officials affectively identify themselves with their way of life. They have a pride of craft which leads them to resist change in established routines; at least, those changes which are felt to be imposed by others. This nonlogical pride of craft is a familiar pattern found even, to judge from Sutherland's *Professional Thief*, among pickpockets who, despite the risk, delight in mastering the prestige-bearing feat of "beating a left breech" (picking the left front trousers pocket).

In a stimulating paper, Hughes has applied the concepts of "secular" and "sacred" to various types of division of labor; "the sacredness" of caste and *Stände* prerogatives contrasts sharply with the increasing secularism of occupational differentiation in our society.[18] However, as our discussion suggests, there may ensue, in particular vocations and in particular types of organization, the *process of sanctification* (viewed as the counterpart of the process of secularization). This is to say that through sentiment-formation, emotional dependence upon bureaucratic symbols and status, and affective involvement in spheres of competence and authority, there develop prerogatives involving attitudes of moral legitimacy which are established as values in their own right, and are no longer viewed as merely technical means for expediting administration. One may note a tendency for certain bureaucratic norms, originally introduced for technical reasons, to become rigidified and sacred, although, as Durkheim would say, they are *laïque en apparence*.[19] Durkheim has touched on this general process in his description of the attitudes and values which persist in the organic solidarity of a highly differentiated society.

PRIMARY VS. SECONDARY RELATIONS

Another feature of the bureaucratic structure, the stress on depersonalization of relationships, also plays its part in the bureaucrat's trained incapacity. The personality pattern of the bureaucrat is nucleated about this norm of impersonality. Both this and the categorizing tendency, which develops from the dominant role of general, abstract rules, tend to produce conflict in the bureaucrat's contacts with the public or clientele. Since functionaries minimize personal relations and resort to categorization, the peculiarities of

[18] E. C. Hughes, "Personality types and the division of labor," *American Journal of Sociology*, 1928, 33, 754–768. Much the same distinction is drawn by Leopold von Wiese and Howard Becker, *Systematic Sociology* (New York: John Wiley & Sons, 1932), 222–225 *et passim*.

[19] Hughes recognizes one phase of this process of sanctification when he writes that professional training "carries with it as a by-product assimilation of the candidate to a set of professional attitudes and controls, *a professional conscience and solidarity. The profession claims and aims to become a moral unit.*" Hughes, *op. cit.*, 762 (italics inserted). In this same connection, Sumner's concept of *pathos*, as the halo of sentiment which protects a social value from criticism, is particularly relevant, inasmuch as it affords a clue to the mechanism involved in the process of sanctification. See his *Folkways*, 180–181.

individual cases are often ignored. But the client who, quite understandably, is convinced of the special features of *his* own problem often objects to such categorical treatment. Stereotyped behavior is not adapted to the exigencies of individual problems. The impersonal treatment of affairs which are at times of great personal significance to the client gives rise to the charge of "arrogance" and "haughtiness" of the bureaucrat. Thus, at the Greenwich Employment Exchange, the unemployed worker who is securing his insurance payment resents what he deems to be "the impersonality and, at times, the apparent abruptness and even harshness of his treatment by the clerks. . . . Some men complain of the superior attitude which the clerks have."[20]

Still another source of conflict with the public derives from the bureaucratic structure. The bureaucrat, in part irrespective of his position within the hierarchy, acts as a representative of the power and prestige of the entire structure. In his official role he is vested with definite authority. This often leads to an actually or apparently domineering attitude, which may only be exaggerated by a discrepancy between his position within the hierarchy and his position with reference to the public.[21] Protest and recourse to other officials on the part of the client are often ineffective or largely precluded by the previously mentioned esprit de corps which joins the officials into a more or less solidary in-group. This source of conflict *may* be minimized in private enterprise since the client can register an effective protest by transferring his trade to another organization within the com-

---

[20] " 'They treat you like a lump of dirt they do. I see a navvy reach across the counter and shake one of them by the collar the other day. The rest of us felt like cheering. Of course he lost his benefit over it. . . . But the clerk deserved it for his sassy way.' " (E. W. Bakke, *The Unemployed Man*, 79–80.) Note that the domineering attitude was *imputed* by the unemployed client who is in a state of tension due to his loss of status and self-esteem in a society where the ideology is still current that an "able man" can always find a job. That the imputation of arrogance stems largely from the client's state of mind is seen from Bakke's own observation that "the clerks were rushed, and had no time for pleasantries, but there was little sign of harshness or a superiority feeling in their treatment of the men." Insofar as there is an objective basis for the imputation of arrogant behavior to bureaucrats, it may possibly be explained by the following juxtaposed statements. "Auch der moderne, sei es öffentliche, sei es private, Beamte erstrebt immer und geniesst meist den Beherrschten gegenüber eine spezifisch gehobene, 'ständische' soziale Schätzung." (Weber, *op. cit.*, 652.) "In persons in whom the craving for prestige is uppermost, hostility usually takes the form of a desire to humiliate others." K. Horney, *The Neurotic Personality of Our Time*, 178–179.

[21] In this connection, note the relevance of Koffka's comments on certain features of the pecking-order of birds. "If one compares the behavior of the bird at the top of the pecking list, the despot, with that of one very far down, the second or third from the last, then one finds the latter much more cruel to the few others over whom he lords it than the former in his treatment of all members. As soon as one removes from the group all members above the penultimate, his behavior becomes milder and may even become very friendly. . . . It is not difficult to find analogies to this in human societies, and therefore one side of such behavior must be primarily the effects of the social groupings, and not of individual characteristics." K. Koffka, *Principles of Gestalt Psychology* (New York: Harcourt, Brace, 1935), 668–669.

petitive system. But with the monopolistic nature of the public organization, no such alternative is possible. Moreover, in this case, tension is increased because of a discrepancy between ideology and fact: the governmental personnel are held to be "servants of the people," but in fact they
are often superordinate, and release of tension can seldom be afforded by
turning to other agencies for the necessary service.[22] This tension is in part
attributable to the confusion of the status of bureaucrat and client; the
client may consider himself socially superior to the official who is at the
moment dominant.[23]

Thus, with respect to the relations between officials and clientele, one
structural source of conflict is the pressure for formal and impersonal treatment when individual, personalized consideration is desired by the client.
The conflict may be viewed, then, as deriving from the introduction of
inappropriate attitudes and relationships. Conflict within the bureaucratic
structure arises from the converse situation, namely, when personalized
relationships are substituted for the structurally required impersonal relationships. This type of conflict may be characterized as follows.

The bureaucracy, as we have seen, is organized as a secondary, formal
group. The normal responses involved in this organized network of social
expectations are supported by affective attitudes of members of the group.
Since the group is oriented toward secondary norms of impersonality, any
failure to conform to these norms will arouse antagonism from those who
have identified themselves with the legitimacy of these rules. Hence, the
substitution of personal for impersonal treatment within the structure is
met with widespread disapproval and is characterized by such epithets as
graft, favoritism, nepotism, apple-polishing, etc. These epithets are clearly
manifestations of injured sentiments.[24] The function of such virtually automatic resentment can be clearly seen in terms of the requirements of bureaucratic structure.

[22] At this point the political machine often becomes functionally significant. As
Steffens and others have shown, highly personalized relations and the abrogation of
formal rules (red tape) by the machine often satisfy the needs of individual "clients"
more fully than the formalized mechanism of governmental bureaucracy.

[23] As one of the unemployed men remarked about the clerks at the Greenwich
Employment Exchange: " 'And the bloody blokes wouldn't have their jobs if it wasn't
for us men out of a job either. That's what gets me about their holding their noses
up.' " Bakke, *op. cit.*, 80. See also H. D. Lasswell and G. Almond, "Aggressive behavior
by clients towards public relief administrators," *American Political Science Review,*
1934, 28, 643–655.

[24] The diagnostic significance of such linguistic indices as epithets has scarcely been
explored by the sociologist. Sumner properly observes that epithets produce "summary
criticisms" and definitions of social situations. Dollard also notes that "epithets frequently
define the central issues in a society," and Sapir has rightly emphasized the importance
of context of situations in appraising the significance of epithets. Of equal relevance is
Linton's observation that "in case histories the way in which the community felt about
a particular episode is, if anything, more important to our study than the actual behavior. . . ." A sociological study of "vocabularies of encomium and opprobrium" should
lead to valuable findings.

Bureaucracy is a secondary group structure designed to carry on certain activities which cannot be satisfactorily performed on the basis of primary group criteria.[25] Hence behavior which runs counter to these formalized norms becomes the object of emotionalized disapproval. This constitutes a functionally significant defence set up against tendencies which jeopardize the performance of socially necessary activities. To be sure, these reactions are not rationally determined practices explicitly designed for the fulfill-ment of this function. Rather, viewed in terms of the individual's interpre-tation of the situation, such resentment is simply an immediate response opposing the "dishonesty" of those who violate the rules of the game. How-ever, this subjective frame of reference notwithstanding, these reactions serve the latent function of maintaining the essential structural elements of bureaucracy by reaffirming the necessity for formalized, secondary relations and by helping to prevent the disintegration of the bureaucratic structure which would occur should these be supplanted by personalized relations. This type of conflict may be generically described as the intrusion of primary group attitudes when secondary group attitudes are institution-ally demanded, just as the bureaucrat-client conflict often derives from interaction on impersonal terms when personal treatment is individually demanded.[26]

[25] *Cf.* Ellsworth Faris, *The Nature of Human Nature* (New York: McGraw-Hill, 1937), 41 ff.

[26] Community disapproval of many forms of behavior may be analyzed in terms of one or the other of these patterns of substitution of culturally inappropriate types of rela-tionship. Thus, prostitution constitutes a type-case where coitus, a form of intimacy which is institutionally defined as symbolic of the most "sacred" primary group relation-ship, is placed within a contractual context, symbolized by the exchange of that most impersonal of all symbols, money. See Kingsley Davis, "The sociology of prostitution," *American Sociological Review*, 1937, 2, 744–755.

PART THREE

GENERAL
SOCIAL PROCESSES

A social system or society is a viable entity which is in a constant state of change. Sometimes a part of the system breaks,
and a revolution follows. Within the changing system men
group themselves, relate to one another, and sometimes attack
one another. We will use the word "processes" to describe
social stratification, mass behavior, and social disorganization,
because these are not things which occur in isolation from
other phenomena, and they are not static.

VII SOCIAL STRATIFICATION

A. Definitions and Concepts

In any society people will differ from one another in intelligence, attractiveness, and physical prowess, among other things. Each society has things in people which it values. It happens that our society thinks thin women more attractive than fat ones. In some societies, however, young women are placed in fattening cages and fed bananas until they have reached weights ranging from two to three hundred pounds. In these societies fat people are beautiful. In our own, money and the consumption products it buys determine to a large extent a person's position in the society. The less of it he has the more likely he is to be at the bottom of some nebulous scale. Other societies have other indicators of worth: it may be the number of sheep or cattle or wives that a person has that places him. Anything can be used as a unit for dividing people or ranking them. Some people will have more of a certain unit, others less. Normally, one's position in the social structure is based on several units, such as wealth, occupation, lineage, morals, or the type of house one lives in. Class is, then, a variable which differs from society to society, and should be viewed as a continuum.

One of the classic ways of dividing the social system is the schema given by Karl Marx, who, for obvious reasons, best represents the conflict approach. Mark adopted the Hegelian dialectic of thesis, antithesis, and synthesis to explain the development of human history by the conflict between classes. His concept of class is determined by relationship to the basic means of production. The following selection gives a detailed account of Marx' treatment.

22   Reinhard Bendix and Seymour Martin Lipset

Karl Marx' Theory of Social Classes

Karl Marx' theory of social classes was of great importance in his work and it has had a profound influence on modern social thought. Yet the writings of Marx, voluminous as they are, do not contain a coherent exposition of that theory. They contain, instead, many scattered fragments on this topic. We have tried to assemble some of these fragments; and by writing a commentary on this series of quotations we attempt to give a view of the theory as a whole. We should add that such a procedure neglects Marx' own intellectual development, for it treats as part of one theory ideas which he expressed at various times in his career. However, in the case of Marx' theory of social classes this difficulty is not a serious one in our judgment.

According to Marx history may be divided roughly into several periods, for example, ancient civilization, feudalism, and capitalism. Each of these periods is characterized by a predominant mode of production and, based upon it, a class structure consisting of a ruling and an oppressed class. The struggle between these classes determines the social relations between men. In particular, the ruling class, which owes its position to the ownership and control of the means of production, controls also, though often in subtle ways, the whole moral and intellectual life of the people. According to Marx, law and government, art and literature, science and philosophy: all serve more or less directly the interests of the ruling class.

In the period of its revolutionary ascendance each class is "progressive" in two senses of that word. Its economic interests are identical with technical progress and hence with increased human welfare. And its efforts to pursue these interests align this class on the side of liberating ideas and institutions and against all who retard technical progress and human welfare. But in time an ascending class may become a ruling class, such as the feudal lords or the capitalists, and then it comes to play a different role. Its economic interests, which originally favored technical progress, call for opposition to it when further change would endanger the economic dominance which it has won. Upon its emergence as a ruling class, it turns from a champion of progress into a champion of reaction. It resists increasingly the attempts to change the social and economic organization of society, which would allow a full measure of the progress that has become technically possible. Such changes would endanger the entrenched position of the ruling class. Hence, tensions and conflicts are engendered that eventually lead to a revolutionary reorganization of society.

. . . the means of production and of exchange, which served as the foundation for the growth of the bourgeoisie, were generated in feudal society. At a certain stage in the development of these means of production and of exchange, the conditions under which feudal society produced and exchanged, the feudal organization of agriculture and manfacturing industry, in a word, the feudal relations of property became no longer compatible with the already developed productive forces; they became so many fetters. They had to be burst asunder; they were burst asunder.

Into their place stepped free competition, accompanied by a social and political constitution adapted to it, and by the economic and political sway of the bourgeois class.

A similar movement is going on before our own eyes. Modern bourgeois society with its relations of production, of exchange, and of property, a society that has conjured up such gigantic means of production and of exchange, is like the sorcerer who is no longer able to control the powers of the nether world whom he has called up by his spells. For many a decade past the history of industry and commerce is but the history of the revolt of modern productive forces against modern conditions of production, against the property relations that are the conditions for the existence of the bourgeoisie and its rule. It is enough to mention the commercial crises that by their periodical return put the existence of the entire bourgeois society on trial, each time more threateningly. In these crises a great part not only of the existing products, but also of the previously created productive forces, are periodically destroyed. In these crises there breaks out an epidemic that, in all earlier epochs, would have seemed an absurdity — the epidemic of overproduction. Society suddenly finds itself put back into a state of momentary barbarism; it appears as if a famine, a universal war of devastation had cut off the supply of every means of subsistence; industry and commerce seem to be destroyed. And why? Because there is too much civilization, too much means of subsistence, too much industry, too much commerce. The productive forces at the disposal of society no longer tend to further the development of the conditions of bourgeois property; on the contrary they have become too powerful for these conditions, by which they are fettered, and no sooner do they overcome these fetters than they bring disorder into the whole of bourgeois society, endanger the existence of bourgeois property. The conditions of bourgeois society are too narrow to comprise the wealth created by them. And how does the bourgeoisie get over these crises? On the one hand by enforced destruction of a mass of productive forces; on the other, by the conquest of new markets, and by the more thorough exploitation of the old one. That is to say, by paving the way for more extensive and more destructive crises, and diminishing the means whereby crises are prevented.

The weapons with which the bourgeoisie felled feudalism to the ground are now turned against the bourgeoisie itself.

But not only has the bourgeoisie forged the weapons that bring death to itself; it has also called into existence the men who are to wield those weapons — the modern working class — the proletarians.[1]

This conception of class conflict and historical change lent itself to a dogmatic interpretation. In particular, the materialist conception of history was often used in a manner which implied that only technical and economic factors were *really* important and that the whole social, political and intellectual realm (what Marx called the "superstructure") was of secondary significance. In two letters, written in 1890, Friedrich Engels, the life-long collaborator of Marx, opposed this "vulgar" interpretation:

> Marx and I are ourselves partly to blame for the fact that the younger writers sometimes lay more stress on the economic side than is due it. We had to emphasize this main principle in opposition to our adversaries, who denied it, and we had not always the time, the place or the opportunity to allow the other elements involved in the interaction to come into their own rights. . . .
>
> . . . the materialist conception of history also has a lot of friends nowadays, to whom it serves as an excuse for *not* studying history. . . .
>
> In general the word *materialistic* serves many of the younger writers in Germany as a mere phrase with which anything and everything is labelled without further study; they stick on this label and they think the question disposed of. But our conception of history is above all a guide to study, not a lever for construction after the manner of the Hegelians. All history must be studied afresh, the conditions of existence of the different formations of society must be individually examined before the attempt is made to deduce from them the political, civil-legal, aesthetic, philosophic, religious, etc., notions corresponding to them. . . .[2]

It is well to keep these reservations in mind. They suggest that Marx and Engels often felt compelled by the exigencies of the social and political struggle, to cast their ideas in extremely pointed formulations. Had they been scholars of the traditional type, they might have avoided at least some of the dogmatic interpretations of their work, though they would have had far less success in spreading their ideas and getting them accepted. Much of the difficulty in obtaining a concise view of Marxian theory stems from the fact that it was meant to be a tool for political action. In reviewing briefly Marx' theory of history and his theory of social class, we shall at first disregard this political implication. We shall consider this implication more directly in the concluding paragraphs of this essay.

A social class in Marx' terms is any aggregate of persons who perform the same function in the organization of production. "Freeman and slave,

---

[1] Karl Marx and Friedrich Engels, *Manifesto of the Communist Party* (New York: International Publishers, 1932), 14–15.

[2] Karl Marx and Friedrich Engels, *Selected Correspondence, 1846–1895* (New York: International Publishers, 1942), 477, 472–473.

patrician and plebeian, lord and serf, guild-master and journeyman, in a word, oppressor and oppressed" (Communist Manifesto) are the names of social classes in different historical periods. These classes are distinguished from each other by the difference of their respective positions in the economy. Since a social class is constituted by the function which its members perform in the process of production, the question arises why the organization of production is the basic determinant of social class. Marx' answer is contained in his early writings on philosophy, especially in his theory of the division of labor.

Fundamental to this theory is Marx' belief that work is man's basic form of self-realization. Man cannot live without work; hence the way in which man works in society is a clue to human nature. Man provides for his subsistence by the use of tools; these facilitate his labor and make it more productive. He has, therefore, an interest in, and he has also a capacity for, elaborating and refining these tools, and in so doing he expresses himself, controls nature and makes history. *If* human labor makes history, then an understanding of the conditions of production is essential for an understanding of history. There are four aspects of production, according to Marx, which explain why man's efforts to provide for his subsistence underlie all change in history.

> (a.) . . . life involves before everything else eating, and drinking, a habitation, clothing and many other things. The first historical act is thus the production of the means to satisfy these needs, the production of material life itself.[3]
>
> (b.) The second fundamental point is that as soon as a need is satisfied (which implies the action of satisfying, and the acquisition of an instrument), new needs are made.[4]
>
> (c.) The third circumstance which, from the very first, enters into historical development, is that men, who daily remake their own life, begin to make other men, to propagate their kind: the relation between man and wife, parents and children, the FAMILY. The family, which to begin with is the only social relationship, becomes later, when increased needs create new social relations and the increased population (creates) new needs, a subordinate one. . . .[5]
>
> (d.) The production of life, both of one's own in labor and of fresh life in procreation, now appears as a double relationship: on the one hand as a natural, on the other as a social relationship. By social we understand the cooperation of several individuals, no matter under what conditions, in what manner and to what end. It follows from this that a certain mode of production, or industrial stage, is always combined with a certain mode of cooperation, or social stage, and this mode of cooperation is itself a "productive

---

[3] Karl Marx and Friedrich Engels, *The German Ideology* (New York: International Publishers, 1939), 16.

[4] *Ibid.*, 16–17.

[5] Marx and Engels, *loc. cit.*

force." Further, that the multitude of productive forces accessible to men determines the nature of society, hence that the "history of humanity" must always be studied and treated in relation to the history of industry and exchange.[6]

There is a logical connection between these four aspects. The satisfaction of man's basic needs makes work a fundamental fact of human life, but it also creates new needs. The more needs are created the more important is it that the "instruments" of production be improved. The more needs are created and the more the technique of production is improved, the more important is it that men cooperate, first within the family, then also outside it. Cooperation implies the division of labor and the organization of production (or in Marx' phrase "the mode of cooperation" as a "productive force") over and above the techniques of production which are employed. It is, therefore, the position which the individual occupies in the social organization of production, that indicates to which social class he belongs. The fundamental determinant of class is the way in which the individual cooperates with others in the satisfaction of his basic needs of food, clothing, and shelter. Other indexes such as income, consumption patterns, educational attainment, or occupation are so many clues to the distribution of material goods and of prestige-symbols. This distribution is a more or less revealing consequence of the organization of production; it is not identical with it. Hence, the income or occupation of an individual is *not*, according to Marx, an indication of his class-position, i.e., of his position in the production process. For example, if two men are carpenters, they belong to the same occupation, but one may run a small shop of his own, while another works in a plant manufacturing pre-fabricated housing; the two men belong to the same occupation, but to different social classes.

Marx believed that a man's position in the production process provided the crucial life experience, which would determine, either now or eventually, the beliefs and the actions of that individual. The experience gained in the effort of making a living, but especially the experience of economic conflict, would prompt the members of a social class to develop common beliefs and common actions. In analyzing the emergence of these beliefs and actions Marx specified a number of variables which would facilitate this process:

1. Conflicts over the distribution of economic rewards between the classes;

2. Easy communication between the individuals in the same class-position so that ideas and action-programs are readily disseminated;

3. Growth of class-consciousness in the sense that the members of the class have a feeling of solidarity and understanding of their historic role;

4. Profound dissatisfaction of the lower class over its inability to control the economic structure of which it feels itself to be the exploited victim;

[6] *Ibid.*, 18.

5. Establishment of a political organization resulting from the economic structure, the historical situation and maturation of class-consciousness.

Thus, the organization of production provides the necessary but not a sufficient basis for the existence of social classes. Repeated conflicts over economic rewards, ready communication of ideas between members of a class, the growth of class-consciousness, and the growing dissatisfaction with exploitation which causes suffering in psychological as much as in material terms: these are the conditions which will help to overcome the differences and conflicts between individuals and groups within the class and which will encourage the formation of a class-conscious political organization.

Marx' discussions of the development of the bourgeoisie and of the proletariat give good illustrations of the manner in which he envisages the emergence of a social class.

> In the Middle Ages the citizens in each town were compelled to unite against the landed nobility to save their skins. The extension of trade, the establishment of communications, led the separate towns to get to know other towns, which had asserted the same interests in the struggle with the same antagonist. Out of the many local corporations of burghers there arose only gradually the burgher *class*. The conditions of life of the individual burghers became, on account of their antagonism to the existing relationships and of the mode of labour determined by these conditions which were common to ᵗhem all and independent of each individual. The burghers had created the conditions in so far as they had torn themselves free from feudal ties, and were created by them in so far as they were determined by their antagonism to the feudal system which they found in existence. When the individual towns began to enter into associations, these common conditions developed into class conditions. The same conditions, the same antagonism, the same interests necessarily called forth on the whole similar customs everywhere. The bourgeoisie itself, with its conditions, develops only gradually, splits according to the division of labour into various fractions and finally absorbs all earlier possessing classes (while it develops the majority of the earlier non-possessing, and a part of the earlier possessing, class into a new class, the proletariat) in the measure to which all earlier property is transformed into industrial or commercial capital.

> The separate individuals form a class only in so far as they have to carry on a common battle against another class; otherwise they are on hostile terms with each other as competitors. On the other hand, the class in its turn achieves an independent existence over against the individuals, so that the latter find their conditions of existence predestined, and hence have their position in life and their personal development assigned to them by their class, become subsumed under it. This is the same phenomenon as the subjection of

> the separate individuals to the division of labour and can only be removed by the abolition of private property and of labour itself. . . .[7]

This passage makes it apparent that Marx thought of social class as a condition of group-life which was constantly generated (rather than simply given) by the organization of production. Essential to this formation of a class was the existence of a common "class enemy," because without it competition between individuals would prevail. Also, this is a gradual process, which depends for its success upon the development of "common conditions" and upon the subsequent realization of common interests. But the existence of common conditions and the realization of common interests are in turn only the necessary, not the sufficient bases for the development of a social class. Only when the members of a "potential" class enter into an association for the organized pursuit of their common aims, does a class in Marx' sense exist.

In discussing the development of the proletariat under capitalism Marx described a process which was essentially similar to that which he had described for the development of the modern bourgeoisie.

> The first attempts of the workers to *associate* among themselves always take place in the form of combinations (unions).
>
> Large-scale industry concentrates in one place a crowd of people unknown to one another. Competition divides their interests. But the maintenance of wages, this common interest which they have against their boss, unites them in a common thought of resistance — combination. Thus combination always has a double aim, that of stopping the competition among themselves, in order to bring about a general competition with the capitalist. If the first aim of the general resistance was merely the maintenance of wages, combinations, at first isolated, constitute themselves into groups as the capitalists in their turn unite in the idea of repression, and in the face of always united capital, the maintenance of the association becomes more necessary to them than that of wages. This is so true that the English economists are amazed to see the workers sacrifice a good part of their wages in favor of associations, which in the eyes of the economists, are established solely in favor of wages. In this struggle — a veritable civil war — are united and developed all the elements necessary for the coming battle. Once it has reached this point association takes on a political character.
>
> Economic conditions had first transformed the mass of the people of the country into workers. The domination of capital has created for this mass a common situation, common interests. This mass is thus already a class as against capital, *but not yet for itself*. In this struggle, of which we have noted only a few phases, this mass becomes united, and constitutes itself as a class for itself. The interests

---

[7] *German Ideology*, 48–49.

it defends become class interests. But the struggle of class against class is a political struggle.[8]

Thus in the case of the proletariat, as in the case of the bourgeoisie, Marx cited several conditions which were essential for the development of a social class: conflict over economic rewards, physical concentration of masses of people and easy communication among them, the development of solidarity and political organization (in place of competition between individuals and organization for purely economic ends).

The antagonism of the workers to the capitalist class and to the prevailing economic system was to Marx not simply a consequence of the struggle for economic advantage. In addition to the conditions mentioned he laid great stress on the human consequences of machine production under capitalism. The social relations which capitalist industry imposed deprived the workers of all opportunities to obtain psychological satisfaction from their work. This complete want of satisfaction Marx called the alienation of human labor. He attributed it to the division of labor in modern industry, which turned human beings into the appendages of the machine.

> The knowledge, the judgment and the will, which though in ever so small a degree, are practiced by the independent peasant or handicraftsman, in the same way as the savage makes the whole art of war consist in the exercise of his personal cunning — these faculties (?) are now required only for the workshop as a whole. Intelligence in production expands in one direction, because it vanishes in many others. What is lost by the detail laborers, is concentrated in the capital that employs them. It is a result of the division of labor in manufactures, that the laborer is brought face to face with the intellectual potencies of the material process of production, as the property of another, and as a ruling power. This separation begins in simple cooperation, where the capitalist represents to the single workman, the oneness and the will of the associated labor. It is developed in manufacture which cuts down the laborer into a detail laborer. It is completed in modern industry, which makes science a productive force distinct from labor and presses it into the service of capital.
>
> In manufacture, in order to make the collective laborer, and through him capital, rich in social productive power, each laborer must be made poor in individual productive powers. "Ignorance is the mother of industry as well as of superstition. Reflection and fancy are subject to err; but a habit of moving the hand or the foot is independent of either. Manufactures, accordingly, prosper most where the mind is least consulted, and where the workshop may . . . be considered as an engine, the parts of which are men." (A. L. Ferguson, p. 280.)[9]

[8] Karl Marx, *The Poverty of Philosophy* (New York: International Publishers, n.d.), 145–146.

[9] Karl Marx, *Capital* (New York: Modern Library, 1936), 396–397.

> . . . within the capitalist system all methods for raising the social productiveness of labor are brought about at the cost of the individual laborer; all means for the development of production transform themselves into means of domination over, and exploitation of the producers; they mutilate the laborer into a fragment of a man, degrade him to the level of an appendage of a machine, destroy every remnant of charm in his work and turn it into a hated toil; they estrange from him the intellectual potentialities of the labor-process in the same proportion as science is incorporated in it as an independent power; they distort the conditions under which he works, subject him during the labor-process to a despotism the more hateful for its meanness; they transform his life time into working-time and drag his wife and child under the wheels of the Juggernaut of capital. But all methods for the accumulation of surplus value are at the same time methods of accumulation; *and every extension of accumulation becomes again a means for the development of those methods. It follows therefore that in proportion as capital accumulates, the lot of the laborer, be his payments high or low, must grow worse.*[10]

Marx believed that the alienation of labor was inherent in capitalism and that it was a major psychological deprivation, which would lead eventually to the proletarian revolution. This theory of why men under capitalism would revolt was based on an assumption of what prompts men to be satisfied or dissatisfied with their work. Marx contrasted the modern industrial worker with the medieval craftsman, and — along with many other writers of the period — observed that under modern conditions of production the worker had lost all opportunity to exercise his "knowledge, judgment and will" in the manufacture of his product. To Marx this psychological deprivation seemed more significant even than the economic pauperism to which capitalism subjected the masses of workers. At any rate, two somewhat conflicting statements can be found in his work. In one he declared that the physical misery of the working classes would increase with the development of capitalism.

> Accumulation of wealth at one pole is, therefore, at the same time accumulation of misery, agony of toil, slavery, ignorance, brutality, mental degradation, at the opposite pole. . . .[11]

But in the other he maintained, that capitalism could result in an absolute increase of the standard of living for the workers, but that it would result nevertheless in the experience of mounting personal deprivation.

> When capital is increasing fast, wages may rise, but the profit of capital will rise much faster. The material position of the laborer

[10] Marx, *op. cit.*, 708–709. (Our emphasis.)
[11] *Ibid.*, 709

> has improved, but it is at the expense of his social position. The
> social gulf which separates him from the capitalist has widened.[12]

And, as we have seen, Marx summarized his analysis of the oppressive
effects of capitalism with a long list of striking phrases, only to conclude
this eloquent recital with the sentence: "It follows therefore that in proportion as capital accumulates, the lot of the labourer, *be his payment high or
low*, must grow worse."

It will be apparent from the preceding discussion that Marx did not
simply identify a social class with the fact that a large group of people
occupied the same objective position in the economic structure of a society.
Instead, he laid great stress on the importance of subjective awareness as
a precondition of organizing the class successfully for the economic and the
political struggle. Marx felt certain that the pressures engendered by capitalism would determine its development in the future. And he believed it
to be inevitable that the masses of industrial workers would come to a
conscious realization of their class-interests. Subjective awareness of class
interests was in his view an indispensable element in the development of a
social class, but he believed that his awareness would inevitably arise along
with the growing contradictions inherent in capitalism. In the preceding
discussion we have cited two of the conditions which made Marx feel sure
of this prediction: the concentration of workers in towns and the resulting
ease of communication between them, and the psychological suffering engendered by the alienation of labor. By way of summarizing Marx' theory
of class we cite his views on the French peasants, who occupy a similar
position in the economic structure but do not thereby provide the basis
for the formation of a social class.

> The small peasants form a vast mass, the members of which live
> in similar conditions, but without entering into manifold relations
> with one another. Their mode of production isolates them from one
> another, instead of bringing them into mutual intercourse. . . . In so
> far as millions of families live under economic conditions of exis-
> tence that divide their mode of life, their interests and their culture
> from those of other classes, and put them into hostile contrast to
> the latter, they form a class. In so far as there is merely a local
> interconnection among these small peasants, and the identity of
> their interests begets no unity, no national union, and no political
> organization, they do not form a class.[13]

That is to say, the peasants occupy the same position in the economic structure of their society. But in their case this fact itself will *not* create similar

---

[12] Karl Marx, "Wage, Labor and Capital," in *Selected Works* (Moscow: Cooperative Publishing Society of Foreign Workers in the U.S.S.R., 1936), I, 273.
[13] Karl Marx, *The Eighteenth Brumaire of Louis Bonaparte* (New York: International Publishers, n.d.), 109.

attitudes and common actions. The peasants do not form a social class in Marx' sense, because they make their living on individual farms in isolation from one another. There is no objective basis for ready communication between them.

In the case of the industrial workers, however, such an objective basis for ready communication existed. They were concentrated in the large industrial towns, and the conditions of factory production brought them into close physical contact with one another. Yet, even then Marx did not believe that the political organization of the working class and the development of class-consciousness in thought and action would be the automatic result of these objective conditions. In his view these objective conditions provided a favorable setting for the development of political agitation. And this agitation was in good part the function of men who were not themselves workers, but who had acquired a correct understanding of historical change, and who were willing to identify themselves with the movement of those who were destined to bring it about.

> . . . in times when the class struggle nears the decisive hour, the process of dissolution going on within the ruling class, in fact within the whole range of old society, assumes such a violent, glaring character, that a small section of the ruling class cuts itself adrift and joins the revolutionary class, the class that holds the future in its hands. Just as, therefore, at an earlier period, a section of the nobility went over to the bourgeoisie, so now a portion of the bourgeoisie goes over to the proletariat, and in particular, a portion of the bourgeois ideologists, who have raised themselves to the level of comprehending theoretically the historical movement as a whole.[14]

There is little question that Marx conceived of his own work as an example of this process. The scientific analysis of the capitalist economy, as he conceived of it, was itself an important instrument by means of which the class-consciousness and the political organization of the workers could be furthered. And because Marx conceived of his own work in these terms, he declared that the detachment of other scholars was spurious, was merely a screen thrown up to disguise the class-interests which their work served. Hence he denied the possibility of a social science in the modern sense of that word. The "proof" of his theory was contained in the actions of the proletariat.

It is apparent that Marx' theory of social classes, along with other parts of his doctrine, involved a basic ambiguity which has bedevilled his interpreters ever since. For, on the one hand, he felt quite certain that the contradictions engendered by capitalism would inevitably lead to a class-conscious proletariat and hence to a proletarian revolution. But on the other hand, he assigned to class-consciousness, to political action, and to his

[14] Karl Marx and Friedrich Engels, *Manifesto of the Communist Party* (New York: International Publishers, 1932), 19.

scientific theory of history a major role in bringing about this result. In his own eyes this difficulty was resolved because such subjective elements as class-consciousness or a scientific theory were themselves a by-product of the contradictions inherent in capitalism. The preceding discussion has sought to elucidate the meaning of this assertion by specifying the general philosophical assumptions and the specific environmental and psychological conditions on the basis of which Marx felt able to predict the *inevitable* development of class-consciousness.[15] To the critics this claim to predict an inevitable future on the basis of assumptions and conditions, which may or may not be valid, has always seemed the major flaw in Marxian theory.

Since the time of Marx and Weber, few sociologists have turned to the task of developing theories of social stratification. The following article created a flurry of activity. Davis and Moore outline a functional *theory of stratification, starting from the premise that stratification is inevitable in any society, and positively functional for that society. (It is functional because each society must have some means of getting its talented individuals to fill those positions which the society needs filled.) Davis and Moore's position has been criticized by many theorists, but often this criticism has proceeded on ideological grounds. For instance, Melvin Tumin, in an article entitled, "Some Principles of Stratification: A Critical Analysis,"[1] pointed out, among other things, that stratification is not inevitable in any society, and examined the theoretical possibilities of a social system in which there would be no "stratification."*

23 KINGSLEY DAVIS AND WILBERT E. MOORE

Some Principles of Stratification

In a previous paper some concepts for handling the phenomena of social inequality were presented. In the present paper a further step in stratifica-

---

[15] On a few occasions Marx allowed for the possibility that the development from capitalism to socialism might occur without a proletarian revolution, especially in England, Holland, and the United States. Properly understood the statement to this effect did not mean that this development was a mere possibility, but that it might take several forms, depending upon the historical situation of each country. By his analysis of the capitalist economy Marx sought to predict major changes, not specific occurrences; but while he allowed for the latter he did not expect them to alter the central tendency of the former.

From *American Sociological Review*, Vol. X (April, 1945), pp. 242–249. Reprinted by permission of the American Sociological Association.

[1] Melvin Tumin, "Some Principles of Stratification: A Critical Analysis," *American Sociological Review*, Vol. 18 (August, 1953), pp. 387–394.

tion theory is undertaken — an attempt to show the relationship between stratification and the rest of the social order. Starting from the proposition that no society is "classless," or unstratified, an effort is made to explain, in functional terms, the universal necessity which calls forth stratification in any social system. Next, an attempt is made to explain the roughly uniform distribution of prestige as between the major types of positions in every society. Since, however, there occur between one society and another great differences in the degree and kind of stratification, some attention is also given to the varieties of social inequality and the variable factors that give rise to them.

Clearly, the present task requires two different lines of analysis — one to understand the universal, the other to understand the variable features of stratification. Naturally each line of inquiry aids the other and is indispensable, and in the treatment that follows the two will be interwoven, although, because of space limitations, the emphasis will be on the universals.

Throughout, it will be necessary to keep in mind one thing — namely, that the discussion relates to the system of positions, not to the individuals occupying those positions. It is one thing to ask why different positions carry different degrees of prestige, and quite another to ask how certain individuals get into those positions. Although, as the argument will try to show, both questions are related, it is essential to keep them separate in our thinking. Most of the literature on stratification has tried to answer the second question (particularly with regard to the ease or difficulty of mobility between strata) without tackling the first. The first question, however, is logically prior and, in the case of any particular individual or group, factually prior.

THE FUNCTIONAL NECESSITY OF STRATIFICATION

Curiously, however, the main functional necessity explaining the universal presence of stratification is precisely the requirement faced by any society of placing and motivating individuals in the social structure. As a functioning mechanism a society must somehow distribute its members in social positions and induce them to perform the duties of these positions. It must thus concern itself with motivation at two different levels: to instill in the proper individuals the desire to fill certain positions, and, once in these positions, the desire to perform the duties attached to them. Even though the social order may be relatively static in form, there is a continuous process of metabolism as new individuals are born into it, shift with age, and die off. Their absorption into the positional system must somehow be arranged and motivated. This is true whether the system is competitive or non-competitive. A competitive system gives greater importance to the motivation to achieve positions, whereas a non-competitive system gives perhaps greater importance to the motivation to perform the duties of the positions; but in any system both types of motivation are required.

If the duties associated with the various positions were all equally pleasant to the human organism, all equally important to societal survival, and all equally in need of the same ability or talent, it would make no difference who got into which positions, and the problem of social placement would be greatly reduced. But actually it does make a great deal of difference who gets into which positions, not only because some positions are inherently more agreeable than others, but also because some require special talents or training and some are functionally more important than others. Also, it is essential that the duties of the positions be performed with the diligence that their importance requires. Inevitably, then, a society must have, first, some kind of rewards that it can use as inducements, and, second, some way of distributing these rewards differentially according to positions. The rewards and their distribution become a part of the social order, and thus give rise to stratification.

One may ask what kind of rewards a society has at its disposal in distributing its personnel and securing essential services. It has, first of all, the things that contribute to sustenance and comfort. It has, second, the things that contribute to humor and diversion. And it has, finally, the things that contribute to self respect and ego expansion. The last, because of the peculiarly social character of the self, is largely a function of the opinion of others, but it nonetheless ranks in importance with the first two. In any social system all three kinds of rewards must be dispensed differentially according to positions.

In a sense the rewards are "built into" the position. They consist in the "rights" associated with the position, plus what may be called its accompaniments or perquisites. Often the rights, and sometimes the accompaniments, are functionally related to the duties of the position. (Rights as viewed by the incumbent are usually duties as viewed by other members of the community.) However, there may be a host of subsidiary rights and perquisites that are not essential to the function of the position and have only an indirect and symbolic connection with its duties, but which still may be of considerable importance in inducing people to seek the positions and fulfil the essential duties.

If the rights and perquisites of different positions in a society must be unequal, then the society must be stratified, because that is precisely what stratification means. Social inequality is thus an unconsciously evolved device by which societies insure that the most important positions are conscientiously filled by the most qualified persons. Hence every society, no matter how simple or complex, must differentiate persons in terms of both prestige and esteem, and must therefore possess a certain amount of institutionalized inequality.

It does not follow that the amount or type of inequality need be the same in all societies. This is largely a function of factors that will be discussed presently.

THE TWO DETERMINANTS OF POSITIONAL RANK

Granting the general function that inequality subserves, one can specify the two factors that determine the relative rank of different positions. In general those positions convey the best reward, and hence have the highest rank, which (1) have the greatest importance for the society and (2) require the greatest training or talent. The first factor concerns function and is a matter of relative significance; the second concerns means and is a matter of scarcity.

Differential functional importance. Actually a society does not need to reward positions in proportion to their functional importance. It merely needs to give sufficient reward to them to insure that they will be filled competently. In other words, it must see that less essential positions do not compete successfully with more essential ones. If a position is easily filled, it need not be heavily rewarded, even though important. On the other hand, if it is important but hard to fill, the reward must be high enough to get it filled anyway. Functional importance is therefore a necessary but not a sufficient cause of high rank being assigned to a position.

Differential scarcity of personnel. Practically all positions, no matter how acquired, require some form of skill or capacity for performance. This is implicit in the very notion of position, which implies that the incumbent must, by virtue of his incumbency, accomplish certain things.

There are, ultimately, only two ways in which a person's qualifications come about: through inherent capacity or through training. Obviously, in concrete activities both are always necessary, but from a practical standpoint the scarcity may lie primarily in one or the other, as well as in both. Some positions require innate talents of such high degree that the persons who fill them are bound to be rare. In many cases, however, talent is fairly abundant in the population but the training process is so long, costly, and elaborate that relatively few can qualify. Modern medicine, for example, is within the mental capacity of most individuals, but a medical education is so burdensome and expensive that virtually none would undertake it if the position of the M.D. did not carry a reward commensurate with the sacrifice.

If the talents required for a position are abundant and the training easy, the method of acquiring the position may have little to do with its duties. There may be, in fact, a virtually accidental relationship. But if the skills required are scarce by reason of the rarity of talent or the costliness of training, the position, if functionally important, must have an attractive power that will draw the necessary skills in competition with other positions. This means, in effect, that the position must be high in the social scale — must command great prestige, high salary, ample leisure, and the like.

How variations are to be understood. In so far as there is a difference between one system of stratification and another, it is attributable to whatever factors affect the two determinants of differential reward — namely, functional importance and scarcity of personnel. Positions important in one society may not be important in another, because the conditions faced by the societies, or their degree of internal development, may be different. The same conditions, in turn, may affect the question of scarcity; for in some societies the stage of development, or the external situation, may wholly obviate the necessity of certain kinds of skill or talent. Any particular system of stratification, then, can be understood as a product of the special conditions affecting the two aforementioned grounds of differential reward.

MAJOR SOCIETAL FUNCTIONS AND STRATIFICATION

Religion. The reason why religion is necessary is apparently to be found in the fact that human society achieves its unity primarily through the possession by its members of certain ultimate values and ends in common. Although these values and ends are subjective, they influence behavior, and their integration enables the society to operate as a system. Derived neither from inherited nor from external nature, they have evolved as a part of culture by communication and moral pressure. They must, however, appear to the members of the society to have some reality, and it is the role of religious belief and ritual to supply and reinforce this appearance of reality. Through belief and ritual the common ends and values are connected with an imaginary world symbolized by concrete sacred objects, which world in turn is related in a meaningful way to the facts and trials of the individual's life. Through the worship of the sacred objects and the beings they symbolize, and the acceptance of supernatural prescriptions that are at the same time codes of behavior, a powerful control over human conduct is exercised, guiding it along lines sustaining the institutional structure and conforming to the ultimate ends and values.

If this conception of the role of religion is true, one can understand why in every known society the religious activities tend to be under the charge of particular persons, who tend thereby to enjoy greater rewards than the ordinary societal member. Certain of the rewards and special privileges may attach to only the highest religious functionaries, but others usually apply, if such exists, to the entire sacerdotal class.

Moreover, there is a peculiar relation between the duties of the religious official and the special privileges he enjoys. If the supernatural world governs the destinies of men more ultimately than does the real world, its earthly representative, the person through whom one may communicate with the supernatural, must be a powerful individual. He is a keeper of sacred tradition, a skilled performer of the ritual, and an interpreter of lore and myth. He is in such close contact with the gods that he is viewed as possessing some of their characteristics. He is, in short, a bit sacred, and hence free from some of the more vulgar necessities and controls.

It is no accident, therefore, that religious functionaries have been associated with the very highest positions of power, as in theocratic regimes. Indeed, looking at it from this point of view, one may wonder why it is that they do not get *entire* control over their societies. The factors that prevent this are worthy of note.

In the first place, the amount of technical competence necessary for the performance of religious duties is small. Scientific or artistic capacity is not required. Anyone can set himself up as enjoying an intimate relation with deities, and nobody can successfully dispute him. Therefore, the factor of scarcity of personnel does not operate in the technical sense.

One may assert, on the other hand, that religious ritual is often elaborate and religious lore abstruse, and that priestly ministrations require tact, if not intelligence. This is true, but the technical requirements of the profession are for the most part adventitious, not related to the end in the same way that science is related to air travel. The priest can never be free from competition, since the criteria of whether or not one has genuine contact with the supernatural are never strictly clear. It is this competition that debases the priestly position below what might be expected at first glance. That is why priestly prestige is highest in those societies where membership in the profession is rigidly controlled by the priestly guild itself. That is why in part at least, elaborate devices are utilized to stress the identification of the person with his office — spectacular costume, abnormal conduct, special diet, segregated residence, celibacy, conspicuous leisure, and the like. In fact, the priest is always in danger of becoming somewhat discredited — as happens in a secularized society — because in a world of stubborn fact, ritual and sacred knowledge alone will not grow crops or build houses. Furthermore, unless he is protected by a professional guild, the priest's identification with the supernatural tends to preclude his acquisition of abundant worldly goods.

As between one society and another it seems that the highest general position awarded the priest occurs in the medieval type of social order. Here there is enough economic production to afford a surplus, which can be used to support a numerous and highly organized priesthood; and yet the populace is unlettered and therefore credulous to a high degree. Perhaps the most extreme example is to be found in the Buddhism of Tibet, but others are encountered in the Catholicism of feudal Europe, the Inca regime of Peru, the Brahminism of India, and the Mayan priesthood of Yucatan. On the other hand, if the society is so crude as to have no surplus and little differentiation, so that every priest must be also a cultivator or hunter, the separation of the priestly status from the others has hardly gone far enough for priestly prestige to mean much. When the priest actually has high prestige under these circumstances, it is because he also performs other important functions (usually political and medical).

In an extremely advanced society built on scientific technology, the priesthood tends to lose status, because sacred tradition and supernaturalism drop into the background. The ultimate values and common ends of the society tend to be expressed in less anthropomorphic ways, by officials who occupy fundamentally political, economic, or educational rather than religious positions. Nevertheless, it is easily possible for intellectuals to exaggerate the degree to which the priesthood in a presumably secular milieu has lost prestige. When the matter is closely examined the urban proletariat, as well as the rural citizenry, proves to be surprisingly god-fearing and priest-ridden. No society has become so completely secularized as to liquidate entirely the belief in transcendental ends and supernatural entities. Even in a secularized society some system must exist for the integration of ultimate values, for their ritualistic expression, and for the emotional adjustments required by disappointment, death, and disaster.

Government. Like religion, government plays a unique and indispensable part in society. But in contrast to religion, which provides integration in terms of sentiments, beliefs, and rituals, it organizes the society in terms of law and authority. Furthermore, it orients the society to the actual rather than the unseen world.

The main functions of government are, internally, the ultimate enforcement of norms, the final arbitration of conflicting interests, and the overall planning and direction of society; and externally, the handling of war and diplomacy. To carry out these functions it acts as the agent of the entire people, enjoys a monopoly of force, and controls all individuals within its territory.

Political action, by definition, implies authority. An official can command because he has authority, and the citizen must obey because he is subject to that authority. For this reason stratification is inherent in the nature of political relationships.

So clear is the power embodied in political position that political inequality is sometimes thought to comprise all inequality. But it can be shown that there are other bases of stratification, that the following controls operate in practice to keep political power from becoming complete: (1) The fact that the actual holders of political office, and especially those determining top policy must necessarily be few in number compared to the total population. (2) The fact that the rulers represent the interest of the group rather than of themselves, and are therefore restricted in their behavior by rules and mores designed to enforce this limitation of interest. (3) The fact that the holder of political office has his authority by virtue of his office and nothing else, and therefore any special knowledge, talent, or capacity he may claim is purely incidental, so that he often has to depend upon others for technical assistance.

In view of these limiting factors, it is not strange that the rulers often have less power and prestige than a literal enumeration of their formal rights would lead one to expect.

Wealth, property, and labor. Every position that secures for its incumbent a livelihood is, by definition, economically rewarded. For this reason there is an economic aspect to those positions (e.g., political and religious) the main function of which is not economic. It therefore becomes convenient for the society to use unequal economic returns as a principal means of controlling the entrance of persons into positions and stimulating the performance of their duties. The amount of the economic return therefore becomes one of the main indices of social status.

It should be stressed, however, that a position does not bring power and prestige *because* it draws a high income. Rather, it draws a high income because it is functionally important and the available personnel is for one reason or another scarce. It is therefore superficial and erroneous to regard high income as the cause of a man's power and prestige, just as it is erroneous to think that a man's fever is the cause of his disease.

The economic source of power and prestige is not income primarily, but the ownership of capital goods (including patents, good will, and professional reputation). Such ownership should be distinguished from the possession of consumers' goods, which is an index rather than a cause of social standing. In other words, the ownership of producers' goods is, properly speaking, a source of income like other positions, the income itself remaining an index. Even in situations where social values are widely commercialized and earnings are the readiest method of judging social position, income does not confer prestige on a position so much as it induces people to compete for the position. It is true that a man who has a high income as a result of one position may find this money helpful in climbing into another position as well, but this again reflects the effect of his initial, economically advantageous status, which exercises its influence through the medium of money.

In a system of private property in productive enterprise, an income above what an individual spends can give rise to possession of capital wealth. Presumably such possession is a reward for the proper management of one's finances originally and of the productive enterprise later. But as social differentiation becomes highly advanced and yet the institution of inheritance persists, the phenomenon of pure ownership, and reward for pure ownership, emerges. In such a case it is difficult to prove that the position is functionally important or that the scarcity involved is anything other than extrinsic and accidental. It is for this reason, doubtless, that the institution of private property in productive goods becomes more subject to criticism as social development proceeds toward industrialization. It is only this pure, that is, strictly legal and functionless ownership, however, that is open to attack; for some form of active ownership, whether private or public, is indispensable.

One kind of ownership of production goods consists in rights over the labor of others. The most extremely concentrated and exclusive of such rights are found in slavery, but the essential principle remains in serfdom, peonage, encomienda, and indenture. Naturally this kind of ownership has the greatest significance for stratification, because it necessarily entails an unequal relationship.

But property in capital goods inevitably introduces a compulsive element even into the nominally free contractual relationship. Indeed, in some respects the authority of the contractual employer is greater than that of the feudal landlord, inasmuch as the latter is more limited by traditional reciprocities. Even the classical economics recognized that competitors would fare unequally, but it did not pursue this fact to its necessary conclusion that, however it might be acquired, unequal control of goods and services must give unequal advantage to the parties to a contract.

Technical knowledge. The function of finding means to single goals, without any concern with the choice between goals, is the exclusively technical sphere. The explanation of why positions requiring great technical skill receive fairly high rewards is easy to see, for it is the simplest case of the rewards being so distributed as to draw talent and motivate training. Why they seldom if ever receive the highest rewards is also clear: the importance of technical knowledge from a societal point of view is never so great as the integration of goals, which takes place on the religious, political, and economic levels. Since the technological level is concerned solely with means, a purely technical position must ultimately be subordinate to other positions that are religious, political, or economic in character.

Nevertheless, the distinction between expert and layman in any social order is fundamental, and cannot be entirely reduced to other terms. Methods of recruitment, as well as of reward, sometimes lead to the erroneous interpretation that technical positions are economically determined. Actually, however, the acquisition of knowledge and skill cannot be accomplished by purchase, although the opportunity to learn may be. The control of the avenues of training may inhere as a sort of property right in certain families or classes, giving them power and prestige in consequence. Such a situation adds an artificial scarcity to the natural scarcity of skills and talents. On the other hand, it is possible for an opposite situation to arise. The rewards of technical position may be so great that a condition of excess supply is created, leading to at least temporary devaluation of the rewards. Thus "unemployment in the learned professions" may result in a debasement of the prestige of those positions. Such adjustments and readjustments are constantly occurring in changing societies; and it is always well to bear in mind that the efficiency of a stratified structure may be affected by the modes of recruitment for positions. The social order itself, however, sets limits to the inflation or deflation of the prestige of experts: an over-supply tends to debase the rewards and discourage recruitment or produce revolution, whereas an under-supply tends to increase the rewards or weaken the society in competition with other societies.

Particular systems of stratification show a wide range with respect to the exact position of technically competent persons. This range is perhaps most evident in the degree of specialization. Extreme division of labor tends to create many specialists without high prestige since the training is short and the required native capacity relatively small. On the other hand it also tends to accentuate the high position of the true experts — scientists, engineers, and administrators — by increasing their authority relative to other functionally important positions. But the idea of a technocratic social order or a government or priesthood of engineers or social scientists neglects the limitations of knowledge and skills as a basis for performing social functions. To the extent that the social structure is truly specialized the prestige of the technical person must also be circumscribed.

VARIATION IN STRATIFIED SYSTEMS

The generalized principles of stratification here suggested form a necessary preliminary to a consideration of types of stratified systems, because it is in terms of these principles that the types must be described. This can be seen by trying to delineate types according to certain modes of variation. For instance, some of the most important modes (together with the polar types in terms of them) seem to be as follows:

(a) *The degree of specialization.* The degree of specialization affects the fineness and multiplicity of the gradations in power and prestige. It also influences the extent to which particular functions may be emphasized in the invidious system, since a given function cannot receive much emphasis in the hierarchy until it has achieved structural separation from the other functions. Finally, the amount of specialization influences the bases of selection. Polar types: *Specialized, Unspecialized.*

(b) *The nature of the functional emphasis.* In general when emphasis is put on sacred matters, a rigidity is introduced that tends to limit specialization and hence the development of technology. In addition, a brake is placed on social mobility, and on the development of bureaucracy. When the preoccupation with the sacred is withdrawn, leaving greater scope for purely secular preoccupations, a great development, and rise in status, of economic and technological positions seemingly takes place. Curiously, a concomitant rise in political position is not likely, because it has usually been allied with the religious and stands to gain little by the decline of the latter. It is also possible for a society to emphasize family functions — as in relatively undifferentiated societies where high mortality requires high fertility and kinship forms the main basis of social organization. Main types: *Familistic, Authoritarian (Theocratic* or sacred, and *Totalitarian* or secular), *Capitalistic.*

(c) *The magnitude of invidious differences.* What may be called the amount of social distance between positions, taking into account the entire scale, is something that should lend itself to quantitative measurement. Considerable differences apparently exist between different societies in this regard, and also between parts of the same society. Polar types: *Equalitarian, Inequalitarian.*

(d) *The degree of opportunity.* The familiar question of the amount of mobility is different from the question of the comparative equality or inequality of rewards posed above, because the two criteria may vary independently up to a point. For instance, the tremendous divergences in monetary income in the United States are far greater than those found in primitive societies, yet the equality of opportunity to move from one rung to the other in the social scale may also be greater in the United States than in a hereditary tribal kingdom. Polar types: *Mobile* (open), *Immobile* (closed).

(e) *The degree of stratum solidarity.* Again, the degree of "class solidarity" (or the presence of specific organizations to promote class interests) may vary to some extent independently of the other criteria, and hence is an important principle in classifying systems of stratification. Polar types: *Class organized, Class unorganized.*

EXTERNAL CONDITIONS

What state any particular system of stratification is in with reference to each of these modes of variation depends on two things: (1) its state with reference to the other ranges of variation, and (2) the conditions outside the system of stratification which nevertheless influence that system. Among the latter are the following:

(a) *The stage of cultural development.* As the cultural heritage grows, increased specialization becomes necessary, which in turn contributes to the enhancement of mobility, a decline of stratum solidarity, and a change of functional emphasis.

(b) *Situation with respect to other societies.* The presence or absence of open conflict with other societies, of free trade relations or cultural diffusion, all influence the class structure to some extent. A chronic state of warfare tends to place emphasis upon the military functions, especially when the opponents are more or less equal. Free trade, on the other hand, strengthens the hand of the trader at the expense of the warrior and priest. Free movement of ideas generally has an equalitarian effect. Migration and conquest create special circumstances.

(c) *Size of the society.* A small society limits the degree to which functional specialization can go, the degree of segregation of different strata, and the magnitude of inequality.

COMPOSITE TYPES

Much of the literature on stratification has attempted to classify concrete systems into a certain number of types. This task is deceptively simple, however, and should come at the end of an analysis of elements and principles rather than at the beginning. If the preceding discussion has any validity, it indicates that there are a number of modes of variation between different systems, and that any one system is a composite of the society's status with reference to all these modes of variation. The danger of trying to classify whole societies under such rubrics as *caste, feudal,* or *open class* is that one or two criteria are selected and others ignored, the result being an unsatisfactory solution to the problem posed. The present discussion has been offered as a possible approach to the more systematic classification of composite types.

B. Processes and Examples

When one thinks of caste he thinks of India, and the East, where a formerly rigid system determined specifically who could marry whom, who was supposed to sweep floors, carry water, be a beggar or a barber. There was no room for movement in this system. An individual was born into a specific caste, and, theoretically, no matter what his worth or talent, he was destined to remain there. Berreman offers us valuable insights into our own country's system by applying his definition of caste to the situation that has prevailed in the southern part of the United States.

24   GERALD D. BERREMAN

Caste in India and the United States[1]

Many writers who have contributed to the vast literature on the caste system in India have emphasized its unique aspects and ignored or denied the qualities it shares with rigid systems of social stratification found in other societies. Others have claimed to find caste systems or caste groups in such widely scattered areas as Arabia, Polynesia, Africa, Guatemala, and Japan.[2] Some observers refer to Negro-white relations in the United States, and

From *American Journal of Sociology,* Vol. LXVI (September, 1960), pp. 120–127. Reprinted by permission of the author and The University of Chicago Press.

[1] Delivered in abbreviated form before the Fifty-eighth Annual Meeting of the American Anthropological Association in Mexico City, December, 1959, and based partly on research carried out in India under a Ford Foundation Foreign Area Training Fellowship during fifteen months of 1957–58 (reported in full in my "Kin, Caste, and Community in a Himalayan Hill Village" [unpublished Ph.D. dissertation, Cornell University, 1959]). I am indebted to Joel V. Berreman and Lloyd A. Fallers for their helpful comments.

[2] E. D. Chapple and C. S. Coon, *Principles of Anthropology* (New York: Henry Holt & Co., 1942), p. 437; S. F. Nadel, "Caste and Government in Primitive Society," *Journal of the Anthropological Society of Bombay,* New Series VIII (September, 1954), 9–22; M. M. Tumin, *Caste in a Peasant Society* (Princeton, N.J.: Princeton University Press, 1952); J. D. Donoghue, "An Eta Community in Japan: The Social Persistence of Outcaste Groups," *American Anthropologist,* LIX (December, 1957), 1000–1017.

particularly in the South, as being those of caste,[3] a usage which others, including C. S. Johnson, Oliver C. Cox, and, more recently, G. E. Simpson and J. M. Yinger, have criticized. This paper will compare the relationship between "touchable," especially twice-born, and "untouchable" castes in India with that between Negroes and whites in the southern United States.

Caste can be defined so that it is applicable only to India, just as it is possible to define narrowly almost any sociocultural phenomenon. Indianists have traditionally held to specific, usually enumerative, definitions. Indeed, the caste system in India has several unique features, among which are its religious aspects, its complexity, and the degree to which the caste is a cohesive group that regulates the behavior of its members. Within India there is considerable variation in the characteristics of, and the relations among, the groups to which the term "caste" is applied.

However, caste can be accurately defined in broader terms. For many purposes similar social facts may be usefully categorized together, despite differences which, while not denied, are not crucial to the purposes at hand. For purposes of cross-cultural comparison this is necessary: for the study of social process, and with the aim of deriving generalizations, caste is a concept which might well be applied cross-culturally. For these purposes a caste system may be defined as a *hierarchy of endogamous divisions in which membership is hereditary and permanent*. Here hierarchy includes inequality both in status and in access to goods and services. Interdependence of the subdivisions, restricted contacts among them, occupational specialization, and/or a degree of cultural distinctiveness might be added as criteria, although they appear to be correlates rather than defining characteristics.

This definition is perhaps best viewed as describing an ideal type at one end of a continuum along which systems of social stratification might be ranged. There can be little doubt that the systems in India and the southern United States would fall far toward the caste extreme of the continuum.[4] It now becomes necessary to look at the differences cited as crucial by those who object to use of the term "caste" in both societies. The objections raised by those interested in structure, relationships, and interaction will be discussed here; the objections of those interested in specific content will be ignored — not because the latter objections are less cogent, but because they are less relevant to the comparison of social systems.[5]

[3] E.g., Allison Davis, Kingsley Davis, John Dollard, Buell Gallagher, Gunnar Myrdal, Kenneth Stampp, Lloyd Warner.

[4] The Tira of Africa, for example, would not fall so far toward this extreme (cf. Nadel, *op. cit.*, pp. 18 ff.).

[5] As a matter of fact, ignorance of the details of content in the patterns of relations between whites and Negroes in the United States has prevented many Indianists from seeing very striking similarities. Two contrasting views of the cross-cultural applicability of the concept of caste have appeared since this paper was written: F. C. Bailey, "For a Sociology of India?" *Contributions to Indian Sociology*, No. 3 (July, 1959), 88–101, esp. 97–98; and E. R. Leach, "Introduction: What Should We Mean by Caste?" in *Aspects of Caste in South India, Ceylon and North-west Pakistan* ("Cambridge Papers in Social Anthropology," No. 2 [Cambridge: Cambridge University Press, 1959]), pp. 1–10.

Johnson sees many similarities in the two systems but objects to identifying both as caste, since "a caste system is not only a separated system, it is a stable system in which changes are socially impossible; the fact that change cannot occur is accepted by all, or practically all, participants. . . . No expenditure of psychological or physical energy is necessary to maintain a caste system."[6] Simpson and Yinger agree with Johnson and further object that, in the United States, "we lack a set of religious principles justifying a rigid system of social stratification and causing it to be willingly accepted by those at all levels."[7] Cox lists a number of features of a caste system (i.e., caste in India) which distinguish it from an interracial situation (i.e., Negro-white relations in America), important among which are its "nonconflictive," "nonpathological," and "static" nature, coupled with absence of "aspiration and progressiveness."[8]

Central to these distinctions is that caste in India is passively accepted and indorsed by all on the basis of religio-philosophical explanations which are universally subscribed to, while Negro-white relations in America are characterized by dissent, resentment, guilt, and conflict. But this contrast is invalid, resulting, as it does, from an idealized and unrealistic view of Indian caste, contrasted with a more realistic, pragmatic view of American race relations; Indian caste is viewed as it is supposed to work rather than as it does work; American race relations are seen as they do work rather than as they are supposed, by the privileged, to work. The traditional white southerner, asked to describe relations between the races, will describe the Negro as happy in his place, which he may quote science and Scripture to justify. This is similar to the explanations offered for the Indian system by the advantaged.

The point here is that ideal intercaste behavior and attitudes in India are much like those in America, while the actual interaction and attitudes are also similar. Commonly, ideal behavior and attitudes in India have been contrasted with real behavior and attitudes in America — a fact which has led to a false impression of difference. Similarly, comparisons of race relations in the rapidly changing urban or industrial South with caste relations in slowly changing rural or agrarian India lead to erroneous conclusions. Valid comparison can be made at either level, but must be with comparable data. The impact on intergroup relations of the social and economic changes which accompany urban life seems to be similar in both societies. Recent literature on village India and on the changing caste functions and caste

[6] C. S. Johnson, *Growing Up in the Black Belt* (Washington, D.C.: American Council on Education, 1941), p. 326.

[7] G. E. Simpson and J. M. Yinger, *Racial and Cultural Minorities* (New York: Harper & Bros., 1953), p. 328.

[8] O. C. Cox, "Race and Caste: A Distinction," *American Journal of Sociology,* L (March, 1945), 360 (see also his *Caste, Class and Race* [Garden City, N.Y.: Doubleday & Co., 1948]).

relations in cities and industrial areas presents a realistic picture which goes far toward counteracting traditional stereotypes of Indian caste.[9]

In a study of caste functioning in Sirkanda, a hill village of northern Uttar Pradesh, India, I was struck by the similarity of relations between the twice-born and untouchable castes to race relations in the southern United States.[10] In both situations there is a genuine caste division, according to the definition above. In the two systems there are rigid rules of avoidance between castes, and certain types of contacts are defined as contaminating, while others are non-contaminating. The ideological justification for the rules differs in the two cultures, as do the definitions of the acts themselves; but these are cultural details. The tabooed contacts are symbolically rather than literally injurious as evidenced by the many inconsistencies in application of the rules.[11] Enforced deference, for example, is a prominent feature of both systems. Lack of deference from low castes is not contaminating, but it is promptly punished, for it implies equality. The essential similarity lies in the fact that the function of the rules in both cases is to maintain the caste system with institutionalized inequality as its fundamental feature. In the United States, color is a conspicuous mark of caste, while in India there are complex religious features which do not appear in America,

---

[9] See, for example, the following community studies: F. G. Bailey, *Caste and the Economic Frontier* (Manchester: University of Manchester Press, 1957); Berreman, *op. cit.*; S. C. Dube, *Indian Village* (Ithaca, N.Y.: Cornell University Press, 1955); Oscar Lewis, *Village Life in Northern India* (Urbana: University of Illinois Press, 1958); McKim Marriott (ed.), *Village India* (American Anthropological Association Memoir No. 83 [Chicago: University of Chicago Press, 1955]); M. E. Opler and R. D. Singh, "The Division of Labor in an Indian Village," in *A Reader in General Anthropology*, ed. C. S. Coon (New York: Henry Holt & Co., 1948), pp. 464–496; M. N. Srinivas, *et al., India's Villages* (Development Department, West Bengal: West Bengal Government Press, 1955). See also, for example, the following studies of caste in the contemporary setting: Bailey, *op. cit.*; N. K. Bose, "Some Aspects of Caste in Bengal," *American Journal of Folklore*, LXXI (July–September, 1958), 397–412; Leach, *op. cit.*; Arthur Niehoff, *Factory Workers in India* ("Milwaukee Public Museum Publications in Anthropology," No. 5 [1959]); M. N. Srinivas, "Caste in Modern India," *Journal of Asian Studies*, XVI (August, 1957), 529–548; and the several articles comprising the symposium on "Caste in India" contained in *Man in India*, XXXIX (April–June, 1959), 92–162.

[10] The following discussion is based not exclusively on the Sirkanda materials but on observations and literature in non-hill areas as well. The hill area presents some distinct regional variations in caste structure, important among which is the absence of intermediate castes — all are either twice-born or untouchable. This leads to a dichotomous situation, as in the United States, but one which differs in that there are important caste divisions on either side of the "pollution barrier" (cf. Bailey, *op. cit.*, p. 8; Berreman, *op. cit.*, pp. 389 ff.). Relations across this barrier do not differ greatly from similar relations among plains castes, although somewhat more informal contact is allowed — pollution comes about less easily — in the hills.

[11] The symbolic acts — the "etiquette" of caste relations — in India and in America are often remarkably similar. The symbolism in America is, of course, not primarily religious as much as it is in India, although the sacred aspects in India are often far from the minds of those engaging in the acts and are not infrequently unknown to them.

but in both cases dwelling area, occupation, place of worship, and cultural behavior, and so on, are important symbols associated with caste status. The crucial fact is that caste status is determined, and therefore the systems are perpetuated, by birth: membership in them is ascribed and unalterable. Individuals in low castes are considered inherently inferior and are relegated to a disadvantaged position, regardless of their behavior. From the point of view of the social psychology of intergroup relations, this is probably the most important common and distinct feature of caste systems.

In both the United States and India, high castes maintain their superior position by exercising powerful sanctions, and they rationalize their status with elaborate philosophical, religious, psychological, or genetic explanations. The latter are not sufficient in themselves to maintain the systems, largely because they are incompletely accepted among those whose depressed position they are thought to justify. In both places castes are economically interdependent. In both there are great differences in power and privilege among, as well as class differences within, castes and elaborate barriers to free social intercourse among them.

Similarities in the two caste systems extend throughout the range of behavior and attitudes expressed in relations among groups. An important and conspicuous area of similarity is associated with competition for certain benefits or "gains" which are personally gratifying and/or socially valued and which by their nature or under the circumstances cannot be enjoyed by all equally. Competitive striving is, of course, not unique to caste organization; it is probably found to some extent in all societies. It is subject to a variety of social controls resulting in a variety of forms of social stratification, one of which is a caste system as defined here. However, the genesis of caste systems is not here at issue.[12]

The caste system in India and in the United States has secured gains for the groups established at the top of the hierarchy. Their desire to retain their position for themselves and their children accounts for their efforts to perpetuate the system. John Dollard, in his discussion of "Southern-town," identifies their gains as economic, sexual, and in prestige.

In the economic field, low-caste dependence is maintained in India as in America by economic and physical sanctions. This assures not only greater high-caste income but a ready supply of free service and cheap labor from the low castes. It also guarantees the continuing availability of the other gains. In India it is the most explicitly recognized high-caste advantage.

The sexual gain for the southern white caste is defined by Dollard, quoting whom I will substitute "high caste" and "low caste" for "white" and "Negro," respectively. In this form his definition fits the Indian caste system equally well.

> In simplest terms, we mean by a "sexual gain" the fact that [high-caste] men, by virtue of their caste position, have access to two

[12] Cf. Nadel, *op. cit.*

classes of women, those of the [high] and [low] castes. The same
condition is somewhat true of the [low-caste] women, except that
they are rather the objects of the gain than the choosers, though it
is a fact that they have some degree of access to [high-caste] men
as well as men of their own caste. [Low-caste] men and [high-caste]
women, on the other hand, are limited to their own castes in sexual
choices.[13]

This arrangement is maintained in the Indian caste system, as it is in
America, by severe sanctions imposed upon any low-caste man who might
venture to defy the code, by the toleration accorded high-caste men who
have relations with low-caste women, and by the precautions which high-
caste men take to protect their women from the low castes.

High-caste people gain, by virtue of their caste status alone, deference
from others, constant reinforcement of a feeling of superiority, and a permanent scapegoat in the lower castes. Dollard has stated the implications
of this gain in prestige, and, again substituting a caste designation for a
racial one, his statement describes the Indian system perfectly:

The gain here . . . consists in the fact that a member of the
[high] caste has an automatic right to demand forms of behavior
from [low-caste people] which serve to increase his own self-esteem.

It must always be remembered that in the end this deference is
demanded and not merely independently given.[14]

Ideally the high-caste person is paternalistic and authoritarian, while the
low-caste person responds with deferential, submissive, subservient behavior. Gallagher might have been describing India rather than America when
he noted: "By the attitudes of mingled fear, hostility, deprecation, discrimination, amused patronage, friendly domination, and rigid authoritarianism,
the white caste generates opposite, and complementary attitudes in the
Negro caste."[15]

An additional high-caste gain in India is the religious tradition which
gives people of high caste promise of greater rewards in the next life than
those of low caste. People can increase their rewards in the next life by
fulfilling their traditional caste duty. For high castes, this generally results
in increasing the economic advantages and prestige acquired in this life,
while it requires that the low castes subordinate their own economic gains
and prestige in this life to the service and honor of high castes. Thus, for

[13] John Dollard, *Caste and Class in a Southern Town* ("Anchor Books" [Garden City,
N.Y.: Doubleday & Co., 1957]), p. 135 (cf. Berreman, *op. cit.*, pp. 470 ff.).

[14] Dollard, *op. cit.*, p. 174. Nadel speaking of caste in general, has noted that "the
lower caste are despised, not only unhappily under-privileged; they bear a stigma apart
from being unfortunate. Conversely, the higher castes are not merely entitled to the
possession of coveted privileges, but are also in some way exalted and endowed with a
higher dignity" (Nadel, *op. cit.*, p. 16).

[15] B. G. Gallagher, *American Caste and the Negro College* (New York: Columbia
University Press, 1938), p. 109.

high-caste people, behavior leading to immediate rewards is consistent with ultimate rewards, while, for low-caste people, behavior required for the two rewards is contradictory.

These advantages are significant and recognized reasons for maintenance of the system by the privileged groups.[16] They are expressed in folklore, proverbs, and jokes; for instance, a story tells that, as the funeral procession of an old landlord passed two untouchable women going for water, one hand of the corpse fell from under the shroud and flopped about. One of the women turned to the other and remarked, "You see, Takur Singh is dead, but he still beckons to us." Other stories recount the avariciousness of Brahmins in their priestly role, the hardheartedness of landlords and the like.

The compensatory gains for low-caste people are cited more often by high-caste advocates of the system than by those alleged to enjoy them. They are gains common to authoritarian systems everywhere and are usually subject to the will of the dominant groups.

As noted above, India is frequently cited as an example of a society in which people of deprived and subject status are content with their lot, primarily justifying it by religion and philosophy. This is the characteristic of caste in India most often cited to distinguish it from hereditary systems elsewhere, notably in the southern United States. On the basis of my research and the literature, I maintain that this is not accurate and therefore not a valid distinction. Its prevalence is attributable in part, at least, to the vested interests of the advantaged and more articulate castes in the perpetuation of the caste system and the maintenance of a favorable view of it to outsiders. The same arguments and the same biases are frequently presented by apologists for the caste system of the southern United States.

In both systems there is a tendency to look to the past as a period of halcyon amity and to view conflict and resentment as resulting from outside disturbances of the earlier normal equilibrium. Alien ideas, or large-scale economic disturbances, or both, are often blamed for reform movements and rebellion. Such explanations may account for the national and regional reform movements which find their advocates and followers primarily among the educated and social elites; they do not account for the recurrent grass-roots attempts, long endemic in India, to raise caste status; for the state of mind which has often led to low-caste defections from Hinduism when the opportunity to do so without fear of major reprisals has presented itself; nor for the chronic resentment and tension which characterizes intercaste relations in even so remote a village as Sirkanda, the one in which I worked.

[16] Cf. Pauline M. Mahar, "Changing Caste Ideology in a North Indian Village," *Journal of Social Issues,* XIV (1958), 51–65, esp. pp. 55–56; Kailash K. Singh, "Intercaste Tensions in Two Villages in North India" (unpublished Ph.D. dissertation, Cornell University, 1957), pp. 184–185; and M. N. Srinivas, "The Dominant Caste in Rampura," *American Anthropologist,* LXI (1959), 1–16, esp. p. 4.

Among the low or untouchable castes in Sirkanda, there was a great deal of readily expressed resentment regarding their caste position. Specific complaints revolved around economic, prestige, and sexual impositions by the high castes. Although resentment was suppressed in the presence of people of the dominant high castes, it was readily expressed where there was no fear of detection or reprisal.[17] Low-caste people felt compelled to express village loyalties in public, but in private acts and attitudes caste loyalties were consistently and intensely dominant when the two conflicted.

Caste, as such, was not often seriously questioned in the village. Objections were characteristically directed not at "caste" but at "my position in the caste hierarchy."

In the multicaste system of India, abolition of the system evidently seems impossible from the point of view of any particular caste, and a change in its rank within the system is viewed by its members as the only plausible means of improving the situation. Moreover, abolition would destroy the caste as a group which is superior to at least some other groups, and, while it would give caste members an opportunity to mingle as equals with their superiors, it would also force them to mingle as equals with their inferiors. Abolition, even if it could be accomplished, would thus create an ambivalent situation for any particular caste in contrast to the clear-cut advantages of an improvement in rank.

In the dual system of the southern United States where the high caste is clearly dominant, abolition of the caste division may be seen by the subordinate group as the only plausible remedy for their deprived position. Furthermore, they have nothing to lose but their inferior status, since there are no lower castes. There are, of course, Negroes and organized groups of Negroes, such as the black supremacist "Muslims" recently in the news in the United States, who want to invert the caste hierarchy; conversely, there are low-caste people in India who want to abolish the entire system. But these seem to be atypical viewpoints. The anticaste religions and reform movements which have from time to time appealed with some success to the lower castes in India, for example, Buddhism, Islam, Christianity, Sikhism, have been unable, in practice, to remain casteless. This seems to be a point of real difference between Indian and American low-caste attitudes, for in America objection is more characteristically directed toward the system as such.[18]

In Sirkanda those low-caste people who spoke most piously against high-caste abuses were likely to be equally abusive to their caste inferiors. However, no low caste was encountered whose members did not seriously

[17] Elaborate precautions were often taken by informants to insure against any possibility that their expressions of feeling might become known to their caste superiors, which is very similar to behavior I have observed among Negroes of Montgomery, Alabama.

[18] Whether this difference in attitude is widely correlated with multiple, as compared to dual, caste systems, or is attributable to other differences in the Indian and American situations, can be established only by further comparative work.

question its place in the hierarchy. A sizable literature is accumulating concerning castes which have sought to alter their status.[19] Such attempts were made in Sirkanda. A more common reaction to deprived status on the part of low-caste people was what Dollard calls "passive accommodation" coupled with occasional ingroup aggression.[20]

In both America and India there is a tendency for the person of low caste to "laugh it off" or to become resigned. In Sirkanda low-caste people could not avoid frequent contacts with their superiors, because of their proximity and relative numbers. Contacts were frequently informal, but status differences and the dangers of ritual pollution were not forgotten. An untouchable in this village who covered up his bitter resentment by playing the buffoon received favors denied to his more sullen caste fellows. The irresponsible, simple-minded untouchable is a widespread stereotype and one which he, like the Negro, has found useful. Similarly, sullen resignation, with the attendant stereotype of lazy shiftlessness, is a common response, typified in the southern Negro axiom, "Do what the man says." This, too, helps him avoid trouble, although it does little for the individual's self-respect. Aggression against the economically and numerically dominant high castes in Sirkanda was too dangerous to be a reasonable alternative. It was discussed by low-caste people in private but was rarely carried out. Even legitimate complaints to outside authority were avoided in view of the general belief that the high-caste's wealth would insure an outcome unfavorable to the low castes — a belief well grounded in experience.

Since they harbored indignation and resentment, a number of rationalizations of their status were employed by low-caste people, apparently as mechanisms to lessen the sting of reality. Thus, they often attributed their caste status to relative wealth and numbers: "If we were wealthy and in the majority, we would make the high castes untouchable."

Three more explanations of their caste status were consistently offered by low-caste people. These had the effect of denying the legitimacy of their low-caste position:

1. Members of the entire caste (or sub-caste) group would deny that they deserved the low status to which they had been assigned. One example:

> Englishmen and Muslims are untouchables because they have an alien religion and they eat beef. This is as it should be. We are Hindus and we do not eat beef, yet we, too are treated as untouchables. This is not proper. We should be accorded higher status.

No group would admit to being lowest in the caste hierarchy.

---

[19] E.g., Opler and Singh, op. cit., p. 476; B. S. Cohn, "The Changing Status of a Depressed Caste," in Marriott (ed.), op. cit., pp. 53–77; and Bailey, op. cit., pp. 220–226.
[20] Dollard, op. cit., p. 253.

2. People might grant that the caste of their clan, lineage, or family was of low status but deny that their particular group really belonged to it. I have not encountered a low-caste group which did not claim high-caste ancestry or origin. Thus a typical comment is:

> Yes, we are drummers by occupation, but our ancestor was a Brahmin who married a drummer woman. By rights, therefore, we should be Brahmins, but in such cases the high castes here go against the usual custom and assign the child the caste of his low-caste parent rather than of his father, from whom a person inherits everything else.

3. A person might grant that his own caste and even his lineage or family were of low status, but his explanation would excuse him from responsibility for it. Such explanations were supplied by Brahmins who, as the most privileged caste and the recipients of religiously motivated charity from all castes, have a vested interest in maintenance of the system and its acceptance by those at all levels. An individual's horoscope would describe him as having been of high caste and exemplary behavior in a previous life and therefore destined for even greater things in the present life. However, in performing some religiously meritorious act in his previous existence, he inadvertently sinned (e.g., he was a raja, tricked by dishonest servants who did not give to the Brahmin the charity he intended for them). As a result he had to be punished in this life with a low rebirth.

Thus, no one said, in effect, "I am of low status and so are my family members and my caste-fellows, and justly so, because of our misdeeds in previous lives." To do so would lead to a psychologically untenable position, though one advocated by high-caste people and by orthodox Hinduism. Rationalizations or beliefs such as these form a consistent pattern — they are not isolated instances. Neither are they unique to the village or culture reported here: the literature reveals similar beliefs elsewhere in North India.[21] They evidently indicate something less than enthusiastic acceptance of caste position and, meanwhile, they perhaps alleviate or divert resentment.

That people remain in an inferior position, therefore, does not mean that they do so willingly, or that they believe it is justified, or that they would do anything in their power to change it, given the opportunity. Rationalizations of caste status which are consistent and convincing to those who are unaffected or who benefit from them seem much less so to those whose deprivation they are expected to justify or explain. Adherence to a religious

---

[21] Cf. E. T. Atkinson, *The Himalayan Districts of the North-Western Provinces of India* (Allahabad: North-Western Provinces and Oudh Press, 1886), III, 446; B. S. Cohn, "The Camars of Senapur: A Study of the Changing Status of a Depressed Caste" (unpublished Ph.D. dissertation, Cornell University, 1954), pp. 112 ff.; and D. N. Majumdar, *The Fortunes of Primitive Tribes* (Lucknow: Universal Publishers Ltd., 1944), p. 193.

principle may not significantly affect the attitudes and behavior to which logic would seem, or to which dogma attempts, to tie it. A comparison of the realities of caste attitudes and interaction in India and the United States suggests that no group of people is content to be low in a caste hierarchy — to live a life of inherited deprivation and subjection — regardless of the rationalizations offered them by their superiors or constructed by themselves. This is one of many points on which further cross-cultural comparison, and only cross-cultural comparison of caste behavior might be conclusive.

It should be evident that the range of similarities between caste in India and race relations in America, when viewed as relations among people, is wide and that the details are remarkably similar in view of the differences in cultural context. Without denying or belittling the differences, I would hold that the term "caste system" is applicable at the present time in the southern United States, if it is applicable anywhere outside of Hindu India, and that it can be usefully applied to societies with systems of hierarchical, endogamous subdivisions whose membership is hereditary and permanent, wherever they occur. By comparing caste situations, so defined, it should be possible to derive further insight, not only into caste in India, but into a widespread type of relations between groups — insight which is obscured if we insist upon treating Indian caste as entirely unique.

Class, as an independent variable, influences a wide variety of behavior, such as voting, church membership, child-rearing patterns, and relationship with relatives. Also related to class, as indicated in the article by Schatzman and Strauss, are patterns of communication and perception. One's perception of the world is shaped by his class-based cognitive makeup, whether this makeup is "deranged" or not. In this classic study by a sociologist, Hollingshead, and a psychiatrist, Redlich, we see how social class is related to psychiatric disorders.

25 A. B. HOLLINGSHEAD AND F. C. REDLICH

Social Stratification and Psychiatric Disorders

The research reported here grew out of the work of a number of men, who, during the last half century, have demonstrated that the social environment in which individuals live is connected in some way, as yet not fully explained, to the development of mental illness.[1] Medical men have approached this problem largely from the viewpoint of epidemiology.[2] Sociol-

From *American Sociological Review,* Vol. XVIII (April, 1953), pp. 163–169. Reprinted by permission of the American Sociological Association.

[1] For example, see, A. J. Rosanoff, *Report of a Survey of Mental Disorders in Nassau County, New York,* New York: National Committee for Mental Hygiene, 1916; Ludwig Stern, *Kulturkreis und Form der Geistigen Erkrankung* (Sammlung Zwanglosen Abshandlungen aus dem Gebiete der Nerven-und-Geisteskrankheiten), X, No. 2, Halle a. S:C. Marhold, 1913, pp. 1–62; J. F. Sutherland, "Geographical Distribution of Lunacy in Scotland," *British Association for Advancement of Science,* Glasgow, Sept, 1901; William A. White, "Geographical Distribution of Insanity in the United States," *Journal of Nervous and Mental Disease,* XXX (1903), pp. 257–279.

[2] For example, see: Trygve Braatoy, "Is It Probable that the Sociological Situation Is a Factor in Schizophrenia?" *Psychiatrica et Neurologica,* XII (1937), pp. 109–138; Donald L. Gerard and Joseph Siegel, "The Family Background of Schizophrenia," *The Psychiatric Quarterly,* 24 (January, 1950), pp. 47–73; Robert W. Hyde and Lowell V. Kingsley, "Studies in Medical Sociology, I: The Relation of Mental Disorders to the Community, Socio-economic Level," *The New England Journal of Medicine,* 231, No. 16 (October 19, 1944), pp. 543–548; Robert W. Hyde and Lowell V. Kingsley, "Studies in Medical Sociology, II: The Relation of Mental Disorders to Population Density," *The New England Journal of Medicine,* 231, No. 17 (October 26, 1944), pp. 571–577; Robert M. Hyde and Roderick M. Chisholm, "Studies in Medical Sociology, III: The Relation of Mental Disorders to Race and Nationality," *The New England Journal of Medicine,* 231, No. 18 (November 2, 1944), pp. 612–618; William Malamud and Irene Malamud, "A Socio-Psychiatric Investigation of Schizophrenia Occurring in the Armed Forces," *Psychosomatic Medicine,* 5 (October, 1943) pp. 364–375; B. Malzberg, *Social and Biological Aspects of Mental Disease,* Utica, N. Y.: State Hospital Press, 1940; William F. Roth and Frank H. Luton, "The Mental Health Program in Tennessee: Statistical Report of a Psychiatric Survey in a Rural County," *American Journal of Psychiatry,* 99 (March, 1943), pp. 662–675; J. Ruesch and others, *Chronic Disease and Psychological Invalidism,* New York: American Society for Research in Psychosomatic Problems, 1946; J. Ruesch and others, *Duodenal Ulcer: A Socio-Psychological Study of Naval Enlisted Personnel and Civilians,* Berkeley and Los Angeles: University of California Press, 1948; Jurgen Ruesch, Annemarie Jacobson, and Martin B. Loeb, "Acculturation and Illness," *Psychological Monographs: General and Applied,* Vol. 62, No. 5, Whole No. 292, 1948 (American Psychological Association, 1515 Massachusetts Ave., N.W., Washington 5, D. C.); C. Tietze, Paul Lemkau and M. Cooper, "A Survey of Statistical Studies on the Prevalence and Incidence of Mental Disorders in Sample Populations," *Public Health Reports,* 1909–27, 58 (December 31, 1943); C. Tietze, P. Lemkau and Marcia Cooper, "Schizophrenia, Manic Depressive Psychosis and Social-Economic Status," *American Journal of Sociology,* XLVII (September, 1941), pp. 167–175.

ogists, on the other hand, have analyzed the question in terms of ecology,[3] and of social disorganization.[4] Neither psychiatrists nor sociologists have carried on extensive research into the specific question we are concerned with, namely, interrelations between the class structure and the development of mental illness. However, a few sociologists and psychiatrists have written speculative and research papers in this area.[5]

The present research, therefore, was designed to discover whether a relationship does or does not exist between the class system of our society and mental illnesses. Five general hypotheses were formulated in our research plan to test some dimension of an assumed relationship between the two. These hypotheses were stated positively; they could just as easily have been expressed either negatively or conditionally. They were phrased as follows:

    I. The *expectancy* of a psychiatric disorder is related significantly to an individual's position in the class structure of his society.

   II. The *types* of psychiatric disorders are connected significantly to the class structure.

  III. The type of *psychiatric treatment* administered is associated with patient's position in the class structure.

  IV. The *psycho-dynamics* of psychiatric disorders are correlative to an individual's position in the class structure.

   V. *Mobility* in the class structure is neurotogenic.

Each hypothesis is linked to the others, and all are subsumed under the theoretical assumption of a functional relationship between stratification in society and the prevalence of particular types of mental disorders among

---

[3] Robert E. L. Faris and H. Warren Dunham, *Mental Disorders in Urban Areas*, Chicago: University of Chicago Press, 1939; H. Warren Dunham, "Current Status of Ecological Research in Mental Disorder," *Social Forces*, 25 (March, 1947), pp. 321–326; R. H. Felix and R. V. Bowers, "Mental Hygiene and Socio-Environmental Factors," *The Milbank Memorial Fund Quarterly*, XXVI (April, 1948), pp. 125–147; H. W. Green, *Persons Admitted to the Cleveland State Hospital*, 1928–1937, Cleveland Health Council, 1939.

[4] R. E. L. Faris, "Cultural Isolation and the Schizophrenic Personality," *American Journal of Sociology*, XXXIX (September, 1934), pp. 155–169; R. E. L. Faris, "Reflections of Social Disorganization in the Behavior of a Schizophrenic Patient," *American Journal of Sociology*, L (September, 1944), pp. 134–141.

[5] For example, see: Robert E. Clark, "Psychoses, Income, and Occupational Prestige," *American Journal of Sociology*, 44 (March, 1949), pp. 433–440; Robert E. Clark, "The Relationship of Schizophrenia to Occupational Income and Occupational Prestige," *American Sociological Review*, 13 (June, 1948), pp. 325–330; Kingsley Davis, "Mental Hygiene and the Class Structure," *Psychiatry*, I (February, 1938), pp. 55–56; Talcott Parsons, "Psychoanalysis and the Social Structure," *The Psychoanalytical Quarterly*, XIX, No. 3 (1950), pp. 371–384; John Dollard and Neal Miller, *Personality and Psychotherapy*, New York: McGraw-Hill, 1950; Jurgen Ruesch, "Social Technique, Social Status, and Social Change in Illness," Clyde Kluckhohn and Henry A. Murray (editors), in *Personality in Nature, Society, and Culture*, New York: Alfred A. Knopf, 1949, pp. 117–130; W. L. Warner, "The Society, the Individual and His Mental Disorders," *American Journal of Psychiatry*, 94, No. 2 (September, 1937), pp. 275–284.

given social classes or strata in a specified population. Although our research was planned around these hypotheses, we have been forced by the nature of the problem of mental illness to study *diagnosed* prevalence of psychiatric disorders, rather than *true* or *total* prevalence.

METHODOLOGICAL PROCEDURE

The research is being done by a team of four psychiatrists,[6] two sociologists,[7] and a clinical psychologist.[8] The data are being assembled in the New Haven urban community, which consists of the city of New Haven and surrounding towns of East Haven, North Haven, West Haven, and Hamden. This community had a population of some 250,000 persons in 1950.[9] The New Haven community was selected because the community's structure has been studied intensively by sociologists over a long period. In addition, it is served by a private psychiatric hospital, three psychiatric clinics, and 27 practicing psychiatrists, as well as the state and Veterans Administration facilities.

Four basic technical operations had to be completed before the hypotheses could be tested. These were: the delineation of the class structure of the community, selection of a cross-sectional control of the community's population, the determination of who was receiving psychiatric care, and the stratification of both the control sample and the psychiatric patients.

August B. Hollingshead and Jerome K. Myers took over the task of delineating the class system. Fortunately, Maurice R. Davie and his students had studied the social structure of the New Haven community in great detail over a long time span.[10] Thus, we had a large body of data we could draw upon to aid us in blocking out the community's social structure.

The community's social structure is differentiated *vertically* along racial, ethnic, and religious lines; each of these vertical cleavages, in turn, is differentiated *horizontally* by a series of strata or classes. Around the sociobiological axis of race two social worlds have evolved: A Negro world and

---

[6] F. C. Redlich, B. H. Roberts, L. Z. Freedman, and Leslie Schaffer.

[7] August B. Hollingshead and J. K. Myers.

[8] Harvey A. Robinson.

[9] The population of each component was as follows: New Haven, 164,443; East Haven, 12,212; North Haven, 9,444; West Haven, 32,010; Hamden, 29,715; and Woodbridge, 2,822.

[10] Maurice R. Davie, "The Pattern of Urban Growth," G. P. Murdock (editor), in *Studies in the Science of Society,* New Haven: 1937, pp. 133–162; Ruby J. R. Kennedy, "Single or Triple Melting-Pot: Intermarriage Trends in New Haven, 1870–1940," *American Journal of Sociology,* 39 (January, 1944), pp. 331–339; John W. McConnell, *The Influence of Occupation Upon Social Stratification,* Unpublished Ph.D. thesis, Sterling Memorial Library, Yale University, 1937; Jerome K. Myers, "Assimilation to the Ecological and Social Systems of a Community," *American Sociological Review,* 15 (June, 1950), pp. 367–372; Mhyra Minnis, "The Relationship of Women's Organizations to the Social Structure of a City," Unpublished Ph.D. Thesis, Sterling Memorial Library, Yale University, 1951.

a white world. The white world is divided by ethnic origin and religion into Catholic, Protestant, and Jewish contingents. Within these divisions there are numerous ethnic groups. The Irish hold aloof from the Italians, and the Italians move in different circles from the Poles. The Jews maintain a religious and social life separate from the gentiles. The *horizontal* strata that transect each of these vertical divisions are based upon the social values that are attached to occupation, education, place of residence in the community, and associations.

The vertically differentiating factors of race, religion and ethnic origin, when combined with the horizontally differentiating ones of occupation, education, place of residence and so on, produce a social structure that is highly compartmentalized. The integrating factors in this complex are two-fold. First, each stratum of each vertical division is similar in its cultural characteristics to the corresponding stratum in the other divisions. Second, the cultural pattern for each stratum or class was set by the "Old Yankee" core group. This core group provided the master cultural mold that has shaped the status system of each sub-group in the community. In short, the social structure of the New Haven community is a parallel class structure within the limits of race, ethnic origin, and religion.

This fact enabled us to stratify the community, for our purposes, with an *Index of Social Position*.[11] This *Index* utilizes three scaled factors to determine an individual's class position within the community's stratificational system: ecological area of residence, occupation, and education. Ecological area of residence is measured by a six point scale; occupation and education are each measured by a seven point scale. To obtain a social class score on an individual we must therefore know his address, his occupation, and the number of years of school he has completed. Each of these factors is given a scale score, and the scale score is multiplied by a factor weight determined by a standard regression equation. The factor weights are as follows: Ecological area of residence, 5; occupation, 8; and education, 6. The three factor scores are summed, and the resultant score is taken as an index of this individual's position in the community's social class system.

This *Index* enabled us to delineate five main social class strata within the horizontal dimension of the social structure. These principal strata or classes may be characterized as follows:

> Class I. This stratum is composed of wealthy families whose wealth is often inherited and whose heads are leaders in the community's business and professional pursuits. Its members live in those areas of the community generally regarded as "the best"; the adults are college graduates, usually from famous private institutions, and

[11] A detailed statement of the procedures used to develop and validate this *Index* will be described in a forthcoming monograph on this research tentatively titled *Psychiatry and Social Class* by August B. Hollingshead and Fredrick C. Redlich.

almost all gentile families are listed in the New Haven *Social Directory,* but few Jewish families are listed. In brief, these people occupy positions of high social prestige.

Class II. Adults in this stratum are almost all college graduates; the males occupy high managerial positions, many are engaged in the lesser ranking professions. These families are well-to-do, but there is no substantial inherited or acquired wealth. Its members live in the "better" residential areas; about one-half of these families belong to lesser ranking private clubs, but only 5 per cent of Class II families are listed in the New Haven *Social Directory.*

Class III. This stratum includes the vast majority of small proprietors, white-collar office and sales workers, and a considerable number of skilled manual workers. Adults are predominantly high school graduates, but a considerable percentage have attended business schools and small colleges for a year or two. They live in "good" residential areas; less than 5 per cent belong to private clubs, but they are not included in the *Social Directory.* Their social life tends to be concentrated in the family, the church, and the lodge.

Class IV. This stratum consists predominantly of semi-skilled factory workers. Its adult members have finished the elementary grades, but the older people have not completed high school. However, adults under thirty-five have generally graduated from high school. Its members comprise almost one-half of the community; and their residences are scattered over wide areas. Social life is centered in the family, the neighborhood, the labor union, and public places.

Class V. Occupationally, Class V adults are overwhelmingly semi-skilled factory hands and unskilled laborers. Educationally most adults have not completed the elementary grades. The families are concentrated in the "tenement" and "cold-water flat" areas of New Haven. Only a small minority belong to organized community institutions. Their social life takes place in the family flat, on the street, or in neighborhood social agencies.

The second major technical operation in this research was the enumeration of psychiatric patients. A Psychiatric Census was taken to discover the number and kinds of psychiatric patients in the community. Enumeration was limited to residents of the community who were patients of a psychiatrist or a psychiatric clinic, or were in a psychiatric institution on December 1, 1950. To make reasonably certain that all patients were included in the enumeration, the research team gathered data from all public and private psychiatric institutions and clinics in Connecticut and nearby states, and all private practitioners in Connecticut and the metropolitan New York area. It received the cooperation of all clinics and institutions, and of all practitioners except a small number in New York City. It can be reasonably assumed that we have data comprising at least 98 per cent of all individuals who were receiving psychiatric care on December 1, 1950.

Forty-four pertinent items of information were gathered on each patient and placed on a schedule. The psychiatrists gathered material regarding symptomatology and diagnosis, onset of illness and duration, referral to the practitioner and the institution, and the nature and intensity of treatment. The sociologists obtained information on age, sex, occupation, education, religion, race and ethnicity, family history, marital experiences, and so on.

The third technical research operation was the selection of a control sample from the normal population of the community. The sociologists drew a 5 per cent random sample of households in the community from the 1951, New Haven *City Directory*. This directory covers the entire communal area. The names and addresses in it were compiled in October and November, 1950 — a period very close to the date of the Psychiatric Census. Therefore there was comparability of residence and date of registry between the two population groups. Each household drawn in the sample was interviewed, and data on the age, sex, occupation, education, religion, and income of family members, as well as other items necessary for our purposes were placed on a schedule. This sample is our Control Population.

Our fourth basic operation was the stratification of the psychiatric patients and of the control population with the *Index of Social Position*. As soon as these tasks were completed, the schedules from the Psychiatric Census and the 5 per cent Control Sample were edited and coded, and their data were placed on Hollerith cards. The analysis of these data is in process.

SELECTED FINDINGS

Before we discuss our findings relative to Hypothesis I, we want to reemphasize that our study is concerned with *diagnosed* or *treated* prevalence rather than *true* or *total* prevalence. Our Psychiatric Census included only psychiatric cases under treatment, diagnostic study, or care. It did not include individuals with psychiatric disorders who were not being treated on December 1, 1950, by a psychiatrist. There are undoubtedly many individuals in the community with psychiatric problems who escaped our net. If we had *true* prevalence figures, many findings from our present study would be more meaningful, perhaps some of our interpretations would be changed, but at present we must limit ourselves to the data we have.

Hypothesis I, as revised by the nature of the problem, stated: *The diagnosed prevalence of psychiatric disorders is related significantly to an individual's position* in the class structure. A test of this hypothesis involves a comparison of the normal population with the psychiatric population. If no significant difference between the distribution of the normal population and the psychiatric patient population by social class is found, Hypothesis I may be abandoned as unproved. However, if a significant difference is found between the two populations by class, Hypothesis I should be entertained until more conclusive data are assembled. Pertinent data for a limited test of Hypothesis I are presented in Table 1. The data included show the number of individuals in the normal population and the psychiatric population, by class level. What we are concerned with in this test is how these two populations are distributed by class.

TABLE 1.   DISTRIBUTION OF NORMAL AND PSYCHIATRIC POPULATION BY SOCIAL CLASS

Social class	Normal population[a]		Psychiatric population	
	Number	Per cent	Number	Per cent
I	358	3.1	19	1.0
II	926	8.1	131	6.7
III	2500	22.0	260	13.2
IV	5256	46.0	758	38.6
V	2037	17.8	723	36.8
Unknown[b]	345	3.0	72	3.7
Total	11,422	100.0	1,963	100.0

Chi square $= 408.16$, P less than .001.

[a] These figures are preliminary. They do not include Yale students, transients, institutionalized persons, and refusals.

[b] The unknown cases were not used in the calculation of chi square. They are individuals drawn in the sample, and psychiatric cases whose class level could not be determined because of paucity of data.

When we tested the reliability of these population distributions by the use of the chi square method, we found a *very significant* relation between social class and treated prevalence of psychiatric disorders in the New Haven community. A comparison of the percentage distribution of each population by class readily indicates the direction of the class concentration of psychiatric cases. For example, Class I contains 3.1 per cent of the community's population but only 1.0 per cent of the psychiatric cases. Class V, on the other hand, includes 17.8 per cent of the community's population, but contribated 36.8 per cent of the psychiatric patients. On the basis of our data Hypothesis I clearly should be accepted as tenable.

Hypothesis II postulated a significant connection between the *type* of psychiatric disorder and social class. This hypothesis involves a test of the idea that there may be a functional relationship between an individual's position in the class system and the type of psychiatric disorder that he may present. This hypothesis depends, in part, on the question of diagnosis. Our psychiatrists based their diagnoses on the classificatory system developed by the Veterans Administration.[12] For the purposes of this paper, all cases are grouped into two categories: the neuroses and the psychoses. The results of this grouping by social class are given in Table 2.

TABLE 2. DISTRIBUTION OF NEUROSES AND PSYCHOSES BY SOCIAL CLASS

| | Neuroses | | Psychoses | |
Social class	Number	Per cent	Number	Per cent
I	10	52.6	9	47.4
II	88	67.2	43	32.8
III	115	44.2	145	55.8
IV	175	23.1	583	76.9
V	61	8.4	662	91.6
Total	449		1,442	

Chi square = 296.45, P less than .001.

A study of Table 2 will show that the neuroses are concentrated at the higher levels and the psychoses at the lower end of the class structure. Our team advanced a number of theories to explain the sharp differences between the neuroses and psychoses by social class. One suggestion was that the low percentage of neurotics in the lower classes was a direct reaction to the cost of psychiatric treatment. But as we accumulated a series of case studies, for tests of Hypotheses IV and V, we became skeptical of this simple interpretation. Our detailed case records indicate that the social distance between psychiatrist and patient may be more potent than economic considerations in determining the character of psychiatric intervention. This question therefore requires further research.

The high concentration of psychotics in the lower strata is probably the product of a very unequal distribution of psychotics in the total population. To test this idea, Hollingshead selected schizophrenics for special study. Because of the severity of this disease it is probable that very few schizophrenics fail to receive some kind of psychiatric care. This diagnostic group comprises 44.2 per cent of all patients, and 58.7 per cent of the psychotics, in our study. Ninety-seven and six-tenths per cent of these schizophrenic patients had been hospitalized at one time or another, and 94 per cent were hospitalized at the time of our census. When we classify these patients by social class we find that there is a very significant inverse relationship between social class and schizophrenia.

Hollingshead decided to determine, on the basis of these data, what the probability of the prevalence of schizophrenia by social class might be in the general population. To do this he used a proportional index to learn whether or not there were differentials in the distribution of the general

[12] *Psychiatric Disorders and Reactions,* Washington: Veterans Administration, Technical Bulletin 10A-78, October, 1947.

population, as represented in our control sample, and the distribution of schizophrenics by social class. If a social class exhibits the same proportion of schizophrenia as it comprises of the general population, the index for that class is 100. If schizophrenia is disproportionately prevalent in a social class the index is above 100; if schizophrenia is disproportionately low in a social class the index is below 100. The index for each social class appears in the last column of Table 3.

TABLE 3. COMPARISON OF THE DISTRIBUTION OF THE NORMAL POPULATION WITH SCHIZOPHRENICS BY CLASS, WITH INDEX OF PROBABLE PREVALENCE

Social class	Normal population		Schizophrenics		Index of prevalence
	No.	Per cent	No.	Per cent	
I	358	3.2	6	.7	22
II	926	8.4	23	2.7	33
III	2,500	22.6	83	9.8	43
IV	5,256	47.4	352	41.6	88
V	2,037	18.4	383	45.2	246
Total	11,077	100.0	847	100.0	

The fact that the Index of Prevalence in Class I is only one-fifth as great as it would be if schizophrenia were proportionately distributed in this class, and that it is two and one-half times as high in Class V as we might expect on the basis of proportional distribution, gives further support to Hypothesis II. The fact that the Index of Prevalence is 11.2 times as great in Class V as in Class I is particularly impressive.

Hypothesis III stipulated that the type of psychiatric treatment a patient receives is associated with his position in the class structure. A test of this hypothesis involves a comparison of the different types of therapy being used by psychiatrists on patients in the different social classes. We encountered many forms of therapy but they may be grouped under three main types; psychotherapy, organic therapy, and custodial care. The patient population, from the viewpoint of the principal type of therapy received, was divided roughly into three categories: 32.0 per cent received some type of psychotherapy; 31.7 per cent received organic treatments of one kind or another; and 36.3 per cent received custodial care without treatment. The percentage of persons who received no treatment care was greatest in the lower classes. The same finding applies to organic treatment. Psychotherapy, on the other hand, was concentrated in the higher classes. Within the psychotherapy category there were sharp differences between the types of psychotherapy administered to the several classes. For example, psychoanalysis was limited to Classes I and II. Patients in Class V who received any psychotherapy were treated by group methods in the state hospitals. The number and percentage of patients who received each type of therapy is given in Table 4. The data clearly support Hypothesis III.

TABLE 4.   DISTRIBUTION OF THE PRINCIPAL TYPES OF THERAPY
BY SOCIAL CLASS

	Psychotherapy		Organic therapy		No treatment	
Social class	Number	Per cent	Number	Per cent	Number	Per cent
I	14	73.7	2	10.5	3	15.8
II	107	81.7	15	11.4	9	6.9
III	136	52.7	74	28.7	48	18.6
IV	237	31.1	288	37.1	242	31.8
V	115	16.1	234	32.7	367	51.2

Chi square = 336.58, P less than .001.

At the moment we do not have data available for a test of Hypotheses IV
and V. These will be put to a test as soon as we complete work on a series
of cases now under close study. Preliminary materials give us the impression that they too will be confirmed.

CONCLUSIONS AND INTERPRETATIONS

This study was designed to throw new light upon the question of how
mental illness is related to social environment. It approached this problem
from the perspective of social class to determine if an individual's position
in the social system was associated significantly with the development of
psychiatric disorders. It proceeded on the theoretical assumption that if
mental illnesses were distributed randomly in the population, the hypotheses designed to test the idea that psychiatric disorders are connected in
some functional way to the class system would not be found to be statistically significant.

The data we have assembled demonstrate conclusively that mental illness, as measured by diagnosed prevalence, is not distributed randomly in
the population of the New Haven community. On the contrary, psychiatric
difficulties of so serious a nature that they reach the attention of a psychiatrist are unequally distributed among the five social classes. In addition,
types of psychiatric disorders, and the ways patients are treated, are
strongly associated with social class position.

The statistical tests of our hypotheses indicate that there are definite
connections between particular types of social environments in which people live, as measured by the social class concept, and the emergence of
particular kinds of psychiatric disorders, as measured by psychiatric diagnosis. They do not tell us what these connections are, nor how they are
functionally related to a particular type of mental illness in a given individual. The next step, we believe, is to turn from the strictly statistical approach to an intensive study of the social environments associated with
particular social classes, on the one hand, and of individuals in these environments who do or do not develop mental illnesses, on the other hand.
Currently the research team is engaged in this next step but is not yet ready
to make a formal report of its findings.

VIII SOCIAL DISORGANIZATION

A. Definitions and Concepts

Every social system is subject to certain types of strains because, obviously, all of its members do not have the same needs or desires. Many times, however, disorganization is viewed as an aberrant phenomenon, which it is not. Sometimes it is also viewed as that which breaks down or destroys the system. This also is not true, as Kai Erikson, a social psychiatrist, indicates. Deviance is, quite simply, what a society chooses to label as deviant. That which is "deviant" in one country will not be in another; the "deviant" at one time will not be deviant at another. The function of the society's labeling is to make disorganization a means for defining the boundaries of the system. In this sense, disorganization can be thought of as system-maintaining.

26 KAI T. ERIKSON

Notes on the Sociology of Deviance

It is general practice in sociology to regard deviant behavior as an alien element in society. Deviance is considered a vagrant form of human activity, moving outside the more orderly currents of social life. And since this type of aberration could only occur (in theory) if something were wrong within the social organization itself, deviant behavior is described almost as if it

From *Social Problems,* Vol. IX, No. 4 (1962), pp. 307–314. Reprinted by permission of the author and The Society for the Study of Social Problems.

were leakage from machinery in poor condition: it is an accidental result of disorder and anomie, a symptom of internal breakdown.

The purpose of the following remarks will be to review this conventional outlook and to argue that it provides too narrow a framework for the study of deviant behavior. Deviation, we will suggest, recalling Durkheim's classic statement on the subject, can often be understood as a normal product of stable institutions, a vital resource which is guarded and preserved by forces found in all human organizations.[1]

I

According to current theory, deviant behavior is most likely to occur when the sanctions governing conduct in any given setting seem to be contradictory.[2] This would be the case, for example, if the work rules posted by a company required one course of action from its employees and the longer-range policies of the company required quite another. Any situation marked by this kind of ambiguity, of course, can pose a serious dilemma for the individual: if he is careful to observe one set of demands imposed upon him, he runs the immediate risk of violating some other, and thus may find himself caught in a deviant stance no matter how earnestly he tries to avoid it. In this limited sense, deviance can be regarded a "normal" human response to "abnormal" social conditions, and the sociologist is therefore invited to assume that some sort of pathology exists within the social structure whenever deviant behavior makes an appearance.

This general approach is clearly more concerned with the *etiology* of deviant behavior than with its continuing social *history* — and as a result it often draws sociological attention away from an important area of inquiry. It may be safe to assume that naive acts of deviance, such as first criminal offenses, are provoked by strains in the local situation. But this is only the beginning of a much longer story, for deviant activities can generate a good deal of momentum once they are set into motion: they develop forms of organization, persist over time, and sometimes remain intact long after the strains which originally produced them have disappeared. In this respect, deviant activities are often absorbed into the main tissue of society and derive support from the same forces which stabilize other forms of social life. There are persons in society, for example, who make career commitments to deviant styles of conduct, impelled by some inner need for continuity rather than by any urgencies in the immediate social setting. There are groups in society which actively encourage new deviant trends, often prolonging them beyond the point where they represent an adaption

---

[1] Emile Durkheim, *The Rules of Sociological Method* (translated by S. A. Solovay and J. H. Mueller), Glencoe: The Free Press, 1958.

[2] The best known statements of this general position, of course, are by Robert K. Merton and Talcott Parsons. Merton, *Social Theory and Social Structures* (revised edition), Glencoe: The Free Press, 1957; and Parsons, *The Social System*, Glencoe: The Free Press, 1951.

to strain. These sources of support for deviant behavior are difficult to visualize when we use terms like "strain," "anomie," or "breakdown" in discussions of the problem. Such terms may help us explain how the social structure creates fresh deviant potential, but they do not help us explain how that potential is later shaped into durable, persisting social patterns.[3] The individual's need for self continuity and the group's offer of support are altogether normal processes, even if they are sometimes found in deviant situations; and thus the study of deviant behavior is as much a study of social organization as it is a study of *dis*organization and anomie.

II

From a sociological standpoint, deviance can be defined as conduct which is generally thought to require the attention of social control agencies — that is, conduct about which "something should be done." Deviance is not a property *inherent in* certain forms of behavior; it is a property *conferred upon* these forms by the audiences which directly or indirectly witness them. Sociologically, then, the critical variable in the study of deviance is the social *audience* rather than the individual *person*, since it is the audience which eventually decides whether or not any given action or actions will become a visible case of deviation.

This definition may seem a little indirect, but it has the advantage of bringing a neglected sociological issue into proper focus. When a community acts to control the behavior of one of its members, it is engaged in a very intricate process of selection. Even a determined miscreant conforms in most of his daily behavior — using the correct spoon at mealtime, taking good care of his mother, or otherwise observing the mores of his society — and if the community elects to bring sanctions against him for the occasions when he does act offensively, it is responding to a few deviant details set within a vast context of proper conduct. Thus a person may be jailed or hospitalized for a few scattered moments of misbehavior, defined as a full-time deviant despite the fact that he had supplied the community with countless other indications that he was a decent, moral citizen. The screening device which sifts these telling details out of the individual's over-all performance, then, is a sensitive instrument of social control. It is important to note that this screen takes a number of factors into account which are not directly related to the deviant act itself: it is concerned with the actor's social class, his past record as an offender, the amount of remorse he manages to convey, and many similar concerns which take hold in the shifting moods of the community. This is why the community often overlooks behavior which seems technically deviant (like certain kinds of white collar graft) or takes sharp exception to behavior which seems essentially harm-

[3] Cf. Daniel Glaser and Kent Rice, "Crime, Age, and Employment," *American Sociological Review*, 24 (1959), pp. 679–686.

less (like certain kinds of sexual impropriety). It is an easily demonstrated fact, for example, that working class boys who steal cars are far more likely to go to prison than upper class boys who commit the same or even more serious crimes, suggesting that from the point of view of the community lower class offenders are somehow more deviant. To this extent, the community screen is perhaps a more relevant subject for sociological research than the actual behavior which is filtered through it.

Once the problem is phrased in this way, we can ask: how does a community decide what forms of conduct should be singled out for this kind of attention? And why, having made this choice, does it create special institutions to deal with the persons who enact them? The standard answer to this question is that society sets up the machinery of control in order to protect itself against the "harmful" effects of deviance, in much the same way that an organism mobilizes its resources to combat an invasion of germs. At times, however, this classroom convention only seems to make the problem more complicated. In the first place, as Durkheim pointed out some years ago, it is by no means clear that all acts considered deviant in a culture are in fact (or even in principle) harmful to group life.[4] And in the second place, specialists in crime and mental health have long suggested that deviance can play an important role in keeping the social order intact — again a point we owe originally to Durkheim.[5] This has serious implications for sociological theory in general.

III

In recent years, sociological theory has become more and more concerned with the concept "social system" — an organization of society's component parts into a form which sustains internal equilibrium, resists change, and is boundary maintaining. Now this concept has many abstract dimensions, but it is generally used to describe those forces in the social order which promote a high level of uniformity among human actors and a high degree of symmetry within human institutions. In this sense, the concept is normatively oriented since it directs the observer's attention toward those centers in social space where the core values of society are figuratively located. The main organizational principle of a system, then, is essentially a centripetal one: it draws the behavior of actors toward the nucleus of the system, bringing it within range of basic norms. Any conduct which is neither attracted toward this nerve center by the rewards of conformity nor compelled toward it by other social pressures is considered "out of control," which is to say, deviant.

This basic model has provided the theme for most contemporary thinking about deviance, and as a result little attention has been given to the

[4] Emile Durkheim, *The Division of Labor in Society* (translated by George Simpson), Glencoe: The Free Press, 1952. See particularly Chapter 2, Book 1.

[5] Emile Durkheim, *The Rules of Sociological Method, op. cit.*

notion that systems operate to maintain boundaries. Generally speaking, boundaries are controls which limit the fluctuation of a system's component parts so that the whole retains a defined range of activity — a unique pattern of constancy and stability — within the larger environment.[6] The range of human behavior is potentially so great that any *social* system must make clear statements about the nature and location of its boundaries, placing limits on the flow of behavior so that it circulates within a given cultural area. Thus boundaries are a crucial point of reference for persons living within any system, a prominent concept in the group's special language and tradition. A juvenile gang may define its boundaries by the amount of territory it defends, a professional society by the range of subjects it discusses, a fraternal order by the variety of members it accepts. But in each case, members share the same idea as to where the group begins and ends in social space and know what kinds of experience "belong" within this domain.

For all its apparent abstractness, a social system is organized around the movements of persons joined together in regular social relations. The only material found in a system for marking boundaries, then, is the behavior of its participants; and the form of behavior which best performs this function would seem to be deviant almost by definition, since it is the most extreme variety of conduct to be found within the experience of the group. In this respect, transactions taking place between deviant persons on the one side and agencies of control on the other are boundary maintaining mechanisms. They mark the outside limits of the area in which the norm has jurisdiction, and in this way assert how much diversity and variability can be contained within the system before it begins to lose its distinct structure, its unique shape.

A social norm is rarely expressed as a firm rule or official code. It is an abstract synthesis of the many separate times a community has stated its sentiments on a given issue. Thus the norm has a history much like that of an article of common law: it is an accumulation of decisions made by the community over a long period of time which gradually gathers enough moral influence to serve as a precedent for future decisions. Like an article of common law, the norm retains its validity only if it is regularly used as a basis for judgment. Each time the community censures some act of deviance, then, it sharpens the authority of the violated norm and re-establishes the boundaries of the group.

One of the most interesting features of control institutions, in this regard, is the amount of publicity they have always attracted. In an earlier day, correction of deviant offenders took place in the public market and gave the crowd a chance to display its interest in a direct, active way. In our own day, the guilty are no longer paraded in public places, but instead we

6 Cf. Talcott Parsons, *The Social System, op. cit.*

are confronted by a heavy flow of newspaper and radio reports which offer much the same kind of entertainment. Why are these reports considered "newsworthy" and why do they rate the extraordinary attention they receive? Perhaps they satisfy a number of psychological perversities among the mass audience, as many commentators have suggested, but at the same time they constitute our main source of information about the normative outlines of society. They are lessons through which we teach one another what the norms mean and how far they extend. In a figurative sense, at least, morality and immorality meet at the public scaffold, and it is during this meeting that the community declares where the line between them should be drawn.

Human groups need to regulate the routine affairs of everyday life, and to this end the norms provide an important focus for behavior. But human groups also need to describe and anticipate those areas of being which lie beyond the immediate borders of the group — the unseen dangers which in any culture and in any age seem to threaten the security of group life. The universal folklore depicting demons, devils, witches and evil spirits may be one way to give form to these otherwise formless dangers, but the visible deviant is another kind of reminder. As a trespasser against the norm, he represents those forces excluded by the group's boundaries: he informs us, as it were, what evil looks like, what shapes the devil can assume. In doing so, he shows us the difference between kinds of experience which belong within the group and kinds of experience which belong outside it.

Thus deviance cannot be dismissed as behavior which *disrupts* stability in society, but is itself, in controlled quantities, an important condition for *preserving* stability.

IV

This raises a serious theoretical question. If we grant that deviant behavior often performs a valuable service in society, can we then assume that society as a whole actively tries to promote this resource? Can we assume, in other words, that some kind of active recruitment process is going on to assure society of a steady volume of deviance? Sociology has not yet developed a conceptual language in which this sort of question can be discussed without a great deal of circularity, but one observation can be made which gives the question an interesting perspective — namely, that deviant activities often seem to derive support from the very agencies designed to suppress them. Indeed, the institutions devised by human society for guarding against deviance sometimes seem so poorly equipped for this task that we might well ask why this is considered their "real" function at all.

It is by now a thoroughly familiar argument that many of the institutions built to inhibit deviance actually operate in such a way as to perpetuate it. For one thing, prisons, hospitals, and other agencies of control provide aid and protection for large numbers of deviant persons. But beyond this, such institutions gather marginal people into tightly segregated groups, give them an opportunity to teach one another the skills and attitudes of a deviant career, and even drive them into using these skills by reinforcing their sense of alienation from the rest of society.[7] This process is found not only in the institutions which actually confine the deviant, but in the general community as well.

The community's decision to bring deviant sanctions against an individual is not a simple act of censure. It is a sharp rite of transition, at once moving him out of his normal position in society and transferring him into a distinct deviant role.[8] The ceremonies which accomplish this change of status, usually, have three related phases. They arrange a formal *confrontation* between the deviant suspect and representatives of his community (as in the criminal trial or psychiatric case conference); they announce some *judgment* about the nature of his deviancy (a "verdict" or "diagnosis," for example); and they perform an act of social *placement*, assigning him to a special deviant role (like that of "prisoner" or "patient") for some period of time. Such ceremonies tend to be events of wide public interest and ordinarily take place in a dramatic, ritualized setting.[9] Perhaps the most obvious example of a commitment ceremony is the criminal trial, with its elaborate ritual and formality, but more modest equivalents can be found almost anywhere that procedures are set up for judging whether or not someone is officially deviant.

An important feature of these ceremonies in our culture is that they are almost irreversible. Most provisional roles conferred by society — like those of the student or citizen soldier, for instance — include some kind of terminal ceremony to mark the individual's movement back out of the role once its temporary advantages have been exhausted. But the roles allotted to the deviant seldom make allowance for this type of passage. He is ushered into the special position by a decisive and dramatic ceremony, yet is retired from it with hardly a word of public notice. As a result, the deviant often returns home with no proper license to resume a normal life in the community. From a ritual point of view, nothing has happened to cancel out the stigmas imposed upon him by earlier commitment ceremonies: the original verdict or diagnosis is still formally in effect. Partly for this reason, the community is apt to place the returning deviant on some form

---

[7] For a good description of this process in the modern prison, see Gresham Sykes, *The Society of Captives,* Princeton: Princeton University Press, 1958. For views of two different types of mental hospital settings, see Erving Goffman, "The Characteristics of Total Institutions," *Symposium on Preventive and Social Psychiatry.* Washington, D.C.: Walter Reed Army Institute of Research, 1957; and Kai T. Erikson, "Patient Role and Social Uncertainty: A Dilemma of the Mentally Ill," *Psychiatry,* 20 (1957), pp. 263–274.

[8] Talcott Parsons, *op. cit.,* has given the classical description of how this role transfer works in the case of medical patients.

[9] Cf. Harold Garfinkel, "Successful Degradation Ceremonies," *American Journal of Sociology,* 61 (1956), pp. 420–424.

of probation within the group, suspicious that he will return to deviant activity upon a moment's provocation.

A circularity is thus set into motion which has all the earmarks of a "self-fulfilling prophecy," to use Merton's fine phrase. On the one hand, it seems obvious that the apprehensions of the community help destroy whatever chances the deviant might otherwise have for a successful return to society. Yet, on the other hand, everyday experience seems to show that these apprehensions are altogether reasonable, for it is a well-known and highly publicized fact that most ex-convicts return to prison and that a large proportion of mental patients require additional treatment after once having been discharged. The community's feeling that deviant persons cannot change, then, may be based on a faulty premise, but it is repeated so frequently and with such conviction that it eventually creates the facts which "prove" it correct. If the returned deviant encounters this feeling of distrust often enough, it is understandable that he too may begin to wonder if the original verdict or diagnosis is still in effect — and respond to this uncertainty by resuming deviant activity. In some respects, this solution may be the only way for the individual and his community to agree what forms of behavior are appropriate for him.

Moreover, this prophecy is found in the official policies of even the most advanced agencies of control. Police departments could not operate with any real effectiveness if they did not regard ex-convicts as an almost permanent population of offenders, a constant pool of suspects. Nor could psychiatric clinics do a responsible job if they did not view former patients as a group unusually susceptible to mental illness. Thus the prophecy gains currency at many levels within the social order, not only in the poorly informed attitudes of the community at large, but in the best informed theories of most control agencies as well.

In one form or another, this problem has been known to Western culture for many hundreds of years, and this simple fact is a very important one for sociology. For if the culture has supported a steady flow of deviant behavior throughout long periods of historical evolution, then the rules which apply to any form of functionalist thinking would suggest that strong forces must be at work to keep this flow intact. This may not be reason enough to assert that deviant behavior is altogether "functional" — in any of the many senses of that term — but it should make us reluctant to assume that the agencies of control are somehow organized to prevent deviant acts from occurring or to "cure" deviant offenders of their misbehavior.[10]

This in turn might suggest that our present models of the social system, with their clear emphasis on harmony and symmetry in social relations,

[10] Albert K. Cohen, for example, speaking for most sociologists, seems to take the question for granted: "It would seem that the control of deviant behavior is, by definition, a culture goal." In "The Study of Social Disorganization and Deviant Behavior," Merton, et al., editors, Sociology Today. New York: Basic Books, 1959, p. 465.

only do a partial job of representing reality. Perhaps two different (and often conflicting) currents are found within any well-functioning system: those forces which promote a high over-all degree of conformity among human actors, and those forces which encourage some degree of diversity so that actors can be deployed throughout social space to mark the system's boundaries. In such a scheme, deviant behavior would appear as a variation on normative themes, a vital form of activity which outlines the area within which social life as such takes place.

As Georg Simmel wrote some years ago:

> An absolutely centripetal and harmonious group, a pure "unification," not only is empirically unreal, it could show no real life process. . . . Just as the universe needs "love and hate," that is, attractive and repulsive forces, in order to have any form at all, so society, too, in order to attain a determinate shape, needs some quantitative ratio of harmony and disharmony, of association and competition, of favorable and unfavorable tendencies. . . . Society, as we know it, is the result of both categories of interaction, which thus both manifest themselves as wholly positive.[11]

V

In summary, two new lines of inquiry seem to be indicated by the argument presented above.

First, this paper attempts to focus our attention on an old but still vital sociological question: how does a social structure communicate its "needs" or impose its "patterns" on human actors? In the present case, how does a social structure enlist actors to engage in deviant activity? Ordinarily, the fact that deviant behavior is more common in some sectors of society than in others is explained by declaring that something called "anomie" or "disorganization" prevails at these sensitive spots. Deviance leaks out where the social machinery is defective; it occurs where the social structure *fails* to communicate its needs to human actors. But if we consider the possibility that deviant persons are responding to the same social forces that elicit conformity from others, then we are engaged in another order of inquiry altogether. Perhaps the stability of some social units is maintained only if juvenile offenders are recruited to balance an adult majority; perhaps some families can remain intact only if one of their members becomes a visible deviant or is committed to a hospital or prison. If this supposition proves to be a useful one, sociologists should be interested in discovering how a social unit manages to differentiate the roles of its members and how certain persons are "chosen" to play the more deviant parts.

Second, it is evident that cultures vary in the way they regulate traffic moving back and forth from their deviant boundaries. Perhaps we could

[11] Georg Simmel, *Conflict* (translated by Kurt H. Wolff), Glencoe: The Free Press, 1955, pp. 15-16.

begin with the hypothesis that the traffic pattern known in our own culture has a marked Puritan cast: a defined portion of the population, largely drawn from young adult groups and from the lower economic classes, is stabilized in deviant roles and generally expected to remain there for indefinite periods of time. To this extent, Puritan attitudes about predestination and reprobation would seem to have retained a significant place in modern criminal law and public opinion. In other areas of the world, however, different traffic patterns are known. There are societies in which deviance is considered a natural pursuit for the young, an activity which they can easily abandon when they move through defined ceremonies into adulthood. There are societies which give license to large groups of persons to engage in deviant behavior for certain seasons or on certain days of the year. And there are societies in which special groups are formed to act in ways "contrary" to the normal expectations of the culture. Each of these patterns regulates deviant traffic differently, yet all of them provide some institutionalized means for an actor to give up a deviant "career" without permanent stigma. The problem for sociological theory in general might be to learn whether or not these varying patterns are functionally equivalent in some meaningful sense; the problem for applied sociology might be to see if we have anything to learn from those cultures which permit re-entry into normal social life to persons who have spent a period of "service" on society's boundaries.

B. Processes and Examples

Try to imagine a system in which there is no conflict; a well-oiled machine that functions with no friction between its moving parts. It will never change; the order and relationship of the parts is forever fixed. A social system with characteristics like this is hard to imagine, but we can feel that it would be boring. Conflict is, as Coser points out, the essence of change. It is a source of creativity and energy for the system. It causes men to dream of and attempt to build better societies. Instead of thinking about how to do away with conflict in systems, some attention should be given to the possible ways of institutionalizing it.

27 Lewis A. Coser

Social Conflict and the Theory of Social Change

This paper attempts to examine some of the functions of social conflict in the process of social change. We shall first deal with some functions of conflict *within* social systems, more specifically with its relation to institutional rigidities, technical progress and productivity, and will then concern ourselves with the relation between social conflict and the changes *of* social systems.

A central observation of George Sorel in his *Reflections on Violence* which has not as yet been accorded sufficient attention by sociologists may serve us as a convenient springboard. Sorel wrote:

> We are today faced with a new and unforeseen fact — a middle class which seeks to weaken its own strength. The race of bold captains who made the greatness of modern industry disappears to make way for an ultracivilized aristocracy which asks to be allowed to live in peace.
>
> The threatening decadence may be avoided if the proletariat hold on with obstinacy to revolutionary ideas. *The antagonistic classes influence each other in a partly indirect but decisive manner.* Everything may be saved if the proletariat, by their use of violence, restore to the middle class something of its former energy.[1]

Sorel's specific doctrine of class struggle is not of immediate concern here. What is important for us is the idea that conflict (which Sorel calls violence, using the word in a very special sense) prevents the ossification of the social system by exerting pressure for innovation and creativity. Though Sorel's call to action was addressed to the working class and its interests, he conceived it to be of general importance for the total social system; to his mind the gradual disappearance of class conflict might well lead to the decadence of European culture. A social system, he felt, was in need of conflict if only to renew its energies and revitalize its creative forces.

This conception seems to be more generally applicable than to class struggle alone. Conflict within and between groups in a society can prevent accommodations and habitual relations from progressively impoverishing creativity. The clash of values and interests, the tension between what is and what some groups feel ought to be, the conflict between vested interests and new strata and groups demanding their share of power, wealth and status, have been productive of vitality; note for example the contrast

From *The British Journal of Sociology*, Vol. 8 (September, 1957), pp. 197–207. Reprinted by permission of the author and publisher.
[1] George Sorel, *Reflections on Violence*, ch. 2, par. 11.

between the "frozen world" of the Middle Ages and the burst of creativity that accompanied the thaw that set in with Renaissance civilization.

This is, in effect, the application of John Dewey's theory of consciousness and thought as arising in the wake of obstacles to the interaction of ⋏groups. "Conflict is the gadfly of thought. It stirs us to observation and memory. It instigates to invention. It shocks us out of sheeplike passivity, and sets us at noting and contriving. . . . Conflict is a *sine qua non* of reflection and ingenuity."[2]

Conflict not only generates new norms, new institutions, as I have pointed out elsewhere,[3] it may be said to be stimulating directly in the economic ⸜and technological realm. Economic historians often have pointed out that much technological improvement has resulted from the conflict activity of trade unions through the raising of wage levels. A rise in wages usually has led to a substitution of capital investment for labour and hence to an increase in the volume of investment. Thus the extreme mechanization of coal-mining in the United States has been partly explained by the existence of militant unionism in the American coalfields.[4] A recent investigation by Sidney C. Sufrin[5] points to the effects of union pressure, "goading management into technical improvement and increased capital investment." Very much the same point was made recently by the conservative British *Economist* which reproached British unions for their "moderation" which it declared in part responsible for the stagnation and low productivity of British capitalism; it compared their policy unfavourably with the more aggressive policies of American unions whose constant pressure for higher wages has kept the American economy dynamic.[6]

This point raises the question of the adequacy and relevancy of the "human relations" approach in industrial research and management practice. The "human relations" approach stresses the "collective purpose of the total organization" of the factory, and either denies or attempts to reduce conflicts of interests in industry.[7] But a successful reduction of industrial conflict may have unanticipated dysfunctional consequences for it may destroy an important stimulus for technological innovation.

It often has been observed that the effects of technological change have

[2] John Dewey, *Human Nature and Conduct*, N.Y.: The Modern Library, 1930, p. 300.

[3] Lewis A. Coser, *The Functions of Social Conflict*, Glencoe, Ill.; London: Routledge and Kegan Paul, 1956.

[4] Cf. McAlister Coleman, *Men and Coal*, N.Y., Farrar and Rinehart, 1943.

[5] *Union Wages and Labor's Earnings*, Syracuse, Syracuse Univ. Press, 1951.

[6] Quoted by Will Herberg, "When Social Scientists View Labor," *Commentary*, Dec. 1951, XII, 6, pp. 590–596. See also Seymour Melman, *Dynamic Factors in Industrial Productivity*, Oxford, Blackwell, 1956, on the effects of rising wage levels on productivity.

[7] See the criticism of the Mayo approach by Daniel Bell, "Adjusting Men to Machines," *Commentary*, Jan. 1947, pp. 79–88; C. Wright Mills, "The Contribution of Sociology to the Study of Industrial Relations," *Proceedings of the Industrial Relations Research Association*, 1948, pp. 199–222.

weighed most heavily upon the worker.[8] Both informal and formal organization of workers represent in part an attempt to mitigate the insecurities attendant upon the impact of unpredictable introduction of change in the factory.[9] But by organizing in unions workers gain a feeling of security through the effective conduct of institutionalized conflict with management and thus exert pressure on management to increase their returns by the invention of further cost-reducing devices. The search for mutual adjustment, understanding and "unity" between groups who find themselves in different life situations and have different life chances calls forth the danger that Sorel warns of, namely that the further development of technology would be seriously impaired.

The emergence of invention and of technological change in modern Western society, with its institutionalization of science as an instrument for making and remaking the world, was made possible with the gradual emergence of a pluralistic and hence conflict-charged structure of human relations. In the unitary order of the medieval guild system, "no one was permitted to harm others by methods which enabled him to produce more quickly and more cheaply than they. Technical progress took on the appearance of disloyalty. The ideal was stable conditions in a stable industry."[10]

In the modern Western world, just as in the medieval world, vested interests exert pressure for the maintenance of established routines; yet the modern Western institutional structure allows room for freedom of conflict. The structure no longer being unitary, vested interests find it difficult to resist the continuous stream of change-producing inventions. Invention, as well as its application and utilization, is furthered through the ever-renewed challenge to vested interests, as well as by the conflicts between the vested interests themselves.[11]

Once old forms of traditional and unitary integration broke down, the clash of conflicting interests and values, now no longer constrained by the rigidity of the medieval structure, pressed for new forms of unification and integration. Thus deliberate control and rationalized regulation of "spontaneous" processes was required in military and political, as well as in economic institutions. Bureaucratic forms of organization with their emphasis

---

[8] See, e.g., R. K. Merton, "The Machine, The Workers and The Engineer," *Social Theory and Social Structure*, Glencoe, Ill., 1949, pp. 317–28; Georges Friedmann, *Industrial Society*, Glencoe, Ill., 1956.

[9] For informal organization and change, see Roethlisberger & Dickson, *Management and the Worker*, Cambridge, 1939, especially pp. 567–68; for formal organization, see Selig Perlman, *The Theory of the Labor Movement;* on general relations between technology and labour, see Elliot D. Smith and Richard C. Nyman, *Technology and Labor,* New Haven, Yale Univ. Press, 1939.

[10] Henri Pirenne, *Economic and Social History of Medieval Europe*, London, Routledge and Kegan Paul, 1949, p. 186.

[11] See W. F. Ogburn, *Social Change*, N.Y.: B. W. Huebsch, 1923, for the theory of "cultural lag" due to "vested interests."

on calculable, methodical and disciplined behaviour[12] arose at roughly the same period in which the unitary medieval structure broke down. But with the rise of bureaucratic types of organization peculiar new resistances to change made their appearance. The need for reliance on predictability exercises pressure towards the rejection of innovation which is perceived as interference with routine. Conflicts involving a "trial through battle" are unpredictable in their outcome, and therefore unwelcome to the bureaucracy, which must strive towards an ever-widening extension of the area of predictability and calculability of results. But social arrangements which have become habitual and totally patterned are subject to the blight of ritualism. If attention is focused exclusively on the habitual clues, "people may be unfitted by being fit in an unfit fitness,"[13] so that their habitual training becomes an incapacity to adjust to new conditions. To quote Dewey again: "The customary is taken for granted; it operates subconsciously. Breach of wont and use is focal; it forms 'consciousness.' "[14] A group or a system which no longer is challenged is no longer capable of a creative response. It may subsist, wedded to the eternal yesterday of precedent and tradition, but it is no longer capable of renewal.[15]

"Only a hitch in the working of habit occasions emotion and provokes thought."[16] Conflict within and between bureaucratic structures provides means for avoiding the ossification and ritualism which threatens their form of organization.[17] Conflict, though apparently dysfunctional for highly rationalized systems, may actually have important latent functional consequences. By attacking and overcoming the resistance to innovation and change that seems to be an "occupational psychosis" always threatening the bureaucratic office holder, it can help to insure that the system does not stifle in the deadening routine of habituation and that in the planning activity itself creativity and invention can be applied.

We have so far discussed change within systems, but changes of systems are of perhaps even more crucial importance for sociological inquiry. Here the sociology of Karl Marx serves us well. Writes Marx in a polemic against Proudhon:

> Feudal production also had two antagonistic elements, which were equally designated by the names of *good side* and *bad side* of feudalism, without regard being had to the fact that it is always the

---

[12] Cf. Max Weber, "Bureaucracy," *From Max Weber,* Gerth and Mills, eds., pp. 196–244. For the pathology of bureaucracy, see R. K. Merton, "Bureaucratic Structure and Personality," *Social Theory and Social Structure, op. cit.,* pp. 151–60.

[13] Kenneth Burke, *Permanence and Change,* N.Y., New Republic, 1936, p. 18.

[14] John Dewey, *The Public and Its Problems,* Chicago, Gateway Books, 1946, p. 100.

[15] This is, of course, a central thesis of Arnold Toynbee's monumental *A Study of History,* Oxford University Press.

[16] John Dewey, *Human Nature and Conduct, op. cit.,* p. 178.

[17] See, e.g., Melville Dalton, "Conflicts Between Staff and Line Managerial Officers," *Am. Soc. R.,* XV (1950), pp. 342–51. The author seems to be unaware of the positive functions of this conflict, yet his data clearly indicate the "innovating potential" of conflict between staff and line.

evil side which finishes by overcoming the good side. It is the bad side that produces the movement which makes history, by constituting the struggle. If at the epoch of the reign of feudalism the economists, enthusiastic over the virtues of chivalry, the delightful harmony between rights and duties, the patriarchal life of the towns, the prosperous state of domestic industry in the country, of the development of industry organized in corporations, guilds and fellowships, in fine of all which constitutes the beautiful side of feudalism, had proposed to themselves the problem of eliminating all which cast a shadow upon this lovely picture — serfdom, privilege, anarchy — what would have been the result? All the elements which constituted the struggle would have been annihilated, and the development of the bourgeoisie would have been stifled in the germ. They would have set themselves the absurd problem of eliminating history.[18]

According to Marx, conflict leads not only to ever-changing relations within the existing social structure, but the total social system undergoes transformation through conflict.

During the feudal period, the relations between serf and lord, between burgher and gentry, underwent many changes both in law and in fact. Yet conflict finally led to a breakdown of all feudal relations and hence to the rise of a new social system governed by different patterns of social relations.

It is Marx's contention that the negative element, the opposition, conditions the change when conflict between the sub-groups of a system becomes so sharpened that at a certain point this system breaks down. Each social system contains elements of strain and of potential conflict; if in the analysis of the social structure of a system these elements are ignored, if the adjustment of patterned relations is the only focus of attention, then it is not possible to anticipate basic social change. Exclusive attention to wont and use, to the customary and habitual bars access to an understanding of possible latent elements of strain which under certain conditions eventuate in overt conflict and possibly in a basic change of the social structure. This attention should be focused, in Marx's view, on what evades and resists the patterned normative structure and on the elements pointing to new and alternative patterns emerging from the existing structure. What is diagnosed as disease from the point of view of the institutionalized pattern may, in fact, says Marx, be the first birth pang of a new one to come; not wont and use but the break of wont and use is focal. The "matters-of-fact" of a "given state of affairs" when viewed in the light of Marx's approach, become limited, transitory; they are regarded as containing the germs of a process that leads beyond them.[19]

---

[18] Karl Marx, *The Poverty of Philosophy*, Chicago, Charles H. Kerr & Co., 1910, p. 132.

[19] For an understanding of Marx's methodology and its relation to Hegelian philosophy, see Herbert Marcuse, *Reason and Revolution*, N.Y., Oxford University Press, 1941. Note the similarity with John Dewey's thought: "Where there is change, there is of

Yet, not all social systems contain the same degree of conflict and strain. The sources and incidence of conflicting behaviour in each particular system vary according to the type of structure, the patterns of social mobility, of ascribing and achieving status and of allocating scarce power and wealth, as well as the degree to which a specific form of distribution of power, resources and status is accepted by the component actors within the different sub-systems. But if, within any social structure, there exists an excess of claimants over opportunities for adequate reward, there arises strain and conflict.

The distinction between changes *of* systems and changes *within* systems is, of course, a relative one. There is always some sort of continuity between a past and a present, or a present and a future social system; societies do not die the way biological organisms do, for it is difficult to assign precise points of birth or death to societies as we do with biological organisms. One may claim that all that can be observed is a change of the organization of social relations; but from one perspective such change may be considered re-establishment of equilibrium while from another it may be seen as the formation of a new system.

A natural scientist, describing the function of earthquakes, recently stated admirably what could be considered the function of conflict. "There is nothing abnormal about an earthquake. An unshakeable earth would be a dead earth. A quake is the earth's way of maintaining its equilibrium, a form of adjustment that enables the crust to yield to stresses that tend to reorganize and redistribute the material of which it is composed. . . . The larger the shift, the more violent the quake, and the more frequent the shifts, the more frequent are the shocks."[20]

Whether the quake is violent or not, it has served to maintain or re-establish the equilibrium of the earth. Yet the shifts may be small changes of geological formations, or they may be changes in the structural relations between land and water, for example.

At what point the shift is large enough to warrant the conclusion that a change *of* the system has taken place, is hard to determine. Only if one deals with extreme instances are ideal types — such as feudalism, capitalism, etc. — easily applied. A system based on serfdom, for example, may undergo considerable change within — *vide* the effects of the Black Death on the social structure of medieval society; and even an abolition of serfdom may not necessarily be said to mark the end of an old and the emergence of a new system, *vide* nineteenth-century Russia.

If "it is necessary to distinguish clearly between the processes *within* the

---

necessity numerical plurality, multiplicity, and from variety comes opposition, strife. Change is alteration, or 'othering' and this means diversity. Diversity means division, and division means two sides and their conflict." *Reconstruction in Philosophy*, N.Y., Mentor Books, 1950, p. 97. See also the able discussion of the deficiencies of Talcott Parsons' sociological theories by David Lockwood, *British Journal of Sociology*, June, 1956.

[20] Waldemar Kaemfert, "Science in Review," *New York Times*, July 27, 1952.

system and processes of change *of* the system," as Professor Parsons has pointed out,[21] an attempt should be made to establish a heuristic criterion for this distinction. We propose to talk of a change *of* system when all major structural relations, its basic institutions, and its prevailing value system have been drastically altered. (In cases where such a change takes place abruptly, as, for example, the Russian Revolution, there should be no difficulty. It is well to remember, however, that transformations of social systems do not always consist in an abrupt and simultaneous change of all basic institutions. Institutions may change gradually, by mutual adjustment, and it is only over a period of time that the observer will be able to claim that the social system has undergone a basic transformation in its structural relations.) In concrete historical reality, no clear-cut distinctions exist. Change *of* system may be the result (or the sum total) of previous changes *within* the system. This does not however detract from the usefulness of the theoretical distinction.

It is precisely Marx's contention that the change from feudalism to a different type of social system can be understood only through an investigation of the stresses and strains *within* the feudal system. Whether given forms of conflict will lead to changes in the social system or to breakdown and to formation of a new system will depend on the rigidity and resistance to change, or inversely on the elasticity of the control mechanisms of the system.

It is apparent, however, that the rigidity of the system and the intensity of conflict within it are not independent of each other. Rigid systems which suppress the incidence of conflict exert pressure towards the emergence of radical cleavages and violent forms of conflict. More elastic systems, which allow the open and direct expression of conflict within them and which adjust to the shifting balance of power which these conflicts both indicate and bring about, are less likely to be menaced by basic and explosive alignments within their midst.

In what follows the distinction between strains, conflicts and disturbances within a system which lead to a re-establishment of equilibrium, and conflicts which lead to the establishment of new systems and new types of equilibria, will be examined.[22] Such an examination will be most profit-

---

[21] Talcott Parsons, *The Social System*, London, Tavistock Publications, 1951, p. 481. I owe much to Prof. Parsons' treatment of this distinction despite a number of major disagreements with his theory of social change.

[22] The concept of *equilibrium* is of great value in social science provided it is used, as by Schumpeter, as a point of reference permitting measurement of departures from it. "The concept of a state of equilibrium, although no such state may ever be realized, is useful and indeed indispensable for purposes of analyses and diagnosis, as a point of reference" (Joseph A. Schumpeter, *Business Cycle*, N.Y., McGraw-Hill, 1939, p. 69). But certain types of sociological functionalism tend to move from this methodological use of the concept to one which has some clearly ideological features. The ideal type of equilibrium, in this illegitimate use, becomes a normative instead of a methodological concept. Attention is focused on the maintenance of a system which is somehow identified with the ethically desirable (see Merton's discussion of this ideological misuse of func-

ably begun by considering what Thorstein Veblen[23] has called "Vested Interests."[24]

Any social system implies an allocation of power, as well as wealth and status positions among individual actors and component sub-groups. As has been pointed out, there is never complete concordance between what individuals and groups within a system consider their just due and the system of allocation. Conflict ensues in the effort of various frustrated groups and individuals to increase their share of gratification. Their demands will encounter the resistance of those who previously had established a "vested interest" in a given form of distribution of honour, wealth and power.

To the vested interests, an attack against their position necessarily appears as an attack upon the social order.[25] Those who derive privileges from a given system of allocation of status, wealth and power will perceive an attack upon these prerogatives as an attack against the system itself.

λ However, mere "frustration" will not lead to a questioning of the legitimacy of the position of the vested interests, and hence to conflict. Levels of aspiration as well as feelings of deprivation are relative to institutionalized expectations and are established through comparison.[26] When social systems have institutionalized goals and values to govern the conduct of component actors, but limit access to these goals for certain members of the society, "departures from institutional requirements" are to be expected.[27]

---

tionalism in *Social Theory and Social Structure, op. cit.*, pp. 38 ff. and 116–17; see also my review of Parsons' Essays, *American Journal of Sociology*, 55, March, 1950, pp. 502–504). Such theorizing tends to look at all behaviour caused by strains and conflict as "deviancy" from the legitimate pattern, thereby creating the perhaps unintended impression that such behaviour is somehow "abnormal" in an ethical sense, and obscuring the fact that some "deviant" behaviour actually serves the creation of new patterns rather than a simple rejection of the old.

23 See especially *The Vested Interests and the State of the Industrial Arts*, N.Y., 1919.

24 Max Lerner ("Vested Interests," *Encyclopaedia of the Social Sciences*, XV, p. 240) gives the following definition: "When an activity has been pursued so long that the individuals concerned in it have a prescriptive claim to its exercise and its profit, they are considered to have a vested interest in it."

25 Veblen has described this aptly: "The code of proprieties, conventionalities, and usages in vogue at any given time and among any given people has more or less of the character of an organic whole; so that any appreciable change in one point of the scheme involves something of a change or readjustment of other points also, if not a reorganization all along the line. . . . When an attempted reform involves the suppression or thoroughgoing remodelling of an institution of first-rate importance in the conventional scheme, it is immediately felt that a serious derangement of the entire scheme would result. . . . Any of these innovations would, we are told, 'shake the social structure to its base,' 'reduce society to chaos,' . . . etc. The aversion to change is in large part an aversion to the bother of making the readjustment which any given change will necessitate" (*The Theory of the Leisure Class*, N.Y., The Modern Library, pp. 201–203).

26 See Robert K. Merton and Alice S. Kitt, "Contributions to the Theory of Reference Group Behaviour" for a development of the concept of "relative deprivation" (originally suggested by Stouffer, et al. in *The American Soldier*) and its incorporation into the framework of a theory of reference groups.

27 This whole process is exhaustively discussed by Merton in his paper on "Social Structure and Anomie," *Social Theory, op. cit.*

Similarly, if certain groups within a social system compare their share in power, wealth and status honour with that of other groups *and* question the legitimacy of this distribution, discontent is likely to ensue. If there exist no institutionalized provisions for the expression of such discontents, departures from what is required by the norms of the social system may occur. These may be limited to "innovation" or they may consist in the rejection of the institutionalized goals. Such "rebellion" "involves a genuine transvaluation, where the direct or vicarious experience of frustration leads to full denunciation of previously prized values."[28] Thus it will be well to distinguish between those departures from the norms of a society which consist in mere "deviation" and those which involve the formation of distinctive patterns and new value systems.

What factors lead groups and individuals to question at a certain point the legitimacy of the system of distribution of rewards, lies largely outside the scope of the present inquiry. The intervening factors can be sought in the ideological, technological, economic or any other realm. It is obvious, moreover, that conflict may be a result just as much as a source of change. A new invention, the introduction of a new cultural trait through diffusion, the development of new methods of production or distribution, etc., will have a differential impact within a social system. Some strata will feel it to be detrimental to their material or ideal interests, while others will feel their position strengthened through its introduction. Such disturbances in the equilibrium of the system lead to conditions in which groups or individual actors no longer do willingly what they have to do and do willingly what they are not supposed to do. Change, no matter what its source, breeds strain and conflict.

Yet, it may be well to repeat that mere "frustration" and the ensuing strains and tensions do not necessarily lead to group conflict. Individuals under stress may relieve their tension through "acting out" in special safety-valve institutions in as far as they are provided for in the social system; or they may "act out" in a deviant manner, which may have serious dysfunctional consequences for the system, and bring about change in this way. This, however, does not reduce the frustrations from which escape has been sought since it does not attack their source.

If, on the other hand, the strain leads to the emergence of specific new patterns of behaviour of whole groups of individuals who pursue "the optimization of gratification"[29] by choosing what they consider appropriate means for the maximization of rewards, social change which reduces the sources of their frustration may come about. This may happen in two ways: if the social system is flexible enough to adjust to conflict situations we will deal with change *within* the system. If, on the other hand, the social system is not able to readjust itself and allows the accumulation of conflict, the "aggressive" groups, imbued with a new system of values which threatens

[28] *Ibid.*, p. 145.
[29] T. Parsons, *The Social System, op. cit.*, p. 498.

to split the general consensus of the society and imbued with an ideology which "objectifies" their claims, may become powerful enough to overcome the resistance of vested interests and bring about the breakdown of the system and the emergence of a new distribution of social values.[30]

In his *Poverty of Philosophy*, Marx was led to consider the conditions under which economic classes constitute themselves:

> Economic conditions have first transformed the mass of the population into workers. The domination of capital created for this mass a common situation and common interest. This mass was thus already a class as against capital, but not for itself. It is in the struggle . . . that the mass gathers together and constitutes itself as a class for itself. The interests which it defends become class interests.[31]

With this remarkable distinction between class *in itself* and class *for itself* (which unfortunately he didn't elaborate upon in later writings though it informs all of them — if not the writings of most latter-day "marxists"), Marx illuminates a most important aspect of group formation: group belongingness is established by an objective conflict situation — in this case a conflict of interests;[32] but only by experiencing this antagonism, that is, by becoming aware of it and by acting it out, does the group (or class) establish its identity.

When changes in the equilibrium of a society lead to the formation of new groupings or to the strengthening of existing groupings that set themselves the goal of overcoming resistance of vested interests through conflict, changes in structural relations, as distinct from simple "maladjustment," can be expected.

What Robert Park said about the rise of nationalist and racial movements is more generally applicable:

> They strike me as natural and wholesome disturbances of the social routine, the effect of which is to arouse in those involved a lively sense of common purpose and to give those who feel them-

---

[30] R. K. Merton, *Social Theory and Social Structure, op. cit.*, pp. 42–43 and 116–17.

[31] Karl Marx, *The Poverty of Philosophy, op. cit.*, pp. 188–89.

[32] This makes it necessary to distinguish between realistic and non-realistic conflict: social conflicts that arise from frustration of specific demands and from estimates of gains of the participants, and that are directed at the presumed frustrating object, may be called realistic conflicts. Non-realistic conflicts, on the other hand, are not occasioned by the rival ends of the antagonists, but by the need for tension release of one or both of them. Some groups may be formed with the mere purpose of releasing tension. Such groups "collectivize" their tensions, so to speak. They can, by definition, only be disruptive rather than creative since they are built on negative rather than positive cathexes. But groups of this kind will remain marginal; their actions cannot bring about social change unless they accompany and strengthen realistic conflict groups. In such cases we deal with an admixture of non-realistic and realistic elements mutually reinforcing each other within the same social movements. Members who join for the mere purpose of tension release are often used for the "dirty work" by the realistic conflict groups.

> selves oppressed the inspiration of a common cause. . . . The effect of this struggle is to increase the solidarity and improve the morale of the "oppressed" minority.[33]

It is this sense of common purpose arising in and through conflict that is peculiar to the behaviour of individuals who meet the challenge of new conditions by a group-forming and value-forming response. Strains which result in no such formations of new conflict groups or strengthening of old ones may contribute to bringing about change, but a type of change that fails to reduce the sources of strain since by definition tension-release behaviour does not involve purposive action. Conflict through group action, on the other hand, is likely to result in a "deviancy" which may be the prelude of new patterns and reward systems apt to reduce the sources of frustration.

If the tensions that need outlets are continually reproduced within the structure, abreaction through tension-release mechanisms may preserve the system but at the risk of ever-renewed further accumulation of tension. Such accumulation eventuates easily in the irruption of destructive unrealistic conflict. If feelings of dissatisfaction, instead of being suppressed or diverted are allowed expression against "vested interests," and in this way lead to the formation of new groupings within the society, the emergence of genuine transvaluations is likely to occur. Sumner saw this very well when he said: "We want to develop symptoms, we don't want to suppress them."[34]

Whether the emergence of such new groupings or the strengthening of old ones with the attendant increase in self-confidence and self-esteem on the part of the participants will lead to a change *of* or *within* the system will depend on the degree of cohesion that the system itself has attained. A well-integrated society will tolerate and even welcome group conflict; only a weakly integrated one must fear it. The great English liberal John Morley said it very well:

> If [the men who are most attached to the reigning order of things] had a larger faith in the stability for which they profess so great an anxiety, they would be more free alike in understanding and temper to deal generously, honestly and effectively with those whom they count imprudent innovators.[35]

[33] Robert E. Park, "Personality and Cultural Conflict," *Publications of the Am. Soc. Soc.*, 25, 1931, pp. 95–110. See p. 107.

[34] Wm. G. Sumner, *War and Other Essays*, p. 241.

[35] John Morley, *On Compromise*, London, Macmillan & Co., 1917, p. 263.

IX MASS BEHAVIOR

A. Definitions and Concepts

At the turn of the century, in this country as well as others, the individual could find his place in society fairly easily. He was a member of a group that was integrated into a community, and life proceeded at a pace that could be comprehended. With the coming of the twentieth century, men began to fill very specialized roles and their participation in the larger society was restricted. There was a breakdown of what some sociologists have referred to as intermediate associations: groups which stood between the individual and the society, such as the church. Daniel Bell, a political sociologist, analyses the concept of mass society.

28   DANIEL BELL

America as a Mass Society: A Critique

. . . a sombre melancholy weighed on people's souls. . . . It would sometimes seem as if this period had been particularly unhappy, as if it had left behind only the memory of violence, of covetousness and moral hatred. . . . The feeling of general insecurity [was heightened] by the chronic form wars were apt to take, by the constant menace of the dangerous classes, by the mistrust of justice. . . . It

Reprinted from *Commentary*, Vol. 22 (July, 1956), pp. 75–83, by permission; copyright © 1956 by the American Jewish Committee.

was, so to say, bad form to praise the world and life openly. It was fashionable to see only its suffering and misery, to discover everywhere the signs of decadence and the near end — in short to condemn the times or to despise them.

J. H. Huizinga, *The Waning of the Middle Ages*

The sense of a radical dehumanization of life which has accompanied events of the past few decades has given rise to the theory of "mass society." One can say that, Marxism apart, it is probably the most influential social theory in the Western world today. While no single individual has stamped his name on it — to the extent that Marx is associated with the transformation of personal relations under capitalism into commodity values, or Freud with the role of the irrational and unconscious in behavior — the theory is central to the thinking of the principal aristocratic, Catholic, or Existentialist critics of modern society. These critics — Ortega y Gasset, Paul Tillich, Karl Jaspers, Gabriel Marcel, Emil Lederer, Hannah Arendt, and others — have been concerned less with the general conditions of freedom in society than with the freedom of the *person* and with the possibility, for some few persons, of achieving a sense of individual self in our mechanized society. And this is the source of their appeal.

The conception of the "mass society" can be summarized as follows: The revolutions in transport and communications have brought men into closer contact with each other and bound them in new ways; the division of labor has made them more interdependent; tremors in one part of society affect all others. Despite this greater interdependence, however, individuals have grown more estranged from one another. The old primary group ties of family and local community have been shattered; ancient parochial faiths are questioned; few unifying values have taken their place. Most important, the critical standards of an educated elite no longer shape opinion or taste. As a result, mores and morals are in constant flux, relations between individuals are tangential or compartmentalized, rather than organic. At the same time, greater mobility, spatial and social, intensifies concern over status. Instead of a fixed or known status, symbolized by dress or title, each person assumes a multiplicity of roles and constantly has to prove himself in a succession of new situations. Because of all this, the individual loses a coherent sense of self. His anxieties increase. There ensues a search for new faiths. The stage is thus set for the charismatic leader, the secular messiah, who, by bestowing upon each person the semblance of necessary grace and of fullness of personality, supplies a substitute for the older unifying belief that the mass society has destroyed.

In a world of lonely crowds seeking individual distinction, where values are constantly translated into economic calculabilities, where in extreme situations shame and conscience can no longer restrain the most dreadful excesses of terror, the theory of the mass society seems a forceful, realistic description of contemporary society, an accurate reflection of the *quality* and *feeling* of modern life. But when one seeks to apply the theory of mass society, analytically, it becomes very slippery. Ideal types, like the shadows in Plato's cave, generally never give us more than a silhouette. So, too, with the theory of "mass society." Each of the statements making up the theory, as set forth in the second paragraph above, might be true, but they do not follow necessarily from one another. Nor can we say that all the conditions described are present at any one time or place. More than that, there is no organizing principle — other than the general concept of a "breakdown of values" — that puts the individual elements of theory together in a logical, meaningful — let alone historical — manner. And when we examine the way the "theory" is used by those who employ it, we find ourselves even more at a loss.

In trying to sort out the ambiguities in the use of the phrase, we can distinguish perhaps five different, and sometimes contradictory, usages:

1. *Mass as undifferentiated number.* As commonly used in the term "mass media," "mass" implies that standardized material is transmitted to "all groups of the population uniformly." As understood generally by sociologists, a *mass* is a heterogeneous and undifferentiated audience, as opposed to a *class*, or any parochial and relatively homogeneous segment. Some sociologists have been tempted to go further and make "mass" a rather pejorative term. Because the mass media subject a diverse audience to a common set of cultural materials, it is argued that these experiences must necessarily lie outside the personal — and therefore meaningful — experiences to which the individual responds directly. A movie audience, for example, is a "mass" because the individuals looking at the screen are, in the words of the American sociologist Herbert Blumer, "separate, detached and anonymous." The mass "has no social organization, no body of custom and tradition, no established set of rules or rituals, no organized group of sentiments, no structure of status roles and no established leadership."

To become part of the mass is to be divorced — or "alienated" — from oneself. And the instruments which project the dominant social values that men (and women and children) choose as their *imago*, or ideal image and desire — television, radio, and the movies — impose a mass response on their audience.

2. *Mass as the judgment by the incompetent.* As first introduced by the late Ortega y Gasset in 1931, in his famous *Revolt of the Masses*, the terms "masses" and "mass" had a far different meaning than the usage implied by the term "mass media" and its invidious connotations. For Ortega, the word "mass" did not designate a group of persons — the masses were not the workers, even though the revolutionary movements of the time had equated the two — but the low *quality* of modern civilization, resulting from the loss of a commanding position by the "gentlemen" who once made up the educated elite. Modern taste, for Ortega, represents the judgment of the

unqualified. Modern life "makes a *tabula rasa* of all classicism." Nothing that is in the past can be "any possible model or standard." Even "the famous Renaissance reveals itself as a period of narrow provincialism — why not use the word? — ordinary." Modern culture, since it disowns the past, seeks a "free expression of its vital desires"; it becomes, therefore, an unrestrained "spoiled child" with no controlling standards, "no limit to its caprice." In Ortega, one finds the most sweeping attack against all "modernity." His is the disdain of the humanist for the vulgar.

3) *Mass as the mechanized society.* In German romanticism, in its idealization of nature and the pastoral, one finds the source of much of the protest against modern life. For these writers — and the poets and critics Ernst and Friedrich George Juenger can be taken as typical — the dehumanizing element is technology. The mass society is a mechanical society. Society has become an "apparatus." The machine impresses its style on man, makes life mathematical and precise; existence takes on a masklike character: the steel helmet and the welder's face-guard symbolize the individual's disappearance into his technical function. The regulated, functional man emerges as a new type, hard and ruthless, a cog in the technological press.

4) *The mass as the bureaucratized society.* Less romantic, but equally critical, are those theorists who see extreme rationalization and extreme bureaucratization — the *over-organization* of life — as the salient features of the mass society. The idea of "rationalization" goes back to Hegel and Marx and along with it the notions of "estrangement" or "alienation," "reification," and the "fetishism of commodities" — all of which express the thought that in modern society man has become a "thing," an object manipulated by society, rather than a subject who can remake life in accordance with his own desires. In our time, Georg Simmel, Max Weber, and Karl Mannheim have developed and elaborated these concepts. In Mannheim's work — notably in his *Man and Society in an Age of Reconstruction* — the diverse strands are all brought together.

Mannheim's argument, put schematically, runs as follows: modern large-scale organization, oriented exclusively to efficiency, creates hierarchies that concentrate all decisions at the top. Even technical decisions are removed from the shop floor and centered in specialized bodies that have no direct contact with work. Since the concern is solely with efficiency, rather than human satisfactions, all solutions to problems are defined in relation to this single value. Mannheim calls this "functional rationality," or direct means-ends relationships, in contrast to "substantial rationality," which is the application of Reason to human affairs.

This concentration of decision-making not only creates conformity but stunts the initiative of subordinates and leaves them unsatisfied in their personal needs for gratification and esteem. (In effect, the demand for submission to extreme rationality deprives the individual of the power to act rationally; i.e., in accordance with reason. This frustration seeks release in irrational ways.) Normally, the routinization of one's job dulls the edge of frustration and provides some security. But when unemployment looms, the helplessness becomes sharpened, and self-esteem is threatened. Since individuals cannot rationally locate the source of their frustration (i.e., the impersonal bureaucratic system itself), they will, under these circumstances, seek scapegoats and turn to fascism.

5. *The mass as mob.* While for Mannheim, and the neo-Marxists, mass society is equated with monolithic bureaucratization, for Emil Lederer and Hannah Arendt it is defined by the elimination of difference, by uniformity, aimlessness, alienation, and the failure of integration.

In Lederer's view, society is made up of many social groups united by function or self-interest, some rational in purpose, some irrational. So long as society is stratified, these groups can impose only partial control, and irrational emotions are restricted. But when the lines dividing social groups break down, the people become volatile and febrile "masses," ready to be manipulated by a leader.

Hannah Arendt, perhaps because she writes a decade later, sees the masses as already overspilling the bounds. The masses are those who, because of indifference or simply sheer number, do not belong to "political parties or municipal governments or professional organizations or trade-unions" — in short, organizations that exist to satisfy a common interest — and they "form the majority of those large numbers of neutral, politically indifferent people who never join a party or hardly ever go to the polls."

Such people already stand "outside" of society. The revolt of the masses is a revolt against the "loss of social status along with which [is] lost the whole sector of communal relationships in whose framework common sense makes sense. . . . The masses [become] obsessed by a desire to escape from reality because in their essential homelessness they can no longer bear its accidental incomprehensible aspects."

And so, because modern life sunders all social bonds, and because the techniques of modern communication have perfected the means whereby propaganda can manipulate the masses, the "age of the masses" is now upon us.

What strikes one first about these varied uses of the concept of mass society is how little they reflect or relate to the complex, richly striated social relations of the real world. Take Blumer's example of the movie audience as "separate, detached, and anonymous." Presumably, a large number of individuals, because they have been subjected to similar experiences, now share some common psychological reality in which the differences between individual and individual become blurred; accordingly we get the sociological assumption that each person is now of "equal weight," and therefore a sampling of what such disparate individuals say they think constitutes "*mass* opinion." But is this so? Individuals are not *tabulae rasae.* They bring varying social conceptions to the same experience and go away with dissimilar responses. They may be silent, separate, detached, and anonymous while watching the movie, but afterward they talk about it with friends and exchange opinions and judgments. They are once again members of particular social groups. Would one say that several hundred or a thousand individuals home alone at night, but all reading the same book, constitute a "mass"?

Because romantic feeling colors critical judgment, the attacks on modern life often have an unduly strong emotional charge. The image of "facelessness," for example, is given a metaphysical twist by Gabriel Marcel: "The individual, in order to belong to the mass . . . has had to . . . divest himself of that substantial reality which was linked to his initial individuality. . . . The incredibly sinister role of the press, the cinema, the radio has consisted in passing that original reality through a pair of flattening rollers to substitute for it a superimposed pattern of ideas, an image with no real roots in the deep being of the subject of this experiment." Perhaps terms like "original reality" and "real roots in the deep being" have a meaning that escapes an empiricist temper, but without the press, the radio, etc., etc. — and they are not monolithic — in what way, short of being everywhere at once, can one learn of events that take place elsewhere? Or should one go back to the happy ignorance of earlier days?

Some of the images of life in the mass society, as presented by its critics, border on caricature. According to Ernest Juenger, traffic demands traffic regulations, and so the public becomes conditioned to automatism. Karl Jaspers has written that in the "technical mass order" the home is transformed "into a lair or sleeping place." Even more puzzling is the complaint against modern medicine. "In medical practice . . . patients are now dealt with in the mass according to the principle of rationalization, being sent to institutes for technical treatment, the sick being classified in groups and referred to this or that specialized department. . . . The supposition is that, like everything else, medical treatment has become a sort of manufactured article."

The attack on the mass society sometimes widens into an attack on science itself. For Ortega, "the scientific man is the prototype of the massman," because science, by encouraging specialization, has made the scientist "hermetic and self-satisfied within his limitations." Ortega draws from this the sweeping conclusion that "the most immediate result of this unbalanced specialization has been that today, when there are more 'scientists' than ever, there are much less 'cultured' men than, for example, about 1750." But how is one to verify such a comparison between 1750 and the present? Even if we could establish comparable categories, surely Ortega would have been the first to shy away from statistical comparisons. Moreover, can we assume that because a man specializes in his work, he is unable, in his leisure and in reflection, to appreciate culture? And what is "culture"?

Would not Ortega admit that we have more knowledge of the world than in 1750 — knowledge not only of nature but of the inner life of man? Is knowledge to be divorced from culture, or is "true culture" a narrow area of classical learning in which eternal truths reside?

One could argue, of course, that reading a book, to cite my previous example, is a qualitatively different experience from going to a movie. But this leads precisely to the first damaging ambiguity in the theory of the mass society. Two things are mixed up in that theory: a judgment regarding the *quality* of modern experience — with much of which any sensitive individual might agree — and a presumed scientific statement concerning the disorganization of society created by industrialization and by the demand of the masses for equality. It is the second of these statements with which this essay quarrels.

Behind the theory of social disorganization lies a romantic — and somewhat false — notion of the past, which sees society as having once been made up of small, "organic," close-knit communities (called *Gemeinschaften* in the terminology of the sociologists) that were shattered by industrialism and modern life, and replaced by a large, impersonal, "atomistic" society (called *Gesellschaft*) that is unable to provide the basic gratifications, and call forth the loyalties, that the older communities knew. These distinctions are, however, completely riddled by value judgments. Everyone is against atomism and for "organic living." But if we substitute, with good logic, the term "total" for "organic," and "individualistic" for "atomistic," the whole argument looks quite different. In any case, a great weakness in the theory is its lack of history-mindedness. The transition to a mass society, if it be such, was not effected suddenly, explosively, within a single lifetime, but took generations to mature. In its sociological determinism, the hypothesis overlooks the human capacity for adaptiveness and creativeness, for ingenuity in shaping new social forms. Such new forms may be trade unions whose leaders rise from the ranks — there are 50,000 trade-union locals in this country that form little worlds of their own — or the persistence under new conditions of ethnic groups and solidarities.

But more than mere contradictions in usage, ambiguities in terminology, and a lack of historical sense are involved in the theory of the mass society. It is at heart a defense of an aristocratic cultural tradition — a tradition that does carry with it an important but neglected conception of liberty — and a doubt that the large mass of mankind can ever become truly educated or acquire an appreciation of culture. Thus, the theory often becomes a conservative defense of privilege. This defense is at times so extreme as to pose a conflict between "culture" and "social justice." The argument (reminiscent of the title of Matthew Arnold's book *Culture and Anarchy*) is made that any attempts of social betterment must harm culture. And, while mainly directed against "bourgeois" society, the theory also strikes at radicalism and its egalitarian notions.

The fear of the "mass" has its roots in the dominant conservative tradition of Western political thought, which in large measure still shapes many of the political and sociological categories of social theory — i.e., in authoritarian definitions of leadership and in the image of the "mindless masses." The picture of the "mass" as capable only of violence and excess originates with Aristotle's *Politics*. In his threefold typology, democracy is equated with the rule of *hoi polloi* — who are easily swayed by demagogues — and which must degenerate into tyranny. This notion of the masses, developed in Hellenistic times, was deepened by the struggles between plebes and aristocracy in the Roman republic, and by the efforts of the Caesars to exploit mob support; and the image of the insensate mob fed by "bread and circuses" became deeply imprinted on history. (From Plutarch, for example, came the description of the fickle masses and the wily tribunes that was drawn upon so directly by Shakespeare in his tragedy *Coriolanus*.) Early Christian theory justified its fear of the masses with a theory about human nature. In the religious terms of Augustine — as, later, in the secularized version of Hobbes — the Earthly City bore an ineradicable stain of blood: in Paradise there was neither private property nor government; property and police were the consequence of the Fall of Man; property and police were signs, therefore, not of man's civilization but of his corruption; they were necessary means of keeping man in check.

But it was the French Revolution that transplanted the image of the "mindless masses" into modern consciousness. The destruction of the *ancien régime* and the rallying cry of "equality" sharpened the fear of conservative, and especially Catholic, critics that traditional values (meaning political, social, and religious dogma) would be destroyed. For a Tocqueville and an Acton, there was an irreducible conflict between liberty and equality; liberty guaranteed each man the right to be different, whereas equality meant a "leveling" of tastes to the lowest common denominator. For a Max Scheler, as well as an Ortega, the mass society meant a "democracy of the emotions," which could unleash only irrational forces. For the Catholic de Maistre, as for the Anglican T. S. Eliot, the equality of men meant the destruction of the harmony and authority so necessary to a healthy, integrated society. From this traditionalist point of view, Nazism has been characterized not as a reaction against, but the inevitable end-product of, democracy. Hitler is seen as a replica of the classical demagogue swaying the mindless masses and leading them in nihilistic revolt against the traditional culture of Europe.

Important as these conceptions are, as reminders of the meaning of liberty, and of excellence, they reflect a narrow conception of human potentialities. The question of social change has to be seen against the large political canvas. The starting point of modern politics, as Karl Mannheim has pointed out, came after the Reformation, when chiliasm, or religiously inspired millennial striving to bring about heaven on earth, became an expression of the demands for social and economic betterment of the lower strata of society. Blind resentment of things as they were was thereby given principle, reason, and eschatological force, and directed to definite political goals. The equality of all souls became the equality of all individuals and the right of everyone, as enlightened by progressive revelation, to make a judgment on society.

Comte, the father of modern sociology, expressed great horror at the idea of this universal right to one's own opinion. No community could exist, he wrote, unless its members had a certain degree of confidence in one another, and this, he said, was incompatible with the right of everyone to submit the very foundations of society to discussion whenever he felt like it. In calling attention to the dangers of free criticism, Comte pointed to the decline in public morals as evidenced by the increase of divorces, the efface-ment of traditional class distinctions, and the ensuing impudence of indi-vidual ambitions. It was part of the function of government, he thought, to prevent the diffusion of ideas and the anarchic spread of intellectual freedom.

Modern society, apparently, does not bear Comte out: though the founda-tions of privilege go on being challenged in the name of justice, society does not collapse. Few moralists would now uphold the bleak view once expressed by Malthus, that "from the inevitable laws of human nature some human beings will be exposed to want. These are the unhappy persons who in the great lottery of life have drawn a blank." The most salient fact about modern life — capitalist and communist — is the ideological commitment to social change. And by change is meant the striving for material, eco-nomic betterment, greater opportunity for individuals to exercise their talents, and an appreciation of culture by wider masses of people. Can any society deny these aspirations?

It is curious that in these "aristocratic" critiques of modern society, re-fracted as they are through the glass of an idealized feudal past, democracy is identified with equality alone. The role of constitutionalism and of the rule of law, which, with universal suffrage, are constituent elements of the Western democratic structure, are overlooked. The picture of modern cul-ture as debauched by concessions to popular taste — a picture that leaves out the great rise in the general appreciation of culture — is equally over-drawn. If it is granted that mass society is compartmentalized, superficial in personal relations, anonymous, transitory, specialized, utilitarian, compet-itive, acquisitive, mobile, and status-hungry, the obverse side of the coin must be shown, too — the right to privacy, to free choice of friends and occupation, status on the basis of achievement rather than of ascription, a plurality of norms and standards, rather than the exclusive and monopo-listic social controls of a single dominant group. For if, as Sir Henry Maine once put it, the movement of modern society has been from status to con-tract, then it has been, in that light, a movement from a fixed place in the world to possible freedom.

The early theorists of the mass society (Ortega, Marcel) focused attention on the "deterioration of excellence," while the later theorists (Mannheim, Lederer, Arendt) called attention to the way in which the over-organization and, at the same time, the disruption of the social fabric facilitated the rise of fascism. Recently, in the light of Communist successes, the argument has been advanced that the mass society, because it cannot provide for the individual's real participation in effective social groups, is particularly vulnerable to Communist penetration, and that the mass organization, because it is so unwieldy, is peculiarly susceptible to Communist penetration and manipulation. Certainly, the Communists have scored enormous successes in infiltration, and their "front organization" may be counted as one of the great political inventions of our century. But without discounting Communist techniques, the real problem here lies less with the "mass society" as such (aside from the excuse it affords disaffected intellectuals for attacks on modern culture) than with the capacity or incapacity of the given social order to satisfy the demands for social mobility and higher standards of living that arise once social change is under way. This is the key to any radical appeal.

It is not poverty per se that leads people to revolt; poverty most often induces fatalism and despair, and a reliance, embodied in ritual and superstitious practices, on supernatural help. *Social tensions are an expression of unfulfilled expectations.* It is only when expectations are aroused that radicalism can take hold. Radical strength is greatest (and here the appeal of communism must be seen as a variant of the general appeal of radicalism) in societies where awareness of class differences runs deep, expectations of social advancement outstrip possibilities, and the establishments of culture fail to make room for aspiring intellectuals.

It is among industrial workers rather than apathetic peasants (in Milan rather than Calabria), among frustrated intellectuals rather than workers long unionized (e.g., India), that radicalism spreads. Resentment, as Max Scheler once noted, is among the most potent of human motives; it is certainly that in politics. It is in the advanced industrial countries, principally the United States, Britain, and northwestern Europe, where national income *has* been rising, where mass expectations of an equitable share in that increase are relatively fulfilled, and where social mobility affects ever greater numbers, that extremist politics have the least hold. It may be, as the late Joseph Schumpeter pessimistically believed, that in newly awakened societies, like Asia's, the impatient expectations of key social strata, particularly the intellectuals, may so exceed the actual possibilities of economic expansion that communism will come to look like the only plausible solution to the majority. Whether this will happen in India and Indonesia is one of the crucial political questions of the next decade. But at any rate it is not the mass society, but the inability, pure and simple, of any society to meet impatient popular expectations that makes for a strong response to radical appeals.

From the viewpoint of the mass-society hypothesis, the United States ought to be exceptionally vulnerable to the politics of disaffection. In our country, urbanization, industrialization, and democratization have eroded older primary and community ties on a scale unprecedented in social history. Yet, though large-scale unemployment during the depression was more prolonged and more severe here than in any country in Western Europe, the Communist movement never gained a real foothold in the United States, nor has any fascist movement on a European model arisen. How does one explain this?

It is asserted that the United States is an "atomized" society composed of lonely, isolated individuals. One forgets the truism, expressed sometimes as a jeer, that Americans are a nation of joiners. There are in the United States today at least 200,000 voluntary organizations, associations, clubs, societies, lodges, and fraternities, with an aggregate (but obviously overlapping) membership of close to 80 million men and women. In no other country in the world, probably, is there such a high degree of voluntary communal activity, expressed sometimes in absurd rituals, yet often providing real satisfactions for real needs.

"It is natural for the ordinary American," wrote Gunnar Myrdal, "when he sees something that is wrong to feel not only that there should be a law against it, but also that an organization should be formed to combat it." Some of these voluntary organizations are pressure groups — business, farm, labor, veterans, trade associations, the aged, etc. — but thousands more are like the National Association for the Advancement of Colored People, the American Civil Liberties Union, the League of Women Voters, the American Jewish Committee, the Parent-Teachers Associations, local community-improvement groups, and so on, each of which affords hundreds of individuals concrete, emotionally shared activities.

Equally astonishing are the number of ethnic group organizations in this country carrying on varied cultural, social, and political activities. The number of Irish, Italian, Jewish, Polish, Czech, Finnish, Bulgarian, Bessarabian, and other national groups, their hundreds of fraternal, communal, and political groups, each playing a role in the life of America, is staggering.

Even in urban neighborhoods, where anonymity is presumed to flourish, the extent of local ties is astounding. Within the city limits of Chicago, for example, there are 82 community newspapers with a total weekly circulation of almost one million; within Chicago's larger metropolitan area, there are 181. According to standard sociological theory, these local papers providing news and gossip about neighbors should slowly decline under the pressure of the national media. Yet the reverse is true. In Chicago, the number of such newspapers has increased 165 per cent since 1910; in those forty years, circulation has jumped 770 per cent. As sociologist Morris Janowitz, who studied these community newspapers, observed: "If society were as impersonal, as self-centered and barren as described by some who are preoccupied with the one-way trend from 'Gemeinschaft' to 'Gesellschaft' seem to believe, the levels of criminality, social disorganization and psycho-pathology which social science seeks to account for would have to be viewed as very low rather than (as viewed now) alarmingly high."

It may be argued that the existence of such a large network of voluntary associations says little about the cultural level of the country concerned. It may well be, as Ortega maintains, that cultural standards throughout the world have declined (in everything? — in architecture, dress, design?), but nonetheless a greater proportion of the population today participates in worthwhile cultural activities. This has been almost an inevitable con-comitant of the doubling — *literally* — of the American standard of living over the last fifty years.

The rising levels of education have meant a rising appreciation of culture. In the United States, more dollars are spent on concerts of classical music than on baseball. Sales of books have doubled in a decade. There are over a thousand symphony orchestras, and several hundred museums, institutes and colleges are purchasing art in the United States today. Various other indexes can be cited to show the growth of a vast middlebrow society. And in coming years, with steadily increasing productivity and leisure, the United States will become an even more active "consumer" of culture. *

It has been argued that the American mass society imposes an excessive conformity upon its members. But it is hard to discern who is conforming to what. The *New Republic* cries that "hucksters are sugarcoating the culture." The *National Review*, organ of the "radical right," raises the ban-ner of iconoclasm against the domination of opinion-making in our society

---

* Some further ambiguity in the use of the mass-society concept derives from the confusions in the use of the anthropological and the humanist meanings of the word "culture." Thus some critics point to the "breakdown" of local folk or regional practices — speech differences, cooking, songs, dances, humor — and their replacement by uni-form national patterns as an indication of the leveling of the mass society and of the decline of culture. These changes, which are real, are meaningful, however, only in anthropological usage, as a change from parochial to more universal cultural forms. But such changes are not *necessarily* a judgment about the humanist quality of the culture. (It is curious that in the past the breakdown of rustic forms was seen as a necessary prelude to the growth of a "high culture." Today the breakdown of the rustic forms is seen as part of the destruction of humanist culture.) The distinctions should be made clear. The anthropological concept of culture is relativistic. It implies no judgment of any one culture and cannot be used as a stick to criticize "high culture." The fact that the nature of satisfactions has changed from country dances and folksy humor to Bra-zilian sambas and Broadway flippancy is analytically a different question than that of the character of the culture. As these criticisms are made, one deals with the presumed disorganization of society, the other with the quality of the culture. Again, it is the pur-pose of this essay to point out that the invocation of the notion of tradition (*Gemein-schaft*, etc.) to make a judgment about the disorganization of the society is scientifically spurious and conceals a value. The other criticism, which is serious, lies outside the scope of this essay. (For a discussion of the issues of "high" vs. "middlebrow" culture, see Clement Greenberg, "The Plight of Our Culture," *Commentary*, June and July, 1953. See also, Mary McCarthy, "America the Beautiful," *Commentary*, September, 1947.)

by "the liberals." *Fortune* decries the growth of "organization man." Each of these tendencies exists, yet in historical perspective there is probably less conformity to an over-all mode of conduct today than at any time within the last half century in America. True, there is less bohemianism than in the twenties (though increased sexual tolerance) and less political radicalism than in the thirties (though the New Deal enacted sweeping reforms). But does the arrival at a political dead center mean the establishment, too, of a dead norm? I do not think so. One would be hard put to find today the "conformity" *Main Street* exacted of Carol Kennicott thirty years ago. With rising educational levels, more individuals are able to indulge a wider variety of interests. ("Twenty years ago you couldn't sell Beethoven out of New York," reports a record salesman. "Today we sell Palestrina, Monteverdi, Gabrielli, and Renaissance and Baroque music in large quantities.")

The curious fact, perhaps, is that no one in the United States defends conformity. Everyone is against it, and probably everyone always was. Thirty-five years ago, you could easily rattle any middle-class American by charging him with being a "Babbitt." Today you can do so by accusing him of conformity. The problem is to know who is accusing whom. In December, 1958, the *Reader's Digest* (circulation twelve million) reprinted an article from *Woman's Day* (circulation five million) with the title, "The Danger of Being Too Well-Adjusted." The point of the article is that great men were not adjusted, and the article quotes a psychiatrist who says that "we've made conformity into a religion"; we ought to remember, however, that each child is different "and ought to be."

Such citation is no proof that there is not "conformity" in the middle class; but if there is, there is also a great deal of anxiety and finger-pointing about it. Certainly those who live on the margin of society — the Upper Bohemians, whose manners soon become the style for the culture — seek frantically to find different ways of emphasizing their non-conformity. In Hollywood, where Pickfair society in the twenties counterfeited a European monarchy (and whose homes crossed Louis XIV with Barnum & Bailey), "non-conformity," according to *Life* magazine (in its jumbo Entertainment issue of December 22, 1958 — readership twenty-five million), "is now the key to social importance and that Angry Middle-Aged man, Frank Sinatra, is its prophet and reigning social monarch." The Sinatra set, *Life* points out, deliberately mocks the old Hollywood taboos and is imitated by a host of other sets that eagerly want to be non-conformist as well. Significantly — a fact *Life* failed to mention — the reigning social set and its leaders, Sinatra, Dean Martin, Sammy Davis, Jr., are all from minority groups and from the wrong side of the tracks. Sinatra and Martin are Italian, Davis a Negro. In earlier times in American life, a minority group, having bulled its way to the top, would usually ape the style and manners of the established status community. In Hollywood, the old status hierarchies have been fragmented, the new sets celebrate their triumph by jeering at the pompous ways of the old.

At the margins of the literary life, and a different social phenomenon, are the Beatniks, a hopped-up, jazzed-up, souped-up, self-proclaimed group of outcasts who are rebelling against the "highly organized academic and literary movement employment agency of the Neoanti-reconstructionist [who form] a dense crust of custom over American cultural life." But the singular fact is, as Delmore Schwartz recently argued, that these Beatniks are imaginary rebels, "since the substance of their work is a violent advocacy of a nonconformism which they already possess . . . since nonconformism of almost every variety had become acceptable and respectable and available to everyone. Unlike the Bohemianism of the past, which had to attack the dominant Puritanism and Victorianism of respectable society in a variety of forms, including the censorship of books, Prohibition and a prudery enforced by the police, the new nonconformism has no genuine enemy . . . hence the new rebel bears a great deal of resemblance to a prize fighter trying to knock out an antagonist who is not in the ring with him." The additional sardonic fact is that the man in the gray flannel suit, the presumed target of the Beatniks, is, as Russel Lynes pointed out, especially if he is in advertising, or the entertainment media, an Upper Bohemian himself. The job is accepted as a means of obtaining an income in order to sport and flaunt his presumed, idiosyncratic tastes in dress, food, travel, and the like.* The problem for all these multiple sets is not conformity but added novelty.

To add one more paradox, the early theorists of mass society (e.g., Simmel) condemned it because in the vast metropolitan honeycombs people were isolated, transient, anonymous to each other. Americans, sensitive as they are to the criticism of others, took the charge to heart and, in building the postwar suburbs, sought to create fraternity, communality, togetherness, only to find themselves accused of conformity. In the new, recent trend of people returning to the city, it is clear that, in recoil, people will once again establish barriers and will thus bring on the charge, in the next

---

* "In the richly appointed Lake Shore Drive apartment of Chicago Financier Albert Newman, the guests chatted animatedly, gazed at the original Picasso on the wall, and the Monet, the Jackson Pollock. On tables and shelves stood Peruvian fertility symbols, jade bracelets, sculptures that looked like the superstructure of a Japanese battleship. . . . [The guests] had come to meet 32-year-old Allen Ginsberg of Paterson, N.J., author of a celebrated, chock-full catalogue called *Howl* ("I saw the best minds of my generation destroyed by madness, starving hysterical naked."). . . . At length Poet Ginsberg arrived wearing blue jeans and a checked black-and-red lumberjacking shirt with black patches. . . . With the crashing madness of a Marx Brothers scene run in reverse, the Beatniks [Ginsberg and two friends] read their poetry, made their pitch for money for a new Beatnik magazine, *The Big Table,* and then stalked out. . . . The trio was an instant hit with the literary upper crust. . . . [The next evening] at the Sherman Hotel, the Beatniks read more poetry for a curious crowd of 700 (who paid $1 and up) . . ." (*Time,* February 9, 1959).

inspection by European sociology, of anonymity, isolation and soullessness, and *anomie*.

One hears the complaint that divorce, crime, and violence demonstrate a widespread social disorganization in the country. But the rising number of divorces may indicate not the disruption of the family but a freer, more individualistic basis of choice and the emergence of the "companionship" marriage. And as regards crime, I have sought to demonstrate . . . that there is actually much *less* crime and violence (though more vicarious violence through movies and TV, and more "windows" onto crime, through the press) than was the case twenty-five and fifty years ago. Certainly Chicago, San Francisco, and New York were much rougher and tougher cities in those years. But violent crime, which is usually a lower-class phenomenon, was then contained within the ecological boundaries of the slum; hence one can recall quiet, tree-lined, crime-free areas and feel that the tenor of life was more even in the past. But a cursory look at the accounts of those days — the descriptions of the gang wars, bordellos, and street-fighting in San Francisco's Barbary Coast, New York's Five Points, or Chicago's First Ward — would show how much more violent the actual life of those cities was in the past.

At this point, it becomes quite apparent that such large-scale abstractions as "the mass society," with the implicit diagnosis of social disorganization and decay that derive from them, are rather meaningless without standards of comparison. Social and cultural change is probably greater and more rapid today in the United States than in any other country, but the assumption that social disorder and *anomie* inevitably attend such change is not borne out in this case.

This may be due to the singular fact that the United States is probably the first large society in history to have change and innovation "built into" its culture. Almost all human societies, traditionalist and habit-ridden as they have been and still are, tend to resist change. The great efforts to industrialize underdeveloped countries, increase worker mobility in Europe, and broaden markets — so necessary to the raising of productivity and standards of living — are again and again frustrated by ingrained resistance to change. Thus, in the Soviet Union, change has been introduced only by dint of wholesale coercion. In the United States — a culture with no feudal tradition, with a pragmatic ethos, as expressed by Jefferson, that regards God as a "workman"; with a boundless optimism and a restless eagerness for the new that have been bred out of the original conditions of a huge, richly endowed land — change, and the readiness to change, have become the norm. This indeed may be why those consequences of change predicted by theorists basing themselves on European precedent find small confirmation.

The mass society is the product of change — and is itself change. It is the bringing of the "masses" into a society, from which they were once excluded. But the *theory* of the mass society affords us no view of the relations of the parts of the society to each other that would enable us to locate the sources of change. We may not have enough data on which to sketch an alternative theory, but I would argue that certain key factors, in this country at least, deserve to be much more closely examined than they have been: the change from a society once geared to frugal saving and now impelled to spend dizzily; the breakup of family capitalism, with the consequent impact on corporate structure and political power; the centralization of decision-making, politically, in the state and, economically, in a group of large corporate bodies; the rise of status and symbol groups replacing specific interest groups — these indicate that new social forms are in the making and, with them, still greater changes in the complexion of life under mass society. With these may well come new status anxieties — aggravated by the threats of war — changed character structures, and new moral tempers.

The moralist may have his reservations or give approval — as some see in the breakup of the family the loss of a source of essential values, while others see in the new, freer marriages a healthier form of companionship — but the singular fact is that these changes emerge in a society that is now providing one answer to the great challenge posed to Western — and now world — society over the last two hundred years: how, within the framework of freedom, to increase the living standards of the majority of people and at the same time maintain or raise cultural levels. For these reasons, the theory of the mass society no longer serves as a description of Western society but as an ideology of romantic protest against contemporary life.

B. Processes and Examples

When people feel themselves threatened by a situation there are many things they can do. They can actively confront those things causing them grief, or they can retreat from them. A notable form of retreatism has characterized the religious cults which withdraw from society and give up worldly pleasures. Sometimes activism takes the form of a political uprising. The means at the individual's disposal for dealing with disorganization in his life are limited by such factors as age, sex, social class, and race. Sometimes the same organization will combine a religious appeal with opportunity for political action, in order to serve the purposes of the individuals who join. Lincoln's study of the Black Muslims, based on surveys and participant observation techniques, traces the development of one group coping in the mass society.

29   C. ERIC LINCOLN

On the Black Muslims

The Black Muslims are probably America's fastest growing racist sect —
100,000 militant "Black Men" who look forward to the day when the white
man in America will be "treated as he ought to be treated." The Movement
is growing rapidly, and it is nationwide; in December 1960, there were
sixty-nine temples or missions in twenty-seven states, from California to
Massachusetts and Florida. Under the leadership of Elijah Muhammad,
who has been hailed by thousands inside and outside the Movement as
"the most fearless Black Man in America," the Black Muslims are demanding — and getting — a hearing from a significant element of the Negro
community. Their ultimate demand — that Black Men be allowed to set
up a separate state within the United States, occupying as much as one-
fifth of the nation's territory — commands little or no attention among non-
Muslim Negroes. But the lashing indictment of the white man that supports
the demand, strikes a responsive, if reluctant, chord in many Negro hearts.

The Black Muslims are neither pacifists nor aggressors. They pay zealous
attention to the requirements of the letter of law regarding peace and
order. They engage in no "sit-ins," test no segregation statutes, participate
in no "marches on Washington" or anywhere else. But they do believe in
keeping the scores even, and they have warned all America that "an eye
for an eye and a tooth for a tooth" is the only effective way to settle racial
differences.

Perhaps the nearest parallel to the Black Muslim Movement was the
Garvey movement of the post-World War I era. The social conditions
which made Garveyism possible were similar to those obtaining at the
present time, if not quite the same. We have had "Little Rock" and "Clin-
ton, Tennessee," though there has been no wholesale murder of Negroes
such as occurred during the infamous "Red Summer" of 1919. There have
been improvements in the Negro's total status since Garvey's day — a
little here, a little there. There have been some breaches in the high, white
wall of segregation. But for Negroes in general, and for the Black Muslims
in particular, these isolated improvements in the Negro's total status are
not enough. The tradition of disprivilege and the continuing formidable
opposition to first-class citizenship are the discouraging elements that
contribute most to the "Muslim mood."

There is a feeling among American Negroes that the non-white world is waiting — waiting to see if they are fit to be counted as men. There is a new determination in the Negro community to "go first class, whatever the cost." For most, "first class" means an unqualified enjoyment of all the rights and duties of citizenship. For others, "first class" means political and social autonomy — a national state for the "Black Man" in America.

For the Black Muslims, theirs is not a "Sunday religion": the Muslim temples hold frequent meetings, and every Muslim is required to attend two (and often more) meetings a week. Nor is it a religion that spares the billfold. The mass of Muslims are from the Negro lower class, with relatively low incomes, and they are encouraged to live respectably and provide for their families. But the men are urged to hold steady jobs; and all Muslims are forbidden to gamble, smoke, drink liquor, overeat, indulge in fripperies or buy on credit. As a result most Muslims enjoy a healthy standard of living and still have enough cash left over to swell the Movement's coffers.

As the Negro community develops its own business and industrial plant, the Muslims' pressure for economic separation is virtually certain to increase. In the not too distant future, this may well take the form of an official boycott against white merchants in the Negro ghettos. In a related move, the Muslims might picket the downtown stores so as to discourage Negroes from entering and shopping there. Such a maneuver would be so explosive that white store-owners and policemen might yearn for the good old days of the tension that accompanied the student sit-ins. Store-owners cannot be expected to take calmly the probable loss of much of their patronage; but the Muslims are neither "passive" nor "loving" toward white men, and any violence on the part of whites would certainly be met with violence. "If it ever happens," said one police official darkly, "that's when we're going to have hell on our hands."

The Black Muslims are not an isolated phenomenon. They are rooted in the whole structure of racial tension. In New York City alone, a score or more organizations operate in the name of black solidarity. Their central theme is always the glorification of black civilization and the deprecation of the white man's culture, which, whenever it has been adopted by the black man, has reduced him to impotence and ignominy.

But, the Black Muslims have gone even further and have made a science of black nationalism. They have made *black* the ideal, the ultimate value; they have proclaimed the Black Man to be the primogenitor of all civilization, the Chosen of Allah, "the rightful ruler of the Planet Earth." And their extreme racist doctrine has attracted more than a hundred thousand adherents — a vivid warning of the deep resentment American Negroes harbor for their status in our society and of the futility they feel about the likelihood of a genuine and peaceful change.

Yet, black nationalism is more than courage and rebellion; it is a way of life. It is an implicit rejection of the "alien" white culture and an explicit rejection of the symbols of that culture, balanced by an exaggerated and undiluted pride in "black" culture. It involves a drastic reappraisal not only of present realities but also of the past and future. The black nationalist revises history (or corrects it, as he would say) to establish that today's black men are descended from glorious ancestors, from powerful and enlightened rulers and conquerors. This reconstruction of history may reach ridiculous extremes; and it can never be accepted by white men, who, to bolster their own security, must perceive history as a record of *white* men's achievements. But a proud history is essential to the black nationalist's self-respect. Essential, too, is the certainty of a brilliant future, in which the inherent superiority of his race will triumph and he will again rule the world.

The main appeal of all black nationalist movements is to the Negro lower class. Here the Negro's resentment is crystallized and open. He has long despaired of the white man's justice and of the trustworthiness of the "acceptable" Negro leaders who court the white man's favor. Moreover, he is already at the bottom of the ladder, so his economic and social position is not vulnerable. An indiscreet word, an admission of hostility or an identification with "radical" or "extremist" groups can cost him nothing. What has he to lose if the demagogues of black nationalism fan his resentment into hatred, openly expressed in defiance of all white men and their compliant Negro "friends"?

The lower-class Negro is ripe for the lure of black nationalism. He is proud to rediscover himself as a Black Man, linked to the great and venerable civilizations of the "single black continent" of Afro-Asia. He is grateful for a mystique, expecially one dignified as a religion, that rationalizes his resentment and hatred as spiritual virtues in a cosmic war of good against evil. And he is jubilant at his new vision of the future — a future not of racial equality, for which he believes the white man has shown himself unfit, but of black supremacy. For "black," to the black nationalist, is a quality and symbol of all that is glorious, triumphant and divine.

In elaborating their doctrines, the Black Muslims have achieved what seems to be a paradox: a rigorously high moral standard of personal and group behavior, laced with a consuming and potentially violent racial and religious hatred. For the Muslims, however, this is no paradox. They urge "peace among brothers" but point out that the white man, having scorned brotherhood with non-whites, "can only be a brother to himself." They urge submission to all authority *except* to the authority of the white man, which, they assert, is not legitimate but is simply "imposed by force and maintained by intimidation." The Muslims' social morality is, in short, an in-group morality. They find no mandate, except that of temporary expediency, for peace and submission between whites and blacks. And from this point of view, it is the religion of the Negro Christian that appears as a paradox, if not an outright hypocrisy or madness. For "it is not possible," says Muhammad's chief spokesman, Malcolm X, "for you to love a man whose chief purpose in life is to humiliate you and still be what is considered a normal human being."

It would be difficult, probably impossible, to separate the Black Muslim teachings on Christianity from those on race. A fundamental tenet of the sect is that all Black Men are Muslims by nature and that Christianity is a white man's religion. Thus there is not even a *possibility* of awakened Black Men accepting Christianity. Nor can the white man accept Islam as taught by Muhammad, for the white man is a devil by nature: "Out of the weak of the Black Nation, the present Caucasian race was created."

These devils were given six thousand years to rule. The allotted span of their rule was ended in 1914, and their "years of grace" will last no longer than is necessary for the chosen of Allah to be resurrected from the mental death imposed upon them by the white man. This resurrection is the task of Muhammad himself, Messenger of Allah and Spiritual Leader of the Lost-Found Nation in the West. The period of grace was seventy years; forty-six have already elapsed.

The Christian religion is the master stratagem for keeping the so-called Negro enslaved. The whites gave him the "poisoned book" and required him to join the "slave religion," which teaches him to love his oppressor and to pray for them who persecute him. It even teaches him that it is God's will that he be the white man's slave!

The Bible is also held in some suspicion because "it is dedicated to King James (a white man) rather than to God." Moreover, "it makes God guilty of an act of adultery by charging him with being the father of Mary's baby; again it charges Noah and Lot with drunkenness and Lot begetting children by his daughter. What a poison book! On the whole, "Christianity is a religion organized and backed by the devils for the purpose of making slaves of black mankind." It "has caused more bloodshed than any other combination of religions. Its sword is never sheathed."

In their day-to-day living, the Black Muslims are governed by a stringent code of private and social morality. Since they do not look forward to an afterlife, this morality is not related to any doctrine of salvation. It is, quite simply, the style of living appropriate to a divine Black Man in his capacity as true ruler of the planet Earth.

The regeneration of criminals and other fallen persons is a prime concern of the Black Muslims, and they have an enviable record of success. Muhammad claims that his Movement has done more to "clean up the so-called Negroes" than all the churches and social agencies combined. Malcolm X scarcely exaggerated when he declared:

> It is a known fact, and sociologists agree that when a man becomes a follower of Mr. Muhammad, no matter how bad his morals or habits were [before], he immediately takes upon himself a pronounced change which everyone admits. He [Muhammad] stops

them from being dope addicts. He stops them from being alcoholics, [and alcohol] is a curse on the so-called Negroes. He has taken men who were thieves, who broke the law — men who were in prison — and reformed them so that no more do they steal, no more do they commit crimes against the government.

There can be no doubt whatever that Muhammad wants to see "every Black Man in America reunited with his own." This means, of course, that every Negro Christian is the target of the Movement. At the present time the Movement is predominantly lower-class, and the Muslims are aware that the middle and upper classes will be harder to reach, for these classes are the "satisfied Black Men who think they have the least to gain." Yet Muhammad declares: "We are trying to reach *all* Black Men, those in the colleges and those in the jails."

Black unity — the "Black Man's one hope for freedom" — is held by the Muslims to be the white man's most haunting fear. And the white man can bring intensely divisive pressures to bear, because the American Negroes, "a nation within a nation," are an "occupied people." The whites control communications, arms and the loyalty of the so-called Negro leadership as thoroughly and effectively as they did during World War II. Operating through "professional Uncle Toms," they have thrown up barriers to black unity; and the divided black people have no way to protect their rights or make themselves heard.

Such, then, is the Muslim vision of a United Front of Black Men — a phalanx of American Negroes no longer torn by dissension but standing shoulder to shoulder, ready for battle. The leader and the enemy are known, but everything else is shrouded in mystery: the methods of combat, the terms of surrender and the new way of life to be established after the victory.

The Black Muslims demand absolute separation of the black and the white races. They are willing to approach this goal by stages — the economic and political links, for example, need not be severed immediately — but all personal relationships between the races must be broken *now*. Economic severance, the next major step, is already under way, and political severance will follow in good time. But only with complete racial separation will the perfect harmony of the universe be restored.

Integration appears only as a stratagem through which the white man hopes to save himself from an inevitable fate. He has sowed the wind, and now he must reap the whirlwind. The ascendancy of the white West is ended. The wheel must turn. When the white man was the undisputed ruler of the earth, who spoke of integration? Now he has seen his empires crumble, his slaves shake off their bonds, his enemies multiply all over the world — "so he is willing to throw his faithful dog the driest bone he has, hoping that dog will once more forget the past and rush out to save his master." But the Negro will still be the loser, for the white man will only "integrate him" where it serves his own advantage, and this will always be at the bottom.

To realize their ends the Muslims have to reach the black masses. Muhammad's strategy has been to put the cult on parade — on the streets, in the press, in the temples, *wherever there are people*. And he has done this with impressive success. For local action, he has had an able corps of ministers in the field; but there were not many at first, and their fight was uphill. The press gave him his first major assist, for it made him "controversial": as a columnist in one of the most important Negro papers in the country, he became a conversation piece for hundreds of thousands of Negroes across America.

People went to the temples to see the man whose columns they read. For the most part they were simply curious, but Muhammad and his ministers are masters at capturing the curious. Muhammad appealed to the newcomers not as individuals but as a crowd. All persons entering a temple were (and still are) searched for weapons as a precaution against the assassination of a minister. This requirement intrigued the curious and excited their sense of personal importance. Inside the temples, they were fascinated by the black-suited young males with the red ties and the military bearing. They were impressed by Muhammad's bold denunciation of the white man, and they were enlightened by hearing for the first time the "truth" about themselves, the Black Nation of Islam.

In pursuit of his goal to make Muslims out of Negro Christians and the unchurched, Muhammad has an ambitious program of recruitment. His ministers go into jails and penitentiaries, pool halls and bars, barbershops and drugstores to talk about Islam. They invade the college campuses, the settlement houses and the YMCA's. Young Muslim brothers pass out literature in front of the Negro Christian churches on Sunday morning, inviting the Christians to attend lectures at the Muslim temples in the afternoon. They speak from street corners and in parks, and they distribute literature wherever large crowds of Negroes are gathered. Invariably, the proselytizers are young, personable, urbane and well-dressed men of confidence and conviction.

On Sunday mornings the crusading brothers may station themselves outside the Christian churches — High-Church or apostolic, cathedral or storefront, it doesn't matter to the self-confident Muslims, for the message they have is ultimately intended for the entire Black Nation. They march silently up and down in front of the churches, passing out handbills inviting the Christians to come to the Muslim temple that afternoon "to hear the truth."

The Black Muslims have spared no effort to contact the Negro masses through every available medium of mass communication. Wherever Muhammad speaks, his audiences are numbered in the thousands; and since 1959 his rallies have been increasingly frequent. For several years, Muhammad's column in the *Pittsburgh Courier* attracted wide attention among

Negroes and stirred a lively debate between those who supported his views and those who were indignant that he was granted space in the paper. During his tenure as a *Courier* columnist, no other single writer drew as many letters to the editor; and the newspaper, which had been steadily losing readers, suddenly found its circulation increasing. This was partially due to the fact that the Muslims took to the street corners and the housing projects to hawk the papers — each brother being assigned a quota.

The fervent activity of the Black Muslims and its rapid growth have become a source of major concern for the recognized Negro leadership. Some of this concern may be attributed to professional jealousy, for each Muslim was once potentially a member of a different Negro organization. But beneath this surface jealousy lie far more serious apprehensions — a recognition of the Muslims as a dangerous threat to the areas of harmony that have been won through years of painstaking interracial negotiation and experimentation.

Negro leadership in America — politicians, intellectuals and businessmen — has been uniformly dedicated to the principle of cooperation with the white man in any attempt to relieve the Negro's condition. Muhammad's harangues on "the truth about the white man" are therefore considered dangerous and destructive, regardless of their truth or falsity. One leader who has spent a lifetime in patient negotiation with the white community declared that Muhammad's allegations are "intemperate enough to be insulting and true enough to be embarrassing."

Because of Muhammad's attacks on Christianity, he has been attacked by some Negro preachers. Yet, because of widespread segregation and other signs of racial bias within the church and throughout the Christian world, many ministers feel vulnerable. They cannot in good conscience flatly reject the Black Muslim position as a whole. Most have taken a position similar to that of The Reverend William M. James, Minister of the Metropolitan Community Methodist Church in Harlem, who repudiated black racism as unjustifiable and unavailing but pointed out that it is rooted in the persecution and the denial of common opportunities to American Negroes.

The Black Muslims are, however, almost unanimously rejected by the orthodox Moslem groups in America. Race is probably not a major factor in this rejection. The rejection is based, rather, on Muhammad's extreme racial views, his emphatic militancy and his unhistoric teachings about the Black Nation. American Moslems do not wish to be identified with such doctrines.

Yet, not all the tensions experienced by the Muslims are from outside the Movement. Some tensions are already perceptible within the Movement, and these seem likely to increase with time. There are problems both of definition and of control. As the Movement solidifies, it will have to make more and more explicit its relationship to both the white American and the international Islamic worlds. For the moment, the Muslim leaders are purposefully vague on these points. When they must declare themselves, the present quiet disagreements within the leadership will most likely become sharp and bitter factionalism. And as the Movement grows in size and influence, it will become more and more a tempting prize for those who covet power. Rivalries within the leadership already exist, as well as a latent reliance on force. These rivalries may erupt quickly when Muhammad dies.

Elijah Muhammad is a hale, energetic and mentally vigorous man, capable of sustaining a grueling workday under very nearly spartan self-discipline. He celebrated his sixty-third birthday in 1960 and seems likely to remain in firm control of his Black Nation for many years to come. Yet flesh is mortal; and even to the Messenger of Allah, death must one day come. So far as is known, Muhammad has not yet named his successor, and we may assume that a struggle for that honor is already under way. The two leading contenders would logically be Malcolm X and Raymond Sharrieff (though one of Muhammad's sons, Wallace D., is also mentioned as a possible heir-apparent). Malcolm is Muhammad's chief lieutenant in the open affairs of the Movement and his emissary to the Islamic nations of Africa and Asia. He is its most articulate spokesman and its most indefatigable organizer, infused with the Messenger's authority and admired by the ministers and the laity alike. Raymond, on the other hand, is Muhammad's son-in-law and his chief lieutenant in the secret affairs of the Movement, manager of its business enterprises and Supreme Captain of the secret army, the Fruit of Islam. Malcolm is undeniably the more popular contender: he would certainly win a resounding mandate in an election by the Muslim faithful. But Muslim affairs are not settled by elections.

The Black Muslim leadership's search for respectability — a concomitant of its desire for rapid growth — may also force an internal showdown on the vehemence and bitterness with which the race issue is to be pressed. At the moment, Muhammad still openly denounces the white man — the entire white race, without exception — in the most scathing language ever heard in the white-dominated nations of the world. These denunciations attract and delight the true believer, but they repel most Negroes, who themselves are daily victims of extreme and irrational racial generalizations.

Yet Muhammad is aware of the paradox that the less respectable he is, the more he is *respected*. His boldness in "saying for millions what millions fear to say for themselves" may elevate him to a recognized position of leadership in the Negro community. Even more important, he feels, it may earn him the respect of the white man, who admires solidarity and determination. And the *respect* of the white man is the key to *respectability* among American Negroes, for "whom the white man respects, the Negro hastens to embrace." Thus, ironically, Muhammad may win by demagogy a seal of approval that he could never win by moderation.

If this gamble pays off, Muhammad may gain respectability for his Movement without retreating an inch on the race issue and without internal dissensions. If it fails, the result may be a tug-of-war between those who cling to respectability and those who cling to hatred. In either case, the Messenger has made his own position clear: "I will never, after having knowledge, love nor befriend the enemies of . . . my Black Nation, whether my people believe as I do or not."

The Black Muslims, however, do exist and are still very much a part of our contemporary scene. They attract the support of the masses and of a small but increasing number of intellectuals. And they will continue to expand as long as racial tension is permitted to flourish in America. True, the Movement in its present form may be crushed by an embarrassed and apprehensive citizenry, white or black. It can be stopped today — and it should be, if it seriously threatens the peace and security of the nation. But in shattering the Movement we shall not eliminate the tension and the need which created and catapulted it to its present momentum. Out of the ashes of the Black Muslims, another "black" specter will inevitably rise to challenge us, for we can destroy the Muslim organization but not the Negro's will to freedom. The essence of the Black Muslim Movement will endure — an extreme expression of the American Negro's rising dissatisfaction with the way things are and his deepening conviction that this is not the way things have to be.

The meaning is clear. We must attack the disease, not its symptoms. We must confront the issue of racism and discrimination. When we have done so with the determination and moral conviction so brutal a problem deserves, there will be no Black Muslims. There will be no need for them.

Gregory Stone is a social psychologist who makes use of the perspective of symbolic interactionism in dealing with a common phenomenon known as Halloween. The mass man has been portrayed as one who lives a life of ritual. To conform to the ritual is painless; it is a means of getting by. By not challenging traditional definitions of situations the individual does not threaten his self; the person who introduces a new perspective into the picture is threatening. Stone's examples of children performing a ritual, and being confronted with a new definition of the situation, which renders them helpless, illustrate these points.

30   GREGORY P. STONE

Halloween and the Mass Child

I set these notes down with a sense of *déjà vu*. Certainly it has all been said before, and I may have read it all somewhere, but I cannot locate the sources. I have often thought about these things in the past. Then, too, as a sociologist, I like to think I am providing observations as well as impressions for my audience. I cannot recall any other counts and tabulations of the very few facts and happenings that I counted and tabulated this year in a small "near southern" town on the traditional hallowed evening.

In brief, I found that Riesman's "other-directed man" may have exported his peculiar life style — tolerance and conformity organized by the prime activity of consumption — from his suburban northeastern habitat to areas westward and southward perilously close to the Mason-Dixon line.[1] The town I speak of is a university town. As such, it has undoubtedly recruited "other-directed's" from the universities of the northeast. For example, I have been there. Moreover, the part of town in which I carried on my quantitative survey (properly speaking, a "pilot study") is a kind of suburb — a sub-village, perhaps an "inner-urb" — the housing section maintained by most large universities where younger faculty are segregated from the rest of the community in World War II officers' quarters. "Other-directed's" are younger and better educated than "inner-directed's."

You will recall the main theme of *The Lonely Crowd:* the very *character* of American life has been revolutionized as the fundamental organizing activity of our waking hours has shifted from production to consumption. We used to work — at least ideally and Protestantly — because work was our life. By our works we were known. Max Weber, among others less careful and profound, has attempted to explain this in his *Protestant Ethic and the Spirit of Capitalism,* showing how a vocabulary of motive was required to consolidate the spread of capitalism in society and arguing that the sheer dialectic of class antagonism was not always sufficient to account for the institution of pervasive economic change. *Every social change requires a convincing rationale.* Protestantism supplied this in part, and its persistence may still be seen in the contrasting attitudes toward gambling

From *American Quarterly,* Vol. 11 (Fall, 1959), pp. 372–379. Reprinted by permission of the author and the publisher.

1 It may well be argued that "other-direction" is, like Babbitry, a midwestern phenomenon. Riesman has probably been unduly and misleadingly cautious in circumscribing his observations as he did. Thus, the notion of "other-direction" as an incipient character type originating in the northeast is probably more a consequence of the locale in which his early investigations were conducted than a reflection of the actual spread of "other-direction" in the United States. I am grateful to David Bakan for the presentation of this point of view.

(*gaming*), for example, held by Protestant and Catholic churches. Only in the 1920's did the American Protestant churches relax their bans on such games, and then it was with the stipulation that they be played for amusement only. Risk and gain were cemented in the context of work; never in the context of play. The place of consumption in the "old" society — the industrial society — may be caricatured by referring to Marx's view that the cost of labor was the money and goods required for laborers to exist and reproduce themselves. Abbreviated: we consumed so that we might work. Today, for the most part, we work to live and live to consume. Abbreviated: we work to consume.

"Trick or Treat" is the contemporary quasi-ritual play and celebration of Halloween. Characteristically, the "trick-or-treater" is rewarded not for his work, but for his play. The practice is ostensibly a vast bribe exacted by the younger generation upon the older generation (by the "other-directed's" upon the "inner-directed's"?). The doorbell rings and is answered. The householder is greeted by a masked and costumed urchin with a bag — significantly, a *shopping* bag — and confronted with dire alternatives: the unknown peril of a devilishly conceived prank that will strike at the very core of his social self — his property; or the "payoff" in candy, cookies or coin for another year's respite from the antisocial incursions of the children. The householder pays.

In his *Psychology of Clothes*, J. C. Flügel has noted that the mask and costume free the individual from social obligation by concealing his identity and cloaking him in the absurd protective anonymity of a mythical or legendary creature — a clown, a ghost, a pirate or a witch. The householder must pay. For, by "dressing out," the urchin is symbolically immunized against those punishments that might ordinarily inhibit the promised violations of property and propriety. Punishment presupposes the identity of the offender.

Nonsense! This conception of "trick or treat" is clearly and grossly in error. In the mass society, the "protection racket" seems as archaic as the concepts of psychoanalysis. To revive either in the analysis of contemporary life betrays the nostalgia of the analyst. Both are but the dusty wreckage of long dead romances. Moreover, as we shall see, the mask invites the ready disclosure of the wearer's identity. Instead of protecting the urchin, the costume is more akin to the Easter bonnet, designed to provoke the uncritical appreciations of the audience.

Even so, we can apprehend the "trick" as a production; the "treat" as a consumption. Just twenty-five years ago, when I was an urchin, Halloween was a time set aside for young tricksters — a time for creative productions. Creativity, I might remind the reader, is inevitably destructive, as it pushes the present into the past. Of course, it is never merely nor exclusively the destruction of established forms. Our destructive productions were immense (I wonder at my adolescence, as Marx wondered at the *bour-*

geoisie!). I don't know now how we managed silently to detach the eave troughs from the house of the neighborhood "crab," remove his porch steps, then encourage him to give chase by hurling those eave troughs, with a terrifying clatter, upon his front porch. I do know it was long, hard and careful *work*. The devices of Halloween were also artfully and craftily produced, like the serrated spool used to rattle the windows of more congenial adults in the neighborhood. We had no conception of being treated by our victims, incidentally, to anything except silence which we hoped was studied, irate words, a chase (if we were lucky), or, most exciting of all, an investigation of the scene by the police whom we always managed to elude. Our masks, we believed, did confound our victims' attempts to identify us.

In sharp contrast to these nostalgic memories are the quantitative findings of my "pilot study." Being a sociologist, I must apologize for my sample first of all. An editorial in a local newspaper warned me that between seventy-five and one hundred children would visit my home on Halloween. Only eighteen urchins bedeviled me that evening, a fact that I attribute to two circumstances. First, I unwittingly left my dog at large early in the evening. A kind animal, a cross between a Weimaraner and some unknown, less nervous breed, she was upset by the curious costumes of the children, and, barking in fright, she frightened away some of the early celebrants. Second, I think that our segregated "inner-urb" was neglected in favor of more imposing, perhaps more lucrative, areas of town. My eighteen respondents ranged in age from about four years to about twelve. Half were girls and half were boys. Two of the six groups — one-third — were mixed. Twenty-five years ago the presence of girls in my own Halloween enterprises was unthinkable.

Was the choice proffered by these eighteen urchins, when they whined or muttered, "Trick or treat?" or stood mutely at my threshold, a choice between production and consumption? Was I being offered the opportunity to decide for these youngsters the ultimate direction they should take in later life by casting them in the role of producer or consumer? Was I located at some vortex of fate so that my very act could set the destiny of the future? Was there a choice at all? No. In each case, I asked, "Suppose I said, 'Trick.' What would you do?" Fifteen of the eighteen (83.3%) answered, "I don't know." The art of statistics, taken half-seriously, permits me to estimate with 95% confidence that the interval, .67–1.00, will include the proportion of children who don't know what a trick is in that "hypothetical universe" for which the eighteen constituted a random sample (this is a ruse employed by some sociologists who find out belatedly that the sample they have selected is inadequate). Yet, it seems that at least two-thirds of the children like those who visited my house on Halloween probably have no conception of producing a trick! They aren't bribing anybody. They grace your and my doorsteps as consumers, pure and simple.

What of the three — the 16.7% — who did not respond, "I don't know"? One said nothing at all. I assume he really didn't know, but, being a careful quantitative researcher, I cannot include him with the others. Another did, in fact say, "I don't know," but qualified his reply. Let me transcribe the dialogue.

> Interviewer: Hello there.
> Respondent: (Silence)
> Interviewer: What do you want?
> Respondent: Trick or treat?
> Interviewer: Supposing I said, "Trick"?
> Respondent: (Silence)
> Interviewer: What would you do, if I said, "Trick"?
> Respondent: *I don't know.* (Long pause.) I'd *probably* go home and get some sand *or something* and throw it on your porch. (Emphasis mine.)
> Field Notes: The porches of the old officers' quarters are constructed from one-by-three slats so that about an inch of free space intervenes between each slat. In short, the porch simply would not hold sand, and the "trick" of the urchin could never be carried off!
> Interviewer: O. K. I'll have to treat, I guess.

The third answered, without prompting, that he'd go home, get a water pistol and squirt my windows (which could have used a little squirting). The "tricks" did not seem so dire, after all! Moreover, the "means of production" — the sand and the water pistol — were left at home, a fact that reminds me of one of Riesman's acute observations to the effect that the home has become a workshop (work is consumed) and the factory, a ranch house (consumption is work).

Did the masks and costumes provide anonymity? To the contrary! I asked each child who he or she was. Happily and trustfully each revealed his or her identity, lifting the mask and disclosing the name. Had they ripped off *my* eave troughs, I would have had the police on them in short order! "Trick or Treat" is a highly personalized affair so that even its ritual quality is lost (for their persistence, rituals depend upon impersonal enactments), and my earlier use of the term, "quasi-ritual," is explained.

On the possibility that the costume might have been a production or a creation, I noted the incidence of ready-to-wear costumes. Two-thirds had been purchased in their entirety. Four of the others were mixed, consisting of homemade costumes and commercial masks. Two were completely homemade: one a ghost outfit, consisting of an old tattle-tale gray sheet with two eye holes; the other, a genuine creation. It was comprised by a mesh wastebasket inverted over an opening in a large cardboard box with armholes. On the front of the box, printed in a firm adult "hand," were the words: Take Me to Your Leader. Occasionally, adults produced, but only to ratify or validate the child in his masquerade as a consumer.

To ascertain the part played by adults in "Trick or Treat," I must, unfortunately, rely on recollections. In preparing my interview schedule and observational data sheets, I had not anticipated the adult, thinking that the celebrants of Halloween would be children. This impression was confirmed by my local newspaper which published the rules of Halloween, stipulating its age-graded character. "Trick or Treat" was set aside for the preadolescents of the town, while teen-agers were obliged to celebrate the event at parties. The rules were apparently enforced, as this news item on the November 1 front page shows:

> Police yesterday afternoon arrested, then released, a youth they said was dressed in a Halloween costume and asking for tricks [*sic*] or treats at downtown stores.
> They said the youth was about 17. He started the rounds of the stores early, he said, because he had to work last night.
> Police said they lectured the youth and explained the traditional [*sic*] trick-or-treat routine is normally reserved for children.

What adults were to do was not clarified by the local press. What many did do was to ease and expedite consumption by clothing their preadolescent children for the role, providing them with shopping bags and, in many instances, accompanying them on the rounds. At least three of the six groups of urchins that called at my house on Halloween were accompanied by adults (the father was always there, one alone!) who lurked uneasily and self-consciously in the darkness where night was mixed with the shadowed shafts cast by my porch light. In one case, a peer group of adults lurked in the shadows and exceeded in number the peer group of children begging on my porch. There they were: agents of socialization, teaching their children how to consume in the tolerant atmosphere of the mass society. The "anticipatory socialization" of the children — accomplished by an enactment of roles not normally played at the time, but roles that would be assumed in the future — was going on before my eyes. I wondered whether the parental preoccupation with the child's adjustment in the larger society could not have been put aside just for Halloween. Perhaps the hiding in the dark allegorically complemented my wish in the tacit expression of shame.

They were teaching a lesson in tolerance, not only a lesson in consumption, encouraging their children to savor the gracious and benign acceptance of their beggary by an obliging adult world. My questions made them nervous. The lone father was silent. He turned his face skywards, studying the stars. One couple spoke rapidly in hushed whispers, punctuating their remarks with nervous laughter. In another couple, the mother said sheepishly, "I wonder what they'll say? They've never been asked that." All the parents were relieved when I tactfully rescued the situation from deterioration by offering to treat the children with (purchased) goodies. Consider a typical protocol.

Field Notes: The bell rings. I go to the door. On the porch are three children between five and nine years old, two boys — one in a clown suit, the other in a pirate suit — and a girl in a Japanese kimono, holding a fan. On the sidewalk are a mother and a father whose faces are hidden in darkness.

Interviewer: Hi!

Respondents: (Silence.)

Interviewer: What do you want?

Respondents: (Silence.)

The clown: Candy.

Interviewer: Why?

Field Notes: The married couple giggles. They shift their feet.

Japanese girl and clown: (Silence.)

Pirate: I don't know.

Field Notes: I look questioningly at the girl and the clown. Each is silent.

Interviewer: What are you supposed to say?

Japanese girl: I don't know.

Interviewer: Have you heard of "Trick or Treat"?

Clown: No.

Field Notes: The married couple is silent. They lean forward expectantly, almost placing their faces in the circle of light arching out and around my porch and open front door, almost telling me who they are.

Interviewer: Well, I guess I'll have to treat.

Field Notes: I get a handful of corn candy from the living room, and divide it among the three outstretched open shopping bags. All the respondents laugh in an appreciative, relieved manner. My study is passed off as a joke. The world has been tolerant after all.

I am reminded of Ortega's remonstrances against the Mass Man, for whom *privileges had become rights*. Standing there, existing, it was the clown's right to receive the treat, the candy. The treat or gift was at one time an act of deference in recognition of esteemed friendship. Herbert Spencer wrote of it in that way — the gift was a privilege. On Halloween, the gift has become the right of every child in the neighborhood, however he or his family is esteemed. Now, rights are not questioned. That such rights would be questioned was hardly anticipated by those who claimed them. It made them ill-at-ease and nervous, perhaps lest the questions betray an indignation — a state of mind more appropriate to an age when people were busy, or perhaps busier, more productive.

Yet, this is not a plea for a return to the "good old days" — ridiculous on the face of it. Certainly, the farther south the tolerance of the mass society creeps, the happier many of us will be. It seems to be unquestionably true that the younger people of the south are less opposed to segregated schools than the adults. There is nothing morally wrong with consumption, per se, as production was often the setting for ruthless destruction. The conformity of "other-direction" (no trick-or-treater came to my door by himself) need not disturb us. Each society must secure conformity from a substantial majority of its members if that society is to persist. Instead, I have tried to show only two things. First, Riesman's character type of "other-direction" may, indeed, be a *prototype* of American character and not some strange mutation in the northeast. Consumption, tolerance and conformity were recognizable in the Halloween masquerade of a near-southern town. Production, indignation and autonomy were not. Second, national holidays and observances may have been transformed into vast staging areas for the anticipatory socialization of mass men. By facilitating this change in life style, they can give impetus to the change in character conceived by Riesman (and many others). I am being very serious when I say that we need studies of what has happened to all these observances — the Fourth of July, Thanksgiving, Christmas and Easter — in all parts of America. After reading this report, you will agree that we need a study of Halloween.

It is not only as a sociologist, however, that I ask for these studies. Something does trouble me deeply about my observations — the "I don't know." Here is the source of our misgivings and dis-ease with respect to the mass man. It is not that he consumes, but, to the profit of the "hidden persuaders," that he consumes, not knowing why or just not knowing. It is not that he is tolerant, but that he is *unreasonably* tolerant. It is not that he conforms, but that he conforms for conformity's sake. *The mass society, like the industrial society, needs a vocabulary of motive — a rationale — to dignify the daily life.* That's what troubles me about my findings on Halloween. It was a rehearsal for consumership without a rationale. Beyond the stuffing of their pudgy stomachs, they didn't know why they were filling their shopping bags.

PART FOUR

QUALITIES OF THE
SOCIAL STRUCTURE

Any society is made up of individuals, some of whom may be members of specific racial or ethnic groups, and live in certain types of communities. These qualities of a social structure are also related, in the sense that race will partly determine the type of community lived in, and even the birth rate within that community. These qualities, then, can, independently, influence human behavior. That is why a sociologist sees them as important variables.

X RACE

A. Definitions and Concepts

*If one were to line up twenty of his acquaintances in front of him
and order them so that the one with the fairest skin was at one end
and the person with the darkest at the other, he could divide them
in the middle and say that one group were Negroes and the other
Caucasians. He could further specify that members from one group
could not intermarry with those from the other, and so forth. Whatever his further refinements, his divisions would remain arbitrary.
In this sense, then, race represents a statistical category of similar
characteristics. Sociologists usually refer to ethnic groups instead of
racial groups, thereby adding the cultural variable. The American
Negro, in his culture, is more like his American Caucasoid counterpart than he is like his African racial group. Carleton Coon, an anthropologist, presents data to show how the separate racial groups
were formed. Coon's conclusion, which is that man evolved five different times in widely separated parts of the globe, was at first the
subject of much controversy.*

31 CARLETON S. COON

New Findings on the Origin of Races

What is race? A myth, as some popular writers would have us believe, or a
rigid division of mankind into superior and inferior groups? A reverse free-

dom rider northward bound? America's greatest and most divisive unsolved problem? The white, black, yellow, red, and brown races pictured in the school geography books? Or a relatively recent and superficial division of mankind?

No. Re-examined in the light of science and history, race is not exactly any of these. It is not a myth, and races are not, as current theory holds, something that evolved into final form about 30,000 years ago and have remained unchanged ever since. In man as in other animals and in plants, a race is a geographically separate division of a species.

A five-year-long study which I have made of every scrap of bone of every fossil man so far discovered — about one thousand pieces — shows rather that the races of man are as old as man himself. The separation of man into races is the work of geography, acting in the guise of natural selection shaping genetically plastic living material.

Races arose as soon as the primitive ancestors of man had dispersed by migrating from the place where they originated — uncertain but possibly in Africa — into all of the warm parts of the Old World (Eurasia and Africa) which could be reached on foot. These earliest humans were not apes, but close relatives of the Australopithecines, the African ape-men with ape-sized brains and essentially manlike bodies.

Between a million and a half-million years ago — in the varied climates and circumstances of regions as widely separated as Morocco and Java — some of the migrants appeared in the form of the oldest known human species, *Homo erectus*. They were already divided into five geographical races and were generally larger of brain, smaller of jaw, and otherwise different in structure from the ape-men.

I. The Australoids. In Java, which was intermittently joined to the Asiatic mainland, *Homo erectus* was already what we now call an Australoid. Later still the Australoids evolved into modern men — *Homo sapiens* — or that part of *Homo sapiens* which includes today's Australian aborigines, Papuans, Melanesians, Negrito dwarfs living from the Philippines to the Andaman Islands, and some of the tribal folk of India.

II. The Mongoloids. In China the early men of the new species, *Homo erectus*, were already Mongoloids. In time they too changed into modern man, siring the numerous peoples of Eastern Asia (except the Ainus) as well as the Polynesians, American Indians, and Eskimos.

III. The Caucasoids. A third race arose somewhere in Western Asia, with the characteristics that were later to be called Caucasoid. By 250,000 years ago some of them had evolved into *Homo sapiens*. From these latter are descended the Europeans and their overseas kin in the Americas and elsewhere; the Middle Eastern whites; most of the people of India; and possibly the Ainus of Japan.

IV. The Capoids. Another race made the transition in North Africa and later, after being pushed south and east, probably evolved into the Bushmen and Hottentots of the race that we call Capoid, after the Cape of Good Hope.

V. The Congoids. A fifth kind of *Homo erectus* appeared in Africa and, as far as we can tell from scanty evidence, it seems to have been related to both Caucasoids and Negroes. I have named it Congoid after the region of the Congo basin. Very late, at a time not exactly known, these people turned into *Homo sapiens* and the modern Negroes and Pygmies.

Homo erectus, as I have shown in my new book, evolved into *Homo sapiens* (our self-named Wise Man), not once but five times, as each subspecies or race living in its own territory passed a critical threshold from a more brutal to a more sapient state.

That such a seeming miracle of transition could occur even once disturbed the smug beliefs of many people when Charles Darwin presented his theory of evolution more than a hundred years ago. My thesis is at variance with the dogmas of 1962, which insist on a single, relatively recent emergence of man. But it is really nothing new. Zoologists and paleontologists have known for some time that the races of a single species can evolve in concert. Only the self-centered folk who cannot see beyond the problems of our own species need be taken aback by this commonplace of zoology.

Nor am I the first to suggest such an origin of races in man. In the 1930's the late Franz Weidenreich, who was studying the bones of *Homo erectus* found in a onetime cave near Peking — Peking Man — noted their Mongoloid character and suggested that the modern Mongoloid races had descended from Peking Man, or Sinanthropus, as he is also called. The idea was immediately attacked and called an impossibility. Critics pointed out that all living men belong to one species, *Homo sapiens.* On the assumption that *Homo sapiens* had originated only once, it was argued that he then spread around the world from the Arctic to Cape Horn and east to west, conveniently extinguishing all archaic species. Only after this dispersal, the argument continued, could the living races of man have developed, each in its own region, and that would have been not much more than 30,000 years ago.

If this were true, I asked, how does it happen that some peoples, like the Tasmanians and many of the Australian aborigines were still living during the nineteenth century in a manner comparable to that of the Europeans of over 100,000 years ago? This would have entailed some major cultural backsliding which the archaeological record does not show. To me there was something pat, dogmatic, and wrong about the anti-Weidenreich point of view.

DRY LAND TO CROSS

To test my thesis that human races were ancient and that they evolved early in five different areas, I undertook the study of all available information on all the fossil remains known from more than three hundred sites. But a theoretical foundation also had to be provided for the facts. What forces exerted pressure on that plastic primate man to make him evolve from a crude to a modern state? To satisfy this need I delved into zoogeography, primate behavior, and social anthropology. At the same time I kept in touch with physiologists studying the mechanisms of adaptation to heat, cold, and altitude, and I went on a field trip with some of them to Chile.

Geography and the rumpled skin of our planet were major shaping elements. From a million to a half-million years ago, the way lay open for the Australopithecine-like ancestors of *Homo erectus* to spread eastward from Africa across the whole range of the Old World tropics. Four of the world's present five continents — Eurasia (Asia and Europe), Africa, and North and South America — were tied together in one fashion or another, but our New World continents were not accessible till later. Low sea levels exposed the Sunda Shelf joining Southeast Asia and the islands of Indonesia. Another now submerged stretch of land, the Sahul Shelf, also stood above the waters to join Australia, Tasmania, New Guinea, and some of the Melanesian Islands. Not only did the shelves serve as dry connections between lands now divided by the seas, but they may also have acted as bellows to suck in and blow out early human populations.

The lesser barriers around the world, such as mountains and deserts, let the dominant animal species, including man, filter through to new territories and favorable breeding grounds. Once there, the populations that had survived the rigors of the journey remained relatively isolated and could evolve in their own ways. New genes brought in from outside, by neighbors or invaders, tended to lose out to those already established by natural selection. However, new genes that were advantageous in all climates and regions, such as those governing higher intelligence, tended to win out everywhere.

In the new lands that the ancestors of the living races reached they encountered many kinds of climate and topography. The newcomers were selected by geographical environment for their ability to resist three kinds of stress in particular — cold, drought, and the thin air of high altitudes. The first entails heat regulation by the human body; the second both heat regulation and the conservation of food and water; and the third, oxygen consumption.

Each race in its own territory independently found its way of surmounting these stresses. The Canoe Indians of Tierra del Fuego at the tip of South America could paddle about without clothing in freezing weather because they have a basal metabolism 160 per cent higher than the norm for whites of the same height and weight. When plunged into cold water, the hands of Alaskan Indians have more blood flow than those of white men.

Selection in another direction enabled the Australian aborigines to take care of cold; they developed insulation in depth of the body core. Members of the Pitjendjera tribe in west central Australia sleep comfortably on the ground in freezing temperatures. They can do this because the outgoing arterial blood in their extremities warms the incoming venous blood.

So far only the Negroes have been shown to possess heat adaptation. American Negroes can tolerate moist heat better than American whites of the same age and background. And so far only Mongoloids, in the Andes and Tibet, are believed to have shown altitude adaptation, in that they have relatively large hearts and large quantities of blood rich in oxygen-carrying red corpuscles. In general, Europeans seem to have no climatic adaptations, but that is probably partly because we use whites as our standard for comparison in studying other peoples.

Among living races many differences may be found in the biochemical realm, such as the tendency of Negroes to be immune to malaria because of possessing sickle cells in their blood, and the tendency of people with blood groups A and B to resist certain contagious diseases; but we can only speculate about the importance of these factors to *Homo erectus* because all we have of him is teeth and bones.

The basic transition from *Homo erectus* to *Homo sapiens* had nothing *directly* to do with adaptation to climate; all that did was to make it possible for man to live in different places and divide into races. The transition was caused by an increase in intelligence and self-control, both of which were needed as men became hunters, had to live in groups of several families in order to get and share their food, had to plan hunts, teach their children how to behave toward others of different sex and age, and needed speech in order to live. These increases were accompanied by an increase in brain size and probably also by changes in endocrine balance. Only the first of these, brain size, left unmistakable marks on the skeleton. A number of criteria, too technical to be explained here briefly, enable us to divide the skeletons of *Homo erectus* from those of *Homo sapiens* in each of the races where adequate remains have been found to make this distinction.*

But two biological problems are central to the question of the origin of races: (1) How did the subspecies or races become differentiated in the first place? This question we have already answered. (2) Why did they not keep on differentiating and become separate species?

The answer to the second question is complicated. In other animals, related species occupying the same territories are kept apart genetically because their members do not feel the desire to breed together, whether or not fertile offspring could be produced if they did. Each has its own set of signals with which it communicates with its kind. In the case of man, we

---

* The designation of a fossil skull as *erectus* or *sapiens* depends on the total configuration, not on brain size alone. But an approximate threshold between the brain-size ranges of *Homo erectus* and *Homo sapiens* can be set at about 1,250 to 1,300 cc, with the expectation that individual differences will occur.

communicate by means of speech, and each group can learn the other's language.

From the earliest times, therefore, there has been gene exchange among groups of people. Wives have been traded or captured, although generally men remain faithful to their own races, at least if their own women are with them. But men traveling alone have no such compunctions, and man is the widest-traveling mammal of them all. So despite racial differences, we are still one species.

One reason why most workers in the fossil man field have failed to realize the vast antiquity of human races is that they have confused two concepts, *grade* and *line*. A grade is an evolutionary level, marked in man by such features as brain size, forehead slope, size of the eyebrow ridges (if any), tooth size, and the presence or absence of a chin. A line is a geographical race, marked by such anatomical details as the shape of the eyebrow ridges, the degree to which the face is either flat or V-shaped, the degree of prominence of the nose, and the structure of the teeth. A skull of any line (race) can belong to any grade (evolutionary level) and vice versa. In most textbooks on human evolution, skulls are lumped together by grade without regard for line, which makes little more sense than confusing bats with birds because both fly.

Inevitably, questions arise as to the modern cultural implications of any discussion of racial differences, but any detailed treatment of this subject will take another book. Briefly, I might say that the Caucasoids and Mongoloids who live today in their homelands and in recently colonized regions, such as North America, did not rise by accident to their present population levels and positions of cultural dominance. They achieved this because their ancestors occupied the most favorable of the earth's zoological regions — regions with challenging climates and ample breeding grounds, centrally located within continental land masses. In our times, the success of these groups is being challenged in many parts of the world as other groups who evolved later learn to use their inventions, especially modern means of communication. And evolution is still taking place, particularly natural selection resulting from crowding and stress.

MAN ON THE THRESHOLD

The oldest adult human skull yet found belongs to the lowest grade of *Homo erectus*, and to the Australoid line. It is known as Pithecanthropus (Ape-Man) Number 4, because it was the fourth of its kind to be found. All four were unearthed in river banks in central Java. Number 4 is about 700,000 years old, and Numbers 1, 2, and 3 between 600,000 and 500,000. We know this because tektites — small, glassy nodules from outer space — were found in the same beds as the first three, and the beds containing Number 4 lay underneath the tektite bed, along with the bones of a more ancient group of animals. These tektites have been picked up in large numbers in Java, the Philippines, and Australia, where they all fell in a single celestial shower. Their age — approximately 600,000 years — has been accurately measured in several laboratories by nuclear chemical analysis, through the so-called argon-potassium method.

Pithecanthropus Number 4 consists of the back part of a skull and its lower face, palate, and upper teeth. As reconstructed by Weidenreich, it is a brutal-looking skull, with heavy crests behind for powerful neck muscle attachments, a large palate, and large teeth, as in apes. The brain size of this skull was about 900 cubic centimeters; modern human brains range from about 1,000 to 2,000 cc with an average of about 1,450 cc. The brains of apes and Australopithecines are about 350 to 650 cc. So Pithecanthropus Number 4 was intermediate in brain size between apes and living men.

His fragmentary skull was not the only find made in the beds it lay in. Nearby were found the cranial vault of a two-year-old baby, already different from those of living infants, and a piece of chinless adult lower jaw. Two other jaws have been discovered in the same deposits which were much larger than any in the world certainly belonging to *Homo erectus*. They are called Meganthropus (Big Man) and may have belonged to a local kind of Australopithecine, but this is not certain. If so, *Homo erectus* coexisted with, or overlapped, the Australopithecines in Java as well as in South Africa, which implies that man did not originate in either place, but somewhere in between.

The three later Pithecanthropus skulls were all faceless, but essentially similar to Number 4, if a little less brutal, and their brains were no larger. A series of eleven more skulls from the Solo River bank, in the same part of Java, carry on this same evolutionary line, but are larger-brained (1,035 to 1,225 cc). They were probably between 150,000 and 75,000 years old, and were still *erectus*, of a higher grade than their predecessors.

The Australoids had begun to cross the threshold from *erectus* to *sapiens* some 40,000 years ago. We know this from a carbon-14 date given a skull found in a cave in North Borneo. In Java itself, the earliest *sapiens* skulls are a pair found at Wadjak, and dated probably no more than 10,000 years ago. These skulls are identical with those of living Australian aborigines.

What happened in Java occurred also in China to a second major race, the Mongoloid. From a series of rock fissures and caves at Choukoutien, near Peking, pieces of the skulls and jaws of about twenty persons and the loose teeth of at least as many more, have been excavated. These specimens, about 360,000 years old, are what is left of a people called Sinanthropus.

Although definitely *Homo erectus* and equal in evolutionary grade to the much less ancient Solo skulls, they differ from the Javanese specimens racially. Instead of sloping gradually, their foreheads stand out sharply from their eyebrow ridges. These persons had cheekbones and jaws which protruded forward, their eyesockets were shallow, and their faces were

SHIFTS OF HUMAN SUBSPECIES, FROM 500,000 TO 10,000 YEARS AGO

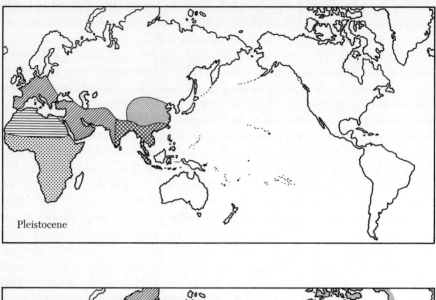

Pleistocene

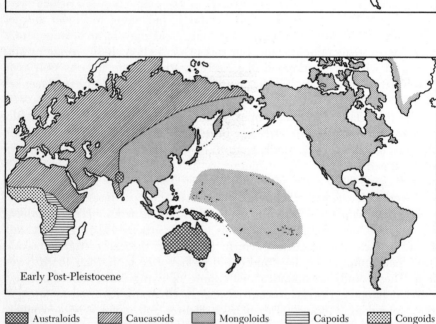

Early Post-Pleistocene

| ▦ Australoids | ▨ Caucasoids | ▦ Mongoloids | ▤ Capoids | ▦ Congoids |

Pleistocene. The five subspecies occupied all of the warm parts of Eurasia and Africa.

Early Post-Pleistocene. The Mongoloids and Caucasoids burst out of their territories. The Mongoloids entered and inhabited America, Southeast Asia, and Indonesia. The Caucasoids thrust northward and into Africa. The Congoids were much reduced, but later evolved rapidly and spread as Negroes over much of Africa.

flattish. Their teeth were the most peculiar of all known in the races of man, particularly the incisors which were not smooth inside as most of ours are, but shaped like shovels, with raised ridges on either side and lumps and teat-like protuberances on the insides of the crowns. These peculiarities are still seen in Mongoloid teeth, from China to Cape Horn.

A series of less ancient skulls also found in China carries the Mongoloid line of descent from Sinanthropus to the modern Chinese, Indonesians, Siberians, Japanese, and American Indians. The earliest of them known to have crossed the evolutionary threshold between *Homo erectus* and *Homo sapiens* is the Tze-Yang skull from Szechuan, Western China, dated at about 150,000 years old. This skull was discovered in 1951 and described in 1957 in a Communist Chinese periodical which few in this country have seen. All the Mongoloid skulls later than Tze-Yang are *sapiens* also. Thus the first ancestors of the American Indians who crossed the Bering Strait more than 10,000 years ago must also have been *sapiens*. *Homo erectus* existed only in the Old World.

MALIGNED NEANDERTHALS

The oldest Caucasoid specimen known is the Heidelberg jaw, about as old as Sinanthropus. Because no braincase was found with it, we do not know whether Heidelberg man was *Homo sapiens* or *Homo erectus* at all. It is chinless, but so are some *sapiens* specimens, and its teeth are of modern size and Caucasoid form.

Two Western European skulls of women, dated at 250,000 years or older, are both *sapiens* and Caucasoid. One is from Swanscombe, England, and the other from Steinheim, Germany. Some of my colleagues have questioned the *sapiens* character of these two skulls, because Swanscombe lacks a face and Steinheim is rather small, and has heavy browridges. But if we are to call all living human beings *Homo sapiens*, then either these ancient women were *sapiens* or else the living Australian aborigines are *erectus*, because Steinheim belonged to the same grade as they do.

From then on all the skulls found in Europe and Western Asia, with one possible exception (Number 5 from the Skhul cave in Palestine, which could have been Australoid) are both *sapiens* and Caucasoid. This statement includes the famous Neanderthals, a much-maligned group of peoples living all the way from France to Uzbekistan, in small, isolated enclaves, during the extremely cold period which lasted from about 75,000 to 40,000 years ago.

The Neanderthals were not stunted, bent over, nor brutal as commonly claimed. Many of them did, however, suffer from arthritis. One skeleton in France is that of an old man who had lost all but two of this teeth, and was too crippled to move about easily. Someone had fed him soft food for years before his death. Another, in Iraq, had been born with a withered arm, which some Neanderthal surgeon had later amputated with a flint knife. People who care for the crippled and aged are not brutes. Furthermore, the Neanderthals were exaggeratedly Caucasoid, with long, pointed faces and beaky noses. The features in which they differed from other Caucasoids were mostly if not entirely due to local inbreeding and adaptation to cold. In Western Europe the Neanderthals were followed by new invaders from the Near East, men indistinguishable from living Europeans.

THOSE WHO FLED

In 1939 in a cave near Tangier, Morocco, I came upon the left half of the upper jaw of a child, in a deposit probably 75,000 years or so old. I took it back to our hotel and showed it to a French physician, who said that it was part of an ape. Later, a distinguished Turkish physical anthropologist, M. S. Şenyürek, labeled it Neanderthal. Finally L. Cabot Briggs, an American anthropologist resident in Algeria, stated that the child had belonged to a previously unidentified local North African race. Briggs' insight was upheld by the discovery, a few years later, of three lower jaws as old as Sinanthropus at Ternefine, Algeria. These jaws also resembled those of Sinanthropus, and so did their teeth. Other specimens from the Moroccan coast filled in the time gap between Ternefine and Tangier, but we have yet to find a braincase.

The Ternefine-Tangier line, as I have called this group of jaws and teeth, resembles the Mongoloid more than any other. Whoever they were, the members of this race were replaced about 10,000 years ago by the Caucasoid ancestors of the living North African Berbers. These invaders came in with an inroad of northern animals — wild cattle, wild sheep, deer, wild boar, and bears — which they had been hunting in Spain or the Near East, and which they pursued into Africa.

Although the evidence is scanty, I believe it likely that the Ternefine-Tangier folk fled into the Sahara and then migrated southward along the East African highlands to the vast paradise of game that was South Africa until the arrival of the Dutch, who began to settle the Cape of Good Hope region about the time that the Pilgrims were landing in Plymouth, Massachusetts. When they first saw the South African natives, the Bushmen and Hottentots, the Dutch thought that they were some kind of Malays or Indonesians, on account of their flat faces and yellowish skins. The Mongoloid features of the Ternefine-Tangier jaws and teeth were thus matched by those of the living Capoids.

ENIGMA OF NEGRO ORIGINS

The fifth major race — the most mysterious of all — is called the Congoid because it includes both the African Negroes and the Pygmies, who share the Congo drainage. The term "Negroid" is to be avoided because it is also used to designate some of the Australoid peoples such as the Melanesians and Negritos. "Negroid" means not a race but a condition (that is, having spiral hair, black skin, etc.), achieved independently in the course of evolution by more than one line of people.

The oldest known Congoid specimen is a skullcap from Olduvai Gorge, Tanganyika, the Grand Canyon of Africa, a rich hunting ground for students of extinct animals as well as for anthropologists. It was found in 1960 by Louis Leakey in a stratum dated at about 400,000 years ago, overlying the layer in which he had previously discovered two kinds of Australopithecines. The Olduvai skullcap is long and relatively narrow, compared to Pithecanthropus, Solo, and Sinanthropus. Unlike these three eastern types, all of which are relatively flat-faced, it has huge eyebrow ridges which sweep backward to either side like bicycle handles. In this respect, and in others, it resembles both the living Caucasoids and Negroes, who have much in common anatomically. This skull clearly belonged to the species *Homo erectus* and probably to the Congoid racial line.

From 400,000 to 40,000 years ago, we have no certain evidence of human evolution in Africa south of the Sahara, although vast quantities of stone implements assure us that people lived their continuously. A skullcap from Saldanha Bay, near Capetown, is probably 40,000 years old or older. It closely resembles the Olduvai specimen. So does a whole skull, minus the lower jaw, from Broken Hill, Northern Rhodesia, which is believed to be no more than 25,000 years old. Sheltered in a cave from death to discovery, it is still in excellent shape. The late Aleš Hrdlička, famed anatomist of the Smithsonian Institution, who was given neither to overstatement nor to displays of unbridled emotion, called it a "comet of man's prehistory" when he saw it in 1930 but, at that time as today, the Rhodesian skull was and remains the only complete specimen of *Homo erectus* yet found, and that may be one reason why it looked so strange. Its browridges, palate, and teeth match in size those of the much earlier Pithecanthropus skulls, but its features are those of Negroes.

After Broken Hill we have no well-dated Negro skulls older than 8,000 to 5,000 years, and these are *sapiens*. Further digging is needed in Africa, particularly in West Africa, whence many Negroes have migrated, both within their own continent and to America, before we will be able to solve the enigma of Negro origins.

But we know, in a general way, the ingredients from which the Negroes may have been blended. One is the old racial line from Olduvai to Broken Hill. A second is the Pygmies of the deep forests, who may be dwarfed descendants of some of the Olduvai-Broken Hill folk. A third is the Capoids, who circled around West Africa and the Congo on their great trek from the Mediterranean to the shores of the Southern Ocean. A fourth is the wave of Caucasoid invaders from North Africa known as the Capsians (after the site of Gafsa in Tunisia) who settled the East African highlands about 5000 b.c., and whose aquiline features may still be seen among the Watussi of Ruanda-Urundi and other spear-brandishing warrior tribes. These four ingredients, combined in varying proportions in different regions and molded by climate and natural selection, probably combined to produce the composite and variable population of black-skinned and curly-

haired peoples known as Negroes who, in 1962, figure prominently in the
national and international news.

Such, then, is the origin of the five living subspecies of man, our human
races, some seen in the broad light of day, others through a dusty glass
darkly. I hope to live long enough to see some of the dust swept away, and
to know where I was right and where wrong and much more important,
where the truth lies.

Quid novi ex Africa?

B. Processes and Examples

*It is well known that different racial and ethnic groups live in ten-
sion with one another in large parts of our society. There is conflict
over housing, employment, and even education. Normally the problems between the various groups have been gradually resolved, but
sometimes the formal procedures for melioration break down and
race riots result. Stanley Lieberson and Arnold Silverman, sociologists and demographers, deal with what they call the precipitants
for race riots, the factors that incite one group to attack another.
Surprisingly enough, when they investigate demographic and housing characteristics as possible causes behind riots in some cities and
absence of them in others, they find that these variables do not
explain differences between cities. It is the structure of the local
governments that is crucial. When a city's government is not so organized that it will mitigate conflict or meet demands by different
racial groups, the potentiality for race riots is greater.*

32 STANLEY LIEBERSON AND ARNOLD R. SILVERMAN

The Precipitants and Underlying Conditions
of Race Riots

The immediate precipitants and underlying conditions of race riots in the
U.S. during the past half century are the subject of this paper. Using both
"hard" and "soft" data, employing journalistic accounts as well as census
data, we consider in a somewhat more systematic fashion the influence of
diverse factors suggested as causes of riots in sociological case studies and

From *American Sociological Review*, Vol. XXX (December, 1965), pp. 887–898. Reprinted by permission of the authors and the *American Sociological Association*.

texts on collective behavior.[1] Riots, as distinguished from lynchings and other forms of collective violence, involve an assault on persons and property simply because they are part of a given subgroup of the community. In contrast, lynchings and other types of violence are directed toward a particular individual as a collective response to some specific act. In practice, this distinction is sometimes difficult to apply, particularly in deciding when a localized racial incident has become a riot.[2] We have excluded some of the housing "riots" from our analysis because they were directed specifically at Negroes attempting to move into an area rather than at Negroes per se or some other more generalized target.

Using the *New York Times Index* for the period between 1913 and 1963, we found 72 different events that might be properly classified as Negro-white race riots. Descriptions of riots in various editions of the *Negro Yearbook* supplemented some of the *Times* reports and also provided reports of four additional riots. In several instances, magazines and local newspapers were used for further information. Finally, we employed the sociological descriptions available for some race riots. Reliance on journalistic accounts for our basic sample of riots means the study is vulnerable to any selectivity in the riots actually reported in the newspaper. Our analysis of the immediate precipitants of race riots is similarly limited by the brevity of some of the descriptive accounts as well as by possible distortions in reporting.[3] For the underlying community conditions of riots, we relied largely on census data.

IMMEDIATE PRECIPITANT

As one might expect, race riots are usually sparked by a provocation involving members of the two races. At most only four of the 76 riots occurred without a precipitating event, and even in these few cases, the apparent

[1] Herbert Blumer, "Collective Behavior," in Alfred McClung Lee (ed.), *New Outline of the Principles of Sociology*, New York: Barnes and Noble, 1951, pp. 165–222; Chicago Commission on Race Relations, *The Negro in Chicago*, Chicago: University of Chicago Press, 1922, pp. 1–78; Allen D. Grimshaw, "Three Major Cases of Colour Violence in the United States," *Race*, 5 (1963), pp. 76–86 and "Factors Contributing to Colour Violence in the United States and Britain," *ibid.*, 3 (May, 1962), pp. 3–19; Allen D. Grimshaw, "Urban Racial Violence in the United States: Changing Ecological Considerations," *American Journal of Sociology*, 66 (1960), pp. 109–119; Kurt Lang and Gladys Engel Lang, *Collective Dynamics*, New York: Thomas Y. Crowell, 1961; Alfred McClung Lee and Norman Daymond Humphrey, *Race Riot*, New York: Dryden Press, 1943; Elliott M. Rudwick, *Race Riot at East St. Louis, July 2, 1917*, Carbondale: Southern Illinois University Press, 1964; Neil J. Smelser, *Theory of Collective Behavior*, New York: Free Press of Glencoe, 1963; Ralph H. Turner and Lewis M. Killian, *Collective Behavior*, Englewood Cliffs, N.J.: Prentice-Hall, 1957; Ralph H. Turner and Samuel J. Surace, "Zoot-Suiters and Mexicans: Symbols in Crowd Behavior," *American Journal of Sociology*, 62 (1956), pp. 14–20.

[2] Lynchings, for example, are sometimes followed by riots. No doubt we would have included some of these events and excluded others had more detail been available.

[3] See, for example, Raoul Naroll, *Data Quality Control — A New Research Technique*, New York: Free Press of Glencoe, 1962.

lack of precipitant may be due to the scantiness of the accounts rather than the absence of an immediate cause. In riots, life and property are treated with an indifference and recklessness contrary to basic values in western society (except in wartime), and it is therefore important to ask what kind of events precipitate such an acute breakdown of social control, and whether these precipitants are uncommon occurrences of an exceptionally provocative nature.

Although lynchings are not riots, data gathered on the immediate causes of the 3,700 lynchings in the U.S. between 1889 and 1930 are illuminating. Of the known accusations, more than a third (37.7 per cent) were murder; in nearly a quarter (23.4 per cent) the accusation was rape or attempted rape; assault was the charge in 5.8 per cent and theft in 7.1 per cent.[4] Compared with the frequency of these felonies in the South, murder and rape — violations of strong social taboos — are greatly over-represented as precipitants of lynchings.

In the same fashion, we suggest, the immediate precipitants of race riots almost always involve some confrontation between the groups in which members of one race are deeply "wronged" in fact or in rumor by members of the other. Precipitants tend to be transgressions of strongly held mores by a representative of the other group. The difficulty is to obtain an independent judgment of the severity of offenses that precipitate riots.

For two rather frequent types of precipitants, we can offer some independent evidence of their intensity. First, riots are often precipitated in the U.S. by crimes — particularly alleged crimes against persons rather than property alone, or the public order. Murder, rape, assault, manslaughter, and theft by means of violence or intimidation arouse the greatest concern and receive the most publicity in the mass media.[5] In 1950, the median sentence received by men found guilty of offenses against persons was 9.9 years, whereas it was 3.9 years for those charged with other felonies.[6] Even excluding murder, sentences for other felonies against persons were more than twice as long as those for offenses solely against property or the public order. Since punishment reflects the public's values with respect to the intrinsic "evil" of various acts, it is in this sense an independent measure of the severity of acts that precipitate race riots.

Another class of events that apparently violate strongly held norms involve Negroes crossing the various segregation barriers erected against

[4] Arthur F. Raper, *The Tragedy of Lynching*, Chapel Hill: University of North Carolina Press, 1933, p. 36.

[5] Marshall B. Clinard, *Sociology of Deviant Behavior*, New York: Holt, Rinehart and Winston, 1957, p. 196. We include robbery as a crime against persons throughout this analysis.

[6] Based on data reported in Federal Bureau of Prisons, *National Prisoner Statistics: Prisoners in State and Federal Institutions, 1950*, Leavenworth, Kansas: U.S. Penitentiary, 1954, Tables 37 and 38. Determinate and maximum indeterminate sentences are combined.

them. Particularly frequent as precipitants in recent years, these acts are "bad" only because Negro-white interaction occurs in a form generally prohibited, e.g., when Negroes use the same swimming pool as whites.[7]

We have classified the 72 riots for which data are available in terms of the nature of the immediate precipitant of the violence. (See Table 1.) The reader should recognize that it is not always clear which event triggered a riot, especially when a chain of inter-related events occurs. Not only is it difficult to specify where the riot begins and the precipitant ends, but often there are several precipitants. In these cases we have determined whether at least some of the events involve offenses against relatively sacred values.

TABLE 1.   IMMEDIATE PRECIPITANTS OF RACE RIOTS, 1913–1963

Rape, murder, attack, or hold-up of white women by Negro men	10
Killings, arrest, interference, assault, or search of Negro men by white police-men	15
Other inter-racial murder or shooting	11
Inter-racial fight, no mention of lethal weapons	16
Civil liberties, public facilities, segregation, political events, and housing	14
Negro strikebreakers, upgrading, or other job-based conflicts	5
Burning of an American flag by Negroes	1
No information available	4
Total Number	76

A sizable majority of the precipitants do involve an actual or rumored violation of one group by a member of the other. The ten cases in which white women were attacked by Negro men are highly inflammatory; apparently these involve violations of an extremely strong taboo. Highly charged acts to begin with, the murder, rape, or assault of women is even more serious an offense when offender and victim are of different races. Negroes were almost half of all persons executed for murder by civil authorities in the United States between 1930 and 1952 and nearly 90 per cent of those executed for rape.[8] In their analysis of the 1943 Los Angeles zoot-suiter riot, Turner and Surace describe sexual assault as the dominant trigger:

> The most prominent charge from each side was that the other had molested its girls. It was reported that sailors became enraged by the rumor that zoot-suiters were guilty of "assaults on female relatives of servicemen." Similarly, the claim against sailors was that

[7] Myrdal hypothesizes a rank order of discrimination in which whites object most strongly to close personal contact with Negroes. See Gunnar Myrdal, *An American Dilemma*, New York: Harper, 1944, pp. 60–61. Although a follow-up study suggested some modifications of this thesis, the areas of highest white resistance to Negroes remained unaltered. See Lewis M. Killian and Charles M. Grigg, "Rank Orders of Discrimination of Negroes and Whites in a Southern City," *Social Forces*, 39 (1961), p. 238.

[8] Federal Bureau of Prisons, *op. cit.*, pp. 30–31.

they persisted in molesting and insulting Mexican girls. While many other charges was reported in the newspapers, including unsubstantiated suggestions of sabotage of the war effort, the sex charges dominated the precipitating context.[9]

The second type of precipitant, offenses committed by white law-enforcement officials against Negroes, involves white transgression of norms no less sacred than those involved in the rape of white women by Negro men. The Harlem riot during World War II started when a Negro woman was arrested by a white policeman for disorderly conduct. A Negro soldier, on leave, tried to stop him and the ensuing fight ended with both men in the hospital, the policeman with a battered head and the soldier with a pistol wound in the shoulder. Of greatest interest here is the account of the incident that spread through the Negro community: a Negro soldier was said to have been shot in the back and killed by a white policeman in the presence of the Negro's mother.[10]

The Harlem riot of July, 1964 was precipitated by a demonstration protesting the slaying of a 15-year-old Negro boy by a white policeman, an act viewed as a wanton exercise of police brutality. The Bedford-Stuyvesant, Rochester, Jersey City, and Philadelphia riots of 1964 — also outside the period covered in our study — were also precipitated by arrests or the presence of police.[11]

Both the fatal shooting of the boy and the rumored treacherous shooting of a soldier during wartime, in front of his mother, are highly inflammatory acts because they arouse some of the strongest sentiments the population holds, and they are especially inflammatory because they were committed by members of one race against another. In addition, offenses committed by white law enforcement officials, highly inflammatory in themselves, are aggravated when they involve actual or alleged wrong-doing on the part of officials expected to uphold and administer the law in an impartial manner. A number of recent race riots over civil-rights issues have been precipitated by police behavior, particularly in breaking up demonstrations.[12] We shall have more to say about the role of the police in our discussion of the underlying conditions of race riots.

The next category of precipitants, "Other inter-racial murder or shooting," calls for little additional comment. The shooting of white policemen by Negro men (three cases), although intrinsically not as inflammatory as inter-racial offenses against women and children, nevertheless involves murder or attempted murder of a representative of the government. The rumored beating to death of a Negro boy in a New York department store after he was seized for shoplifting, and the rumors of brutal assaults on

[9] Turner and Surace, *op. cit.*, pp. 16–17.
[10] *Time*, August 9, 1943, p. 19; *New Republic*, August 16, 1943, pp. 220–222.
[11] "Background of Northern Negro Riots," *New York Times*, September 27, 1964, p. 81.
[12] This is particularly evident in the South.

women and children that circulated among both races during the Detroit race riot of World War II, are clearly in accord with our thesis that the precipitants tend to be violations of important mores. In two cases rumors of impending violence precipitated actual riots. In one instance there was a rumor of a forthcoming riot and in the other, anticipation of a lynching. In both instances, the rumors involved inter-racial violation of rights widely accepted as fundamental. Finally, two of the other four inter-racial murders or shootings were accompanied by Negro offenses against white women: as we noted earlier, more than one element may be involved in the precipitation of a race riot. In one of these incidents, a white man was murdered by three Negroes and a rumor arose that he had been trying to protect a white woman from these men.[13] In the other, a Negro had made derogatory statements about a white woman over whom a Negro had been lynched some weeks before.[14]

Most of the 16 race riots precipitated by inter-racial fights without the use of lethal weapons do not appear to involve offenses of the most intense nature. One difficulty here is that the accounts of these riots are so scanty that we do not know whether rumors existed, over what issue the fights started, or other features that may have made the incident especially inflammatory, e.g., a young adult attacking an elderly person or a cripple. A fairly common element in riots with this type of precipitant is a chain of events in which members of each racial group come to the assistance of others already engaged in the fight. This tends to excite the onlookers who arrive after the initial provocation, particularly if members of one race appear to be receiving the worst part of the battle.

"Civil liberties, public facilities, segregation, political events, and housing" is a residual category involving diverse precipitants. Some of the precipitants fit the thesis that sacred values were violated. For example, a riot in upstate New York in the mid-thirties was precipitated by whites attempting to break up a meeting called to rally support for a Negro accused of attacking a white girl.[15] From the white point of view this involves the not uncommon theme of sexual molesting; from the other side, it is a white attempt to prevent Negroes' efforts to insure fair treatment for a Negro accused of a provocative act. A riot in Athens, Ala. in 1946 involved whites protesting police favoritism after a brawl for which two whites had been arrested and a Negro escaped.[16] But for the most part, it is difficult to establish conclusively the extent to which the precipitants in this category were offenses against inter-racial mores. In some cases we are tempted to

[13] *New York Times*, September 21, 1920, p. 1; *Chicago Daily Tribune*, September 21, 1920, pp. 1–2.
[14] Monroe N. Work (ed.), *Negro Year Book, 1921–1922*, Tuskegee Institute, Ala.: Negro Year Book Publishing Co., p. 75.
[15] *New York Times*, August 28, 1934, p. 3.
[16] Charles R. Lawrence, Jr., "Race Riots in the United States 1942–1946" in Jessie Parkhurst Guzman (ed.), *Negro Year Book, 1941–46*, Tuskegee Institute, Ala.: Department of Records and Research, 1947, pp. 253–254.

say that they were — the two just mentioned, or the Negro boy attempting to dance with a white girl at a city-sponsored dance — but in others, we are less certain about the nature of the acts.

Of the five job-based riots, three involved the allegation that Negroes were or had been strikebreakers, one was over the up-grading of jobs held by Negroes, and one was simply in an industrial setting. Taking a conservative stance, we would not be inclined to label these as violations of sacred norms.

Burning an American flag is a different type of offense, for it violates neither the person nor any segregation taboo, but it is clearly an offense against one of the nation's most sacred symbols. We shall say more about this type of precipitant, which is unusual for riots in the U.S., when we discuss racial and ethnic riots elsewhere in the world.

In brief, at least a sizable proportion of the immediate precipitants of race riots appear to involve inter-racial violations of intense societal norms. Noteworthy are the large number of events in which bodily injury is the precipitant as well as the smaller number of cases precipitated by violations of inter-racial segregation taboos.

UNDERLYING CONDITIONS

Applying Durkheim's typology, we observe that many of the immediate precipitants were acts that call for repressive sanctions, that is, they "consisted essentially in an act contrary to strong and defined states of the common conscience."[17] Repressive sanctions are normally administered under penal law by courts in the U.S. For example, murder, rape, and other acts of physical violence are strongly disapproved and severely punished in our society. Many, though not all, of the violations of segregation taboos in the period studied were also punishable through law enforcement, but in these instances, at least some members of either or both racial populations were unable to accept the institutions normally used for handling such offenses. Instead a riot occurred, involving, by definition, a generalized response directed at a collectivity rather than the offender — indeed, the actual offender was often untouched.

Although the immediate precipitants were highly inflammatory, we may still ask why a riot occurred rather than the normal processes of arrest, trial, and punishment, for inter-racial friction occurs far more often than the small number of occasions that erupted into race riots indicates. Why did violence break out where it did rather than at other places where similar incidents occurred? Or to put it another way, the types of violation described earlier probably occur almost daily, yet in most instances they do not lead to collective violence. Are there special circumstances that increase or decrease the chances of a riot ensuing?

[17] Emile Durkheim, *The Division of Labor in Society,* Glencoe, Ill.: Free Press, 1933, p. 105.

One possible interpretation of the location and timing of riots is simply that riots are randomly distributed. Any precipitating incident of this type increases the chances of a riot, but there is no systematic reason why riots occur when and where they do, other than possible differences among cities in the frequency of precipitating incidents. A second approach is based on the notion that certain social conditions in the community increase the probability that a precipitating incident will lead to a riot. From this perspective, we can ask whether cities experiencing riots differ from other cities with regard to the institutional conditions suggested as increasing the chances of a riot.

TABLE 2. RACE RIOTS: ACTUAL AND EXPECTED FREQUENCIES

By year			By city		
Riots per year (1)	Observed frequency (2)	Poisson frequency (3)	Riots per year (4)	Observed frequency (5)	Poisson frequency (6)
0	26	11.4	0	300	281.2
1	10	17.1	1	25	47.2
2	7	12.8	2	3	4.3
3	2	6.4	3	3	0.3
4	1	2.4	4	1	0.0
5	0	0.7	5–14	1	0.0
6	0	0.2			
7	2	0.0			
8	1	0.0			
9	1	0.0			
10	0	0.0			
11	1	0.0			
Total years	51	51.0	Total cities	333	333.0

Poisson distribution. To evaluate the first interpretation, that is, whether riots are randomly distributed in time and place, we used the Poisson distribution, which the low frequency of race riots (1.5 per year between 1913 and 1963) makes appropriate for comparing the actual frequency of riots with what would be expected in a random distribution.[18] Columns 2 and 3 of Table 2 show, respectively, the actual and expected number of riots per year in the 51 years from 1913 through 1963. Inspection indicates that the Poisson distribution yields a poor fit. For example, in 26 of the years no riot was reported though the theoretical distribution would lead us to expect only 11 such years. Applying the appropriate chi-square test

---

[18] For discussions of the application of the Poisson distribution, see G. Udny Yule and M. G. Kendall, *An Introduction to the Theory of Statistics*, London: Charles Griffin, 1950, pp. 189–194; M. J. Moroney, *Facts From Figures*, Harmondsworth, Middlesex: Penguin Books, 1951, Ch. 8.

for goodness of fit, we conclude that we cannot accept the assumption that the probability of riots is equal each year.[19]

In similar fashion, we can consider the concentration of riots in cities. Restricting ourselves to the 333 cities with 50,000 or more population in 1960, we have compared the actual and expected frequencies of cities experiencing a specified number of riots. There are more cities without any riots, and more with several, than would be expected on the basis of the Poisson distribution (columns 5 and 6): riots occurred in only 33 of these cities. The goodness-of-fit test confirms our impression that the theoretical distribution does not fit the actual distribution of riots in cities.

Two types of sampling bias may have influenced these results. First, newspapers probably fluctuate in their propensity to report riots, so that the frequency of riots at a given point in time increases the probability that riots occurring shortly afterwards will be reported. This is analogous to the tendency of newspapers to make the frequency of rapes or other events into a crime wave when in fact the major variable is the frequency of reporting such events.[20] A second possible bias arises from the fact that our primary source is the *New York Times*. Milder forms of racial violence in metropolitan New York and the mid-Atlantic area are more likely to be covered than riots of equivalent severity elsewhere. This would lead to a distribution of repeated riots different from that expected on the basis of the Poisson formula. Also, note that our test refers only to riots, not to precipitating incidents per se. Therefore we can reach no conclusions with respect to the distribution of precipitants by time or place. These difficulties notwithstanding, the results give us no reason to think riots are random with respect to time and place.

A COMPARATIVE ANALYSIS

Since the type of event that precipitates riots is far more common than actual riots, we ask whether this form of collective violence is due to underlying conditions that keep at least one segment of the population from accepting the normal institutional response to a provocative incident. From this perspective, precipitants are a necessary but not sufficient cause of riots.

A rather wide-ranging array of interpretations have been advanced after the occurrence of riots in particular communities. Such factors as rapidly expanding Negro population, economic hardships, police brutality, job ceilings, Negro competition with whites, slums, unsympathetic city officials, contagion, communist elements, agitators, warm weather, unruly elements, and others have figured in popular and semi-popular interpretations of race

[19] Our computation of chi-square is based on the adjustments suggested in Helen M. Walker and Joseph Lev, *Statistical Inference,* New York: Henry Holt, 1953, pp. 105–107.
[20] See, for example, Nahum Z. Medalia and Otto N. Larsen, "Diffusion and Belief in a Collective Delusion: The Seattle Windshield Pitting Epidemic," *American Sociological Review,* 23 (1958), pp. 180–186.

riots. Although case studies of race riots are extremely valuable where they provide an accurate description of events before and during a riot, obviously it is impossible to determine which factors are critical on the basis of one city's experience.

When we move from the presentation of *plausible* reasons to a systematic empirical test of the actual importance of various attributes in increasing the chances of riots, we encounter serious difficulties. Not only do we have a plethora of independent variables, but their actual significance is very difficult to test. Quantitative data on many of these characteristics are scarce, and in any case it is difficult to know how much causal significance to attribute anyway. For example, a riot may occur in a city containing a Negro slum area. The cruel truth is that housing conditions for Negroes are inferior in virtually every city in the U.S. To infer a causal link, one must determine not whether Negro slums exist in the riot city, but whether that city is worse in this respect than others where no riots occurred. Similarly, in any large city unemployed whites and Negroes might respond to an opportunity for a racial riot. Again the question is whether an unusually large number of such people live in one community compared with another.

Our requirements for quantitative data covering at least part of a 50-year span limit the causal hypotheses we can test. For the most part we have relied on U.S. censuses of the past six decades for data bearing on some of the propositions encountered in case studies and popular interpretations of race riots. This part of our study, therefore, necessarily has a certain ad hoc quality.

Method. To examine the influence of variables others have suggested as underlying causes of race riots, we used a paired-comparison analysis. Each city experiencing a riot was compared with a city as similar as possible in size and region which had no riot in the ten years preceding or following the riot date.[21] Preference was given to the city in the same state closest in population size, with the provision that it have at least half but no more than twice the population of the riot city. Where no such city existed we selected the city closest in size in the same subregion or region.[22] We compared the very largest cities, such as New York, Chicago, and Los Angeles, with other leading centers in the nation closest in population, regardless of region.

Using the nonparametric sign test, we evaluated the extent to which riot cities differ from their control cities in the direction hypothesized. When a given city experienced more than one riot, it was included as many times as the number of riots. Because census data by size of place and decade were not always available, our "N" in most cases is considerably less than

---

[21] For the most recent riots we could not apply the ten-year limit into the future in selecting control cities, but such cities were included in our analysis.

[22] See U.S. Bureau of the Census, *U.S. Census of Population: 1960. Selected Area Reports, Standard Metropolitan Statistical Areas.* Washington, D.C.: U.S. Government Printing Office, 1963, pp. xvi–xvii.

the 76 riots discussed earlier. For convenience in presentation, we have divided the hypotheses into four major categories: population growth and composition; work situation; housing; and government.

DEMOGRAPHIC FACTORS

The rapid influx of Negroes and sometimes whites into cities is certainly one of the most frequently cited reasons for the occurrence of race riots. Although large-scale migration is not usually viewed as a sufficient cause for a riot, it is commonly considered important because rapid influx disrupts the on-going social order and creates various problems in the Negro community. For 66 riots we could determine the growth of the Negro and white populations between the census years preceding and following the race riot, for each riot city and for a comparable community selected at the beginning of the decade. We thus have data for 66 pairs of cities, each pair consisting of a riot city and a control city.

In about half the cases, percentage increases in both total and white population were smaller in the riot cities than in the non-riot cities. Moreover, in 56 per cent of the comparisons the control cities experienced greater percentage increases in Negro population than the riot cities did. Our results clearly fail to support the contention that rapid population change accompanies riots. For the years between 1917 and 1921 — a period marked by both Negro migration and numerous riots — we found no sizable difference between riot and control cities in their percentage gains in Negro population during the decades. Also contrary to expectation are the differences in racial composition of riot and control cities. Again for 66 pairs, we find that in exactly half the comparisons, the proportion of Negroes is smaller in the riot city than in its control city.

Since this comparative approach is used with succeeding hypotheses, we should consider briefly the implications of these findings. First, we draw no conclusions about whether Negro population growth in riot cities differs from its growth elsewhere in the U.S. Riot cities have experienced more rapid growth than the remainder of the nation simply because Negro population movement has been largely from rural to urban areas. Similarly, since our method is designed to compare riot cities only with other cities similar in size and region, we make no inferences about differences between riot cities and all other U.S. cities. What we do conclude is that riot cities do not differ from non-riot cities of the same size and region in their rates of population increase, and therefore that increases in population fail to explain the occurrence of outbreaks in one city rather than another.[23]

[23] See Robin Williams, Jr., in collaboration with John P. Dean and Edward A. Suchman, *Strangers Next Door*, Englewood Cliffs, N.J.: Prentice-Hall, 1964, pp. 135–137. In a study based on a nationwide sample of cities, they find the general level of race conflict and tension no higher in cities with rapid population growth and high mobility than in those with relatively stable populations. In short, our method gets at the question of why riots occur in the particular cities they do, rather than in comparable urban centers.

WORK SITUATION

Traditional occupations. The occupational world of Negroes is far more restricted than that of whites. In particular, certain occupational pursuits have been more or less "traditional" for urban Negroes. These are generally lower in both status and income. Accordingly, wherever possible we determined the proportion of Negro men in the labor force who are employed either as laborers or in domestic and service occupations. Needless to say, we were forced to use some rather crude measures as well as broad categories which undoubtedly include some occupations outside the "traditional" rubric. A serious difficulty is created by contradictory hypotheses that depend on which group appears to be the aggressor. On the one hand, we might expect greater antagonism on the part of Negroes in cities where they are relatively restricted in occupational opportunities, i.e., where most Negroes are in traditional pursuits. On the other hand, we might well expect that where Negroes fare relatively well in their efforts to break through the job restrictions, whites' hostility might be greater and hence riots more likely to ensue.

For 43 riots we were able to determine the Negro occupational distribution in both the riot and control city during the closest census period. In 65 per cent of these paired comparisons (N = 28), the percentage of Negro men holding traditional occupations is lower in the riot city.[24] This suggests that riots are due to the relative threat to whites where Negroes are less concentrated in their traditional pursuits. If such were the case, then we might expect the white and Negro percentages in these occupations to be more alike in the riot city than in the control city. This is precisely what we find: in 30 of the 43 paired comparisons, the *difference* between whites and Negroes, in proportions engaged in laboring, domestic, and service occupations, is smaller in the riot city.[25] The encroachment of Negroes in the white occupational world evidently tends to increase the chances of a riot, although we must also consider the possibility that Negro militancy increases as Negroes move out of their traditional niche.

Store owners. A more specific occupational factor sometimes associated with riots — particularly ghetto riots — is the low frequency of store ownership in Negro areas and the consequent resentment of white store owners in these areas. We are unable to get at these data directly. If we assume, however, that virtually all Negro store owners are located in the ghetto, then we can simply examine the percentage of employed Negro men who are self-employed in various facets of retail trade, such as store, restaurant, or tavern owners. Although differences between riot and control cities tend to be slight, nevertheless in 24 of 39 riots, the percentage of Negroes who are store owners is larger in the nonriot city.[26] Results might be even

---

[24] Using a two-tailed test, p = .0672.
[25] p = .0073, single-tailed test.
[26] These differences are significant at the .10 level.

stronger had it been possible to subcategorize riots. For instance, the absence of Negro store owners would presumably contribute to Negroes' rioting but would contribute relatively little to white assaults.

Unemployment. As was the case for traditional occupations, unemployment presents contradictory possibilities, so that we might well expect riots when either Negroes or whites have relatively high unemployment rates. Our analysis is even cruder here, since unemployment is far more volatile from year to year, and we are able to use data only for the closest census year.[27] First, the white unemployment rate appears to have no influence on the likelihood of a riot. In 12 comparisons white unemployment rates were higher in the city experiencing the riot, and in 13 cases, higher in the control city. For Negro unemployment, results tend to run counter to what we might expect. Negro unemployment is higher in the control than in the riot city in 15 out of 25 comparisons. And Negro-white *differences* are lower in the riot than in the control city in 15 out of 25 comparisons.[28]

These results do not confirm our expectations: high white unemployment apparently does not increase the chances of a riot, nor is high Negro unemployment associated with riots in the direction expected. On an aggregate basis, the number of riots during the Great Depression of the thirties was not unusually large. In view of the weakness of the data — particularly the fact that we do not have unemployment rates for the specific year in which the riots take place — all we can conclude is that we have failed to confirm the hypothesis, not that we have disproved it.

Income. Since the influence of income on riots may reflect either group's position, our problem is similar to that discussed in connection with Negro occupational composition. Median income data are available for only 12 riots and their controls. In six comparisons Negro income is higher in the control city and in the other six it is higher in the riot city. In 11 of the 12 cases, however, white income in the riot city is lower than in the control.[29] The *difference* between Negro and white income was larger in the city without a riot in ten of the 12 cases.[30] The small number precludes analysis of these findings in greater detail, but we can observe that riots tend to occur in cities where white income is lower than that of whites in comparable areas. The lower white income also means that Negro-white differences tend to be smaller in these cities than in the control areas. Thus, the results, though extremely limited in time and place, do not support the notion that race riots are a consequence either of low Negro income or of relatively large Negro-white discrepancies in income.

[27] Although data are available for other years, to our knowledge none can be obtained by race for specific cities.

[28] $p = .212$, single-tailed test.

[29] $p < .01$, single-tailed test.

[30] $p = .038$, two-tailed test.

HOUSING

Ghetto riots in particular are often attributed to the poor housing conditions of Negroes, but our data fail to disclose any tendency whatsoever for housing to be of lower quality in cities that have experienced riots. For 20 paired comparisons we could determine which city had a larger percentage of Negro families in sub-standard housing (using the census categories of. "dilapidated" in 1950 and 1960 and "needing major repairs" in 1940). In ten cases the non-riot city had poorer Negro housing than the riot city. Although obviously not all riots could be considered ghetto riots, surely we should find some tendency for Negroes in cities experiencing riots to have poorer dwellings than they do in cities without riots, if it were true that poorer housing quality increases the likelihood of a race riot. Very likely, Negro housing is poor in so many locales that it cannot distinguish cities experiencing riots from those that do not.

GOVERNMENT

Police. Local government is one of the most important institutions to consider in an analysis of race riots. Municipal policies, particularly with respect to police, can greatly influence the chances of a race riot. Earlier, we observed that many of the precipitating incidents involve white police behavior toward Negroes, and adequate police training and tactics often prevent incipient riots from developing.[31] Moreover, police activities reflect the policies, sympathies, and attitudes of the local municipal government.

One often-cited factor in race riots is the lack of Negro policemen. First, one major complaint on the part of Negroes is that of white police brutality. So far as the police are Negroes, actual brutality will probably not arouse strong racial feelings. Second, police in some riots have encouraged or tolerated white violence toward Negroes, so that we might expect stronger police control where the force is mixed, as well as greater confidence in police protection among Negroes. Finally, since the number of Negro policemen is for the most part controlled by the city administration, the representation of Negroes is an indicator of city policies toward race relations in general.

Data are hard to obtain and for 1950 and 1960 we have been obliged to use census reports for entire metropolitan areas. Also, for some decades policemen are not reported separately from closely related occupations such as sheriffs and marshals. Nevertheless, of 38 pairs of cities, in 24 the city without the riot had more Negro policemen per thousand Negroes than did the matched city that experienced a riot.[32] Although differences be-

---

[31] Joseph D. Lohman, *The Police and Minority Groups,* Chicago: Chicago Park District, 1947, pp. 80–93; Smelser, *op. cit.,* pp. 261–268.

[32] $p = .07$, single-tailed test.

tween riot and control cities are rather slight, these results do suggest that police force composition influences the likelihood of a riot.

City council. We hypothesize that the manner in which councilmen are elected and the relative size of the city council will influence the occurrence of riots. Our reasoning is based on several assumptions. The election of councilmen at large gives numerically smaller groups a greater handicap in expressing their interests than they encounter in communities where councilmen are elected directly from spatial districts.[33] In cities where the average size of a councilman's constituency is small, we assume that representatives are more responsive to the wishes of the population and therefore that members of the community have a more adequate mechanism for transmitting their interests and concerns. This implies that more diverse interests will be expressed in the city's governing body.

Our hypothesis is that the more direct the relation between voter and government, the less likely are riots to occur. A more responsive government makes riots less likely because it provides regular institutional channels for expressing grievances. Small districts provide more responsive government than large districts, and large districts, more than elections at large. In comparisons between a city with a city-wide election system and one where councilmen are elected both at large and by district, we classified the latter situation as the less likely to lead to riots. Where both cities have the same form of election, we computed the mean population per councilman. (Comparisons involving Deep South cities were based on the white population only.) Thus, we gave form of election priority over size of constituency in our causal hypothesis.

In 14 of 22 pairs, population per councilman was larger in the city experiencing the riot than in the control city, or elections at large were used in the riot city and direct election of representatives in the control city.[34] Considering our inability to take into account the degree of gerrymandering in cities with direct representation, these results offer an encouraging degree of support for our hypothesis.

DISCUSSION

Our analysis of the precipitating and underlying conditions of race riots suggests several generalizations about their evolution. First, precipitating incidents often involve highly charged offenses committed by members of one group against the other, such as attacks on women, police brutality and interference, murder, and assault. In recent years, violation of segregation taboos by Negroes as well as white resistance have been increasingly frequent precipitants. Riots are generalized responses in which there is categorical assault on persons and property by virtue of their racial mem-

---

[33] James Q. Wilson, *Negro Politics*, Glencoe, Ill.: Free Press, 1960, pp. 25–33.
[34] Though p is not significant (.143), the relationship is in the predicted direction.

bership. Such violence is not restricted and may even exclude the specific antagonists responsible for the precipitating event.

The diffuse response generated by the precipitating event, as well as the fact that often the alleged offenses are of the sort normally dealt with by appropriate communal institutions, suggests that additional factors channel the inflammatory act into a riot. Since there are usually a number of factors that could have contributed to a riot in any given community, we used a comparative approach to determine why riots occur in some cities and not in others of comparable size and location.

Going beyond our data and trying to place our findings in a broad framework, we suggest that riots are more likely to occur when social institutions function inadequately, or when grievances are not resolved, or cannot be resolved under the existing institutional arrangements. Populations are predisposed or prone to riot; they are not simply neutral aggregates transformed into a violent mob by the agitation or charisma of individuals. Indeed, the immediate precipitant simply ignites prior community tensions revolving about basic institutional difficulties. The failure of functionaries to perform the roles expected by one or both of the racial groups, crosspressures, or the absence of an institution capable of handling a community problem involving inter-racial relations will create the conditions under which riots are most likely. Many riots are precipitated by offenses that arouse considerable interest and concern. When members of the victimized race are dubious about the intention or capacity of relevant functionaries to achieve justice or a "fair" solution, then the normal social controls are greatly weakened by the lack of faith in the community's institutions.

Our evidence supports the proposition that the functioning of local community government is important in determining whether a riot will follow a precipitating incident. Prompt police action can prevent riots from developing; their inaction or actual encouragement can increase the chances of a race riot. Riot cities not only employ fewer Negro policemen, but they are also communities whose electoral systems tend to be less sensitive to the demands of the electorate. Local government illustrates the possibility that riots occur when a community institution is malfunctioning, from the perspective of one or both racial segments.

Our finding that Negroes are less likely to be store owners in riot cities illustrates the problem arising when no social institution exists for handling the difficulties faced by a racial group. Small merchants require credit, skill and sophistication in operating and locating their stores, ability to obtain leases, and so on. To our knowledge no widely operating social institution is designed to achieve these goals for the disadvantaged Negro. Similarly, our finding that riots are more likely where Negroes are closer to whites in their proportions in "traditional" Negro occupations, and where Negro-white income differences are smaller, suggests that a conflict of interests between the races is inherent in the economic world.

Our use of significance tests requires further comment. Many of the relationships are in the direction predicted but fail to meet the normal standards for significance. Several extenuating circumstances help account for this. First, many of our hypotheses refer to specific types of riots: for example, some riots are clearly "white riots"; others, equally clearly, are Negro; and many are both, in the sense that extensive attacks are directed at both groups. Were the data in an ideal form, we could separate the ghetto riots, the white assaults, and the inter-racial warfare into separate categories, and then apply our hypotheses to specific subsets of riots. Because our sample is small and the accounts of many riots are very scanty, we are prepared to accept these weaker associations as at least consistent with our approach to the underlying conditions of race riots.

Several implications of our results are relevant to riots elsewhere. Racial and ethnic incidents in other parts of the world are also frequently precipitated by physical violence. Dahlke's description of the Kishinew pogrom in Russia ascribes considerable importance as a precipitant to the widespread legend that Jews annually kill Christian children, as a part of their religious rites.[35] The extensive riots in Ceylon in 1958 included a number of highly provocative rumors of inter-ethnic violations. For example, "a Sinhalese baby had been snatched from its mother's arms and immersed in a barrel of boiling tar."[36] The Durban riots of 1949 were precipitated by an incident in which an African youth was knocked over by an Indian trader.[37]

A number of other riots, however, are precipitated by violations of symbols rather than persons or taboos. The burning of an American flag by Negroes triggered a race riot in the United States. Our impression is that this type of precipitant is more common in some other parts of the world. Riots in Kashmir, West Bengal, and East Pakistan in late 1963 and early 1964, for example, were precipitated by the theft of a hair of the prophet Mohammed from a Mosque in Kashmir.[38] One of the precipitants of the Chinese-Thai riots of 1945, the Yaorawat Incident, was the Chinese tendency to fly Chinese flags without also flying the Thai flag of the nation.[39] Jews tore down the czar's crown from the town hall and damaged portraits of various rulers prior to Kiev's pogrom in 1905.[40]

[35] H. Otto Dahlke, "Race and Minority Riots — A Study in the Typology of Violence," *Social Forces*, 30 (1952), p. 421.

[36] Tarzie Vittachi, *Emergency '58: The Story of the Ceylon Race Riots*, London: Andre Deutsch, 1958, p. 48.

[37] Anthony H. Richmond, *The Colour Problem* (rev. ed.), Harmondsworth, Middlesex: Pelican Books, 1961, p. 123.

[38] *New York Times*, January 16, 1964, p. 17; January 19, p. 6; January 20, p. 6; January 24, p. 2; January 26, p. 15.

[39] G. William Skinner, *Chinese Society in Thailand: An Analytical History*, Ithaca, N.Y.: Cornell University Press, 1957, p. 279.

[40] From the diary of Shulgin, in *Source Book for History 2.1*, Vol. 2, "History of Western Civilization," Brooklyn, N.Y.: Brooklyn College, Department of History, 1949, Ch. 31.

Our results also suggest that race riots are frequently misunderstood. We have encountered a number of accounts in the popular literature attributing riots to communist influence, hoodlums, or rabble-rousers. Although lower-class youths and young adults are undoubtedly active during riots, potential participants of this type are probably available in almost any community. What interests us is the community failure to see the riot in terms of institutional malfunctioning or a racial difficulty which is not met — and perhaps cannot be — by existing social institutions. Many riots in other parts of the world revolve about national political institutions such that a disadvantaged segment is unable to obtain recognition of its interests and concerns through normal political channels. While this type of riot is not common in the U.S., the same basic conditions exist when either whites or Negroes are unable to use existing institutions to satisfy their needs and interests.

XI COMMUNITIES

A. Definitions and Concepts

Early sociological theoreticians were concerned with developing typologies for studying and classifying behavior. One example was the idea of the primary group and the secondary group (see page 175). Communities were studied in essentially the same manner when the urban setting, with its breakdown of warm, personal ties, was contrasted with the village, which still possessed these ties. Entire societies were dealt with in a discussion of "folk" and "urban" societies. Gideon Sjoberg, a demographer, shows how the terms might be refined, in his comparison of feudal societies and folk societies.

33 GIDEON SJOBERG

Folk and "Feudal" Societies

Until the past decade sociologists in the United States directed only a small portion of their efforts toward a comparative study of society. As a result, the distinctions between folk and feudal orders and the differential effects of the process of industrialization and urbanization on the two kinds of society have been little perceived. This oversight is, of course, understandable in the light of American history; only incipient forms of "feudalism" have been evidenced in this country. Attention therefore was not turned

From *American Journal of Sociology*, Vol. LVIII (November, 1952), pp. 231–239. Reprinted by permission of the author and The University of Chicago Press.

toward feudalism, even on the world scene. Recent political changes, however, have placed the United States in a position of world leadership; reform programs are being carried out in many "backward" countries. Through failure to interpret correctly the functionings of other societies, a number of these plans have been naïvely conceived. At the same time, sociologists and anthropologists are becoming increasingly concerned with the comparative study of sociocultural systems; a critical evaluation, therefore, of present-day perspectives is requisite.

The primary purpose of this paper is to formulate a typology of the feudal social system in contradistinction to that of the folk order. Then, through an analysis of the differential effects on folk and feudal societies of social change resulting from the industrial-urban process, justification is offered for their separation. Although other sets of typologies are logically possible, the study should contribute toward the development of a comparative sociology.

It is not suggested here that the concept "folk society" should be discarded. Actually it serves many useful purposes. Yet its indiscriminate application to communities in all nonindustrialized areas has given rise to serious misinterpretations of existing conditions. Although no one society need correspond exactly to the constructed type, the value of the "model" for understanding and interpreting social action is enhanced if it does not diverge too widely from reality.

Redfield,[1] employing the ideal-type method, has provided us with one of the most careful and logically consistent formulations of the folk order. This is a small, isolated, nonliterate, and homogeneous society with a strong sense of solidarity. The primary group ties — those of kinship in particular — are of crucial importance to its effective functioning. Furthermore, a minimum of division of labor is present, from which it can be deduced that stratification in terms of social classes is unknown. Finally, the value orientation is sacred, and the actions of the members tend toward strict conformance to the norms of the folk.

The so-called "primitive" societies most nearly correspond to this folk typology; some isolated tribal communities fit the constructed type rather well. On the other hand, the concept is much less meaningful for interpreting complex societies in Asia, Europe, and even Latin America. Although a few writers[2] have recognized certain distinctions between "folk and peasant" and "nonliterate and literate" societies, no systematic presentation of these differences and their implications for social change seems to be extant.

---

[1] Robert Redfield, "The Folk Society," *American Journal of Sociology*, LII (1947), 293–308; see also Alvin Boskoff, "Structure, Function, and Folk Society," *American Sociological Review*, XIV (1949), 749–58.

[2] See, e.g., A. L. Kroeber, *Anthropology* (rev. ed.; New York: Harcourt, Brace & Co., 1948), p. 284, and Robert Bierstedt, "The Limitations of Anthropological Methods in Sociology," *American Journal of Sociology*, LIV (1948), 22–30.

THE FEUDAL SOCIETY

Both feudal and folk societies are static and have sacred-value orientations; consequently, the action patterns of their members are clearly defined. But the feudal society is far more heterogeneous and complex than is the folk order. Their essential differences can best be stated in terms of the respective social structures. The feudal order is characterized by rigid class or castelike stratification and complex state, educational, and economic institutions — all of which necessitate an extensive division of labor. Furthermore, it has a relatively large population and an extended territorial base.

It should be noted before proceeding, however, that the concept "feudalism" has been used in several ways. Historians conventionally have taken as their criteria certain restricted institutional patterns of medieval Europe, especially the lord-vassal relationship.[3] Although this structural arrangement may have existed at times in other societies also,[4] the application of the concept in this manner is too limited for sociological analysis. The formulations of Boeke, Weber, and Rüstow,[5] although quite incomplete, more nearly fulfil our requirements. The more inclusive meaning given herein to the concept "feudalism" avoids the pitfalls of historicism and the resultant emphasis on uniqueness.

The structural arrangement of the feudal society is outlined below. In order to demonstrate a degree of empirical plausibility for this typology, brief references are made to social situations which correspond rather closely to its criteria.[6]

Typically, feudalism is predicated on a large peasant population. These individuals live in small village settlements and gain their livelihood primarily from intensive cultivation of the soil through the use of a simple technology. Scattered about the countryside, they form the backbone of the feudal system. But the peasant villages, significantly, are not isolated from

---

[3] F. L. Ganshof, *Qu'est-ce que la Féodalité?* (2nd ed.; Neuchâtel: Éditions de la Baconnière, 1947); Otto Hintze, "Wesen und Verbreitung des Feudalismus," *Sitzungsberichte der Preussischen Akademie der Wissenschaften, philosophisch-historische Klasse* (1929), pp. 321–47; Carl Stephenson, *Mediaeval Feudalism* (Ithaca: Cornell University Press, 1942).

[4] Ch'i Ssu-ho, "A Comparison between Chinese and European Feudal Institutions," *Yenching Journal of Social Studies*, IV (1948), 1–13.

[5] J. H. Boeke, *The Interests of the Voiceless Far East* (Leiden: Universitaire Pers Leiden, 1948), pp. 1–8; Max Weber, *Wirtschaft und Gesellschaft* (Tübingen: J. C. B. Mohr, 1925), III, Part 2, 724 ff.; Alexander Rüstow, *Ortsbestimmung der Gegenwart: Eine universalgeschichtliche Kulturkritik*. I: *Ursprung der Herrschaft* (Erlenbach-Zürich: Eugen Rentsch Verlag, 1950).

[6] In constructing any typology, a mass of descriptive material is essential. Many sociologists fail to recognize that Weber, the popularizer of the ideal-type method, relied heavily upon a great accumulation of historical materials for his typologies. The author has avoided constructing types about merely one historical situation; special study was made of China, Japan, India, and France, and surveys of other areas were read to check the generalizations offered.

one another. Field studies which have focused strictly upon the local community have often lost sight of the total sociocultural setting.

Unlike the members of a folk order, the peasants provide sufficient surplus food to sustain a limited number of population concentrations — the focal points of the feudal society. Towns spring up as political, religious, and trading centers, and although only a small portion of the total populace inhabit these communities, their social significance extends far beyond mere numbers. That these towns are quite unlike industrial cities is obvious: feudal towns do not exhibit the social disorganization and individualization commonly associated with present-day industrial-urban centers.[7] However, it must not be inferred that life in the feudal town is not distinct from that in the feudal village. These towns, moreover, are linked to one another. But inasmuch as transportation and communication still are relatively undeveloped, the contacts between the various communities are not comparable to those in industrial-urban societies.

Within the towns reside many of the elite, particularly its most important members. The ruling stratum is at the very least composed of a governmental bureaucracy and a priestly and/or scholar group. In addition, a nobility, a landlord group, and militarists or warriors, among others, may be present in various combinations. The unique cultural-historical development of a given social order determines the exact composition of the elite; it varies not only among societies but from time to time within a society.

But the significant feature of the stratification pattern is its bifurcation — a small minority supported by and "exploiting" a large subservient populace which passively accepts its role. The traditional Chinese society evidenced this most strikingly. To be sure, hierarchical gradations occur in both the upper stratum and the masses, but these are slight when compared to the basic cleavage within the society as a whole. The upper class is differentiated in terms of its monopoly of power and authority, the "correct" kinship groupings, and the highly valued achievements. Particularly important in this context are institutionalized differences in personal attributes. Distinctive dress, speech, and manners render the elite easily recognizable at all times.[8] And inasmuch as an individual's status within the elite or the masses is ascribed, social mobility is minimized.

A closer examination of the ruling minority is essential. As noted, polit-

---

[7] See, e.g., Morton H. Fried, "Some Preliminary Considerations of Larger Units in Chinese Social Organization," *Transactions of the New York Academy of Sciences*, Ser. 2, XI (1949), 121–26; Roger Le Tourneu, *Fès: Avant le Protectorat* (Casablanca: Société Marocaine de Librairie et d'Édition, 1949). The latter study, which has received no formal recognition by sociologists in this country, is a most detailed description of a feudal city.

[8] An illuminating discussion of personal attributes in a feudal order may be found in Cornelius Osgood, *The Koreans and Their Culture* (New York: Ronald Press Co., 1951), chap. viii. This discusses the city of Seoul at the end of the nineteenth century.

ical functionaries are one of the constituent elements. For in a feudal society a complex and highly institutionalized state system extends its control directly or indirectly over the masses. Among other forms, this state
system may be a monarchy or possibly a theocracy such as existed in
medieval Europe. Aside from exerting legal control, the political functionaries exact some kind of tribute from the peasantry. This serves to perpetuate the elite and support such groups as an army, which protects the
society from external aggression. Political functionaries are recruited from
the upper class and thus reflect an inherently conservative tradition which
is gauged to preserve the status quo.

Scholars and priests are another integral element of the elite. Usually
they merge into one group, for the educational and religious institutions
are characteristically identical. In addition, some of these individuals may
be political bureaucrats. The scholar's prime qualification is his knowledge
of the sacred writings and traditions of the past; these govern the actions
of the present. Memorization and understanding of the ancient thoughtways are preconditions for his assumption of a role in the highly institutionalized educational system. Scholarship is notable for its compiling and
preserving qualities and not for any degree of originality. This aspect of
the typology is empirically attested by the characteristics of such groups as
the Chinese literati, the Indian Brahmins, and the medieval European
clergy.

The scholar-priests perform an important function as official carriers of
the classical written tradition which provides the social system with a
sophisticated and elaborate justification for its existence and continued
survival. Inconsistencies (present in all societies) are explained away.
Through the sacred writings a continuity is achieved and the past more
easily retained. This is not possible among the folk, whose history is perpetuated solely by oral transmission. The ideology of the sacred writings,
by standardizing the action patterns of the elite, also establishes solidarity
over a broad geographic area. As a result, the homogeneity of the upper
class is typically greater than that of the masses.[9] Finally, the scholar-
priest's existence as a member of the elite brings about a striking diver-
gence of his religious actions from those of the masses, who comprehend
little of the philosophical basis of the religion they practice.

Landlords often constitute part of the elite class — for example, in China
and in medieval Europe. But the landlord faction per se is not an essential
component of feudalism as conceived herein. At times the political bureaucrats assume functions similar to those of the landlords; this occurred in
India before the arrival of the British. The strength of the landlord stems

[9] On this point see E. Shouby, "The Influence of the Arabic Language on the Psychology of the Arabs," *Middle East Journal*, V (1951), 284–302, and Gerald F. Win-
field, *China: The Land and the People* (New York: William Sloane Associates., Inc.,
1948), p. 184.

from his direct control over the peasantry and concomitantly over the surplus food supply. Finally, other special groups may comprise the elite; for example, in Japan prior to the Meiji Restoration the topmost position of prestige and power was commanded by the military, or *samurai*, but some of these also doubled as governmental leaders.

Economically and politically the elite class dominates the mass populace. The latter supply the ruling minority with food, goods, and services but receive little in return. The trading relations of the city, therefore, are not with the countryside but with other towns, sometimes in quite distant regions. The relationship between the upper stratum and the masses is not entirely one-sided, however. Guidance is offered in the "moral" or religious sphere — the elite's ideal patterns are those emulated by the masses. Protection from outside attack and conquest is also the responsibility of the upper stratum. But more concrete functions may be performed — for example, the Chinese bureaucrats had an important duty in water control, chiefly for purposes of irrigation.

The peasants are not the only components of the masses. Characteristic of a feudal economic system is handicraft manufacturing based on a household economy. This requires skilled artisans. Most typically they reside in the towns, although some may be village-dwellers, where commonly they are also part-time farmers. The characteristic organizational units of artisans in the towns are guilds, each of which embraces a different occupational grouping: potters, weavers, metal workers, and carpenters, among others.

Not only do the guilds maintain a monopolistic control over recruitment through the apprenticeship system, but they also establish the norms of work. Furthermore, the actions of the members are prescribed down to the family level; in time of crisis the guild functions as a welfare agency. The artisans are instrumental in providing the elite with the luxury goods and services for the "conspicuous consumption" which clearly differentiates the latter from the disadvantaged members in the society.

Finally, another group within the feudal order must be considered. Typically, a small minority (or minorities) reside in the feudal society but occupy a marginal position, not being fully integrated into the social system. These persons are ranked even lower than peasants and artisans. Feudal orders often have scorned the merchant: he usually has too much contact with foreigners and is therefore a transmitter of "dangerous" ideas. Other outsiders have been slaves, the "untouchables" of India and the Eta class of Japan. These groups provide special goods and perform those services considered degrading by members of the morally valued occupations. In this way, they are functionally important to the entire society, particularly the elite.

To recapitulate: folk and feudal societies are similar in that both are relatively static and possess a sacred-value orientation. As such, the action patterns of their members are predictable, for there exists a minimum of internal conflict and disorder. In their structural arrangements, however, they differ perceptibly.

IMPLICATIONS FOR SOCIAL CHANGE

What are the implications of separating folk and feudal societies for sociological interpretation? A clearer understanding of contemporary social change follows from treating these as distinct social systems.

That industrial urbanization is bringing about change in the sociocultural organization of many societies is obvious.[10] But the resistance of the feudalistic structure to this process has been equally significant. Recent evidence for this is overwhelming: only a few exemplary cases are presented here. Authorities on China have often commented on how the elite in that country during the twentieth century has held firmly to the Confucianist ideology, the feudalistic governmental structure, the traditional family system, and even the feudal economic organization, although the forces making for change have been formidable.[11] (That the present Chinese regime will eradicate the feudalistic past is most doubtful.) And the tenacity of feudalism in Europe has only recently come to public consciousness. France is a case in point, although other countries (e.g., Germany and Italy) might also be cited. Despite the fact that France has experienced industrial urbanization for over a century, many feudalistic institutions have survived: a kind of handicraft system is still an important element in the economy, the pro-monarchical group continues to reassert itself in one form or another, and the feudalistic church and family systems are still in evidence.[12] All this has fostered the schisms and conflicts so typical of France since the Revolution.

Even the material coming to light on Russia reveals that the Soviets, though using forceful persuasion, have found it difficult to subdue at least one of the feudalistic subsystems within their borders — a Moslem group in Central Asia. The persistence of the Moslem religion, with its month of fasting (Ramadan), and the latent power of the old aristocracy have served

[10] The industrial-urban process is not the only factor which has induced change in "backward" areas. The state system per se, including colonial government, could be considered. Yet, to deal primarily with industrialization and urbanization is not unreasonable, even though these are being carried forward by the state. It is the industrial factor which makes the present-day state so potent.

[11] See, e.g., Marion J. Levy, Jr., and Shih Kuo-heng, *The Rise of the Modern Chinese Business Class* (New York: Institute of Pacific Relations, 1949), pp. 8–17, 34 ff.; John King Fairbank, *The United States and China* (Cambridge: Harvard University Press, 1948), pp. 240 ff.; *Far Eastern Culture and Society* ("Princeton University Bicentennial Conferences," Ser. 2, Conference 7) (Princeton: Princeton University Press, 1946), p. 21.

[12] For two excellent discussions of this subject see: Edward Mead Earle (ed.), *Modern France* (Princeton: Princeton University Press, 1951), esp. John E. Sawyer, "Strains in the Social Structure of Modern France," chap. xvii; Donald C. McKay, *The United States and France* (Cambridge: Harvard University Press, 1951), chaps. vii and viii.

as stumbling blocks to the efficient industrialization of this regime.[13] (As a matter of fact, the Soviet power complex is itself a reincarnation, loosely speaking, of the feudal regime which existed prior to the 1917 revolution.) Evidence for the survival of feudalistic patterns in the Middle East and India[14] is also readily obtainable.

On the other hand, the rapid disintegration and, at times, loss of cultural identity of folk, or "primitive," societies is common knowledge. Examples can be found in the Americas and in Australia, Africa, and various parts of Asia. Specifically, India comes to mind. There the feudal order has maintained itself, whereas the tribal units, much to the concern of many anthropologists and government officials, are being "detribalized."[15]

The question now arises: How is the feudalistic social structure able to survive in the face of industrial urbanization? For one thing, the elite strives to retain its traditional advantages at all cost. The elite is assumed to have "everything to lose and nothing to gain" from social change. The following discussion points to some of the conditions which make this resistance possible.

The upper stratum's ability to ward off the consequences of industrial urbanization first arises from its command of technical intelligence. To insure the continuance of the society, positions in the complex governmental and educational institutions must be staffed; the alternative is chaos. A modicum of order must be maintained by all ruling groups if they are to preserve their positions of power (this is true even of revolutionary elements). Reliance upon the feudal functionaries who possess the necessary knowledge to sustain a degree of efficient organization is therefore mandatory. As a result, feudal political or educational bureaucrats, because of this strategic location, are able to veto (either formally or informally) any proposed radical change.[16]

[13] Mark Alexander, "Tensions in Soviet Central Asia," *The Twentieth Century*, CL (1951), 192–200.

[14] See, e.g., Lewis V. Thomas and Richard N. Frye, *The United States and Turkey and Iran* (Cambridge: Harvard University Press, 1951); Halford L. Hoskins, "Point Four with Reference to the Middle East," *Annals of the American Academy of Political and Social Science*, CCLXVIII (1950), 85–95; J. A. Curran, Jr., *Militant Hinduism in Indian Politics: A Study of the R.S.S.* (New York: Institute of Pacific Relations, 1951); Radhakamad Mukerjee *et al.*, *Inter-Caste Tensions: A Survey under the Auspices of UNESCO* (Lucknow, India: Lucknow University Press, 1951); Kingsley Davis, *The Population of India and Pakistan* (Princeton: Princeton University Press, 1951), *passim*.

[15] D. N. Majumdar, *Races and Cultures of India* (2d rev. ed.; Lucknow, India: Universal Publishers, Ltd., 1950), pp. 97, 179, 187; J. H. Hutton, "Primitive Tribes" in L. S. S. O'Malley (ed.), *Modern India and the West* (London: Oxford University Press, 1941), pp. 415–44; and various issues of the *Eastern Anthropologist*, published in Lucknow, India, esp. Vol. III, September, 1949.

[16] An interesting situation has evolved in the case of colonial rule. Inasmuch as members of the elite have commanded the important governmental and educational posts, their contact with the foreign rulers has been far more extensive than that of the masses. The upper-class individuals, especially those who are able to accommodate somewhat, gain access to the implements of the foreigner's power — education, technological knowledge, etc. Actually, this reinforces their status and increases their possibilities for survival; this in turn aids in the preservation of feudal traits.

The survival of the elite, particularly within governmental and educational and/or religious institutions, is greatly enhanced by the prevailing language patterns. The speech of the upper class markedly differs from that of the folk. But more important is the nature of the written language — the medium by which officialdom conducts its affairs. It may be a completely different one from that spoken by the masses — for example, Latin in medieval Europe — or, as in the case of the Chinese and Japanese scripts, most difficult to master. In any event, knowledge of the literary language requires much leisure — the prerogative of the elite. Few of the folk are able to gain access to the sacred knowledge possessed by the political and intellectual leaders; thus, criticism or rejection of the elite's moral ideals is quite unlikely. Through this monopoly of the written language the elite seals itself off from the masses. And these written languages have a remarkable survival quality. Latin is a striking example. In addition, the Arabic literary language and the Chinese and Japanese scripts display an inflexibility which assures their continued usage for some time to come, despite the various attempts at reform.[17]

The written tradition, especially as embodied in the sacred literature, is the product of the privileged group. As such, it prescribes the ideal action patterns in family, religious, and interpersonal situations. Many of these rules are carried over into the urban-industrial society through enacted legislation. For example, many of the law norms which are applied to the contemporary industrial-urban communities of India stem from the sacred writings of the Hindus and thus perpetuate the ideal norms not of the lower castes but of the Brahmins.[18] This pattern has no correlate in folk orders. Among the folk, once the oral traditions are lost, they can never be recovered.

Although it is difficult to express the following in strictly objective terms, research reveals that the superiority-inferiority structure is tenacious. Possibly one reason for this is the rationalization it receives in the religious writings. Yet, whatever the explanation, empirical materials lend credence to the "toughness" of this structural nexus in a society. In Japan after World War II, lower-class individuals when asked by pollsters for their opinions would refer the interviewer to upper-class leaders who would speak for them.[19] Employer-employee relations in feudal countries now undergoing industrialization also reflect the continuance of earlier traditions. In southeast Asia, China, and Japan, the employer-laborer relationship exhibits a

[17] Shouby, op. cit.; John De Francis, Nationalism and Language Reform in China (Princeton: Princeton University Press, 1950).

[18] Benjamin Lindsay, "Law," in O'Malley, op. cit., pp. 107–37; Dinshah Fardunji Mulla, Principles of Hindu Law (10th ed.; Calcutta: Eastern Law House, Ltd., 1946), chap. ii.

[19] Frederick S. Hulse, "Some Effects of the War upon Japanese Society," Far Eastern Quarterly, VII (1947), 37.

direct correspondence to the elite-mass system of feudalism.[20] And the prestige of the European nobility has died slowly, even in a country as democratic as England.

Up to this point, only resistance to the industrial-urban complex has been examined. An objection could be raised: Did not the elite in Japan actually instigate the industrialization of the nation? The rebuttal to such an argument is that industrial urbanization was only partially accepted. Many of the value orientations and structural arrangements which ordinarily are correlated with it were summarily rejected. The feudalistic ruling group who retained control of the governmental bureaucracy impeded the "modernization" of women's role in society and the development of a small-family system. Consequently, an overpopulation problem was fostered which may ultimately threaten the whole industrial-urban structure. Furthermore, the state was able to perpetuate many feudal traditions by maintaining rigid control over the educational system and by keeping the workers in a position of subservience.[21]

Recent happenings in a number of folk orders testify to the significance of an elite class. The ability of "primitive" societies to adjust to, or frequently combat, industrial urbanization and the kind of social organization which ordinarily accompanies it is dependent upon the development of an elite which is sufficiently trained to comprehend the implications of what is transpiring. This is strikingly evident in Negro Africa. In the Belgian Congo the government contributed toward the formation of an educated *noire élite;* only then did formal resistance to "modernization" arise.[22] And the incipient opposition of the Natives in South Africa and in British West Africa[23] is being led by the educated among them. Only these are able to utilize such mediums as books, newspapers, and the radio — and thus publicize the "evils" of the prevailing social change. In other words, the growth

[20] See, e.g., Bruno Lasker, *Human Bondage in Southeast Asia* (Chapel Hill: University of North Carolina Press, 1950), *passim;* John Campbell Pelzel, "Social Stratification in Japanese Urban Economic Life" (unpublished Ph.D. dissertation, Harvard University, Department of Social Relations, 1950); Shih Kuo-heng, *China Enters the Machine Age* (ed. and trans. Hsiao-tung Fei and Francis L. K. Hsu) (Cambridge: Harvard University Press, 1944), pp. 116 ff.

[21] Some works discussing the persistence of feudalism in Japan and its effects are: Nobutaka Ike, *The Beginnings of Political Democracy in Japan* (Baltimore: Johns Hopkins Press, 1950), Parts 3 and 4; Hugh Borton (ed.), *Japan* (Ithaca: Cornell University Press, 1950), esp. chaps. viii and xii; Warren S. Thompson, "Future Adjustments of Population to Resources in Japan," in *Modernization Programs in Relation to Human Resources and Population Problems* (New York: Milbank Memorial Fund, 1950), pp. 142–53.

[22] See recent issues of the journal *La Voix du Congolais*, particularly Vol. VI (1950).

[23] Ellen Hellmann (ed.), *Handbook on Race Relations in South Africa* (Cape Town: Oxford University Press, 1949), chap. xx; also see various issues of the journal *Race Relations* (published in Johannesburg, South Africa), esp. Vol. XVI, No. 3 (1949), and Vernon McKay, "Nationalism in British West Africa," *Foreign Policy Reports,* XXIV (1948), 2–11.

of an institutional apparatus, one not found among the folk, is essential if this society is to preserve its identity. Interestingly enough, anthropologists may place themselves in a position of a "neo-elite" when studying "primitive" peoples. For only after the folk customs have been recorded is it possible for governments to make adjustments in their policies to prevent the disappearance of those groups which lack an educated and political elite.[24]

Among the masses in the feudal order the artisans or craftsmen constitute a group which has a vested interest in keeping the situation stabilized. Although in some countries their resistance has not been noticeably effective, nevertheless the artisans play a role in checking the diffusion of the industrial-urban complex. For if and when it occurs, it does so at the expense of this group. Should a society desire to maintain a minimum of order, the artisans must not be destroyed too rapidly. Furthermore, they are at times active in repelling the intrusion of the new type of economic system.[25]

Second, modern feudal societies are typically overpopulated. In contrast, folk societies are by nature small and are not faced with this problem. Kingsley Davis[26] has offered what is perhaps the most plausible set of explanations showing how overpopulation acts as a deterrent to industrial-urban expansion. Overpopulation, for one thing, focuses economic effort on consumption goods rather than on heavy industry, discounting future for present advantage. The situation of low capitalization is apparent first in agriculture, where land becomes increasingly scarce and expensive. Moreover, a high ratio of farm population to agricultural resources results in the production of food crops for sustenance rather than export crops for investment surplus. As a result of overpopulation, labor is immediately cheaper than machinery, which discourages the rationalization of industry. Finally, rapid population growth implies a high fertility and a somewhat lower, though still high, death rate. This creates an unusually heavy burden of young dependents.

One of the most crucial problems now faced by many countries, especially those in Asia, is how to combat the great inertia inherent in overpopulation. This is further complicated by the resistance of the feudal elite, who impede the process of industrial urbanization sufficiently to facilitate a progressive increase in the population.

An ideal typology has been constructed in contradistinction to that of the folk. One essential of the former is the two-class system — a small elite supported by a large peasant population. Even more significant are the

24 This is apparent in the United States government-sponsored surveys of non-literate peoples of Oceania after World War II, as well as in studies of American Indians during the last fifty years.

25 Levy and Shih Kuo-heng, op. cit., p. 35; R. G. Kakade, A Socio-Economic Survey of Weaving Communities in Sholapur (Poona: Gokhale Institute of Politics and Economics, 1947), passim.

26 Davis, op. cit., pp. 218–19.

existent and highly developed state and educational and/or religious institutions — through dominant positions in these structures the elite class
controls the society. The feudal manufacturing system is much more elaborate than that within the folk order: for example, handicraft workers are
present. All this implies an extensive division of labor. Although both
feudal and folk societies have a sacred-value orientation and exhibit a
minimum of internal change, their social structures are markedly divergent.
An understanding of the effects of the industrial-urbanization process in
many areas of the world is possible only if these two typologies are separated; too often the distinctions have not been emphasized.

Other implications stem from the foregoing discussion; only a few are
mentioned here. First, many sociologists and anthropologists have given
undue emphasis to the local community, especially when this is a mere
segment of the larger sociocultural setting. Community-bound research
stresses the family unit and neglects the study of governmental and educational institutions, through which the family necessarily must work in order
to achieve its power and influence. From this it follows that, methodologically, the lumping-together of folk and feudal societies is often not justified. Doubts might legitimately be expressed concerning the validity of
such a technique as the "cross-cultural survey" when generalizations are
attempted beyond the area of family or kinship system.

Finally, more attention needs to be devoted to the effects of industrial
urbanization upon feudalistic societies. Few problems are of greater significance. In Asia, particularly, conflicts of great magnitude have been
evidenced as the industrial-urban complex has spread into that region.
Europe has been experiencing a similar fate for many decades.

Obviously, despite the resistance of the feudal structure, the industrialization and urbanization process has been moving forward. However, instead of encompassing the whole society (which is now almost the case
in the United States), in the feudal order the industrial-urbanized society
will in all probability be superimposed upon the existing structure, with
the latter remaining to some degree intact. Bifurcation within the society
would therefore still persist, although in quite different form and with
quite different effects. This possibility has found empirical expression in
such countries as France and Italy, where enclaves of peasants still perpetuate the feudal organization. Overpopulation combined with the resistance to change inherent among the elite have contributed to this situation.
A similar co-existence of two societies was deliberately planned by the
Netherlands government in its rule over the Netherlands East Indies. The
Dutch envisaged a "plural" economy, which also meant a bifurcated social
structure.[27] Industrial urbanization has thus led to a modification rather

---

[27] J. S. Furnivall, *Netherlands India* (Cambridge: Cambridge University Press,
1939), esp. pp. 446 ff.

than a destruction of feudal societies (folk orders, in contrast, seem to be disappearing). Though any attempt at generalization is fraught with difficulties, such an adjustment in feudal countries is not unlikely for a long time to come. But whatever the outcome, the imposition of the industrial-urban society upon an already highly developed social organization such as that found in feudalism will unquestionably be accompanied by disorganization, severe strains, and conflict.

B. Processes and Examples

One image of the urban area sees it as composed of atomistic individuals having little or no relationship to one another. The city is seen as composed of several basic homogeneous areas. Greer, a demographer, concentrates on urbanism as a way of life, and shows that the traditional measures for characterizing urban environments are inadequate. It should not be forgotten that communities are viable entities and represent a viable adaptation to their environment. This is no less true in the urban setting than it is in the rural.

34 SCOTT GREER

Urbanism Reconsidered: A Comparative Study of Local Areas in a Metropolis

The investigation of the internal differentiation of urban population has been concerned chiefly with economic rank and ethnic diversity, and with the differences which accompany variations in these factors. Such studies throw little light upon the broad, non-ethnic, cultural differences generated in the metropolitan environment, i.e., upon "urbanism as a way of life." While there has been much concern, theoretically, with the effects of the metropolitan ambit upon all social relationships, most of the empirical basis of urban theory has been the study of small "natural areas" or the study of gross regularities in census data, arranged spatially for analysis.

Perhaps the best evidence bearing upon this larger question of "urbanism" has been the study of urban neighborhoods. The work of Donald Foley, for example, indicates that in a sample of Rochester residents (1) the neighborhood pattern still exists to some degree, but, (2) many indi-

From *American Sociological Review,* Vol. XXI (February, 1956), pp. 19–25. Reprinted by permission of the author and the American Sociological Association.

viduals do not neighbor and do not consider their local area to be a social community.[1] Such studies approach the propositions that urban society is functionally rather than spatially organized and that urbanites are mobile, anonymous, and lacking in identification with their local area.

To gauge the generality of Foley's conclusions, however, one needs to know where the neighborhoods he studied fit in an array of neighborhoods. Because wide variation exists, the relation between the area studied and others is crucial for the hypothesis tested; most of Rochester may be much more neighborhood oriented, or much less so, than the area studied.

The Shevky-Bell typology of urban sub-areas is useful in this connection, for it allows any census tract to be located in three different arrays by means of three indices constructed from census data.[2] It is hypothesized that these represent three dimensions within urban social space, each statistically unidimensional and independent of the others. The dimensions are social rank, segregation, and urbanization.[3] The last largely measures differences in family structure, and, it is assumed, indicates corollary differences in behavior. Thus, when social rank and segregation are controlled, differences in the index of urbanization for specific tract populations should indicate consistent variations in social behavior. One purpose of the present research was to determine the nature of such corollary differences, and particularly differences in social participation.

This report is based upon a pilot study of differences in social participation between sample populations in two Los Angeles areas (census tracts 35 and 63).[4] The two tract populations are nearly identical with respect to two of the indices (social rank and segregation) and differ on the third, urbanization. For simplicity in presentation the tract with the higher urbanization index score (tract 63) will hereafter be called the high-urban tract, the other (tract 35) the low-urban tract.

The two sample tracts compare as follows. *History:* the low-urban tract is in an area that thirty years ago was separately incorporated for a brief time; the high-urban tract has always been a part of Los Angeles proper. *Location:* the low-urban tract is approximately fifteen minutes from the city

[1] Donald L. Foley, "Neighbors or Urbanites? The Study of a Rochester District," *The University of Rochester's Studies of Metropolitan Rochester,* Rochester, New York, 1952.

[2] Eshref Shevky and Wendell Bell, *Social Area Analysis,* Stanford, California: Stanford University Press, 1955. See also, Eshref Shevky and Marilyn Williams, *The Social Areas of Los Angeles,* Berkeley and Los Angeles: The University of California Press, 1948.

[3] For a description of the statistical analysis and testing of the typology, see Wendell Bell, "Economic, Family, and Ethnic Status," *American Sociological Review,* 20 (February, 1955), pp. 45–52.

[4] The extension of the study to include two additional sample tracts will be reported later; results are generally consistent with the findings reported here. Rank and segregation are the same in the added tract samples, but the new tracts extend to the extremes of the urbanization index.

center by auto; the high-urban tract is about half as far. (The low-urban tract is adjacent to the competing centers of Glendale and Pasadena.) *Social rank:* both tracts fall within the large middle range, being slightly above the median for the County. The social rank index for the low-urban tract is 68, for the high-urban tract, 66, as of the 1950 census of population, based upon the standard scores developed by Shevky with 1940 census data. *Ethnicity:* in neither tract does the foreign-born and non-white population amount to more than 5 per cent. *Urbanization:* the two tracts represent the extremes of the middle range of the urbanization index, within which a majority of the Los Angeles County census tracts lie. The low-urban tract had an urbanization index of 41, the high-urban tract, 57. There are much more highly urban tracts at middle rank, and much lower ones, in the County. The sample is weighted against the instrument, so that if striking and consistent variations appear in this middle range, they probably indicate more extreme variations at the poles.

THE FIELD PROCEDURE AND THE SAMPLE

The field study included scheduled interviews on the participation of adult members of households in formal organizations, neighboring, cultural events, visiting, domestic activities, the mass media, the kin group, and other social structures.

Visiting was measured by questions concerning friends or relatives who were visited regularly at least once a month. The respondent was asked to give the address of the residence visited, both as a control over the accuracy of the information, and as a clue to social space position in the Shevky-Bell typology. Neighboring was measured by Wallin's "Neighborliness Scale," which was developed for a similar population in Palo Alto, California.[5] The scale assumes that neighborliness is unidimensional and can be measured by a small battery of questions referring to the degree of interaction with neighbors. The reproducibility for the present sample has not yet been determined. Cultural events were recorded and categorized in the manner devised by Queen, in his studies of social participation in St. Louis.[6] Individuals were asked about their attendance in the past month at movies, classes and study groups, athletic contests, lectures and speeches, museums and exhibits, musical events, and stage shows. They were also asked the location of the event and who accompanied them. Special schedules of questions were developed for the purpose of describing participation in formal organizations of various sorts, definitions of the local area, domestic participation, neighborhood play of children, and other aspects of participation which will not be reported here.

[5] Paul Wallin, "A Guttman Scale for Measuring Women's Neighborliness," *American Journal of Sociology*, 49 (November, 1953), pp. 243–246.

[6] Stuart A. Queen, "Social Participation in Relation to Social Disorganization," *American Sociological Review*, 14 (April, 1949), pp. 251–256.

An area random sample was interviewed in each tract, with 161 respondents in the low-urban tract, 150 in the high-urban tract. These households represented approximately 7 per cent of the populations of the two census tracts chosen. The housewife was the respondent, and the response rate was over 85 per cent, being higher in the low-urban area. Interviewers were advanced and graduate students at Occidental College, and the average interview time was approximately one hour.

The two samples of households compare as follows:

> *Income:* 20 per cent of the households in each area had less than $3,000 annually; 37 per cent in the low-urban area and 31 per cent in the high-urban area had annual incomes between $3,000 and $5,000; 35 per cent in the low-urban area and 38 per cent in the high-urban area had over $5,000 annually. Those who did not know or declined to state were 8 per cent in the low-urban area, 11 per cent in the high-urban area. The chief difference was a preponderance of middle income households in the low-urban area, with somewhat more heterogeneity in the high-urban area. *Occupation:* using the blue collar-white collar break, the samples were identical. In both areas, 72 per cent of the employed respondents were white-collar. Seventy-two per cent of the husbands in each area were in clerical jobs or higher.
>
> *Education:* if education is divided into three classes, elementary or less, some high school or completed high school, and some college or more, the low-urban sample is slightly more homogeneous. Both respondents and husbands are 60 per cent high-school educated, with approximately 15 per cent below and 25 per cent above this class. In the high-urban sample the middle category accounted for only 50 per cent, with approximately 25 per cent below and 25 per cent above this class.

Such differences are not great but seem to indicate a consistent tendency towards somewhat more heterogeneity in the high-urban sample. It includes a slightly higher proportion of low-income, low-education persons, and also a slightly higher proportion of high-income, high-education persons. The high-urban sample is also more heterogeneous with respect to ethnicity. Although the percentage of non-white and foreign-born is similar in the two samples (9 for the low-urban sample, 11 for the high-urban) differences in religious affiliation indicate more ethnic diversity in the high-urban sample.

The low-urban area sample is much more homogeneous and Protestant in affiliation and preference. The high-urban sample, however, includes sizeable representations of the minority American religious beliefs: Jews and Roman Catholics are, together, only 20 per cent of the low-urban sample; they are 37 per cent of the high-urban sample. This heterogeneous and non-Protestant population in the high-urban sample is probably, to a large degree, made up of second and later generation ethnic individuals.

Since the census tracts with high indexes of segregation in middle economic ranks are usually found in the more highly urbanized areas of the Shevky-Bell grid, it is likely that "later generation ethnics" (not identified in census data) are also concentrated in the more highly urbanized tracts of the middle social rank.

Such a correlation between second and later generation ethnic populations and urbanization, however, does not allow the reduction of the urbanization dimension to the ethnic component. In truth, many of these individuals are in process of leaving their ethnic status behind. Instead, it may be said that one of the attributes indicated by the urbanization index is apt to be the presence of second and later generation ethnics in the midst of acculturation. Such heterogeneity between faiths and within faiths is one of the conditions that give highly urbanized populations their particular characteristics.

EMPIRICAL FINDINGS

Table 1 gives differences in participation between two areas with respect to the localization of community. The low-urban sample differed sharply and consistently in the direction of more participation in the local community. Their neighboring score was higher, they were more apt to have friends in the local area, and these constituted a larger proportion of all close friends, i.e., those visited at least once a month. They were more apt to go to cultural events such as movies, athletic contests, stage shows, and study groups, in the local area, and they were more apt to use local commercial facilities of certain types.

The low-urban sample had a higher rate of membership and participation in formal organizations other than church, and, more important, a larger proportion of their organizations were local in nature. A large majority of the respondents' organizations held meetings in the local area, and although the husbands' organizations usually met outside the area, still a much larger proportion met locally than did in the high-urban sample. Furthermore, the members of formal organizations to which the low-urban sample belonged were more apt to live in the immediate local community. In the high-urban sample other members were most apt to be scattered over the metropolis as a whole.

Further indication of the differential importance the local based organization had for these two samples is the greater familiarity of the low-urban sample with local community leaders. (See Table 2.)

While the samples were equally able (and unable) to name Los Angeles leaders, there was a significantly higher proportion who could name local leaders in the low-urban area sample. This probably indicates a uniform engagement of the middle-rank populations in the affairs of the metropolis as a whole, but definite variations in their interest and involvement with respect to local affairs.

TABLE 1. LOCAL COMMUNITY PARTICIPATION IN TWO URBAN AREAS

Type of social participation	Low urban[a]	High urban[a]	Type of social participation	Low urban[a]	High urban[a]
Percentage of respondents with high neighboring scores (Scale types 2 through 5)	67[b]	56[b]	Percentage of respondents' formal organizations with the majority of members residing in:		
N of respondents	(162)	(150)	Local area	57	33
Percentage of respondents with friends in the local area	50	29	Other area	18	18
			Scattered over the city	23	45
N of respondents	(162)	(150)	No response	2	4
			N of organizations	(126)	(67)
Percentage of all respondents' friends who live in local area	41	25	Percentage of husbands' formal organizations (as reported by respondent) which meet in:		
N of all friends	(441)	(316)			
Percentage of respondents attending cultural events in local area, of those attending any cultural events	45	18	Local area	21[c]	5[c]
			Other areas	73	86
			No response	6	9
N attending any events	(101)	(92)	N of husbands' organizations	(104)	(57)
Percentage of respondents' formal organizations which meet in:			Percentage of husbands' formal organizations (as reported by respondent) with the majority of members residing in:		
Local area	62	26			
Other areas	35	71			
No response	3	3			
N of organizations	(126)	(67)	Local area	25	10
			Other area	23	12
			Scattered over the city	45	77
			No response	7	1
			N of husbands' organizations	(104)	(57)

[a] P (χ^2) < .01, with exceptions noted below.
[b] P (χ^2) slightly above .05 level: $\chi^2 = 3.77$.
[c] P (χ^2) between .01 and .02 levels.

Table 2. Respondents' Ability to Name Leaders of the Local Area and of Los Angeles

	Low urban	High urban
Percentage of respondents who could name at least one local leader	32[a]	21[a]
N of respondents	(162)	(150)
Percentage of respondents who could name at least one Los Angeles leader	38[b]	37[b]
N of respondents	(162)	(150)

[a] P (χ^2) between .02 and .05 levels.
[b] Difference not significant.

Table 3. Kin Visiting in Two Urban Areas

Percentage visiting kin	Low urban[a]	High urban[a]
Once a week or more often	49	55
At least once a month, but less than once a week	24	21
A few times a year, but less than once a month	11	8
Never	5	9
No kin in Los Angeles	1J	7
N of respondents	(162)	(150)

[a] No significant difference between low and high urban area samples.

It is sometimes stated, almost as an axiom, that the urban milieu results in the extreme attrition of kin relations. The present study indicates this to be questionable. The most important single kind of social relationship for both samples is kinship visiting. A large majority of both samples visit their kin at least once a month, and *half of each sample visit their kin at least once a week.* These data, reported in Table 3, are consistent with the findings of Bell in his comparable study of social areas in the San Francisco Bay Region.[7]

Both samples indicated complacency with their neighborhood and said they were satisfied with it as a home, but in giving their reasons for liking it, they tended to differ. The low-urban sample described their area as a "little community," like a "small town," where "people are friendly and neighborly." The high-urban sample, on the other hand, most frequently mentioned the "convenience to downtown and everything," and spoke often of the "nice people" who "leave you alone and mind their own business." The high-urban sample seemed less committed to remaining in their present area — a higher proportion stating that there were other neighborhoods in the city in which they would rather live.

A tendency toward differential association with populations at a similar level of urbanization is indicated in the visiting patterns of the two samples outside their local areas. The residences of close friends and the meeting places of social circles are almost mutually exclusive for the two samples.

[7] Wendell Bell (with the assistance of Maryanne Force and Marion Boat), "People of the City" (processed), Stanford University Survey Research Facility, Stanford, California, 1954.

Furthermore, when the census tracts in which are located the homes of the friends they visit are categorized by urbanization scores, clear differences appear. The low-urban sample is more apt to have friends in other low-urban areas, while the high-urban sample is apt to visit in other high-urban areas. (See Table 4.)

TABLE 4. RESIDENCE OF FRIENDS
VISITED, OUTSIDE OF THE LOCAL AREA,
BY URBANIZATION INDEX SCORE[a]

	Low urban[b]	High urban[b]
Percentage of friends living in tracts with urbanization index score of		
1–20	13	12
21–40	35	25
41–60	41	33
61–80	8	19
81–100	3	11
N of friends visited	(180)	(162)

[a] Friends' addresses which could not be coded (80 in the low-urban area, 65 in the high-urban) are excluded.
[b] $P(\chi^2) < .001$.

When it is recalled that these two samples are almost identical with respect to social rank and segregation, the importance of the urbanization dimension is underlined. These visiting patterns refer to well structured friendship relations of probable importance. Such differential association may result from proximity, as well as selective visiting by levels of urbanization. The relative importance of proximity will be measured through the use of the intervening opportunities model. However, even if such differential association is to a large degree a function of spatial proximity, its significance in certain respects would remain. For, if populations at given levels of urbanization interact more intensely within those levels than with other populations, such interactions should result in fairly stable networks of informal communication and influence. The content of such communication should vary with urbanization.

SUMMARY AND INTERPRETATION

In order to investigate empirically the complex of notions surrounding the nature of urban social behavior, the Shevky-Bell typology, applied to subareas in Los Angeles County, was used to select two neighborhoods which differed clearly on the index of urbanization. Social rank was not used as the chief factor accounting for differential social participation, as was the case in the studies of Komarovsky, Goldhamer, and others.[8] Instead, rank was controlled, and the urbanization dimension was tested for broad differences in social participation.

It should be noted that this study investigates the effects of urbanization at a *particular* level of rank and segregation; at other levels, the effects of urbanization remain problematical. It is hoped that future studies will clarify, for example, the effects of differential urbanization at higher and lower social ranks, as well as in segregated populations. The Shevky-Bell typology, based upon a three dimensional attribute-space model of urban society, calls attention not only to three separate factors, but also to the possibility that the particular effects of one may be transformed as either or both of the others vary.

However, the urbanization dimension was the focus of the present study. It was not identified with the older notion of urbanism which implies that all city populations are changing in the direction of atomistic, mass society.[9] Instead, it was assumed that there is a continuum of alternative life-styles at the same economic level and that these are concentrated in different urban sub-areas. In this framework, the low-urban areas are just as characteristic of modern urban society as are the high-urban areas. Both types continue to be alternatives in the urban complex. In this view, the Shevky-Bell index of urbanization is a putative means of identifying such variations in "ways of life." Instead of concentrating on urbanism as *a* way of life, the present study was focused upon the variations possible.

Two social aggregates, inhabiting tracts with similar economic rank and ethnicity but varying with respect to the urbanization index, were sampled. The sample populations were then studied by means of reported social participation.

The findings are consistent with the hypothesis that, where rank and ethnicity are equal, differences in the urbanization index will indicate differences in social behavior. Had the index identified populations not significantly different, doubt would have been cast upon its utility at the level of individual social behavior, for the urbanization dimension of modern society, as conceived by Shevky in his theoretical structure, implies such differences in social behavior.[10] However, the present study indicates that the index, constructed primarily with items related to family structure, does identify differences in social participation which are associated with variations in family structure but not derived solely from them. The general

---

[8] Mirra Komarovsky, "The Voluntary Associations of Urban Dwellers," *American Sociological Review*, 11 (December, 1946), pp. 868–896; Herbert Goldhamer, "Voluntary Associations in the United States," unpublished Ph.D. thesis, University of Chicago, 1942.

[9] See Louis Wirth, "Urbanism as a Way of Life," *The American Journal of Sociology*, 44 (July, 1938), pp. 1–24.

[10] Shevky and Bell, *op. cit.,* especially Chapter II.

validity of the hypothesis must rest upon further studies in Los Angeles and other urban complexes. Although this study and that of Bell indicate the urbanization dimension does affect social participation to an impressive degree, the regularity with which these differences form a continuum at this intersection of social rank and segregation, and the nature of the hypothesized continuum, remain to be spelled out. Still, in the interpretation of the findings here reported, the following implications come to mind:

1. The local area in the contemporary American metropolis may be viewed as attracting population, not only by the economic rank and ethnic composition of the population already in the area, but also by the degree of urbanization characteristic of the area — the way of life common to the older inhabitants.

2. Such areas may attract populations on at least two different functional bases: (1) the demographic and the cultural characteristics of the older settlers, who give the area its "tone," may attract people, as seems true in the low-urban sample, or, (2) the area as a socially neutral, but convenient, base of operations for various segmental interests, may attract people as in the high-urban sample. Such different principles of attraction would tend to produce greater homogeneity of background and interest in low-urban areas, and from this similarity a higher degree of community-type behavior and of conformity would be expected.

3. A continuum is hypothesized for nonsegregated, middle-rank areas. At one pole lie the local areas which select a predominantly "old American" population with similar jobs, aspirations, incomes, who wish to raise children, neighbor, participate in local community groups, and, in brief, carry on a life in many ways similar to that of the small towns described by Warner and his associates.[11] At the other pole lie those areas of the city which are more heterogeneous, with fewer children and little interest in the local area as a social arena. Such areas may approach, in many ways, the ideal type of urban environment hypothesized by Wirth.[12]

4. In this perspective, the local area is important as a framework for interaction, as a "social fact," just where it is least representative of the total urban society. The small community, as studied by Warner and others, is a very poor example of the urban complex, since it will include the fewest elements of urban society as a whole. At the same time, the high-urban tract as a sample of urban society is only slightly less biased, for in it the local area as a social fact disappears altogether. Thus it is not possible to use either the model of a small, spatially enclosed community or the stereotype of the continually more atomistic mass society in describing social participation in the contemporary metropolis.

[11] See, for example, W. Lloyd Warner and associates, *Democracy in Jonesville*, New York: Harper and Brothers, 1949.
[12] Wirth, *op. cit.*

There are, however, certain common structural threads running through the fabric of modern society. As Paul Hatt noted, the indices developed by Warner and others to measure social status may be generalized to the total society, since the various methods correlate highly with one universal attribute — occupation.[13] The present approach is, then, to ask: How does this attribute become defined and organized, how does it influence participation, in different sub-areas of the metropolis?

A tentative answer is that the individual's social position is defined differently and his social participation is patterned differently as the focus shifts from the low-urban populations to the high-urban populations. One may envisage the low-urban areas as somewhere between the small town and the conventional picture of metropolitan living. Where the local area is a social fact, where common interests and associations obtain, generalizations derived from small community studies may have validity. For here the individual's status will result, in part, from participation in a known and used local organizational structure and from family ties that are publicly understood.

When, however, high-urban populations are considered, social participation is organized around position in other organizational contexts, as for example, the corporation, politics, the labor union, or perhaps, as Riesman has suggested, categories derived from the popular culture of the mass media.[14] Here also are many individuals whose life, aside from work, is ordered by participation in small informal groups, and informal groups only, floating within the vast culture world of the market and the mass media. In such populations the locally defined community is largely irrelevant to status and participation. Associations are spread geographically, but ordered and concentrated in terms of selected interests. Family, in this context, is still important. It is slightly more important in the high-urban sample described. But it is probably much more private in its reference. In fact, kin relations may be seen as growing in importance just because of the diminished reliance placed upon neighborhood and local community.

What has been sketched above is a tentative model which will allow the use of contributions from earlier research (studies of small cities, natural areas, the apartment house family, the suburban fringe) within a framework which integrates and orders them in relation to one another. Such a frame of reference also relates, eventually, to the increasing importance of large-scale organizations in a society which allows many alternative life patterns for individuals at the same functional and economic level.

[13] Paul K. Hatt, "Stratification in the Mass Society," *American Sociological Review*, 15 (April, 1950), pp. 216–222.

[14] David Riesman, in collaboration with Reuel Denny and Nathan Glazer, *The Lonely Crowd, A Study of the Changing American Character*, New Haven: Yale University Press, 1950, especially Chs. X, XI, XII.

PART FIVE

SELECTED
INSTITUTIONS

An institution can be defined as an organized form of group behavior, relating to specific events, and generally recognized as fundamental to the society. Thus, the family represents events such as mating, birth, and child rearing, which are organized and recognized by the society at large as important. It is society's way of coping with the problem of procreating the species. There are other basic organized systems of behavior, such as the polity, which "solves" the problem of conflict resolution, or religion, which satisfies spiritual needs. We have chosen to limit ourselves to these three complexes of values and behavior. Since the individual simultaneously participates in more than one institution, we will also deal with their relationship to one another.

XII THE FAMILY

A. Definitions and Concepts

A subject of controversy throughout the ages has been the family. Some philosophers have seen the family as the basic unit in the political system, and have stressed its importance in maintaining strong characters and a healthy society. Other theorists have, with just as much vigor, condemned the family for corrupting the child with its reactionary values. Though people have quarrelled over the form the family ought to take, they have usually assumed that it has always existed, and always will exist. Spiro, an anthropologist, raises the question of its universality, in analyzing the kibbutz.

35 MELFORD E. SPIRO

Is the Family Universal? — The Israeli Case

The universality of the family has always been accepted as a sound hypothesis in anthropology; recently, Murdock has been able to confirm this hypothesis on the basis of his important cross-cultural study of kinship. Moreover, Murdock reports that the "nuclear" family is also universal, and that typically it has four functions: sexual, economic, reproductive, and educational. What is more important is his finding that no society "has succeeded

Reproduced by permission of the author and the American Anthropological Association from the *American Anthropologist*, Vol. 56 (Oct.–Dec. 1954), pp. 839–846. The 1958 Addendum on pages 391–394 is reprinted by permission of the authors and The Macmillan Company from *A Modern Introduction to the Family*, Norman W. Bell and Ezra F. Vogel, eds. © The Free Press, a Corporation, 1960.

in finding an adequate substitute for the nuclear family, to which it might transfer these functions." In the light of this evidence, there would be little reason to question his prediction that "it is highly doubtful whether any society ever will succeed in such an attempt, utopian proposals for the abolition of the family to the contrary notwithstanding."

The functions served by the nuclear family are, of course, universal prerequisites for the survival of any society, and it is on this basis that Murdock accounts for its universality.

Without provision for the first and third (sexual and reproductive), society would become extinct; for the second (economic), life itself would cease; for the fourth (educational), culture would come to an end. The immense social utility of the nuclear family and the basic reason for its universality thus begins to emerge in strong relief.

Although sexual, economic, reproductive, and educational activities are the functional prerequisites of any society, it comes as somewhat of a surprise, nevertheless, that all four functions are served by the same social group. One would normally assume, on purely a priori grounds, that within the tremendous variability to be found among human cultures, there would be some cultures in which these four functions were distributed among more than one group. Logically, at least, it is entirely possible for these functions to be divided among various social groups within a society; and it is, indeed, difficult to believe that somewhere man's inventive ingenuity should not have actualized this logical possibility. As a matter of fact this possibility has been actualized in certain utopian communities — and it has succeeded within the narrow confines of these communities. The latter, however, have always constituted subgroups within a larger society, and the basic question remains as to whether such attempts could succeed when applied to the larger society.

Rather than speculate about the answer to this question, however, this paper presents a case study of a community which, like the utopian communities, constitutes a subgroup within a larger society and which, like some utopian communities, has also evolved a social structure which does not include the family. It is hoped that an examination of this community — the Israeli *kibbutz* — can shed some light on this question.

A *kibbutz* (plural, *kibbutzim*) is an agricultural collective in Israel whose main features include communal living, collective ownership of all property (and hence, the absence of "free enterprise" and the "profit motive"), and the communal rearing of children. Kibbutz culture is informed by its explicit, guiding principle, "from each according to his ability, to each according to his needs." The family, as that term is defined in *Social Structure*, does not exist in the kibbutz, in either its nuclear, polygamous, or extended forms. It should be emphasized, however, that the kibbutzim are organized into three separate national federations, and though the basic structure of kibbutz society is similar in all three, there are important differences among them. Hence, the term kibbutz, as used in this paper, refers exclusively to those kibbutzim that are members of the federation studied by the author.

As Murdock defines it, the family is a social group characterized by common residence, economic co-operation, and reproduction. It includes adults of both sexes, at least two of whom maintain a socially approved sexual relationship, and one or more children, own or adopted, of the sexually cohabiting adults. The social group in the kibbutz that includes adults of both sexes and their children, although characterized by reproduction, is not characterized by common residence or by economic co-operation. Before examining this entire social group, however, we shall first analyze the relationship between the two adults in the group who maintain a "socially approved sexual relationship," in order to determine whether their relationship constitutes a "marriage."

Murdock's findings reveal that marriage entails an interaction of persons of opposite sex such that a relatively permanent sexual relationship is maintained and an economic division of labor is practiced. Where either of these behavior patterns is absent, there is no marriage. As Murdock puts it:

> Sexual unions without economic co-operation are common, and there are relationships between men and women involving a division of labor without sexual gratification . . . but marriage exists only when the economic and the sexual are united in one relationship, and the combination occurs only in marriage.

In examining the relationship of the couple in the kibbutz who share a common marriage, and whose sexual union is socially sanctioned, it is discovered that only one of these two criteria — the sexual — applies. Their relationship does not entail economic co-operation. If this be so — and the facts will be examined in a moment — there is no marriage in the kibbutz, if by marriage is meant a relationship between adults of opposite sex, characterized by sexual and economic activities. Hence, the generalization that, "marriage, thus defined, exists in every known society," has found an exception.

A kibbutz couple lives in a single room, which serves as a combined bedroom-living room. Their meals are eaten in a communal dining room, and their children are reared in a communal children's dormitory. Both the man and the woman work in the kibbutz, and either one may work in one of its agricultural branches or in one of the "service" branches. The latter include clerical work, education, work in the kitchen, laundry, etc. In actual fact, however, men preponderate in the agricultural branches, and women in the service branches of the economy. There are no men, for example, in that part of the educational system which extends from infancy to the junior-high level. Nor do women work in those agricultural branches that require the use of heavy machinery, such as trucks, tractors, or combines. It should be noted, however, that some women play major roles in agricultural branches, such as the vegetable garden and the fruit orchards; and some men are indispensable in service branches such as the high school. Nevertheless, it is accurate to state that a division of labor based on sex is characteristic of the kibbutz society as a whole. This division of labor, however, does not characterize the relationship that exists between couples. Each mate works in some branch of the kibbutz economy, and each, as a member (*chaver*) of the kibbutz, receives his equal share of the goods and services that the kibbutz distributes. Neither, however, engages in economic activities that are exclusively directed to the satisfaction of the needs of his mate. Women cook, sew, launder, etc., for the entire kibbutz, and not for their mates exclusively. Men produce goods, but the economic returns from their labor go to the kibbutz, not to their mates and themselves, although they, like all members of the kibbutz, share in these economic returns. Hence, though there is economic co-operation between the sexes within the community as a whole, this co-operation does not take place between mates because the social structure of this society precludes the necessity for such co-operation.

What then is the nature of the relationship of the kibbutz couple? What are the motives for their union? What functions, other than sex, does it serve? What distinguishes such a union from an ordinary love affair?

In attempting to answer these questions, it should first be noted that premarital sexual relations are not taboo. It is expected, however, that youth of high-school age refrain from sexual activity; sexual intercourse between high-school students is strongly discouraged. After graduation from high school, however, and their election to membership in the kibbutz, there are no sanctions against sexual relations among these young people. While still single, kibbutz members live in small private rooms, and their sexual activities may take place in the room of either the male or the female, or in any other convenient location. Lovers do not ask the kibbutz for permission to move into a (larger) common room, nor, if they did, would this permission be granted if it were assumed that their relationship was merely that of lovers. When a couple asks for permission to share a room, they do so — and the kibbutz assumes that they do so — not because they are lovers, but because they are in love. The request for a room, then, is the sign that they wish to become a "couple" (*zug*), the term the kibbutz has substituted for the traditional "marriage." This union does not require the sanction of a marriage ceremony, or of any other event. When a couple requests a room, and the kibbutz grants the request, their union is *ipso facto* sanctioned by society. It should be noted, however, that all kibbutz couples eventually "get married" in accordance with the marriage laws of the state — usually just before, or soon after, their first child is born — because children born out of wedlock have no legal rights according to state law.

But becoming a couple affects neither the status nor the responsibilities of either the male or the female in the kibbutz. Both continue to work in whichever branch of the economy they had worked in before their union. The legal and social status of both the male and the female remain the same. The female retains her maiden name. She not only is viewed as a member of the kibbutz in her own right, but her official registration card in the kibbutz files remains separate from that of her "friend" (chaver) — the term used to designate spouses.

But if sexual satisfaction may be obtained outside of this union, and if the union does not entail economic co-operation, what motivates people to become couples? It seems that the motivation is the desire to satisfy certain needs for intimacy, using that term in both its physical and psychological meanings. In the first place, from the sexual point of view, the average chaver is not content to engage in a constant series of casual affairs. After a certain period of sexual experimentation, he desires to establish a relatively permanent relationship with one person. But in addition to the physical intimacy of sex, the union also provides a psychological intimacy that may be expressed by notions such as comradeship, security, dependency, succorance, etc. And it is this psychological intimacy, primarily, that distinguishes couples from lovers. The criterion of the couple relationship, then, that which distinguishes it from a relationship between adults of the same sex who enjoy psychological intimacy, or from that of adults of opposite sex who enjoy physical intimacy, is love. A couple comes into being when these two kinds of intimacy are united in one relationship.

Since the kibbutz couple does not constitute a marriage because it does not satisfy the economic criterion of marriage, it follows that the couple and their children do not constitute a family, economic co-operation being part of the definition of the family. Furthermore, as has already been indicated, this group of adults and children does not satisfy the criterion of common residence. For though the children visit their parents in the latter's room every day, their residence is in one of the children's houses (*bet yeladim*), where they sleep, eat, and spend most of their time.

More important, however, in determining whether or not the family exists in the kibbutz is the fact that the physical care and the social rearing of the children are not the responsibilities of their own parents. But these responsibilities, according to Murdock's findings, are the most important functions that the adults in the family have with respect to the children.

Before entering into a discussion of the kibbutz system of collective education (*chinuch meshutaf*), it should be emphasized that the kibbutz is a child-centered society, par excellence. The importance of children, characteristic of traditional Jewish culture, has been retained as one of the primary values in this avowedly antitraditional society. "The parents' crown" is the title given to the chapter on children in an ethnography of the Eastern European Jewish village. The authors of this ethnography write:

> Aside from the scriptural and social reasons, children are welcomed for the joy they bring beyond the gratification due to the

parents — the pleasure of having a child in the house. A baby is a toy, the treasure, and the pride of the house.

This description, except for the scriptural reference, applies without qualification to the kibbutz.

But the kibbutz has still another reason for cherishing its children. The kibbutz views itself as an attempt to revolutionize the structure of human society and its basic social relations. Its faith in its ability to achieve this end can be vindicated only if it can raise a generation that will choose to live in this communal society, and will, thus, carry on the work that was initiated by the founders of this society — their parents.

For both these reasons the child is king. Children are lavished with attention and with care to the point where many adults admit that the children are "spoiled." Adult housing may be poor, but the children live in good houses; adult food may be meager and monotonous, but the children enjoy a variety of excellent food; there may be a shortage of clothes for adults, but the children's clothing is both good and plentiful.

Despite this emphasis on children, however, it is not their own parents who provide directly for their physical care. Indeed, the latter have no responsibility in this regard. The kibbutz as a whole assumes this responsibility for all its children. The latter sleep and eat in special children's houses, they obtain their clothes from a communal store; when ill, they are taken care of by their "nurses." This does not mean that parents are not concerned about the physical welfare of their own children. On the contrary, this is one of their primary concerns. But it does mean that the active responsibility for their care has been delegated to a community institution. Nor does it mean that parents do not work for the physical care of their children, for this is one of their strongest drives. But the fruits of their labor are not given directly to their children; they are given instead to the community which, in turn, provides for all the children. A bachelor or a couple without children contribute as much of the children's physical care as a couple with children of their own.

The family's responsibility for the socialization of children, Murdock reports, is "no less important than the physical care of the children."

> The burden of education and socialization everywhere falls primarily upon the nuclear family. . . . Perhaps more than any other single factor collective responsibility for education and socialization welds the various relationships of the family firmly together.

But the education and socialization of kibbutz children are the function of their nurses and teachers, and not of their parents. The infant is placed in the infants' house upon the mother's return from the hospital, where it remains in the care of nurses. Both parents see the infant there; and the mother when she feeds it, the father upon return from work. The infant is not taken to its parents' room until its sixth month, after which it stays with them for an hour. As the child grows older, the amount of time he spends with his parents increases, and he may go to their room whenever he chooses during the day, though he must return to his children's house before lights-out. Since the children are in school most of the day, however, and since both parents work during the day, the children — even during their school vacations — are with their parents for (approximately) a two-hour period in the evening — from the time that the parents return from work until they go to eat their evening meal. The children may also be with their parents all day Saturday — the day of rest — if they desire.

As the child grows older, he advances through a succession of children's houses with children of his own age, where he is supervised by a nurse. The nurse institutes most of the disciplines, teaches the child his basic social skills, and is responsible for the "socialization of the instincts." The child also learns from his parents, to be sure, and they too are agents in the socialization process. But the bulk of his socialization is both entrusted, and deliberately delegated, to the nurses and teachers. There is little doubt but that a kibbutz child, bereft of the contributions of his parents to his socialization, would know his culture; deprived of the contributions of his nurses and teachers, however, he would remain an unsocialized individual.

As they enter the juvenile period, pre-adolescence, and adolescence, the children are gradually inducted into the economic life of the kibbutz. They work from an hour (grade-school students) to three hours (high-school seniors) a day in one of the economic branches under the supervision of adults. Thus, their economic skills, like most of their early social skills, are taught them by adults other than their parents. This generalization applies to the learning of values, as well. In the early ages, the kibbutz values are inculcated by nurses, and later by teachers. When the children enter junior high, this function, which the kibbutz views as paramount in importance, is delegated to the "homeroom teacher," known as the "educator" (*mechanech*), and to a "leader" (*madrich*) of the inter-kibbutz youth movement. The parents, of course, are also influential in the teaching of values, but the formal division of labor in the kibbutz has delegated this responsibility to other authorities.

Although the parents do not play an outstanding role in the socialization of their children, or in providing for their physical needs, it would be erroneous to conclude that they are unimportant figures in their children's lives. Parents are of crucial importance in the *psychological* development of the child. They serve as the objects of his most important identifications, and they provide him with a certain security and love that he obtains from no one else. If anything, the attachment of the young children to their parents is greater than it is in our own society. But this is irrelevant to the main consideration of this paper. Its purpose is to call attention to the fact that those functions of parents that constitute the *conditio sine qua non* for the existence of the "family" — the physical care and socialization of children — are not the functions of the kibbutz parents. It can only be concluded that in the absence of the economic and educational functions of the typical family, as well as of its characteristic of common residence, that the family does not exist in the kibbutz.

It is apparent from this brief description of the kibbutz that most of the functions characteristic of the typical nuclear family have become the functions of the entire kibbutz society. This is so much the case that the kibbutz as a whole can almost satisfy the criteria by which Murdock defines the family. This observation is not meant to imply that the kibbutz is a nuclear family. Its structure and that of the nuclear family are dissimilar. This observation does suggest, however, that the kibbutz can function without the family, because it functions as if it, itself, were a family; and it can so function because its members perceive each other as kin, in the psychological implications of that term. The latter statement requires some explanation.

The members of the kibbutz do not view each other merely as fellow citizens, or as coresidents in a village, or as co-operators of an agricultural economy. Rather they do view each other as *chaverim,* or comrades, who comprise a group in which each is intimately related to the other, and in which the welfare of the one is bound up with the welfare of the other. This is a society in which the principle, "from each according to his ability, to each according to his needs," can be practiced, not because its members are more altruistic than the members of other societies, but because each member views his fellow as a kinsman, psychologically speaking. And just as a father in the family does not complain because he works much harder than his children, and yet he may receive no more, or even less, of the family income than they, so the kibbutz member whose economic productivity is high does not complain because he receives no more, and sometimes less, than a member whose productivity is low. This principle is taken for granted as the normal way of doing things. Since they are all chaverim, "it's all in the family," psychologically speaking.

In short, the kibbutz constitutes a *gemeinschaft.* Its patterns of interaction are interpersonal patterns; its ties are kin ties, without the biological tie of kinship. In this one respect it is the "folk society," in almost its pure form. The following quotation from Redfield could have been written with the kibbutz in mind, so accurately does it describe the social-psychological basis of kibbutz culture.

> The members of the folk society have a strong sense of belonging together. The group . . . see their own resemblances and feel correspondingly united. Communicating intimately with each other, each has a strong claim on the sympathies of the others. . . . The personal and intimate life of the child in the family is extended, in the folk society, into the social world of the adults. . . . It is not merely that relations in such a society are personal; it is also that they are familial. . . . The result is a group of people among whom prevail the personal and categorized relationships that characterize the families as we know them, and in which the patterns of kinship

> tend to be extended outward from the group of genealogically connected individuals into the whole society. The kin are the type persons for all experience.

Hence it is that the bachelor and the childless couple do not feel that an injustice is being done them when they contribute to the support of the children of others. The children *in* the kibbutz are viewed as the children *of* the kibbutz. Parents (who are much more attached to their own children than they are to the children of others) and bachelors, alike, refer to all the kibbutz children as "our children."

The social perception of one's fellows as kin, psychologically speaking, is reflected in another important aspect of the kibbutz behavior. It is a striking and significant fact that those individuals who were born and raised in the kibbutz tend to practice group exogamy, although there are no rules that either compel or encourage them to do so. Indeed, in the kibbutz in which our field work was carried out, all such individuals married outside their own kibbutz. When they are asked for an explanation of this behavior, these individuals reply that they cannot marry those persons with whom they have been raised and whom they, consequently, view as siblings. This suggests, as Murdock has pointed out, that "the kibbutz to its members *is* viewed psychologically as a family to the extent that it generates the same sort of unconscious incest-avoidance tendencies" (private communication).

What is suggested by this discussion is the following proposition: although the kibbutz constitutes an exception to the generalization concerning the universality of the family, structurally viewed, it serves to confirm this generalization, functionally and psychologically viewed. In the absence of a specific social group — the family — to whom society delegates the functions of socialization, reproduction, etc., it has become necessary for the entire society to become a large extended family. But only in a society whose members perceive each other psychologically as kin can it function as a family. And there would seem to be a population limit beyond which point individuals are no longer perceived as kin. That point is probably reached when the interaction of its members is no longer face-to-face; in short, when it ceases to be a primary group. It would seem probable, therefore, that only in a "familial" society, such as the kibbutz, is it possible to dispense with the family.

ADDENDUM, 1958

This is, quite obviously, an essay in the interpretation, rather than in the reporting of data. After rereading the paper in 1958, I realized that the suggested interpretation follows from only one conception of the role which definitions play in science. Starting with Murdock's inductive — based on a sample of 250 societies — definitions of marriage and family, I concluded that marriage and the family do not exist in the kibbutz, since no single group or relationship satisfies the conditions stipulated in the definitions. If I were writing this essay today, I would wish to explore alternative interpretations as well — interpretations which, despite Murdock's definitions, would affirm the existence of marriage and the family in the kibbutz. Hence, I shall here very briefly outline the direction which one alternative interpretation would take.

The kibbutz, it should be noted first, does not practice — nor does it sanction — sexual promiscuity. Each adult member is expected to form a more-or-less permanent bisexual union; and this union is socially sanctioned by the granting of a joint room to the couple. The resulting relationship is different from any other adult relationship in the kibbutz in a number of significant features. (1) It alone includes common domicile for persons of opposite sex. (2) It entails a higher rate of interaction than is to be found in any other bisexual relationship. (3) It involves a higher degree of emotional intimacy than is to be found in any other relationship. (4) It establishes (ideally) an exclusive sexual relationship. (5) It leads to the deliberate decision to have children. These characteristics which, separately and severally, apply uniquely to this relationship, not only describe its salient features but also comprise the motives for those who enter into it. The couple, in short, viewed either objectively or phenomenologically, constitutes a unique social group in the kibbutz.

What, then, are we to make of this group? Since economic co-operation is not one of its features, we can, using Murdock's cross-cultural indices, deny that the relationship constitutes marriage. This is the conclusion of the foregoing paper. In retrospect, however, this conclusion does not leave me entirely satisfied. First, although we deny that the relationship constitutes a marriage, it nevertheless remains, both structurally and psychologically, a unique relationship within the kibbutz. Moreover, it is, with the exception of the economic variable, similar to those distinctive relationships in other societies to which the term marriage is applied. Hence, if I were writing this paper today, I should want to ask, before concluding that marriage is not universal, whether Murdock's inductive definition of marriage is, in the light of the kibbutz data, the most fruitful, even for his large sample; and if it were agreed that it is, whether it ought not to be changed or qualified so as to accommodate the relationship between kibbutz "spouses." Here I can only briefly explore the implications of these questions.

If the stated characteristics of the kibbutz relationship are found in the analogous relationship (marriage) in other societies — and I do not know that they are — it is surely apposite to ask whether Murdock's definition could not or should not stipulate them, as well as those already stipulated. For if they are found in other societies, on what theoretical grounds do we assign a higher priority to sex or economics over emotional intimacy, for example? Hence, if this procedure were adopted (and assuming that the characteristics of the kibbutz relationship were to be found in the marriage relationship in other societies) we would, since the kibbutz relationship satisfies all but one of the cross-cultural criteria, term the kibbutz relationship "marriage."

Alternatively, we might suggest that Murdock's definition of marriage, as well as the one suggested here, are unduly specific; that cross-cultural research is most fruitfully advanced by means of analytic, rather than substantive or enumerative, definitions. Thus, for example, we might wish to define marriage as "any socially sanctioned relationship between non-sanguineally related cohabiting adults of opposite sex which satisfied felt needs — mutual, symmetrical, or complementary." A non-enumerative definition of this type would certainly embrace all known cases now termed "marriage" and would, at the same time, include the kibbutz case as well.

In the same vein, and employing similar definitional procedures, alternative conclusions can be suggested with respect to the family in the kibbutz. Although parents and children do not comprise a family, as Murdock defines family, they nevertheless constitute a unique group within the kibbutz, regardless of the term with which we may choose to designate it. (1) Children are not only desired by kibbutz parents, but, for the most part, they are planned. (2) These children — and no others — are called by their parents "sons" and "daughters"; conversely, they call their parents — and no other adults — "father" and "mother." (3) Parents and children comprise a social group in both an interactional and an emotional, if not in a spatial, sense. That is, though parents and children do not share a common domicile, they are identified by themselves and by others as a uniquely cohesive unit within the larger kibbutz society; this unit is termed a *mishpacha* (literally, "family"). (4) The nature of their interaction is different from that which obtains between the children and any other set of adults. (5) The rate of interaction between parents and children is greater than that between the children and any other set of adults of both sexes. (6) The psychological ties that bind them are more intense than those between the children and any other set of adults of both sexes.

Here, then, we are confronted with the same problem we encountered with respect to the question of kibbutz marriage. Because the parent-child relationship in the kibbutz does not entail a common domicile, physical care, and social rearing — three of the stipulated conditions in Murdock's definition of family — we concluded that the family does not exist in the kibbutz. But, since parents and children comprise a distinct and differentiated social group within the kibbutz, I am now not entirely satisfied with a conclusion which seems, at least by implication, to ignore its presence. For, surely, regardless of what else we might do with this group, we cannot simply ignore it. We can either perceive it, in cross-cultural perspective, as a unique group, and invent a new term to refer to it, or we can revise Murdock's definition of family in order to accommodate it.

Should the latter alternative be preferred, it could be effected in the following way. The stipulation of "common residence" could be qualified to refer to a reference, rather than to a membership, residence; and this is what the parental room is, for children as well as for parents. When, for example, they speak of "my room" or "our room," the children almost invariably refer to the parental room, not to their room in the communal children's house. If, moreover, the educational and economic functions of the family were interpreted as responsibilities for which parents were either immediately or ultimately responsible, the kibbutz parent-child unit would satisfy these criteria as well. For, though parents do not provide immediately for the physical care of their children, neither do they renounce their responsibility for them. Rather, they seek to achieve this end by working jointly rather than separately for the physical welfare of all the children — including, of course, their own.

Similarly, though the parents have only a minor share in the formal socialization process, they do not simply give their children to others to be raised as the latter see fit. Rather, socialization is entrusted to specially designated representatives, nurses and teachers, who rear the children, not according to their own fancy, but according to rules and procedures established by the parents. In short, though parents do not themselves socialize their children, they assume the ultimate responsibility for their socialization. Interpreted in this way, the relationship between kibbutz parents and children satisfies Murdock's definition of family.

To conclude, this addendum represents an alternative method of interpreting the kibbutz data concerning the relationship between spouses, and among parents and children. I am not suggesting that this interpretation is necessarily more fruitful than the one adopted in the paper. Certainly, however, I should want to examine it carefully before concluding, as I previously did, that marriage and the family are not universal.

B. Processes and Examples

Why did she marry him, or he her, has been asked by sociologists as well as backyard gossips. Regardless of the questioner's motives, the answer is important. It is useful to be able to predict whether or not a couple is likely to make a good adjustment and whether their family situation is likely to be stable. Kerckhoff and Davis, in one of the more important articles on marriage and the family, deal with three major variables: social status, value consensus, and need complementarity. The first variable, composed of things like age, sex, social class, limits one's choice of spouse to someone with matching characteristics. The necessity for agreeing about specific values is discussed under the second variable. The authors indicate that need complementarity is the final stage in spouse selection. The submissive girl or man will marry someone who is dominant.

36 ALAN C. KERCKHOFF AND KEITH E. DAVIS

Value Consensus and Need Complementarity in Mate Selection

One of the continuing interests in family research has been the attempt to define the factors which lead to a lasting relationship between a man and a woman. The two major concerns in such research have been with the process through which mates are chosen and the characteristics of mates which are predictive of "success" in the marital relationship. A considerable body of knowledge has been assembled based on data gathered in both the premarital and postmarital periods.[1] Although there have been somewhat

From *American Sociological Review*, Vol. XXVII (June, 1962), pp. 295–303. Reprinted by permission of the authors and the American Sociological Association.

[1] Relevant studies involving subects in the premarital period are C. E. Bowerman and B. R. Day, "A Test of the Theory of Complementary Needs as Applied to Couples During Courtship," *American Sociological Review*, 21 (October, 1956), pp. 602–605; Joseph S. Himes, Jr., "Value Consensus in Mate Selection Among Negroes," *Marriage and Family Living*, 14 (November, 1952), pp. 317–321.

Studies utilizing married couples only are R. J. Corsini, "Understanding and Similarity in Marriage," *Journal of Abnormal and Social Psychology*, 52 (May, 1956), pp. 327–332; A. B. Hollingshead, "Cultural Factors in the Selection of Marriage Mates," *American Sociological Review*, 15 (October, 1950), pp. 619–627; I. Katz, S. Glucksberg, and R. Krauss, "Need Satisfaction and Edwards PPS Scores in Married Couples," *Journal of Consulting Psychology*, 24 (June, 1960), pp. 205–208; E. L. Kelly, "Consistency of the Adult Personality," *American Psychologist*, 10 (November, 1955), pp. 659–681; T. Ktsanes, "Mate Selection on the Basis of Personality Type: A Study Utilizing an Empirical Typology of Personality," *American Sociological Review*, 20 (October, 1955), pp. 547–551; R. F. Winch, T. Ktsanes, and V. Ktsanes, "A Theory of Complementary Needs in Mate Selection: An Analytic and Descriptive Study," *American Sociological Review*, 19 (June, 1954), pp. 241–249; R. F. Winch, "The Theory of Complementary Needs in Mate Selection: Final Results on the Test of the General Hypothesis," *American Sociological Review*, 20 (October, 1955), pp. 552–555; R. F. Winch, *Mate-Selection*, New York: Harper & Bros., 1958.

Some studies have employed subjects in both the premarital and married stages of the relationship: J. A. Schellenberg and L. S. Bee, "A Re-Examination of the Theory of Complementary Needs in Mate Selection," *Marriage and Family Living*, 22 (August, 1960) pp. 227–232; J. A. Schellenberg, "Homogamy in Personal Values and the 'Field of Eligibles'," *Social Forces*, 39 (December, 1960), pp. 157–162; E. W. Burgess, and P. Wallin, "Homogamy in Personality Characteristics," *Journal of Abnormal and Social Psychology*, 39 (October, 1944), pp. 475–484.

There are also quite a number of studies bearing on the general issues of factors determining selective association. Among the most relevant of these are: J. Altrocchi, "Dominance as a Factor in Interpersonal Choice and Perception," *Journal of Abnormal and Social Psychology*, 59 (November, 1959), pp. 303–308; L. R. Hoffman, "Similarity in Personality: A Basis for Interpersonal Attraction?" *Sociometry*, 21 (December, 1958), pp. 300–308; C. E. Izard, "Personality Similarity and Friendship," *Journal of Abnormal and Social Psychology*, 51 (July, 1960), pp. 47–51; E. E. Jones and B. N. Daugherty, "Political Orientation and the Perceptual Effect of Anticipated Interaction," *Journal of Abnormal and Social Psychology*, 59 (November, 1959), pp. 340–349; G. Lindzey and inconsistent results at times, the most general conclusion suggested by these data is that individuals who are similar to each other are most likely to choose each other as mates and are most likely to be successful in the relationship. Similarities have been noted in a large number of characteristics such as area of residence, socioeconomic level, religious affiliation and activity, and many kinds of attitudes and values. This tendency toward homogamy in mate selection, however, is not the only tendency noted in the literature. A strong case has been made, for instance, for the proposition that heterogamy or complementarity of personality needs is an important principle of selection. Winch[2] has indicated that those variables normally associated with the theory of homogamy in mate selection simply define the "field of eligibles" from which each individual then chooses a mate who is likely to complement himself on the personality level.

The present study is intended as a contribution to this body of knowledge. The major innovation it introduces is a longitudinal perspective during the selection period so that further knowledge of the actual selection process is gained. This is in contrast to most of the earlier studies which have compared a number of cases at a single point in time. The present study attempts to examine the relationship between progress in the mate selection process in the premarital period and measures of homogamy and complementarity.

J. A. Urdan, "Personality and Social Choice," *Sociometry*, 17 (February, 1954), pp. 47–63; T. M. Newcomb, "Varieties of Interpersonal Attraction," in D. Cartwright and A. Zander, editors, *Group Dynamics*, Evanston, Ill.: Row, Peterson, 1960, pp. 104–119; J. A. Precker, "Similarity of Valuings as a Factor in Selection of Peers and Near-authority Figures," *Journal of Abnormal and Social Psychology*, 47 (April, 1952), pp. 406–414; W. C. Schutz, *FIRO: A Three-Dimensional Theory of Interpersonal Behavior*, New York: Rinehart, 1958; H. Zimmer, "Motivational Factors in Dyadic Interaction," *Journal of Personality*, 24 (March, 1956), pp. 251–262.

In addition to the discussions to be found in the empirical studies, important theoretical analyses relevant to the problem of selective association may be found in A. M. Katz and R. Hill, "Residential Propinquity and Marital Selection: A Review of Theory, Method, and Fact," *Marriage and Family Living*, 20 (February, 1958), pp. 27–35; I. Rosow, "Issues in the Concept of Need-Complementarity," *Sociometry*, 20 (September, 1957), pp. 216–223; J. W. Thibaut and H. H. Kelley, *The Social Psychology of Groups*, New York: Wiley, 1959, pp. 31–50.

Other relevant studies would include: H. M. Richardson, "Studies of Mental Resemblance Between Husbands and Wives and Between Friends," *Psychological Bulletin*, 36 (February, 1939), pp. 104–120; P. F. Lazarsfeld and R. K. Merton, "Friendship as a Social Process," in M. Berger, T. Abel, and C. H. Page, editors, *Freedom and Control in Modern Society*, New York: Van Nostrand, 1954, pp. 18–66; E. Gross, "Symbiosis and Consensus as Integrative Factors in Small Groups," *American Sociological Review*, 21 (April, 1956), pp. 174–179; W. Kernodle, "Some Implications of the Homogamy-Complementary Needs Theories of Mate Selection for Sociological Research," *Social Forces*, 38 (December, 1959), pp. 145–152.

[2] *Op. cit.*, 1958.

METHOD

In October, 1959 an attempt was made to enlist the cooperation of a number of women students at Duke University as participants in this study. This was done both through calling a meeting for this purpose and through making the study instruments available in the dormitories. Women who were engaged, pinned or "seriously attached" were asked to participate. The latter term was used to refer to those who were seriously considering marriage even though not actually pinned or engaged. Since the women were told that the man would be asked to take part also, we assume the group was limited to those who were fairly confident of the relationship. The women filled out an extended questionnaire (including materials not reported here) and gave us the names and addresses of their fiancés or boy-friends. The same questionnaire was sent to the men by mail. One hundred and sixteen women filled out the questionnaire, and 103 of their boy-friends returned completed questionnaires. In May of 1960 both members of the 103 couples on whom we had complete October data were sent another short questionnaire. Data for the present report on 94 couples[3] were derived from these returns.

Four factors were considered in the analysis. The dependent variable was the degree of movement toward a permanent union between October and May. The two independent variables were: (1) the degree of consensus between the man and woman on family values, and (2) the degree of need complementarity. In addition, the length of time the couple had been going together was used as a control variable since it was expected that the relationship of either or both of the independent variables with the dependent variable might differ at different stages of the mate selection process.

Two hypotheses guided the analysis:

1. Degree of value consensus is positively related to progress toward a permanent union.

2. Degree of need complementarity is positively related to progress toward a permanent union.

The variables were measured as follows:

Progress toward a permanent union. In May the subjects were asked: "Is the relationship (between you two) different from what it was last fall when you filled out the first questionnaire?" There were three possible re-

---

[3] An examination of the data on the thirteen women whose partners did not respond indicates that no systematic bias was apparent. However, it seems likely that these thirteen men were not as serious about the relationship as were those who did respond. It is also likely that most of the nine couples for whom we do not have complete information in May are cases of "failures," although this could not be clearly predicted from the October data.

sponses: "Yes, we are farther from being a permanent couple," "No, it is the same," and "Yes, we are nearer to being a permanent couple." Since only twelve gave the first response, the sample was divided into those who said they were *closer* to being a permanent couple (56 couples) vs. all others (38 couples). This factor will be referred to as "progress toward permanence."[4]

Value consensus. Bernard Farber's "index of consensus" was used for this purpose. As in Farber's original work, both members of the couple were asked (in October) to rank order ten standards by which family success might be measured.[5] The rank correlation between the two sets of rankings was the index of consensus. The distribution of correlation coefficients is presented in Table 1.

TABLE 1. DISTRIBUTION OF SPEARMAN RANK CORRELATION
COEFFICIENTS FOR VALUE CONSENSUS

Coefficient	Frequency	
Below — .40	1	
— .21 to — .40	3	
— .01 to — .20	10	Low
.00 to .19	11	
.20 to .39	21	
.40 to .59	25	
.60 to .79	14	High
.80 & above	9	
Total	94	

Need complementarity. William Schutz's FIRO-B scales were used in the October questionnaire.[6] There are six of these scales consisting of nine items each. Each scale is concerned with one of the content variables which Schutz calls "inclusion," "control," and "affection," and each is also concerned with either the desire to have others act in some way toward one's self or the desire to act in some way toward others. These two directions are called "wanted" and "expressed" by Schutz. Before computing the complementarity scores for each couple, the scalability of the six scales was tested. It was found that it was necessary to reduce the size of the scales to five items each in order to arrive at equal-sized scales which met the

---

4 Here, as in all other such cases, if the man and woman did not agree, the most conservative choice was made. That is, if one said they were closer to being a permanent couple and the other said the relationship was the same, the couple was recorded as *not* closer to being permanent. Although there were not many such cases, they are an indication of the problems encountered when using individual responses to form a group response. The decision made here was based on the argument that if either of them was in doubt about being closer, it was questionable that they were in fact closer.

5 The items are published in: "An Index of Marital Integration," *Sociometry,* 20 (June, 1957), pp. 117–134.

6 *Op. cit.,* pp. 58–65.

scaling criteria[7] for both men and women separately.[8] Using the scale scores on the six five-item scales, need complementarity was computed using Schutz's formula for what he calls "reciprocal compatibility." The formula is $rk_{ij} = | e_i - w_j | + | e_j - w_i |$ where e_i and w_i are the expressed and wanted scores of the man and e_j and w_j are the expressed and wanted scores of the woman. A separate rk was computed for each need area (inclusion, control, and affection). Since the scale scores varied from 0 to 5, it was possible for rk to assume values of from 0 to 10, lower values indicating greater complementarity.[9] The distribution of these scores is shown in Table 2.

Length of association. For the purposes of this analysis, couples were divided into approximately equal groups, the "long-term" group having gone together for 18 months or more, the "short-term" group having gone together less than 18 months.

RESULTS

Since the dependent variable was a dichotomy and since the independent variables could not be assumed to be more than ordinal scales, the form of analysis used was the test of significance of the difference in the proportions of couples showing progress toward permanence in the categories defined by the hypotheses. In all tests, the distributions of cases on the in-

[7] The scaling method used and the criteria applied are those outlined by Robert N. Ford, "A Rapid Scoring Procedure for Scaling Attitude Questions," in Matilda White Riley, John W. Riley, Jr., and Jackson Toby, editors, *Sociological Studies in Scale Analysis,* New Brunswick, New Jersey: Rutgers University Press, 1954.

[8] This reduction was also effected because we were in doubt about the justifiability of including in the same scale two items which differed only in the form of the response categories and the cut points among these categories. For instance, Schutz uses the following as two separate items in the same scale, the slash line indicating the cut point: "I like people to act close toward me: most people, many people, / some people, a few people, one or two people, nobody." "I like people to act close toward me: usually, / often, sometimes, occasionally, rarely, never." All such duplications were left out of the final five-item scales.

[9] Schutz also offers two other compatibility formulae. One is called "interchange compatibility," the formula for which is: $xk = (e_i + w_i) - (e_j + w_j)$. The second is called "originator compatibility," the formula for which is: $ok = (e_i - w_i) + (e_j - w_j)$. The possible range of the first, using our scales, is 0 to 10, the possible range for the second is −10 to +10. Neither of these measures seems to involve the reasoning normally used in discussions of need complementarity. The first simply takes the overall quantity of a particular need area (wanted *and* expressed) for one person and compares it with the overall quantity for the other person. Thus, for instance, a woman's high need for control by others can be balanced off with the man's high need for control by others, which would be the opposite of what is normally called complementarity. The second formula gives the balance between the *excess* of e or w one person has in an area and the excess of the other person. It includes the confounding factor of balance *within* each individual which is of doubtful utility for our purposes. In contrast, the formula we used seems to be exactly the kind of measure called for by the concept of complementarity. As Winch puts it, two people are complementary "when A's behavior in acting out A's need X is gratifying to B's need Y and B's behavior in acting out B's need Y is gratifying to A's need X." (*Op. cit.,* 1958, p. 93.)

TABLE 2. DISTRIBUTION OF NEED COMPLEMENTARITY
SCORES OF CONTENT AREA

Score	Inclusion	Control	Affection	
0	6	6	2	⎫
1	12	13	12	⎬ High
2	13	18	23	⎭
3	22	20	21	⎫
4	15	12	16	⎪
5	13	11	7	⎪
6	9	10	9	⎬ Low
7	3	3	2	⎪
8	1	1	1	⎪
9	0	0	1	⎪
10	0	0	0	⎭
Total	94	94	94	

TABLE 3. PROPORTIONS OF COUPLES INDICATING PROGRESS BY VALUE CONSENSUS
AND NEED COMPLEMENTARITY COMBINED   (TOTAL $P = .596$)

(A) *Value consensus and inclusion complementarity*

	High consensus	Low consensus	Groups compared	Significance of difference
High comp.	.760 (25)	.571 (28)	HH > LL	.01
			HH > HL	—
			HH > LH	.10
Low comp.	.696 (23)	.278 (18)	HL > LL	.01
			LH > LL	.10

(B) *Value consensus and control complementarity*

	High consensus	Low consensus	Groups compared	Significance of difference
High comp.	.692 (26)	.636 (11)	HH > LL	.05
			*HH < HL	—
			HH > LH	—
Low comp.	.773 (22)	.400 (35)	HL > LL	.01
			LH > LL	.10

(C) *Value consensus and affection complementarity*

	High consensus	Low consensus	Groups compared	Significance of difference
High comp.	.750 (16)	.571 (21)	HH > LL	.01
			HH > HL	—
			HH > LH	—
Low comp.	.718 (32)	.360 (25)	HL > LL	.01
			LH > LL	.10

Note: The cell frequency is presented in parentheses in each cell. In the cell comparisons the value consensus measure is listed first in all cases. Thus, HL means high consensus, low complementarity.

* The asterisk marks the single reversal of direction of relationship from that predicted.

TABLE 4. PROPORTIONS OF COUPLES INDICATING PROGRESS BY VALUE CONSENSUS, NEED COMPLEMENTARITY AND LENGTH OF ASSOCIATION (TOTAL $P = .596$)

(A) *Value consensus*

	High consensus	Low consensus	Significance of difference
Short-term	.783 (23)	.350 (20)	.01
Long-term	.680 (25)	.538 (26)	—
Total	.729 (48)	.457 (46)	.01

(B) *Inclusion complementarity*

	High comp.	Low comp.	Significance of difference
Short-term	.560 (25)	.611 (18)	—
Long-term	.750 (28)	.435 (23)	.02
Total	.660 (53)	.512 (41)	.10

(C) *Control complementarity*

	High comp.	Low comp.	Significance of difference
Short-term	.588 (17)	.577 (26)	—
Long-term	.750 (20)	.516 (31)	.05
Total	.676 (37)	.544 (57)	.10

(D) *Affection complementarity*

	High comp.	Low comp.	Significance of difference
Short-term	.588 (17)	.577 (26)	—
Long-term	.700 (20)	.548 (31)	—
Total	.649 (37)	.561 (57)	—

Note: The n on which each proportion is based is presented in parentheses after the proportion.

dependent and control variables were dichotomized as close to the median as possible. One-tailed tests were used.

When the simple relationships between the independent and the dependent variables were tested, only that between value consensus and progress in the relationship proved to be statistically significant at the .05 level or better. Two of the measures of complementarity (inclusion and control) approached this level of significance, however, and the third relationship was in the predicted direction. (These relationships are reported in the "Total" rows of Table 4.) Although these findings lead to the tentative acceptance of the first hypothesis and the rejection of the second, further analysis presents a somewhat different picture.

As we have noted, all four of the differences in the "Totals" rows of Table 4 are in the predicted direction. It may also be argued that *if* the two hypotheses being tested are true, we should find a general pattern of relationships among the categories of couples defined by a combination of the two types of independent variables (homogamy and complementarity). This pattern should be: HH > Mixed > LL. (Since the original hypotheses did not include a statement about the relative importance of the two independent variables, there is no basis for predicting a difference between the HL and LH cases within the Mixed category.) Table 3 indicates that, with one exception, this pattern is found in each of the combinations of value consensus with one of the complementarity measures. In all three sets of comparisons, the difference between the HH and the LL cases approaches significance.[10] Although this table does not provide unequivocal support for the hypotheses, it does present a rather consistent pattern of relationships which may be derived from those hypotheses.

The introduction of the control variable of length of association provides even more information about the adequacy of the hypotheses. The data relevant here are provided in Table 4. In all four cases, the introduction of the control variable points up a difference in the pattern for short-term and long-term couples. Most interesting is the fact that the pattern is consistently different for value consensus and the three measures of need complementarity.

The relationship between value consensus and progress toward permanence is still significant for the short-term couples as it was for the total sample. However, for the long-term couples, although the direction of the relationship remains the same, the degree of significance falls even below the .10 level. On the other hand, when the relationships between progress toward permanence and the three measures of complementarity are examined, the reverse is true. For the short-term couples there is no hint of a relationship between complementarity and progress toward permanence. But for the long-term couples the relationship is significant at the .02 level in the inclusion area and at the .05 level in the control area. In the affection area the direction of the relationship is the same, but it is not statistically significant.[11]

Although it had originally been considered necessary to control for length of association while examining the relationship between the independent and dependent variables, the particular pattern of relationships which was

[10] The consistency of the pattern is of particular note given the fact that the three complementarity values are not highly correlated. The Pearsonian coefficient for Inclusion-Affection is .332, for Inclusion-Control it is − .105, and for Affection-Control it is − .018. Only the first deviates significantly from zero.

[11] It may be worth noting also that both long-term and short-term couples experienced progress toward permanence in about the same proportions. This may seem surprising at first since we would expect that the long-term couples were originally more committed to the relationship and would have less "distance" to move in the seven months. However, when one remembers that the measure of progress is a subjective one, it becomes apparent that, even if the long-term couples were objectively closer to a permanent union in October, their sense of progress would be a function of the expectations for *that* stage of the mate selection process. Not only would we expect that objective and subjective "distances" might not be directly comparable, it is also important to remember that the measure is a very crude one differentiating only between progress and no progress rather than between amounts of progress or "distances."

found had not been hypothesized. The original hypotheses simply dealt with the overall relationship between progress toward permanence and value consensus and the three measures of complementarity. Thus, it is not possible to state that the original hypotheses were clearly either confirmed or denied by the data, although value consensus was significantly related to progress toward permanence for the total sample.

DISCUSSION

If we accept the pattern of relationships discussed above as significant for the research enterprise, two further issues remain: (1) How do we interpret or explain the pattern of relationships noted? (2) How does this research fit into the body of knowledge about the process of mate selection?

Turning to the first question, it is necessary to argue on a somewhat ad hoc basis since the specific pattern of relationships found had not been explicitly predicted. However, the pattern does fit rather well with some earlier work in the field of inquiry. It was noted above that Winch speaks of the "field of eligibles" from which one presumably chooses a spouse who complements one's personality needs. In his discussion of the concept "field of eligibles" Winch says:

> There is a set of variables upon which homogamy has been shown to function: race, religion, social class, broad occupational grouping, location of residence, income, age, level of education, intelligence, etc. It is my opinion that these variables function to select for each of us the sort of people with whom we shall be most likely to interact, to assure that the people with whom we otherwise associate are more or less like us with respect to that set of variables and also with respect to cultural interests and values.[12]

Although neither this particular passage nor others in Winch's writings make the point explicit, he seems to be lumping social structure variables and attitude and value variables together in his discussion. The expectation that the two kinds of variables would be highly correlated is a reasonable one, but, we would argue, further understanding of the selection process might be gained if we examined the concept "field of eligibles" more closely.

The present study indicates that such a blanket statement concerning the homogamy variables may give a misleading image of the mate selection process. The homogamy variable discussed above is value consensus. However, other measures of homogamy were also made in this study, such as education, religion, and father's occupation. It is of interest to note that such social categories did not discriminate effectively among the couples. That is, the subjects of this study were very homogamous with respect to

[12] *Op. cit.,* p. 14.

social attributes.[13] On the other hand, the use of the more individual measure of values reported here led to a much clearer discrimination among the couples, as indicated in Table 1, although even here the degree of homogamy is notable.

Thus, a different kind of homogamy is evidently represented by family value consensus than by similarity in social characteristics. Evidently the couples of the present study had *already* limited their field of eligibles with respect to social characteristics but were far from having limited it with respect to value consensus.

This leads us to the tentative suggestion that there are various "filtering factors" operating during the mate selection period. The social attributes presumably operate at an early stage, but values and needs are more clearly operative later on.

Our data do not fit neatly into the logic of a serial set of filtering factors, however. If they did, and if we assume that social attributes, value consensus, and complementarity operate in that order, we would expect a significantly higher proportion of high value consensus couples in the long-term group, since many of the low consensus couples would have broken up (been filtered out) in the early stages of courtship. This is not the case. What we do find is that *if* the couple survives the earlier stages despite having low value consensus, they are more likely than short-term low consensus couples to progress toward permanence, and this greater likelihood is largely explained by the variable of complementarity.

This may be seen in part from the fact (see Table 4) that long-term low consensus couples show progress more often than short-term low consensus couples (.538 *vs.* .350). If the low consensus couples are sorted according to *both* length of association *and* one measure of complementarity, however, it is even more striking. Table 5 shows this analysis. In the case of each measure of complementarity, there is a negligible difference in the short-term row but a very sizeable difference in the long-term row. Thus, complementarity evidently does have a differential effect in long-term and short-term low consensus couples. What remains unspecified is the mechanism through which some short-term low consensus couples manage to stay together.

---

[13] The degree of homogamy is evidenced by the following: (1) Seventy per cent of the couples had the same level of education. If we accept as homogamous those cases in which the man has graduated from college and is no longer in school and the woman is still in college, only fourteen remain. Of these fourteen, ten are cases of men in graduate school and women in college and only four are cases of women in college and men who are high school graduates. (2) Eighty-seven per cent of the couples are members of the same religious groups (Protestant, Catholic, Jew). Forty per cent report the same rate of attendance at services and 83 per cent are within one category on a five-point scale ranging from "never attend" to "four or more times a month." (3) Using Hollingshead's seven-category classification of occupations, the fathers of the man and woman are in the same category in 45 per cent of the cases; in 76 per cent of the cases they are in the same or adjacent categories.

TABLE 5. PROPORTIONS OF LOW CONSENSUS COUPLES SHOWING PROGRESS BY LENGTH OF ASSOCIATION AND NEED COMPLEMENTARITY (TOTAL P = .467)

	Inclusion		Control		Affection	
	High	Low	High	Low	High	Low
Short term	.357 (14)	.333 (6)	.400 (5)	.333 (15)	.333 (9)	.364 (11)
Long term	.786 (14)	.250 (12)	.833 (6)	.450 (20)	.750 (12)	.357 (14)

Note: The n on which each proportion is based is presented in parentheses after the proportion.

However, even if this question were answered adequately, our data raise another question about the order of influence of these filtering factors, namely: How does it happen that the filtering effects of need complementarity are not noticeable until the later stages of courtship? Although our data do not provide a wholly satisfactory answer to this question either, some light may be shed on the issue. One of the measures used in the October questionnaire was the other half of Farber's "Index of Marital Integration," the measure of value consensus being the first half. This second measure involves the rating of one's self and of one's partner on a set of personality characteristics. Some of these characteristics are "negative," such as "irritable," "stubborn," "easily excited," etc. Scores are computed for each person according to the number and intensity of such negative personality traits he attributes to his partner. If we sum the two scores for the couple, we have a measure of negative person perception in the couple or what Farber calls "an index of role tension."

When we analyze these scores according to the length of association, we find that short-term couples have much lower scores than long-term couples. That is, short-term couples were less likely to attribute negative personality characteristics to each other than were long-term couples. Also, there is a greater tendency for the person perception scores of short-term couples to become *more* negative between October and May, even when we hold original scores constant. This seems to be in keeping with the point so often stressed in the literature that couples go through a period of idealization and perception distortion which may lead to disillusionment (or "reality shock") at a later date.

In the light of our other findings, we would interpret this to mean that the short-term couples were likely to be responding to an idealized version of the love object which would make the effectiveness of any personality complementarity less probable. They were responding to a stylized role relationship rather than to another personality. Not until the idealization is destroyed can they interact at the more realistic level of personality, and only then can need complementarity "make a difference" in the relationship.

We may now turn to our other question: How does this research fit into the body of knowledge about the process of mate selection? First, the research gives added support for both the homogamy and complementarity theories, and it provides a tentative statement of the relationship between these two during the selection process.

Second, rather than simply comparing married or engaged couples with a random pairing of other individuals in order to show greater complementarity in the couples, this study attempts to demonstrate that complementarity "makes a difference" in the actual selection process. So far as we know, this is the first time such a longitudinal perspective has been provided.

Third, this is the first study of mate selection in which paper and pencil measures have pointed to a significant contribution of complementarity in the selection process. One of the criticisms of Winch's work has been that his measures were not adequately freed of rater bias.[14] On the other hand, one of Winch's criticisms of other attempts to test the importance of complementarity with paper and pencil instruments has been that such instruments are not sufficiently sensitive to tap the relevant need area.[15] Although there may be some disagreement over the adequacy of our operational definitions of the needs involved, the fact remains that this study has been more successful in showing a contribution of complementarity than any other of its kind.[16]

Finally, although the present study has added to our knowledge, it still leaves many unanswered questions which are also left unanswered by earlier studies. One of the most critical of these is the question of the importance or the salience of the needs being studied. In order for complementarity to make much of a difference in the selection process, one would expect that the needs involved must be of some importance to the individuals. Neither the present study nor the earlier ones has provided a means of determining the salience of the needs. It would be possible with the present measuring devices to use the intensity dimension of Guttman scaling as a measure of salience, but with such a small sample the simultaneous control of another variable in addition to those already included would not be feasible.

SUMMARY

We have reported on the findings of a study in which measures of value consensus and need complementarity have been shown to be related to a sense of progress toward permanence during a seven-month interval in the mate selection period. Although only value consensus was related to pro-

[14] Cf. H. Zimmer, op. cit.

[15] Winch, op. cit., 1958, p. 83, footnote. Winch is referring to the Edwards Personal Preference Schedule here, but presumably his point is a more general one.

[16] We have purposely avoided a discussion of the concept "need" in this article. It is defined in so many different ways in the literature that we feel it best to let the operational definition stand on its own feet rather than attempting to add still another definition. Let it suffice to note that Schutz refers to his scales as measures of "interpersonal needs," but they are certainly a very different kind of measure than that provided by the TAT.

gress toward permanence for the sample as a whole, when the sample was divided into long-term and short-term couples, value consensus was related to progress for the short-term couples and two of three measures of complementarity were related to progress for the long-term couples. These findings are interpreted as indicating that a series of "filtering factors" operate in mate selection at different stages of the selection process. Our data generally support the idea that social status variables (class, religion, etc.) operate in the early stages, consensus on values somewhat later, and need complementarity still later. Our interpretation of the delay in the operation of the complementarity factor is that such personality linkages are often precluded by the unrealistic idealization of the loved one in the early stages of courtship.

C. Relationships with Other Institutions

It is inconceivable to many that a major social institution could pass from the scene. Everyone is raised in some sort of a family and probably believes that everyone else ought to be. Courts still talk about the importance of keeping the child in the home, whether it be foster or kindred. The rapidly rising divorce rates, however, call all this in question. Is the family, as we know it, inevitable? Barrington Moore asks this question and others. It can be seen that changes in other institutions radically affect the functions of the family.

37 BARRINGTON MOORE, JR.

Thoughts on the Future of the Family

Among social scientists today it is almost axiomatic that the family is a universally necessary social institution and will remain such through any foreseeable future. Changes in its structure, to be sure, receive wide recognition. The major theme, however, in the appraisal American sociologists present is that the family is making up for lost economic functions by providing better emotional service. One work announces as its central thesis that "the family in historical times has been, and at present is, in transition from an institution to a companionship." In the past, the authors explain, the forces holding the family together were external, formal, and authoritarian, such as law, public opinion, and the authority of the father. Now, it is claimed, unity inheres in the mutual affection and comradeship of its members. Another recent work by a leading American sociologist makes a similar point. The trend under industrialism, we are told, does not constitute a decline of the family as such, but mainly a decline of its importance in the performance of economic functions. Meanwhile, the author tells us, the family has become a more specialized agency for the performance of other functions, namely, the socialization of children and the stabilization of adult personalities. For this reason, the author continues, social arrangements corresponding rather closely to the modern family may be expected to remain with us indefinitely.

In reading these and similar statements by American sociologists about other aspects of American society, I have the uncomfortable feeling that the authors, despite all their elaborate theories and technical research devices, are doing little more than projecting certain middle-class hopes and ideals onto a refractory reality. If they just looked a little more carefully at what was going on around them, I think they might come to different conclusions. This is, of course, a very difficult point to prove, though C. Wright Mills, in a brilliant essay, has shown how one area of American sociology, the study of crime, is suffused with such preconceptions. While personal observations have some value, one can always argue that a single observer is biased. Here all I propose to do, therefore, is to raise certain questions about the current sociological assessment of the family on the basis of such evidence as has come my way rather casually. In addition, I should like to set this evidence in the framework of an intellectual tradition, represented, so far as the family is concerned, by Bertrand Russell's *Marriage and Morals,* that sees the family in an evolutionary perspective, and raises the possibility that it may be an obsolete institution or become one before long. I would suggest then that conditions have arisen which, in many cases, prevent the family from performing the social and psychological functions ascribed to it by modern sociologists. The same conditions may also make it possible for the advanced industrial societies of the world to do away with the family and substitute other social arrangements that impose fewer unnecessary and painful restrictions on humanity. Whether or not society actually would take advantage of such an opportunity is, of course, another question.

It may be best to begin with one observation that is not in itself conclusive but at least opens the door to considering these possibilities. In discussions of the family, one frequently encounters the argument that Soviet experience demonstrates the necessity of this institution in modern society. The Soviets, so the argument runs, were compelled to adopt the family as a device to carry part of the burden of making Soviet citizens, especially after they perceived the undesirable consequences of savage homeless children, largely the outcome of the Civil War. This explanation is probably an accurate one as far as it goes. But it needs to be filled out by at least two further considerations that greatly reduce its force as a general argument. In the first place, the Soviets, I think, adopted their conservative policy toward the family *faute de mieux*. That is to say, with their very limited resources, and with other more pressing objectives, they had no genuine alternatives. Steel mills had to be built before crèches, or at least before crèches on a large enough scale to make any real difference in regard to child care. In the meantime the services of the family, and especially of grandma (*babushka*), had to be called upon. In the second place, with the consolidation of the regime in the middle thirties, Soviet totalitarianism may have succeeded in capturing the family and subverting this institution to its own uses. At any rate the confidence and vigor with which the regime supported this institution from the early thirties onward suggests such an explanation. Thus the Soviet experience does not constitute by itself very strong evidence in favor of the "functional necessity" of the family.

If the Soviet case does not dispose of the possibility that the family may be obsolete, we may examine other considerations with greater confidence, and begin by widening our historical perspective. By now it is a familiar observation that the stricter Puritan ethics of productive work and productive sex have accomplished their historical purposes in the more advanced sections of the Western world. These developments have rendered other earlier elements of Western culture and society, such as slavery, quite obsolete, and constitute at least prima facie evidence for a similar argument concerning the family. Let us ask then to what extent may we regard the family as a repressive survival under the conditions of an advanced technology? And to what extent does the modern family perform the function of making human beings out of babies and small children either badly or not at all?

One of the most obviously obsolete features of the family is the obligation to give affection as a duty to a particular set of persons on account of the accident of birth. This is a true relic of barbarism. It is a survival from human prehistory, when kinship was the basic form of social organization. In early times it was expedient to organize the division of labor and affection in human society through real or imagined kinship bonds. As civilization became technically more advanced, there has been less and less of a tendency to allocate both labor and affection according to slots in a kinship system, and an increasing tendency to award them on the basis of the actual qualities and capacities that the individual possesses.

Popular consciousness is at least dimly aware of the barbaric nature of the duty of family affection and the pain it produces, as shown by the familiar remark, "You can choose your friends, but you can't choose your

relatives." Even if partly concealed by ethical imperatives with the weight
of age-old traditions, the strain is nevertheless real and visible. Children
are often a burden to their parents. One absolutely un-Bohemian couple
I know agreed in the privacy of their own home that if people ever talked
to each other openly about the sufferings brought on by raising a family
today, the birth rate would drop to zero. It is, of course, legitimate to wonder how widespread such sentiments are. But this couple is in no sense
"abnormal." Furthermore, a revealing remark like this made to a friend
is worth more as evidence than reams of scientific questionnaires subjected
to elaborate statistical analyses. Again, how many young couples, harrassed
by the problems of getting started in life, have not wished that their parents could be quietly and cheaply taken care of in some institution for the
aged? Such facts are readily accessible to anyone who listens to the conversations in his own home or among the neighbors.

The exploitation of socially sanctioned demands for gratitude, when the
existing social situation no longer generates any genuine feeling of warmth,
is a subtle and heavily tabooed result of this barbaric heritage. It is also
one of the most painful. Perhaps no feeling is more excruciating than the
feeling that we ought to love a person whom we actually detest. The Greek
tragedians knew about the problem, but veiled it under religion and mythology, perhaps because the men and women of that time felt there was no
escape. In the nineteenth century the theme again became a dominant one
in European literature, but with the clear implication that the situation was
unnecessary. Even these authors, Tolstoi, Samuel Butler, Strindberg, and
Ibsen, in exposing the horrors and hypocrisies of family life, wove most of
their stories around the marital relationship, where there is an element of
free choice in the partner selected. Kafka's little gem, *Das Urteil*, is a significant exception. With magnificent insight into the tragedy on both sides,
it treats the frustrations of a grown-up son forced to cherish a helpless but
domineering father. Henry James' short story, *Europe*, is an effective treatment of the same relationship between a mother and her daughters. Despite some blind spots and limitations, the artists, it appears, have seen vital
aspects of the family that have largely escaped the sociologists.

In addition to these obsolete and barbaric features one can point to certain trends in modern society that have sharply reduced rather than
increased the effectiveness of the home as an agency for bringing up children. In former times the family was a visibly coherent economic unit, as
well as the group that served to produce and raise legitimate children. The
father had definite and visible economic tasks, before the household became separated from the place of work. When the children could see what
he did, the father had a role to be copied and envied. The source and justification of his authority was clear. Internal conflicts had to be resolved. This
is much less the case now.

It is reasonably plain that today's children are much less willing than those of pre-industrial society to take their parents as models for conduct. Today they take them from the mass media and from gangs. Radio and television heroes, with their copies among neighborhood gangs, now play a vital part in the socialization process. Parents have an uphill and none too successful struggle against these sources. Like adult mobs, children's groups readily adopt the sensational, the cruel, and the most easily understood for their models and standards. These influences then corrupt and lower adult standards, as parents become increasingly afraid to assert their own authority for fear of turning out "maladjusted" children.[1]

The mass media have largely succeeded in battering down the walls of the social cell the family once constituted in the larger structure of society. Privacy has greatly diminished. Newspapers, radios, and television have very largely destroyed the flow of private communications within the family that were once the basis of socialization. Even meals are now much less of a family affair. Small children are frequently plumped down in front of the television set with their supper on a tray before them to keep them quiet. Since the family does less as a unit, genuine emotional ties among its members do not spring up so readily. The advertising campaign for "togetherness" provides rather concrete evidence that family members would rather not be together.

The mother, at least in American society, is generally supposed to be the homemaker and the center of the family. Has she been able to take up the slack produced by the change in the father's role? Is she, perhaps, the happy person whose face smiles at us from every advertisement and whose arts justify the sociologists' case? A more accurate assessment may be that the wife suffers most in the modern middle-class family, because the demands our culture puts upon her are impossible to meet. As indicated by advertisements, fiction, and even the theories of sociologists, the wife is expected to be companion, confidante, and ever youthful mistress of her husband.

If the demands could be met, many wives might feel very happy in this fulfillment of their personality. The actual situation is very different. The father is out of the house all day and therefore can be neither overlord nor companion. With the father absent, radio and television provide the mother with a watery substitute for adult companionship. A young colleague told me recently that his wife leaves the radio on all day merely to hear the sound of a grown-up voice. The continual chatter of little children can be profoundly irritating, even to a naturally affectionate person. The absence of servants from nearly all American middle-class households brings the

---

[1] It is sometimes claimed that the modern family still represents a bulwark against mass and totalitarian pressures. No doubt this is true in the best cases, those few where parents are still able to combine authority and affection. These are, however, mainly a relic of Victorian times. By and large it seems more likely that the family constitutes the "transmission belt" through which totalitarian pressures toward conformity are transmitted to the parents through the influence of the children.

wife face to face with the brutalizing features of motherhood and house-work. If she had the mentality of a peasant, she might be able to cope with them more easily. Then, however, she could not fulfill the decorative functions her husband expects. As it is now, diapers, dishes, and the state of the baby's bowels absorb the day's quota of energy. There is scarcely any strength left for sharing emotions and experiences with the husband, for which there is often no opportunity until the late hours of the evening. It is hardly a wonder that the psychiatrists' anterooms are crowded, or that both husband and wife seek escapes from psychological and sexual bore-dom, the cabin fever of the modern family. For the wife, either a job or an affair may serve equally well as a release from domesticity.

A further sign of the modern family's inadequacy in stabilizing the human personality may be seen in the troubled times of adolescence. This stage of growing up has been interpreted as a rejection of adult standards of responsibility and work by youngsters who are about to enter adult life. It seems to me that this period is more significantly one of pseudo-rebellion, when the youngsters copy what they see to be the real values of adult life instead of the professed ones. Even in the more extreme forms of youthful rebellion, relatively rare among respectable middle-class children, such as roaring around in noisy cars to drinking and seduction parties, the adolescents are aping actual adult behavior. Adolescents then do things they know many grown-ups do when the latter think they are escaping the observant eyes of the young. A "hot-rod" is, after all, nothing but an immature Cadillac. Where the Cadillac is the symbol of success, what else could be expected? Adult standards too are made tolerable through com-mercialized eroticism that lures us on to greater efforts and greater consump-tion from every billboard and magazine cover. Thus the whole miasma of sexual and psychological boredom in the older generation, pseudo-rebellion and brutality in the younger one, is covered over by a sentimental and sug-gestive genre art based on commercial sentiment.

No doubt many will think that these lines paint too black a picture. Statistics could perhaps be accumulated to show that families such as the type sketched here are far from a representative cross-section of American middle-class life. Such facts, however, would not be relevant to the argu-ment. As pointed out elsewhere in these essays, the representative character of certain types of social behavior is not necessarily relevant to estimates of current and future trends. This kind of statistical defense of the status quo represents that of a certain maiden's virtue by the claim, "After all, she is only a little bit pregnant."

To refute the appraisal offered in these pages it would be necessary to demonstrate that they misrepresent basic structural trends in the family in advanced industrial countries. The most important argument of this type that I have encountered asserts that the proportion of married people in the population has steadily risen while the proportion of single individuals has steadily dropped. Therefore, people obviously prefer family life to bachelorhood, and the gloomy picture sketched above must be nothing more than vaporings of sour-bellied intellectuals thrown on the dumpheap by the advance of American society.

Before discussing the question further, let us look at some of the relevant facts. The table below shows changes in the proportions of single, married, and divorced persons in the United States from the age of fourteen onward. The source, an authoritative and very recent statistical survey of the American family, has standardized the proportions for age, using the 1940 age distribution as a standard, in order to eliminate changes due merely to shifts in the age composition of our population, which would merely confuse the issue. The figures do show a rise in the proportion of married persons and a decline in the proportion of single ones. They also show that the proportion of married persons is overwhelmingly larger than the number of divorced ones. But the biggest change has been in the proportion of divorced people. For men it has risen ninefold since 1890 and for women more than fivefold. A bigger proportion of people are married now than in 1890, but a *much* bigger proportion have abandoned the marital state. In the long run, the latter change might turn out to be the more important one.

PERCENTAGE DISTRIBUTION OF PERSONS 14 YEARS AND OVER BY MARITAL STATUS AND SEX IN THE CIVILIAN POPULATION, 1890–1954

Year	Single	Male Married	Divorced	Single	Female Married	Divorced
1954	28.4	66.7	1.8	22	65.8	2.2
1950	29.4	65.5	1.5	22.5	64.8	2.1
1940	34.8	59.7	1.2	27.6	59.5	1.6
1930	34.7	59.1	1.1	26.9	59.7	1.3
1890	36.7	57.9	0.2	27.8	57.7	0.4

Even the statistical evidence, in other words, does not uphold in a completely unambiguous manner the sociologists' argument for the family. Sometimes an attempt to save the case is made by interpreting the rise in divorce as something that allows greater freedom for the individual to choose marital partners on the basis of congeniality. Thereby divorce allegedly strengthens the family's function as a source of emotional support. By talking about greater freedom for the individual in this fashion one has already taken a long step toward the opponents' view that marriage as such may be superfluous.

The point cannot be considered merely in the light of the facts as they exist now or have existed in the past. To do this in social questions is basically unscientific. Those who dismiss negative appraisals of the family with the crude observation that they reflect personal bias or mere "European decadence" deserve an equally crude reply: "So what if Americans prefer to get married! That simply shows how stupid they are."

Acrimony here unfortunately conceals a genuine issue. It is perfectly possible that conditions exist, perhaps even now, that permit better institutional arrangements than most people would be willing to accept. The word better, of course, implies a definite standard of judgment. One can debate such standards endlessly, and perhaps cannot reach agreement without at some point making arbitrary assumptions. I shall not enter this debate here except to say that any social institution is a bad one that imposes more suffering on people than is necessary when they have sufficient material resources and scientific knowledge to do away with this suffering. This standard, anthropologists tell us, is that not only of Western culture, but of all culture.

What then, are the prospects for the future? We need not take a completely determinist view. Indeed, the perceptions that both plain people and opinion makers have about the present enter in as a significant component among the forces shaping the future and thereby provide an entering wedge for rational adaptation.

Among those who accept a substantial part of the preceding image of the family as basically correct, one frequently hears the prescription that what American culture really needs is a higher evaluation of the social role of the housewife and of motherhood. The trouble with this prescription, I would suggest, is that it merely increases the element of self-deception already so prevalent in our culture. Under present conditions motherhood is frequently a degrading experience. There is nothing to be gained by concealing the facts in the manner of an advertising campaign designed to raise the prestige of a particular occupation. We would not think of trying to eliminate the hazards of coal mining in this way. Why should we try to do it with motherhood? If it is true that under present circumstances the experience of motherhood narrows and cramps the personality rather than promotes the development of its capacities, some other way will have to be found if it is to be a real solution.

The trend towards a continually more efficient technology and greater specialization, which dominates the rest of our culture, may conceivably provide an answer. In regard to the division of labor it is important to recall one widely known but neglected fact. In the past, whenever human beings have acquired sufficient resources and power, as among aristocracies, they have put the burden of child-rearing on other shoulders. Twenty years ago Ralph Linton pointed out that "aristocrats the world over . . . are reluctant to take care of their own children. Anyone who has had to take care of two or three infants simultaneously will understand why. This arduous business is turned over to slaves or servants. . . ."

Since the decline of slavery, a basic trend in European society has been to transfer to machines more and more tasks formerly carried out by slaves.

By and large, this change has been accompanied by the growth of large organizations to perform tasks formerly scattered among many small groups. This trend may well affect the family. Specialized human agencies, developing from such contemporary forms as the crèche, play school, and boarding school, might assume a much larger share of the burden of child rearing, a task that could in any case be greatly lightened by machinery for feeding and the removal of waste products. Can one sensibly argue that the technical ingenuity and resources required to solve this problem are greater than those necessary for nuclear warfare? Are we to regard as permanent and "natural" a civilization that develops its most advanced technology for killing people and leaves their replacement to the methods of the Stone Age?

Against this viewpoint it is usually argued that human infants require some minimum of human affection, even fondling, if they are to survive, and that therefore some form of the family is bound to remain. The premises may be correct, but the conclusion does not follow. A nurse can perform these tasks of giving affection and early socialization just as well as the parents, often better. The argument does not prove anything therefore about the inevitable necessity of the family.

At the same time this point of view does call attention to certain important problems. Industrial society is not likely to produce household nurses, or any form of "servant class" in abundance. On the other hand, as everyone knows who has been in a hospital, nurses in a bureaucratic setting have a strong tendency to treat persons under their care "by the book," without much regard for their individual tasks and requirements. This is a well-known trait of bureaucracy, which tends to treat people and situations alike in order to achieve precision and efficiency. Infants and small children on the contrary require individual attention. For some years they may need to feel that they are the center of the universe. How then can the characteristics of bureaucracy be brought in line with those of maternal affection?

Though this may be the most difficult problem facing any qualitative transformation of the family, it is not necessarily insoluble. In the first place, as Bertrand Russell points out, a good institutional environment may be better for the development of the human personality than a bad family one. In the second place, an increase in the resources allocated to a bureaucratic organization can greatly increase its flexibility and capacity to satisfy variations in individual temperament. Any first-class hotel knows how to cope with this problem. In a few of the best ones in Europe the guest can have privacy and the illusion of being the center of the universe. Finally, one might legitimately expect that the persons who are drawn to serve in any such child-rearing institutions of the future would have more than the average amount of fondness for children, as well as general human warmth and kindliness. Under proper circumstances and management such institutions could give full scope to these benevolent sentiments.

Certain other considerations suggest an alternative that has at least the merit of being much more palatable to the vast majority of people today, since it is more in line with our deep-rooted cultural traditions. These considerations are essentially two. One is the possibility of some innate biological trait roughly resembling the "maternal instinct." The other lies in technological developments that might allow for wider dissemination of machinery to lighten household tasks and to take over the more routine aspects of child rearing. The dish-washing machine, laundromat, and, as a much more extreme device, the "Skinner box" represent prototypes of this technological development that could strengthen decentralized arrangements for rearing children.

I do not know what students of human physiology now believe about the maternal instinct. Common observation is enough to show that it cannot be an instinct like sex or hunger. There are many women who never become fond of children, or who soon cease to be fond of them. For them the institutional outlet just sketched would be the most satisfactory way of providing for their offspring. But for others, possibly the majority, the gestation period with its trials and burdens may be enough to create in the mother a desire to retain the infant under her care, after which she could become reluctant to give it up. If machinery were available to lighten child-rearing and household tasks on a far wider scale than is now the case, mothers might be able to satisfy the more positive desires of motherhood. One that seems to be quite important in the middle class is the desire to mold the child according to some ideal image, though it is now contradicted by fears of damaging the child that derive from superficial popularizations of Freud.

For the home to become again the place where human beings take the first important steps toward realizing their creative potentialities, parents would have to become willing once more to assert their authority. In turn this authority would have to acquire a rational and objective basis, freed of current attempts to revive religious taboos. Thus there would have to be a philosophical as well as a social revolution whose implications we cannot here pursue. One aspect, nevertheless, deserves to be stressed. Rational arguments can be given only to persons competent to understand them. For obvious reasons children are not able to absorb all rational arguments at once, though the present system of education undoubtedly postpones the development of this faculty where it does not destroy it altogether. Therefore parents will have to learn not to be afraid of saying to a child, "You are not old enough yet to understand why you have to do this. But you must do it anyway." The "progressive" family, where every decision turns into an incoherent and rancorous debate, actually contributes to reactionary tendencies in society by failing to equip the next generation with adequate standards of judgment.

There are, however, some grounds for doubting that this conservative

solution will eventually prevail as the dominant one. The disappearance of
the wider economic functions of the family would make it very difficult,
and probably impossible, to restore the emotional atmosphere of a cooperative group in which the father has a respected authority. Furthermore, the
bureaucratic division of labor has proved the most effective way of solving
recurring and routine problems in other areas of life. Though a considerable part of the task of raising children is not routine, a very great portion
is repetitive. For these reasons one may expect that semi-bureaucratic arrangements will continue to encroach on the traditional structure of the
family. No doubt many individual variations, combinations, and compromises will remain for some time to come. Yet one fine day human society
may realize that the part-time family, already a prominent part of our social
landscape, has undergone a qualitative transformation into a system of
mechanized and bureaucratized child rearing, cleansed of the standardized
overtones these words now imply. As already pointed out, an institutional
environment can be warm and supporting, often warmer than a family torn
by obligations its members resent.

Such a state of affairs, if it comes at all, is well over the visible horizon
now. Quite possibly it may never come at all. If it does come, there is not
the slightest guarantee that it will solve all personal problems and land
us in a state of air-conditioned euphoria. Values that many people hold
high today may go by the board, such as the affection older couples show
for one another who have shared the same pains in life until they have
grown but a single scar. It is also possible that a world of reduced family
burdens might be one of shallow and fleeting erotic intrigues, based really
on commercial interests. Hollywood could conceivably be the ugly prototype of such a future world, especially in its earlier transitional phases. The
most that might be claimed by any future apologist for such institutions, if
they ever come to pass, is that they gave greater scope to the development
of the creative aspects of the human personality than did the family, which
had begun to damage rather than develop this personality under advancing
industrialism. And the most that can be claimed for the arguments supporting this possibility is that they correspond to some important trends visible
in the family itself as well as in the rest of society. Nevertheless, it would
appear that the burden of proof falls on those who maintain that the family
is a social institution whose fate will differ in its essentials from that which
has befallen all the others.

XIII   THE POLITY

A. Definitions and Concepts

Alexis de Tocqueville's Democracy in America, *published in 1835, was one of the first major attempts at an analysis of power in the United States. De Tocqueville concluded that a tyranny of the majority existed, and rejected the notion that equality necessarily led to freedom. The question of who in America should have power, and how much, is still being asked. Our political institutions are organized around the general principles of a republic, but some theorists have seen the republic as controlled by a small elite, whereas others believe that it is controlled by a variety of special interest groups. Kornhauser, a political sociologist, describes two opposing positions and sets up criteria for analyzing power.*

38   WILLIAM KORNHAUSER

"Power Elite" or "Veto Groups"?

I

In the 50's two books appeared purporting to describe the structure of power in present-day America. They reached opposite conclusions: where C. Wright Mills found a "power elite," David Riesman found "veto groups." Both books have enjoyed a wide response, which has tended to divide

Reprinted with permission of the Macmillan Company from *Culture and Social Character,* edited by Seymour Martin Lipset and Leo Lowenthal. © The Free Press of Glencoe, Inc., 1961.

along ideological lines. It would appear that *The Power Elite* has been most favorably received by radical intellectuals, and *The Lonely Crowd* has found its main response among liberals. Mills and Riesman have not been oblivious to their differences. Mills is quite explicit on the matter: Riesman is a "romantic pluralist" who refuses to see the forest of American power inequalities for the trees of short-run and discrete balances of power among diverse groups. [244][1] Riesman has been less explicitly polemical, but he might have had Mills in mind when he spoke of those intellectuals "who feel themselves very much out of power and who are frightened of those who they think have the power," and who "prefer to be scared by the power structures they conjure up than to face the possibility that the power structure they believe exists has largely evaporated." [257–258][2]

I wish to intervene in this controversy just long enough to do two things: (1) locate as precisely as possible the items upon which Riesman and Mills disagree; and (2) formulate certain underlying issues in the analysis of power that have to be met before such specific disagreements as those between Riesman and Mills can profitably be resolved.

We may compare Mills and Riesman on power in America along five dimensions:

1. Structure of power: how power is distributed among the major segments of present-day American society.

2. Changes in the structure of power: how the distribution of power has changed in the course of American history.

3. Operation of the structure of power: the means whereby power is exercised in American society.

4. Bases of the structure of power: how social and psychological factors shape and sustain the existing distribution of power.

5. Consequences of the structure of power: how the existing distribution of power affects American society.

1. Structure of power. It is symptomatic of their underlying differences that Mills entitles his major consideration of power simply "the power elite," whereas Riesman has entitled one of his discussions "who has the power?" Mills is quite certain about the location of power, and so indicates by the assertive form of his title. Riesman perceives a much more amorphous and indeterminate power situation, and conveys this view in the interrogative form of his title. These contrasting images of American power may be diagrammed as two different pyramids of power. Mills' pyramid of power contains three levels.

[1] Page references in the text for remarks by C. Wright Mills refer to *The Power Elite,* New York: Oxford University Press, 1956.

[2] Page references in the text for remarks by David Riesman refer to *The Lonely Crowd,* New York: Doubleday Anchor, 1953.

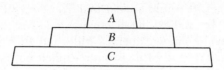

The apex of the pyramid (A) is the "power elite": a unified power group composed of the top government executives, military officials, and corporation directors. The second level (B) comprises the "middle levels of power": a diversified and balanced plurality of interest groups, perhaps most visibly at work in the halls of Congress. The third level (C) is the "mass society": the powerless mass of unorganized and atomized people who are controlled from above.

Riesman's pyramid of power contains only two major levels. The two

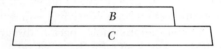

levels roughly correspond to Mills' second and third levels, and have been labeled accordingly. The obvious difference between the two pyramids is the presence of a peak in the one case and its absence in the other. Riesman sees no "power elite," in the sense of a single unified power group at the top of the structure, and this in the simplest terms contrasts his image of power in America with that of Mills. The upper level of Riesman's pyramid (B) consists of "veto groups": a diversified and balanced plurality of interest groups, each of which is primarily concerned with protecting its jurisdiction by blocking efforts of other groups that seem to threaten that jurisdiction. There is no decisive ruling group here, but rather an amorphous structure of power centering in the interplay among these interest groups. The lower level of the pyramid (C) comprises the more or less unorganized public, which is sought as an ally (rather than dominated) by the interest groups in their maneuvers against actual or threatened encroachments on the jurisdiction each claims for itself.

2. *Changes in the structure of power.* Riesman and Mills agree that the American power structure has gone through four major epochs. They disagree on the present and prospective future in the following historical terms: Mills judges the present to represent a fifth epoch, whereas Riesman judges it to be a continuation of the fourth.

The first period, according to Mills and Riesman, extended roughly from the founding of the republic to the Jacksonian era. During this period, Riesman believes America possessed a clearly demarcated ruling group, composed of a "landed-gentry and mercantilist-money leadership." [239] According to Mills, "the important fact about these early days is that social life, economic institutions, military establishment, and political order coincided, and men who were high politicians also played key roles in the economy and, with their families, were among those of the reputable who made up local society." [270]

The second period extended roughly from the decline of Federalist leadership to the Civil War. During this period power became more widely dispersed, and it was no longer possible to identify a sharply defined ruling group. "In this society," Mills writes, "the 'elite' became a plurality of top groups, each in turn quite loosely made up." [270] Riesman notes that farmer and artisan groups became influential, and "occasionally, as with Jackson, moved into a more positive command." [240]

The third period began after the Civil War and extended through McKinley's administration in Riesman's view [240] and until the New Deal according to Mills. [271] They agree that the era of McKinley marked the high point of the unilateral supremacy of corporate economic power. During this period, power once more became concentrated, but unlike the Federalist period and also unlike subsequent periods, the higher circles of economic institutions were dominant.

The fourth period took definite shape in the 1930's. In Riesman's view this period marked the ascendancy of the "veto groups," and rule by coalitions rather than by a unified power group. Mills judges it to have been so only in the early and middle Roosevelt administrations: "In these years, the New Deal as a system of power was essentially a balance of pressure groups and interest blocs." [273]

Up to World War II, then, Mills and Riesman view the historical development of power relations in America along strikingly similar lines. Their sharply contrasting portrayal of present-day American power relations begins with their diverging assessments of the period beginning about 1940. Mills envisions World War II and its aftermath as marking a new era in American power relations. With war as the major problem, there arises a new power group composed of corporate, governmental, and military directors.

> The formation of the power elite, as we may know it, occurred during World War II and its aftermath. In the course of the organization of the nation for that war, and the consequent stabilization of the war-like posture, certain types of man have been selected and formed, and in the course of these institutional and psychological developments, new opportunities and intentions have arisen among them.[3]

Where Mills sees the ascendancy of a power elite, Riesman sees the opposite tendency toward the dispersal of power among a plurality of organized interests:

> There has been in the last fifty years a change in the configuration of power in America, in which a single hierarchy with a ruling

[3] C. Wright Mills, "The Power Elite," in A. Kornhauser, editor, *Problems of Power in American Society*, Detroit: Wayne University Press, 1957, p. 161.

class at its head has been replaced by a number of "veto groups" among which power is dispersed. [239]

The shifting nature of the lobby provides us with an important clue as to the difference between the present American political scene and that of the age of McKinley. The ruling class of business-men could relatively easily (though perhaps mistakenly) decide where their interests lay and what editors, lawyers, and legislators might be paid to advance them. The lobby ministered to the clear leadership, privilege, and imperative of the business ruling class. Today we have substituted for that leadership a series of groups, each of which has struggled for and finally attained a power to stop things conceivably inimical to its interests and, within far narrower limits, to start things. [246–247]

In short, both Mills and Riesman view the current scene from an histor-ical perspective; but where one finds a hitherto unknown *concentration* of power, the other finds an emerging *indeterminacy* of power.

3. *Operation of the structure of power.* Mills believes the power elite sets all important public policies, especially foreign policy. Riesman, on the other hand, does not believe that the same group or coalition of groups sets all major policies, but rather that the question of who exercises power varies with the issue at stake: most groups are inoperative on most issues, and all groups are operative primarily on those issues that vitally impinge on their central interests. This is to say that there are as many power struc-tures as there are distinctive spheres of policy. [256]

As to the modes of operation, both Mills and Riesman point to increasing *manipulation,* rather than command or persuasion, as the favored form of power play. Mills emphasizes the secrecy behind which important policy-determination occurs. Riesman stresses not so much manipulation under the guise of secrecy as manipulation under the guise of mutual tolerance for one another's interests and beliefs. Manipulation occurs, according to Riesman, because each group is trying to hide its concern with power in order not to antagonize other groups. Power relations tend to take the form of "monopolistic competition": "rules of fairness and fellowship [rather than the impersonal forces of competition] dictate how far one can go." [247] Thus both believe the play of power takes place to a considerable extent backstage; but Mills judges this power play to be under the direction of one group, while Riesman sees it as controlled by a mood and structure of accommodation among many groups.

Mills maintains that the mass media of communication are important instruments of manipulation: the media lull people to sleep, so to speak, by suppressing political topics and by emphasizing "entertainment." Riesman alleges that the mass media give more attention to politics and problems of public policy than their audiences actually want, and thereby convey the false impression that there is more interest in public affairs than really exists in America at the present time. Where Mills judges the mass media of communication to be powerful political instruments in American society [315–316], Riesman argues that they have relatively little significance in this respect. [228–231]

4. *Bases of the structure of power.* Power tends to be patterned according to the structure of interests in a society. Power is shared among those whose interests coincide, and divides along lines where interests diverge. To Mills, the power elite is a reflection and solidification of a *coincidence of interests among* the ascendant institutional orders. The power elite rests on the "many interconnections and points of coinciding interests" of the corporations, political institutions, and military services. [19] For Riesman, on the other hand, there is an amorphous power structure, which reflects a *diversity of interests* among the major organized groups. The power structure of veto groups rests on the divergent interests of political parties, business groups, labor organizations, farm blocs, and a myriad of other organized groups. [247]

But power is not a simple reflex of interests alone. It also rests on the capabilities and opportunities for cooperation among those who have similar interests, and for confrontation among those with opposing interests. Mills argues in some detail that the power elite rests not merely on the coincidence of interests among major institutions but also on the "psychological similarity and social intermingling" of their higher circles. [19] By virtue of similar social origins (old family, upper-class background), religious affiliations (Episcopalian and Presbyterian), education (Ivy League college or military academy), and the like, those who head up the major institutions share codes and values as well as material interests. This makes for easy communication, especially when many of these people already know one another, or at least know many people in common. They share a common way of life, and therefore possess both the will and the opportunity to integrate their lines of action as representatives of key institutions. At times this integration involves "explicit co-ordination," as during war. [19–20] So much for the bases of power at the apex of the structure.

At the middle and lower levels of power, Mills emphasizes the lack of independence and concerted purpose among those who occupy similar social positions. In his book on the middle classes,[4] Mills purports to show the weakness of white-collar people that results from their lack of economic independence and political direction. The white-collar worker simply follows the more powerful group of the moment. In his book on labor leaders,[5] Mills located the alleged political impotence of organized labor in its dependence on government. Finally, the public is conceived as composed of atomized and submissive individuals who are incapable of engaging in effective communication and political action. [302 ff.]

Riesman believes that power "is founded, in large measure, on inter-

---

[4] *White Collar*, New York: Oxford University Press, 1951.
[5] *The New Men of Power*, New York: Harcourt, Brace, 1948.

personal expectations and attitudes." [253] He asserts that in addition to the diversity of interest underlying the pattern of power in America there is the psychocultural fact of widespread feelings of weakness and dependence at the top as well as at the bottom of the power structure: "If businessmen feel weak and dependent they do in actuality become weaker and more dependent, no matter what material resources may be ascribed to them." [253] In other words, the amorphousness of power in America rests in part on widespread feelings of weakness and dependence. These feelings are found among those whose position in the social structure provides resources that they could exploit, as well as among those whose position provides less access to the means of power. In fact, Riesman is concerned to show that people at all levels of the social structure tend to feel weaker than their objective position warrants.

The theory of types of conformity that provides the foundation of so much of Riesman's writings enters into his analysis of power at this point. The "other-directed" orientation in culture and character helps to sustain the amorphousness of power. The other-directed person in politics is the "inside-dopester," the person who possesses political competence but avoids political commitment. This is the dominant type in the veto groups, since other-direction is prevalent in the strata from which their leaders are drawn. "Both within the [veto] groups and in the situation created by their presence, the political mood tends to become one of other-directed tolerance." [248] However, Riesman does not make the basis of power solely psychological:

> This does not mean, however, that the veto groups are formed along the lines of character structure. As in a business corporation there is room for extreme inner-directed and other-directed types, and all mixtures between, so in a veto group there can exist complex "symbiotic" relationships among people of different political styles. . . . Despite these complications, I think it fair to say that the veto groups, even when they are set up to protect a clearcut moralizing interest, are generally forced to adopt the political manners of the other-directed. [249]

Riesman and Mills agree that there is widespread apathy in American society, but they disagree on the social distribution of political apathy. Mills locates the apathetic primarily among the lower social strata, whereas Riesman finds extensive apathy in higher as well as lower strata. Part of the difference may rest on what criteria of apathy are used. Mills conceives of apathy as the lack of political meaning in one's life, the failure to think of personal interests in political terms, so that what happens in politics does not appear to be related to personal troubles.[6] Riesman extends the notion of apathy to include the politically uninformed as well as the polit-

---

[6] *White Collar,* p. 327.

ically uncommitted.[7] Thus political indignation undisciplined by political understanding is not a genuine political orientation. Riesman judges political apathy to be an important *basis* for amorphous power relations. Mills, on the other hand, treats political apathy primarily as a *result* of the concentration of power.

5. *Consequences of the structure of power.* Four parallel sets of consequences of the structure of power for American society may be inferred from the writings of Mills and Riesman. The first concerns the impact of the power structure on the interests of certain groups or classes in American society. Mills asserts that the existing power arrangements enhance the interests of the major institutions whose directors constitute the power elite. [276 ff.] Riesman asserts the contrary: no one group or class is decisively favored over others by the culminated decisions on public issues. [257]

The second set of consequences concerns the impact of the structure of power on the quality of politics in American society. Here Mills and Riesman are in closer agreement. Mills maintains that the concentration of power in a small circle, and the use of manipulation as the favored manner of exercising power, lead to the decline of politics as public debate. People are decreasingly capable of grasping political issues, and of relating them to personal interests.[8] Riesman also believes that politics has declined in meaning for large numbers of people. This is not due simply to the ascendancy of "veto groups," although they do foster "the tolerant mood of other-direction and hasten the retreat of the inner-directed indignants." [251] More important, the increasing complexity and remoteness of politics make political self-interest obscure and aggravate feelings of impotence even when self-interest is clear.[9]

The third set of consequences of the American power structure concerns its impact on the quality of power relations themselves. Mills contends that the concentration of power has taken place without a corresponding shift in the bases of legitimacy of power: power is still supposed to reside in the public and its elected representatives, whereas in reality it resides in the hands of those who direct the key bureaucracies. As a consequence, men of power are neither responsible nor accountable for their power. [316–317] Riesman also implies that there is a growing discrepancy between the facts of power and the images of power, but for the opposite reason from Mills: power is more widely dispersed than is generally believed. [257–258]

Finally, a fourth set of consequences concerns the impact of the power structure on democratic leadership. If power tends to be lodged in a small group that is not accountable for its power, and if politics no longer in-

[7] David Riesman and Nathan Glazer, "Criteria for Political Apathy," in Alvin W. Gouldner, editor, *Studies in Leadership,* New York: Harper, 1950.

[8] *White Collar,* pp. 342–350.

[9] "Criteria for Political Apathy," p. 520.

TWO PORTRAITS OF THE AMERICAN POWER STRUCTURE

	Mills	Riesman
Levels	a. Unified power elite	a. No dominant power elite
	b. Diversified and balanced plurality of interest groups	b. Diversified and balanced plurality of interest groups
	c. Mass of unorganized people who have practically no power over elite	c. Mass of unorganized people who have some power over interest groups
Changes	a. Increasing concentration of power	a. Increasing dispersion of power
Operation	a. One group determines all major policies	a. Who determines policy shifts with the issue
	b. Manipulation of people at the bottom by group at the top	b. Monopolistic competition among organized groups
Bases	a. Coincidence of interests among major institutions (economic, military, governmental)	a. Diversity of interests among major organized groups
		b. Sense of weakness and dependence among those in higher as well as lower status
Consequences	a. Enhancement of interests of corporations, armed forces, and executive branch of government	a. No one group or class is favored significantly over others
	b. Decline of politics as public debate	b. Decline of politics as duty and self-interest
	c. Decline of responsible and accountable power — loss of democracy	c. Decline of capacity for effective leadership

volves genuine public debate, then there will be a *severe weakening of democratic institutions,* if not of leadership (the power elite exercises leadership in one sense of the term, in that it makes decisions on basic policy for the nation). Mills claims that power in America has become so concentrated that it increasingly resembles the Soviet system of power:

> Official commentators like to contrast the ascendancy in totalitarian countries of a tightly organized clique with the American system of power. Such comments, however, are easier to sustain if one compares mid-twentieth-century Russia with mid-nineteenth-century America, which is what is often done by Tocqueville-quoting Americans making the contrast. But that was an America of a century ago, and in the century that has passed, the American elite have

> not remained as patrioteer essayists have described them to us. The
> "loose cliques" now head institutions of a scale and power not then
> existing and, especially since World War I, the loose cliques have
> tightened up. [271]

If, on the other hand, power tends to be dispersed among groups that
are primarily concerned to protect and defend their interests rather than
to advance general policies and their own leadership, and if at the same
time politics has declined as a sphere of duty and self-interest, then there
will be a *severe weakening of leadership.* Thus Riesman believes that
"power in America seems to [be] situational and mercurial; it resists attempts to locate it." [257] This "indeterminacy and amorphousness" of
power inhibits the development of leadership: "Where the issue involves
the country as a whole, no individual or group leadership is likely to be
very effective, because the entrenched veto groups cannot be budged."
[257] "Veto groups exist as defense groups, not as leadership groups."
[248] Yet Riesman does not claim that the decline of leadership directly
threatens American democracy, at least in the short run: the dispersion of
power among a diversity of balancing "veto groups" operates to support
democratic institutions even as it inhibits effective leadership. The long
run prospects of a leaderless democracy are of course less promising.

II

In the second part of this paper, I wish to raise certain critical questions
about Riesman's and Mills' images of power. One set of questions seeks to
probe more deeply the basic area of disagreement in their views. A second
set of questions concerns their major areas of agreement.

Power usually is analyzed according to its distribution among the several
units of a system. Most power analysts construe the structure of power as
a *hierarchy* — a rank-order of units according to their amount of power.
The assumption often is made that there is only one such structure, and
that all units may be ranked vis-à-vis one another. Units higher in the
hierarchy have power over units lower in the structure, so there is a one-
way flow of power. Mills tends to adopt this image of the structure of
power.

Riesman rejects this conception of the power structure as mere hierarchy:

> The determination of who [has more power] has to be made all
> over again for our time: we cannot be satisfied with the answers
> given by Marx, Mosca, Michels, Pareto, Weber, Veblen, or Burn-
> ham. [255]
>
> The image of power in contemporary America presented [in *The
> Lonely Crowd*] departs from current discussions of power which
> are usually based on a search for a ruling class. [260]

Riesman is not just denying the existence of a power elite in contemporary American society; he is also affirming the need to consider other aspects of power than only its unequal distribution. He is especially concerned to analyze common responses to power:

> If the leaders have lost the power, why have the led not gained it? What is there about the other-directed man and his life situation which prevents the transfer? In terms of situation, it seems that the pattern of monopolistic competition of the veto groups resists individual attempts at power aggrandizement. In terms of character, the other-directed man simply does not seek power; perhaps, rather, he avoids and evades it. [275]

Whereas Mills emphasizes the *differences* between units according to their power, Riesman emphasizes their *similarities* in this respect. In the first view, some units are seen as dominated by other units, while in the second view, all units are seen as subject to constraints that shape and limit their use of power *in similar directions.*

The problem of power is not simply the differential capacity to make decisions, so that those who have power bind those who do not. Constraints also operate on those who are in decision-making positions, for if these are the places where acts of great consequence occur, so are they the targets for social pressures. These pressures become translated into restrictions on the alternatives among which decision-makers can choose. Power may be meaningfully measured by ascertaining the range of alternatives that decision-makers can realistically consider. To identify those who make decisions is not to say how many lines of action are open to them, or how much freedom of choice they enjoy.

A major advance in the study of power is made by going beyond a formal conception of power, in which those who have the authority to make decisions are assumed to possess the effective means of power and the will to use it. Nor can it be assumed that those not in authority lack the power to determine public policy. The identification of effective sources of power requires analysis of how *decision-makers are themselves subject to various kinds of constraint.* Major sources of constraint include (1) opposing elites and active publics; and (2) cultural values and associated psychological receptivities and resistances to power. A comparison of Mills and Riesman with respect to these categories of constraint reveals the major area of disagreement between them.

Mills implies that both sources of constraint are by and large inoperative on the highest levels of power. (1) There is little opposition among the top power-holders. Since they are not in opposition to one another, they do not constrain one another. Instead, they are unified and mutually supportive. Furthermore, there are few publics to constrain the elite. Groups capable of effective participation in broad policy determination have been replaced by atomized masses that are powerless to affect policy, since they lack the social bases for association and communication. Instead, people in large numbers are manipulated through organizations and media controlled by the elite. (2) Older values and codes no longer grip elites, nor have they been replaced by new values and codes that could regulate the exercise of power. Top men of power are not constrained either by an inner moral sense or by feelings of dependence on others. The widespread permissiveness toward the use of expedient means to achieve success produces "the higher immorality," that is to say, elites that are irresponsible in the use of power.

In sharp contrast to Mills, Riesman attaches great importance to both kinds of constraints on decision-makers. (1) There is a plethora of organized groups, "each of which has struggled for and finally attained a power to stop things conceivably inimical to its interests." [247] Furthermore, there is extensive opportunity for large numbers of people to influence decision-makers, because the latter are constrained by their competitive relations with one another to bid for support in the electoral arena and more diffusely in the realm of public relations. (2) The cultural emphasis on "mutual tolerance" and social conformity places a premium on "getting along" with others at the expense of taking strong stands. People are psychologically disposed to avoid long-term commitments as a result of their strong feelings of dependence on their immediate peers. "Other-directed" persons seek approval rather than power.

In general, the decisive consideration in respect to the restraint of power is the presence of multiple centers of power. Where there are many power groups, not only are they mutually constrained; they also are dependent on popular support, and therefore responsive to public demands. Now, there are many readily observable cases of institutionalized opposition among power groups in American society. In the economic sphere, collective bargaining between management and labor is conflict of this kind; and to the extent that "countervailing power" among a few large firms has been replacing competition among many small firms in the market place, there is a de facto situation of opposition among economic elites. In the political sphere, there is a strong two-party system and more or less stable factionalism within both parties, opposition among interest blocs in state and national legislatures, rivalry among executive agencies of government and the military services, and so forth.

Mills relegates these conflicting groups to the middle levels of power. Political parties and interest groups, both inside and outside of government, are not important units in the structure of power, according to Mills. It would seem that he takes this position primarily with an eye to the sphere of foreign policy, where only a few people finally make the big decisions. But he fails to put his argument to a decisive or meaningful test: he does not examine the pattern of decisions to show that foreign policy not only is made *by* a few people (this, after all, is a constitutional fact), but that it is made *for their particular interests*. Mills' major premise seems to be that all decisions are taken by and for special interests; there is no action oriented toward the general interests of the whole community. Furthermore, Mills seems to argue that because only a very few people occupy key decision-making *positions*, they are free to decide on whatever best suits their particular interests. But the degree of *autonomy* of decision-makers cannot be inferred from the *number* of decision-makers, nor from the *scope* of their decisions. It is determined by the character of decision-making, especially the dependence of decision-makers on certain kinds of *procedure* and *support*.

Just as Mills is presenting a distorted image of power in America when he fails to consider the pressures on those in high positions, so Riesman presents a biased picture by not giving sufficient attention to *power differentials* among the various groups in society. When Riesman implies that if power is dispersed, then it must be relatively equal among groups and interests, with no points of concentration, he is making an unwarranted inference. The following statement conjures up an image of power in America that is as misleading on its side as anything Mills has written in defense of his idea of a power elite.

> One might ask whether one would not find, over a long period of time, that decisions in America favored one group or class . . . over others. Does not wealth exert its pull in the long run? In the past this has been so; for the future I doubt it. The future seems to be in the hands of the small business and professional men who control Congress, such as realtors, lawyers, car salesmen, undertakers, and so on; of the military men who control defense and, in part, foreign policy; of the big business managers and their lawyers, finance-committee men, and other counselors who decide on plant investment and influence the rate of technological change; of the labor leaders who control worker productivity and worker votes; of the black belt whites who have the greatest stake in southern politics; of the Poles, Italians, Jews, and Irishmen who have stakes in foreign policy, city jobs, and ethnic, religious and cultural organizations; of the editorializers and storytellers who help socialize the young, tease and train the adult, and amuse and annoy the aged; of the farmers — themselves a warring congeries of cattlemen, corn men, dairymen, cotton men, and so on — who control key departments and committees and who, as the living representatives of our inner-directed past, control many of our memories; of the Russians and, to a lesser degree, other foreign powers who control much of our agenda of attention; and so on. [257]

It appears that Riesman is asking us to believe that power differentials do not exist, but only differences in the spheres within which groups exercise control.

If Riesman greatly exaggerates the extent to which organized interests possess equal power, nevertheless he poses an important problem that Mills brushes aside. For Riesman goes beyond merely noting the existence of opposition among "veto groups" to suggest that they operate to smother one another's initiative and leadership. It is one thing for interest groups to constrain one another; it is something else again when they produce stalemate. Riesman has pointed to a critical problem of pluralist society: the danger that power may become fragmented among so many competing groups that effective general leadership cannot emerge.

On Mills' side, it is indisputable that American political institutions have undergone extensive centralization and bureaucratization. This is above all an *institutional* change wrought by the greatly expanded scale of events and decisions in the contemporary world. But centralization cannot be equated with a power elite. There can be highly centralized institutions and at the same time a fragmentation of power among a multiplicity of relatively independent public and private agencies. Thus Riesman would appear to be correct that the substance of power lies in the hands of many large organizations, and these organizations are not unified or coordinated in any firm fashion. If they were, surely Mills would have been able to identify the major mechanisms that could produce this result. That he has failed to do so is the most convincing evidence for their nonexistence.

To complete this analysis, we need only remind ourselves of the fundamental area of agreement between our two critics of American power relations. Both stress *the absence of effective political action* at all levels of the political order, in particular among the citizenry. For all of their differences, Mills and Riesman agree that there has been a decline in effective political participation, or at least a failure of political participation to measure up to the requirements of contemporary events and decisions. This failure has not been compensated by an increase in effective political action at the center: certainly Riesman's "veto groups" are not capable of defining and realizing the community's general aspirations; nor is Mills' "power elite" such a political agency. Both are asserting the inadequacy of political associations, including public opinion, party leadership, Congress, and the Presidency, even as they see the slippage of power in different directions. In consequence, neither is sanguine about the capacity of the American political system to provide responsible leadership, especially in international affairs.

If there is truth in this indictment, it also may have its sources in the very images of power that pervade Mills' and Riesman's thought. They are both inclined toward a negative response to power; and neither shows a willingness to confront the idea of a political system and the ends of power in it. Riesman reflects the liberal suspicion of power, as when he writes "we have come to realize that men who compete primarily for wealth are relatively harmless as compared with men who compete primarily for power." That such assertions as this may very well be true is beside the point. For certainly negative consequences of power can subsist alongside of positive ones. At times Riesman seems to recognize the need for people to seek and use power if they as individuals and the society as a whole are to develop to the fullest of their capacities. But his dominant orientation toward power remains highly individualistic and negative.

Mills is more extreme than Riesman on this matter, since he never asks what is socially required in the way of resources of power and uses of power, but instead is preoccupied with the magnitude of those resources and the (allegedly) destructive expropriation of them by and for the higher circles of major institutions. It is a very limited notion of power that construes it only in terms of coercion and conflict among particular interests. Societies require arrangements whereby resources of power can be effectively used and supplemented for public goals. This is a requirement for government, but the use of this term should not obscure the fact that government either commands power or lacks effectiveness. Mills does not concern himself with the *ends* of power, nor with the conditions for their attainment. He has no conception of the bases of political order, and no theory of the functions of government and politics. He suggests nothing that could prevent his "power elite" from developing into a full-blown totalitarianism. The logic of Mills' position finally reduces to a contest between anarchy and tyranny.

The problem of power seems to bring out the clinician in each of us. We quickly fasten on the pathology of power, whether we label the symptoms as "inside-dopesterism" (Riesman) or as "the higher immorality" (Mills). As a result, we often lose sight of the ends of power in the political system under review. It is important to understand that pivotal decisions increasingly are made at the national level, and that this poses genuine difficulties for the maintenance of democratic control. It is also important to understand that a multiplicity of public and private agencies increasingly pressure decision-makers, and that this poses genuine difficulties for the maintenance of effective political leadership. But the fact remains that there have been periods of centralized decision-making *and* democratic control, multiple constraints on power *and* effective leadership. There is no simple relationship between the extent to which power is equally distributed and the stability of democratic order. For a democratic order requires strong government as well as public consent by an informed citizenry. Unless current tendencies are measured against both sets of needs, there will be little progress in understanding how either one is frustrated or fulfilled. Finally, in the absence of more disciplined historical and comparative analysis, we shall continue to lack a firm basis for evaluating such widely divergent diagnoses of political malaise as those given us by Mills and Riesman.

B. Processes and Examples

For Marxians, the hope for a classless society lay with the workers. The working class was supposed to possess the true ideology. When the workers realized this, they were to take action to build a new society. The worker has often been characterized as the "noble savage," a person without guile or malice, with simple motives and desires. On the basis of characteristics like these, utopias could be built. The fact remains that workers, like members of other classes, have supported a variety of political ideologies, whether fascist, democratic, or socialistic. Seymour M. Lipset was one of the first sociologists to emphasize that authoritarianism is extensive among the working classes. Lipset has been criticized for his definitions of authoritarianism, his ideology, and his interpretation of data. The fact remains, however, that the working classes have not always supported the tenets of a democratic, let alone communal, way of life.

39 Seymour Martin Lipset

Working Class Authoritarianism

The gradual realization that extremist and intolerant movements in modern society are more likely to be based on the lower classes than on the middle and upper classes has posed a tragic dilemma for those intellectuals of the democratic left who once believed the proletariat necessarily to be a force for liberty, racial equality, and social progress. The Socialist Italian novelist Ignazio Silone has asserted that "the myth of the liberating power of the proletariat has dissolved along with that other myth of progress. The recent examples of the Nazi labor unions, like those of Salazar and Peron . . . have at last convinced of this even those who were reluctant to admit it on the sole grounds of the totalitarian degeneration of Communism."[1]

Dramatic demonstrations of this point have been given recently by the southern workers' support of White Citizens' Councils and segregation in the United States and by the the active participation of many British

From *Political Man* by Seymour Martin Lipset, pp. 87–126. Copyright © 1960 by Seymour Martin Lipset. Reprinted by permission of the author and Doubleday & Company, Inc.

[1] "The Choice of Comrades," *Encounter*, 3 (December 1954), p. 25. Arnold A. Rogow writing in the Socialist magazine *Dissent* even suggests that "the liberal and radical approach has always lacked a popular base, that in essence, the liberal tradition has been a confined minority, perhaps elitist, tradition." "The Revolt Against Social Equality," *Dissent*, 4 (1957), p. 370.

workers in the 1958 race riots in England. A "Short Talk with a Fascist Beast" (an eighteen-year-old casual laborer who took part in the beating of Negroes in London), which appeared in the left socialist *New Statesman,* portrays graphically the ideological syndrome which sometimes culminates in such behavior. "Len's" perspective is offered in detail as a prelude to an analytical survey of the authoritarian elements of the lower-class situation in modern society.

> "That's why I'm with the Fascists," he says. "They're against the blacks. That Salmon, he's a Communist. The Labour Party is Communist too. Like the unions." His mother and father, he says, are strict Labour supporters. Is he against the Labour Party? "Nah, I'm for them. They're for y'know — us. I'm for the unions too." Even though they were dominated by Communists? "Sure," he says. "I like the Communist Party. It's powerful, like." How can he be for the Communists when the fascists hate them?
>
> Len says, "Well, y'know, I'm for the fascists when they're against the nigs. But the fascists is really for the rich people y'know, like the Tories. All for the guv'nors, people like that. But the Communists are very powerful." I told him the Communist Party of Britain was quite small.
>
> "But," he says, "they got Russia behind them." His voice was full of marvel. "I admire Russia. Y'know, the people. They're peaceful. They're strong. When they say they'll do a thing, they do it. Not like us. Makes you think: they got a weapon over there can wipe us all out, with one wave of a general's arm. Destroy us completely and totally. Honest, those Russians. When they say they'll do a thing, they do it. Like in Hungary. I pity those people, the Hungarians. But did you see the Russians went in and stopped them. Tanks. Not like us in Cyprus. Our soldiers got shot in the back and what do we do? The Communists is for the small man."[2]

Such strikingly visible demonstrations of working-class ethnic prejudice and support for totalitarian political movements have been paralleled in studies of public opinion, religion, family patterns, and personality structure. Many of these studies suggest that the lower-class way of life produces individuals with rigid and intolerant approaches to politics.

At first glance the facts of political history may seem to contradict this. Since their beginnings in the nineteenth century, workers' organizations and parties have been a major force in extending political democracy, and in waging progressive political and economic battles. Before 1914, the classic division between the working-class left parties and the economically privileged right was not based solely upon such issues as redistribution of income, status, and educational opportunities, but also rested upon civil liberties and international policy. The workers, judged by the policies of

[2] Clancy Sigal in the *New Statesman,* October 4, 1958, p. 440.

their parties, were often the backbone of the fight for greater political democracy, religious freedom, minority rights, and international peace, while the parties backed by the conservative middle and upper classes in much of Europe tended to favor more extremist political forms, to resist the extension of the suffrage, to back the established church, and to support jingoistic foreign policies.

Events since 1914 have gradually eroded these patterns. In some nations working-class groups have proved to be the most nationalistic sector of the population. In some they have been in the forefront of the struggle against equal rights for minority groups, and have sought to limit immigration or to impose racial standards in countries with open immigration. The conclusion of the anti-fascist era and the emergence of the cold war have shown that the struggle for freedom is not a simple variant of the economic class struggle. The threat to freedom posed by the Communist movement is as great as that once posed by Fascism and Nazism, and Communism, in all countries where it is strong, is supported mainly by the lower levels of the working class, or the rural population.[3] No other party has been as thoroughly and completely the party of the working class and the poor. Socialist parties, past and present, secured much more support from the middle classes than the Communists have.

Some socialists and liberals have suggested that this proves nothing about authoritarian tendencies in the working class, since the Communist party often masquerades as a party seeking to fulfill the classic Western-democratic ideals of liberty, equality, and fraternity. They argue that most Communist supporters, particularly the less educated, are deceived into thinking that the Communists are simply more militant and efficient socialists. I would suggest, however, the alternative hypothesis that, rather than being a source of strain, the intransigent and intolerant aspects of Communist ideology attract members from that large stratum with low incomes, low-status occupations, and low education, which in modern industrial societies has meant largely, though not exclusively, the working class.

The social situation of the lower strata, particularly in poorer countries with low levels of education, predisposes them to view politics as black and white, good and evil. Consequently, other things being equal, they should be more likely than other strata to prefer extremist movements which suggest easy and quick solutions to social problems and have a rigid outlook.

The "authoritarianism" of any social stratum or class is highly relative, of course, and often modified by organizational commitments to democracy and by individual cross-pressures. The lower class in any given country may be more authoritarian than the upper classes, but on an "absolute" scale all the classes in that country may be less authoritarian than any class in another country. In a country like Britain, where norms of tolerance are

[3] The sources of variation in Communist strength from country to country . . . in relation to the level and speed of economic development [should be noted].

well developed and widespread in every social stratum, even the lowest class may be less authoritarian and more "sophisticated" than the most highly educated stratum in an underdeveloped country, where immediate problems and crises impinge on every class and short-term solutions may be sought by all groups.[4]

Commitments to democratic procedures and ideals by the principal organizations to which low-status individuals belong may also influence these individuals' actual political behavior more than their underlying personal values, no matter how authoritarian.[5] A working class which has developed an early (prior to the Communists) loyalty to democratic political and trade-union movements which have successfully fought for social and economic rights will not easily change its allegiance.

Commitments to other values or institutions by individuals (cross-pressures) may also override the most established predispositions. For example, a French, Italian, or German Catholic worker who is strongly anticapitalist may still vote for a relatively conservative party in France, Italy, or Germany, because his ties to Catholicism are stronger than his resentments about his class status; a worker strongly inclined toward authoritarian ideas may defend democratic institutions against fascist attack because of his links to anti-fascist working-class parties and unions. Conversely, those who are not inclined toward extremist politics may back an extremist party because of certain aspects of its program and political role. Many persons supported the Communists in 1936 and 1943 as an anti-fascist internationalist party.

The specific propensity of given social strata to support either extremist or democratic political parties, then, cannot be predicted from a knowledge of their psychological predispositions or from attitudes inferred from survey data.[6] Both evidence and theory suggest, however, that the lower strata are relatively more authoritarian, that (again, other things being equal) they will be more attracted to an extremist movement than to a moderate and

[4] See Richard Hoggart, *The Uses of Literacy* (London: Chatto and Windus, 1957), pp. 78–79 and 146–48, for a discussion of the acceptance of norms of tolerance by the British working class. E. T. Prothro and Levon Melikian, in "The California Public Opinion Scale in an Authoritarian Culture," *Public Opinion Quarterly*, 17 (1953), pp. 353–63, have shown, in a study of 130 students at the American University in Lebanon, that they exhibited the same association between authoritarianism and economic radicalism as is found among workers in America. A survey in 1951–52 of 1,800 Puerto Rican adults, representative of the entire rural population, found that 84 per cent were "somewhat authoritarian," as compared to 46 per cent for a comparable U.S. population. See Henry Wells, "Ideology and Leadership in Puerto Rican Politics," *American Political Science Review*, 49 (1955), pp. 22–40.

[5] The southern Democrats were the most staunch opponents of McCarthy and his tactics, not because of any deep opposition to undemocratic methods, but rather because of an organizational commitment to the Democratic party.

[6] For a detailed discussion of the fallacy of attempting to suggest that political behavior is a necessary function of political attitudes or psychological traits, see Nathan Glazer and S. M. Lipset, "The Polls on Communism and Conformity," in Daniel Bell, ed., *The New American Right* (New York: Criterion Books, 1955), pp. 141-66.

democratic one, and that, once recruited, they will not be alienated by its lack of democracy, while more educated or sophisticated supporters will tend to drop away.[7]

DEMOCRACY AND THE LOWER CLASSES

The poorer strata everywhere are more liberal or leftist on economic issues; they favor more welfare state measures, higher wages, graduated income taxes, support of trade-unions, and so forth. But when liberalism is defined in non-economic terms — as support of civil liberties, internationalism, etc. — the correlation is reversed. The more well-to-do are more liberal, the poorer are more intolerant.[8]

Public opinion data from a number of countries indicate that the lower classes are much less committed to democracy as a political system than are the urban middle and upper classes. In Germany, for example, a study conducted by the UNESCO Institute at Cologne in 1953 asked a systematic sample of 3,000 Germans: "Do you think that it would be better if there were one party, several parties, or no party?" The results analyzed according to occupational status indicate that the lower strata of the working class and the rural population were less likely to support a multi-party system (a reasonable index of democratic attitudes in Westernized countries) than the middle and upper strata. (See Table 1.)

TABLE 1. RESPONSES OF DIFFERENT GERMAN OCCUPATIONAL GROUPS TO PREFERRED PARTY SYSTEM IN PERCENTAGES[a] (MALES ONLY)

Occupational group	Several parties	One party	No party	No opinion	Total number of persons
Civil servants	88	6	3	3	111
Upper white-collar	77	13	2	8	58
Free professionals	69	13	8	10	38
Skilled workers	65	22	5	8	277
Artisans	64	16	9	11	124
Lower white-collar	62	19	7	12	221
Businessmen (small)	60	15	12	13	156
Farmers	56	22	6	16	241
Semiskilled workers	49	28	7	16	301
Unskilled workers	40	27	11	22	172

[a] Computed from IBM cards supplied to author by the UNESCO Institute at Cologne.

[7] The term "extremist" is used to refer to movements, parties, and ideologies. "Authoritarian" refers to the attitudes and predispositions of individals (or of groups, where a statistical aggregate of *individual* attitudes, and not group characteristics as such, are of concern). The term "authoritarian" has too many associations with studies of attitudes to be safely used to refer also to types of social organizations.

[8] See two articles by G. H. Smith, "Liberalism and Level of Information," *Journal of Educational Psychology,* 39 (1948), pp. 65–82; and "The Relation of 'Enlightenment' to Liberal-Conservative Opinions," *Journal of Social Psychology,* 28 (1948), pp. 3–17.

Comparable results were obtained in 1958 when a similar question was asked of national or regional samples in Austria, Japan, Brazil, Canada, Mexico, West Germany, the Netherlands, Belgium, Italy, and France. Although the proportion favoring a multi-party system varied from country to country, the lower classes within each nation were least likely to favor it.[9]

Surveys in Japan, Great Britain, and the United States designed to secure general reactions to problems of civil liberties, or the rights of various minorities, have produced similar results. In Japan, the workers and the rural population were more authoritarian and less concerned with civil liberties than the middle and upper classes.[10]

In England, the psychologist H. J. Eysenck found comparable differences between people who were "tough-minded" and those who were "tender-minded" in their general social outlook. The first group tended to be intolerant of deviations from the standard moral or religious codes, to be anti-Negro, anti-Semitic, and xenophobic, while the "tender-minded" were tolerant of deviation, unprejudiced, and internationalist.[11] Summing up his findings, based on attitude scales given to supporters of different British parties, Eysenck reported that "middle-class Conservatives are more tender-minded than working-class Conservatives; middle-class Liberals are more tender-minded than working-class Liberals; middle-class Socialists are more tender-minded than working-class Socialists; and even middle-class Communists are more tender-minded than working-class Communists."[12]

The evidence from various American studies is also clear and consistent — the lower strata are the least tolerant.[13] In the most systematic of these,

[9] Based on as yet unpublished data in the files of the World Poll, an organization established by International Research Associates which sponsors comparable surveys in a number of countries. The question asked in this survey was: "Suppose there was a political party here which corresponds to your own opinions — one you would more or less consider 'your' party. Would you wish this to be the only party in our country with no other parties besides, or would you be against such a one-party system?" Similar correlations were found between low status and belief in the value of a strong leader.

[10] See Kotaro Kido and Masataka Sugi, "A Report of Research on Social Stratification and Mobility in Tokyo" (III), *Japanese Sociological Review*, 4 (1954), pp. 74–100; and National Public Opinion Institute of Japan, Report No. 26, *A Survey Concerning the Protection of Civil Liberties* (Tokyo, 1951).

[11] See H. J. Eysenck, *The Psychology of Politics* (London: Routledge and Kegan Paul, 1954), p. 127.

[12] *Ibid.*, p. 137: for a critique of the methodology of this study which raises serious questions about its procedures see Richard Christie, "Eysenck's Treatment of the Personality of Communists," *Psychological Bulletin*, 53 (1956), pp. 411–30.

[13] See Arnold W. Rose, *Studies in Reduction of Prejudice* (Chicago: American Council on Race Relations, 1948), for a review of the literature bearing on this point prior to 1948. Several studies have shown the key importance of education and the independent effect of economic status, both basic components of low status. See Daniel J. Levenson and R. Nevitt Sanford, "A Scale for the Measurement of Anti-Semitism," *Journal of Psychology*, 17 (1944), pp. 339–70, and H. H. Harlan, "Some Factors Affecting Attitudes toward Jews," *American Sociological Review*, 7 (1942), pp. 816–27, for data on attitudes toward one ethnic group. See also James G. Martin and Frank R. Westie, "The Tolerant Personality," *American Sociological Review*, 24 (1959), pp. 521–

based on a national sample of nearly 5,000 Americans, Samuel A. Stouffer divided his respondents into three categories, "less tolerant, in-between, and more tolerant," by using a scale based on responses to questions about such civil liberties as the right of free speech for Communists, critics of religion, or advocates of nationalization of industry, and the like. As the data presented in Table 2 demonstrate, tolerance increases with moves up the social ladder. Only 30 per cent of those in manual occupations are in the "most tolerant" category, as contrasted with 66 per cent of the professionals, and 51 per cent of the proprietors, managers, and officials. As in Germany and Japan, farmers are low in tolerance.

TABLE 2. PROPORTION OF MALE RESPONDENTS WHO ARE "MORE TOLERANT" WITH RESPECT TO CIVIL LIBERTIES ISSUES[a]

Professional and semiprofessional	66%	(159)
Proprietors, managers, and officials	51	(223)
Clerical and sales	49	(200)
Manual workers	30	(685)
Farmers or farm workers	20	(202)

[a] Samuel A. Stouffer, *Communism, Conformity and Civil Liberties* (New York: Doubleday & Co., 1955), p. 139. The figures for manual and farm workers were calculated from IBM cards kindly supplied by Professor Stouffer.

The findings of public opinion surveys in thirteen different countries that the lower strata are less committed to democratic norms than the middle classes are reaffirmed by the research of more psychologically oriented investigators, who have studied the social correlates of the "authoritarian personality."[14] Many studies in this area, summarized recently, show a consistent association between authoritarianism and lower-class status.[15] One survey of 460 Los Angeles adults reported that "the working class contains a higher proportion of authoritarians than either the middle or the upper class," and that among workers, those who explicitly identified themselves as "working class" rather than "middle class" were more authoritarian.[16]

Recent research further suggests the possibility of a *negative* correlation between authoritarianism and neuroticism within the lower classes. In general, those who deviate from the standards of their group are more likely to be neurotic than those who conform, so if we assume that authoritarian

28. For a digest of recent research in the field of race relations in the U.S.A., see Melvin M. Tumin, *Segregation and Desegregation* (New York: Anti-Defamation League of B'nai B'rith, 1957).

[14] See Theodore Adorno, *et al.*, *The Authoritarian Personality* (New York: Harper & Bros., 1950). This, the original study, has less consistent results on this point than the many follow-up studies. The authors themselves (p. 178) point to the inadequacy of their sample.

[15] Richard Christie and Peggy Cook, "A Guide to Published Literature Relating to the Authoritarian Personality," *Journal of Psychology*, 45 (1958), pp. 171–99.

[16] W. J. McKinnon and R. Centers, "Authoritarianism and Urban Stratification," *American Journal of Sociology*, 61 (1956), p. 618.

traits are more or less standard among low-status people, then the more liberal members of this group should also be the more neurotic.[17] As two psychologists, Anthony Davids and Charles Eriksen, point out, where the "standard of reference on authoritarianism is quite high," people may be well adjusted *and* authoritarian.[18] And the fact that this is often the case in lower-class groups fits the hypothesis that authoritarian attitudes are "normal" and expected in such groups.[19]

EXTREMIST RELIGIONS AND THE LOWER CLASSES

Many observers have called attention to a connection between low social status and fundamentalist or chiliastic religion. This suggests that extremist religion is a product of the same social forces that sustain authoritarian political attitudes. The liberal Protestant churches, on the other hand, have been predominantly middle class in membership. In the United States, this has created a dilemma for the liberal Protestant clergy, who have tended to be liberal in their politics as well as their religion and, hence, have often wanted to spread their social and religious gospel among the lower strata. But they have found that these classes want ministers who will preach of hell-fire and salvation rather than modern Protestant theology.[20]

In the early period of the Socialist movement, Engels observed that early Christianity and the revolutionary workers' movement had "notable points of resemblance," particularly in their millennial appeals and lower-class base.[21] Recently, Elmer Clark, a student of small sects in contemporary America, has noted that such sects, like early Christianity, "originate mainly among the religiously neglected poor." He writes that when "the revolts of the poor have been tinged with religion, which was nearly always the case until recent times, millennial ideas have appeared, and . . . these notions are prominent in most of the small sects which follow the evangelical tradition. Premillenarianism is essentially a defense mechanism of the dis-

[17] Too much of contemporary psychological knowledge in this area has been gained from populations most convenient for the academic investigator to reach — university students. It is often forgotten that personality and attitude syndromes may be far different for this highly select group than for other segments of the total population.

[18] See Anthony Davids and Charles W. Eriksen, "Some Social and Cultural Factors Determining Relations Between Authoritarianism and Measures of Neuroticism," *Journal of Consulting Psychology,* 21 (1957), pp. 155–59. This article contains many references to the relevant literature.

[19] The greater compatibility of the demands of Communist party membership and working-class background as indicated by Almond's finding that twice as many of the middle-class party members as of the working-class group in his sample of Communists had neurotic problems hints again at the normality and congruence of extremist politics with a working-class background. Gabriel Almond, *The Appeals of Communism* (Princeton: Princeton University Press, 1954), pp. 245–46.

[20] See Liston Pope, *Millhands and Preachers* (New Haven: Yale University Press, 1942), pp. 105–16.

[21] See Friedrich Engels, "On the Early History of Christianity," in K. Marx and F. Engels, *On Religion* (Moscow: Foreign Languages Publishing House, 1957), pp. 312–20.

inherited; despairing of obtaining substantial blessings through social processes, they turn on the world which has withheld its benefits and look to its destruction in a cosmic cataclysm which will exalt them and cast down the rich and powerful."[22]

Ernst Troeltsch, the major historian of sectarian religion, has characterized the psychological appeal of fundamentalist religious sects in a way that might as appropriately be applied to extremist politics: "It is the lower classes which do the really creative work, forming communities on a genuine religious basis. They alone unite imagination and simplicity of feeling with a nonreflective habit of mind, a primitive energy, and an urgent sense of need. On such a foundation alone is it possible to build up an unconditional authoritative faith in a Divine Revelation with simplicity of surrender and unshaken certainty. Only within a fellowship of this kind is there room for those who have a sense of spiritual need, and who have not acquired the habit of intellectual reasoning, which always regards everything from a relative point of view."[23]

Jehovah's Witnesses, whose membership in the United States runs into the hundreds of thousands, is an excellent example of a rapidly growing sect which "continues to attract, as in the past, the underprivileged strata."[24] The Witnesses' principal teaching is that the Kingdom of Heaven is at hand: "The end of the age is near. Armageddon is just around the corner, when the wicked will be destroyed, and the theocracy, or rule of God, will be set up upon the earth."[25] And like the Communists, their organization is "hierarchical and highly authoritarian. There is little democratic participation in the management or in the formation of policies of the movement as a whole."[26]

Direct connections between the social roots of political and of religious extremism have been observed in a number of countries. In Czarist Russia, the young Trotsky recognized the relationship and successfully recruited

[22] Elmer T. Clark, *The Small Sects in America* (New York: Abingdon Press, 1949), pp. 16, 218–19. According to Bryan Wilson, "insecurity, differential status, anxiety, cultural neglect, prompt a need for readjustment which sects may, for some, provide. The maladjusted may be communities, or occupational groups, or dispersed individuals in similar marginal positions." See "An Analysis of Sect Development," *American Sociological Review*, 24 (1959), p. 8, and the same author's *Minority Religious Movements in Modern Britain* (London: Heinemann, 1960).

[23] Ernst Troeltsch, *The Social Teaching of the Christian Churches* (London: George Allen and Unwin, 1930), Vol. 1, p. 44.

[24] See Charles S. Braden, *These Also Believe. A Study of Modern American Cults and Minority Religious Movement* (New York: Macmillan, 1949), p. 384.

[25] *Ibid.*, p. 370.

[26] *Ibid.*, p. 363. It may be suggested that, as in authoritarian political movements, the intolerant character of most of the sects is an attractive feature and not a source of strain for their lower-class members. Although no systematic evidence is available, this assumption would help account for the lack of tolerance for factionalism within these sects, and for the endless schisms, with the new groups as intolerant as the old, since the splits usually occur over the issue of *whose* intolerant views and methods shall prevail.

the first working-class members of the South Russian Workers' Union (a revolutionary Marxist organization of the late 1890's) from adherents to religious sects.[27] In Holland and Sweden, recent studies show that the Communists are strongest in regions which were once centers of fundamentalist religious revivalism. In Finland, Communism and revivalist Christianity often are strong in the same areas. In the poor eastern parts of Finland, the Communists have been very careful not to offend people's religious feelings. It is reported that many Communist meetings actually begin with religious hymns.[28]

This is not to imply that religious sects supported by lower-class elements necessarily or usually become centers of political protest. In fact, such sects often drain off the discontent and frustration which would otherwise flow into channels of political extremism. The point here is that rigid fundamentalism and dogmatism are linked to the same underlying characteristics, attitudes, and predispositions which find another outlet in allegiance to extremist political movements.

In his excellent study of the sources of Swedish Communism, Sven Rydenfelt analyzed the differences between two socially and economically comparable northern counties of Sweden — Vasterbotten and Norrbotten — in an attempt to explain the relatively low Communist vote in the former (2 per cent) and the much larger one in the latter (21 per cent). The Liberal party, which in Sweden gives much more support than any other party to religious extremism, was strong in Vasterbotten (30 per cent) and weak in Norrbotten (9 per cent). Since the total extremist vote in both was almost identical — 30 and 32 per cent — he concluded that a general predisposition toward radicalism existed in both counties, containing some of the poorest, most socially isolated, and rootless groups in Sweden, but that its expression differed, taking a religious form in one county and a Communist in the other: "The Communists and the religious radicals, as for instance, the Pentecostal sects, seem to be competing for the allegiance of the same groups."[29]

THE SOCIAL SITUATION OF THE LOWER CLASSES

A number of elements contribute to authoritarian predispositions in lower-class individuals. Low education, low participation in political or voluntary

---

[27] See Isaac Deutscher, *The Prophet Armed, Trotsky, 1879–1921* (London: Oxford University Press, 1954), pp. 30–31.

[28] See Sven Rydenfelt, *Kommunismen i Sverige. En Samhallsvetenskaplig Studie.* (Kund: Gleerupska Universitetsbokhandeln, 1954), pp. 296, 336–37; Wiardi Beckman Institute, *Verkiezingen in Nederland* (Amsterdam, 1951, mimeographed), pp. 15, 93–94; Jaako Novsiainen, *Kommunism Kuopion lää nissä* (Helsinki: Joensuu, 1956).

[29] See W. Phillips Davison's extensive review of Sven Rydenfelt, *op. cit.,* which appeared in the *Public Opinion Quarterly,* 18 (1954–55), pp. 375–88. Quote is on p. 382.

organizations of any type, little reading, isolated occupations, economic insecurity, and authoritarian family patterns are some of the most important. These elements are interrelated, but they are by no means identical.

There is consistent evidence that degree of formal education, itself closely correlated with social and economic status, is also highly correlated with undemocratic attitudes. Data from the American sociologist Samuel Stouffer's study of attitudes toward civil liberties in America and from the UNESCO Research Institute's survey of German opinion on a multi-party system (Tables 3 and 4) reveal this clearly.

These tables indicate that although higher occupational status within each educational level seems to make for greater tolerance, the increases in

TABLE 3. THE RELATIONSHIP BETWEEN OCCUPATION, EDUCATION, AND POLITICAL TOLERANCE IN THE UNITED STATES, 1955[a]

| | Percentages in the two "most tolerant" categories | | | |
| | Occupation | | | |
Education	Low manual	High manual	Low white collar	High white collar
Grade school	13 (228)	21 (178)	23 (47)	26 (100)
Some high school	32 (99)	33 (124)	29 (56)	46 (68)
High school grad	40 (64)	48 (127)	47 (102)	56 (108)
Some college	— (14)	64 (36)	64 (80)	65 (37)
College grad	— (3)	— (11)	74 (147)	83 (21)

[a] Computed from IBM cards kindly supplied by Samuel A. Stouffer from his study, *Communism, Conformity and Civil Liberties* (New York: Doubleday & Co., Inc., 1955).

TABLE 4. THE RELATIONSHIP BETWEEN OCCUPATION, EDUCATION, AND SUPPORT OF A DEMOCRATIC PARTY SYSTEM IN GERMANY—1953[a]

| | Percentage favoring the existence of several parties | |
| | Educational level | |
Occupation	Elementary school	High school or higher
Farm laborers	29 (59)	—
Manual workers	43 (1439)	52 (29)
Farmers	43 (381)	67 (9)
Lower white collar	50 (273)	68 (107)
Self-employed business	53 (365)	65 (75)
Upper white collar	58 (86)	69 (58)
Officials (govt.)	59 (158)	78 (99)
Professions	56 (18)	68 (38)

[a] Same source as Table 1, p. 437.

tolerance associated with higher educational level are greater than those related to higher occupational level, other factors being constant.[30] Inferior education and low occupational position are of course closely connected, and both are part of the complex making up low status, which is associated with a lack of tolerance.[31]

Low-status groups are also less apt to participate in formal organizations, read fewer magazines and books regularly, possess less information on public affairs, vote less, and in general, take less interest in politics.[32] The available evidence suggests that each of these attributes is related to attitudes toward democracy. The 1953 UNESCO analysis of German data found that, at every occupational level, those who belonged to voluntary associations were more likely to favor a multi-party system than a one-party one.[33] American findings, too, indicate that authoritarians "do not join many community groups" as compared with nonauthoritarians.[34] And it has been discovered that people poorly informed on public issues are more likely to be both *more liberal* on economic issues and *less liberal* on noneconomic ones.[35] Nonvoters and those less interested in political matters are much more intolerant and xenophobic than those who vote and have political interests.[36]

The "hard core" of "chronic know-nothings" comes disproportionately from the less literate, lower socioeconomic groups, according to a study by two American social psychologists, Herbert Hyman and Paul Sheatsley. These people are not only uninformed, but "harder to reach, no matter what the level or nature of the information." Here is another hint of the complex character of the relationship between education, liberalism, and status. Noneconomic liberalism is not a simple matter of acquiring educa-

[30] A study based on a national sample of Americans reported that education made no difference in the extent of authoritarian responses on an "authoritarian personality" scale among workers, but that higher educational attainment reduced such responses among the middle class. The well-educated upper-middle class were least "authoritarian." Morris Janowitz and Dwaine Marvick, "Authoritarianism and Political Behavior," *Public Opinion Quarterly*, 17 (1953), pp. 195–96.

[31] The independent effect of education even when other social factors are least favorable has special long-range significance in view of the rising educational level of the population. Kornhauser and his associates found that auto workers with an eighth-grade education were more authoritarian than those with more education. See A. Kornhauser, A. L. Sheppard, and A. J. Mayer, *When Labor Votes* (New York: University Books, 1956), for further data on variations in authoritarianism *within* a working-class sample.

[32] The research showing the social factors such as education, status and income (themselves components of an over-all class or status index) associated with political participation is summarized in Chap. 6 [of *Political Man*].

[33] Data computed for this study.

[34] F. H. Sanford, *Authoritarianism and Leadership* (Philadelphia: Stevenson Brothers, 1950), p. 168. See also Mirra Komarovsky, "The Voluntary Associations of Urban Dwellers," *American Sociological Review*, 11 (1946), p. 688.

[35] G. H. Smith, *op. cit.*, p. 71.

[36] G. M. Connelly and H. H. Field, "The Non-Voter, Who He Is, and What He Thinks," *Public Opinion Quarterly*, 8 (1944), p. 179; Samuel A. Stouffer, *op. cit.*, passim, and F. H. Sanford, *op. cit.*, p. 168. M. Janowitz and D. Marvick, *op. cit.*, p. 200.

tion and information; it is at least in part a basic attitude which is actively discouraged by the social situation of lower-status persons.[37] As Genevieve Knupfer, an American psychiatrist, has pointed out in her revealing "Portrait of the Underdog," "economic underprivilege is psychological underprivilege: habits of submission, little access to sources of information, lack of verbal facility . . . appear to produce a lack of self-confidence which increases the unwillingness of the low-status person to participate in many phases of our predominantly middle-class culture. . . ."[38]

These characteristics also reflect the extent to which the lower strata are *isolated* from the activities, controversies, and organizations of democratic society — an isolation which prevents them from acquiring the sophisticated and complex view of the political structure which makes understandable and necessary the norms of tolerance.

In this connection it is instructive to examine once again, as extreme cases, those occupations which are most isolated, in every sense, from contact with the world outside their own group. Manual workers in "isolated occupations" which require them to live in one-industry towns or areas — miners, maritime workers, forestry workers, fishermen, and sheep-shearers — exhibit high rates of Communist support in most countries.[39]

Similarly, as all public opinion surveys show, the rural population, both farmers and laborers, tends to oppose civil liberties and multi-party systems more than any other occupational group. Election surveys indicate that farm owners have been among the strongest supporters of fascist parties, while farm workers, poor farmers, and share-croppers have given even

[37] See Herbert Hyman and Paul B. Sheatsley, "Some Reasons Why Information Campaigns Fail," *Public Opinion Quarterly*, 11 (1947), p. 413. A recent survey of material on voluntary association memberships is contained in Charles L. Wright and Herbert Hyman, "Voluntary Association Memberships of American Adults: Evidence from National Sample Surveys," *American Sociological Review*, 23 (1958), pp. 284–94.

[38] Genevieve Knupfer, "Portrait of the Underdog," *Public Opinion Quarterly*, 11 (1947), p. 114.

[39] The greatest amount of comparative material is available on the miners. For Britain, see Herbert G. Nicholas, *British General Election of 1950* (London: Macmillan, 1951), pp. 318, 342, 361. For the United States, see Paul F. Brissenden, *The IWW: A Study of American Syndicalism* (New York: Columbia University Press, 1920), p. 74, and Harold F. Gosnell, *Grass Roots Politics* (Washington, D.C.: American Council on Public Affairs, 1942), pp. 31–32. For France see François Goguel, "Geographie des élections sociales de 1950–51," *Revue française de science politique*, 3 (1953), pp. 246–71. For Germany, see Ossip K. Flechtheim, *Die Kommunistische Partei Deutschlands in der Weimarer Republik* (Offenbach am Main: Bollwerk-Verlag Karl Drott, 1948), p. 211. Data are also available for Australia, Scandinavia, Spain, and Chile.

Isolation has also been linked with the differential propensity to strike of different industries. Violent strikes having the character of a mass grievance against society as a whole occur most often in isolated industries, and probably have their origins in the same social situations as those which produce extremism. See Clark Kerr and Abraham Siegel, "The Interindustry Propensity to Strike: An International Comparison," in *Industrial Conflict*, eds., A. Kornhauser, R. Dubin, and A. M. Ross (New York: McGraw-Hill Book Co., 1954), pp. 189–212.

stronger backing to the Communists than has the rest of labor in countries like Italy, France, and India.[40]

The same social conditions are associated with middle-class authoritarianism. The groups which have been most prone to support fascist and other middle-class extremist ideologies have been, in addition to farmers and peasants, the small businessmen of the smaller provincial communities — groups which are also isolated from "cosmopolitan" culture and are far lower than any other nonmanual-labor group in educational attainment.[41]

A second and no less important factor predisposing the lower classes toward authoritarianism is a relative lack of economic and psychological security. The lower one goes on the socioeconomic ladder, the greater economic uncertainty one finds. White-collar workers, even those who are not paid more than skilled manual workers, are less likely to suffer the tensions created by fear of loss of income. Studies of marital instability indicate that this is related to lower income and income insecurity. Such insecurity will of course affect the individual's politics and attitudes.[42] High states of tension require immediate alleviation, and this is frequently found in the venting of hostility against a scapegoat and the search for a short-term solution by support of extremist groups. Research indicates that the unemployed are less tolerant toward minorities than the employed, and more likely to be Communists if they are workers, or fascists if they are middle class. Industries which have a high rate of Communists in their ranks also have high economic instability.

The lower classes' insecurities and tensions which flow from economic

[40] According to Carl Friedrich, agricultural groups are more emotionally nationalistic and potentially authoritarian politically because of the fact that they are more isolated from meeting people who are different than are urban dwellers. See "The Agricultural Basis of Emotional Nationalism," *Public Opinion Quarterly*, 1 (1937), pp. 50–51. See also Rudolf Heberle, *From Democracy to Nazism: A Regional Case Study on Political Parties in Germany* (Baton Rouge, Louisiana: Louisiana State University Press, 1945), pp. 32 ff., for a discussion of the appeal of Nazism to the German rural population, and K. Kido and M. Sugi, *op. cit.*, for similar survey findings in Japan.

[41] Statistical data indicate that German and Austrian Nazism, French Poujadism, and American McCarthyism have all drawn their heaviest nonrural support from the small businessmen of provincial small communities, particularly those with little education.

[42] In addition to the insecurity which is normally attendant upon lower-class existence, special conditions which uproot people from a stable community life and upset the social supports of their traditional values make them receptive to extremist chiliastic ideologies which help to redefine their world. Rydenfelt in his study of Swedish Communism suggests that "rootlessness" is a characteristic of individuals and occupations with high Communist voting records. See W. Phillips Davison, *op. cit.*, p. 378. Engels also called attention in the 1890's to the fact that chiliastic religions and social movements, including the revolutionary socialist one, attracted all the deviants or those without a place in society: "all the elements which had been set free, i.e., at a loose end, by the dissolution of the old world came one after the other into the orbit of [early] Christianity . . . [as today] all throng to the working-class parties in all countries." F. Engels, *op. cit.*, pp. 319–20. See also G. Almond, *op. cit.*, p. 236, and Hadley Cantril, *The Psychology of Social Movements* (New York: John Wiley & Sons, 1941), Chaps. 8 and 9.

instability are reinforced by their particular patterns of family life. There is a great deal of direct frustration and aggression in the day-to-day lives of members of the lower classes, both children and adults. A comprehensive review of the many studies of child-rearing patterns in the United States completed in the past twenty-five years reports that their "most consistent finding" is the "more frequent use of physical punishment by working-class parents. The middle class, in contrast, resorts to reasoning, isolation, and . . . 'love-oriented' techniques of discipline. . . . Such parents are more likely to overlook offenses, and when they do punish they are less likely to ridicule or inflict physical pain."[43] A further link between such child-rearing practices and adult hostility and authoritarianism is suggested by the finding of two investigations in Boston and Detroit that physical punishments for aggression, characteristic of the working class, tend to increase rather than decrease aggressive behavior.[44]

LOWER-CLASS PERSPECTIVES

Acceptance of the norms of democracy requires a high level of sophistication and ego security. The less sophisticated and stable an individual, the more likely he is to favor a simplified view of politics, to fail to understand the rationale underlying tolerance of those with whom he disagrees, and to find difficulty in grasping or tolerating a gradualist image of political change.

Several studies focusing on various aspects of working-class life and culture have emphasized different components of an unsophisticated perspective. Greater suggestibility, absence of a sense of past and future (lack of a prolonged time perspective), inability to take a complex view, greater difficulty in abstracting from concrete experience, and lack of imagination (inner "reworking" of experience), each has been singled out by numerous students of quite different problems as characteristic of low status. All of these qualities are part of the complex psychological basis of authoritarianism.

[43] See Urie Bronfenbrenner, "Socialization and Social Class Through Time and Space," in E. E. Maccoby, T. M. Newcomb, and E. L. Hartley, eds., *Readings in Social Psychology* (New York: Henry Holt, 1958), p. 419. The sociologist Allison Davis has summarized in a similar vein research findings relating to intra-family relations in different classes: "The lower classes not uncommonly teach their children and adolescents to strike out with fists or knife and to be certain to hit first. Both girls and boys at adolescence may curse their father to his face or even attack him with fists, sticks, or axes in free-for-all family encounters. Husbands and wives sometimes stage pitched battles in the home; wives have their husbands arrested, and husbands try to break in or burn down their own homes when locked out. Such fights with fists or weapons, and the whipping of wives occur sooner or later in many lower-class families. They may not appear today, nor tomorrow, but they *will* appear if the observer remains long enough to see them." Allison Davis, "Socialization and Adolescent Personality," in Guy E. Swanson, *et al.*, eds., *Readings in Social Psychology* (New York: Henry Holt, 1954), p. 528. (Emphasis in original.)

[44] Some hint of the complex of psychological factors underlying lower-class authoritarianism is given in one study which reports a relationship between overt hostility and authoritarianism. See Saul M. Siegel, "The Relationship of Hostility to Authoritarianism," *Journal of Abnormal and Social Psychology*, 52 (1956), pp. 368–72.

The psychologist Hadley Cantril considered suggestibility to be a major psychological explanation for participation in extremist movements.[45] The two conditions for suggestibility are both typical of low-status persons: either the lack of an adequate frame of reference or general perspective, or a fixed, rigid one. A poorly developed frame of reference reflects a limited education, a paucity of the rich associations on a general level which provide a basis for evaluating experience. A fixed or rigid one — in a sense the opposite side of the same coin — reflects the tendency to elevate whatever general principles are learned to absolutes which even experience may fail to qualify and correct.

The stimulating book by the British journalist Richard Hoggart, *The Uses of Literacy*, makes the same point in another way. Low-status persons without rich and flexible perspectives are likely to lack a developed sense of the past *and* the future. "Their education is unlikely to have left them with any historical panorama or with any idea of a continuing tradition. . . . A great many people, though they may possess a considerable amount of disconnected information, have little idea of an historical or ideological pattern or process. . . . With little intellectual or cultural furniture, with little training in the testing of opposing views against reason and existing judgments, judgments are usually made according to the promptings of those group apothegms which come first to mind. . . . Similarly, there can be little real sense of the future. . . . Such a mind is, I think, particularly accessible to the temptation to live in a constant present."[46]

This concern with the present leads to a concentration on daily activities, without much inner reflection, imaginative planning of one's future, or abstract thinking unrelated to one's daily activities. One of the few studies of lower-class children which used projective techniques found that "these young people are making an adjustment which is orientated toward the outside world rather than one which rests on a developing acquaintance with their own impulses and the handling of these impulses by fantasy and introspection. . . . They do not have a rich inner life, indeed their imaginative activity is meagre and limited. . . . When faced with a new situation, the subjects tend to react rapidly, and they do not alter their original impressions of the situation which is seen as a crude whole with little intellectual discrimination of components."[47]

---

[45] See Hadley Cantril, *op. cit.*, p. 65.

[46] Richard Hoggart, *op. cit.*, pp. 158–59.

[47] B. M. Spinley, *The Deprived and the Privileged* (London: Routledge and Kegan Paul, 1953), pp. 115–16. These conclusions were based on Rorschach tests given to 60 slum-area children. The last point is related to that made by another British scholar, that working-class people are not as likely as those with middle-class backgrounds to perceive the *structure* of an object, which involves thought on a more abstract level of relationships, but have an action-oriented reaction to the *content* of an object. For more discussion of this point, see B. Bernstein, "Some Sociological Determinants of Perception," *The British Journal of Sociology*, 9 (1958), pp. 160 ff.

Working-class life as a whole emphasizes the concrete and immediate. As Hoggart puts it, "if we want to capture something of the essence of working-class life . . . we must say that it is the 'dense and concrete' life, a life whose main stress is on the intimate, the sensory, the detailed and the personal. This would no doubt be true of working-class groups anywhere in the world."[48] Hoggart sees the concreteness of working-class perceptions as the main difference between them and middle-class people, who more easily meet abstract and general questions. The sharp British working-class distinction between "Us" and "Them," he notes, is "part of a more general characteristic of the outlook of most working-class people. To come to terms with the world of 'Them' involves, in the end, all kinds of political and social questions, and leads eventually beyond politics and social philosophy to metaphysics. The question of how we face 'Them' (whoever 'They' are) is, at last, the question of how we stand in relation to anything not visibly and intimately part of our local universe. The working-class splitting of the world into 'Us' and 'Them' is on this side a symptom of their difficulty in meeting abstract or general questions."[49] Hoggart is careful to emphasize that probably most persons in *any* social class are uninterested in general ideas, but still "training in the handling of ideas or in analysis" is far more characteristic of the demands of middle-class parents and occupations.[50]

A recent analysis by the British sociologist Basil Bernstein of how differences in ways of perceiving and thinking in the different classes lead to variations in social mobility also underlines the manner in which different family patterns affect authoritarianism. The middle-class parent stresses "an awareness of the importance between means and long-term ends, cognitively and affectually regarded . . . [and has] the ability to adopt appropriate measures to implement the attainment of distant ends by a purposeful means-end chain. . . . The child in the middle classes and associative levels grows up in an environment which is finely and extensively controlled; the space, time and social relationships are explicitly regulated

---

[48] Richard Hoggart, *op. cit.*, p. 88. This kind of life, like other social characteristics of human beings, has different consequences for different areas of society and social existence. It may be argued, though I personally doubt it, that this capacity to establish personal relationships, to live in the present, may be more "healthy" (in a strictly medical, mental-health sense) than a middle-class concern with status distinctions, one's own personal impact on one's life situation, and a preoccupation with the uncertain future. But on the political level of consequences, the problem of concern here, this same action-oriented, nonintellectualistic aspect of working-class life seems to prevent the realities of long-term social and economic trends from entering working-class consciousness, simply because such reality can enter only through the medium of abstractions and generalizations.

[49] *Ibid.*, p. 86.

[50] *Loc. cit.*

within and outside the family group."[51] The situation in the working-class family is quite different:

> The working-class family structure is less formally organized than the middle-class in relation to the development of the child. Although the authority within the family is explicit, the values which it expresses do not give rise to the carefully ordered universe spatially and temporally of the middle-class child. The exercise of authority will not be related to a stable system of rewards and punishments but may often appear arbitrary. The specific character of long-term goals tends to be replaced by more general notions of the future, in which chance, a friend or a relative plays a greater part than the rigorous working out of connections. Thus present, or near-present, activities have greater value than the relation of the present activity to the attainment of a distant goal. The system of expectancies, or the time-span of anticipation, is shortened and this creates different sets of preferences, goals, and dissatisfactions. The environment limits the perception of the developing child of and in time. Present gratifications or present deprivations become absolute gratifications or absolute deprivations, for there exists no developed time continuum upon which present activity can be ranged. Relative to the middle-classes, the postponement of present pleasure for future gratifications will be found difficult. By implication *a more volatile patterning of affectual and expressive behavior will be found in the working-classes.*[52]

This emphasis on the immediately perceivable and concern with the personal and concrete is part and parcel of the short time perspective and the inability to perceive the complex possibilities and consequences of actions which often result in a general readiness to support extremist political and religious movements, and a generally lower level of liberalism on noneconomic questions.[53]

Even within extremist movements these differences in the perceptions and perspectives of working-class as against middle-class persons affect their experiences, readiness to join a "cause," and reasons for defecting. The American political scientist Gabriel Almond's study of 221 ex-Communists

---

[51] B. Bernstein, *op. cit.*, pp. 161, 165.

[52] *Ibid.*, p. 168 (my emphasis).

[53] This hypothesis has suggestive implications for a theory of trade-union democracy, and possible strains within trade-union organizational life. Working-class union members may not be at all as concerned with dictatorial union leadership as are middle-class critics who assume that the rank and file would actively form factions, and critically evaluate union policies if not constrained by a monolithic structure imposed by the top leadership. On the other hand, the more educated, articulate staff members (on a union newspaper, for example) may want to include more literate and complex discussions of issues facing the union but feel constrained by the need to present simple, easily understood propagandistic slogans for rank-and-file consumption. The "house organ" type of union newspaper may not be due entirely to internal political necessities.

in four countries provides data on this point. He distinguishes between the "exoteric" (simple, for mass consumption) and "esoteric" (complex, for the inner circle) doctrines of the party. In contrast to middle-class members "relatively few working-class respondents had been exposed to the esoteric doctrine of the party before joining, and . . . they tended to remain unindoctrinated while in the party."[54] The middle-class recruits "tended to come to the party with more complex value patterns and expectations which were more likely to obstruct assimilation into the party. . . . The working-class member, on the other hand, is relatively untroubled by doctrinal apparatus, less exposed to the media of communication, and his imagination and logical powers are relatively undeveloped."[55]

One aspect of the lower classes' lack of sophistication and education is their anti-intellectualism (a phenomenon Engels long ago noted as a problem faced by working-class movements). While the complex esoteric ideology of Communism may have been one of the principal features attracting middle-class people to it, the fundamental anti-intellectualism which it shares with other extremist movements has been a source of strain for the "genuine" intellectuals within it. Thus it has been the working-class rank and file which has been least disturbed by Communism's ideological shifts, and least likely to defect.[56] Their commitment, once established, cannot usually be shaken by a sudden realization that the party, after all, does not conform to liberal and humanistic values.

This helps to explain why socialist parties have been led by a high proportion of intellectuals, in spite of an original ideological emphasis on maintaining a working-class orientation, while the Communists have alienated their intellectual leaders and are led preponderantly by those with working-class occupations.[57] Almond's study concluded that ". . . while the party is open to all comers, working-class party members have better prospects of success in the party than middle-class recruits. This is probably due both to party policy, which has always manifested greater confidence in the reliability of working-class recruits, and to the difficulties of assimilation into the party generally experienced by middle-class party members."[58]

[54] G. Almond, *op. cit.*, p. 244.

[55] *Ibid.*, p. 177.

[56] *Ibid.*, pp. 313 ff., 392.

[57] For French data from 1936 to 1956 see Mattei Dogan, "Les Candidats et les élus," in L'Association française de science politique, *Les Élections du 2 janvier* (Paris: Librairie Armand Colin, 1956), p. 462, and Dogan, "L'origine sociale du personnel parlementaire français," in *Parties politique et classes sociales en France,* edited by Maurice Duverger (Paris: Librairie Armand Colin, 1955), pp. 291–329. For a comparison of German Social Democratic and Communist parliamentary leadership before Hitler see Viktor Engelhardt, "Die Zusammensatzung des Reichstage nach Alter, Beruf, und Religionsbekenntnis," *Die Arbeit,* 8 (1931), p. 34.

[58] G. Almond, *op. cit.*, p. 190. This statement was supported by analysis of the biographies of 123 Central Committee leaders of the Party in three countries, as well as by interviews with 221 ex-Communists (both leaders and rank-and-file members) in four countries, France, Italy, Great Britain, and the United States.

MAKING OF AN AUTHORITARIAN

To sum up, the lower-class individual is likely to have been exposed to punishment, lack of love, and a general atmosphere of tension and aggression since early childhood — all experiences which tend to produce deep-rooted hostilities expressed by ethnic prejudice, political authoritarianism, and chiliastic transvaluational religion. His educational attainment is less than that of men with higher socioeconomic status, and his association as a child with others of similar background not only fails to stimulate his intellectual interests but also creates an atmosphere which prevents his educational experience from increasing his general social sophistication and his understanding of different groups and ideas. Leaving school relatively early, he is surrounded on the job by others with a similarly restricted cultural, educational, and family background. Little external influence impinges on his limited environment. From early childhood, he has sought immediate gratifications, rather than engaged in activities which might have long-term rewards. The logic of both his adult employment and his family situation reinforces this limited time perspective. As the sociologist C. C. North has put it, isolation from heterogeneous environments, characteristic of low status, operates to "limit the source of information, to retard the development of efficiency in judgment and reasoning abilities, and to confine the attention to more trivial interests in life."[59]

All of these characteristics produce a tendency to view politics and personal relationships in black-and-white terms, a desire for immediate action, an impatience with talk and discussion, a lack of interest in organizations which have a long-range perspective, and a readiness to follow leaders who offer a demonological interpretation of the evil forces (either religious or political) which are conspiring against him.[60]

It is interesting that Lenin saw the character of the lower classes, and the tasks of those who would lead them, in somewhat these terms. He specified as the chief task of the Communist parties the leadership of the broad masses, who are "slumbering, apathetic, hidebound, inert, and dormant." These masses, said Lenin, must be aligned for the "final and decisive battle" (a term reminiscent of Armageddon) by the party which alone can present an uncompromising and unified view of the world, and an immediate program for drastic change. In contrast to "effective" Communist

[59] C. C. North, *Social Differentiation* (Chapel Hill: University of North Carolina Press, 1926), p. 247.

[60] Most of these characteristics have been mentioned by child psychologists as typical of adolescent attitudes and perspectives. Werner Cohn, in an article on Jehovah's Witnesses, considers youth movements as a prototype of all such "proletarian" movements. Both "adolescent fixation and anomie are causal conditions" of their development (p. 297), and all such organizations have an "aura of social estrangement" (p. 282). See Werner Cohn, "Jehovah's Witnesses as a Proletarian Movement," *The American Scholar*, 24 (1955), pp. 281–99.

leadership, Lenin pointed to the democratic parties and their leadership as "vacillating, wavering, unstable" elements — a characterization that is probably valid for any political group lacking ultimate certainty in its program and willing to grant legitimacy to opposition groups.[61]

The political outcome of these predispositions, however, is not determined by the multiplicity of factors involved. Isolation, a punishing childhood, economic and occupational insecurities, and a lack of sophistication are conducive to withdrawal, or even apathy, and to strong mobilization of hostility. The same underlying factors which predispose individuals toward support of extremist movements under certain conditions may result in total withdrawal from political activity and concern under other conditions. In "normal" periods, apathy is most frequent among such individuals, but they can be activated by a crisis, especially if it is accompanied by strong millennial appeals.[62]

EXTREMISM AS AN ALTERNATIVE: A TEST OF A HYPOTHESIS

The proposition that the lack of a rich, complex frame of reference is the vital variable which connects low status and a predisposition toward extremism does not necessarily suggest that the lower strata will be authoritarian; it implies that, other things being equal, they will choose the least complex alternative. Thus in situations in which extremism represents the more complex rather than the less complex form of politics, low status should be associated with *opposition* to such movements and parties.

This is in fact the case wherever the Communist party is a small party competing against a large reformist party, as in England, the United States, Sweden, Norway, and other countries. Where the party is small and weak, it cannot hold out the promise of immediate changes in the situation of the most deprived. Rather, such small extremist parties usually present the

[61] The quotes from Lenin are in his *Left Wing Communism: An Infantile Disorder* (New York: International Publishers, 1940), pp. 74–75. Lenin's point, made in another context, in his pamphlet, *What Is to Be Done?* that workers left to themselves would never develop socialist or class consciousness, and that they would remain on the level of economic "day to day" consciousness, unless an organized group of revolutionary intellectuals brought them a broader vision, is similar to the generalizations presented here concerning the inherent limited time perspective of the lower strata.

[62] Various American studies indicate that those lower-class individuals who are non-voters, and who have little political interest, tend to reject the democratic norms of tolerance. See Samuel A. Stouffer, *op. cit.,* and G. M. Connelly and H. H. Field, *op. cit.,* p. 182. Studies of the behavior of the unemployed in countries in which extremist movements were weak, such as the United States and Britain, indicate that apathy was their characteristic political response. See E. W. Bakke, *Citizens Without Work* (New Haven: Yale University Press, 1940), pp. 46–70. On the other hand, German data suggest a high correlation between working-class unemployment and support of Communists, and middle-class unemployment and support of Nazis. In France, Italy, and Finland today, those who have been unemployed tend to back the large Communist parties of those countries. See Erik Allardt, *Social Struktur och Politisk Aktivitet* (Helsingfors: Söderstrom Förlagsaktiebolag, 1956), pp. 84–85.

fairly complex intellectual argument that in the long run they will be strengthened by tendencies inherent in the social and economic system.[63] For the poorer worker, support of the Swedish Social Democrats, the British Labor party, or the American New Deal is a simpler and more easily understood way of securing redress of grievances or improvement of social conditions than supporting an electorally insignificant Communist party.

The available evidence from Denmark, Norway, Sweden, Canada, Brazil, and Great Britain supports this point. In these countries, where the Communist party is small and a Labor or Socialist party is much larger, Communist support is stronger among the better paid and more skilled workers than it is among the less skilled and poorer strata.[64] In Italy, France, and Finland, where the Communists are the largest party on the left, the lower the income level of workers, the higher their Communist vote.[65] A comparison of the differences in the relative income position of workers who vote Social Democratic and those who back the Communists in two neighboring Scandinavian countries of Finland and Sweden shows these alternative patterns clearly (Table 5). In Finland, where the Communists are very strong, their support is drawn disproportionately from the poorer workers,

[63] Recent research on the early sources of support for the Nazi party challenges the hypothesis that it was the apathetic who came to its support prior to 1930, when it still represented a complex, long-range alternative. A negative rank-order correlation was found between the per cent increase in the Nazi vote and the increase in the proportion voting in the German election districts between 1928 and 1930. Only after it had become a relatively large party did it recruit the previously apathetic, who now could see its immediate potential.

[64] For Denmark, see E. Høgh, *Vaelgeradfaerdi Danmark* (Ph.D. thesis, Sociology Institute, University of Copenhagen, 1959), Tables 6 and 9. For Norway, see Allen Barton, *Sociological and Psychological Implications of Economic Planning in Norway* (Ph.D. thesis, Department of Sociology, Columbia University, 1957); and several surveys of voting behavior in Norway conducted by Norwegian poll organizations including the 1949 FAKTA Survey, and the February 1954 and April 1956, NGI Survey, the results of which are as yet unpublished. Data from the files of the Canadian Gallup Poll for 1945, 1949, and 1953 indicate that the Labor-Progressive (Communist) party drew more support from the skilled than the unskilled sections of the working class. For Brazil, see A. Simao, "O voto operario en São Paulo," *Revista Brasilieras estudos politicos*, 1 (1956), p. 130–41.

[65] For a table giving precise statistics for Italy and France, see Hadley Cantril, *The Politics of Despair* (New York: Basic Books, 1958), pp. 3–10. In pre-Hitler Germany, where the Communists were a large party, they also secured their electoral strength much more from the less skilled sections of the workers than from the more skilled. See Samuel Pratt, *The Social Basis of Nazism and Communism in Urban Germany* (M.A. thesis, Department of Sociology, Michigan State College, 1948), pp. 156 ff.

An as yet unpublished study by Dr. Pertti Pesonen, of the Institute of Political Science of the University of Helsinki, of voting in the industrial city of Tampere reports that the Communist voters were more well to do than the Social Democrats. On the other hand, Communists were much more likely to have experienced unemployment during the past year (21 per cent) or in their entire work history (46 per cent) than Social Democrats (10 per cent and 23 per cent). This study suggests that the experience of recent unemployment in the family is the most important determinant of a Communist vote in Tampere.

TABLE 5. THE INCOME COMPOSITION OF THE WORKING-CLASS SUPPORT OF THE SOCIAL DEMOCRATIC AND COMMUNIST PARTIES IN FINLAND AND SWEDEN[a]

| | Finland—1956 | |
Income class in Markkaa	Social Democrats	Communists
Under 100	8%	13%
100–400	49	50
400–600	22	29
600+	21	8
(N)	(173)	(119)

| | Sweden—1946 | |
Income class in Kroner	Social Democrats	Communists
Under 2,000	14%	9%
2,001–4,000	43	40
4,001–6,000	34	35
6,001+	9	15
(N)	(4832)	(819)

a The Finnish data were secured from a special run made for this study by the Finnish Gallup Poll. The Swedish statistics were recomputed from data presented in Elis Hastad, *et al.*, eds., *"Gallup" och den Svenska Valjarkaren* (Uppsala: Hugo Gebers Forlag, 1950), pp. 175-76. Both studies include rural and urban workers.

while in Sweden, where the Communists are a minor party, they have considerably more success with the better paid and more skilled workers than they do with the unskilled and lowly paid.[66]

This holds true in all countries for which data exist.[67] One other country, India, offers even better evidence. In India, the Communists are a major

[66] Or to present the same data in another way, in Finland, 41 per cent of all workers earning less than 100 markkaa a month vote Communist, as compared with only 12 per cent among those earning over 600 markkaa. In Sweden, 7 per cent of the workers earning less than 2,000 kroner a year vote Communist, as compared with 25 per cent among those earning over 8,000.

[67] It may be noted, parenthetically, that where the Socialist party is small and/or new, it also represents a complex alternative, and attracts more middle-class support proportionately than when it is a well-established mass party which can offer immediate reforms. On the other hand, when a small transvaluational group does *not* offer an intellectually complex alternative, it should draw disproportionate support from the lower strata. Such groups are the sectarian religions whose millennial appeals have no developed rationale. Some extremely slight evidence on this point in a political contest is available from a recent Norwegian poll which shows the composition of the support for various parties. Only eleven persons supporting the Christian party, a party which appeals to the more fundamentalist Lutherans who are comparable to those discussed earlier in Sweden, were included in the total sample, but 82 per cent of these came from lower-income groups (less than 10,000 kroner per year). In comparison 57 per cent of the 264 Labor party supporters, and 39 per cent of the 21 Communist supporters earned less than 10,000 kroner. Thus the small Communist party as the most complex transvaluational alternative drew its backing from relatively high strata, while the fundamentalist Christians had the economically poorest social base of any party in the country. See the February 1954 NGI Survey, issued in December 1956 in preliminary mimeographed form.

party, constituting the government or the major opposition (with 25 per cent or more of the votes) in two states, Kerala and Andhra. While they have substantial strength in some other states, they are much weaker in the rest of India. If the proposition is valid that Communist appeal should be substantially for the lower and uneducated strata where the Party is powerful, and for the relatively higher and better educated ones where it is weak, the characteristics of Party voters should vary greatly in different parts of India, and this is in fact precisely what Table 6 below shows.[68]

TABLE 6. COMMUNIST AND SOCIALIST PREFERENCES IN INDIA, BY CLASS AND EDUCATION[a]

Communist party preferences in Kerala and Andhra		Rest of India	Preferences for Socialist parties in All-India
Class			
Middle	7%	27%	23%
Lower-middle	19	30	36
Working	74	43	41
Education			
Illiterate	52%	43%	31%
Under-matric.	39	37	43
Matric. plus	9	20	26
(N)	(113)	(68)	(88)

[a] These figures have been computed from tables presented in the *Indian Institute of Public Opinion, Monthly Public Opinion Surveys*, Vol. 2, Nos. 4, 5, 6, 7 (Combined Issue), New Delhi, January–April, 1957, pp. 9–14. This was a pre-election poll, not a report of the actual voting results. The total sample was 2,868 persons. The Socialist party and the Praja-Socialist party figures are combined here, since they share essentially the same moderate program. The support given to them in Andhra and Kerala was too small to be presented separately.

Where the Indian Communist party is small, its support, like that of the two small moderate socialist parties, comes from relatively well-to-do and better educated strata. The picture shifts sharply in Kerala and Andhra, where the Communists are strong. The middle class provides only 7 per cent of Communist support there, with the working class supplying 74 per cent.[69] Educational differences among party supporters show a similar pattern.

[68] These data were located after the hypothesis was formulated, and thus can be considered an independent replication.

[69] The hypothesis presented here does not attempt to explain the growth of small parties. Adaptations to major crisis situations, particularly depressions and wars, are probably the key factors initially increasing the support for a small "complex" party. For an analysis of the change in electoral support of a Socialist party as it moved up to major party status see S. M. Lipset, *Agrarian Socialism* (Berkeley: University of California Press, 1950), esp. pp. 159–78.

HISTORICAL PATTERNS AND DEMOCRATIC ACTION

Despite the profoundly antidemocratic tendencies in lower-class groups, workers' political organizations and movements in the more industrialized democratic countries have supported *both* economic and political liberalism.[70] Workers' organizations, trade-unions and political parties played a major role in extending political democracy in the nineteenth and early twentieth centuries. However, these struggles for political freedom by the workers, like those of the middle class before them, took place in the context of a fight for economic rights.[71] Freedom of organization and of speech,

[70] There have been many exceptions to this. The Australian Labor party has been the foremost supporter of a "white Australia." Similarly, in the United States until the advent of the ideological New Deal in the 1930's, the lower-class-based Democratic party has always been the more anti-Negro of the two parties. The American labor movement has opposed nonwhite immigration, and much of it maintains barriers against Negro members.

When the American Socialist party was a mass movement before World War I, its largest circulation newspapers, such as the Milwaukee *Social Democratic Herald* and the *Appeal to Reason* opposed racial integration. The latter stated explicitly, "Socialism will separate the races." See David A. Shannon, *The Socialist Party of America* (New York: Macmillan, 1955), pp. 49–52. Even the Marxist Socialist movement of Western Europe was not immune to the virus of anti-Semitism. Thus, before World War I there were a number of anti-Semitic incidents in which Socialists were involved, some avowedly anti-Semitic leaders connected with different socialist parties, and strong resistance to committing the socialist organizations to opposition to anti-Semitism. See E. Silberner, "The Anti-Semitic Tradition in Modern Socialism," *Scripta Hierosolymitana,* III (1956), pp. 378–96. In an article on the recent British race riots, Michael Rumney points out the working-class base of the anti-Negro sentiment and goes so far as to predict that "the Labour party will become the enemy of the Negro as time goes on." He reports that "while the Conservative party has been able to stand behind the police and take any means it feels necessary to preserve the peace, the Labour party has been strangely silent. If it speaks it will either antagonize the men who riot against West Indians, or forfeit its claim to being the party of equal rights." See "Left Mythology and British Race Riots," *The New Leader* (September 22, 1958), pp. 10–11.

British Gallup Poll surveys document these judgments. Thus in a survey completed in July 1959, the poll asked whether Jews "have more or less power than they should really have," and found, when respondents were compared according to party choice, that the anti-Semitic response of "more power" was given by 38 per cent of the Labor voters, 30 per cent of the Tories, and 27 per cent of the Liberals. Seven per cent of the Laborites, 8 per cent of the Conservatives, and 9 per cent of the Liberals thought that Jews have too little power. The same organization has reported a 1958 survey in which fewer Laborites and lower class people said that they would vote for a Jew if their party nominated one than did upper class and Conservative voters. But in all fairness it must also be noted that almost every Jew in the House of Commons represents the Labor party, and that almost all of the approximately twó dozen Jews represent overwhelmingly non-Jewish constituencies.

[71] Actually there are some striking similarities between the behavior of various middle-class strata when they constituted the lower strata within a predominantly aristocratic and feudal society, and the working class in newly industrialized societies who have not yet won a place in society. The affinities of both for religious and economic "radicalism," in the same sense, are striking. Calvin's doctrine of predestination, as Tawney points out, performed the same function for the eighteenth-century *bourgeoisie* as did Marx's theory of the inevitability of socialism for the proletariat in the nineteenth. Both "set their virtue at their best in sharp antithesis with the vices of the established

together with universal suffrage, were necessary weapons in the battle for a better standard of living, social security, shorter hours, and the like. The upper classes resisted the extension of political freedom as part of their defense of economic and social privilege.

Few groups in history have ever voluntarily espoused civil liberties and freedom for those who advocate measures they consider despicable or dangerous. Religious freedom emerged in the Western world only because the contending powers each found themselves unable to destroy the other without destroying the entire society, and because in the course of the struggle itself many men lost faith and interest in religion, and consequently the desire to suppress dissent. Similarly, universal suffrage and freedom of organization and opposition developed in many countries either as concessions to the established strength of the lower classes, or as means of controlling them — a tactic advocated and used by such sophisticated conservatives as Disraeli and Bismarck.

Once in existence, however, and although originating in a conflict of interests, democratic norms became part of the institutional system. Thus the Western labor and socialist movement has incorporated these values into its general ideology. But the fact that the movement's ideology is democratic does not mean that its supporters actually understand the implications. The evidence seems to indicate that understanding of and adherence to these norms are highest among leaders and lowest among followers. The general opinions or predispositions of the rank and file are relatively unimportant in predicting behavior as long as the organization to which they are loyal continues to act democratically. In spite of the workers' greater authoritarian propensity, their organizations which are anti-Communist still function as better defenders and carriers of democratic values than parties based on the middle class. In Germany, the United States, Great Britain, and Japan, individuals who support the democratic left party are more likely to support civil liberties and democratic values than people *within* each occupational stratum who back the conservative parties. Organized social democracy not only defends civil liberties but influences its supporters in the same direction.[72]

---

order at its worst, taught them to feel that they were a chosen people, made them conscious of their great destiny in the Providential and resolute to realize it." The Communist party, as did the Puritans, insists on "personal responsibility, discipline and asceticism," and although the historical contents differ, they may have the same sociological roots: in isolated, status-deprived occupational groups. See R. H. Tawney, *Religion and the Rise of Capitalism* (New York: Penguin Books, 1947), pp. 9, 99. For a similar point see Donald G. MacRae, "The Bolshevik Ideology," *The Cambridge Journal*, 3 (1950), pp. 164–77.

[72] A striking case in point occurred in Australia in 1950. During a period of much agitation about the dangers of the Communist party, a Gallup Poll survey reported that 80 per cent of the electorate favored outlawing the Communists. Shortly after this survey, the Conservative government submitted a proposal to outlaw the party to referen-

Conservatism is especially vulnerable in a political democracy since, as Abraham Lincoln said, there are always more poor people than well-to-do ones, and promises to redistribute wealth are difficult to rebut. Consequently, conservatives have traditionally feared a thoroughgoing political democracy and have endeavored in most countries — by restricting the franchise or by manipulating the governmental structure through second chambers or overrepresentation of rural districts and small towns (traditional conservative strongholds) — to prevent a popular majority from controlling the government. The ideology of conservatism has frequently been based on elitist values which reject the idea that there is wisdom in the voice of the electorate. Other values often defended by conservatives, like militarism or nationalism, probably also have an attraction for individuals with authoritarian predispositions.[73]

It would be a mistake to conclude from the data presented here that the authoritarian predispositions of the lower classes necessarily constitute a threat to a democratic social system; nor should similar conclusions be drawn about the antidemocratic aspects of conservatism. Whether or not a given class supports restrictions on freedom depends on a wide constellation of factors of which those discussed here are only a part.

The instability of the democratic process in general and the strength of the Communists in particular, as we have seen, are closely related to national levels of economic development, including national levels of educational attainment. The Communists represent a mass movement in the poorer countries of Europe and elsewhere, but are weak where economic development and educational attainment are high. The lower classes of the less developed countries are poorer, more insecure, less educated, and relatively more underprivileged in terms of possession of status symbols than are the lower strata of the more well-to-do nations. In the more developed, stable democracies of Western Europe, North America, and Australasia the lower classes are "in the society" as well as "of it" — that is, their isolation from the rest of the culture is much less than the social isolation of the

---

dum. During the referendum electoral campaign, the Labor party and the trade-unions came out vigorously against the proposal. Considerable shifting took place after this, to the point that the measure to outlaw the Communists was actually defeated by a small majority, and Catholic workers who had overwhelmingly favored the outlaw measure when first questioned by the Gallup Poll eventually followed the advice of their party and unions and voted against it. See Leicester Webb, *Communism and Democracy in Australia: A Survey of the 1951 Referendum* (New York: Frederick A. Praeger, 1955).

[73] A study of the 1952 elections in the United States revealed that at every educational level (grammar school, high school, and college) individuals who scored high on an "authoritarian personality" scale were much more likely to vote for Eisenhower rather than Stevenson. Robert Lane, "Political Personality and Electoral Choice," *American Political Science Review,* 49 (1955), pp. 173–90. In Britain, a study of working-class anti-Semitism found that the small group of Conservatives in the sample were much more anti-Semitic than the Liberals and the Laborites. See James H. Robb, *Working-class Anti-Semite* (London: Tavistock Publications, 1954), pp. 93–94.

poorer groups in other countries, who are cut off by abysmally low incomes and very low educational levels, if not by widespread illiteracy. This incorporation of the workers into the body politic in the industrialized Western world has reduced their authoritarian tendencies greatly, although in the United States, for example, McCarthy demonstrated that an irresponsible demagogue who combines a nationalist and anti-elitist appeal can still secure considerable support from the less educated.[74]

While the evidence as to the effects of rising national standards of living and education permits us to be hopeful about working-class politics and behavior in those countries in which extremism is weak, it does suggest pessimistic conclusions with regard to the less economically developed, unstable democracies. Where an extremist party has secured the support of the lower classes — often by stressing equality and economic security at the expense of liberty — it is problematic whether this support can be taken away from it by democratic methods. The Communists, in particular, combine the two types of a chiliastic view of the world. Whether democratic working-class parties, able to demonstrate convincingly their ability to defend economic and class interests, can be built up in the less stable democracies is a moot question.

[74] "The history of the masses, however, has been a history of the most consistently anti-intellectual force in society. . . . It was the American lower classes, not the upper, who gave their overwhelming support to the attacks in recent years on civil liberties. It is among the working people that one finds dominant those sects and churches most hostile to the free spirit." Lewis S. Feuer, Introduction to *Marx and Engels, Basic Writings on Politics and Philosophy* (New York: Doubleday Anchor Books, 1959), pp. xv–xvi. And in another wealthy country, white South Africa, Herbert Tingsten points out that "industrialization and commercialization . . . have formed that social class now constituting the stronghold of Boer nationalism: workers, shop assistants, clerks, lower grades of civil servants. Here, as in the United States, these 'poor whites' — more correctly, whites threatened by poverty — are the leading guardians of prejudice and white supremacy." *The Problem of South Africa* (London: Victor Gollancz, Ltd., 1955), p. 23.

C. Relationships with Other Institutions

*It is almost axiomatic that college students will rebel, whether
against their parents, the university, the church, or society in general.
If a student does rebel against his parents' political attitudes, in
what direction does he go? Middleton and Putney, showing the relationship between the institution of the family and that of the polity,
address themselves to this question. Their findings are significant in
that they show in what direction American political traditions might
go and the increasing "conservatism" or "liberalism" of our politics.
(Notice that Putney and Middleton present data bearing on attitudes in college. They do not know whether or not the students
who have rebelled ultimately return to the political position of their
parents.)*

40 RUSSELL MIDDLETON AND SNELL PUTNEY

Student Rebellion Against Parental Political Beliefs

The nation's press has proclaimed a surge of political interest among American college students. The beat, silent, apolitical generation of the 1950's
is said to have been succeeded by a politically awakened, impatient, and
iconoclastic generation of college students in the 1960's. This popular image
is based both upon the proliferation of political clubs on college campuses[1]
and upon an increasing tendency for students to engage in direct political
action — sit-ins, freedom rides, peace marches, and demonstrations against
the House Committee on Un-American Activities.

Traditionally it has been assumed that the usual political pattern was a
liberal or radical rebellion during youth, followed by a gradual return to
conservative orthodoxy in later life. As Robert Frost expressed it, "I never
dared be radical when young/For fear it would make me conservative
when old." At least two studies, however, have cast doubt on the assumption that conservatism increases with age. Lazarsfeld and associates found
that older people were not necessarily more conservative than younger
people, but were merely more closely aligned with the political attitudes
prevalent in their ethnic or religious group,[2] and Centers failed to find a

From *Social Forces,* Vol. 41 (May, 1963), pp. 377–383. Reprinted by permission of the
authors and publisher.

[1] *Time* reported that in 1961 on 353 campuses a total of 315 new political groups
were formed — 169 conservative and 146 liberal — and that the pace was even faster
in 1962. "The Need to Speak Out," *Time,* 79 (February 23, 1962), p. 74.

[2] Paul F. Lazarsfeld, Bernard Berelson, and Hazel Gaudet, *The People's Choice*
(New York: Harcourt Brace, 1952), p. 44.

tendency for older people to be more conservative than younger people among laboring groups, although there was a slight tendency in this direction among the upper occupational groups.[3]

But whether or not youthful liberal rebellion has predominated in the past, most of the nation's press sees a reversal of this pattern today. It is contended that there is an upsurge of conservatism among students, who are rebelling from what is described as the current liberal establishment. The keynote was sounded by *Time:*

> The new trend is youth's natural rebellion against conformity, and to many the liberalism of their New Deal-bred elders is the most ironbound conformity. "My parents thought Franklin D. Roosevelt was one of the greatest heroes who ever lived," says Y.A.F. Chairman, Yale Law Student Robert Schuchman, 22. "I'm rebelling from that concept." Says President Roger Claus of Wisconsin's Conservative Club: "You walk around with your Goldwater button, and you feel the thrill of treason."[4]

The same theme has been stressed by a number of other news magazines and authors as well.[5]

Elms, on the other hand, writing in *The Nation,* maintains that there has been no mass conversion to conservatism among college students. The greater interest in conservatism, he argues, is merely a part of a wider political awakening among youths, and it is overshadowed by a stronger but less publicized resurgence of liberalism on the campus. He also suggests that most student conservatives come from solidly conservative families and conservative milieux: "Conformity to socio-economic class roles is a more likely reason for student conservatism than reaction against the conformity of liberalism."[6]

---

[3] Richard Centers, *The Psychology of Social Class* (Princeton: Princeton University Press, 1949), p. 165.

[4] "Campus Conservatives," *Time,* 77 (February 10, 1961), pp. 34, 37.

[5] Raymond Moley, "Youth Turns to the Right," *Newsweek,* 57 (March 13, 1961), p. 100; "Conservatism in the U.S. . . . And Its Leading Spokesman," *Newsweek,* 57 (April 10, 1961), pp. 28–38; "Behind the 'Conservative' Movement in Colleges," *U.S. News and World Report,* 51 (December 25, 1961), p. 64; and M. Stanton Evans, *Revolt on the Campus* (Chicago: Henry Regnery Co., 1961).

[6] Alan C. Elms, "The Conservative Ripple," *Nation,* 192 (May 27, 1961), pp. 458–460, 468. George Gallup has recently commented in a similar vein: "We hear it said that there is a 'great, conservative movement' sweeping the college and university campuses today. We find no evidence of any great conservative movement on the campuses. That doesn't mean that if Goldwater, who is an interesting and exciting person, came to a campus he wouldn't draw a big crowd. He most certainly would. But right-wing Republicans, I believe, are engaging in wishful thinking." "Opinion Polls: Interviews by Donald McDonald with Elmo Roper and George Gallup," pamphlet issued by the Center for the Study of Democratic Institutions, Santa Barbara, California, 1962, p. 34. Michael Harrington also sees little evidence of any conservative trend among college students: "From reading the journals one might think that there is a wave of campus conservatism. As far as I can tell, that is simply not true. I have been North, South, East and West, and I have yet to find a chapter of Young Americans for Freedom

Lacking comparable data from an earlier period, we cannot here determine whether college students are more interested in politics than formerly, or whether students are less inclined to rebel toward liberalism than in the past. However, it is possible to shed some light on the controversy between Elms and the Editors of *Time* by comparing the political viewpoints of college students with those of their parents. Accordingly, this study is focused on two questions: (1) Is the prevailing direction of political rebellion among college students today toward conservatism? and (2) Is there evidence that those who espouse conservative viewpoints are predominantly rebels against liberal parents?

METHODS

The data for this study were collected by means of anonymous questionnaires administered during 1961 to classes of students in 16 colleges and universities in the United States. The sample of institutions includes a private university, a private liberal arts college, a state college, and a state university in each of four regions: Far West, Middle West, Northeast, and South. Four of the eight private institutions are church affiliated. Thus the students represent a variety of regions and types of institutions although intact classes were selected within the institutions and caution should be used in generalizing the findings of this study to all American college and university students.

Completed and usable questionnaires were obtained from 824 males and 616 females, a total of 1,440 students. Approximately 28 per cent of the students were freshmen, 23 per cent sophomores, 23 per cent juniors, 21 per cent seniors, and 5 per cent graduate students.

A major problem in any study of political attitudes is the definition of a continuum of political positions. Political party preference is a questionable index because of the wide range of ideological variation within American parties. Another approach, often used in the past, is a scale based on certain substantive issues, such as the role of government in the regulation of the economy. A typical example is the Politico-Economic Conservatism Scale developed in the California studies of the authoritarian personality.[7] Although such a scale may be of considerable utility for classifying people in regard to the substantive issues, the broader significance of these may be problematic. The components of variation in the political spectrum are both complex and controversial, and many substantive issues are not related in a linear fashion to a political continuum ranging from extreme left to ex-

---

which is playing a really vital role on campus. . . . Generally speaking, YAF is less of a force on the big campuses than the Young Peoples Socialist League — and no one has been writing about a socialist sweep among the young. . . . The young conservatives are the product of some good copy writers, not the campus scene." Michael Harrington, "The American Campus: 1962," *Dissent*, 9 (Spring 1962), p. 167.

[7] T. W. Adorno, et al., *The Authoritarian Personality* (New York: Harper, 1950), pp. 163, 169.

treme right. Moreover, many people who have political views nevertheless have no crystallized position on specific issues, particularly if they are complex.

At the other extreme, McClosky has developed a conservatism scale which taps an underlying conservatism in the personality structure, but is so far removed from particular political issues that many aspects of ideological variation are likely to be obscured.[8]

In this study we sought to avoid the problems inherent in the use of party identification or inferential scales by utilizing a set of familiar political labels, or categories, and asking the subject to choose the one most closely corresponding to his own political views. Although most Americans are by no means ideologues, they frequently think in terms of political labels and they appear to have much less difficulty in categorizing their own position than in spelling out their substantive views.

However, selecting categories which are familiar and meaningful to American college students and at the same time are free of evaluative bias is no simple task. Several sets of categories were tried and discarded during the pretesting. One set, for example, presented a series of current political figures ranging from left to right, and the subjects were asked with which figure they most closely agreed. The results, however, were distorted by the students' lack of familiarity with even major political figures, their ignorance of the political positions of figures whom they did know, and the purely personal appeal of some of the figures. In one pretest involving a class of seniors and graduate students in social science, for example, 25 per cent said that they were not familiar enough with Senator Hubert Humphrey to classify his political position, even though he had conducted a vigorous and much publicized campaign for the Democratic nomination for President less than a year before. Another 14 per cent classified him as a conservative. Similarly, 21 per cent classified Senator Barry Goldwater as a liberal. President Kennedy, enjoying great personal popularity immediately following his election (this pretest was in the spring of 1961), attracted support from all camps — socialists, liberals, and conservatives.

It was necessary to avoid labels which are often used in a pejorative sense or as epithets. The labels "fascist" and "communist" are obvious examples, and the label "reactionary" failed to attract a single student during the pretesting (though some applied it to their parents). Despite evident pejoration the label "socialist" appeared to retain utility: a plausible minority of students applied it to themselves, and only rarely was it applied to others in an implausible manner (e.g., "most people in the United States are socialist").

---

[8] Herbert McClosky, "Conservatism and Personality," *American Political Science Review*, 52 (March 1958), pp. 27–45.

The set of categories which proved to be most meaningful to American college students was an extremely simple left-to-right continuum. The students were presented with socialist, liberal, and conservative categories, the latter two being further subdivided by a qualifying adverb. Thus each subject was asked, "Which of these political positions is closest to your own views?"

(1) Socialist
(2) Highly liberal
(3) Moderately liberal
(4) Moderately conservative
(5) Highly conservative
(6) I have no political views.

The final category was added to avoid forcing the student with no real political views to make a choice which would not have been meaningful. Any Communists who might have been included in the sample would probably have been willing to accept the socialist label. Reactionaries, or members of the "radical right," generally refer to themselves as conservatives,[9] and they would seem most likely to choose the highly conservative category.

The meanings attached to these labels, particularly the moderately liberal and moderately conservative labels, may vary considerably from one individual to another. However, the problem of this study does not require the definition of an objective political continuum which is interpreted in precisely the same way by all subjects. It is sufficient that the subject be able to compare his position on the continuum with the positions he attributes to others, particularly his parents. It is not even essential that this attribution be accurate; for the purposes of this study what the parents or others actually believe is far less important than what the student thinks that they believe.

Many investigators have concentrated merely on the influence of one parent.[10] This procedure greatly simplifies the analysis, but as Hyman points out, ". . . familial influence involves a contribution from each of the parents."[11] We therefore developed the following classification of ways in

[9] See Senator Barry Goldwater's statement of philosophy, *The Conscience of a Conservative* (New York: Hillman Books, 1960), the title of which indicates his choice of political labels. Far from advocating the conservation of the status quo, however, Senator Goldwater argues for radical political changes: "I have little interest in streamlining government or in making it more efficient, for I mean to reduce its size. I do not undertake to promote welfare, for I propose to extend freedom. My aim is not to pass laws, but to repeal them. It is not to inaugurate new programs, but to cancel old ones that do violence to the Constitution, or that have failed in their purpose, or that impose on the people an unwarranted financial burden" (p. 23).

[10] See, for example, Robert E. Lane, "Fathers and Sons: Foundations of Political Belief," *American Sociological Review*, 24 (August 1959), pp. 502–511.

[11] Herbert H. Hyman, *Political Socialization* (Glencoe, Ill.: Free Press, 1959), p. 82.

which the views of the students could be related to those they attribute to their parents:

> 1. *Rebels to the left of parents.* The student places himself to the left of both parents, or to the left of one parent when the other parent has no political views or when his views are unknown to the student.
>
> 2. *Rebels to the right of parents.* The student places himself to the right of both parents, or to the right of one parent when the other parent has no political views or when his views are unknown to the student.
>
> 3. *Conformists.* The student shares the beliefs of one or both of his parents or takes a compromise position between the views of disagreeing parents.
>
> 4. *Independent crystallizers.* The student has arrived at a political position although both his parents either have no political views or have views of which he is unaware.
>
> 5. *Uncrystallized.* The student has no explicit political views.

This classification of students in relation to their parents forms the basis of most of the analysis which follows. The chi-square test of significance was applied throughout the analysis, and the rejection level for the null hypothesis was set at .05.

FINDINGS

The distribution of the political views of the students, and of the viewpoints they perceive in their mothers and fathers, is presented in Table 1. The great bulk of the cases are moderately liberal or moderately conservative, the former constituting the modal category for students and the latter the modal category attributed to parents. Relatively few cases are to be found in the extreme categories — socialist and highly conservative. The students tend to be farther to the left politically than they think their parents are, either fathers (P < .001) or mothers (P < .001). Male students are farther to the left than female students (P < .001), and the females are more likely than males to have no crystallized political views (P < .001). The distributions for fathers and mothers are similar although the fathers show more tendency toward the extreme positions than do the mothers (P < .02).

In Table 2 the views of the students are compared to the views they attribute to their parents. In terms of the categories defined above, approximately two-fifths of the students are rebels, about an equal number are conformists, and the remaining fifth are about equally divided between the independent crystallizers and the uncrystallized. The students are far more likely to move to the left of their parents than to the right (P < .001), and this is true for both males (P < .001) and females (P < .001). Our findings thus contrast with those of Nogee and Levin who found in a 1956 study of

Table 1.   Political Views of Students and Perceptions of Parental Views

Political views	Percent holding views			Percentage perceived to hold views	
	Male students	Female students	Total students	Fathers	Mothers
Socialist	2.7	.8	1.9	.8	.4
Highly liberal	13.7	6.5	10.6	5.8	3.6
Moderately liberal	46.8	49.2	47.8	24.7	24.0
Moderately conservative	29.2	29.9	29.5	37.4	38.1
Highly conservative	3.3	2.6	3.0	13.1	10.0
No political views	4.3	11.0	7.2	1.4	6.5
Unaware of views	—	—	—	16.8	17.4
Total	100.0	100.0	100.0	100.0	100.0
N	824	616	1440	1440	1440

Table 2.   Political Views of Students in Relation to Perceived Parental Views

Relation of student views to perceived parental views	Percentage of students		
	Males	Females	Total
Rebels to left of parents	37.3	27.3	33.0
Rebels to right of parents	8.0	7.0	7.6
Conformists	41.4	44.3	42.6
Independent crystallizers	9.1	10.4	9.7
Uncrystallized	4.2	11.0	7.1
Total	100.0	100.0	100.0
N	824	616	1440

314 Boston University students that those who deviated from the political party preference of their parents were as likely to do so in a conservative direction as in a liberal direction.[12]

It is also evident from Table 2 that male students are more likely to rebel to the left than are female students (P < .001), and that female students are more likely than males to remain uncrystallized (P < .001). Otherwise the patterns for males and females are not significantly different.

In Table 3 the students adhering to each political position are broken down into rebels to the right, rebels to the left, conformists, etc. About one-half of the highly conservative students are conforming to the position held by their parents. On the other hand, only about one-sixth of the socialists and highly liberal students are conforming to the position of their parents. Thus, highly conservative students are far more likely to be conformists than socialist and highly liberal students (P < .001).

[12] Philip Nogee and M. B. Levin, "Some Determinants of Political Attitudes among College Voters," *Public Opinion Quarterly*, 22 (Winter 1958-59), pp. 449–463. As Hyman points out, however, political party preference is probably more subject to family influence than political ideology, and this may account for part of the difference. Hyman, *op. cit.*, pp. 74–76.

Table 3.   Political Views of Students in Relation
to Perceived Parental Views

	Percentage of students				
				Moder-	
			Moder-	ately	Highly
Relation of student views to		Highly	ately	conser-	conser-
perceived parental views	Socialist	liberal	liberal	vative	vative
Rebels to left of parents	81.5	73.2	43.1	10.4	—[a]
Rebels to right of parents	—[a]	.7	4.4	13.6	46.5
Conformists	11.1	18.3	40.8	66.4	46.5
Independent crystallizers	7.4	7.8	11.7	9.6	7.0
Total	100.0	100.0	100.0	100.0	100.0
N	27	153	689	425	43

[a] No cases possible by definition.

Moreover, about two-thirds of the highly conservative students who are rebels had parents who were themselves moderately conservative rather than liberal. It is possible that such deviation should be viewed more as over conformity than as rebellion. The moderately conservative group of students also shows by far the greatest degree of conformity, with two-thirds of the students agreeing with at least one parent or taking an intermediate position between disagreeing parents.

In contrast, the largest single group of socialist students — 37 per cent — report that their fathers are highly conservative. Among highly liberal students only 7 per cent say that their fathers are highly conservative, but another 33 per cent consider their fathers to be moderately conservative. Thus highly conservative students, even when rebels, are more likely than socialist or highly liberal students to have parents who are on the same end of the political continuum.

Most of the students claim to be at least moderately interested in politics. About 26 per cent say that they are very much interested in political matters all of the time, 48 per cent are moderately interested most of the time, 22 per cent are only slightly interested most of the time, and 4 per cent admit that they are not at all interested in politics most of the time. Interest in politics is strongly associated with rebellion from parental political beliefs, as is shown in Table 4. The greater their interest in politics, the greater is the likelihood that the students are rebels from the political views of their parents ($P < .001$). Those with little or no interest in politics tend to accept their parents' political positions or fail to develop any identifiable position at all, whereas more than half of those who are very much interested in political matters reject the views of their parents in favor of other views.

It might be expected that the direction of rebellion from parental beliefs would be influenced by the student's conceptions of the predominant or conventional political position. Thus, if his parents diverged from the con-

TABLE 4. STUDENT POLITICAL REBELLION, BY INTEREST IN POLITICS

| Degree of interest in politics | N | Percentage of students | | Total |
		Political rebels	Political nonrebels	
Very much interested	368	54.6	45.4	100.0
Moderately interested	687	40.0	60.0	100.0
Slightly interested	307	29.6	70.4	100.0
Not interested	59	18.6	81.4	100.0

TABLE 5. STUDENT POLITICAL REBELLION, BY PARENTAL AGREEMENT WITH PERCEIVED CONVENTIONAL POLITICAL VIEWS IN THE UNITED STATES

| Relation of perceived parental views to perceived conventional political views | N | Percentage of students | | Total |
		Political rebels	Political conformists	
One or both parents in agreement with perceived conventional position	534	44.0	56.0	100.0
Neither parent in agreement with perceived conventional position	550	55.3	44.7	100.0

ventional, he might rebel from their views as a means of conforming to the society around him. In a somewhat parallel study of rebellion of college students from the religious views of their parents, we found a clear tendency for rebels against parental beliefs to move toward a more conventional position than that of their parents.[13]

Analysis of the data in Table 5 reveals that students are less likely to rebel against the political views of their parents when at least one parent holds what the student regards as the conventional position, than when neither parent is seen as conventional ($P < .001$). However, analysis of the data in Table 6 reveals that when students do rebel against the political position of their parents, they tend to move away from the position which they perceive as conventional ($P < .001$). This pattern was present for both male rebels ($P < .01$) and female rebels ($P < .01$). Students are thus less likely to rebel politically if their parents seem to hold conventional views, but those who do rebel are likely to move away from the conventional position rather than towards it. Conformity to the society around them does not emerge as a basic factor in student rebellion against parental political beliefs, as it did in the case of rebellion against parental religious beliefs. A possible interpretation of this finding would be that students tend to rebel religiously largely as a means of adjusting themselves to society,

[13] Snell Putney and Russell Middleton, "Rebellion, Conformity, and Parental Religious Ideologies," *Sociometry*, 24 (June 1961), pp. 125–135.

TABLE 6. STUDENT POLITICAL REBELLION, BY RELATION TO PERCEIVED
CONVENTIONAL POLITICAL VIEWS IN THE UNITED STATES

Direction of rebellion on conventionality continuum	Percentage of students		
	Males	Females	Total students
Rebellion toward perceived conventional position	36.5	33.2	35.3
Rebellion away from perceived conventional position	50.1	50.7	50.3
Rebellion to position equidistant from perceived conventional position	7.0	6.2	6.7
No perception of conventional position	6.4	9.9	7.7
Total	100.0	100.0	100.0
N	373	211	584

whereas political rebellion is more likely to be associated with a generalized disenchantment with their social milieu.

CONCLUSION

In this sample of 1,440 American college students we find that nearly as
many deviate from their parents' political views as conform to them.
Rebellion is particularly likely among those students most interested in
politics and among those students who see their parents as holding uncon-
ventional political views. There is no evidence in this study that the prevailing direction of political rebellion is toward conservatism, the contentions
of the popular press to the contrary notwithstanding. Indeed, the students
are considerably more liberal than their parents due largely to the fact that
rebels are about five times as likely to move to the left as to the right.
Lacking comparable data from the past, we cannot rule out the possibility
that rebellion to the right is increasing, but the prevailing direction of rebellion today would seem distinctly leftward.

Neither is there evidence in this study to support the contention that the
current campus conservatives are predominantly the offspring of liberal
parents. A few of them are, but the great majority of the conservatives in
our sample came from conservative family backgrounds, and those who
have rebelled at all have usually moved only from "moderately conservative" to "highly conservative." The greater vigor which has been observed
among conservative student organizations is probably due primarily to an
awakening of latent political interest among conservative students from
conservative backgrounds, not to recruitment of students from liberal backgrounds. The student rebels do tend to move away from the position they
regard as conventional, but it is typically the conservative position that they
see in this light.

XIV RELIGION

A. Definitions and Concepts

The topic of religion and its role in peoples' lives has been claimed as the province of sociologists, psychologists, theologians, and philosophers, among others. Religion as an institution has been vital in every society, for none has been without religion; each contains a group with rituals and ethical prescriptions that relate to the supernatural. Max Weber wished, generally, to explain the development of Western civilization, especially its economic system, which is quite different from those of the Orient. To do so he began a comparative study of the religions of such countries as China, India, and Europe. The selection which follows is taken from a small part of the larger study described above. Weber's thesis has been the subject of much debate, part of it due to a misunderstanding of what Weber was trying to do. In brief, his aim in The Protestant Ethic *was to see whether Calvinism contributed to the development of capitalism.*

41 MAX WEBER

The Protestant Ethic and the Spirit of Capitalism

A product of modern European civilization, studying any problem of universal history, is bound to ask himself to what combination of circumstances the fact should be attributed that in Western civilization, and in

Adapted and reprinted with the permission of Charles Scribner's Sons and George Allen & Unwin, Ltd. from *The Protestant Ethic and the Spirit of Capitalism,* pp. 13–27 and 155–181 by Max Weber, translated by Talcott Parsons.

Western civilization only, cultural phenomena have appeared which (as we like to think) lie in a line of development having *universal* significance and value.

Only in the West does science exist at a stage of development which we recognize today as valid. Empirical knowledge, reflection on problems of the cosmos and of life, philosophical and theological wisdom of the most profound sort, are not confined to it, though in the case of the last the full development of a systematic theology must be credited to Christianity under the influence of Hellenism, since there were only fragments in Islam and in a few Indian sects. In short, knowledge and observation of great refinement have existed elsewhere, above all in India, China, Babylonia, Egypt. But in Babylonia and elsewhere astronomy lacked — which makes its development all the more astounding — the mathematical foundation which it first received from the Greeks. The Indian geometry had no rational proof; that was another product of the Greek intellect, also the creator of mechanics and physics. The Indian natural sciences, though well developed in observation, lacked the method of experiment, which was, apart from beginnings in antiquity, essentially a product of the Renaissance, as was the modern laboratory. Hence medicine, especially in India, though highly developed in empirical technique, lacked a biological and particularly biochemical foundation. A rational chemistry has been absent from all areas of culture except the West.

Similar statements can be made about other fields. There was printing in China. But a printed literature, designed *only* for print and only possible through it, and, above all, the press and periodicals, have appeared only in the Occident. Institutions of higher education of all possible types, even some superficially similar to our universities, or at least academies, have existed (China, Islam). But a rational, systematic, and specialized pursuit of science, with trained and specialized personnel, has only existed in the West in a sense at all approaching its present dominant place in our culture. Above all is this true of the trained official, the pillar of both the modern State and of the economic life of the West. He forms a type of which there have heretofore only been suggestions, which have never remotely approached its present importance for the social order. Of course the official, even the specialized official, is a very old constituent of the most various societies. But no country and no age has ever experienced, in the same sense as the modern Occident, the absolute and complete dependence of its whole existence, of the political, technical, and economic conditions of its life, on a specially trained *organization* of officials. The most important functions of the everyday life of society have come to be in the hands of technically, commercially, and above all legally trained government officials.

And the same is true of the most fateful force in our modern life, capitalism. The impulse to acquisition, pursuit of gain, of money, of the greatest possible amount of money, has in itself nothing to do with capitalism. This impulse exists and has existed among waiters, physicians, coachmen, artists, prostitutes, dishonest officials, soldiers, nobles, crusaders, gamblers, and beggars. One may say that it has been common to all sorts and conditions of men at all times and in all countries of the earth, wherever the objective possibility of it is or has been given. Capitalism is identical with the pursuit of profit, and forever *renewed* by profit, by means of continuous, rational, capitalistic enterprise. For it must be so: in a wholly capitalistic order of society, an individual capitalistic enterprise which did not take advantage of its opportunities for profit-making would be doomed to extinction.

Now, however, the Occident has developed capitalism in types, forms, and directions which have never existed elsewhere. All over the world there have been merchants, wholesale and retail, local and engaged in foreign trade. Loans of all kinds have been made, and there have been banks with the most various functions, at least comparable to ours of, say, the sixteenth century. Whenever money finances of public bodies have existed, money-lenders have appeared, as in Babylon, Hellas, India, China, Rome. They have financed wars and piracy, contracts and building operations of all sorts. This kind of entrepreneur, the capitalistic adventurer, has existed everywhere. With the exception of trade and credit and banking transactions, their activities were predominantly of an irrational and speculative character, or directed to acquisition by force, above all the acquisition of booty, whether directly in war or in the form of continuous fiscal booty by exploitation of subjects.

But in modern times the Occident has developed, in addition to this, a very different form of capitalism which has appeared nowhere else: the rational capitalistic organization of (formally) free labour. Only suggestions of it are found elsewhere.

Rational industrial organization, attuned to a regular market, and neither to political nor irrationally speculative opportunities for profit, is not, however, the only peculiarity of Western capitalism. The modern rational organization of the capitalistic enterprise would not have been possible without two other important factors in its development: the separation of business from the household, which completely dominates modern economic life, and closely connected with it, rational bookkeeping.

These peculiarities of Western capitalism have derived their significance in the last analysis only from their association with the capitalistic organization of labour. Even what is generally called commercialization, the development of negotiable securities and the rationalization of speculation, the exchanges, etc., is connected with it. For without the rational capitalistic organization of labour, all this, so far as it was possible at all, would have nothing like the same significance, above all for the social structure and all the specific problems of the modern Occident connected with it. Exact calculation — the basis of everything else — is only possible on a basis of free labour.

Hence in a universal history of culture the central problem for us is not, in the last analysis, even from a purely economic viewpoint, the development of capitalistic activity as such, differing in different cultures only in form: the adventurer type, or capitalism in trade, war, politics, or administration as sources of gain. It is rather the origin of this sober bourgeois capitalism with its rational organization of free labour. Or in terms of cultural history, the problem is that of the origin of the Western bourgeois class and of its peculiarities, a problem which is certainly closely connected with that of the origin of the capitalistic organization of labour, but is not quite the same thing. For the bourgeois as a class existed prior to the development of the peculiar modern form of capitalism, though, it is true, only in the Western hemisphere.

Now the peculiar modern Western form of capitalism has been, at first sight, strongly influenced by the development of technical possibilities. Its rationality is today essentially dependent on the calculability of the most important technical factors. But this encouragement was derived from the peculiarities of the social structure of the Occident. We must hence ask, from what parts of that structure was it derived, since not all of them have been of equal importance?

Among those of undoubted importance are the rational structures of law and of administration. For modern rational capitalism has need, not only of the technical means of production, but of a calculable legal system and of administration in terms of formal rules. Without it adventurous and speculative trading capitalism and all sorts of politically determined capitalisms are possible, but no rational enterprise under individual initiative, with fixed capital and certainty of calculations. Such a legal system and such administration have been available for economic activity in a comparative state of legal and formalistic perfection only in the Occident. We must hence inquire where that law came from. Among other circumstances, capitalistic interests have in turn undoubtedly also helped, but by no means alone nor even principally, to prepare the way for the predominance in law and administration of a class of jurists specially trained in rational law. But these interests did not themselves create that law. Quite different forces were at work in this development. And why did not the capitalistic interests do the same in China or India? Why did not the scientific, the artistic, the political, or the economic development there enter upon that path of rationalization which is peculiar to the Occident? For in all the above cases it is a question of the specific and peculiar rationalism of Western culture. Now by this term very different things may be understood. There is, for example, rationalization of mystical contemplation, that is of an attitude which, viewed from other departments of life, is specifically irrational, just as much as there are rationalizations of economic life, of technique, of scientific research, or military training, of law and administration. Furthermore, each one of these fields may be rationalized in terms of very different ultimate values and ends, and what is rational from one point of view may well be irrational from another. Hence rationalizations of the most varied character have existed in various departments of life and in all areas of culture. To characterize their differences from the viewpoint of cultural history it is necessary to know what departments are rationalized, and in what direction. Every such attempt at explanation must, recognizing the fundamental importance of the economic factor, above all take account of the economic conditions. But at the same time the opposite correlation must not be left out of consideration. For though the development of economic rationalism is partly dependent on rational technique and law, it is at the same time determined by the ability and disposition of men to adopt certain types of practical rational conduct. When these types have been obstructed by spiritual obstacles, the development of rational economic conduct has also met serious inner resistance. The magical and religious forces, and the ethical ideas of duty based upon them have in the past always been among the most important formative influences on conduct. In particular, it is our contention that there is a direct connection of the spirit of modern economic life with the rational ethics of ascetic Protestantism.

In order to understand the connection between the fundamental religious ideas of ascetic Protestantism and its maxims for everyday economic conduct, it is necessary to examine some of the beliefs of the early Puritans. Waste of time is the first and in principle the deadliest of sins. The span of human life is infinitely short and precious to make sure of one's own election. Loss of time through sociability, idle talk, luxury, even more sleep than is necessary for health, six to at most eight hours, is worthy of absolute moral condemnation. Inactive contemplation is also valueless, or even directly reprehensible if it is at the expense of one's daily work. For it is less pleasing to God than the active performance of His will in a calling.

The usefulness of a calling, and thus its favour in the sight of God, is measured primarily in moral terms, and thus in terms of the importance of the goods produced in it for the community. But a further, and, above all, in practice the most important, criterion is found in private profitableness. For if that God, whose hand the Puritan sees in all the occurrences of life, shows one of His elect a chance of profit, he must do it with a purpose. Hence the faithful Christian must follow the call by taking advantage of the opportunity. "If God show you a way in which you may lawfully get more than in another way (without wrong to your soul or to any other), if you refuse this, and choose the less gainful way, you cross one of the ends of your calling, and you refuse to be God's steward, and to accept His gifts and use them for Him when He requireth it: you may labour to be rich for God, though not for the flesh and sin." Wealth is thus bad ethically only in so far as it is a temptation to idleness and sinful enjoyment of life, and its acquisition is bad only when it is with the purpose of later living merrily and without care. But as a performance of duty in a calling it is not only morally permissible, but actually enjoined. The parable of the servant who was rejected because he did not increase the talent which was entrusted to him seemed to say so directly. To wish to be poor was, it was often argued, the same as wishing to be unhealthy; it is objectionable as a glorification of works and derogatory to the glory of God. Especially begging, on the part of one able to work, is not only the sin of slothfulness, but a violation of the duty of brotherly love according to the Apostle's own word.   (material)

The emphasis on the ascetic importance of a fixed calling provided an ethical justification of the modern specialized division of labour. In a similar way the providential interpretation of profit-making justified the activities of the business man.

Let us now clarify the points in which the Puritan idea of the calling and the premium it placed upon ascetic conduct was bound directly to influence the development of a capitalistic way of life. This asceticism turned with all its force against one thing: the spontaneous enjoyment of life and all it had to offer. Its attitude was thus suspicious and often hostile to the aspects of culture without any immediate religious value. The theatre was obnoxious to the Puritans, and with the strict exclusion of the erotic and of nudity from the realm of toleration, a radical view of either literature or art could not exist. The conceptions of idle talk, of superfluities, and of vain ostentation, all designations of an irrational attitude without objective purpose, thus not ascetic, and especially not serving the glory of God, but of man, were always at hand to serve in deciding in favour of sober utility as against any artistic tendencies. This was especially true in the case of decoration of the person, for instance clothing. That powerful tendency toward uniformity of life, which today so immensely aids the capitalistic interest in the standardization of production, had its ideal foundations in the repudiation of all idolatry of the flesh.

Finally, on the side of the production of private wealth, asceticism condemned both dishonesty and impulsive avarice. What was condemned as covetousness, Mammonism, etc., was the pursuit of riches for their own sake. For wealth in itself was a temptation. But here asceticism was the power "which ever seeks the good but ever creates evil"; what was evil in its sense was possession and its temptations. For, in conformity with the Old Testament and in analogy to the ethical valuation of good works, asceticism looked upon the pursuit of wealth as an end in itself as highly reprehensible; but the attainment of it as a fruit of labour in a calling was a sign of God's blessing. And even more important: the religious valuation of restless, continuous, systematic work in a worldly calling, as the highest means to asceticism, and at the same time the surest and most evident proof of rebirth and genuine faith, must have been the most powerful conceivable lever for the expansion of that attitude toward life which we have here called the spirit of capitalism.

When the limitation of consumption is combined with this release of acquisitive activity, the inevitable practical result is obvious: accumulation of capital through ascetic compulsion to save. The restraints which were imposed upon the consumption of wealth naturally served to increase it by making possible the productive investment of capital. As far as the influence of the Puritan outlook extended, under all circumstances — and this is, of course, much more important than the mere encouragement of capital accumulation — it favoured the development of a rational bourgeois economic life; it was the most important, and above all the only consistent influence in the development of that life. It stood at the cradle of the modern economic man.

Thus, a specifically bourgeois economic ethic had grown up. With the consciousness of standing in the fullness of God's grace and being visibly blessed by Him, the bourgeois business man, as long as he remained within the bounds of formal correctness, as long as his moral conduct was spotless and the use to which he put his wealth was not objectionable, could follow his pecuniary interests as he would and feel that he was fulfilling a duty in doing so. The power of religious asceticism provided him in addition with sober, conscientious, and unusually industrious workmen, who clung to their work as to a life purpose willed by God.

One of the fundamental elements of the spirit of modern capitalism, and not only of that but of all modern culture: rational conduct on the basis of the idea of the calling, was born from the spirit of Christian asceticism. The idea that modern labour has an ascetic character is of course not new. Limitation to specialized work, with a renunciation of the Faustian universality of man which it involves, is a condition of any valuable work in the modern world; hence deeds and renunciation inevitably condition each other today.

The Puritan wanted to work in a calling; we are forced to do so. For when asceticism was carried out of monastic cells into everyday life, and began to dominate worldly morality, it did its part in building the tremendous cosmos of the modern economic order. This order is now bound to the technical and economic conditions of machine production which to-day determine the lives of all the individuals who are born into this mechanism, not only those directly concerned with economic acquisition, with irresistible force. Perhaps it will so determine them until the last ton of fossilized coal is burnt. In Baxter's view the care for external goods should only lie on the shoulders of the "saint like a light cloak, which can be thrown aside at any moment." But fate decreed that the cloak should become an iron cage.

B. Processes and Examples

The distinction between a sect and a church was first made by Ernst Troeltsch in The Social Teaching of the Christian Churches. *In the United States we find hundreds of sects, small religious groups characterized usually by tension with the larger society. One of the major reasons for their proliferation is that the main source of ethical beliefs for these groups, the Bible, can be interpreted in various ways. The sect has been characterized as offering refuge to the downtrodden in a mass society. Some sects, however, have grown into the stature of churches, because of their dogma and orientation to the world. Benton Johnson, a sociologist of religion, stresses that certain sects stress ascetic norms which are similar to those of the dominant society.*

42 BENTON JOHNSON

Do Holiness Sects Socialize in Dominant Values?

INTRODUCTION

It is the thesis of this paper that one of the most important functions of the Holiness movement in American Protestantism is the socializing of marginal, lower class groups in the values commonly called middle class, or more broadly, in the dominant, institutionalized values of the larger society. This thesis cannot now be conclusively proved, but enough evidence exists to give it substantial credibility. Some of this evidence has been gathered by other investigators in the course of research on other problems involving Holiness groups. Much of the evidence was gathered by the author in his own research on Holiness sects.[1] For the most part the available material requires us to limit whatever generalizations are drawn to the group of white Holiness adherents in the South.

From *Social Forces*, Vol. 39 (May, 1961), pp. 309–316. Reprinted by permission of the author and publisher.

[1] G. Benton Johnson, Jr., "A Framework for the Analysis of Religious Action with Special Reference to Holiness and Non-Holiness Groups" (Unpublished doctoral dissertation, Harvard University, 1953). The purpose of this research was to compare the religious values of Holiness groups with those of non-Holiness evangelical groups on the same socio-economic level and in the same locality. A set of value conflict questions was asked verbally of 20 subjects with high religious commitment. Half of these were Holiness and half of them were non-Holiness in affiliation. The research sites, which were both rural and urban and included some mill villages, were in North Carolina. Evidence directly substantiating the present thesis was not deliberately gathered by this previous research, but much of what was gathered does uphold it.

At first glance there seems to be much evidence to support a contrary view. Holiness church life is markedly different from upper and middle class Protestant church life. For example, Holiness groups encourage their members to display strong, uninhibited religious feelings at their public meetings. This striking emotionalism is not at all like the staid and dignified tone of worship at higher social levels. Holiness groups are fundamentalist in theology and other-worldly in outlook, and this too is counter to the less dogmatic, less other-worldly tone of belief in many Protestant churches. Finally, the legalistic approach to "morals" of the Holiness bodies contrasts with the increasingly permissive and tolerant attitude toward such matters that is characteristic of the middle and upper classes. It is our contention, however, that these differences should not be allowed to obscure the more fundamental fact of similarity of basic value orientation between Holiness groups and the more privileged classes. We will show that many of the strikingly different features of the Holiness groups probably function as mechanisms of socialization. And we will see that there is evidence that the values in which Holiness adherents are socialized are similar to the dominant, institutionalized values of the larger society.

Most previous research conducted on Holiness groups has not been concerned with the present problem. Broadly speaking, previous sociological investigation has presented the following picture of the Holiness movement: (1) it offers an other-worldly, escapist, and emotional compensation for low socio-economic status; (2) the movement is not interested in attacking directly the institutional causes of this low status, and is hence indifferent to the major social and economic problems of the time. We have no quarrel with this exposition as far as it goes, but we do insist that it is only a partial sociological analysis. In a very few places in the present literature there are allusions to the phenomenon which we shall treat. Boisen states that Holiness sects give their members "hope and courage and strength to keep going in the face of difficulties," and adds that "Insofar as they succeed in doing this, their economic and social status is likely to be raised."[2] Holt remarks, after characterizing the social views of Holiness groups as "reactionary" rather than "revolutionary or constructive," that nevertheless, these sects "are successful in inspiring hope and a type of behavior in individuals which may raise their individual or group status above that of their class."[3] Somewhat more to the present point, Yinger briefly states that "Many individual adherents are helped, by the self-discipline that the sect encourages, to improve their own status," but immediately adds that "the sect is irrelevant to the social and cultural causes that continue to create

---

[2] Anton T. Boisen, "Economic Distress and Religious Experience," *Psychiatry*, 2 (May 1939), p. 194.

[3] John B. Holt, "Holiness Religion: Cultural Shock and Social Reorganization," *American Sociological Review*, 5 (October 1940), p. 741.

such disprivileged individuals."[4] The emphasis in all but one of these statements is on courage in the face of adversity, and the consequence, in all the statements, is considered to be upward social mobility.

In contrast, our emphasis will be on the fact that the Holiness groups encourage an orientation toward the world that constrains their members to adopt both motivationally and behaviorally an outlook similar in many respects to that of higher, more privileged social strata. Upward mobility may be an important long-term consequence of this orientation, but more fundamental is the possession of the orientation itself, which governs the believer's behavior toward the secular world. This orientation which the Holiness sects espouse is a variant of what Weber has called the ethic of inner-worldly asceticism.[5] Most authorities concede that there is an important connection between this orientation toward the world and the values and structure of industrial capitalism, specifically, and the dominant values of American society, more broadly. These values have been described frequently by sociologists.[6] Central to all descriptions is the emphasis on individual achievement of concrete goals by the consistent application of appropriate means. Closely related to the central achievement theme is the emphasis on democracy, individualism, mobility, and moral respectability. We will argue that the specifically religious values of Holiness groups converge with several features of the secular value system. If this is so, it will be plausible to suggest that a latent function of Holiness groups is the socialization of their adherents in the dominant societal values.

Theologically, the Holiness movement is a part of a larger movement within American Protestantism that has reacted against the austerities of Calvinism and has instead stressed the general availability of salvation and the possibility of the believer's achieving a kind of spiritual perfection. Of Arminian and Wesleyan parentage, Holiness theology has gone on to elaborate the stages by which the believer attains perfection. The so-called Pentecostal branch of the Holiness movement, to which nowadays the term Holiness is popularly applied, conceives of three such stages. The mandatory "initial evidence" of arriving at the third and last stage is the believer's utterance of syllables of an unknown tongue. The Holiness movement is also heir to the tradition of revivalism. Many well known orgiastic or emotional phenomena are common in Holiness meetings and some demonstra-

---

[4] J. Milton Yinger, *Religion, Society, and the Individual* (New York: The Macmillan Company, 1957), p. 173.

[5] Max Weber, *The Protestant Ethic and the Spirit of Capitalism*, Trans. by Talcott Parsons (New York: Charles Scribner's Sons, 1930). See especially Chap. 4, "The Religious Foundations of Worldly Asceticism," pp. 95–154.

[6] See especially the following works: Robin M. Williams, Jr., *American Society* (New York: Alfred Knopf, 1951), pp. 388–442; Clyde Kluckhohn and Florence R. Kluckhohn, "American Culture: Generalized Orientations and Class Patterns," in Lyman Bryson, Louis Finkelstein, and R. M. McIver (eds.), *Conflicts of Power in Modern Culture* (New York: Harper & Bros. 1947), pp. 106–128.

tion of strong feeling is considered an appropriate sign of attaining the various stages of perfection. The Holiness movement is fragmented into numerous sects. Some of these sects are congregational in polity but a number of them are episcopally organized.

Our concern will be with the Holiness groups of Pentecostal persuasion. We will also restrict ourselves to a consideration of the formally organized denominations in the Pentecostal tradition. There are many small groups, some confederated, some existing as individual "store front" congregations, that are in the Pentecostal movement. They seem especially prevalent among Negroes. We will not be concerned with these groups. It is freely admitted that the sociological generalizations which we hope to draw as to the effect of the Holiness movement on the value orientations of its adherents may not apply to the isolated "store front" variety of Pentecostal religion.

THE EMPHASIS ON CONVERSION

The great majority of the members of these newer Holiness sects of the Pentecostal persuasion are of low socio-economic status.[7] But it has also been established that lower class persons tend to be less involved in religious activities than any other class of the population.[8] Holiness groups are especially strong in the southern states.[9] Now it is probably accurate to assume that the southern white lower class is less imbued with the dominant values of the society than any other large group of native non-Catholic whites in the country. Writing on this class in Old City, Davis and Gardner note:

> By and large, lower-class behavior and ideology may be said to be characterized by a disdain for the government and laws which they see as creations of the upper class and middle class, a disdain for churches and associations and for the moral and religious values.[10]

The ordinary lower class person, and especially in the South, is not exposed

[7] See Liston Pope, "Religion and the Class Structure," *Annals of the American Academy of Political and Social Science,* 56 (March 1948), pp. 84–91; also Walter Goldschmidt, "Class Denominationalism in Rural California Churches," *American Journal of Sociology,* 49 (January 1944), pp. 348–355.

[8] Hadley Cantril, "Educational and Economic Composition of Religious Groups: An Analysis of Poll Data," *American Journal of Sociology,* 48 (March 1943), p. 577; Frank D. Alexander, "Religion in a Rural Community of the South," *American Sociological Review,* 6 (April 1944), p. 245.

[9] Holt, *op. cit.,* p. 742.

[10] Allison Davis, Burleigh B. Gardner, and Mary R. Gardner, *Deep South* (Chicago: University of Chicago Press, 1941), p. 80. See also pp. 79–83 and 118–136 [of *Social Forces*]. For other portrayals of the values of the southern white lower class, see W. J. Cash, *The Mind of the South* (New York: Alfred Knopf, 1941), pp. 42–44, 44–53, 308–309, etc.; also Leonard W. Doob, "Poor Whites: A Frustrated Class," in John Dollard, *Caste and Class in a Southern Town* (New York: Harper & Brothers, 1937), pp. 445–484.

to a constant set of socializing pressures emphasizing middle class work and achievement values, as is the person at higher social levels. In view of his initial commitment to values that are different from those of higher social classes, the lower class person if he is to adhere to these higher values, must make a "decision" or a reformulation of motivations, considerably more hard for him than for the middle class person who has really never had any serious choice to make. The borderline that he must cross is a sharp one. It is not chiefly an economic or occupational borderline but an evaluational and motivational borderline. And it is a borderline which, in view of his background and possible continued participation in lower class circles, the individual is in danger of crossing again in the opposite direction.

The great attention that Holiness and other sects pay to the phenomenon of conversion is highly suggestive of the fact that these groups endeavor to reorient the individual's motivations and values in fundamental ways. Holiness believers usually insist that they and their colleagues are "changed" at the time of conversion. Most of these groups draw a sharp and rigid line between the converted and the unconverted. Like the emphasis on conversion, the drawing of this line again suggests that a value conflict of some importance is involved.

What impels individuals to become members of Holiness sects and, we assume, to cross a value orientational borderline? Prior to any important reformulation of motives there is likely to be an experience of heightened frustration or deprivation. A number of observers of the Holiness groups suggest that many join in order to compensate for the frustration occasioned by their low socio-economic position. As Holt points out, the areas within the South that have experienced the greatest growth of Holiness groups have been those characterized by an expanding economy, chiefly of an industrial nature, but also of an agricultural and recreational character.[11] It is very likely, as some have suggested,[12] that in these areas the awareness among lower class persons that they are underprivileged has been sharpened as they have increasingly been obliged to earn a livelihood in fairly regimented organizations under the supervision of persons of higher status than themselves. In view of this heightened sense of being on the bottom of society, Holiness religion enables the lower class individual to deny that he is really on the bottom in any meaningful sense. As Liston Pope has put it, Holiness religion allows the individual to "substitute religious status for social status."[13] Or, as Goldschmidt has written, Holiness religion "denies the existence of this world and its woes; it denies the values in terms of which they [the adherents] are the underprivileged and sets up in their

[11] Holt, *op. cit.*, pp. 742–743.
[12] *Ibid.*, p. 745; also Yinger, *op. cit.*, p. 167.
[13] Liston Pope, *Millhands and Preachers* (New Haven: Yale University Press, 1942), p. 137.

stead a putative society in the Kingdom of God, where, because of their special endowments . . . they are the elite."[14]

THE ACCEPTANCE OF SECULAR SOCIETY

That important reformulations of values or motives take place when a person joins a Holiness sect seems pretty well agreed on. But we have not yet established the direction which this reformulation takes other than to note that most observers emphasize that the other-worldliness of Holiness belief inclines the individual to make a kind of fantasy-like retreat from what many would call social reality.

Let us grant that Holiness sects place great emphasis on getting to heaven and correspondingly devalue the pursuit of empirical, social ends as ultimate goals in themselves. Still, we assume that these sects are obliged to adopt some orientation toward secular activities. Basically, such an orientation must reject or accept the values and institutions of society.

Yinger, Pope, and others have rightly pointed out that although Holiness groups preach against "worldliness" they do not attempt an organized protest against any important features of the social system.[15] Now if a group espouses values in considerable opposition to those of the larger society, that group *must* face the problem of its relation to that society and the problem of how, specifically, to institutionalize its own values. This leads it to formulate a social policy aimed at securing these values in the face of opposition. The two possible polar types of such a social policy are outright attack on the larger social structure and a relatively total withdrawal from that society into exclusive religious communities. Holiness groups are not interested in "social action" or in attempts to reform society broadly so as to make it more "Christian" in any structural sense. Neither are they interested in forming themselves into segregated, tightly knit, self-sufficient communities.

Either the social action orientation or the withdrawal orientation would seem to be necessary adaptations if Holiness groups were seriously at odds with secular society. This leaves the alternative that Holiness groups basically accept society as constituted. There is evidence which can be immediately noted in support of the view that some kind of acceptance pattern characterizes the adaptation of these sects to the larger society. Even when we consider the many rules to which Holiness sects hold their members, these members are still for the most part left entirely free to participate in ordinary secular life. The church does not in any significant way attempt to be a regulator or coordinator of all its members' activities. Although the Holiness believer is held to certain distinct standards, he is able to pursue

[14] Goldschmidt, *op. cit.*, p. 354.
[15] Pope, *Millhands and Preachers*, pp. 164–166; Holt, *op. cit.*, p. 741; Yinger, *op. cit.*, pp. 170–173.

any legitimate private interest without being answerable to the congregation.

Although Holiness adherents are inclined to emphasize their distinctiveness and particularly their separation from "the things of this world," an examination of what they usually mean by this sentiment fails to reveal a sweeping rejection of secular norms. What Holiness people usually mean when they speak of their anti-worldliness is that they are opposed to religious disbelief and to a violation of their own normative standards. One Holiness pastor, when asked by the author to describe the chief evils of modern times, complained that "women will go downtown nude — I mean not wearing anything you'd call decent dress." Another pastor was concerned with "the material outlook on life . . . playing it high, wide and handsome." As we shall see, however, his objection is not to involvement in money-making activities per se, but to involvement without proper motivation and discipline.

Further evidence of the very restricted nature of the Holiness opposition to the ways of contemporary society is seen in the interest which some of our respondents showed in being respected in their own communities. An eagerness to be acknowledged as a legitimate movement by outsiders may be taken as a sign that the movement is not really so "different" and that it embodies beliefs and norms that outsiders might admire. A minister of the Pentecostal Holiness Church expressed great pride that he had been invited to sit on the platform at the public high school commencement exercises along with the usual group of Baptist, Methodist, and Presbyterian ministers. He acknowledged that when a Holiness church is founded in a community, ill will and opposition often arise. "They'll point us out and not want to have anything to do with us. . . . Call us liars and funny people," he said. This attitude is based on ignorance, according to the pastor, for "after they see what we really are they usually quiet down." Holiness people are simply "clean and decent folks" in his opinion. The emphasis on winning respect and acceptance of the non-Holiness community by showing them "what we really are," namely "clean and decent folks," seems to imply that there are important normative similarities between Holiness people and non-Holiness people.

THE PRIMACY OF ASCETIC NORMS

Still, acceptance of secular values can be a passive matter or it can be positive. There is evidence for the view that the Holiness acceptance of much of society and its values is of a positive and not of a passive nature. We make this statement because of the predominating influence of a form of Calvinist inner-worldly asceticism in determining the Holiness orientation toward the world. This asceticism underlies the specific norms to which Holiness adherents are held. These norms closely correspond, both in general orientation and in particulars, to the rules commonly incumbent on members of the older revivalistic denominations at an earlier stage of their development. Members of Holiness sects are forbidden to consume alcoholic beverages, to dance, to gamble or to play cards, to "smoke, dip or chew" tobacco. They may not attend places of "worldly amusement" such as plays, movies, fairs, ball games, or poolrooms. They may not engage in mixed bathing; women may not use makeup or wear short skirts, short sleeves, short hair or ornamental jewelry. Profanity is forbidden, and strict Sabbath observance is enjoined. Obligations, including debts, must be faithfully discharged. There are a few other specific commandments varying from denomination to denomination and from congregation to congregation, but the above list is the hard core of those categorical behavioral injunctions, chiefly of a prohibitive nature, to which most Holiness sects subscribe.

Almost all these rules are directed toward the suppression of the esthetic, the erotic, the irrational chance-taking or immediately pleasurable aspects of life. As Weber has argued, the "destruction of spontaneous, impulsive enjoyment"[16] implied in such ascetic rules is related to the attempt which certain religious systems make to induce their adherents to devote their lives to the systematic pursuit of overriding ends.[17] We assume that in general asceticism is a mechanism of the regulation of the gratification needs of individuals. It is especially important in a situation where behavior patterns stressing rational, purposeful activity are being inculcated. By cultivating the attitude of affective neutrality which is appropriate to any goal attainment process asceticism keeps the actor's gratification needs focused on the *ultimate* goal of action (salvation) by avoiding distracting or tempting gratifications that might enhance regressive tendencies or reinforce alienative motivations.

What is the relationship of these ascetic norms to the general observation that Holiness adherents are emotionally uninhibited? Much has been written about the fact that the emotionalism of Holiness meetings is erotically charged, that it appeals to persons who are emotionally "starved," and that it serves for lower class persons what more sublimated pursuits of immediate gratification serve for middle and upper class persons. No doubt all this is true, but from our standpoint the principal consequence of Holiness emotionalism is to secure and maintain the motivational commitment of individuals to the kind of life implied by the ascetic rules.

This commitment to asceticism is secured by playing on the individual's desire to escape punishment and find reward. The punishment is Hell. The reward is Heaven. The traditional Christian conception of man, destined without grace to go to Hell to suffer eternal torment, is usually presented at Holiness meetings. At the same time a "way out" is offered that promises

[16] Weber, *The Protestant Ethic,* p. 119.
[17] *Ibid.,* pp. 105, 166–169.

eternal joy instead. These alternatives are portrayed in the most vivid manner so as to induce the hearers actually to experience the extremes involved. Very likely the promise of immediate relief from a sense of general deprivation and meaninglessness is especially attractive to members of socially depressed strata. The "blessed assurance" of salvation is held to be attainable forthwith, as a kind of "foretaste of glory divine." Although Holiness religion does encourage a person to become satiated with the joy that he is saved, if he is to enter into full membership in the sect he must pay a price for this joy. The price is that he must frame his life according to the ascetic norms of the congregation. Hence for the full sect member the emotional permissiveness of Holiness meetings is likely to be seen as an opportunity to strengthen commitment to the obligatory norms of the group.

It is the ascetic norms and not the experiencing of a state of spiritual exaltation that are the substance of the day-to-day religious role of the Holiness believer. There are a number of common features of Holiness sects which attest to this fact. First, whereas an individual believer is only required to experience the initial stage of grace, that is of conversion itself, *all* members are required to abide by the set of ascetic rules which is typically referred to as the "discipline." Secondly, it is largely infraction of these rules that calls forth strong negative sanctions on the part of the congregation. Holiness sects are not typically lenient where infraction is concerned. They often practice a form of excommunication known as "disfellowshipping" or reading the offender out of the congregation. Finally, it is not possible among Holiness sects for an individual to claim a kind of spiritual exemption from these rules owing to his having received higher spiritual or emotional blessings. Quite the contrary: despite the fact that he may have received such a blessing, he is subject to negative sanctions if he fails to abide by the "discipline" of the sect. This policy is not the subject of controversy in Holiness circles and it is theologically supported by the Wesleyan doctrine of the possibility of a fall from grace.[18]

THE EFFECTS OF HOLINESS COMMITMENT

So far we have argued that far from being diffusely alienated from secular society, Holiness sectarians are positively oriented to it in terms of an ethic of inner-worldly asceticism. This ethic is regarded as having made its most significant secular impact on the economy. Therefore, it is important to investigate whether Holiness adherents tend to possess traits or attitudes

[18] These and other considerations have led the author to the conclusion that most Holiness sects are *ethical* in the sense in which this term has been defined by Weber. According to Weber, an ethical religion is one that stresses the ordering of everyday life according to a set of supernaturally legitimated norms. Such a religion stands in contrast to one that stresses contemplative or orgiastic union with the supernatural. See Max Weber, "The Social Psychology of the World Religions," in *From Max Weber: Essays in Sociology* (Trans. and ed. by Hans H. Gerth and C. Wright Mills) (New York: Oxford University Press, 1946), pp. 287–291.

which make for their successful integration into productive enterprises. Liston Pope has pointed to the fact that many mills in the South encourage the establishment of churches among their workers by giving land, buildings, and financial support. From the mills' standpoint this encouragement has been more than a pious gesture. It has been given with the expectation that the churches will produce a more dependable kind of worker, in short, that they will inculcate traits in laborers that are desirable from a managerial or production point of view. Almost without exception the churches so subsidized are Protestant and in the tradition of inner-worldly asceticism. Pope states:

> There is no doubt in the minds of employers that churches have succeeded, and still succeed, in providing better workers for the mills. Statements by employers in Gaston County may be taken as representative of employers throughout the brief history of the Southern textile industry.[19]

Although at the time of Pope's research in 1939 the mills tended predominantly to support non-Holiness evangelical denominations such as the Baptists, he did note an increasing tendency for them also to support Holiness sects, apparently as the employers came to recognize that these sects did not "upset the routine of the life of workers."[20]

Pope's interest in the mills' encouragement of churches was centered about the opportunities for control of the workers by the mill management that this situation affords and in the generally conservative social doctrine espoused by most churches whether subsidized or not.[21] This is a legitimate, and we think, valid analysis. But our interest here is in the simple fact that Protestant churches are directly encouraged by industrial concerns which feel it to be "good business" in the sense of enhancing the profit opportunities of the firm by providing a disciplined labor supply. A mill pastor very frankly spoke of this to the author in the following manner:

> Take these mills around here. They figure that church people make a better type than other people and they know what they're saying. X Mills, for instance, they invest from 50 to 100 thousand dollars a year in churches. . . . They say it's a good investment because the fellow who goes to church regularly is a more efficient worker in the long run. Maybe here is a better workman, but he gets drunk. Well, he spends his weekend drinking and he's no good on Monday. A company can't have half of its force staying out on Monday. . . . Some people don't wait for the weekends either, they go out on a spree every night. In other words, the Christian man

---

[19] Pope, *Millhands and Preachers,* p. 29.
[20] *Ibid.,* p. 140.
[21] See especially Pope's chapter on "Churches and Sects," pp. 117–140, and his chapter on "The Control of Churches by Mills," pp. 143–161, both in *Millhands and Preachers.*

in the long run would prove the more efficient workman because he can be depended on.

The emphasis is on efficiency and steadiness, and a direct connection between these virtues and the ascetic norm of abstention from alcohol is noted. Pope notes that southern mill officials lay particularly strong emphasis on the fact that the churchgoing employee is thought to be a steady and reliable worker. Nonchurchgoing employees may be as efficient, but they are more prone to absenteeism and to quitting the job, both of which have been serious problems to the southern textile industry.[22] We have argued before that asceticism is associated with a generally methodical long-term devotion to concrete tasks. The evidence presented by Pope establishes the plausibility of the proposition that the Holiness and other inner-worldly ascetic sects in the South actually do produce workers who consistently apply themselves to the tasks set for them in the industrial work situation.

Consistent self-application to one's work is not only a vital condition for building and maintaining a highly productive economy, it is one of the oft-mentioned characteristics of the dominant American value system. Self-application can be, and in many unskilled work roles possibly must be, essentially a routine matter requiring little initiative or independent decision-making. According to Weber, however, a further distinguishing characteristic of the ethic of inner-worldly asceticism is the concept of the *calling*. Self-direction, mastery, and positive achievement in occupational tasks are its central themes. Such an orientation is more appropriate to managerial and entrepreneurial roles than to lower level occupational positions. If, as we argue, the Holiness sects socialize in dominant values through the medium of an emphasis on the ethic of inner-worldly asceticism, they should produce values which stress mastery and self-direction.

What evidence is there that this is so? The author asked ten Holiness ministers in intensive interviews a question in which they were required to choose between two conflicting, generalized orientations toward life. One of these orientations was a statement of the self-direction and mastery theme of the ethic of the calling. The other orientation was stated so as to imply a less achievement-minded, more cautious outlook on life, and possibly to imply (if the respondent so chose) a rejection of the goal attainment process altogether. The question is reproduced below as it was read to the respondents:

> Two young Christian men are talking about what they are going to do with their lives. One of them says that in his life he is going to aim high. He is going to use his opportunities as they come to him day by day, he is going to develop his talents to the utmost; he is even going to risk failure by setting his own aims so far beyond that he may only partly attain them. The other man says, no, that

[22] Pope, *Millhands and Preachers*, pp. 29–30.

> in his life he isn't going to bite off more than he can chew, that
> he would rather do a little bit all right than make a big mess out of
> something that he can't handle. Now if you had to give aid and en-
> couragement to one of these two young men, which one would you
> agree with?

Only one respondent to this question tended in any manner to deny the
desirability of positive goal attainment in the occupational area. All the rest
of the informants, regardless of whether they chose the first or second
orientational alternative, demonstrated a positive approval of the goal attainment process. Almost all of those who chose the second orientational
alternative called attention to the importance of ascetic or traditional moral
norms. They did so, however, in order to set guides and limits to the
achievement process and not in order to pose asceticism as a complete way
of life. One minister of the Assemblies of God was disturbed at the prospect
of "going after success for its own sake." A minister of the Pentecostal Holiness Church did not want a man's overriding ambition to cause him to
"*push* himself anywhere that he wasn't prepared for." Still, this same minister held that "the higher positions will come if we've been consistent with
our self-improvement."

Half the respondents voiced the kind of enthusiastic endorsement of the
occupational goal attainment process that would have gratified an investigator such as Max Weber. All of them showed a clear comprehension and
acceptance of the ethic of the calling. The following response was given by
a Church of God pastor:

> I think it pays to have a vision. That's a wonderful thing to have.
> If you have God in your life then I think you'll always go forward
> and never backward. You have to stress your goal and what you're
> aiming for and go forth to get it. . . . If you ain't got no vision
> then you're going to say, "No I can't do it." You're going to say
> good enough is good enough. Determine what you want to do,
> then press on, don't be defeated.

A minister of the same denomination echoed similar sentiments when
he stated, "Where there's no aspiration, there's nothing done, there's no
heights taken." Still another minister of the Church of God said that he had
advised his son in school not to be "content with being in the middle of that
class or at the tail end of it — be at the very top of it." He went on to remark that people "ought to desire to excel in their work," and "make up
their minds to do well."

In many ways the most striking response was made by the minister of
the Assemblies of God whose stricture against "material things" was noted
above. In the present context he said:

> Well, I believe God has a plan for every one of us. If we accept
> Him then we're obligated to follow that plan for the glory of God.
> . . . When we're doing what God has planned for us we ought to

give God our very best. We ought to aim high, like the man said.
If you had a call to the grocery business, then you ought to be
ambitious for the glory of God, to be successful for Christ's sake.
That other man is a drifter. He's not interested in the glory of God.
He's not industrious, just doesn't care. I'm trying to think of some
Scripture. One that comes to mind is, "Be not slothful in business."
. . . When I went into the painting business I said I was going to
be the best in the business. And I was.

If we add this pastor's views on greed and worldly pleasures as well as
his joy over his salvation and spiritual perfection, we can round out our
presentation of the Holiness orientation toward life: It is other-worldly in
the sense of expecting the greatest personal joy in the hereafter, but it involves as a condition of this the devotion to doing the will of God in this
world. This will can be realized in almost any kind of activity, but it demands consistent output of effort, a denial of distracting pleasures, and a
focus on achievement. The positive emphasis on self-application, consistency, and achievement, are the principal Holiness themes that directly
converge with dominant American values.

C. Relationships with Other Institutions

*A church is, to some extent, a primary group. It is a place where
people come to meet with one another frequently and intimately.
Since members of a social class associate with each other, it is unlikely that people from diverse social classes would be found in any
given church. Undoubtedly, the class composition will vary from
community to community, but within the given community it is
quite homogeneous. Certain racial and ethnic groups were historically found in specific religious groups, and these patterns persist.
It is for such reasons that Liston Pope, a professor of social ethics,
can draw a neat relationship between religion and the class structure.
Religion is related to other institutions through the family, through
religion's role in social action and politics, and in other ways.*

43   LISTON POPE

Religion and the Class Structure

Archibald MacLeish once said that he divides people into two classes: those who divide people into classes, and those who do not. The doctrine of equalitarianism reflected in his statement has been central not only in the modern democratic ethos, but also in the Judaeo-Christian heritage from which modern democracy derived and secularized most of its basic values. Like democratic nations, however, Western religious communities have affirmed egalitarianism more clearly in theory than in practice, and at times they have modified even their theory — generally in terms of a doctrine of hierarchy or of "station" — in such fashion as to sanction social stratification.

BACKGROUND IN AMERICA

Almost from the beginning, Protestantism has tended to be the religion of the ruling and advantaged groups in the United States. In the early New England theocracies, church membership and the political franchise were closely associated, and both were restricted to a small minority. At the time of the first Federal census in 1790, less than 10 per cent of the population were church members; less than 10 per cent of the church members were Roman Catholics. By this time, most of the formal ties between religious affiliation and political power had been broken, but church membership continued to be confined largely to the more privileged groups.

The great Protestant revivals during the nineteenth century broadened the social base of church affiliation immensely. So did the waves of immigration during the latter half of the century; most of the new immigrants after 1880 were Roman Catholics, and their arrival greatly increased the strength of the Catholic Church in the United States, and also gave that church close connections with the growing mass of urban industrial workers. During the same period, Protestant churches were gaining strength in the rural population, among the American Negroes, and in the middle and upper classes of the rising cities. These broad tendencies in the relation of religion to social classes have gradually developed into the present patterns.

NATIONAL PATTERNS BEFORE THE WAR

The popular myth that America has no social classes is obscurantist but not entirely empty — it is hardly a greater misrepresentation than is the Marxist

From *The Annals of the American Academy of Political and Social Science,* Vol. 256 (March, 1948), pp. 84–91. Reprinted by permission of the author and publisher.

dogma at the other extreme.[1] Social stratification in the United States has
been proceeding rapidly for several decades, but according to most indices
American society still has the character of a continuum rather than of several discrete planes; it more nearly resembles a ramp than a staircase.
Further, the degree and modes of stratification vary considerably by region,
by size of town, by the economic and ethnic bases of the community, and
perhaps by other factors.[2]

There is no clearly defined national pattern of social classes, except as
one may be arbitrarily constructed in terms of income classes or other general criteria — and such procedure falsifies the picture of the actual stratification in most American communities. The most accurate studies of social
classes have therefore been pitched at the community level, and generalizations for the Nation as a whole must be rather tentative and abstract.

The over-all pattern for religion and the class structure can be pieced
together from information gathered in public opinion polls.[3] Using data
gathered from approximately 14,000 persons in 1939–40, Hadley Cantril
employs a threefold class scheme: upper, middle, and lower.[4] His material
(adapted in Table 1) indicates that there was at that time far less difference in class affiliation between Protestants and Catholics in the Nation as
a whole than had been commonly supposed, though differences become
more apparent when data from the South are segregated. For every upper-
class Protestant in the South, there were six lower-class Protestants; in the
other regions of the country, the percentage classified as upper class ranged
from 14 to 18 per cent, and the percentage in the lower class ranged from
25 to 32 per cent, leaving a majority in each region in the middle class.

In comparison, the Roman Catholic Church was composed of a smaller
percentage of upper-class members (ranging from 6 to 15 per cent in the
various regions) and a larger percentage of lower-class adherents (varying
from 30 to 51 per cent). But the net results of Cantril's study indicate that
Protestantism had a larger representation from the lower class and Catholi-

---

[1] Gunnar Myrdal, looking at American society as a European social scientist, found
an impressive degree of social fluidity and mobility still present. An American Dilemma
(New York, 1944), p. 670.

[2] All these facts are reflected in a continuing debate among social scientists over the
validity of various criteria for the study of class alignments, the number of social classes,
and so forth.

[3] It is not certain that these polls are entirely adequate for description of religious or
class patterns, even when "social" rather than "voting" samples are used. For one thing,
the distribution by religious denominations in their samples seldom coincides with the
established proportions of these denominations in relation either to the total population
or to the total church membership. Similarly, regional distribution of various religious
groups is not always reflected accurately. Further, classification of interviewees into
social classes generally rests on rather superficial and subjective methodology; in most
cases, the interviewer makes the classification in terms of general impressions as to the
type of neighborhood, occupation, house furnishings, dress, and so on.

[4] Hadley Cantril, "Educational and Economic Composition of Religious Groups,"
American Journal of Sociology, Vol. 47, No. 5 (March 1943), pp. 574–79.

Table 1.   Class Composition of Catholics and Protestants, 1939–40[a]

	Percentage distribution		
	Upper class	Middle class	Lower class
Protestants			
In US	14	52	34
In South[b]	8	48	44
In remainder of US	17	54	29
Catholics			
In US	9	50	41
In South[c]	10	42	48
In remainder of US	9	51	40

[a] Constructed from data given by Hadley Cantril, "Educational and Economic Composition of Religious Groups," *American Journal of Sociology*, Vol. 47, No. 5 (March 1943), p. 576, Table 2. Cantril used "social" samples.

[b] The South is overwhelmingly Protestant, and the ratio of church membership to population is higher there than in any other region (see Howard W. Odum, *Southern Regions of the United States* [Chapel Hill, 1936], p. 141). The South is also notoriously poor in comparison with other regions, and has proportionately smaller middle and upper classes. Gross inclusion of its figures in national studies therefore results in considerable distortion of the picture for other regions of the country.

[c] Cantril's sample of Southern Catholics is too small — only 165 cases — to support confident generalizations.

cism had more middle-class members than popular generalizations have assumed.

Cantril also discovered that the proportion of Protestants to Catholics rises as one moves up the educational scale. Protestants have had more schooling in every section of the country, and outside the South the percentage of college graduates is almost twice as high for Protestants as for Catholics. Further, "those who are not church members (whether Protestant or Catholic) are found in increasing numbers as either income or education decreases" — and vice versa.

PRESENT PATTERNS

Cantril's conclusions must be thoroughly revised in the light of a series of studies of similar data gathered more recently. A breakdown of four polls taken in 1945–46 has been made for the Department of Research and Education of the Federal Council of Churches by the same office from which the data for 1939–40 were obtained — the Office of Public Opinion Research at Princeton University, of which Dr. Cantril is director. The contrast between Cantril's earlier data and these more recent studies indicates either that information gathered in these various public opinion polls is not reliable for interpretation of the relation of religion to class structure, or else that a profound class realignment has occurred in religious denominations during the war years or that class lines themselves have shifted significantly.

TABLE 2.   CLASS COMPOSITION OF RELIGIOUS BODIES, 1945–46[a]

Body	Upper class	Middle class	Lower class
	Percentage distribution		
Entire sample	*13*	*31*	*56*
Catholic	9	25	66
Jewish	22	32	46
Methodist	13	35	52
Baptist	8	24	68
Presbyterian	22	40	38
Lutheran	11	36	53
Episcopalian	24	34	42
Congregational	24	43	33

[a] Derived from a breakdown of four polls taken by the American Institute of Public Opinion in 1945-46, covering approximately 12,000 cases. Each poll covered a "voting sample" of approximately 3,000 cases. See note 3.

TABLE 3.   OCCUPATIONAL CATEGORIES, AND TRADE UNION MEMBERSHIP, IN MAJOR RELIGIOUS BODIES, 1945–46[a]

Body	Business and professional	White collar	Urban manual workers[b]	Farmers	Percentage belonging to trade unions
	Percentages by occupational categories				
Entire sample	*19*	*20*	*44*	*17*	*19*
Catholic	14	23	55	8	28
Jewish	36	37	27	0.6	23
Methodist	19	19	39	23	14
Baptist	12	14	52	22	16
Presbyterian	31	21	31	17	13
Lutheran	13	18	43	26	20
Episcopalian	32	25	36	7	13
Congregational	33	19	28	20	12

[a] For source of data, see note to Table 2. Figures given above pertain to "the principal breadwinner" in the case of each family interviewed, where the interviewee was not personally employed.

[b] This category includes urban manual workers of all grades of skill, and also incorporates a rather diverse group of "service occupations" that are primarily manual in character (such as domestic servants, policemen, firemen). A great deal of variation is represented within each of the categories in this table, and their relative class status varies from community to community.

The class composition of various religious bodies as revealed by these more recent studies is indicated in Table 2. If these figures reflect the actual situation, all the major religious bodies in the United States now draw a far higher percentage of their members from the lower class than they did before World War II. There remains a significant difference between the Catholic constituency and all others except the Baptist, which parallels it almost precisely in stratification. Distribution of the Jewish group is very much like that of the Episcopalians; a majority of the members of both still come from the middle and upper classes, and this is even more largely the case for the Presbyterians and the Congregationalists.

The Federal Council studies also provide information on the relation of religious adherents to certain occupational groups, to membership in trade unions, to educational status, to political preferences in 1944, and to other indices of class affiliation. Space permits only a few generalizations derived from the studies.[5]

Occupational affiliations. Occupation is considered one of the most reliable indices of class affiliation; Table 3 attempts to correlate major religious bodies with certain categories of occupation. The categories are too gross in character to permit exact comparison with Table 2, and the class rank of many occupations varies by social context. The most surprising revelation in Table 3 is the number of trade union members in the churches, and especially the number in the Protestant churches, which have been considered to be largely divorced from industrial workers.[6] The proportion

TABLE 4. EDUCATIONAL LEVELS IN RELIGIOUS BODIES, 1945–46[a]

	Percentage distribution		
Body	*High school incomplete (or less)*	*High school graduates (or more)*	*College graduates*
Entire sample	52	48	*11*
Catholic	57	43	7
Jewish	37	63	16
Methodist	49	51	12
Baptist[b]	65	35	6
Presbyterian	37	63	22
Lutheran	56	44	8
Episcopalian	35	65	22
Congregational	29	71	21

[a] For source, see note to Table 2.

[b] As the data for this table were drawn from a *voting* cross section, virtually no Southern Negro Baptists are represented in these figures.

[5] Access to this material has generously been made available by the Department of Research and Education of the Federal Council of Churches, and parts of it are used here by permission. . . .

[6] Trade union leaders are also more characteristically Protestant than many Protestants realize. A survey of two hundred top American Federation of Labor (AFL) and Congress of Industrial Organizations (CIO) leaders was made in 1945 by the Bureau of Applied Social Research at Columbia University. Fifty-one per cent of the leaders designated their religious preference as Protestant, 35 per cent Catholic, and 4 per cent Jewish. There were no significant differences between AFL and CIO leaders in this respect. Twelve per cent of the AFL leaders and 6 per cent of the CIO leaders had no religious affiliation.

of union members is considerably higher, however, in the Catholic and Jewish groups.

Educational levels. The Federal Council studies of poll data concerning religious affiliation and educational achievement confirm — and refine — the general conclusions reached by Cantril, as is indicated in Table 4. But significant differences within Protestantism are depicted by this table, ranging from the least-educated Baptists to the most-educated Congregationalists. Measured against the Protestant scale in this respect, the Catholics are above the Baptists and almost on a par with the Lutherans; the Jews are near the top, almost precisely on the same level as the Presbyterians. Other data indicate that denominational differences in educational level prevail in all class groups, though they are somewhat less pronounced in the middle and upper classes than in the lower.

TABLE 5.   POLITICAL PREFERENCES IN RELIGIOUS BODIES, 1944[a]

	Percentage voting for Dewey	Percentage voting for Roosevelt
Entire sample	32	42
Catholic	20	54
Jewish	6	75
Methodist	38	37
Baptist	24	42
Presbyterian	48	32
Lutheran	42	35
Episcopalian	44	36
Congregational	56	26

[a] For source of data, see note to Table 2.

Political preferences. Several studies have shown that religion and class status are important variables in the study of political behavior, and that they often cut across each other, exposing individuals to "cross pressures."[7] Table 5 summarizes the Federal Council poll data covering political preferences of religious groups in the 1944 election. The Catholics and the Jews voted heavily for the Democratic candidate; the Protestants split more evenly, but in most denominations a majority of the votes went to the Republican candidate, with significant variations between the denominations. From the political standpoint, the raw data reveal that 25 per cent of all Mr. Roosevelt's votes came from the Catholic group, as did 12.5 per cent of Mr. Dewey's.

Summary. All told, information derived from public opinion polls indicates that Protestant and Jewish adherents come more largely from the middle and upper classes than do Catholics, with significant differences be-

[7] Paul F. Lazarsfeld, Bernard Berelson, and Hazel Gaudet, *The People's Choice* (New York, 1944); Gerhart H. Saenger, "Social Status and Political Behavior," *American Journal of Sociology*, Vol. 51, No. 2 (Sept. 1945), pp. 103–13.

tween the major Protestant denominations in this respect. At the same time, Protestants are more largely represented in the lower class than has been commonly supposed; a significant change in this respect may have occurred during World War II. Protestants, and Jews even more largely, come typically from business, professional, white collar, and service occupations; Catholics are more typically workers; Catholics, Jews, and Episcopalians have comparatively few farmers. Each major religious body has a sizable percentage of trade unionists in its membership. In the over-all picture, Protestants and Jews have had more education than Catholics. Catholics and Jews gave large majorities of their votes to Mr. Roosevelt in 1944; the Protestants divided, with a majority in most denominations voting for Mr. Dewey.

COMMUNITY STUDIES

There have been a number of close studies of social stratification in particular American communities in the last twenty-five years, and they yield more precise information concerning religion and the class structure than can be deduced from public opinion polls. Their findings are too varied in detail (this is their great merit) to permit summary here, but generalizations based on them would include the following:

Social stratification. 1. Every American community, from the most rural to the most urban, from Plainville through Middletown to Metropolis, has some pronounced pattern of social stratification, and religious institutions and practices are always very closely associated with this pattern. The number of classes, or layers, varies from community to community; Old City in the Deep South differs in important respects from Yankee City in New England; not all social hierarchies call their bottom class, as do the residents of Plainville, "people who live like the animals." However much details may differ, the stratification is found in all American communities, and religion is always one of its salient features.

2. Differentiation within Protestantism corresponds fairly closely to class divisions. Individual Protestant churches tend to be "class churches," with members drawn principally from one class group. Even where membership cuts across class lines, control of the church and its policies is generally in the hands of officials drawn from one class, usually the middle class.

Protestant denominations in their total outreach touch nearly all sections of the population. But each denomination tends also to be associated with a particular social status. Such denominations as the Congregational, Episcopal, and Presbyterian are generally associated in local communities with the middle and upper classes; the Methodist, Baptist, and Disciples of Christ denominations are more typically associated with the middle classes. The Lutheran denominations are harder to classify, because of their closer association with farmers, with particular ethnic backgrounds, and with skilled workers.

Though all of these major denominations have adherents from the lower classes, the religious expression of the latter has increasingly taken place in the last quarter-century through the new Pentecostal and holiness sects, which represent on the one hand a protest (couched in religious form) against social exclusion and on the other a compensatory method (also in religious form) for regaining status and for redefining class lines in religious terms. Some of these sect groups are already beginning to repeat the age-old transition toward establishment as respected churches, moving up the social scale (in terms of the class status of their adherents) as they do so. Christianity itself began among the poor, who accepted it less because they were poor than because they were marginal; most of its branches have long since permeated the higher classes of their societies and have relatively neglected the poor.

Ethnic division. 3. Internal differentiation in the Catholic Church tends to follow ethnic lines more largely than economic lines.[8] Ethnic divisions cut across the organization of Catholic parishes by geographical districts, though the latter have often themselves reflected the residential propinquity of immigrants from a particular country. Thus the local Catholic churches in a community may include a French Catholic church, a Polish Catholic church, an Irish Catholic church, and the like.

"Nationality churches" are found in Protestantism also, but they tend to be exceptional and to be associated more clearly with social (and often spatial) isolation than is the case in Catholicism. There is a great deal of evidence that nationality churches, whether Protestant or Catholic, are gradually losing their peculiar ethnic connections. As the number of foreign born has declined, sermons in English have been introduced to supplement — or to replace — the mother tongue.

The institution has found it very difficult to bridge effectively the cultural gap between its older and younger members. Of most importance, intermarriage is increasingly modifying ethnic divisions in urban centers, though some groups (especially the Jewish, Italian, and Polish) remain more endogamous than others; such intermarriage, however, "is not general and indiscriminate but is channeled by religious barriers; and groups with the same religions tend to intermarry."[9] Religious divisions may therefore become even more important indices of stratification in the future. Meanwhile, the nationality church continues to serve as a cohesive force, at least for its older members, and at the same time it helps to insulate them against disruptive and assimilative influences.

4. Differentiation within Judaism corresponds to a combination of ethnic

8 See John W. McConnell, *The Evolution of Social Classes,* Washington, 1942; Elin Anderson, *We Americans: A Study of Cleavage in an American City,* Cambridge, Mass., 1938; W. Lloyd Warner and Leo Srole, *The Social Systems of American Ethnic Groups,* New Haven, 1945.

9 Ruby Jo Reeves Kennedy, "Single or Triple Melting-Pot? Intermarriage Trends in New Haven, 1870–1940," *American Journal of Sociology,* Vol. 49, No. 4 (Jan. 1944), pp. 331–39.

and class pressures, with the latter probably stronger in the large. Higher-class and better-educated Jews tend to leave Orthodox synagogues and to join Conservative or Reform congregations, or to become secularized. Studies of this alignment are inadequate, but the general trend appears clear. This trend has not prevailed, incidentally, among the Jews of Great Britain.

Church of the middle class. 5. Religious organizations decline in influence at both extreme ends of the social scale, among the most privileged (though there is some contrary evidence) and among the most disadvantaged. In this very general sense, the churches are associated especially with the middle classes.

NEGRO STRATIFICATION

A few statistics will summarize the relation of Negro churchmen to the white religious institutions.[10] Of the more than 14 million Negroes in the United States, about 6.8 million belong to some church. Of these, about 300 thousand are Catholics; two-thirds of the Negro Catholics are in segregated or separate churches. Of the 6.5 million Negro Protestants, about half a million belong to the predominantly white denominations. While Negroes are integrated into denominational affairs to varying degree in higher ecclesiastical bodies (synods, presbyteries, general conferences, and so forth), there is almost no mixing of whites and Negroes at the level of the individual congregation. According to unpublished studies by Frank Loescher, Dwight Culver, and others, less than 1 per cent of the white congregations have any Negro members (and each of these generally has only two or three), and less than one-half of 1 per cent of the Negro Protestants who belong to "white denominations" worship regularly with white persons.

The remaining six million Negro churchmen belong to all-Negro denominations. Nearly all of them are Methodists or Baptists. There are social classes within the Negro community, though the criteria differ from those operative in the white community. Religion tends to be associated with Negro class divisions in a particular context, however, much as it does among whites.[11]

DYNAMICS OF RELIGION AND CLASS

There has been a long debate over whether religion or class is primary in social structure and change, with the other as a function or a secondary manifestation. Max Weber and Karl Marx represent extreme views; Bergson appears to be more nearly correct in the light of evidence accumulated recently.[12] Religion, despite the close association of its institutions with the

[10] For fuller details, see the articles by John LaFarge and by the present writer in *Survey Graphic*, Vol. 36, No. 1 (Jan. 1947), pp. 59 and 61.

[11] V. E. Daniel, "Ritual and Stratification in Chicago Negro Churches," *American Sociological Review*, Vol. 7, No. 3 (June 1942), pp. 352–61.

[12] Henri Bergson, *The Two Sources of Morality and Religion* (New York, 1935).

class structure, is neither simply a product nor a cause, a sanction nor an enemy, of social stratification. It may be either or both, as it has been in various societies at various times.

There is little evidence that religion will operate in the near future to change American class structure appreciably. Several opinion polls have shown ministers to be discontent with many aspects of social organization in this country, and church leaders — of all faiths — are more concerned about racial patterns in America than ever before. (There is less concern about class lines than about race barriers.) But unless a drastic transformation comes about in the churches, they will probably continue for the most part to adapt to class divisions — and even to intensify them — as they have done in the past.

XV RELATIONSHIP OF INSTITUTIONS

We have listed articles which deal with one institution in relation to another, but have not indicated the subtle interplays among them all. Bellah, a sociologist of religion and social theorist, traces the changes that took place in the religious value systems, which in turn influenced other institutions, when modernization began in Turkey and Japan.

44 ROBERT N. BELLAH

Religious Aspects of Modernization in Turkey and Japan

The process of modernization of the "backward" nations such as Turkey and Japan, which will be considered here, involves changes in the value system as well as economic, political, and social changes. In traditional societies the value system tends to be what Howard Becker calls "prescriptive."[1] A prescriptive system is characterized by the comprehensiveness and specificity of its value commitments and by its consequent lack of flexibility. Motivation is frozen, so to speak, through commitment to a vast range of relatively specific norms governing almost every situation in life. Most of these specific norms, usually including those governing social institutions,

From *American Journal of Sociology*, Vol. LXIV (July, 1958), pp. 1–5. Reprinted by permission of the author and The University of Chicago Press.
[1] For a recent definition of "prescriptive" and "principial" see Howard Becker, "Current Sacred-Secular Theory and Its Development," in Howard Becker and Alvin Boskoff (eds.), *Modern Sociological Theory in Continuity and Change* (New York: Dryden Press, 1957).

are thoroughly integrated with a religious system which invokes ultimate
sanctions for every infraction. Thus changes in economic or political institutions, not to speak of family and education, in traditional societies tend
to have ultimate religious implications. Small changes will involve supernatural sanctions.

Yet such a society, when faced with grave dislocations consequent to
Western contact, must make major changes in its institutional structure if
it is to survive. What changes must be made in the organization of the
value system so that these structural changes may go forward?

We may say that the value system of such a society must change from a
prescriptive type to a "principial" type, to borrow again from Becker. Traditional societies, as we have said, tend to have a normative system, in
which a comprehensive, but uncodified, set of relatively specific norms
governs concrete behavior. But in a modern society an area of flexibility
must be gained in economic, political, and social life in which specific
norms may be determined in considerable part by short-term exigencies in
the situation of action, or by functional requisites of the relevant social sub-
systems. Ultimate or religious values lay down the basic principles of social
action; thus such a normative system is called "principial," but the religious
system does not attempt to regulate economic, political, and social life in
great detail, as in prescriptive societies. Looking at this process another
way, we may say that there must be a differentiation between religion and
ideology, between ultimate values and proposed ways in which these values
may be put into effect. In traditional prescriptive societies there is no such
discrimination. Difference of opinion on social policy is taken to imply difference as to religious commitment. The social innovator necessarily becomes a religious heretic. But in modern society there is a differentiation
between the levels of religion and social ideology which makes possible
greater flexibility at both levels.

How is the normative system in a traditional society to be changed from
prescriptive to principial, and how is the differentiation of the religious and
ideological levels to be effected, especially in the face of the concerted
effort of the old system to avoid any changes at all? I would assert that
only a new religious initiative, only a new movement which claims religious
ultimacy for itself, can successfully challenge the old value system and its
religious base. The new movement, which arises from the necessity to make
drastic social changes in the light of new conditions, is essentially ideological and political in nature. But, arising as it does in a society in which the
ideological level is not yet recognized as having independent legitimacy,
the new movement must take on a religious coloration in order to meet the
old system on its own terms. Even when such a movement is successful in
effecting major structural changes in the society and in freeing motivation
formerly frozen in traditional patterns so that considerable flexibility in

economic and political life is attained, the problems posed by its own partly
religious origin and its relation to the traditional religious system may still
be serious indeed.

Let us turn to the example of Turkey.[2]

Ottoman Turkey in the eighteenth century was a traditionalistic society
with a prescriptive value system. Virtually all spheres of life were theoretically under the authority of the religious law, the Shari'ah. Indeed, the
government was supposed to have an area of freedom within the law. But
this freedom had become narrowly restricted. Precedents of governmental
procedure were tacitly assimilated to the religious law.

Beginning with Selim III in the late eighteenth century, a series of reforming sultans and statesmen attempted to make major changes in Turkish
society in an effort to cope with increasingly desperate internal and external conditions. While some changes were made, especially in areas remote
from the central strongholds of the religious law, the reforming party was
unable to attain any ultimate legitimation in the eyes of the people, and,
although Turkish society was shaken to its foundations, periods of reform
alternated with periods of blind reaction in which reformers were executed
or banished.

The last of these reactionary periods was that of the rule of the despotic
Sultan Abdul Hamid II, who was overthrown in 1908 by a coup of young
army officers whom we know as the "Young Turks." By this time it had
become clear to leading intellectuals that more was needed than another
interim of liberal reform. They saw that a basic change in the cultural
foundation of Turkish society was demanded if the long-delayed changes
in economic, political, and social structure were to be effected. Some felt
that a modern purified Islam could provide the new cultural basis, but
orthodox Islam was so deeply imbedded in the fabric of traditional society
that the Islamic modernists found little response in the religious party.
Others looked to Western liberal democracy as a satisfactory foundation.
Those sensitive to the mind of the Turkish masses, however, pointed out
that the Turkish people would never accept a value system so obviously
"made abroad" and which could so easily be condemned by the conservatives with the stigma of unbelief.

It was Ziya Gökalp, a sociologist much influenced by Durkheim, who
ardently championed Turkish nationalism as the only satisfactory cultural
foundation for the new Turkey. Gökalp found the referent for all symbols
of ultimate value in society itself. His answer to the religious conservatives
was that the true Islam was that of the Turkish folk, not of the effete religious hierarchy which was largely educated in the Arabic and Persian

[2] Throughout the discussion of Turkey I shall rely heavily on lectures and unpublished material of Niyazi Berkes, of the Islamic Institute at McGill University, who is
undertaking a pioneering study of Turkish modernization.

languages rather than the Turkish language. Here at last was an ideology to which people could respond with emotion and which could challenge religious conservatism on its own grounds.

But the course of world history did as much as Gökalp's eloquence to decide in favor of the nationalist alternative for Turkey. Not only did World War I shear Turkey of her empire, but the subsequent invasions of Anatolia threatened the very life of the nation itself. Mustafa Kemal, who led the ultimately successful effort of national resistance, partly chose and partly was impelled to make the nation the central symbol in his subsequent drive for modernization. As a result, the highest value and central symbol for the most articulate sections of the Turkish people became not Islam but Turkism, or nationalism, or Kemalism, or, simply, "the Revolution." Having a strong national and personal charismatic legitimacy, Mustafa Kemal, later known as "Ataturk," was able to create a far-reaching cultural revolution in which the place of religion in the society was fundamentally altered. We may note some of the landmarks in this revolution. In 1924 the office of caliph was abolished. In the same year all religious schools were closed or converted into secular schools. The most important change of all took place in 1926: the Muslim Civil Law was abandoned and the Swiss Civil Code adopted almost without change. Finally, in 1928, the phrase in the constitution stating that the religion of Turkey is Islam was deleted, and Turkey was declared a secular state.

That the Turks were deeply conscious of what they were doing is illustrated by the following quotation from Mahmud Essad, the minister of justice under whom the religious law was abandoned:

> The purpose of laws is not to maintain the old customs or beliefs which have their source in religion, but rather to assure the economic and social unity of the nation.
>
> When religion has sought to rule human societies, it has been the arbitrary instrument of sovereigns, despots, and strong men. In separating the temporal and the spiritual, modern civilization has saved the world from numerous calamities and has given to religion an imperishable throne in the consciences of believers.[3]

This quotation illustrates well enough the transition from prescriptive to principial society and the differentiation of religion and ideology as two distinct levels. It is clear that the great advances of Turkish society in economic, political, and social life are based on this new cultural foundation. But implicit in Essad's words are some of the yet unsolved problems about that new cultural pattern.

For Essad and other Turkish reformers "the Revolution" was a criterion for everything, even for the place of religion in society, and thus, whether

[3] Quoted in Henry E. Allen, *The Turkish Transformation* (Chicago: University of Chicago Press, 1935), p. 34.

consciously or not, they gave the revolution an ultimate, a religious, significance. The six principles upon which the constitution is based — republicanism, nationalism, populism, étatism, secularism, and revolution — are taken as self-subsisting ultimates. Thus the religious implications of the political ideology remain relatively unchecked. These express themselves in party claims to ultimate legitimacy and in an inability on the part of the party in power to accept the validity of an opposition, which are not in accord with the flexibility appropriate in a modern principial society.

On the other hand, Islam in Turkey has not on the whole been able to redefine its own self-image and face the theological issues involved in becoming a religion primarily, in Essad's words, "enthroned in men's consciences." Nor has it been able to provide a deeper religious dimension of both legitimation and judgment of the six principles which are the basis of the new social life. It remains, on the whole, in a conservative frame of mind in which the ideological claims are considerable, thus still posing a threat, possibly a great one, to return the society to a less differentiated level of social organization. Considering the trend of the last forty years, however, we seem to be observing a differentiation in the process of becoming, but it is too soon to say that it has been entirely accomplished.

Japan, while illustrating the same general processes as Turkey, does so with marked differences in important details.[4] Premodern Japan was a traditionalistic society with a prescriptive normative system closely integrated with a religious system composed of a peculiar Japanese amalgam of Shinto, Confucianism, and Buddhism. In the immediate premodern period, however, a conjuncture of the Confucian stress on loyalty and a revived interest in Shinto began to have explosive consequences. The actual rule at this time was in the hands of a military dictator, or Shogun, hereditary in the Tokugawa family. The emperor was relegated to purely ceremonial functions in the palace at Kyoto. But, as economic and social conditions deteriorated under Tokugawa rule, important elements in the population became alienated from the political status quo. They proved extremely receptive to the religious message of the revival Shintoists and legitimist Confucians, who insisted that the true sovereign was the emperor and that the Shogun was a usurper. According to their conception, the emperor is divine, descended from the sun-goddess, and his direct rule of the Japanese people could be expected to bring in a virtually messianic age.

This movement was already vigorous when Perry's ships moved into Tokyo Bay in 1853. The inability of the Tokugawa government to keep foreigners from desecrating the sacred soil of Japan added the last fuel to the flames of resentment, and, with the slogan "Revere the Emperor; expel the barbarians," a successful military coup overthrew the Tokugawa and restored the emperor to direct rule.

---

[4] For a more extensive treatment of the Japanese case, especially the premodern background see my *Tokugawa Religion* (Glencoe, Ill.: Free Press, 1957).

I would suggest that Japan was at this point, in 1868, virtually at the beginning of serious Western influence, in a position that Turkey reached only in the early 1920's under Mustafa Kemal. But she reached it in quite a different way. Unlike Turkey, one of the very foundations of the old traditional order in Japan, the divine emperor, provided the main leverage for the radical reorganization of that order. The young samurai who put through the Meiji Restoration used the central value of loyalty to the emperor to legitimize the immense changes they were making in all spheres of social life and to justify the abandoning of many apparently sacred prescriptions of the traditional order. No other sacredness could challenge the sacredness inherent in the emperor's person.

Here we see an ideological movement, essentially political in nature, whose aim was the strengthening and thus the modernizing of Japan, taking a much more openly religious coloration than was the case in Turkey. There was in the early Meiji period an attempt to make Shinto into the national religion and a determined effort to root out all rival religions. Christianity was sharply discouraged, but it was on Buddhism, the chief native religious tradition with little relation to the imperial claims to divinity, that the ax fell. The Buddhist church was disestablished, and all syncretism with Shinto prohibited. In the words of D. C. Holtom:

> Members of the royal family were debarred from continuing in Buddhist orders; Buddhist ceremonials in the imperial palace were prohibited; Buddhist temples all over the land were attacked and destroyed. A blind fury of misplaced patriotic zeal committed precious Buddhist writings, fine scuptures, bronzes, wood-carvings and paintings to the flames, broke them in pieces, cast them away, or sold them for a pittance to whosoever would buy. Buddhist priests were prohibited from participating in Shinto ceremonies. They were subjected to beatings and threatened with military force. Monks and nuns in large numbers were obliged to take up secular callings.[5]

Grave foreign protests on the subject of Christianity plus serious unrest among the masses devoted to Buddhism forced the abandonment of the policy of religious persecution. Liberal elements within the country agitated for the complete separation of church and state, and the Meiji leaders were brought to understand that religious freedom was a principle of the modern society they were trying to establish. Consequently, the government included in the constitution of 1889 a clause guaranteeing freedom of religion. At the same time it continued its support of the state Shinto cult, whose main aim was the veneration of the emperor. It solved this seeming contradiction by declaring that state Shinto was not a religion but merely an expression of patriotism. Nevertheless, the existence of the national cult

[5] D. C. Holtom, *Modern Japan and Shinto Nationalism* (Chicago: University of Chicago Press, 1947), p. 127.

imposed a real limitation on the independence and effectiveness of the private religious bodies. Though in the 1920's there was a strong tendency to differentiate religion and ideology, in times of stress such as the late 1930's and early 1940's religion was completely subordinated to and fused with a monolithic ideology, an ideology which had demonic consequences both for Japan and for the rest of the world. The new, 1946, constitution, by disestablishing Shinto and deriving sovereignty from the people rather than from the sacred and inviolable emperor, theoretically completed the process of secularization.

But, in fact, serious religious problems remain. All religious groups with the exception of the Christians were compromised by their connection with the nationalistic orgy. In the absence of any really vigorous religious life, except for the popular faith-healing cults and the small Christian community, the religious impulses of the Japanese people find expression for the more radical in the symbol of socialism, for the conservatives in a longing for a new and more innocent version of state Shinto. Here, as in Turkey, the differentiation between religion and ideology remains to be completed.

Other examples of the processes we have been discussing come readily to mind. Communism is an example of a secular political ideology which successfully came to power in the prescriptive, religiously based societies of Russia and China. But communism itself makes an ultimate religious claim, and here, as in the case of Japan, a secular ideology claiming religious ultimacy has embarked on courses of action which hinder, rather than further, the transition to modern principial society. It is perhaps safe to say that alongside the serious political and economic problems which communism faces today is the perhaps even more serious cultural problem, the problem of the differentiation of the religious and ideological levels.

In conclusion, it seems worthwhile to stress that the process of secularization, which is in part what the transition from prescriptive to principial society is, does not mean that religion disappears. The function of religion in a principial society is different from that in a prescriptive society, but it is not necessarily less important. Moreover, in the very process of transition religion may reappear in many new guises. Perhaps what makes the situation so unclear is its very fluidity. Even in highly differentiated societies, such as our own, traditional religion, so deeply associated with the prescriptive past, is still in the process of finding its place in modern principial society.

PART SIX

THE DISCIPLINE

Early American sociology had its roots in a social meliorism that is still present in some contemporary sociological work, where it takes the form of a humanistic approach to materials. Here, the fundamental purpose of studying man is felt to be gaining understanding that will allow him to live in harmony with himself and his fellows. There are many variations on this theme, but the main thread runs strong.

Along with a basic concern for meliorism came the attempt to build a scientific discipline, which led eventually to problems in gathering and analyzing materials. In the search for laws and principles, some sociologists came to concentrate primarily on quantifying materials and techniques of measurement. Often, as a result, the questions asked and their answers were of a restricted nature, since it was possible only on a very limited scale to control variables and have precise measures of phenomena. Other sociologists turned from quantification and attempted to construct theoretical models which would explain the behavior of entire societies and the groups within them. Building theory on such a grand level produced many interesting theologies, but few empirically tested dogmas.

509

It is evident that either approach was severely limiting. What good is methodology, if the questions asked have little significance for society in general or the study of human behavior? What good is theory, if it can't be tested? There has been a gradual wedding of these two positions, though each still absorbs many a sociologist.

If sociology got its impetus in this country from social meliorism, it is still a source of problems for both methodologists and theorists. Should sociologists concentrate on putting their findings to use and bettering the lot of man? Or should they just publish their findings and let others do what they will?

A profession does not spring into being, but for a long time attempts to develop boundaries which define its subject matter, methods, and use of data. As we shall see in the following articles, sociology is still making this attempt.

XVI APPROACHES

One of the problems of the grand theorist is that he too often lacks an awareness of the means by which his theories might be tested. Recently, courses have been introduced into departments of sociology which try to show the relationship between the theoretical and methodological approaches. One cannot just go out and gather a random assortment of data; he must have a theoretical framework in order to make the data meaningful. A scientist is concerned with the relationships between phenomena. Further, if one develops a theoretical model without considering the problems involved in testing his schema, he ends up with a framework that cannot be verified and therefore, by definition, is operationally untrue. Mills discusses these problems in the following article.

45 C. Wright Mills

Two Styles of Research in Current Social Studies

When in the course of our work we are uncertain, we sometimes become more concerned with our methods than with the content of our problems. We then try to clarify our conceptions and tighten our procedures. And as we re-examine studies that we feel have turned out well, we create conscious models of inquiry with which we try to guide our own work-in-progress.

From *Philosophy of Science*, Vol. 20 (1953), pp. 265–275. Copyright © 1953, The Williams & Wilkins Co., Baltimore, Md. 21202, U.S.A. Reprinted by permission of the author and publisher.

It is in terms of these models that we sometimes gain that sense of craftsmanship that is one subjective yield of work well done.

Modern men have generally been happier in their sense of craftsmanship when they have felt that they were at least approximating the generalized model of the laboratory. "Every step in science," Charles Peirce wrote, "has been a lesson in logic." In our search for a general model of inquiry, we have usually seized upon the supposed Method of Physical Science, and we have often fetichized it.

In the sociological disciplines, this grateful acceptance of "Science" is often more formal than operative and always more ambiguous than clear-cut. As a going concern, in the social studies, scientific empiricism means many things, and there is no one accepted version, much less any systematic use of any one model of science. The same work, admired by some as "great," is disparaged by others as "journalism." Professional expectations about method are quite confused, and our sense of craftsmanship may be realized in terms of quite different modes of inquiry.

There are, in fact, at least two working models of inquiry now available in current social studies, and accordingly two senses of craftsmanship in terms of which work is judged, and on the basis of which controversies over method occur.

ONE

The first of these two research-ways might be called the macroscopic. It has a venerable history, reaching notable heights, for example, in the work of Weber and Ostrogorski, Marx and Bryce, Michels, Simmel and Mannheim. These men like to deal with total social structures in a comparative way; their scope is that of the world historian; they attempt to generalize types of historical phenomena, and in a systematic way, to connect the various institutional spheres of a society, and then relate them to prevailing types of men and women. How did the Crusades come about? Are Protestantism and the rise of capitalism related? If so, how? Why is there no socialist movement in the U.S.?

The other way of sociological research might be called the molecular. It is, at first glance, characterized by its usually small-scale problems and by its generally statistical models of verification. Why are 40 per cent more of the women who give marketing advice to their neighbors during a given week on a lower income level than those who gave it during another week? Molecular work has no illustrious antecedents, but, by virtue of historical accident and the unfortunate facts of research finance, has been developed a great deal from studies of marketing and problems connected with media of mass communication. Shying away from social philosophy, it often appears as technique and little else.

Everyone involved in the social studies will recognize these two styles, and by now, a good many will readily agree that "we ought to get the two together." Sometimes this program is put in terms of the statement that the sociologist's ideal task during the next decades is to unite the larger problems and theoretical work of the 19th century, especially that of the Germans, with the research techniques predominant in the 20th century, especially that of the Americans. Within this great dialectic, it is felt, signal and continuous advances in masterful conception and rigorous procedure will be made.

If we inquire more closely into just how the two research-ways differ, we find that there is sometimes a confusion of differences that are non-logical with those that are logical in character. This is revealed, for example, in statements of the difference between the two styles as a political and intellectual dilemma: the more socially or politically significant our problems and work (the more macroscopic), the less rigorous is our solution and the less certain our knowledge (the less molecular).

There is much social truth in such statements; as they have so far been used these two styles of thought do differ in their characteristic value-relevance and political orientation. But this does not mean that any political orientation is inherent in the logic of either style of thought. The evaluative choice of problems characteristic of each of the two methods has not been *necessarily* due to logical capabilities or limitations of either. Molecular work of great political relevance is logically possible; and macroscopic work is not necessarily of broad significance, as a glance at many "political science" monographs proves all too well. No, many of the differences between the two styles are not logical, but social.

From the standpoint of the individual researcher, the choice of problems in either style of work may be due to academic timidity, political disinterest, or even cowardice; but above all it is due to the institutional facts of the financial life of molecular research. Molecular work requires an organization of technicians and administrators, of equipment and money, and, as yet, of promoters. It can not proceed until agencies of research are sufficiently developed to provide detailed materials. It has arisen in definite institutional centers: in business, since the twenties among marketing agencies, and since the thirties, in the polling agencies; in academic life at two or three research bureaux; and in research branches of government. Since World War II the pattern has spread, but these are still the centers.

This institutionalization of the molecular style has involved the applied focus, which has typically been upon specific problems, presented so as to make clear alternatives of practical — which is to say, pecuniary and administrative — action. It is *not* true that only as general principles are discovered can social science offer "sound practical guidance"; often the administrator needs to know certain detailed facts and relations, and that is all he needs to know.

The sociologist in the applied focus no longer addresses "the public"; more usually he has specific clients with particular interests and perplexities. This shift from public to client, clearly destroys the idea of objectivity as aloofness, which perhaps meant responsiveness to vague, unfocused pressures, and thus rested more on the individual interests of the researcher. In applied research of the molecular style, the client's social operations and economic interests have often supplied the sometimes tacit but always present moral meaning and use to the problem and to its solution. This has meant that most molecular work of any scale has been socially guided by the concerns and worries set by practical government and business interests and has been responsible to them. Accordingly, there is little doubt that the applied focus has tended to lower the intellectual initiative and to heighten the opportunism of the researcher. However technically free he may be, his initiative and interest are in fact usually subordinate to those of the client, whether it be the selling of pulp magazines or the administration of an army's morale.

Very little except his own individual limitations has stood between the individual worker and macroscopic work of the highest order. But the rise of the molecular style means that the unattached man cannot pursue such research on any scale, for such work is dependent upon organization and money. If we would "solve" the problem raised by the coexistence of these two styles we must pay attention to the design of work that is possible for the unattached men who still comprise the bulk of those claiming membership in the sociological community.

The rise of applied molecular work, as it is now being organized, makes questions of moral and political policy of the social studies all the more urgent. As a bureaucratization of reflection, the molecular style is quite in line with dominant trends of modern social structure and its characteristic types of thought. I do not wish to consider these problems here except to say that they should not be confused with any differences of a logical character between the two styles of inquiry.

TWO

There are at least three relative differences of a logical sort between the macroscopic and the molecular styles of work as they are now practiced: the molecular is more objective; it is more open to cumulative development; and it is more open to statistical quantification.

Objectivity means that the work is so done and so presented that any other qualified person can repeat it, thus coming to the same results or showing that the results were mistaken. Subjectivity means the reverse, and thus that there is usually a persistent individual variation of procedure — and of solution. Under this difference lies the fact that when work is objective the procedures used are systematized or even codified and hence are available to any qualified operator; whereas in subjective work the procedures are often not systematized, much less standardized or codified.

This in turn means that in objective work there is a more distinct possibility of cumulation — or at least replication! — both in terms of empirical solutions and in terms of the procedures used. In the more subjective macroscopic work the sensitivity and talent of the individual worker weigh more heavily and although there may be those who "take up where he left off," this is usually a continuity of subject-matter, general ideas, and approach rather than an accumulation of procedure. It is possible within a few years to train competent persons to repeat a Sandusky job;[1] it is not so possible to train them to repeat a Middletown study. Another sample of soldiers in another war can be located on a morale scale and comparisons built up; Max Weber's analytic and historical essay on bureaucracy has not been repeated or checked in the same way, however much it has been criticized and "used." Macroscopic work has not experienced the sort of cumulative development that molecular work during the current generation of sociologists has.

It is descriptively true that the molecular style has been heavily statistical, whereas the macroscopic has not. This, again, is an aspect of the greater codification and the lower level of abstraction that molecular work entails. And it can be confidently supposed that as macroscopic work is made more systematic it will become more quantitative — at least as a general form of thought. For example, Darwin's *Origin* as well as many of Freud's theories are quantitative models of reflection.

Each of these three points is underpinned by the fact that molecular procedures can be, and have been, more explicitly codified than those of the macroscopic style; and by the fact that molecular terms are typically on a lower level of abstraction than most macroscopic conceptions.

Insofar as the logical differences between the two styles concern *procedures*, they are differences in the degree of systematic codification. Insofar as they involve *conceptions*, they are differences in level of abstraction.

THREE

When we say that molecular terms are on *lower* levels of abstraction we mean that they isolate from larger contexts a few precisely observed elements; in this sense they are of course quite abstract. When we say that macroscopic concepts are on *higher* levels of abstraction, we mean that they are more generalized, that the number of single variables which they cover are more numerous. The molecular term is narrow in scope, and specific in reference: it deals with a few discrete variables; the macroscopic researcher gains his broader scope by using concepts that cover, usually less specifically, a much larger number of variables.

There is no one clear-cut variable, the presence or absence of which allows application of the concept, "capitalism": under such concepts there is likely to be a pattern of interrelated variables. Thus, such concepts are not only high-level but their index structure is an elaborately compounded affair. Put technically, most big macroscopic concepts already have under them rather elaborate, and often unsystematic, cross-tabulations of several

[1] Paul F. Lazarsfeld, et al., *The People's Choice* (New York: Duell, Sloan and Pearce, 1944).

variables; most molecular terms stand for single variables useful for the stubs of such tables.

We can consider a term in its relation to some empirical item(s) — that is, its semantic dimension; and we can consider a term in its relation to other terms — that is, its syntactical dimension, or if you like, its conceptual implications.[2] It is characteristic of molecular terms that their semantic dimensions are pronounced, although syntactical relations may also be there. It is characteristic of macroscopic terms that their syntactical dimensions are pronounced, although semantical relations may also be available.

The higher macroscopic levels are more syntactically elaborate; semantically they involve a hierarchy of compounded indices pointing to whole gestalts of attributes. Macroscopic concepts are often sponge-like and unclarified in their semantic dimensions. Sometimes, in fact, they do not have any index structure that enables us to touch empirically observable facts or relations.[3] They have under them only a vague kind of many-dimensional indicator rather than an index. Yet, with all this, it may be that whether a statement is macroscopic or molecular is a matter of degree — a question of at what level we introduce our syntactical elaboration.

FOUR

Our choice of level of abstraction occurs, if I may simplify the matter, in at least two distinct junctions of our research act: The character and scope of the unit that we take as problematic, the what-is-to-be-explained;[4] and the model of explanation — the concepts we use in the solution of the problem.[5]

---

[2] We can also consider it in relation to its users — the pragmatic dimension — which I am not here considering. These are the three dimensions of meaning which Charles M. Morris has systematized in his "Foundations of the Theory of Signs," *International Encyclopedia of Unified Science*, Volume I: Number 2. University of Chicago Press, 1938.

[3] To sort out the dimensions of a macroscopic concept requires us to elaborate it syntactically, while keeping our eyes open for semantic indices for each implication so elaborated. To translate each of these points into molecular terms requires us to trace the hierarchy of inference down to single, clear-cut variables. In assertions using macroscopic concepts, we must watch for whether or not the assertion (1) states a proposition, or (2) unlocks an implication. The guide-rule is whether the statement involves one empirical factor or at least two. If it involves only one factor, then it simply "spells out" or specifies one of the conceptual implications of that one factor; its meaning is syntactical. If the assertion involves two factors, it may be a proposition, a statement of a relation which can be true or false; its meaning is semantical.

[4] In either style, one may of course start with a simple declaration of descriptive intent, finding more precisely-put problems as one goes along. In either style, too, the assembly of stray facts without any general significance or interconnection may be found; the new (molecular) ideography is no different in this respect from the older macroscopic kind. Both are composed of details not connected with any problem and entailing no evident syntactical implications.

[5] The difference here is not a difference in the general logic of explanation: in both styles of work a third factor (or fourth or fifth factor) is appealed to in the explanation of some relation observed.

The explanatory intent of the macroscopic style is to *locate* the behavior to be explained within a structural totality or a cultural milieu; it finds its explanation in this

The grand tradition in social studies has been to state both problem and explanation in more or less macroscopic terms. In contrast, the *pure* molecular student goes through the whole research act on the molecular level. In the simplest scheme of observation and explanation there are four possibilities:

	Observations to be explained:	
Explanations	Macroscopic	Molecular
Macroscopic	I	II
Molecular	III	IV

I. Both what is to be explained and its explanation can be on the macroscopic level. E.g.: Why do many people follow Hitler? Answer: Because in the bureaucratization of modern society, life-plans are taken over by centralized bureaucracies in such a way that when crises occur, people are disoriented and feel that they need guidance. Bureaucracy has thus resulted in a trained incapacity of people to steer themselves. In crises the bureaucratic routine that trained them is gone: they therefore follow Hitler. Etc.

II. When the problematic observations are molecular, but the explanation macroscopic, the question is thought to be too general and figures on the vote, pro-Hitler sentiment, and urban residence, for example, are taken as what is to be explained. Then they are explained macroscopically, although usually in a more modest way because of the molecular problem-setting. E.g.: The urban people were more disoriented and thus in need of the image of a Father who would promise to plan their lives and take care of them. They therefore voted pro-Hitler. Etc.

III. The problematic observations may be macroscopic and the explanation molecular. Why do some people follow Hitler? Answer: We know that only 5 per cent of the population went to college: this is a fact pointing to social ignorance, which is further confirmed by the correlation of education and political information, revealed in all our polls. Ignorance, thus established, goes far to explain why some people follow Hitler. Etc.

IV. In this type of procedure, both phases are held to the molecular level. E.g.: The question is too general to be appropriately answered, it must be rephrased: 30 per cent of the adult population voted for Hitler in a given election. Why? Answer: When we take into account the rural-urban distribution, the religious, and the income level of the population, we find that 80 per cent of the rural, Protestant, high income level voted pro-Hitler, only 15 per cent of the urban, Catholic, low income. These three factors in the combination indicated seem to explain something about why certain people voted pro-Hitler and others did not. Etc.[6]

"meaningful location" — which means that it seeks to interpret in the terms of a highly intricate, interrelated complex of variables.

The explanatory intent of the molecular student is to break down the behavior of the individuals involved into component parts and to find the explanation in the association of further simplified attributes of these individuals.

[6] All illustrative facts and figures in this paper are products of the imagination.

Notice the following characteristics of these four models of thought:

The inadequacies of the purely macroscopic and the purely molecular (I & IV) are tied in with the fact that in both cases there is no shuttle between levels of abstraction. Since rigorous proof only exists empirically on the molecular levels, in the pure macroscopic there is no proved connection between problematic observation and explanation; when you are persuaded by such work, it is only because "it makes so much sense," it is syntactically convincing. On the purely molecular level there is a connection proved between problematic observation and explanatory observation, yet here the larger implications and meaning of that association are neither explored nor explained. When you are unsatisfied with such work it is because, although it is "neat" and "ingenious," you feel "there is more to it all."

In procedures II & III there is a shuttle between the macroscopic and molecular levels but it does *not* occur in the same phase of the total research act: we do not move from macroscopic to molecular inside the problematic phase, and we do not do so inside the explanatory phase. This means that the problematic observation and the explanation are not logically connected.

When the problem is molecular and the explanation macroscopic (II), there is an error of *falsely concretizing a concept:* in explaining some molecular observation by appealing, ad hoc, to a macroscopic concept, that concept tends to be handled in discussion as if it were a definite variable statistically related to the molecular observation.

When the problem is macroscopic and the solution molecular (III), the error might be called *unduly stretching an index:* in explaining some macroscopic observation by appealing to a molecular variable, that variable is unduly generalized and handled in discussion as if it were a carefully built index. The molecular explanation is *imputed* to explain the macroscopic observation, not connected.[7]

What all this (II and III) amounts to is the use of statistics to illustrate general points, and the use of general points to illustrate statistics. The general points are not tested, nor necessarily enlarged; they are conveniently adapted to the figures, as the arrangement of figures are cleverly adapted to them. The general points and explanations can be used with other figures too; so can the figures be used with other points.

Perhaps there is nothing especially wrong in all this; it is almost respectable procedure in some circles. But it does fall short of what is coming to be our vision of what social inquiry might be.

---

[7] In some research shops, the term "bright" is frequently applied when molecular facts or relations are cogently explained by macroscopic suppositions (II).

When further molecular variables, whose meaning is generalized very far — i.e., stretched — are brought in to explain, and they work, the result may be referred to as a "cute" table (III).

I mention this only to indicate that there is slowly emerging a shop language to cover the procedures I am trying to assert.

FIVE

I have discussed these research-ways at length in order to be able to set forth an "ideal" procedure, which we can use as a sort of lordly measuring rod for any piece of work in current social studies. The inadequacies indicated above may be summarized in one positive statement: If our work is to be clarified, we must be able to shuttle between levels of abstraction *inside each phase* of our simplified two-step act of research. This, of course, is simply another way of referring to the problem of indices and their place in the research process. Examine this simplified chart:

	Problematic	*Explanatory*
Macroscopic	1	2
Molecular	3	4

Only by moving grandly on the macroscopic level can we satisfy our intellectual and human curiosities. But only by moving minutely on the molecular level can our observations and explanations be adequately connected. So, if we would have our cake and eat it too, we must shuttle between macroscopic and molecular levels in instituting the problem *and* in explaining it — developing the molecular index structure of general concepts and the general conceptual implications of molecular variables. We move from macroscopic to molecular in both problem and in solution phase (1 to 3 and 2 to 4); then we relate the two on the molecular level (3 and 4); then we go back to the macroscopic (3 to 1 and 4 to 2). After that we can speak cautiously (i.e., bearing in mind the shuttles made), of relations on the macroscopic level (1 and 2).

To illustrate these shuttles, we may now design one ideal way of asking and answering a general question: Why *do* some people follow Hitler?

First, we accept the question macroscopically, and without losing any of its intended meaning, break it into more manageable (molecular) parts: "following Hitler" means: Expressing pro-Hitler sentiments to an interviewer, consistently voting for him, going out on the street to demonstrate when he or his agents request it, urging others to follow Hitler. Etc.

Each individual in a cross-section of the population may be classified in terms of a table composed of such items, and the tables reduced to a scale of types. Thus we build an index for "following Hitler"; our observation of what-is-to-be-explained is molecularly translated: transparent and specific indices are available.

We also accept, as a rather complicated hypothesis, the macroscopic statements (A) that people follow Hitler because of an inability to plan their own life-ways, (B) that this inability has been trained into them by work and life in bureaucratic structures, (C) that it was the crises and collapse of these bureaucracies that precipitated their allegiance to Hitler, whom, (D) they see as the big planner of their little lives.

Now this is somewhat tangled, although ordering it into these four assertions helps some. We have set ourselves quite some work, in translating and interpreting molecularly each of the four parts of the hypothesis. To short-cut it: for (A) we develop an index for "inability to plan life-ways." Perhaps we ask each individual about details of his daily routine and his weekly and yearly cycle, scoring each detail as to its indication of ability or inability to plan. We also ask directly about the images or lack of them that they have about the future and their future, etc. Then we carefully relate these scores, and come out again with a scale of types: at one end are those most able to plan their life-ways, at the other end those least able.

Then we go to segment (B) of the hypothesis, building indices to work and leisure within bureaucracies. And so on, with (C) and (D).

Finally, we interrelate our molecular indices to all four features of our hypothesis, reduce them, and emerge with a master scale: at its top are people who seem unable to plan their own lives, have been duly exposed to and "trained" by bureaucracies,[8] who began to be pro-Hitler in the major crises in Weimar society, and who have an image of Hitler as an omnipotent regulator and giver of satisfactory life-plans.

Given the crude state of our empirical technique and the clumsiness of our index building, we would probably finish with five cases in our extreme types, but that in itself has no logical meaning: what we are doing is translating an elaborate macroscopic explanation into molecular terms, and this must be done if we are serious about relating problematic observation to explanation. If we have other macroscopic explanations we must handle them in the same way; in our design we must think through their index structure.

Now we run our observations to be explained against our explanation, and this is what we obtain:

Observation of Hitler sentiment	Predisposition according to bureaucratic hypothesis		
	High	Intermediate	Low
Pro-Hitler	80%	20%	5%
Intermediate	15	60	15
Anti-Hitler	5	20	80
Total	100%	100%	100%

Maybe. But if so —

After controlling all the possible other variables we can think of, the reader might agree that we have earned the right to discuss, on the macroscopic level, bureaucracy, dictatorship and the character traits of modern mass-man. That is, to shuttle between macroscopic observations and macroscopic explanations.[9]

[8] For simplicity of presentation, I skip here the causal links between, e.g., B and A implied in the hypothesis.
[9] Of course, by the time we had gone through the three steps outlined, surely Hitler would have us in his clutches; but that is an irrelevant incident, and of no concern or consequence to the *designer* and methodologist of research, however inconvenient it might be to the research worker.

SIX

Even this brief discussion of this sketchy model suggests general rules of procedure for interpenetrating more neatly molecular terms and macroscopic concepts. We must build up molecular terms; we must break down macroscopic conceptions. For, as matters now stand, the propositional meaning of many macroscopic statements is ambiguous and unclear; the conceptual meaning of many molecular statements is often barren.

Any macroscopic statement that makes sense *can be* reduced to a set of molecular assertions — by untangling its dimensions and clarifying the index structure of each of them. Any molecular statement can presumably be built up to macroscopic levels of abstraction — by combining it with other molecular indices and elaborating it syntactically — although many of them are probably not worth it, except as a formal exercise in ingenuity.

Every macroscopic study runs the risk of being confused by the wealth of materials that come into its scope. In order to decrease the chance of ambiguity in the semantic dimension of macroscopic conceptions, we must strain towards a clarification of their index structure and, while making them as clear as possible, we must work towards an increased codification of how we are using them.

Every molecular study involves a series of guesses about the important variables that may characterize and explain a phenomena. In order to increase the chance that our focus will be upon key variables, we must strain towards possible levels of macroscopic concepts in our molecular work, but not stretch indices of explanatory variables, or at least do so only with an awareness of our speculative posture.

The sociological enterprise requires macroscopic researchers to imagineer more technically, as well as with scope and insight; it requires technicians to go about their work with more imaginative concern for macroscopic meaning, as well as with technical ingenuity. Perhaps we cannot hope, except in rare instances, to have combined in one man all the skills and capacities required. We must proceed by means of a division of labor that is self-guided, in each of its divisions, by an understanding of and a working agreement upon a grand model. When as individuals we specialize in one or the other phases of this model, we must do so with a clear consciousness of the place of that phase within the model, and thus perform our specialist role in a manner most likely to aid another specialist in the architectonic endeavor. The development of such clear consciousness, in fact, is the complete and healthy significance of discussions of the method of the social studies.

XVII USES OF SOCIOLOGY

> When sociological data are used for such things as evidence to sup-
> port the advisability of desegregation, most sociologists think it a
> good thing. Similarly, sociologists working with cities on urban
> planning, or as consultants on federal projects on problems of aging,
> crime, delinquency, or mental health, are approved of. There is a
> general tendency in the profession, however, to disparage the per-
> son who "sells out" to business and becomes a consultant for a
> marketing firm or some other private agency. Business makes use of
> the published materials of sociology quite frequently, but that is,
> supposedly, not active participation by the sociologists. Irving Horo-
> witz, editor of Trans-Action, spells out some of the problems that
> occurred when sociologists organized a research project funded by
> the Department of Defense. This was one of the largest grants ever
> awarded to a group of sociologists. The project was eventually
> disbanded.

46 IRVING LOUIS HOROWITZ

The Life and Death of Project Camelot

In June of this year — in the midst of the crisis over the Dominican Republic — the United States Ambassador to Chile sent an urgent and angry
cable to the State Department. Ambassador Ralph Dungan was confronted
with a growing outburst of anti-Americanism from Chilean newspapers and
intellectuals. Further, left-wing members of the Chilean Senate had accused the United States of espionage.

From *Trans-Action*, Vol. 3 (November–December, 1965), pp. 3–7, 44–47. Reprinted
by permission of the author and publisher.

The anti-American attacks that agitated Dungan had no direct connection with sending U.S. troops to Santo Domingo. Their target was a mysterious and cloudy American research program called Project Camelot.

Dungan wanted to know from the State Department what Project Camelot was all about. Further, whatever Camelot was, he wanted it stopped because it was fast becoming a *cause célèbre* in Chile (as it soon would throughout capitals of Latin American and in Washington) and Dungan had not been told anything about it — even though it was sponsored by the U.S. Army and involved the tinderbox subjects of counter-revolution and counter-insurgency in Latin America.

Within a few weeks Project Camelot created repercussions from Capitol Hill to the White House. Senator J. William Fulbright, chairman of the Foreign Relations Committee, registered his personal concern about such projects as Camelot because of their "reactionary, backward-looking policy opposed to change. Implicit in Camelot, as in the concept of 'counter-insurgency,' is an assumption that revolutionary movements are dangerous to the interests of the United States and that the United States must be prepared to assist, if not actually to participate in, measures to repress them."

By mid-June the State Department and Defense Department — which had created and funded Camelot — were in open contention over the project and the jurisdiction each department should have over certain foreign policy operations.

On July 8, Project Camelot was killed by Defense Secretary Robert McNamara's office which has a veto power over the military budget. The decision had been made under the President's direction.

On that same day, the director of Camelot's parent body, the Special Operations Research Organization, told a Congressional committee that the research project on revolution and counter-insurgency had taken its name from King Arthur's mythical domain because "It connotes the right sort of things — development of a stable society with peace and justice for all." Whatever Camelot's outcome, there should be no mistaking the deep sincerity behind this appeal for an applied social science pertinent to current policy.

However, Camelot left a horizon of disarray in its wake: an open dispute between State and Defense; fuel for the anti-American fires in Latin America; a cut in U.S. Army research appropriations. In addition, serious and perhaps ominous implications for social science research, bordering on censorship, have been raised by the heated reaction of the executive branch of government.

GLOBAL COUNTER-INSURGENCY

What was Project Camelot? Basically, it was a project for measuring and forecasting the causes of revolutions and insurgency in underdeveloped areas of the world. It also aimed to find ways of eliminating the causes, or coping with the revolutions and insurgencies. Camelot was sponsored by the U.S. Army on a four to six million dollar contract, spaced out over three to four years, with the Special Operations Research Organization (SORO). This agency is nominally under the aegis of American University in Washington, D.C., and does a variety of research for the Army. This includes making analytical surveys of foreign areas; keeping up-to-date information on the military, political, and social complexes of those areas; and maintaining a "rapid response" file for getting immediate information, upon Army request, on any situation deemed militarily important.

Latin America was the first area chosen for concentrated study, but countries on Camelot's four-year list included some in Asia, Africa, and Europe. In a working paper issued on December 5, 1964, at the request of the Office of the Chief of Research and Development, Department of the Army, it was recommended that "comparative historical studies" be made in these countries:

Latin America. Argentina, Bolivia, Brazil, Colombia, Cuba, Dominican Republic, El Salvador, Guatemala, Mexico, Paraguay, Peru, Venezuela.
Middle East. Egypt, Iran, Turkey.
Far East. Korea, Indonesia, Malaysia, Thailand.
Others. France, Greece, Nigeria.

"Survey research and other field studies" were recommended for Bolivia, Colombia, Ecuador, Paraguay, Peru, Venezuela, Iran, Thailand. Preliminary consideration was also being given to a study of the separatist movement in French Canada. It, too, had a code name: Project Revolt.

In a recruiting letter sent to selected scholars all over the world at the end of 1964, Project Camelot's aims were defined as a study to "make it possible to predict and influence politically significant aspects of social change in the developing nations of the world." This would include devising procedures for "assessing the potential for internal war within national societies" and "identify(ing) with increased degrees of confidence, those actions which a government might take to relieve conditions which are assessed as giving rise to a potential for internal war." The letter further stated:

> The U.S. Army has an important mission in the positive and constructive aspects of nation-building in less developed countries as well as a responsibility to assist friendly governments in dealing with active insurgency problems. Such activities by the U.S. Army were described as "insurgency prophylaxis" rather than the "sometimes misleading label of counter-insurgency."

Project Camelot was conceived in late 1963 by a group of high ranking Army officers connected with the Army Research Office of the Department of Defense. They were concerned about new types of warfare springing up around the world. Revolutions in Cuba and Yemen and insurgency movements in Vietnam and the Congo were a far cry from the battles of World War II and also different from the envisoned — and planned for — apocalypse of nuclear war. For the first time in modern warfare, military establishments were not in a position to use the immense arsenals at their disposal — but were, instead, compelled by force of a geopolitical stalemate to increasingly engage in primitive forms of armed combat. The questions of moment for the Army were: Why can't the "hardware" be used? And what alternatives can social science "software" provide?

A well-known Latin American area specialist, Rex Hopper, was chosen as director of Project Camelot. Hopper was a professor of sociology and chairman of the department at Brooklyn College. He had been to Latin America many times over a thirty-year span on research projects and lecture tours, including some under government sponsorship. He was highly recommended for the position by his professional associates in Washington and elsewhere. Hopper had a long-standing interest in problems of revolution and saw in this multi-million dollar contract the possible realization of a life-long scientific ambition.

THE CHILEAN DEBACLE

How did this social science research project create a foreign policy furor? And, at another level, how did such high intentions result in so disastrous an outcome?

The answers involve a network spreading from a professor of anthropology at the University of Pittsburgh, to a professor of sociology at the University of Oslo, and yet a third professor of sociology at the University of Chile in Santiago, Chile. The "showdown" took place in Chile, first within the confines of the university, next on the floor of the Chilean Senate, then in the popular press of Santiago, and finally, behind U.S. embassy walls.

It was ironic that Chile was the scene of wild newspaper tales of spying and academic outrage at scholars being recruited for "spying missions." For the working papers of Project Camelot stipulated as a criterion for study that a country "should show promise of high pay-offs in terms of the kinds of data required." Chile did not meet these requirements — it is not on the preliminary list of nations specified as prospects.

How then did Chile become involved in Project Camelot's affairs? The answer requires consideration of the position of Hugo G. Nutini, assistant professor of anthropology at Pittsburgh, citizen of the United States and former citizen of Chile. His presence in Santiago as a self-identified Camelot representative triggered the climactic chain of events.

Nutini, who inquired about an appointment in Camelot's beginning stages, never was given a regular Camelot appointment. Because he was planning a trip to Chile in April of this year — on other academic business — he was asked to prepare a report concerning possibilities of cooperation from Chilean scholars. In general, it was the kind of survey which has mild results and a modest honorarium attached to it (Nutini was offered $750). But Nutini had an obviously different notion of his role. Despite the limitations and precautions which Rex Hopper placed on his trip, especially Hopper's insistence on its informal nature, Nutini managed to convey the impression of being an official of Project Camelot with the authority to make proposals to prospective Chilean participants. Here was an opportunity to link the country of his birth with the country of his choice.

At about the same time, Johan Galtung, a Norwegian sociologist famous for his research on conflict and conflict resolution in underdeveloped areas, especially in Latin America, entered the picture. Galtung, who was in Chile at the time and associated with the Latin American Faculty of Social Science (FLACSO), received an invitation to participate in a Camelot planning conference scheduled for Washington, D.C., in August 1965. The fee to social scientists attending the conference would be $2,000 for four weeks. Galtung turned down the invitation. He gave several reasons. He could not accept the role of the U.S. Army as a sponsoring agent in a study of counterinsurgency. He could not accept the notion of the Army as an agency of national development; he saw the Army as managing conflict and even promoting conflict. Finally, he could not accept the asymmetry of the project — he found it difficult to understand why there would be studies of counter-insurgency in Latin America, but no studies of "counter-intervention" (conditions under which Latin American nations might intervene in the affairs of the United States). Galtung was also deeply concerned about the possibility of European scholars being frozen out of Latin American studies by an inundation of sociologists from the United States. Furthermore, he expressed fears that the scale of Camelot honoraria would completely destroy the social science labor market in Latin America.

Galtung had spoken to others in Oslo, Santiago, and throughout Latin America about the project, and he had shown the memorandum of December, 1964, to many of his colleagues.

Soon after Nutini arrived in Santiago, he had a conference with Vice-Chancellor Alvaro Bunster of the University of Chile to discuss the character of Project Camelot. Their second meeting, arranged by the vice-chancellor, was also attended by Professor Eduardo Fuenzalida, a sociologist. After a half-hour of exposition by Nutini, Fuenzalida asked him point-blank to specify the ultimate aims of the project, its sponsors, and its military implications. Before Nutini could reply, Professor Fuenzalida, apparently with some drama, pulled a copy of the December 4 circular letter from his briefcase and read a prepared Spanish translation. Simultaneously, the authorities at FLACSO turned over the matter to their associates in the Chilean Senate and in the left-wing Chilean press.

In Washington, under the political pressures of State Department officials and Congressional reaction, Project Camelot was halted in midstream, or more precisely, before it ever really got under way. When the ambassador's communication reached Washington, there was already considerable official ferment about Project Camelot. Senators Fulbright, Morse, and McCarthy soon asked for hearings by the Senate Foreign Relations Committee. Only an agreement between Secretary of Defense McNamara and Secretary of State Rusk to settle their differences on future overseas research projects forestalled Senate action. But in the House of Representatives, a hearing was conducted by the Foreign Affairs Committee on July 8. The SORO director, Theodore Vallance, was questioned by committee members on the worth of Camelot and the matter of military intrusion into foreign policy areas.

That morning, even before Vallance was sworn in as a witness — and without his knowledge — the Defense Department issued a terse announcement terminating Project Camelot. President Johnson had decided the issue in favor of the State Department. In a memo to Secretary Rusk on August 5 the President stipulated that "no government sponsorship of foreign area research should be undertaken which in the judgment of the Secretary of State would adversely affect United States foreign relations."

The State Department has recently established machinery to screen and judge all federally financed research projects overseas. The policy and research consequences of the Presidential directive will be discussed later.

What effect will the cancellation of Camelot have on the continuing rivalry between Defense and State departments for primacy in foreign policy? How will government sponsorship of future social science research be affected? And was Project Camelot a scholarly protective cover for U.S. Army planning — or a legitimate research operation on a valid research subject independent of sponsorship?

Let us begin with a collective self-portrait of Camelot as the social scientists who directed the project perceived it. There seems to be general consensus on seven points.

First, the men who went to work for Camelot felt the need for a large-scale, "big picture" project in social science. They wanted to create a sociology of contemporary relevance which would not suffer from the parochial narrowness of vision to which their own professional backgrounds had generally conditioned them. Most of the men viewed Camelot as a bona fide opportunity to do fundamental research with relatively unlimited funds at their disposal. (No social science project ever before had up to $6,000,000 available.) Under such optimal conditions, these scholars tended not to look a gift horse in the mouth. As one of them put it, there was no desire to inquire too deeply as to the source of the funds or the ultimate purpose of the project.

Second, most social scientists affiliated with Camelot felt that there was actually more freedom to do fundamental research under military sponsorship than at a university or college. One man noted that during the 1950's there was far more freedom to do fundamental research in the RAND corporation (an Air Force research organization) than on any campus in America. Indeed, once the protective covering of RAND was adopted, it was almost viewed as a society of Platonist elites or "knowers" permitted to search for truth on behalf of the powerful. In a neoplatonic definition of their situation, the Camelot men hoped that their ideas would be taken seriously by the wielders of power (although, conversely, they were convinced that the armed forces would not accept their preliminary recommendations).

Third, many of the Camelot associates felt distinctly uncomfortable with military sponsorship, especially given the present United States military posture. But their reaction to this discomfort was that "the Army has to be educated." This view was sometimes cast in Freudian terms: the Army's bent toward violence ought to be sublimated. Underlying this theme was the notion of the armed forces as an agency for potential social good — the discipline and the order embodied by an army could be channeled into the process of economic and social development in the United States as well as in Latin America.

Fourth, there was a profound conviction in the perfectibility of mankind; particularly in the possibility of the military establishment performing a major role in the general process of growth. They sought to correct the intellectual paternalism and parochialism under which Pentagon generals, State Department diplomats, and Defense Department planners seemed to operate.

Fifth, a major long-range purpose of Camelot, at least for some of its policy-makers, was to prevent another revolutionary holocaust on a grand scale, such as occurred in Cuba. At the very least, there was a shared belief that *Pax Americana* was severely threatened and its future could be bolstered.

Sixth, none of them viewed their role on the project as spying for the United States government, or for anyone else.

Seventh, the men on Project Camelot felt that they made heavy sacrifices for social science. Their personal and professional risks were much higher than those taken by university academics. Government work, while well compensated, remains professionally marginal. It can be terminated abruptly (as indeed was the case) and its project directors are subject to a public scrutiny not customary behind the walls of ivy.

In the main, there was perhaps a keener desire on the part of the directing members of Camelot not to "sell out" than there is among social scientists with regular academic appointments. This concern with the ethics of social science research seemed to be due largely to daily confrontation of the problems of betrayal, treason, secrecy, and abuse of data, in a critical situation. In contrast, even though a university position may be created by federally-sponsored research, the connection with policy matters is often too remote to cause any *crise de conscience*.

THE INSIDERS REPORT

Were the men on Camelot critical of any aspects of the project?

Some had doubts from the outset about the character of the work they would be doing, and about the conditions under which it would be done. It was pointed out, for example, that the U.S. Army tends to exercise a far more stringent intellectual control of research findings than does the U.S. Air Force. As evidence for this, it was stated that SORO generally had fewer "free-wheeling" aspects to its research designs than did RAND (the Air Force-supported research organization). One critic inside SORO went so far as to say that he knew of no SORO research which had a "playful" or unregimented quality, such as one finds at RAND (where for example, computers are used to plan invasions but also to play chess). One staff member said that "the self-conscious seriousness gets to you after a while." "It was all grim stuff," said another.

Another line of criticism was that pressures on the "reformers" (as the men engaged in Camelot research spoke of themselves) to come up with ideas were much stronger than the pressures on the military to actually bring off any policy changes recommended. The social scientists were expected to be social reformers, while the military adjutants were expected to be conservative. It was further felt that the relationship between sponsors and researchers was not one of equals, but rather one of superordinate military needs and subordinate academic roles. On the other hand, some officials were impressed by the disinterestedness of the military, and thought that far from exercising undue influence, the Army personnel were loath to offer opinions.

Another objection was that if one had to work on policy matters — if research is to have international ramifications — it might better be conducted under conventional State Department sponsorship. "After all," one man said, "they are at least nominally committed to civilian political norms." In other words, there was a considerable reluctance to believe that the Defense Department, despite its superior organization, greater financial affluence, and executive influence, would actually improve upon State Department styles of work, or accept recommendations at variance with Pentagon policies.

There seemed to be few, if any, expressions of disrespect for the intrinsic merit of the work contemplated by Camelot, or of disdain for policy-oriented work in general. The scholars engaged in the Camelot effort used two distinct vocabularies. The various Camelot documents reveal a military vocabulary provided with an array of military justifications; often followed (within the same document) by a social science vocabulary offering social science justifications and rationalizations. The dilemma in the Camelot literature from the preliminary report issued in August 1964 until the more advanced document issued in April 1965, is the same: an incomplete amalgamation of the military and sociological vocabularies. (At an early date the project had the code name SPEARPOINT.)

POLICY CONFLICTS OVER CAMELOT

The directors of SORO are concerned that the cancellation of Camelot might mean the end of SORO as well in a wholesale slash of research funds. For while over $1,000,000 was allotted to Camelot each year, the annual budget of SORO, its parent organization, is a good deal less. Although no such action has taken place, SORO's future is being examined. For example, the Senate and House Appropriations Committee blocked a move by the Army to transfer unused Camelot funds to SORO.

However, the end of Project Camelot does not necessarily imply the end of the Special Operations Research Office, nor does it imply an end to research designs which are similar in character to Project Camelot. In fact, the termination of the contract does not even imply an intellectual change of heart on the part of the originating sponsors or key figures of the project.

One of the characteristics of Project Camelot was the number of antagonistic forces it set in motion on grounds of strategy and timing rather than from what may be called considerations of scientific principles.

The State Department grounded its opposition to Camelot on the basis of the ultimate authority it has in the area of foreign affairs. There is no published report showing serious criticism of the projected research itself.

Congressional opposition seemed to be generated by a concern not to rock any foreign alliances, especially in Latin America. Again, there was no statement about the project's scientific or intellectual grounds.

A third group of skeptics, academic social scientists, generally thought that Project Camelot, and studies of the processes of revolution and war in general, were better left in the control of major university centers, and in this way, kept free of direct military supervision.

The Army, creator of the project, did nothing to contradict McNamara's order cancelling Project Camelot. Army influentials did not only feel that they had to execute the Defense Department's orders, but they are traditionally dubious of the value of "software" research to support "hardware" systems.

Let us take a closer look at each of these groups which voiced opposition to Project Camelot. A number of issues did not so much hinge upon, as swim about, Project Camelot. In particular, the "jurisdictional" dispute between Defense and State loomed largest.

State vs. Defense. In substance, the debate between the Defense Department and the State Department is not unlike that between electricians and bricklayers in the construction of a new apartment house. What "union" is responsible for which purposes? Less generously, the issue is: who controls what? At the policy level, Camelot was a tool tossed about in a larger power struggle which has been going on in government circles since the end of World War II, when the Defense Department emerged as a competitor for honors as the most powerful bureau of the administrative branch of government.

In some sense, the divisions between Defense and State are outcomes of the rise of ambiguous conflicts such as Korea and Vietnam, in contrast to the more precise and diplomatically controlled "classical" world wars. What are the lines dividing political policy from military posture? Who is the most important representative of the United States abroad: the ambassador or the military attaché in charge of the military mission? When soldiers from foreign lands are sent to the United States for political orientation, should such orientation be within the province of the State Department or of the Defense Department? When undercover activities are conducted, should the direction of such activities belong to military or political authorities? Each of these is a strategic question with little pragmatic or historic precedent. Each of these was entwined in the Project Camelot explosion.

It should be plain therefore that the State Department was not simply responding to the recommendations of Chilean left-wingers in urging the cancellation of Camelot. It merely employed the Chilean hostility to "interventionist" projects as an opportunity to redefine the balance of forces and power with the Defense Department. What is clear from this resistance to such projects is not so much a defense of the sovereignty of the nations where ambassadors are stationed, as it is a contention that conventional political channels are sufficient to yield the information desired or deemed necessary.

Congress. In the main, congressional reaction seems to be that Project Camelot was bad because it rocked the diplomatic boat in a sensitive area. Underlying most congressional criticisms is the plain fact that most congressmen are more sympathetic to State Department control of foreign affairs than they are to Defense Department control. In other words, despite military sponsored world junkets, National Guard and State Guard pressures from the home State, and military training in the backgrounds of many congressmen, the sentiment for political rather than military control is greater. In addition, there is a mounting suspicion in Congress of varying kinds of behavioral science research stemming from hearings into such matters as wire-tapping, uses of lie detectors, and truth-in-packaging.

Social Scientists. One reason for the violent response to Project Camelot, especially among Latin American scholars, is its sponsorship by the Department of Defense. The fact is that Latin Americans have become quite accustomed to State Department involvements in the internal affairs of various nations. The Defense Department is a newcomer, a dangerous one, inside the Latin American orbit. The train of thought connected to its activities is in terms of international warfare, spying missions, military manipulations, etc. The State Department, for its part, is often a consultative party to shifts in government, and has played an enormous part in either fending off or bringing about coups d'état. This State Department role has by now been accepted and even taken for granted. Not so the Defense Department's role. But it is interesting to conjecture on how matter-of-factly Camelot might have been accepted if it had had State Department sponsorship.

Social scientists in the United States have, for the most part, been publicly silent on the matter of Camelot. The reasons for this are not hard to find. First, many "giants of the field" are involved in government contract work in one capacity or another. And few souls are in a position to tamper with the gods. Second, most information on Project Camelot has thus far been of a newspaper variety; and professional men are not in a habit of criticizing colleagues on the basis of such information. Third, many social scientists doubtless see nothing wrong or immoral in the Project Camelot designs. And they are therefore more likely to be either confused or angered at the Latin American response than at the directors of Project Camelot. (At the time of the blowup, Camelot people spoke about the "Chilean mess" rather than the "Camelot mess.")

The directors of Project Camelot did not "classify" research materials, so that there would be no stigma of secrecy. And they also tried to hire, and even hired away from academic positions, people well known and respected for their independence of mind. The difficulty is that even though the stigma of secrecy was formally erased, it remained in the attitudes of many of the employees and would-be employees of Project Camelot. They unfortunately thought in terms of secrecy, clearance, missions, and the rest of the professional nonsense that so powerfully afflicts the Washington scientific as well as political ambience.

Further, it is apparent that Project Camelot had much greater difficulty hiring a full-time staff of high professional competence, than in getting part-time, summertime, weekend, and sundry assistance. Few established figures in academic life were willing to surrender the advantages of their positions for the risks of the project.

One of the cloudiest aspects to Project Camelot is the role of American University. Its actual supervision of the contract appears to have begun and ended with the 25 per cent overhead on those parts of the contract that a university receives on most federal grants. Thus, while there can be no question as to the "concern and disappointment" of President Hurst R. Anderson of the American University over the demise of Project Camelot, the reasons for this regret do not seem to extend beyond the formal and the financial. No official at American University appears to have been willing to make any statement of responsibility, support, chagrin, opposition, or anything else related to the project. The issues are indeed momentous, and must be faced by all universities at which government sponsored research is conducted: the amount of control a university has over contract work; the role of university officials in the distribution of funds from grants; the relationships that ought to be established once a grant is issued. There is also a major question concerning project directors: are they members of the faculty, and if so, do they have necessary teaching responsibilities and opportunities for tenure as do other faculty members.

The difficulty with American University is that it seems to be remarkably unlike other universities in its permissiveness. The Special Operations Research Office received neither guidance nor support from university officials. From the outset, there seems to have been a "gentleman's agreement" not to inquire or interfere in Project Camelot, but simply to serve as some sort of camouflage. If American University were genuinely autonomous it might have been able to lend highly supportive aid to Project Camelot during the crisis months. As it is, American University maintained an official silence which preserved it from more congressional or executive criticism. This points up some serious flaws in its administrative and financial policies.

The relationship of Camelot to SORO represented a similarly muddled organizational picture. The director of Project Camelot was nominally autonomous and in charge of an organization surpassing in size and importance the overall SORO operation. Yet at the critical point the organizational blueprint served to protect SORO and sacrifice what nominally was its limb. That Camelot happened to be a vital organ may have hurt, especially when Congress blocked the transfer of unused Camelot funds to SORO.

Military. Military reaction to the cancellation of Camelot varied. It should be borne in mind that expenditures on Camelot were minimal in the Army's overall budget and most military leaders are skeptical, to begin with, about the worth of social science research. So there was no open protest about the demise of Camelot. Those officers who have a positive attitude toward social science materials, or are themselves trained in the social sciences, were dismayed. Some had hoped to find "software" alternatives to the "hardware systems" approach applied by the Secretary of Defense to every military-political contingency. These officers saw the attack on Camelot as a double attack — on their role as officers and on their professional standards. But the Army was so clearly treading in new waters that it could scarcely jeopardize the entire structure of military research to preserve one project. This very inability or impotence to preserve Camelot — a situation threatening to other governmental contracts with social scientists — no doubt impressed many armed forces officers.

The claim is made by the Camelot staff (and various military aides) that the critics of the project played into the hands of those sections of the military predisposed to veto any social science recommendations. Then why did the military offer such a huge support to a social science project to begin with? Because $6,000,000 is actually a trifling sum for the Army in an age of multi-billion dollar military establishment. The amount is significantly more important for the social sciences, where such contract awards remain relatively scarce. Thus, there were differing perspectives of the importance of Camelot: an Army view which considered the contract as one of several forms of "software" investment; a social science perception of Project Camelot as the equivalent of the Manhattan Project.

WAS PROJECT CAMELOT WORKABLE?

While most public opposition to Project Camelot focused on its strategy and timing, a considerable amount of private opposition centered on more basic, though theoretical, questions: was Camelot scientifically feasible and ethically correct? No public document or statement contested the possibility that, given the successful completion of the data gathering, Camelot could have, indeed, established basic criteria for measuring the level and potential for internal war in a given nation. Thus, by never challenging the feasibility of the work, the political critics of Project Camelot were providing back-handed compliments to the efficacy of the project.

But much more than political considerations are involved. It is clear that some of the most critical problems presented by Project Camelot are scientific. Although for an extensive analysis of Camelot, the reader would, in fairness, have to be familiar with all of its documents, salient general criticisms can be made without a full reading.

The research design of Camelot was from the outset plagued by ambiguities. It was never quite settled whether the purpose was to study counter-insurgency possibilities, or the revolutionary process. Similarly, it was difficult to determine whether it was to be a study of comparative social structures, a set of case studies of single nations "in depth," or a study of social structure with particular emphasis on the military. In addition, there was a lack of treatment of what indicators were to be used, and whether a given social system in Nation A could be as stable in Nation B.

In one Camelot document there is a general critique of social science for failing to deal with social conflict and social control. While this in itself is admirable, the tenor and context of Camelot's documents make it plain that a "stable society" is considered the norm no less than the desired outcome. The "breakdown of social order" is spoken of accusatively. Stabilizing agencies in developing areas are presumed to be absent. There is no critique of U.S. Army policy in developing areas because the Army is presumed to be a stabilizing agency. The research formulations always assume the legitimacy of Army tasks — "if the U.S. Army is to perform effectively its parts in the U.S. mission of counter-insurgency it must recognize that insurgency represents a breakdown of social order. . . ." But such a proposition has never been doubted — by Army officials or anyone else. The issue is whether such breakdowns are in the nature of the existing system or a product of conspiratorial movements.

The use of hygienic language disguises the anti-revolutionary assumptions under a cloud of powder puff declarations. For example, studies of Paraguay are recommended "because trends in this situation (the Stroessner regime) may also render it 'unique' when analyzed in terms of the transition from 'dictatorship' to political stability." But to speak about changes from dictatorship to stability is an obvious ruse. In this case, it is a tactic to disguise the fact that Paraguay is one of the most vicious, undemocratic (and like most dictatorships, stable) societies in the Western Hemisphere.

These typify the sort of hygienic sociological premises that do not have scientific purposes. They illustrate the confusion of commitments within Project Camelot. Indeed the very absence of emotive words such as revolutionary masses, communism, socialism, and capitalism only serves to intensify the discomfort one must feel on examination of the documents — since the abstract vocabulary disguises, rather than resolves, the problems of international revolution. To have used clearly political rather than military language would not "justify" governmental support. Furthermore, shabby assumptions of academic conventionalism replaced innovative orientations. By adopting a systems approach, the problematic, open-ended aspects of the study of revolutions were largely omitted; and the design of the study became an oppressive curb on the study of the problems inspected.

This points up a critical implication for Camelot (as well as other projects). The importance of the subject being researched does not per se determine the importance of the project. A sociology of large-scale relevance and reference is all to the good. It is important that scholars be willing to risk something of their shaky reputations in helping resolve major world social problems. But it is no less urgent that in the process of addressing major problems, the autonomous character of the social science disciplines — their own criteria of worthwhile scholarship — should not be abandoned. Project Camelot lost sight of this "autonomous" social science character.

It never seemed to occur to its personnel to inquire into the desirability for successful revolution. This is just as solid a line of inquiry as the one stressed — the conditions under which revolutionary movements will be able to overthrow a government. Furthermore, they seem not to have thought about inquiring into the role of the United States in these countries. This points up the lack of symmetry. The problem should have been phrased to include the study of "us" as well as "them." It is not possible to make a decent analysis of a situation unless one takes into account the role of all the different people and groups involved in it; and there was no room in the design for such contingency analysis.

In discussing the policy impact on a social science research project, we should not overlook the difference between "contract" work and "grants." Project Camelot commenced with the U.S. Army; that is to say, it was initiated for a practical purpose determined by the client. This differs markedly from the typical academic grant in that its sponsorship had "built-in" ends. The scholar usually *seeks* a grant; in this case the donor, the Army, promoted its own aims. In some measure, the hostility for Project Camelot may be an unconscious reflection of this distinction — a dim feeling that there was something "non-academic," and certainly not disinterested, about Project Camelot, irrespective of the quality of the scholars associated with it.

THE ETHICS OF POLICY RESEARCH

The issue of "scientific rights" versus "social myths" is perennial. Some maintain that the scientist ought not penetrate beyond legally or morally sanctioned limits and others argue that such limits cannot exist for science. In treading on the sensitive issue of national sovereignty, Project Camelot reflects the generalized dilemma. In deference to intelligent researchers, in recognition of them as scholars, they should have been invited by Camelot to air their misgivings and qualms about government (and especially Army sponsored) research — to declare their moral conscience. Instead, they were mistakenly approached as skillful, useful potential employees of a higher body, subject to an authority higher than their scientific calling.

What is central is not the political motives of the sponsor. For social scientists were not being enlisted in an intelligence system for "spying" purposes. But given their professional standing, their great sense of intellectual honor and pride, they could not be "employed" without proper deference for their stature. Professional authority should have prevailed from beginning to end with complete command of the right to thrash out the moral and political dilemmas as researchers saw them. The Army, however respectful and protective of free expression, was "hiring help" and not openly and honestly submitting a problem to the higher professional and scientific authority of social science.

The propriety of the Army to define and delimit all questions, which Camelot should have had a right to examine, was never placed in doubt. This is a tragic precedent; it reflects the arrogance of a consumer of intellectual merchandise. And this relationship of inequality corrupted the lines of authority, and profoundly limited the autonomy of the social scientists involved. It became clear that the social scientist savant was not so much functioning as an applied social scientist as he was supplying information to a powerful client.

The question of who sponsors research is not nearly so decisive as the question of ultimate use of such information. The sponsorship of a project, whether by the United States Army or by the Boy Scouts of America, is by itself neither good nor bad. Sponsorship is good or bad only insofar as the intended outcomes can be pre-determined and the parameters of those intended outcomes tailored to the sponsor's expectations. Those social scientists critical of the project never really denied its freedom and independence, but questioned instead the purpose and character of its intended results.

It would be a gross oversimplification, if not an outright error, to assume that the theoretical problems of Project Camelot derive from any reactionary character of the project designers. The director went far and wide to select a group of men for the advisory board, the core planning group, the summer study group, and the various conference groupings, who in fact were more liberal in their orientations than any random sampling of the sociological profession would likely turn up.

However, in nearly every page of the various working papers, there are assertions which clearly derive from American military policy objectives rather than scientific method. The steady assumption that internal warfare is damaging disregards the possibility that a government may not be in a position to take actions either to relieve or improve mass conditions, or that such actions as are contemplated may be more concerned with reducing conflict than with improving conditions. The added statements about the United States Army and its "important mission in the positive and constructive aspects of nation building . . ." assumes the reality of such a function in an utterly unquestioning and unconvincing form. The first rule of the scientific game is not to make assumptions about friends and enemies in such a way as to promote the use of different criteria for the former and the latter.

The story of Project Camelot was not a confrontation of good versus evil. Obviously, not all men behaved with equal fidelity or with equal civility. Some men were weaker than others, some more callous, and some more stupid. But all of this is extrinsic to the heart of the problem of Camelot: what are and are not the legitimate functions of a scientist?

In conclusion, two important points must be clearly kept in mind and clearly apart. First, Project Camelot was intellectually, and from my own perspective, ideologically unsound. However, and more significantly, Camelot was not cancelled because of its faulty intellectual approaches. Instead, its cancellation came as an act of government censorship, and an expression of the contempt for social science so prevalent among those who need it most. Thus it was political expedience, rather than its lack of scientific merit, that led to the demise of Camelot because it threatened to rock State Department relations with Latin America.

Second, giving the State Department the right to screen and approve government-funded social science research projects on other countries, as the President has ordered, is a supreme act of censorship. Among the agencies that grant funds for such research are the National Institutes of Mental Health, the National Science Foundation, the National Aeronautics and Space Agency, and the Office of Education. Why should the State Department have veto power over the scientific pursuits of men and projects funded by these and other agencies in order to satisfy the policy needs —

or policy failures — of the moment? President Johnson's directive is a gross violation of the autonomous nature of science.

We must be careful not to allow social science projects with which we may vociferously disagree on political and ideological grounds to be decimated or dismantled by government fiat. Across the ideological divide is a common social science understanding that the contemporary expression of reason in politics today is applied social science, and that the cancellation of Camelot, however pleasing it may be on political grounds to advocates of a civilian solution to Latin American affairs, represents a decisive setback for social science research.

If sociology has had its failures, as in Operational Camelot, it has also had its successes. The following article by Lewis Killian, a sociologist, traces sociology's role in preparing the first desegregation brief.

47 LEWIS M. KILLIAN

The Social Scientist's Role in the Preparation of the Florida Desegregation Brief

One of the significant features of the 1954 desegregation cases was the extensive, even though indirect, involvement of social scientists in both the arguments and the decisions. Social science work had been cited previously in cases involving racial segregation, but never before had it played so important and influential a part. In the further hearings of the cases, at least two of the briefs, that of the NAACP and the *amicus curiae* brief of the Attorney General of Florida, relied heavily upon social science findings for their arguments. Once again the problem of the role conflicts that the social scientist encounters when he enters the field of applied research presented itself for analysis.

This problem is of particular interest when it involves the collaboration of social scientists with legal authorities rather than with administrators. The ad hoc team of the lawyer and the social scientist constitutes a structure of roles which the occupants themselves usually try to keep clearly separated. The lawyer is first and foremost the advocate; the social scientist constantly guards against becoming an advocate. It seems evident that

From *Social Problems*, Vol. 3, No. 4 (April, 1956), pp. 211–214. Reprinted by permission of the author and publisher.

much of the desegregation process will transpire in the arena of the law, as it already has. If social scientists are not to remain aloof from this process as it develops, they must risk encountering such role conflicts and must examine realistically the implications for them as both scientists and citizens. The participation of the writer in the preparation of the Florida brief provides material for a case study of collaboration between social scientist and government official.

HOW THE BRIEF WAS PREPARED

The prime mover and the leader in the group that collaborated in preparing the Florida brief was the state Attorney General. It was he who decided that his state should file a brief and that this brief should be based upon a scientific study of the problems of desegregation. In his hands rested the final decision as to what should go into the brief as a legal document.

The Florida Attorney General felt that the answers to the questions asked by the Supreme Court could be found only in the types of data social scientists were accustomed to collecting. Therefore, he organized a biracial committee of eighteen people to plan and conduct such research. The committee included social scientists, educational administrators, personnel from the state's Department of Education, and lawyers from the Attorney General's office. This committee was asked to recommend the kind of research which would produce the best answers to the Court's questions IV and V, concerning the pace and manner in which the decision was to be executed. It was also entrusted with the responsibilities of selecting personnel to carry out the research, analyzing the findings, and presenting conclusions to the Attorney General for his consideration in writing the brief.

The committee decided that the most feasible and meaningful research would be a study of the opinions and attitudes of officials and prestige leaders at the local level whose responsibility it would be to implement whatever decision the Court handed down. It was felt that this group of subjects would include both opinion leaders and people who would be acquainted with the problems which desegregation would create for local communities. Briefly, the research findings seemed to support the argument of the Attorney General, made before the Court, that a program of gradual integration under the supervision of lower courts should be ordered.

The writer occupied the key role in the Research Supervisory Committee, as Coordinator of Research. He designed the research, with the broad, general advice and direction of the entire committee. He carried it out, with the assistance of a paid staff, and wrote the final research report. The research was designed and completed before the writing of the legal portion of the brief, the argument, was begun. The Coordinator's research report and conclusions were reviewed and approved by the entire Research Supervisory Committee before they were presented to the Attorney General as the official findings of the group, but the major part of the interaction during the entire process took place between the Attorney General and the Coordinator of Research.

THE ROLE OF THE ATTORNEY GENERAL

The Attorney General himself was confronted with a definite role conflict. In his capacity as Attorney General, he is the chief legal officer of the state. He pleads the case of the state when it is in court, much the same as any counsel does for his client. As an elected official, however, he has another role — that of the politician, responsive to the will of his constituency. While the layman may think of the lawyer's and the politician's roles as being almost identical, there was a definite conflict here.

The shrewd lawyer desires to present the best plea for his client that he can, even though sometimes this plea may be "guilty." As an effective legal advisor, he is not completely responsive to the wishes and hopes of his client — he is an advisor, not just a mouthpiece. The wise lawyer knows also that a good case rests on sound, unimpeachable evidence. Hence it was very much to the interest of the Attorney General, as a lawyer, to obtain honest, independent findings and advice from his social science advisors.

The politician, "good" or "bad," usually wants to keep his job. If a "good" politician, he may wish to keep it not simply for the sake of personal gains but so that a "worse" politician will not dispossess him. An elected attorney general must, in deciding how to plead a case, reach conclusions that will be acceptable to his constituency and state them in a language which will not furnish ammunition to his political enemies.

The Attorney General of Florida was certainly caught in the conflict between the lawyer's and the politician's roles, but he did not seek to escape from it. In the South it seems to be a widespread assumption that the politically safe course at this time was to ignore or defy the Supreme Court. When the Attorney General accepted the Court's premise that the propositions stated in IV A and IV B were the only available alternatives — i.e., that segregation be abolished either "forthwith" or gradually — he closed this door. The possibility remained that the research findings might show a "forthwith" decision to be the evident answer to the Court's question. Were this to be the case, the only choices would be to relinquish the role of politician or simply not present a brief. That he might follow the latter course remained a real possibility until the research was completed and the data analyzed.

THE ROLE OF THE SOCIAL SCIENTIST

The sociologist finds himself in strange company when he works with lawyers, providing them with data which he knows will be used — or not used — in support of a legal argument. The most obvious problem for him as a social scientist is that which presents itself in any applied, "bought" research. He knows that his conclusions are to be evaluated in terms of political expediency and of a policy over which he has little or no control. He will always ask himself — but will never know — to what extent his research is subtly colored by his knowledge of what conclusions would best serve the consumer.

Yet the social scientist should not assume that in conducting applied research, direct attempts will always be made to dictate his conclusions. As has been pointed out, the capable counsel or administrator recognizes that it is in his best interest to get independent, objective findings. There are other pressures on the social scientist, however, which are direct and obvious.

The nature of these pressures makes very clear the meaning of the term "independent research." One of these pressures was that of having to design and execute research in the glare of publicity. Any significant social science research has some news interest, but the scientist usually has control over what information will be released to the press and when it will be released. Often, indeed, he has to arouse the press's interest in order to get the publicity which he may desire. But when a sociologist studies such a controversial issue as desegregation, and does it under governmental auspices, he does not have to look for newspapermen. Public policy, as well as the insistence of the press, requires that all operations be open to public scrutiny. At every step of the research the Coordinator had to ask the question, "What if the newspapers get hold of this?" This can be an annoying handicap to such operations as formulating instruments and pre-testing them. Even when the instruments reached final form, there remained the danger that the subjects on whom they were to be used might be fore-warned that they would be subjects, an eventuality hardly guaranteed to produce spontaneous responses. The possibility that subjects would be "contaminated" before they could be interviewed was increased by the desire of the press to publish the instruments themselves. At the very conclusion of the research the committee was hampered by the presence of newspapermen at the meeting in which it discussed the Coordinator's conclusions, to decide whether the data supported them. It would have provided a juicy item for the newspapers had the committee itself begun to wrangle over the significance of the findings.

The pressure of publicity is intensified by the fact that in this sort of research the social scientist is perforce a public relations man. This is not to say that good public relations are not always important in research with human subjects. In this case, however, the Coordinator was public relations man not only for himself, as social scientist, but for the Attorney General as a politician. In planning his research he was dealing with laymen who knew neither the theory nor the methods of social science. The political official is, in turn, highly sensitive to the expectations of a public of laymen. For the subjects, too, had a dual role: they were subjects, but they were

also voters and political leaders. If offended by the technique of an interviewer or the content of a question, they might not only refuse to cooperate
but might also retaliate politically. This circumstance inevitably influenced
the type of questions that could be asked, the wording of the questions,
and the language of the conclusions.

Selection of subjects was affected, too, as to both number and identity.
For instance, questionnaires were sent to more people than the requirements of social science would demand, for sheer numbers of subjects impress the lay public. Even then, some groups in the state were offended
because they were not polled. The need for a research project of such large
dimensions brought pressure of another sort upon the research workers.
The scope of the study could not be tailored strictly in terms of the time
available for efficient research. The scope had to be determined on the
basis of good public relations, and the time found to do it on this scale with
a minimum of error.

ADVANTAGES TO THE SOCIAL SCIENTIST OF STATE-SPONSORED RESEARCH

Myrdal has dissuaded us of the belief in the possibility of a sterile objectivity in social science research. Yet the social scientist still prefers to do
independent research, designed and executed only in terms of the best principles of scientific methodology. Obviously when he engages in applied
research for a political agency, he sacrifices some of this independence and
thereby runs the risk of reducing even further his already imperfect objectivity. Perhaps the wise course is to remain "simon-pure," staying clear of
such applied, sponsored research. No doubt there will be many situations
where this is the only ethical course to follow. But to follow this course in
every case would mean that the sociologist, particularly in the South, would
completely forego an opportunity to have some influence on governmental
policy on such an issue as desegregation.

There is no doubt that, in terms of his occupational ethos, the sociologist
is expected to take a position in opposition to "gradualism" if that means
simply delay or evasion. Even if he adopts a "gradualist" position, he still
risks the charge of suffering from the conservative bias of the southern culture. On the other hand, even gradualism is considered radical by many
southern politicians; hence, sociologists in the South have rarely had the
opportunity to set foot inside state capitols — unless they were under investigation! It may be argued that when the doors are opened to him, the
social scientist should be prepared to take a calculated risk by working
with government officials. The Florida experience seems to show two reasons why taking such a risk may be justified.

The first of these is that government officials do not always want simply
to "use" the social scientist. As has been indicated, it may be to the best
interest of the client to give a scientist as much independence as possible.

More important, in cooperating with government officials, the academician gets an opportunity to bring social science theory and findings to bear on policy at the top level. He can never be sure that these theories will be accepted or how they will be used, but he does gain an audience.

It represents a marked advance in the South when social scientists are regarded as competent in the field of race relations, when they come to be viewed as "experts" rather than as "agitators." One of the most important byproducts of the legal fight against school segregation will be the education of the public in race relations. Operating under the auspices of duly elected government officials, sociologists may get an even larger audience. Not as a sociologist nor as a college professor, but as consultant to the Attorney General, the writer has had countless opportunities in recent months to address a wide variety of audiences. In the role of consultant to a state official, as well as in the role of the objective social scientist, he has been precluded from advocating any particular course of action with reference to school desegregation. Yet as an objective, scientific "expert," he has been able to present a broad range of social science findings in race relations to a greatly extended audience.

XVIII NEW DIRECTIONS

One pleasant feature of a growing discipline not set in its ways is the variety in its approaches to, and interpretations of, its data. Nisbet, a social theorist, is interested in showing that many of the discoveries of sociology have come about through the "creative process" rather than the "scientific method." In other words, insight or intuition rather than a rigid deductive process leads to a discovery of new things. This position of Nisbet's is not unique. Several philosophers of science have recognized that, after all, deduction deals with closed systems; one can never get any more out of a closed system than he starts with.

48 ROBERT A. NISBET

Sociology as an Art Form

I admit readily that both by temperament and academic background I have always been more interested in the non-uses of our discipline than the uses. I admit further to believing that theories should be tested as much by their reach as their grasp, their importance as their validity, and their elegance as their congruence with such facts as may be at hand. It is my major contention that the science of sociology makes its most significant intellectual advances under the spur of stimuli and through processes that it largely shares with art; that whatever the differences between science and art, it is what they have in common that matters most in discovery and creativeness.

From *Pacific Sociological Review*, Vol. 5 (Fall, 1962), pp. 67–74. Reprinted by permission of the author and publisher.

Nothing I say is intended to imply that sociology is not a science. I am quite willing, for present purposes, to put sociology on the same line with physics and biology, applying to each of these the essence of what I say about sociology. Each is indeed a science, but each is also a form of art, and if we forget this we run the risk of losing the science, finding ourselves with a sandheap empiricism or methodological narcissism, each as far from science as art is from billboard advertisements.

My interest in sociology as an art form was stimulated recently by some reflections on ideas that are by common assent among the most distinctive that sociology has contributed to modern thought. Let me mention these: *mass society, alienation, anomie, rationalization, community, disorganization.* I will have more to say about these ideas and their contexts a little later. Here it suffices to note that all of them have had lasting effect upon both the theoretical and empirical character of sociology. And all have exerted notable influence on other fields of thought, scientific and humanistic.

It occurred to me that not one of these ideas is historically the result of the application of what we are today pleased to call scientific method. If there is evidence that any one of these ideas as first set forth in the writings of such men as Tocqueville, Weber, Simmel, and Durkheim, is the result of problem-solving thought, proceeding rigorously and self-consciously from question to hypothesis to verified conclusion, I have been unable to discover it. On the contrary, each of these profound and seminal ideas would appear to be the consequence of intellectual processes bearing much more relation to the artist than the scientist, as the latter tends to be conceived by most of us. Apart from processes of intuition, impressionism, iconic imagination (the phrase is Sir Herbert Read's), and even objectification, it seems unlikely that any one of these ideas would have come into being to influence generations of subsequent thought and teaching.

For a few, no doubt, this conclusion, if believed at all, may seem like throwing vile suspicion on trusted ancestors: like a child's discovery that his father is a member of the John Birch society or his mother a descendant of the Jukes or Kallikaks. It may smack of an anthropologist's gratuitous demonstration to a pentecostal communicant of the totemistic origins of Christianity. But let us withhold further comment on this aspect of our subject, turning instead for a few moments to a more fundamental and inclusive matter — the habit of treating science as though it were substantively and psychologically different from art.

It is a deeply rooted habit, but by no means universal in the history of modern thought. We need go back no further than the Renaissance to discover a time when art and science were universally regarded as but different manifestations of the same form of creative consciousness. We know that Leonardo da Vinci thought of his paintings and his ingenious works in physiology and mechanics as, equally, art and science. The type of thought and even the outcome in each did not seem significantly different from the other. And, three centuries later, Goethe seems to have felt the same way. He did not suppose that one type of thought operated while he was writing *Faust* and another during his remarkable inquiries in geology and botany. In both the Renaissance and Enlightenment a radical distinction between art and science would have been incomprehensible.

When, then, did the change take place that produced self-consciousness in the scientist and the artist, so like that of Adam and Eve after the Fall? Like a few other things that plague us, it was, I think, in the nineteenth century. Beginning with social movements generated by the French Revolution, and closely connected with processes of division of labor introduced by the industrial revolution, we find a growing tendency in the nineteenth century to assume that the artist and scientist work in ways that are alien, even antagonistic to one another. Gilbert and Sullivan were but giving lyric expression to what everyone knew when they wrote that the scientist is "a matter-of-fact young man, an alphabetical, arithmetical, every-day young man" whereas the artist is "a crotchety, cracked young man, an ultra-poetical, super-aesthetical, out-of-the-way young man."

In art there had developed, by the end of the nineteenth century, the view that creation works through some inscrutable process called genius or inspiration, never through technique and experimental work. We see this vividly in Romanticism and especially in the *fin de siècle*. Associated with this stereotype was the equally fundamental one that the artist is not concerned with reality or truth, but only beauty — timeless supra-terrestrial beauty. And, forming the context of both of these, was the fateful view of the artist's role in society. Far from admitting any continuity with, or dependence on, society, the Romantic artist emphasized instead the gulf between him and society, seeking in solitary escape the anodyne that his medieval and Renaissance forebears had found in fellowship and social purpose. His rejection of the world that was being created by the industrial revolution was total.

But while art was becoming mythicized in this fashion, science was succumbing to another myth, one of reverse character and of equal influence on the popular mind. This was the myth, not of inspiration, but of method. Here, as in the case of art, we are dealing with something related to the industrial revolution. But, whereas art was generally repelled by the new industrial society, science was virtually absorbed by it. Just as industry began to dominate technology, technology dominated science, making it not what it had been for centuries, primarily a pursuit of the reflective mind, but a profession governed by rules and by criteria of service, all of a piece with law, engineering, and medicine.

The new universities in both Europe and America gave immense impetus to science but, to a very large extent, it was science of the applied type. In the United States the rise of the Land Grant colleges, based in their earliest years on an unrelieved vocationalism, was a major step in the union of science and industry and in the cultivation of the stereotype that science, like industry, is practical, the very opposite of art. The "mechanic arts" became, for several generations, the prime conception of everything scientific, placing their stamp upon the type of science done and respected at large. It was Thomas Edison who became the archetype of the scientist in the United States. A Willard Gibbs was simply overlooked.

Gradually the idea spread that science, unlike art, flows along the same methodical and systematic channels that business or law or medicine does. What is crucial, it was felt, was not free reflection, intuition, and imagination but rigorous adherence to procedure. The machine in the factory was proof that skill could be transferred from man to technology, making human ingenuity an expendable item. Could not method be the analogue of the machine? Several generations of Americans thought that it could, and schools and colleges were filled with students doggedly learning what was thought to be scientific method — not, alas, as an aid to ratiocination but as a substitute for it.

It is little wonder, given the overwhelmingly practical and methodical character of American science that Europeans looked for a long time with scant respect upon American science. It is a safe generalization that had it not been for the European institutes to which Americans in rising number went for advanced work, thus acquiring a truer conception of science, American science would never have burst forth from its shell of useful mediocrity. To be sure, there were those of like mind in Europe, especially England; those for whom science was profession, subject to and limited by rules and techniques. But in Europe, where the humanistic tradition was stronger as the result of a much older predemocratic, preindustrial past, and where a mind of the stature of Faraday's could reject for himself the title of physicist, preferring that of philosopher, and be understood and honored for it, there was less likelihood of science becoming mired in unrelieved method and technique.

II

The worst result of the nineteenth-century separation of art and science is not one of historical interpretation. It is the continuing belief in many classrooms and laboratories that the objectives as well as thought processes are different. At its worst, this view tells us that science alone is concerned with reality; that art's function is simply to titillate the senses in a kind of aimless quest of the decorative and eye-pleasing.

Nothing could be further from the truth. Any art form that is serious, be it the novel, poem, or painting, is concerned first and foremost with reality. It is interested in throwing light upon reality, and in somehow communicating this light to others. And this, basically, is what science — as contrasted with technology — is concerned with. I venture the judgment that there is more in common between Picasso and Einstein — in objective, in inspiration, and mode of fulfillment — than there is between Picasso and, say, Norman Rockwell or between Einstein and any of the stolid practitioners of what A. N. Whitehead once called "dustbowl empiricism." Both the artist and the scientist are driven by the desire to understand, to interpret, and to communicate their understanding to the rest of the world.

The artist, let it be trumpeted, is *not* interested in decoration, and it is only because Non-Artists have worked as though decoration, fatuous reminiscence, and eye titillation were the highest ends of art that many persons still find themselves accepting or rejecting an art work largely in terms of whether it is beautiful to the eye. Of course art can be beautiful, but not if it seeks beauty as its chief end. So, let it be remembered, can science be beautiful though no one would suppose that even a mathematician is actuated fundamentally by the goal of beauty.

"The essential nature of art," writes Sir Herbert Read, "will be found neither in the production of objects to satisfy practical needs, nor in the expression of religious or philosophical ideas, but in its capacity to create a synthetic and self-consistent world: a world which is neither the world of practical needs and desires, nor the world of dreams and fantasy, but a world compounded of these contradictions: a convincing representation of the totality of experience: a mode therefore of envisaging the individual's perception of some aspect of universal truth. In all its essential activities art is trying to tell us something: something about the universe, something about nature, about man, or about the artist himself. . . . It is only when we have clearly recognized the function of art as a mode of knowledge parallel to the other modes by which man arrives at an understanding of his environment that we can begin to appreciate its significance in the history of mankind."[1]

The artist's interest in form is the scientist's interest in structure. In each the desire for vision and understanding is dominating. Each works empirically; each strives to communicate what it finds through a pattern or formal structure requiring technique for its mastery. It is worth noting that the word "theory" comes from the same Greek root as the word "theater." It means, basically, looking fixedly at, contemplation. It is allied with the word imagination — that is, literally, internalizing the outer world to an image that the mind holds tenaciously. Both art and science, in short, depend upon the capacity for detachment and upon the ability to hold back from commitment. The essence of each, wrote Santayana, "is the steady contemplation of things in their order and worth."

In truth, science and art have had a profoundly important cultural relationship for the greater part of the history of man. Eugene Rabinowitch,

---

[1] Sir Herbert E. Read, *Art and Society,* London: William Heinemann, Limited, 1937, pp. x–xii.

distinguished chemist and science editor, has recently written some words that might fittingly hang in every hall of learning.

> The evolution of the human mind is a single process, revealed with different intensity, different clarity, and different timing — in its various manifestations — in art, science, philosophy, social and political thought. It is like a fugue, or an oratorio, in which different instruments or voices enter in turn. The voice of the artist is often the first to respond. The artist is the most sensitive individual in society. His feeling for change, his apprehension of new things to come, is likely to be more acute than of the slower-moving, rational, scientific thinker. It is in the artistic production of a period, rather than in its thinking, that one should search for shadows cast in advance by coming events, for prophetic anticipation. I do not mean the forecast of future events, but rather the revelation, in the framework of artistic production, of the mental attitudes which only later will become apparent in other fields of human endeavour. Thus the impending breakdown of the existing order of things, of the generally accepted system of values, should be — and often is — first recognizable in a revolt against the values and canons that had dominated artistic creation; a revolution in art precedes the revolution in society.[2]

Repeatedly, the history of the West has shown these words to be true. Historians of both ancient and modern European culture have emphasized the directive role played by the artist's mind: how philosophical and scientific images of man were preceded by those to be seen first in the drama, the sonnet, and in painting or sculpture. This first became a vivid truth for me several years ago while going through the great Uffizi gallery in

---

[2] Eugene Rabinowitch, "Integral Science and Atomized Art," *Bulletin of the Atomic Scientists*, 15 (February, 1959), p. 64. The entire issue is organized around the theme, science and art, and contains a number of highly perceptive pieces by both scientists and artists. Particularly valuable are those by Rabinowitch, Marston Morse, Carl Holty, and Martin Kamen and Beka Doherty.

Some prolonged, if unsystematic, personal questioning of scientists suggests to me that there is a stratification of acceptance of the art element in creative science. Mathematicians and theoretical physicists, currently high in the status system of modern science, are prone to accept immediately the reality of intuitive and nonlogical elements in scientific discovery. So, for the most part, are those working in such relatively new and highly creative areas as biophysics and biochemistry. Geologists, today low in the pecking order of science, appear least likely to accept or understand the art element in science, although they have much company in the more established and formalized areas of other disciplines, including biology and physics and chemistry. In the behavioral sciences generally there is a greater insistence upon rigor and logic of method — and preoccupation with method itself — than is true of the physical sciences. There are differences, of course, by field. Thus the educationists are more likely to fluff their scientific feathers than are the anthropologists in whose number unabashed artists have always flourished and who have, on the whole, spent least time on matters of abstract methodology. Similarly, my experience indicates, acceptance of the art element in science seems to follow the curve of personal distinction. I am told that one Nobel laureate, a chemist, dismissing method, describes scientific discovery as "rape followed by seduction."

Florence. Here it is possible to trace, in hall after hall, standing for age after age, the historically evolving images of man in Western Europe: from the spiritual, almost mystical and transcendent representations of man to be found in the Italian Primitives, through transitional manifestations that are both divine and human in appearance, to the frankly human, self-contained, and overwhelmingly terrestrial men and women of the Renaissance and Baroque. It is a development that plainly precedes the analogous transitions of image in philosophy and science. It was art with its swift, encompassing, and iconic vision that formed the bridge from medieval asceticism and corporatism to modern humanism; from organism to the obsessing problem of man's relation to society and values.

It was indeed in the Renaissance — and what else was the Renaissance but the conception of man and society as works of art? — that the whole modern view came into existence. This is a view that has since been modified in countless ways — now enhanced, now vulgarized; now made tragic, now trivial; sometimes ennobled, sometimes debased — but never really changed after the late fourteenth century in Italy. Whether the objective was the building of a cathedral or a bridge, the planning of a tapestry or a voyage to the Indies, the forming of a guild or the state itself, Renaissance man saw the world around him from the vantage point of the artist-scientist; not as something to worship or to manipulate but to understand and master even as Michelangelo mastered the marble he worked or Marco Polo the route to Cathay.

The problems and answers that form the core of modern culture are the work, not of the Usefuls in society but of the Visionaries, those who are lost in wonder and who, not knowing where they are going, go therefore the farthest. The same impulse to reality and its communication drove Michelangelo and Machiavelli alike — the one to the majestic *David*, the other to the Renaissance state — each a product of the artist-scientist.

The basic affinity between the artist and the scientist is, as the mathematician Marston Morse has told us, psychological and spiritual. "The first essential bond between mathematics and the arts is found in the fact that discovery in mathematics is not a matter of logic. It is rather the result of mysterious powers which no one understands, and in which the unconscious recognition of. beauty must play an important part. Out of an infinity of designs a mathematician chooses one pattern for beauty's sake, and pulls it down to earth, no one knows how. Afterward the logic of words and of forms sets the pattern right. Only then can one tell someone else. The first pattern remains in the shadows of the mind."[3]

[3] Marston Morse, "Mathematics and the Arts," *Bulletin of the Atomic Scientists, op. cit.,* 56–57. Two recent literary studies have shown, with impressive imagination and learning, how unreason and reason, unconscious and conscious, hunch and hypothesis, have worked together historically. See Wayne Shumaker, *Literature and the Irrational,* Englewood Cliffs, N.J.: Prentice-Hall, Inc., 1960, and Ernest Tuveson, *Imagination as a Means of Grace: Locke and the Aesthetics of Romanticism,* Berkeley: University of California Press, 1960.

These are important words, burning words. They might hang over the entrance to every methodology seminar as a prophylaxis to pedantry. Too many sociologists have assumed that because scientific thought is by definition rational and logical in expression, its psychological roots must therefore be limited to strictly empirical and logical processes. Only that is scientific — so runs the folklore of scientism — that proceeds from an unambiguous and precisely delimited problem, drawn from statistically aseptic data, to a carefully tailored hypothesis. All else is, by definition, art or philosophy. It is hard to think of a better way to apotheosize the routine and insignificant.

Of course science is concerned with problems, with questions rooted in empirical observation as well as reflection. Like the artist, the scientist is interested in understanding the world around him and in discovering significant relationships. But from the large and incontestable truth that scientific thought is ultimately rooted in a preoccupation with the unknown, in a gnawing desire to reduce the tensions of uncertainty, it does not follow that scientific discovery is wholly, or even largely, the simple consequence of problem-defining and problem-solving thought. Such a conclusion has done much to drive sociology into areas of study chosen not because of their intrinsic intellectual importance, but because in them quantitative methodologies can work frictionlessly.

The late Florian Znaniecki foresaw, a generation ago, the trend that things are taking. He was referring to the already manifest influence of methodology courses. "This influence consists in substituting tabulating technique for intellectual methods, and thus eliminating theoretical thinking from the process of scientific research. . . . A condition can be foreseen — indeed, it has almost been reached — when anybody who has learned by heart the various technical rules and formulae of statistics, with no other education whatsover and no more intelligence than a moron, will be able to draw from a given material all the conclusions which statistical problematization makes possible. . . . The role of creative thinking in science, according to this conception, will be reduced to the function of formulating hypotheses which are to be tested by technical means. But we have seen that the only hypotheses statisticians ever have formulated, and ever can formulate, in view of the unavoidable limitations of their method, are no more than superficial generalizations of common-sense practical reflection. There is little place for creative thought and even for scientific progress in this kind of problematization."[4]

Despite the candor of many distinguished scientists in telling about their work, and despite what we are on the way to learning about processes of creativity in general, there is still a great deal that we do not know about how scientists arrive at their problems, do the really crucial work on them, and draw their basic insights. But this much is clear. Such problems and

[4] Florian Znaniecki, *The Method of Sociology*, New York: Holt, Rinehart & Winston, Inc., 1934, pp. 234–235.

ideas, from all that we can presently learn, seem to come as often from the unconscious as the conscious mind; from wide and extraneous reading, or from buried experience, as from the data immediately in view; from the "left-handed" processes of feeling and intuition as from the "right-handed" imperatives of logic and reason. Therefore, may we not draw this conclusion?: Anything that shrinks the field of experience and imagination, that in any way diminishes the sources of inspiration, that routinizes the workings of the intelligent mind, is to be regarded with suspicion.

III

It is time to return to the ideas in sociology I referred to at the outset of my paper. Let me describe them briefly again, for they are indubitably the most distinctive and illuminating contributions of sociology to the study of culture and society. There is, first, the view of human association as containing endemic processes of disorganization, dysfunction, call them what we will. Second, there is the view of the individual as alienated and anomic. Third, there is the perspective of community — in contrast to rationalistic and contractual forms of relationship — involving the key concepts of hierarchy and status. Fourth, we have the great theme of rationalization as a process in history and in the whole structure of modern society.

We know where these ideas came from: from the writings of four or five remarkable minds in the late nineteenth century: Tocqueville, Weber, Simmel, Tönnies, and Durkheim. I need not enlarge upon their formulations of the ideas. I am more interested in the processes by which the ideas came into being: that is, the contexts in which the ideas were uttered, the traditions they came out of, and, if it were possible, the mental states behind the ideas. Obviously, we are limited in what we can say positively, but I believe certain points are clear.

There is, first, the manifest discontinuity of these ideas in the history of modern social thought. Not one of them could have been deduced from the propositions of rationalism on human behavior that flourished in the Enlightenment. The true heritage of the Enlightenment is to be found, not in sociology, but in classical economics, individual psychology, and utilitarian political science. What we find in sociology — that is, in its distinctive currents — is a revolt against the rationalist view of man and society.

The second point is this. Not only are the key ideas of sociology unrelated to prior "scientific" ideas; they have their closest affinity with an art movement, Romanticism. In the same way that the Renaissance image of man proceeded from prior currents in art, so, I argue, the sociological image arises in the first instance from visions which had their earliest and most far reaching appeal in Romantic art.[5]

[5] I have discussed this at greater length in an article "Conservatism and Sociology," *American Journal of Sociology*, 134 (September, 1952), 167–175. See also Leon Bramson's interesting discussion in his *The Political Context of Sociology*, Princeton, N.J.: Princeton University Press, 1961, Chap. 1.

Weber has somewhere likened his own concept of rationalization to the poet Schiller's earlier view of the "disenchantment of the world." He was candid and accurate. Tocqueville, Simmel, and Durkheim might well have done likewise. From the first burst of the Romantic spirit in the late eighteenth century — rising to do battle with the classicist-rationalist view — we find luminously revealed two central visions: (1) the estrangement of the individual from a growingly impersonal and disorganized society (and the consequent spiritual inaccessibility of modern institutions — city, factory, mass society); (2) a celebration of status and community — whether rural, religious, or moral — in contrast to the individualistic and contractual society of the *philosophes.*

Third, and most important, even if most elusive, are the psychological affinities between the Romantic artists and the sociologists. It is impossible, as I have already suggested, to entertain seriously the thought that these major ideas were arrived at in a manner comparable to what we think of as scientific methodology. Can you imagine what would have happened had any one of them been subjected, at the moment following its inception, to a rigorous design analysis? Can anyone believe that Weber's vision of rationalization in history, Simmel's vision of metropolis, or Durkheim's vision of *anomie,* came from logico-empirical analysis as this is understood today? Merely to ask the question is to know the answer. Plainly, these men were not working with finite and ordered problems in front of them. They were not problem-solving at all. Each was, with deep intuition, with profound imaginative grasp, reacting to the world around him, even as does the artist, and, also like the artist, objectifying internal and only partly conscious states of mind.

Consider one example: the view of society and man that underlies Durkheim's great study of suicide. Basically, it is the view of the artist as much as that of the scientist. Background, detail, and characterization blend into something that is iconic in its grasp of an entire social order. How did Durkheim get his controlling idea? We may be sure of one thing: he did not get it, as the stork story of science might have it, from a preliminary examination of the vital registers of Europe, any more than Darwin got the idea of natural selection from his observations during the voyage of the *Beagle.* The idea, the plot, and the conclusion of *Suicide* were well in his mind before he examined the registers. Where, then, did he get the idea? We can only speculate. He might have got it from reading Tocqueville, who could certainly have got it from Lamennais, who could have got it from Bonald or Chateaubriand. Or, it could have come from personal experience — from a remembered fragment of the Talmud, from an intuition born of personal loneliness and marginality, a scrap of experience in Paris. Who can be sure? But one thing is certain. The creative blend of ideas behind *Suicide* — a blend from which we still draw in our scientific labors — was reached in ways more akin to those of the artist than to those of the data processor, the logician, or the technologist.

It is not different with the ideas and perspectives of Simmel — in many ways the most imaginative and intuitive of all the great sociologists. His treatment of fear, love, conventionality, power, and friendship show the mind of the artist-essayist, and it is no distortion of values to place him with such masters as Montaigne and Bacon. Remove the artist's vision from the treatments of the stranger, the dyad, and the role of secrecy, and you have removed all that gives life. In Simmel there is that wonderful tension between the esthetically concrete and the philosophically general that always lies in greatness. It is the esthetic element in Simmel's work that makes impossible the full absorption of his sociological substance by anonymous, systematic theory. One must go back to Simmel himself for the real insight. As with Darwin and Freud, it will always be possible to derive something of importance from the man directly that cannot be gleaned from impersonal statements in social theory.

This leads to another important fact. Our dependence upon these ideas and their makers is akin to the artist's dependence upon the artists who precede him. In the same way that the novelist will always be able to learn from a study and restudy of Dostoevski or James — to learn a sense of development and form, as well as to draw inspiration from the creative source — so the sociologist can forever learn from a rereading of such men as Weber and Simmel.

It is this element that separates sociology from some of the physical sciences. There is, after all, a limit to what the young physicist can learn from even a Newton. Having once grasped the fundamental points of the *Principia,* he is not likely to draw very much as a physicist from rereadings (though he could as a historian of science). How different is the relation of the sociologist to a Simmel or Durkheim. Always there will be something to be gained from a direct reading; something that is informative, enlarging, and creative. This is precisely like the contemporary artist's return to the study of medieval architecture, the Elizabethan sonnet, or the paintings of Matisse. This is the essence of the history of art, and why the history of sociology is so different from the history of science.

IV

That such men as Weber, Durkheim, and Simmel fall in the scientific tradition is unquestioned. Their works, for all the deep artistic sensitivity and intuition, no more belong in the history of art than the works of Balzac or Dickens do in the history of social science. The conclusion we draw is not that science and art are without differences. There are real differences, as there are among the arts and among the sciences.[6] No one

---

[6] Charles Morris, the philosopher, has suggested that the major difference is this: although both science and art communicate by the use of ideas and representations not completely describable in terms of sense experience, science typically seeks to make its communications capable of identification or verification by the largest number of indi-

asks a Picasso to verify one of his visions by repeating the process; and, conversely, we properly give short shrift to ideas in science that no one but the author can find supported by experience. The ideas of Durkheim may, as I have suggested, be dependent upon thought processes like those of the artist, but none of them would have survived in sociology or become fruitful for others were it not for criteria and modes of communication that differ from those in art.

The conclusion, then, is not that science and art are, or should be, alike. It is the simpler but more fundamental conclusion that in both art and science the same type of creative imagination works. And everything that impedes or frustrates this imagination strikes at the source of the discipline itself. This unhappily is what is happening today in large areas of sociological instruction and research. It is a recurrent phenomenon in philosophy and science.

All too often in the history of thought we find techniques, methods, and doctrines becoming puny earthworks, hiding the view of the Olympian

---

viduals, whereas art tends to insist that each individual translate the original vision into something peculiarly his own creation.

There are probably also interesting role differences between artists and scientists, though this is, so far as I can discover, a relatively unexplored area of study. Martyl Landsdorf, an artist, and Cyril S. Smyth, a scientist, in a joint article in the *Bulletin of the Atomic Scientists* already cited, say: "In many contacts with humanist and scientific friends we have noticed only one consistent difference of professional attitudes — the scientists are jealous of their ideas; the humanists do not seem to mind if someone appropriates their ideas but are outraged by a plagiarism of form." This is an important insight, but I judge that it has more relevance to painters and sculptors, and possibly poets, than to novelists and playwrights who are certainly as jealous of ideas, and as secretive, as are the scientists. Legal battles over plots are not unknown.

One commonly alleged difference between scientists and artists deserves critical comment. It is an old stereotype of the scientist, sedulously cultivated in many a seminar, that the scientist, simply because he is scientist and not artist, is preconditioned to a willingness, even a desire, to be displaced by the work of students and others. But this stereotype says more about the ideal world of science than it does about actual scientists. The desire for self-preservation is surely as strong among scientists as among artists, and the evidence suggests that in such matters as protection of personal theories, hoarding of data, and secretiveness of intent, there may not be very significant role differences.

Passion for self-preservation may be more functional in scientific thought than is commonly supposed. Marston Morse, in the article referred to above, is of this view so far as mathematics is concerned. He cites the famous feud between Poincaré and his young colleague Lebesque, suggesting the similarity of conflict and outcome to the revolt of Philipp Emanuel Bach against the work of his father, Johann Sebastian. In each case the reactions were dictated by instincts of self-preservation which, as Professor Morse points out, were clearly to the advantage of posterity.

On one point the evidence is clear. Scientists have a far higher sense of priority — though not of competitiveness — than artists. This would seem to follow from the broad differences of context. It is highly unlikely that anything in the history of art resembles what Robert Merton has emphasized in his studies of priority in science or what Frederick Reif has described as prevailing practice among physicists in an article, "The Competitive World of the Pure Scientist," *Science*, 134 (December 15, 1961), pp. 1957–1962.

heights. How many mute, inglorious Simmels, how many village Cooleys lie today buried in required sequences of curriculum and in the computer rooms, their talents occupied not by development of ideas and insights but by the adaptation of trivial or well-worn ideas to the language of the machine or by the endless replication of studies that often shouldn't have been done in the first place? Such servitude is justified on the false and appalling ground that the student can thus be taught the "method" of science. One may observe cynically that he sees no Simmels and Durkheims walking the campus today. I venture the statement that there would have been none in their day had certain curricular requirements and terminological fashions been then in existence.

Which leads me to my final observations. I have stressed the art element in sociology not because I think the villain is the machine — any more than it is the machine tender who occasionally walks like a social scientist. The danger, if I may indulge myself in the presidential prerogative of the sermon, is nontechnological; it is sociological; it is the systematics and the dogmatics that always threaten to seep into the cellars of intellectual disciplines, thus driving out the art elements. For art's war is with system building, not with science. I know of no better way of expressing this than in the form that Francis Bacon chose three centuries ago. That is, in the form of the Idols of the Mind. Let us call them the Idols of the Profession.

There are, first, you will remember, the Idols of the Tribe. These are the inclinations, perspectives, and modes of perception that are common to all; they are unavoidable, but must nevertheless be allowed for. The mere fact that we are sociologists — instead of biologists or economists — means that there are certain endemic, uniting ways of seeing the world around us. They are valuable and unavoidable, but not final.

Second, there are the Idols of the Cave — those that come, not from the character of the profession as a whole, but of that small part of the profession each of us lives in. Here we have the idols of specialization; the human but nevertheless dangerous tendency to reduce the richness and variety of the whole to the specialized perspectives and techniques that each of us operates with and that always threaten to become as rigid and fixed as the skills of technicians.

Third, we have the Idols of the Market Place — words, phrases, and neologisms that become substitutes for ideas. Who among us has not learned to his advantage or disadvantage of the hypnotic fascination that is exerted upon foundations, research committees, and certain editors, by phraseology? And who does not know of the ease with which the words conveying the concept become the thing itself — with resulting inability to go beyond the words?

But, the greatest and most formidable of the Idols are those of the Theater. Here Bacon had reference to systems of thought, systems which become, like bureaucracies, their own reason for being; where original goals have become displaced, leaving only the goals of systematic survival and self-maintenance. It seems to be the mark of all systems that their very degree of initial success leads before long to an almost ritualistic conclusion. We have all laughed at the teacher of classics who saw in the *Antigone* "a veritable treasure house of grammatical peculiarities." And for this teacher's students the classics were indeed killed. But why do we not laugh also at the teacher of sociology who introduces his students not to the rich and endlessly diversified field of social and cultural experience but to dull and potentially alienating analyses of fashionable systems and methodologies. Is not at least part of the attraction today of the natural sciences for the gifted student the assurance that he will be introduced immediately to the materials and problems of science and not to the locutions of systems? Systems so easily become bureaucracies of the spirit, subject to the same pettifogging rules and regulations.

Art abhors systems, and so does all creativity. History is the graveyard of systems, and this is precisely why Simmel and Cooley and Sumner remain fresh and valuable for us today and why few read Spencer or Ward. How often do system-builders produce students who are themselves creative and viable? The system killeth, the insight giveth life. What remains today of nominalism, realism, sensationalism, pragmatism, and all the other systems that once paraded over the landscape of Europe? Dead, all dead. God lives, Blake wrote, in the details. I amend this to say he lives in the insights, the intuitions, the imaginations of the artist. I cannot better conclude than with one final excerpt from Marston Morse:

> The creative scientist lives in "the wildness of logic" where reason is the handmaiden and not the master. I shun all monuments that are coldly legible. I prefer the world where the images turn their faces in every direction, like the masks of Picasso. It is the hour before the break of day when science turns in the womb, and, waiting, I am sorry that there is between us no sign and no language except by mirrors of necessity. I am grateful for the poets who suspect the twilight zone.
>
> The more I study the interrelations of the arts the more I am convinced that every man is in part an artist. Certainly as an artist he shapes his own life, and moves and touches other lives. I believe that it is only as an artist that man knows reality. *Reality is what he loves, and if his love is lost it is his sorrow.*[7]

[7] Morse, *op. cit.*, p. 58.

One of the most useful tools of the working sociologist is the digital computer. Computers are efficient means of comparing large quantities of data, computing statistical measures, and doing anything else involving the manipulation of symbols. Computers can even take data written longhand on a questionnaire, compare responses, and do a content analysis of them. Some theoretically inclined sociologists have shied away from using computers, because they have an image of them as turning out only meaningless correlations. The Gullahorns, both sociologists, describe the uses of HOMUNCULUS, a computer model of social behavior, and show the value of the computer for manipulating and generating theoretical models.

49   JOHN T. GULLAHORN AND JEANNE E. GULLAHORN

Some Computer Applications in Social Science

The modern electronic digital computer has revolutionized data analysis in social science and in other fields as well, but its general symbol-manipulating capacities suggest other less obvious and as yet less explored applications. A computer can read symbols, store them in memory, compare them, erase them, and associate them by allowing access to one symbol when another is given. Combinations of these basic information-processing functions yield powerful resources for developing and verifying social theory through formalization, objectification and analysis of symbolic representations of theoretical constructs.[1]

Some of the advantages of expressing a theory in the form of a computer program are analogous to those derived from formalizing a theory in mathematical terms. The systematization allows comparisons between sets of generalizations — comparisons which may not be obvious, given the structure of verbal formulation. In consequence, one can explore more adequately the logical implications of verbal propositions. Furthermore, the very process of translation to programming language forces one to be precise about variables and their relationships, thus helping one recognize ambiguities in expression and implicit assumptions in the verbal model. For example, if the verbal formulation contains qualifying phrases such as "other things being equal," in programming one must define precisely what these "other things" are and what it means for them to be "equal."

From *American Sociological Review*, Vol. XXX (June, 1965), pp. 353–365. Reprinted by permission of the authors and the American Sociological Association.

[1] A more detailed discussion of uses of computers for theory development appears in John T. Gullahorn and Jeanne E. Gullahorn, "The Computer as a Tool for Theory Development," in Dell Hymes (ed.), *Uses of Computers in Anthropology*, The Hague: Mouton, in press.

Because of the computer's step-by-step mode of operation, the complexity of a model is not a serious obstacle; one can complicate the steps in a program to test more elaborate hypotheses or to introduce additional variables. Aside from these advantages, the computer is a unique instrument for developing stronger theory — precise theory, possessing dynamic potentiality, because programmed concepts actually generate consequences. In computer simulation, in which a symbolic representation of theoretical processes is programmed for machine manipulation, one can determine whether the static classificatory assertions of conventional theory really do evolve as logical outcomes. With a computer model one can actually set theoretical processes in motion, generate data as logical consequences of hypothesized processes, and thereby realize the theory's extended consequences. Furthermore, the data generated during a computer run are the direct and exclusive results of operationalizing the hypotheses and involve no extraneous unverbalized — or unprogrammed — influences.

Perhaps the strongest impetus to computer applications using the modern digital computer's general symbol-manipulating capacities to test hypotheses in social science has come from the joint efforts of the RAND-Carnegie Tech group. Development of Information Processing Language, Version V (IPL-V) by Allen Newell and his colleagues has provided a powerful tool for social theorists interested in simulation.[2] In IPL-V, both data and routines for manipulating them are written in the form of lists. Complex information can be handled efficiently through the use of list structures, or hierarchies of lists containing as many sublists as needed, and description lists, which associate with any symbol a list of its attributes and their values.

A pioneering demonstration of the feasibility of computer simulation appeared in 1957 when Newell, Shaw, and Simon published a description of their Logic Theorist program, which proved theorems in elementary symbolic logic — a feat previously accomplished only by humans.[3] Among subsequent applications of information processing programs to classical problems of psychological theory are Feigenbaum's Elementary Perceiver and Memorizer, a computer model of verbal rote memorization; Feldman's simulation of the behavior of subjects in a binary-choice experiment, and Hovland and Hunt's model of human concept formulation.[4] Lindsay ex-

[2] Allen Newell, Fred M. Tonge, Edward A. Feigenbaum, Bert F. Green, Jr., and George H. Mealy, *Information Processing Language-V Manual* (2nd ed.), Englewood Cliffs, N.J.: Prentice-Hall, 1964.

[3] Allen Newell, J. Clifford Shaw, and Herbert A. Simon, "Empirical Explorations of the Logic Theory Machine: A Case Study in Heuristics," *Proceedings of the Western Joint Computer Conference* (1957), New York: Institute of Radio Engineers, 1957, pp. 218–230.

[4] Edward A. Feigenbaum, "The Simulation of Verbal Learning Behavior"; Julian Feldman, "Simulation of Behavior in the Binary Choice Experiment"; and Earl B. Hunt and Carl I. Hovland, "Programming a Model of Human Concept Formulation," in Edward A. Feigenbaum and Julian Feldman (eds.), *Computers and Thought,* New York: McGraw-Hill, 1963, pp. 297–309; 329–346 and 310–325.

plores another facet of cognitive activity in his computer processing of syntactic and semantic information to analyze communications in Basic English, and Bert Green and associates have programmed a machine to respond to questions phrased in ordinary English.[5] Still another aspect of human decision-making appears in Clarkson's model of the trust investment process.[6] At a more general level, Newell, Shaw, and Simon have programmed an information processing theory of human problem solving, a model whose output has been compared systematically with that of human problem solvers.[7] Reitman has incorporated elements of this general problem-solving system in simulating the complex creative activity involved in musical composition.[8]

While early applications of information processing models focus on relatively logical aspects of human behavior, recent simulation models incorporate emotional responses. Concerned by the singlemindedness of cognitive activity programmed in the Newell, Shaw, and Simon General Problem Solver, Reitman and associates recently have programmed a Hebbian-type model of human thinking that is not in complete control of what it remembers and forgets, being subject to interruption and to conflict.[9] Kenneth Colby, a psychiatrist, has developed a computer model for simulating therapeutic manipulation of emotions as well as a patient's responses.[10] In HOMUNCULUS, our computer model of elementary social behavior, simulated subjects may at times emit anger or guilt reactions, or they may suppress aggression and later vent it against a less threatening figure than the one who violated norms regarding distributive justice.[11]

All of the diverse operating information processing models cited thus far are programmed in IPL-V. Models to be discussed next are written in

[5] Robert K. Lindsay, "The Reading Machine Problem," unpublished Ph.D. dissertation, Carnegie Institute of Technology, Pittsburgh, 1961; and Bert F. Green, Jr., Alice K. Wolf, Carol Chomsky, and Kenneth Laughery, "Baseball: An Automatic Question-Answerer," *Proceedings of the Western Joint Computer Conference*, New York: Institute of Radio Engineers, 1961, pp. 219–224.

[6] Geoffrey P. E. Clarkson, *Portfolio Selection: A Simulation of Trust Investment,* Englewood Cliffs, N.J.: Prentice-Hall, 1962.

[7] Allen Newell, J. Clifford Shaw, and Herbert A. Simon, "Report on a General Problem-Solving Program," *Information Processing,* Proceedings of the International Conference on Information Processing, Paris: UNESCO, 1960, pp. 256–264; and Allen Newell and Herbert A. Simon, "Computer Simulation of Human Thinking," *Science,* 134 (December 22, 1961), pp. 2011–2017.

[8] Walter R. Reitman, "Programming Intelligent Problem Solvers," *IRE Transactions of the Professional Group on Human Factors in Electronics,* 2 (1961), pp. 27–33.

[9] Walter R. Reitman, Richard B. Grove, and Richard G. Shoup, "Argus: An Information-Processing Model of Thinking," *Behavioral Science,* 9 (July, 1964), pp. 270–281.

[10] Kenneth M. Colby, "Computer Simulation of a Neurotic Process," in Silvan S. Tomkins and Samuel Messick (eds.), *Computer Simulation of Personality,* New York: Wiley, 1963, pp. 165–179.

[11] John T. Gullahorn and Jeanne E. Gullahorn, "A Computer Model of Elementary Social Behavior," in Feigenbaum and Feldman, *op. cit.,* pp. 375–386; also reprinted in *Behavioral Science,* 8 (October, 1963), pp. 354–362.

several different computer languages. Among other computer applications involving considerations of emotional behavior are Coe's simulation of responses to frustration and conflict, Loehlin's simulation of socialization, and Abelson's design for computer simulation of "hot," affect-laden cognition.[12] Imaginative computer simulations of voting behavior have been done by Robert Abelson, William McPhee, and their associates. Using the fluoridation controversies as a case in point, Abelson and Bernstein blend theories from several disciplines and from both field and experimental phenomena in constructing their model.[13] Simulated individuals are assigned characteristics known to be relevant, and the programmed model specifies the processes by which they may change during the fluoridation campaign.

In their theory of informal social influence, McPhee, Smith, and Ferguson model the process by which children are socialized so that a majority adopt the same political affiliation as their parents, and their model accounts for deviants as well.[14] Using the same basic model McPhee accurately simulated the Wisconsin Presidential primary election involving Kennedy, Humphrey, and Nixon. In contrast to the research of the Simulmatics Project,[15] whose goal is specifically prognostication, the Abelson and McPhee computer models just described are designed to contribute to social science theory and not only to predict voting outcomes. More recently McPhee's student, Robert B. Smith, has undertaken a simulation of Selvin's analysis of leadership patterns, a project with broad implications for data processing as well as simulation.[16]

Probably the most active center for computer research in sociology is at Johns Hopkins University. Interactions in a triad have been simulated in one study.[17] Assuming only that (1) if two persons find interaction with each other rewarding they will tend to interact more frequently, and (2)

[12] Rodney M. Coe, "Conflict, Interference, and Aggression: Computer Simulation of a Social Process," *Behavioral Science*, 9 (April, 1964), pp. 186–197; John C. Loehlin, "A Computer Program that Simulates Personality," and Robert P. Abelson, "Computer Simulation of 'Hot' Cognition," in Tomkins and Messick, *op. cit.*, pp. 189–211 and 277–298.

[13] Robert P. Abelson, and Alex Bernstein, "A Computer Simulation Model of Community Referendum Controversies," *Public Opinion Quarterly*, 27 (Spring, 1963), pp. 93–122.

[14] William N. McPhee, *Formal Theories of Mass Behavior*, New York: Free Press of Glencoe, 1963.

[15] Ithiel de Sola Pool and Robert P. Abelson, "The Simulmatics Projects," *Public Opinion Quarterly*, 25 (Summer, 1961), pp. 167–183. A popularization of this research appears in Thomas B. Morgan, "The People-Machine," *Harper's*, 222 (1961), pp. 53–57.

[16] Robert B. Smith, "Leadership, Participation, and Anomie: A Model Simulating the Effects of Leadership," unpublished manuscript reporting preliminary steps toward programming a simulation of the research reported in Hanan C. Selvin, *The Effects of Leadership*, Glencoe, Ill.: Free Press, 1959.

[17] James S. Coleman, "Analysis of Social Structures and Simulation of Social Processes with Electronic Computers," in Harold Guetzkow (ed.), *Simulation in Social Science: Readings*, Englewood Cliffs, N.J.: Prentice-Hall, 1962, pp. 61–69.

time available for interaction is limited, the investigators have simulated interactions producing a dyad and an isolate, a group in which one person dominates interaction, and groups with balanced interaction. In another study one of Coleman's students, Raymond Breton, has simulated a restriction-of-output situation.[18] According to this model, under most conditions pressures from fellow workmen result in a more homogeneous output, presumably in conformity with the norm. When motivation for monetary reward is intensified, however, some simulated workers develop negative sentiments toward those attempting to apply constraints, and variability of output increases.

Simulations of reference group behavior by the Johns Hopkins group involve a programmed representation of a social system composed of the high school students Coleman surveyed in an earlier study.[19] Responses to questionnaires administered at two points in time are used to calculate parameters for the computer model of the social system. During a simulation run, the programmed reference group processes operate on the input data to produce changes in attitudes and in friendships, indicating the impact of friendship on attitude consistency and the contribution of attitude consistency to the maintenance of friendship. The friendship and attitude data resulting from one computer run are then used as parameters to represent a new state of the social system, and further simulations generate data predicting future states of the system. (To validate the model additional surveys of the same sample would be necessary, so that data procured at subsequent periods could be compared with results from the computer simulation runs, but as yet the Coleman group has not reported such a study.)

HOMUNCULUS

As a detailed illustration of the utility of computer simulation in clarifying hypotheses and generating data that follow as logical results of postulated processes, we shall describe a recent application of HOMUNCULUS,[20] our computer model based largely on Homans' theory of elementary social be-

---

[18] Reported in James S. Coleman, "The Use of Computers in the Study of Social Organization," paper presented to the Sociological Research Association, Los Angeles, 1963.

[19] Simulations of reference group behavior are discussed in Coleman's chapter in Guetzkow, *op. cit.*, as well as in Frank Waldorf and James S. Coleman, "Analysis and Simulation of Reference Group Processes," paper presented at the American Psychological Association meetings, St. Louis, 1962. The data for the simulation studies come from research reported in James S. Coleman, *Adolescent Society*, Glencoe, Ill.: Free Press, 1961.

[20] A description of the full model appears in John T. Gullahorn and Jeanne E. Gullahorn, "Computer Simulation of Human Interaction in Small Groups," in American Federation of Information Processing Societies Conference Proceedings, 1964 *Spring Joint Computer Conference*, Baltimore: Spartan Books, 1964, pp. 103–113. Also reprinted in *Simulation*, 4 (January, 1965), pp. 50–61.

TABLE 1. ROLE CONFLICT QUESTIONNAIRE:
SAMPLE PAGE AND PERCENTAGE DISTRIBUTION OF RESPONSES

Assume you are an officer of the Employees' Club, which is largely supported by the company. You believe strongly in the union and attend meetings regularly. Your fellow workers have chosen you to be their Chief Steward, and you wonder whether you should resign from the club office so you can devote your time to the job of Chief Steward. *You really haven't time to do both jobs well.* You feel responsible for the continued success of a program which you have started for the club, and at the same time you feel obligated to do a good job as Chief Steward.

	I would be most likely to do the following		
In each of the following situations, please check the appropriate space to indicate the action you would be most likely to take.	*Resign from club office*	*Retain both positions*	*Resign from position of chief steward*
An officer of the company tells you that if you continue your good work in the Employees' Club it may lead to a management position. What if —			
1. Both the union executive committee and the people you represent as Chief Steward want you to keep the club office.	19	44	37
2. The executive committee wants you to keep the club office — the people you represent want you to serve as steward.	42	36	22
3. The executive committee wants you to serve as steward — the people you represent want you to keep the club office.	29	39	32
4. Both the executive committee and the people you represent want you to serve as steward.	61	24	15
Your work as Chief Steward will give you more chance to make a favorable showing before management than will the club office. What if —			
5. Both the executive committee and the people you represent want you to keep the club office.	30	40	30
6. The executive committee wants you to keep the club office — the people you represent want you to serve as steward.	55	32	13
7. The executive committee wants you to serve as steward — the people you represent want you to keep the club office.	39	39	22
8. Both the executive committee and the people you represent want you to serve as steward.	71	22	7
N = 148; Average percentages:	43	35	22

havior.[21] In keeping with Homans' theory the computer model incorporates principles from Skinnerian psychology and classical economics, envisaging an individual's responses as a function of the quantity and quality of reward and punishment his actions elicit. In computer routines operationalizing the theoretical formulation, simulated individuals are programmed to identify social stimuli, retrieve data regarding the past reinforcement value of alternative responses, assess their current level of satiation or deprivation with reference to expected reactions to their responses, select socially profitable activities, and modify their behavior in accord with feedback from interaction partners. For example, in a computer-generated social exchange based on Blau's observations of behavior in a bureaucracy,[22] two simulated office workers carry out a sequence of interactions in which one requests help from the other, receives assistance, gives approval and respect as reinforcement, and so on until the helper terminates the interaction because the cost of time taken from his own work exceeds the value of further approval from his colleague.

TABLE 2. PERCENTAGE WHO WOULD RESIGN

Source of pressure	From employees' club office under pressure to keep:			From union chief stewardship under pressure to keep:		
	Union stewardship	Club office	Difference	Union stewardship	Club office	Difference
Persons represented	57	29	28	14	30	16
Executive committee	50	37	13	19	25	6
Management	49	38	11	18	26	8

While such interaction sequences appear to be reasonable examples of social exchange, plausibility is a weak test of the model's validity. For a more stringent assessment of routines operationalizing Homans' conceptualization of the effects of value, cost, and profit on social behavior, we designed a computer simulation of questionnaire data concerning role conflict resolution.

THE ROLE CONFLICT FIELD STUDY

One page of a questionnaire included in the senior author's field research on role conflict among labor union leaders posed a situation involving two roles — a union chief stewardship and a responsible position in the com-

[21] George C. Homans, *Social Behavior: Its Elementary Forms*, New York: Harcourt, Brace & World, 1961.

[22] Peter M. Blau, *The Dynamics of Bureaucracy*, Chicago: University of Chicago Press, 1955.

pany-sponsored employees' club (see Table 1).[23] An attempt was made to establish the respondent's moral commitment to each role. Then moral and practical sanctions for each position were introduced and systematically varied by qualifying pressures from three reference groups. The respondent was invited to withdraw from one role or the other or, as an alternative, to "Retain both positions." This third course was plainly labeled a decision of desperation, for he was told, "You really haven't time to do both jobs well." Responses in the middle column are thus a rough index of unresolved felt role conflict.

Union members responding to the questionnaire expressed a stronger commitment to the chief stewardship than to the employees' club position. Under the eight combinations of reference group pressures, almost twice as many (an average of 43 per cent) would resign from the employees' club office as would give up the chief stewardship (22 per cent).

Three reference groups exerted pressures on the respondents, and all three introduced consistent differences in response. The greatest shift came from yielding to persons represented by the respondent in his capacity as chief steward; the union executive committee was no more influential than management. Table 2 presents the percentage who would resign from each position under each source and direction of pressure.

If a person feels more strongly committed to one of two competing roles, then role conflict will increase in intensity as reference group pressures build up in favor of the other role. For respondents who favored retaining the chief stewardship, increasing pressures towards retaining the club office should increase the intensity of felt role conflict.

The possibility that unresolved role conflict produces an increasing tendency to view the situation unrealistically, to attempt more than one can accomplish, was tested in the field study by offering the respondents an opportunity to reject either of the roles or to retain both although they would not have time to do both jobs well. We expected increased pressures in favor of the employees' club to cause a higher percentage to choose the "retain both positions" category.

Interviews with union members as well as observations of meetings suggested the following rank-order of the three reference groups in terms of power: (1) persons represented; (2) the executive committee; (3) management. (Actually, as indicated in Table 2, the latter two groups did not differ essentially in this questionnaire situation.) On the basis of these expectations concerning pressure effectiveness we predicted the rank orderings of responses to the questionnaire items shown in Table 3. We expected item number 1, with all three groups aligned in favor of the employees' club office (the generally less desirable position according to the members' per-

[23] John T. Gullahorn, "Measuring Role Conflict," *American Journal of Sociology*, 61 (January, 1956), pp. 299–303.

TABLE 3. PREDICTED AND OBSERVED RANK ORDERINGS OF QUESTIONNAIRE ITEMS: PERCENTAGES WHO WOULD

Item no.[a]	Groups favoring employees' club:	Resign from club office rank ordering		Retain both positions rank ordering		Resign from stewardship rank ordering	
		Predicted	Observed	Predicted	Observed	Predicted	Observed
1.	All three groups	8	8	1	1	1	1
5.	Persons represented and executive committee	7	6	2	2	2	3
3.	Persons represented and management	6	7	3	4	3	2
7.	Persons represented	5	5	4	3	4	4
2.	Executive committee and management	4	4	5	5	5	5
6.	Executive committee	3	3	6	6	6	7
4.	Management	2	2	7	7	7	6
8.	None	1	1	8	8	8	8
		$r_s = .98^b$ ($p < .01$)		$r_s = .98^b$ ($p < .01$)		$r_s = .95^b$ ($p < .01$)	

[a] Item numbers refer to Table 1. Rank in this table is based on the amount of pressure exerted by reference groups to retain the club office.

[b] Spearman rank correlation coefficient.

sonal preferences), to produce the highest number of responses in the middle, "retain both positions," category. We expected a coalition of pressures for the club office from persons represented and the executive committee (item 5) to be ranked second in intensity of induced role conflict, as reflected in decisions to retain both positions; a combination of pressures from persons represented and management (item 3) to be third, and so on. Comparison of our predicted rank ordering with that observed in the questionnaire response frequencies indicates that the data support our expectations (Table 3).

THE SIMULATION STUDY

From the field research, we formulated certain hypotheses about the information processing involved in the observed decisions for role conflict resolution.[24] Programming a digital computer to simulate a portion of the questionnaire study enabled us to state these hypotheses explicitly and to generate data resulting directly from the programmed processes. Figure 1 is a flow diagram summarizing the sequential processing.

The executive routine selects a simulated respondent to "answer" the questionnaire (Figure 1, Box 1). In the role-conflict situation a labor-union member is rewarded by role behavior in a selected position as well as by approval from certain relevant reference groups; he has a history of reinforcement from activities involving both the employees' club and the local union. Since the reward value of each of these activities varies among members, the program assigns to each simulated respondent an individual set of reward values for the club office and the chief stewardship, using a random number generator (Box 2). The average value of the numbers generated by this Monte Carlo technique equals the averages from the observed data from labor union members — i.e., 43 points for the chief stewardship and 22 points for the employees' club office.[25]

Interview data from union members indicated that a few made their decisions without detailed assessment of reference group pressures when the perceived reward value of one or both statuses was so high that the respondent was unwilling to sacrifice it. In simulating the processing leading to these short-cut decisions (Boxes 3 through 8 in Figure 1), we therefore assign as cut-off points 81 per cent of the possible maximum value for the chief stewardship position and 93 per cent of the possible maximum value for the employees' club office. These figures correspond to the data presented in Table 1: even with all reference group pressures aligned in favor

[24] John T. Gullahorn and Jeanne E. Gullahorn, "Role Conflict and Its Resolution," *Sociological Quarterly*, 4 (Winter, 1963), pp. 32–48.

[25] Monte Carlo techniques are not inherent in simulation models. Indeed, HOMUNCULUS is generally a deterministic computer model. In the present situation we did not have data indicating individual values for relevant parameters; therefore we resorted to a Monte Carlo procedure to generate random values over a range that seemed reasonable on the basis of interview and other data from the field study.

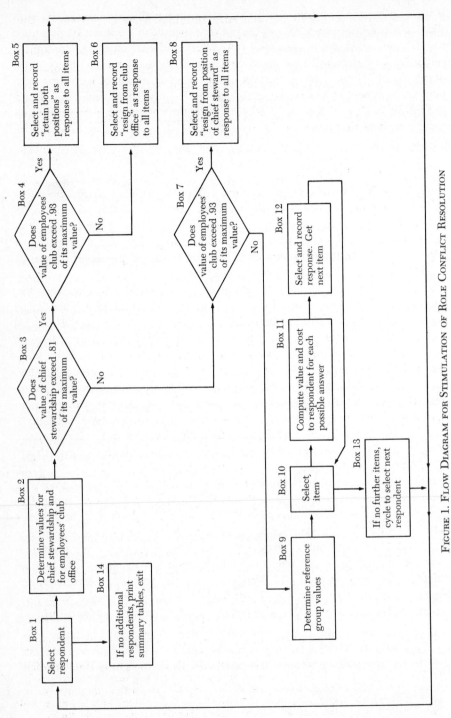

Figure 1. Flow Diagram for Stimulation of Role Conflict Resolution

Box 1
Select respondent

Box 2
Determine values for chief stewardship and for employees' club office

Box 3
Does value of chief stewardship exceed .81 of its maximum value?

Box 4
Does value of employees' club exceed .93 of its maximum value?

Box 5
Select and record "retain both positions" as response to all items

Box 6
Select and record "resign from club office" as response to all items

Box 7
Does value of employees' club exceed .93 of its maximum value?

Box 8
Select and record "resign from position of chief steward" as response to all items

Box 9
Determine reference group values

Box 10
Select item

Box 11
Compute value and cost to respondent for each possible answer

Box 12
Select and record response. Get next item

Box 13
If no further items, cycle to select next respondent

Box 14
If no additional respondents, print summary tables, exit

of the employees' club, 19 per cent still resigned from it in favor of the chief stewardship; and with all pressures favoring the chief stewardship, 7 per cent nonetheless rejected it in favor of the employees' club office. Thus, when a synthetic respondent's assigned value for one and only one of the positions exceeds the cut-off point, he is made to resign from the other position without further processing. If his values for both positions exceed the cut-off points, he selects the middle course and resigns from neither. In this situation the net profit from choosing one alternative is lower than the value of either position. Our model follows Homans' definition of cost and profit: the cost of an activity is the value of an alternative foregone in pursuing the activity.[26] In this case, the cost of selecting one role is the value of the rejected alternative. The net social profit of an activity is simply its reward value minus its cost.[27]

Only a small proportion of our simulated sample of respondents make a decision at this point. For the majority, the choice involves consideration of the individual's sensitivity to pressure from each of the three reference groups. Assuming that the simulated respondents — like the real union members — have past histories of reinforcement involving interaction with each group, we used a Monte Carlo method to generate random numbers and assigned these as individual values for each group. The average values of the numbers so generated equal the observed sensitivities to pressures represented by the "Difference" columns of Table 2.

After reference groups have been given their values (Box 9), the first item from the questionnaire is presented to the simulated subject (Box 10) for processing (Box 11) leading to selection of a response (Box 12). Using the values for each position involved and for sensitivity to each reference group's pressure, the program computes both the reward value and the cost of each possible course of action. The simulated respondent's decision strategy is to select the alternative yielding the greatest profit. After each item has been answered and the choice recorded, the program cycles back to the executive routine, which selects the next respondent and repeats the same process.

As noted previously, we hypothesized that as role conflict increased, respondents increasingly would choose to retain both positions, though they were aware that they could not do both jobs well. In our initial formulation regarding role conflict resolution,[28] we considered adoption of the "retain both positions" alternative a residual decision — a choice by default resulting from inability to decide between the conflicting roles. This hypothesis is not inconsistent with Homans' theory of elementary social behavior, the basis for HOMUNCULUS. In a situation involving cross-pressures from highly valued reference groups, the personal cost of foregoing the expected

[26] Homans, *op. cit.*, p. 58.
[27] *Ibid.*, p. 61.
[28] Gullahorn, *op. cit.*

rewards from incumbency in either position may be so high as to preclude the respondent's realizing a profit from favoring one role at the expense of the other. In such a case we predicted that the respondent would choose what we considered a desperate alternative by retaining both positions under the stated conditions, without actively considering the potential rewards and costs ensuing from such a course of action.

TABLE 4.   CONSEQUENCES OF DECISION-BY-DEFAULT STRATEGY

	Spearman rank order correlations for		
	Resign from club office	Retain both positions	Resign from stewardship
Computer with theory	1.00	.74	.95
Computer with people	.98	.76	1.00
	Percentages responding in each category		
Computer-simulated respondents	42	45	13
Labor union members	43	35	22

An alternative formulation is also consistent with Homans' theory, however. Rather than making the decision to retain both positions by default, the respondent resolves his dilemma by comparing the expected social profit of this choice with the expected profits from a decision in favor of either one of the positions, selecting the most profitable of the three courses of action.

Our survey data supported our prediction that as pressures mounted in favor of the less favored position, respondents increasingly would decide to retain both roles rather than choose between them (Table 3). But through conventional methods of analysis we could not assess the adequacy of either of our hypotheses regarding decision strategies leading to the observed results. In programming a sequence of computer instructions, however, we could state precisely the information processing necessitated by each strategy; and in simulation runs executing the instructions operationalizing each formulation, we obtained data generated as direct logical outcomes of each strategy. Let us consider the results of these computer runs.

Figure 2 summarizes the process for testing our hypothesis that retaining both positions is a decision by default. Such a decision occurs when the expected profit from the favored position is less than the reward value of the less valued position. As the data in Table 4 indicate, rank orderings of the frequencies of responses to items by simulated respondents agree with the observed item rank orderings from union members as well as with the predicted item rank orderings. While the rank order correlations are satisfactory, on seven of the eight individual items the distribution of choices by simulated respondents differs significantly from that by union members (see Table 5).

Let V1 = Total value of retaining chief stewardship, including rewards of approval from reference groups.

Let V3 = Total value of retaining employees' club office, including rewards of approval from reference groups.

Let |Diff| = Absolute value of V1 - V3.

Then:

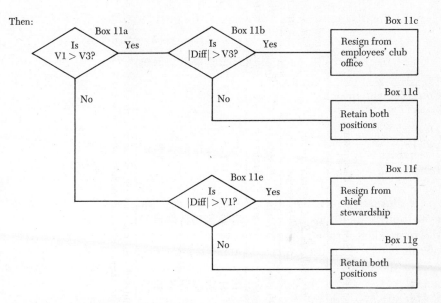

FIGURE 2. FLOW DIAGRAM FOR "RETAINING BOTH JOBS" AS A DECISION BY DEFAULT

Let us turn now to our other formulation regarding decision strategies. Figure 3 summarizes the process involved when each respondent computes the reward and cost of all three decision alternatives before choosing among them. Only half of the flow diagram is shown to describe decisions made when the respondent values the chief stewardship more than he does the employees' club (S1 is greater than S3). The other half of the diagram (when S3 is greater than S1) is not depicted here, since it is simply the obverse of what is presented. (We shall discuss presently the integrity and consonance scores referred to in Figure 3.) As indicated in Table 6, the computer output corresponds very closely to both the predicted item rank orderings and the observed data from union members, but on six of the eight individual items the distribution of choices by simulated respondents differs significantly from that of union members (Table 5). We conclude, therefore, that while our hypothesis that respondents evaluate the social profit of all response alternatives is more adequate, in general, than our decision-by-default hypothesis, some aspects of the decision process are still neglected in our model.

Table 5. Percentage Distribution of Responses from Simulated Respondents in Terms of Three Decision-Making Hypotheses

Item no.	Hypothesis 1: Decision by Default			Hypothesis 2: Compute profit for each response			Hypothesis 3: Hypothesis 2 plus consonance and integrity values		
	Resign office	Retain both	Resign as steward	Resign office	Retain both	Resign as steward	Resign office	Retain both	Resign as steward
1.	21	46	33	16	51	33	20	46	34
2.	42	50	8*	41	45	14*	45	35	20
3.	27	51	22*	20	50	30*	23	44	33
4.	57	39	4*	62	31	7*	63	24	13
5.	26	55	19*	20	54	26*	23	47	30
6.	54	42	4*	58	35	7*	61	28	11
7.	37	53	10*	33	50	17*	36	40	24
8.	69	27	4*	70	25	5	70	19	11

* Comparisons were made between the computer-simulated subjects' responses to each item and the responses of labor union members to the item (as reported in Table 1). For each set of three responses marked with an asterisk χ^2 with 2 degrees of freedom > 5.991 ($p < .05$).

Let S1   = Personal value of chief stewardship to respondent.
Let S3   = Personal value of employees' club office.
Let RG1 = Reference group pressures in favor of chief stewardship.
Let RG3 = Reference group pressures in favor of employees' club office.
Let V1   = Total value of chief stewardship. Let V2 = Total value of retaining both jobs.
Let V3   = Total value of employees' club office.

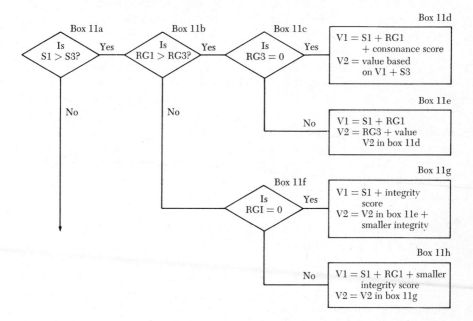

FIGURE 3. FLOW DIAGRAM FOR DECISION INCORPORATING INTEGRITY AND CONSONANCE SCORES

TABLE 6.   CONSEQUENCES OF EVALUATING PROFIT
FROM ALL THREE RESPONSE ALTERNATIVES

	Spearman rank order correlations for		
	Resign from club office	*Retain both positions*	*Resign from stewardship*
Computer with theory	1.00	.98	.95
Computer with people	1.00	.95	1.00
	Percentages responding in each category		
Computer-simulated respondents	40	43	17
Labor union members	43	35	22

To explain the results of one of Gerard's small group experiments,[29] Homans postulates four important influences on individual behavior: personal preference, social approval, cognitive consonance, and personal integ-

[29] Harold B. Gerard, "The Anchorage of Opinions in Face-to-Face Groups," *Human Relations*, 7 (November, 1954), pp. 313–325.

rity. With these, he provides a cogent analysis of data Gerard could not explain.[30] In the runs described thus far, our computer model incorporates only two of these influences on decision making — personal preference and social approval (involved in the sensitivity to reference group pressures). Using Homans' framework, we can postulate that cognitive consonance will lead a respondent to increase the value of his preferred choice if reference group pressures support it. On the other hand, maintenance of personal integrity will make him reluctant to yield to pressure.

Consonance scores for each simulated individual are determined as follows. The respondent's personal valuation for the chief stewardship is added to that for the employees' club office. The difference between these two scores is then subtracted from their sum to obtain a maximum value. The consonance score is a random number between zero and the value just obtained, or $0 \leqslant RN \leqslant MaxVal$; $MaxVal = S1 + S3 - |S1 - S3|$. Using this method to compute the score, we assume that the importance to an individual of having others agree with him is inversely proportional to the difference between the two roles in their personal value to him. Consequently, if he favors the chief stewardship over the employees' club office only slightly, reference group support is more likely to be decisive.

We have assumed, as Homans does, that a cost is incurred in lost personal integrity when one changes a decision because of pressure rather than conviction. When all relevant reference groups oppose an individual's personal choice, maximum pressure is exerted on him to change to agree with everybody; thus maintenance of integrity has its highest value. If most of the pressure that can be exerted in a decision situation opposes a person's choice, but if some groups support him, yielding involves a smaller loss of integrity. Having some support for either decision, one will not necessarily be surrendering just because of pressure.

Scores representing the value of maintaining integrity are computed as follows. When all reference groups oppose an individual's personal preference, an integrity value is added to his personal evaluation of his favored role, and a smaller increment is added to the value of retaining both positions. Assuming that the greatest value for integrity follows from not yielding at all, we add a high increment to that decision — in fact, the value of the respondent's favored alternative is doubled. Since some value accrues when a respondent's integrity is not completely compromised — when he retains the position he values most but yields enough also to keep the position urged by reference groups — then a smaller increment is made to the alternative of keeping both positions. This value then becomes the sum of reference group pressures opposed to the respondent plus an integrity score represented by a random number between zero and the sum of the respondent's valuations for the two positions, that is S1 plus S3.

[30] Homans, *op. cit.*, pp. 93–102.

When over half, but not all, of the reference group pressure is in opposition to the respondent's preference, the integrity increment for both his personal preference and for retaining both positions is a random number between zero and S1 plus S3. Integrity scores, of course, are added to different base scores for each action. Note that while "all reference group pressures" will usually mean pressures from all three groups, this is not necessarily the case. One or even two of the groups may be exerting no pressure, or, on occasion, one group's pressure may outweigh that of both others.

The effects of including cognitive consonance and personal integrity in the computer program are indicated in Boxes 11d, 11g, and 11h of Figure 3. Incorporating these additional influences on rewards and costs produces the computer-generated results summarized in Table 7.

Table 7. Consequences of Evaluating Profit from All Three Response Alternatives and Incorporating Consonance and Integrity Considerations

	Spearman rank order correlations for		
	Resign from club office	Retain both positions	Resign from stewardship
Computer with theory	.98	.98	.95
Computer with people	1.00	.95	1.00
People with theory	.98	.98	.95
	Percentages responding in each category		
Computer-simulated respondents	42	36	22
Labor union members	43	35	22

In addition to the close correspondence indicated by the rank order correlations in Table 7, computer-generated responses and labor union members' decisions do not differ significantly on any of the eight individual questionnaire items (see Table 5). Data from both the computer-simulated respondents and the human respondents support theoretical predictions, and this version of the model regarding decision strategy produces data that are remarkably close to living persons' responses, even in the variations from predictions.

SUMMARY

In our discussion of computer models in general, and a portion of our own program in particular, we have tried to demonstrate that computer simulation contributes to the development and verification of social theory. Formulating a theory as a computer model creates a relatively tractable representation and possibly a more meaningful conceptualization, since the clarification of concepts required for programming increases precision.

This organizing function of the model is further enhanced by the computer's predictive dynamic capacity to set theoretical processes in motion and generate data that follow as logical results of hypothesized processes.

To illustrate a social-psychological application of computer simulation, we have described a validation study involving a portion of our computer model, HOMUNCULUS. We programmed routines that operationally expressed alternative hypotheses concerning profit-oriented decision strategies for resolving role conflict, incorporating each of these decision making routines in the portion of HOMUNCULUS involving considerations of expected rewards and costs. Since the data generated by each computer run represented the logical results of the hypotheses operating in that run, it thus was possible to assess each programmed formulation by comparing the simulated responses with the actual decisions of the respondents in the original survey. Such flexibility and dynamic capacity, added to the increased precision and tractability of a computer model, amply compensate the social theorist for the cost of translating from verbal formulations.